CAP JULUCA

Cap Juluca is an award-winning, 179 acre retreat with eighteen very private Moorish-style beachfront villas comprising 58 spacious rooms and junior suites, seven suites and six pool villas. All rooms lead out onto the mile-long, white-sand beach of Maunday's Bay and overlook the Caribbean Sea and the mountains of St Martin. Cap Juluca is a member of The Leading Small Hotels of the World.

Cap Juluca
P.O. Box 240
Maunday's Bay
Anguilla
Leeward Islands
British West Indies

Tel: +1 264 497 6666
Fax: +1 264 497 6617
Email: capjuluca@anguillanet.com
Website: www.capjuluca.com

Cap Juluca is pleased to support the publication of
75 Years of West Indies Cricket, 1928 - 2003

75 YEARS OF
WEST INDIES CRICKET
1928 - 2003

Albert
Hope you enjoy
the info in this
book.
Best Wishes

[signature] 21/7/04

75 YEARS OF
WEST INDIES CRICKET
1928 - 2003

RAY GOBLE

and

KEITH A.P. SANDIFORD

HANSIB

First published in Great Britain in 2004
by Hansib Publications Limited
London: PO Box 34621, London E17 4GL
Hertfordshire: Orchard Road, Royston, Hertfordshire SG8 5HA

Email: info@hansib-books.com. Website: www.hansib-books.com

ISBN 1 870518 78 0

Design and Production by Books of Colour, Hertfordshire, England

Cover design by Graphic Resolutions, Hertfordshire, England

Printed and bound by Interprint, Malta

Cover images:
Learie Constantine, Sonny Ramadhin, Garry Sobers, Viv Richards and Brian Lara

Supported by the University of the West Indies, St Augustine, Trinidad
and Cap Juluca, Maunday's Bay, Anguilla, British West Indies

CONTENTS

PART I

PART II

Also published by Hansib

50 Great Westindian Test Cricketers (1983)
100 Great Westindian Test Cricketers: From Challenor to Richards (1988)
Indo-Westindian Cricket (1988)
The Rise of Westindian Cricket: From Colony to Nation (1996)
Cornered Tigers: The History of Pakistan's Cricket (1997)
Black Pearls: The A-Z of Black Footballers in the English Game (1999)

PUBLISHER'S INTRODUCTION

THE WEST INDIES CRICKET TEAM HAS COME A LONG WAY SINCE its first match (as West Indies XI) on 15 February 1897 at Queen's Park in Port of Spain, Trinidad. And since its first Test match at Lord's in June 1928, and its first Test victory in February 1930 at Bourda in British Guiana, the West Indies has developed into a world-class, world-beating team.

Since these early days, the Caribbean region has produced some of the world's finest cricketers, and created a West Indies team that reached its peak in the early 1980s and maintained its dominance of world cricket for fifteen years. The seventy-five-year period from 1928 is littered with world records and landmark achievements from such players as Garry Sobers (8,032 Test runs and 235 Test wickets), Gordon Greenidge (37,354 First Class runs), Courtney Walsh (1807 First Class wickets) and Deryck Murray (740 catches and 108 stumpings).

Even the Caribbean cricket grounds have had their part to play. The West Indians are among the most passionate supporters of the game and it is at these grounds that their devotion is most fervently expressed. From the Kensington Oval in Barbados, where the first Test match in the West Indies was held in January 1930, to the Queens Park Oval in Trinidad and Sabina Park in Jamaica; from Bourda in Guyana where the West Indies achieved their first Test victory in February 1930, to Antigua's Recreation Ground, St Vincent's Arnos Vale and the Beausejour Stadium in St Lucia, there are few sporting occasions more spectacular than an international Caribbean cricket match in full swing.

Although the final years of the twentieth century and the early years of the twenty-first century have seen a slump in team fortunes, the recent arrival of new and talented young players such as Ian Bradshaw and Dwayne Smith (Barbados), Dwayne Bravo and Ravindranath Rampaul (Trinidad and Tobago) and Darren Sammy (the first St Lucian to be selected to play for the West Indies), may breathe new life into the squad. Perhaps Brian Lara's record-breaking 400 not out against England at the Antigua Recreation Ground in April 2004 may signal the start of things to come.

ACKNOWLEDGEMENTS

THE IDEA TO PUBLISH A BOOK COMMEMORATING SEVENTY-FIVE years of West Indies cricket came about in the mid-1990s. Having known Ray Goble for many years, and been fully aware of his knowledge of West Indian cricket and his authority as a statistician, the project was discussed at length on many occasions. During these discussions, Ray had made the suggestion that a colleague of his would be an ideal co-author to provide the historical background for this particular title. Following Ray's recommendation, Keith Sandiford agreed to provide Part I of *75 Years of West Indies Cricket, 1928-2003*.

I should like to offer my thanks and appreciation to the following: The University of the West Indies, St Augustine, Trinidad, especially Pro Vice Chancellor Dr Bhoendradatt Tewarie who recognised the importance of the book; the directors of the luxury resort, Cap Juluca in Anguilla, whose General Manager, Eustace "Guish" Guishard, is a great and committed supporter of West Indies cricket in Anguilla and beyond, and Managing Director, John Mezzanotte; Kash Ali, who managed the project and designed and produced the book; Isha Persaud for her dedication; Shareef Ali of Graphic Resolutions; Richard Painter of Print Resources; Alan Cross, Susan Andrews, Brendan Ali, Dr Phyllis Fleming-Banks, Clive Lloyd, Professor Baldwin Mootoo, Professor Brinsley Samaroo, Alan Pryer and Lord's Cricket Ground for their help with the launch, Interprint in Malta, and Clive Porter, editor of The Journal of Cricket Society, for his kind permission to reprint passages of this study which previously appeared in that journal.

And finally, you cannot record seventy-five years of West Indies cricket without acknowledging the sponsors over the years – Shell, Red Stripe, Busta, Carib, Texaco, Heineken, Banks, Gillette, Guinness, Cable & Wireless, Sandals, Geddes Grant and Harrison Line – and the lesser-known local businesses and individuals who supported up-and-coming players, and the sport in general, to ensure that Caribbean cricket achieved world-class status.

Arif Ali
June 2004

PREFACE

THIS IS A VERY COMPREHENSIVE TREATMENT OF THE FIRST seventy-five years of West Indies Cricket. Statistics and basic information is well documented and, for the first time, the full first-class record of all West Indian Test cricketers is fully presented.

The material is located in the context of an evolving society from plantocracy to independence linking cricketing achievement with the role and influence of church, school, club, and political evolution in the individual territories.

The chronological treatment of Test records also shows the organic growth of West Indies cricket and it is fascinating to read, for example, that the highest aggregate of Test runs at the Queen's Park Oval in Trinidad, held by Rohan Kanhai since 1974, was in turn a replacement of the previous mark set by Everton Weekes in 1958; or that the highest aggregate by a Test batsman at Bridgetown, Barbados, was that of Garry Sobers (914, in 1974) to be surpassed successively by Viv Richards (959) and Desmond Haynes (1210).

This work is an indispensable addition to publications on West Indies cricket, combining the more readily available Test match statistics with the full first-class records of all West Indian players. For completeness and a wider understanding of the impact of the West Indies on world cricket, a chapter on West Indians who have represented other countries is included.

By focusing on the contribution of the players on a territorial basis this book provides useful insights on the evolutionary trends of the various sub-units and in addition gives us a better appreciation of the development of the administrative structures that has led to the present West Indies Cricket Board Inc.

The authors are to be commended on the immense effort involved in putting together the statistics in this unique way, combining it with sociological narrative that make for a deeper understanding of West Indies cricket achievements and doing so in a readily readable style – it is an essential addition to West Indies cricket literature.

Baldwin S. Mootoo
Professor Emeritus
University of the West Indies

THE AUTHORS

RAY GOBLE

Ray Goble provided the comprehensive statistics for this book. He is now retired, and is still living in the Chichester area of West Sussex in England where he was born, and worked as a company representative all his working life.

He first started taking an interest in West Indies cricket in 1950 after watching them play for the first time, and has been keeping records and collecting all manner of material on them ever since.

He is co-author of *The Complete Record of West Indian Test Cricketers* (1991). He has been a member of the Association of Cricket Statisticians since 1986, and was also a founder member of the Association of Football Statisticians, and a life long supporter of Manchester City. He is author of *The Complete Record of Manchester City FC* (1987 & 1992). He has also supplied statistics to many other books and magazines over the years.

KEITH A.P. SANDIFORD

A native of Barbados, Dr Keith A.P. Sandiford is a graduate of Combermere School, the University of the West Indies and the University of Toronto. After lecturing in modern history for more than thirty years at the University of Toronto, York University in Ontario and the University of Manitoba in Winnipeg, he retired in 1998 and was elevated to the status of Professor Emeritus.

He is a prolific and wide-ranging author whose numerous books and articles address such subjects as Black Studies, Victorian politics and diplomacy, Barbadian sport and education, the professionalisation of modern cricket and the impact of Caribbean immigration on the development of Manitoba. A regular contributor to *Cricket Lore* and *The Journal of the Cricket Society*, Professor Sandiford has also written seven monographs in the 'Famous Cricketers' series published by the Association of Cricket Statisticians and Historians.

Once an avid bridge player, he is a Life Master of the American Bridge League (ACBL) and a recognised Scrabble expert. A superb and enthusiastic fieldsman in his youth, he volunteered to serve for several years as the twelfth man in the famous Combermere teams of the early 1950s which included such promising stars as Rawle Brancker, Wes Hall, Frank King, Peter Lashley and Lionel Williams.

FOREWORD

IT IS AN HONOUR TO PRESENT THE FOREWORD TO A LANDMARK volume that accurately chronicles the rich history of West Indies cricket. As someone who has been intimately involved with international cricket in the Caribbean for virtually all of adult life, this book, *75 Years of West Indies Cricket, 1928-2003*, is an important initiative and a validation of the unique skill and talent of gifted athletes, from Headley to Lara, and the imaginative leadership that has effected the West Indies' meteoric rise in World Cricket.

For all of its flamboyance and its phenomenal accomplishments over the years, West Indies cricket has not been sufficiently documented. In my view, this publication is therefore not just symbolic but timely.

Comprehensively, *75 Years of West Indies Cricket, 1928-2003* not only provides perspective for its historical statistical data, but in effect, reflects the fun, excitement and the ebullience of men playing a boys' game on a field of dreams that stretches from Bridgetown to Brisbane, from Kingston to Karachi, and from Mumbai to Manchester.

This book is a remarkable collaborative effort of Professor Keith Sandiford and Ray Goble. Historically, it presents a mosaic game that transcends its boundaries to unity and elevates the Caribbean community as no other sport, cultural or political entity has done. As it relates to the body politic, cricket flourishes with promise and possibility for the Caribbean - a region that is too often diminished by the myopia of insularity.

However, *75 Years of West Indies Cricket, 1928-2003* is an uplifting account of the growth and maturity of West Indies cricket that will undoubtedly inspire prospective young cricketers in the Caribbean.

I was extremely fortunate to have had the opportunity, along with a number of dedicated team-mates, to make a contribution to the enhancement of West Indies cricket as it reached its zenith.

I am confident that this book, which eloquently portrays the history of West Indies cricket, will not only be well received in the Caribbean but by fans throughout the cricket world.

Clive Lloyd, CBE, OA, OR
I.C.C. Match Referee
Captain of the West Indies, 1974-1985

INTRODUCTION

THIS BOOK CELEBRATES THE 75TH ANNIVERSARY (2003) OF THE achievement of Test match status on the part of the West Indies who played their inaugural Test against England in June 1928. It is intended to be a companion study to *100 Great Westindian Test Cricketers: from Challenor to Richards*, written by Bridgette Lawrence and Reg Scarlett and released by Hansib in 1988, to commemorate the 60th anniversary of West Indian Test cricket.

The men from the Caribbean began with three consecutive losses in the summer of 1928 and were destined to lose their first four Tests on English soil, but they gradually became competitive. At home, they defeated England 2-1 in 1934/35 and 2-0 in 1947/48. By 1950, they were strong enough to defeat England 3-1 in a series in England. By 1965, they had become for the first time the unofficial champions of Test cricket, having shown a marked superiority over Australia and England, the perennial great powers of the sport. During the period 1980-95, the West Indies bestrode the cricketing world like some mighty colossus, going undefeated in an unprecedented 29 successive series.

Since 1995, the West Indian record has been much less impressive as they have been consistently embarrassed abroad, even by such teams as New Zealand, Pakistan and Sri Lanka who are not normally regarded as cricketing giants. But even though they have recently returned to earth with a resounding thud, the West Indian overall record in Test cricket is still outstanding. Of the 401 Tests they have played thus far, the West Indies have won 147, lost 115 and drawn 138. They were also fortunate enough to participate in the very first tie in the history of Test cricket.

These peaks and valleys of West Indian cricket are traced in this study in a novel fashion. Rather than the simple chronological approach, detailing success and failure in successive series, West Indian cricket is analysed from region to region. The contributions of each island/territory are addressed in detail, following an opening chapter on West Indian cricket which serves as the necessary backdrop. This book is thus different in scope and conception from *100 Great Westindian Test Cricketers* which focused more sharply on individual players. The various world records of West Indian teams and individuals are then set forth in a separate chapter. This section shows that the West Indies have set and/or broken an almost incredible number of important records in Test cricket.

In addition to the 253 players who have represented the West Indies in their first 75 years of Test cricket, the Caribbean basin produced thirteen others who played at the highest level for different countries. Brief profiles are provided of these emigrants even though the West Indies do not appear to have suffered from the talent-drain.

The individual statistics of all West Indian players are presented here, for the very first time, in Part II – serving as additional evidence of the enormous impact that many West Indians have made on the development of the sport. While the team records and individual statistics are accurate up to 30 November 2003 in Part I, the date of 30 September 2003 was used as a cut-off point for the statistics appearing in Part II.

The Select Bibliography at the end of the book is meant as an aid to those readers who wish to pursue further research on Caribbean cricket.

PART I

PART I

CHAPTER ONE

CRICKET IN THE WEST INDIES, 1928-2003

FROM 1980 TO 1995 THE WEST INDIES DOMINATED INTERNATIONAL cricket in a most spectacular fashion, going undefeated in an unprecedented 29 consecutive series. They played 115 Test matches during this phenomenal streak and lost only 15 of them. They won 59 and were often prevented by the weather from doing likewise in the majority of the 41 remaining Tests that were left drawn. Clive Lloyd, Viv Richards and Richie Richardson all won more than 45 percent of their games as captain, while losing 25 percent or fewer, and Richards retired in 1991 with the enviable distinction of having never captained the West Indies in a losing series. Such individual players as Eldine Baptiste of Antigua, Carlisle Best of Barbados, Winston Davis of St Vincent, Jeffrey Dujon and Patrick Patterson of Jamaica, Roger Harper of Guyana, and Gus Logie of Trinidad had the enormous satisfaction of having never participated in a Test rubber that was lost.

Sports sociologists everywhere are still marvelling at this miracle which defies adequate analysis or explanation. The most that can be said is that the West Indies have traditionally attached greater significance to cricket than to any other activity and most certainly than do any other communities. They see cricket as the one area in which they can compete effectively on the international stage. The territories have neither the material nor human resources to make an impact in such fields as agriculture, commerce, industry or technology. Cricket has therefore been their main focus for several decades and the success of their composite teams has created a certain momentum which fuels their nationalistic fires in a way in which no other sport, activity or development has yet been able to do. The West Indies were also most fortunate in producing a veritable galaxy of outstanding cricket stars who peaked during the wonderful decade of the 1980s.

One might have expected this cricket cult to suffer irrevocably in the early days from such destructive forces as parochialism, racism and snobbery. Divisions between and among islands, classes, races and colours had been so deep that most other activities were simply stifled. But cricket flourished in this environment in a most uncanny manner. The various units in the region, all emulating their imperial masters, adopted cricket as their 'national' game and took particular pride in their accomplishments in it. The Caribbean Whites, meanwhile, played cricket largely to prove their gentility, while the Browns and Blacks did so to prove their equality. All across the region, cricket clubs were established to cater to the needs of specific constituencies. Such cricket clubs as Kingston, Lucas and Melbourne in Jamaica, for instance, long remained very careful and inordinately jealous about their membership and composition. In Trinidad, the great C.L.R. James knew, long before he left school, with which cricket club he was expected to be associated and which (among Queen's Park, Maple, Shannon, Shamrock and Stingo) he simply could or could not join. In Barbados, too, while Pickwick and Wanderers initially admitted only the white and wealthy, Spartan spoke for middle class Blacks and Mulattoes, and it was left to Empire to cater to the lower middle-income families.

All that such racial, ethnic and class distinctions accomplished was the sharpening of the competitive edge, so that cricket matches all across the Caribbean became integral features of the unending quest for group authority, respectability and identity. Honour was constantly at stake in such matches as Maple v Shamrock, Pickwick v Wanderers, Empire v Spartan and Kingston v Lucas. Thus it was that Caribbean Browns, Blacks, Mulattoes and Whites all honed their cricketing skills in a sequence of epic clashes along the way during the whole period leading up to Independence and sometimes beyond. Cricketing excellence became a badge of honour and was one of the most effective keys a West Indian could use to unlock some otherwise stubborn social doors. As late as the 1940s and 1950s, the ability to play good cricket could tilt the scales when a young man was applying for a job even as a civil servant or a teacher. Until very recently, the headmasters of secondary schools in Barbados, for example, were anxious to invite scholar/cricketers to join their teaching staff. Famous schoolboy athletes, like Harold Gittens Brewster, G. Harry Sealy and J.E. Derek Sealy, were all appointed to the Combermere School staff largely on the strength of their cricketing skills. Such was the awesome power of the cricket cult.

The result (which is itself partly a cause) is that most Caribbean institutions have consistently supported cricket in the region in one fashion or another. Governments have generally considered it more worthy of material assistance than any other sport, while churches and schools have historically seen cricket as a useful and character-building activity. Banks and other commercial houses have continued to sponsor it with more enthusiasm than they do other sports. This single-minded focus on cricket meant that the West Indies were among the leaders in the professionalisation of this sport, especially after the Packer Revolution of the late 1970s. They appointed a full-time physiotherapist, Dennis Waight of Australia, to ensure that their players remained in excellent physical shape and began to make regular use of chiropractors, dentists and general physicians. Their emphasis on mental sharpness and physical fitness paid such huge dividends that their opponents were compelled to follow their example.

OUTDONE BY THEIR OWN IMITATORS

By the mid-1990s, other communities had learnt the West Indian lessons very well indeed. Cricket academies began to sprout up in such countries as Australia and South Africa, and all professional teams began to make greater use of such technologies as video replay to study the technical strengths and weaknesses of individual opponents. The West Indies also pioneered the fearsome four-pronged pace attack which has influenced most countries to put less faith in spin bowling. Even on the sub-continent, where spinners had long been in the ascendant, India and Pakistan began to produce speedsters of the quality of Kapil Dev, Abey Kuruvilla, Venkatesh Prasad, Wasim Akram and Waqar Younis. West Indian opponents have also apparently copied the Caribbean methods of wicket-preparation to produce livelier and bouncier strips to assist their pacers. The resultant irony has been that the West Indies in recent years have been out-gunned by their own kinds of ammunition. They lost all three Tests in their tour of Pakistan in 1997/98 and suffered the humiliation of a 5-0 'whitewash' at the hands of South Africa in 1998/99 and Australia in 2000/2001. In fact, since 1995, they have lost every series on foreign soil quite convincingly, apart from their victories against the weak opposition provided by Bangladesh and Zimbabwe.

There is considerable concern in the West Indian camps these days because the general public cannot accept defeat on the cricket field. They see the modern game almost as a peculiar kind of Caribbean gift to the rest of the world and have become spoilt and sometimes too sanguine as a result of the 'Wonder Years'. The older folk (as usual) have begun to complain about the lack of dedication on the part of the youth, the tendency of the younger generation to become too captivated by such American sports as basketball and tennis, and the return of that pernicious brand of parochialism which once made a mockery of West Indian attempts at unity and co-operation. The loss of all three Test matches in Sri Lanka in 2001/02 was a particularly bitter pill to swallow since that country is a relative newcomer to Test cricket.

It is true that West Indian youth are less committed to cricket than their parents and grandparents. They are now being exposed to a much wider variety of sports and recreations. The schools, churches and businesses are no longer bent on the monolithic cultivation of cricketers. In Barbados, for instance, most of the physical education teachers have been trained in American colleges and are preparing their students to compete in a larger cluster of sports. While cricket may well have suffered as a result, Barbados can claim to have improved significantly in such disciplines as athletics, golf, hockey, swimming, football and tennis. But this does not mean that the cricket fires have ceased to burn. The universal outpouring of joy which accompanied the two West Indian victories in the 1999 series against Australia is proof enough of that. The establishment of the Centre for Cricket Research (CCR) on the Cave Hill Campus of the University of the West Indies is another significant indicator. So too is

5

the appearance of a cricket academy in Grenada and a cricket centre in Antigua. The wailing and gnashing of teeth which accompanies every cricket loss or disappointment provides further testimony.

What the West Indian public must recognise is that sporting triumphs generally move in cycles. No one community can expect to monopolise a particular craft or discipline indefinitely. The Glory Years were, in effect, a magnificent aberration. The Australians have always taken cricket very seriously indeed and have generally played it much better than their opponents. Even during the nineteenth century, when they were outnumbered some 10-1 by the inhabitants of England and Wales, Australians were able to compete on even terms with the 'Mother Country'. During the twentieth century, they often dominated the 'Ashes' series, but Australia has known its ups and downs too. It went through very lean times during most of the 1980s. Cricket champions tend to remain at the top of the heap for about four to five years, on average, before being dethroned. The Australians, it is true, once held the Ashes from 1934 to 1953, but that period included a lengthy interregnum of eight years (1938-46), thanks to the Second World War. Even when the West Indies themselves became acknowledged as world champions for the first time, their reign (1965-68) ended with the passage of a single generation of Test players.

Since cricket stars tend to reach their best form in their mid-twenties and decline within the next ten years before retiring altogether, it is almost impossible for countries or clubs to extend their dominance indefinitely. What set the West Indies apart from the norm during the 1980s was their extraordinary ability to reconstruct their Test XIs without apparently breaking stride when their older stars declined and/or retired. When, for instance, Alvin Kallicharran disqualified himself from Test cricket by touring South Africa in 1982, he was promptly replaced by another left-hander, Larry Gomes, who accumulated more than 3,000 runs in his 60 Tests. Lloyd amassed 7,515 runs in 110 Tests, but Richards who succeeded him as captain proceeded to reach 8,540 in 121. Even before these men had departed, Richie Richardson and Gus Logie had arrived.

When Roy Fredericks, Guyana's finest opening batsman, retired relatively early from the international stage, he was immediately replaced by Desmond Haynes who reached even greater heights, exceeding 7,000 Test runs in the next sixteen years. Trinidad's Deryck Murray had proven himself one of the best wicket-keepers of his generation. David Murray, his Barbadian successor, was a superior batsman and not any less capable with the gloves. Then came Jamaica's Jeffrey Dujon, unquestionably a greater player than either of them. He effected a West Indian record number of dismissals (272) and scored over 3,000 runs in his 81 Tests. His acrobatic athleticism behind the stumps often proved an excellent complement to the West Indian fast attack.

6

Malcolm Marshall, perhaps West Indies' finest fast bowler, seen here in action on 19 August 1984

THE AGE OF UNCEASING FIRE

The rapid succession of West Indian fast bowlers was even more incredible. In 1976, Wayne Daniel, Vanburn Holder, Michael Holding and Andy Roberts literally took England by storm. Roberts wound up his Test career with 202 wickets in 47 matches. His regular partner with the new ball was Holding who finished with 249 wickets in 60 Tests. When Roberts retired, his place was taken by Malcolm Marshall who established a West Indian record of 376 wickets in 81 Tests and is generally regarded as one of the finest bowlers the world has seen. Joel Garner, meanwhile, usurped Daniel's place and went on to capture 259 wickets in 58 Tests. Colin Croft, breathing forth sheer brimstone and malevolence, took 125 wickets in 27 Tests before curtailing his own career by making an ill-advised visit to South Africa. That allowed Courtney Walsh to step forward and bowl his way to a world-record 519 Test wickets, demolishing Marshall's West Indian record as he did so. When the Barbadian 'Big Bird', Garner, called it quits in 1988, he was succeeded by Antigua's Curtly Ambrose, an even bigger bird, who claimed 405 victims in his stellar Test career.

This ability to churn out great fast bowlers in such profusion is one of the wonders of modern cricket. With Marshall gone and Patrick Patterson going, Ian Bishop and Kenny Benjamin stepped forward in the early 1990s. A sizeable number of others, including Ian Allen, Sylvester Clarke, Cameron Cuffy, Winston Davis, Ezra Moseley and Milton Small, who were good enough to have represented many another country, have been left to lament the fact that they arrived at the worst possible time. Meanwhile, such promising speedsters as Hendy Bryan, Pedro Collins, Corey Collymore, Mervyn Dillon, Nixon McClean, Reon King and Franklyn Rose were left waiting impatiently in the wings. Although the quality is not at present as impressive as the quantity, the fast bowling cupboard is still full and there are many successors (like Jermaine Lawson and Adam Sanford) vying for a place now that those two ancient war-horses, Ambrose and Walsh, have hung up their boots.

To explain this remarkable phenomenon, one well-known English journalist once expressed the view, in a famous documentary, that the fury of the Caribbean fast bowlers is a product of the abject poverty within their homes. They see fast bowling not only as a means of escape from destitution but as a legitimate form of rebellion against the society that spawned them. They are, in a word, little more than angry and hungry urchins seeking some form of respectable identity in the only avenue open to them. Such a morbid and unkind view does not take properly into account the amount of dedication and practice necessary to achieve the standards of excellence that the Caribbean pacers reached.

The superb fast bowling produced by Garner, Holding, Marshall and Roberts required not only hard physical labour but considerable cricket acumen. Fast bowlers must not only be malevolent but very efficient, very astute and very accurate. It must also be emphasised that no member of that particular quartet came from desperately poor homes. Bob Willis, who was himself an excellent fast bowler in his prime, simply concluded that, "It seems ingrained in the West Indian psyche that it is good to see a batsman hopping around and ducking under spectacularly fast bowling, even though it sometimes does not get wickets".

Caribbean fast bowling can never be seriously regarded as the simple offspring of plebeian ferocity. The tradition of excellent fast bowling dates back to the nineteenth century when Blacks were encouraged to bowl as fast as they could to the white batsmen who, like all good Anglo-Saxons of that era, regarded fast bowling and wicket-keeping as menial tasks beneath the dignity of gentlemen. The majority of West Indian fast bowlers have consequently been Black, and it is worthy of note that, as long ago as 1898, Pelham Warner

Learie Constantine, the greatest West Indian all-rounder during the inter-war years

thought it necessary to insist that his white friends in the Caribbean take a few 'professionals' with them on their first tour of England. Warner's considered view was that unless the West Indies selected such fast bowlers as Archie Cumberbatch and 'Float' Woods, who had performed so brilliantly against English touring teams in the late 1890s, "it would be absurd to attempt to play the first class counties". He was sure that a combination of nine players and five Blacks could give the majority of English counties very stiff competition indeed. Without the work of Tommie Burton and Woods, the West Indies might not have won a single match in their 1900 tour. Had Cumberbatch also been selected, they would certainly have won many more.

THE ABSENCE OF SPIN

Until the sudden arrival of Sonny Ramadhin and Alfred Valentine in 1950, in fact, the West Indies did not produce a single spinner of any quality, apart perhaps from Bertie Clarke and Wilfred Ferguson. Most of their bowling successes of the inter-war years were achieved by such speedsters as Learie Constantine, George Francis, Herman Griffith, George John and 'Mannie' Martindale. This left their own batsmen at a serious disadvantage when they encountered clever spin bowling in their trips abroad. Thus, for instance, when they came up against A.P. 'Tich' Freeman in England in 1928, they found themselves totally at sea. He mesmerised them to such an extent that he finished with 22 wickets (av: 13.72) in the three Tests that year. Significantly, Freeman,

9

who could claim no more than 66 wickets (av: 25.86) in his whole Test career, was never so successful against the more experienced Australians. The English selectors therefore thought it prudent to allow that Kentish spinner only 12 Test matches altogether.

There are no rational explanations for the dearth of Caribbean spin in those days. In an era before the covering of wickets became routine, West Indian pitches were notoriously sticky when it rained. This ought to have encouraged their bowlers to resort to spin rather than to swerve. It, however, did not. Perhaps it might be said that the spinners were generally discouraged by the groundsmen's tendency in those days to prepare featherbed pitches which gave spin bowlers no help at all. Few spinners therefore caught the public imagination prior to 1950. Apart from the very popular 'Puss' Achong in Trinidad (1929-35) and 'Puss' Parris in Barbados (1926-47), West Indian spin bowlers were seldom idolised.

It was the constant preparation of unresponsive pitches, geared to ensure that the bat remained supreme over the ball, which also discouraged West Indian fast bowlers throughout the period 1935-55. Huge scores were the result in inter-colonial matches and the batsmen enjoyed themselves enormously. With the solitary exception of Frank King, no top-class fast bowler appeared on the Caribbean scene between the careers of E.A.V. 'Foffie' Williams and Wesley Hall. To make matters worse, the myopic selectors confined themselves to the so-called 'Big Four' (Barbados, British Guiana, Jamaica and Trinidad) and lost the chance, during the early 1950s, to make use of the skills of such promising cricketers as Hubert Anthonyson of Antigua and Frank Mason of St Vincent.

RESORT TO MEDIUM PACE

Traditions, however, always die hard, if they die at all. Whereas the West Indies had to use such medium-pacers as Gerry Gomez and Frank Worrell to open the bowling for most of the early 1950s, they soon found themselves with a superabundance of firepower.

Young men keen on making the West Indian Test XI gradually recognised that they could hardly be expected to compete with such great stroke-players as Robert Christiani, Jack Holt, Roy Marshall, Clyde Walcott, Everton Weekes and Frank Worrell. They steadily shifted their focus and some of them even decided to retool. Both Wes Hall and Charlie Griffith, who began their careers as wicket-keeper/batsmen in the early 1950s, shifted to fast bowling in their late teens. They might never otherwise have represented Barbados, much less the West Indies. Their decision bore remarkable fruit. Within a few years, they had made themselves, by dint of assiduous toil, two of the world's most feared fast bowlers. They became role models not only for West Indians but for others as well. That great Australian fast bowler, Dennis Lillee for instance, has often admitted that Hall was his main source of inspiration.

Frank Worrell (left) and Everton Weekes go out to resume their record-making innings against England at Trent Bridge in 1950

Ironically, it was the lack of fast bowling that prevented the West Indies from reaching the top of the international ladder for about fifteen years. After the Second World War, they had emerged as a powerful batting side with three fine openers in Roy Marshall, Allan Rae and Jeffrey Stollmeyer and at least five superb middle-order batsmen in Christiani, Holt and the 'Three Terrible Ws'. They also possessed two magnificent spin bowlers in Ramadhin and Valentine. But, curiously, there was no fast bowling to give the team the necessary balance. Had John Trim been properly used in Australia in 1951/52, or had Frank King been selected for that tour, the results might well have been much different.

A QUESTION OF BALANCE

It was this question of balance that hampered the West Indies at every turn before the 1960s. In the early days, they failed to find (or to select when one was available) a competent wicket-keeper. Indeed, in 1900, they toured England without a recognised stumper at all. Their policy for many years was to select a batsman who could keep wicket rather than a specialist for the position. Thus, such batsmen as Robert Christiani, Rohan Kanhai, Karl Nunes and Clyde Walcott were often pressed into service. This seriously weakened their out-cricket and, particularly during the 1930s, their fast bowlers suffered from too many missed chances behind the stumps.

Imbalance was sometimes the product of the senseless 'quota' system which was routinely used from 1900 until about 1950. This policy meant the selection of a roughly equal number of players from the four leading cricket territories irrespective of their relative strengths. As a consequence, the best team was seldom chosen for overseas tours and some critical mistakes were inevitable. In 1923, for instance, Herman Griffith was bypassed even though he was arguably the finest fast bowler in the West Indies at that time. Similarly, in 1933, Derek Sealy was inexplicably omitted from the touring team to England. As late as 1948/49, such an excellent all-rounder as John Lucas could find no place among the sixteen who travelled to India. When he was excluded again from the tour to England in 1950, he gave up in despair and emigrated to Canada. It is hard to believe that a batsman who scored 1,030 runs (av: 64.37) in 12 matches for Barbados was not good enough to gain a single Test cap for the West Indies.

The 'quota' system and the sad neglect of the so-called 'smaller islands' were not the only impediments to West Indian cricket success prior to the 1960s. The old-fashioned racist policy of 'white captaincy' also left the islanders considerably hamstrung. Until the appointment of Frank Worrell to lead the team to Australia in 1960/61, the West Indies seldom selected their best captain. Such fine players as Constantine, Griffith and Headley, who possessed keen cricketing brains, were never considered appropriate candidates for the captaincy. Even when Headley was appointed, at the age of almost 40, to lead the West Indies in the first Test against England at Bridgetown in January 1948, it was understood that the system of 'rotating headship', which had often been used in the past, would be tried again. Thus, Gerry Gomez captained the side in Trinidad and John Goddard led it in the final two Tests. During the 1929/30 series against England, four local Whites had led the West Indies at the different locations. It was an absurd policy which ought never to have been conceived.

While these wounds were largely self-inflicted, there were other basic difficulties over which the West Indians had less control. Until the inception of the Shell Shield in 1965/66, there was no regular, annual competition in the territory. First-class matches were haphazardly arranged and West Indians routinely entered Test cricket without the necessary experience of having played several first-class matches. All Caribbean cricketers were Saturday afternoon club players, in effect, who had to adjust rapidly to the regular grind of first-class cricket six days a week when they undertook tours to England and elsewhere. This left them at a considerable disadvantage and helps to explain why they so often failed to do justice to their natural talents.

THE ROOTS OF CALYPSO CRICKET

Saturday afternoon club cricket requires the swift accumulation of runs and there are few opportunities for patient grafting. On their tours abroad, the West Indians consequently became notorious for scoring about 20 to 30 beautiful runs and losing their concentration after about an hour's toil. The expression, 'Calypso Cricket', steadily gained regular usage to describe their bright and breezy approach. But it also conveyed negative messages as it denoted an almost innate or congenital inability (on the part of Blacks and Browns) to remain focused for very long. Of all their earlier batsmen, only George Challenor, Tim Tarilton and George Headley seemed prepared to stay at the crease for any considerable length of time. Some pundits simply put all of this down to basic flaws in Caribbean technique as well as African temperament.

Most critical observers now agree, however, that there seemed very little wrong with the temperament or the batting technique of Derek Sealy, the Barbadian child prodigy, who fashioned a stylish century against the MCC in its 1929/30 tour of the Caribbean and proceeded to represent the West Indies in a Test match at the unprecedentedly young age of seventeen years, 122 days. This world record has since been eclipsed by fourteen players from Bangladesh, India and Pakistan but Sealy is still the youngest cricketer ever to represent the West Indies in a Test match. He scored a superb 58 on his debut and produced a number of very fine innings thereafter. There can be no question about his ability to bat and to do so in critical situations. At the end of the day, however, he could show a batting average of only 28.11 from his nineteen innings in eleven Tests.

EFFECTS OF FIRST-CLASS INEXPERIENCE
Other classic examples of the result of first-class cricket inexperience are the careers of Learie Constantine and C.R. 'Snuffie' Browne. These two fine all-rounders had the capacity to defeat many a county side entirely single-handed and they often did so. But their approach was totally inappropriate for Test cricket and they consequently left very mediocre statistics indeed as batsmen at this level of the game. Constantine boasted a batting average of 19.24 runs in his 18 Test matches and 'Snuffie' 25.14 in his eight Test innings.

How crucial was this whole question of first-class cricket inexperience and lack of practice was amply demonstrated as late as 1951/52 during the West Indian tour of Australia. In the first Test at Brisbane, on what everyone agreed was a batsman's wicket, the tourists won the toss and succumbed before the end of the first day for 216 runs although only Rae and Walcott, among their specialist batsmen, had failed. No fewer than six of them settled down and reached a promising 20, yet not a single one advanced to a half-century. None of these batsmen, apart from Rae and Walcott who were completely undone by Ray Lindwall's exceptional pace, had really been defeated by the bowler. They had all behaved in the unintelligible manner of proverbial lemmings after batting for about an hour. Not a single partnership yielded 50 runs, although Goddard scored 45, Worrell 37, Weekes 35, Marshall 28 and Gomez 22. If any one of these great players had resolved to occupy the crease for as long as possible, the West Indies could easily have batted themselves into a winning position. In their second innings, five batsmen again exceeded

20 runs; Weekes struck a brilliant 70; Gomez a defiant 55; and Marshall a promising 30. But the West Indies could manage only 245 runs altogether. Had Weekes been patient enough to complete his century, or had Marshall been less anxious to score at breakneck speed, the visitors would clearly have put the match beyond Australia's reach. They lost that Test by 3 wickets and could still have won it had they accepted the many chances provided by the wizardry of Ramadhin and Valentine.

When the West Indies lost the second Test of that series at Sydney, the pattern was distressingly similar. Rae (17), Stollmeyer (36), Worrell (64), Walcott (60), Christiani (76), Gomez (54) and Goddard (33) all settled down and looked, from the Australian point of view, ominously comfortable. Yet each of them suddenly and inexplicably lost his way and the whole side was dismissed for 362 on a batsman's paradise. In their second innings (trailing by 155 runs after some very amateurish out-cricket), six players scored 20 runs or better; Weekes (56), Christiani (30), Gomez (41) and Goddard (57 not out) collared the bowling, but the final tally still fell ten runs short of 300 and the West Indies lost again, this time by seven wickets, having suffered from impatient batting, incompetent fielding, deplorable catching and uninspiring leadership. Years later, Gomez put his finger squarely on the nub of the difficulty when he reflected that if any one of the West Indian batsmen had made a significant score in each of the Tests, the tourists could easily have won the series, which was so much more closely contested than the 4-1 margin indicated. One Test was lost by three wickets and another by one wicket (when the last pair were allowed to scratch and claw their way to a tenth wicket partnership of 38 runs).

These scores and results should never be dismissed as mere details or cricket trivia. They are, in fact, enormously instructive. They tell us very little about 'calypso cricket', even though the Caribbean batsmen had all demonstrated an abundance of attractive strokes. They speak eloquently to the matter of *approach* and *experience*. It is highly unlikely that that same team, opposing the same Australians in 1990, would have lost any of those matches at all. It is not enough simply to say that batsmen the stamp of Christiani, Goddard, Gomez, Marshall, Rae, Stollmeyer, Walcott, Weekes and Worrell were all defective in either temperament or technique, or both. The more telling consideration is that their background, their training and their instincts were not in keeping with the demands of a five-day Test match.

Prior to the 1960s, therefore, the West Indies struggled on what was far from a level playing field. All of their opponents had established local, annual first-class competitions long before the inception of the Caribbean Shell Shield in 1965/66. Regular and organised county cricket in England, for example, went back at least as far as 1873. The Australians began to compete for their Sheffield Shield as long ago as 1892/93, after some 40 years of regular 'inter-colonial' jousting. The Currie Cup competition in South Africa dates back to 1889/90. New Zealand's Plunket Shield competition, replaced by the Shell

The West Indies cricket team during their British tour in 1950. Standing (l-r): W. Ferguson (scorer), C.L. Walcott, A. Valentine, H.H. Johnson, P. Jones, L. Pierre and S. Ramadhin. Seated (l-r): Roy Marshall, R.J. Christiani, G.E. Gomez, J.D. Goddard (captain), E. Weekes, C.B. Williams and A.F. Rae

Trophy competition in 1974, began in 1921/22. India's Ranji Trophy had its origins in 1934/35, while the Pakistanis began their annual quest for the Quaid-E-Azam Trophy in the 1953/54 season. Whatever the quality of the cricket, these competitions taught cricketers how to play at the first-class level for several days on end and the situation was thus very much different from club matches played very casually on weekends.

RESULTS OF EARLY TOURS TO ENGLAND

It is consequently not surprising that the West Indies achieved relatively few successes in Test cricket during the inter-war years. That they were playing good cricket, no one could deny. Their results against English touring teams were generally satisfactory and if their first tours to England in 1900 and 1906 had, on the whole, been disappointing, their results in 1923 were most promising indeed. That summer they played 26 matches, won twelve, lost seven and drew seven. Their success was based to a large extent on Challenor's magisterial batting and the quality of fast bowling produced by George Francis and George John, whom many pundits were then willing to compare with the famous Australian duo of Jack Gregory and Ted McDonald who had wrought such havoc during their tour of England in 1921. Challenor scored 1,556 runs at an average of 51.86 per innings, registering six centuries and finishing third in the national averages behind only 'Patsy' Hendren and Phil Mead. Francis, who had played not a single first-class match prior to the tour but had been personally

15

hand-picked by the captain, H.B.G. (later Sir Harold) Austin, captured 82 wickets at less than sixteen runs each, and the ageing John (now somewhere in the vicinity of forty years old) took 49 at less than twenty.

It was the performance of the tourists during this triumphant summer that led directly to the general conviction that the West Indies deserved serious consideration for Test match status. This impression was strengthened by the performance of the islanders during the MCC tour of the Caribbean in 1925/ 26. This visit was one of the important turning-points in the history of West Indian cricket. It was the first time that the MCC sent out to the islands a team that was almost representative of England's true strength. Led by F.S. Gough-Calthorpe, it included such fine professionals as Ewart Asgill, George Collins, Walter Hammond, Percy Holmes, Roy Kilner, Fred Root, 'Tiger' Smith and F.B. Watson. It was, nevertheless, the first time that an MCC squad would return to England with but two paltry victories to show for its pains.

ADVENT OF THE WICBC

By 1927, West Indian friends in Britain, including Pelham Warner, a native of Trinidad who had been educated at Harrison College in Barbados, were encouraging the islanders to prepare themselves for Test cricket by establishing more formal administrative structures in the region. Similar suggestions were made by Lord Hawke, the president of the Yorkshire County Cricket Club, and the Hampshire captain, Hon. L.H. Tennyson, who was so impressed with Jamaica that he visited that island twice in consecutive winters during 1926-28.

Caribbean cricketers had long felt a need for an establishment of this kind. There was no central organisation to co-ordinate the regular inter-colonial tournaments, to select composite West Indian XIs and to arrange West Indian tours to England and elsewhere. The geography and culture of the Caribbean territories militated against the foundation of a centralised framework. It took all the diplomatic skills of an influential MCC member, Richard Mallett, to bring the territories together immediately after Calthorpe's tour. Mallett was a great friend of West Indian cricket. It was he who had managed their tours to England in 1906 and 1923 and who was destined to manage their first ever visit to Australia in 1930/31. Representatives of the 'Big Four' finally got together, under Mallett's direction, to create the West Indian Cricket Board of Control (WICBC) in 1927.

Social historians still know too little about the formation and early workings of the WICBC. It is known that a small group of wealthy individuals held a preliminary meeting in Bridgetown, Barbados, in 1926 out of which an informal structure (the West Indies Cricket Conference) emerged, holding its first official meeting at the Bridgetown Club on 22 January 1927. This meeting was attended by George Challenor (Barbados), W.E. Dolly (Windward Islands), Fred Grant (Trinidad), R.H. Mallett (England), A.C. O'Dowd (Demerara), Joseph Schoult (Trinidad), Tim Tarilton (Barbados) and C.V. Wight (Demerara). The duties of secretary were performed by H.A. (later Sir Archibald) Cuke of Barbados. In

16

H.B.G. Austin's absence, L.T. Yearwood, vice chairman of the Barbados Cricket Committee, presided. Delegates had been invited from Jamaica and the Leeward Islands but unfortunately were unable to attend.

It was this group of ten, of whom four were Barbadians, who resolved to create the WICBC, which would include a president, a secretary, two delegates each from Barbados, Demerara, Jamaica and Trinidad, and one representative each from the Leeward and Windward Islands. The WICBC's first meeting was held in Port of Spain, Trinidad, on 17 and 18 June 1927, under the presidency of Harold Austin, the Barbadian cricketer who had captained the West Indian teams to England in 1906 and 1923. Also present on that historic occasion were H.N. Leacock and L.T. Yearwood (Barbados), A.C. O'Dowd and O. Webber (Demerara), F.G. Grant (representing Jamaica), A. Cory-Davies and J.G. Kelshall (Trinidad) and C.A. Child (representing the Windward Islands in W.E. Dolly's absence). Unable to send a delegate to the meeting, the Leeward Islands were represented by Yearwood. Jack Kidney of Barbados was appointed the first honorary secretary/treasurer. Thus, as in the January meeting of the short-lived West Indies Cricket Conference, the WICBC was dominated by the Barbadians and the Trinidadians who comprised no fewer than seven of the ten executive members.

Apart from Mallett and Austin, the guiding forces behind the establishment of the WICBC appear to have been the Hon. Laurie T. Yearwood, Fred Grant and Alty O'Dowd. Lacking the necessary financial resources, the WICBC was little more than a small, almost unofficial body, comprised entirely of members of the white elite in the territories. Problems of distance and money often meant that representatives of Jamaica and the smaller islands could not attend meetings that invariably were held in Bridgetown and Port of Spain. The Barbadians and Trinidadians tended consequently to dominate the majority of the early meetings. The WICBC naturally adopted very conservative attitudes from the very beginning and was, in any case, much too weak to impose its will on local clubs or associations. Its main concern in 1927 was preparation for the tour of 1928 which the West Indies were invited to make. It discussed the problem of quotas and attempted to embark on a more progressive policy by arranging a series of trial matches in Barbados between teams from the 'Big Four'.

The WICBC was determined that the West Indies, having now been promoted to full Test match status, should make a good showing in England in 1928. It discussed the important matter of professional fees and agreed to offer £3 per Test match in addition to the weekly allowance of 30 shillings to each member to cover out-of-pocket expenses. It also devised a scheme providing for talent money to be paid to individuals for outstanding feats in first-class games. These decisions marked an obvious advance in West Indies cricket, but they could not bridge the huge gap between hardened county players, accustomed to cricket six days every week, and Saturday amateurs who were afforded too few opportunities for first-class play.

Such enormous handicaps could not be overcome by three trial matches played in Bridgetown during December and January 1927/28. Despite all attempts to avoid the quota system, the structure of the West Indies team that toured England in 1928 was not much different from its predecessors. Among the seventeen players finally chosen were five Barbadians, four Trinidadians, four from British Guiana, and four Jamaicans. This distribution was as even as one could manage, and once again there was no specialist wicket-keeper among the group. No provision having been made for the Leewards and Windwards to participate in the Bridgetown trials, the squad did not include a single player from the smaller islands. The captain had, of course, to be a wealthy white cricketer, whatever his other qualifications, and the lack of funds militated against the selection of more than a few so-called professionals.

TEST MATCH STATUS AT LAST

With too much depending on its veteran players, like George Challenor and Herman Griffith, whose best years were behind them, the team failed to repeat the exploits of 1923. All three of the Tests were easily lost and only five of the 30 first-class matches were won, as against twelve defeats. This was not an auspicious start to West Indian Test cricket, but it must be said in the tourists' defence that they had the ill fortune to confront three England XIs that were very powerful indeed. Even had West Indian fielding been brilliant and its wicket-keeping competent, it is difficult to see how they could have defeated a squad which included such stars as A.P. Chapman, George Duckworth, 'Tich' Freeman, Walter Hammond, Jack Hobbs, Douglas Jardine, Vallance Jupp, Harold Larwood, Herbert Sutcliffe and Maurice Tate. It is difficult to conceive of a stronger England XI than the one which overwhelmed the West Indies at The Oval in August 1928. This same combination, led by Chapman, proceeded in the following winter to defeat the Australians in Australia by a margin of four Tests to one. England thus won seven consecutive Tests before yielding to Australia at Melbourne in March 1929.

Thanks in large measure to the emergence of Donald George Bradman, Australia shortly rebounded from its four straight defeats and so too did the West Indies, who regrouped to square the series against England in the West Indies in 1929/30. They lost the second Test at Port of Spain but won the third at Georgetown and drew the first and fourth. By this time, they had discovered an exceptional talent in George Alphonso Headley, who announced his arrival on the international scene by becoming the first batsman to score four Test centuries in his very first series and to do so before reaching the age of 21. At Georgetown, in February 1930, he also became the first batsman under 21 to register centuries in both innings of a Test match. At Kingston, two months later, Headley scored a superb 223 to save his side from certain defeat in the infamous 'timeless' Test. At twenty years, 315 days, he remained the youngest batsman in the world to score a double-century in a Test innings until Javed

The West Indies cricket team of 1933. Standing (l-r): J.M. Kidney, H.C. Griffith, C. Christiani, I. Barrow, E. Achong, C. Merry, E.A. Martindale, C.A. Wiles, G. Headley. Seated (l-r): G.C. Grant (Captain), C.A. Roach, B. Sealy, V.A. Valentine, O. Dacosta

Miandad of Pakistan accomplished the feat at nineteen years, 141 days, against New Zealand in November 1976.

That the West Indies should have rebounded against England at home in 1929/30 is not at all surprising when the facts are considered. England actually sent two teams abroad that winter, with the other visiting New Zealand simultaneously. This was a clear indication that both the West Indians and the New Zealanders were regarded as no better than second-class opponents at that time. From the side which played in the Caribbean that winter, such stars as Chapman, Freeman, Hammond, Hobbs, Jardine, Larwood, Sutcliffe and Tate (who had inflicted so much pain on the West Indies in 1928) were conspicuously absent. Even so, the arrival of Ivan Barrow, Headley and Sealy seemed to indicate much better prospects for the future.

The huge gap between the West Indies and the established 'Big Two', however, was again demonstrated during their first tour of Australia in 1930/31 when they managed to win only five of their sixteen first-class games while losing eight. They salvaged some of their pride by winning the fifth Test after losing the first four, but their inability to cope with the spin bowling of Clarrie Grimmett and Bert Ironmonger was embarrassingly manifest and Headley, who exceeded 1,000 runs on the tour, was the only batsman who enhanced his reputation. Griffith (at 37) was their most successful bowler and although Constantine enjoyed some triumphant days in the field, his performances in the

Tests were woefully disappointing. The West Indian bowlers tamed the mighty Bradman somewhat by confining him to two centuries in the series but he still managed to average almost 75 runs per innings. Although that was something like 25 runs below par for the great man from Bowral, he would certainly have fared a lot worse, had a simple slip catch off Constantine's bowling been held when he was only four in the third Test at Brisbane. Bradman went on to score 223, then the highest score ever made by an Australian in a Test match at home.

When the West Indies returned to England in 1933, they profited from the brilliant cricket of Headley with the bat and Martindale with the ball. The former scored 2,320 runs at an average of almost 67 per innings and the latter claimed 103 wickets at less than 21 runs apiece. Headley's aggregate that summer still stands as a record for a West Indian batsman touring England and his achievement of seven centuries in a single season was not surpassed by another West Indian tourist until Gordon Greenidge struck nine in 1976. But nine defeats against only five victories in 30 first-class matches was one of the West Indies' worst records while on tour. Their fielding continued to be inept and, with the exception of Headley, their batsmen again failed to cope satisfactorily with the spinning ball. Such was their discomfiture against slow bowling that Charles 'Father' Marriott, in his only Test, was allowed to take eleven wickets for 96 runs with his leg-breaks and googlies at The Oval in August. The whole sad tale allowed *Wisden* to observe that the West Indies "did not convey the impression of being fitted temperamentally for matches of such an important

22 August 1939: Martindale (left) and Sealy leave the Oval each carrying a stump after their match against England on the last day of the last Test before the outbreak of the Second World War

nature". The Test series was easily lost 0-2, with the only bright spot being the drawn encounter at Old Trafford, where the West Indies broke their sequence of four Test losses in England by registering their highest total (375) in that country up to that time.

Notwithstanding the one-sided nature of the 1933 series, England sent a much more powerful squad to the Caribbean in 1934/35 than they had done five years before. Their side included such stars as Leslie Ames, Ken Farnes, Hendren, Hammond, Eric Hollies, Errol Holmes, Maurice Leyland and Bob Wyatt. The West Indies could therefore derive immense satisfaction from their very first triumph in a Test series. At Bridgetown, they lost a truly crazy match which witnessed three declarations and an aggregate of 309 runs on a devilish pitch. Asked to make 73 runs for victory, England stumbled to 48/6 before Hammond and Wyatt saved the day. 'Jackie' Grant, the captain, probably lost this Test by his refusal to bowl Derek Sealy who was well-known in Barbados as 'the best bowler on a bad wicket in the entire world'. He persisted with Leslie Hylton as Martindale's partner in the second innings when the Jamaican speedster was obviously not at his best. While Martindale was capturing 5/22, Hylton's eight untidy overs cost 48 runs and yielded only one wicket. Hammond finally finished the proceedings with a mighty six off the third ball of Martindale's ninth over. This was destined to be the last time that the West Indies would lose a Test match at the Kensington Oval until March 1994.

WINNING AT HOME

The West Indies proceeded to win the second Test at Port of Spain by 217 runs and the fourth at Kingston by an innings and 161. The low-scoring match at Georgetown was marred by rain and left drawn. The victory at Sabina Park was by far their most impressive to date. Their 2-1 success in the series was based again on the excellent bowling of Martindale who captured nineteen wickets for 239 runs (av: 12.57) and the brilliant batting of Headley who scored 485 runs (av: 97.00), including a superb 270 not out at Sabina Park (which remained a West Indian Test record until 1958). Useful contributions also came from Constantine, who took fifteen wickets at just over thirteen runs each, and Sealy who averaged 45 runs in his six innings. This series seemed to mark a turning-point for the West Indies who derived considerable confidence from its result. They could also boast of having confined the leading batsman on the opposing side (Hendren) to a Test average of 28.85. Even the mighty Hammond could do no better than 25.00 from his eight innings, though left unbeaten in one of them.

This increased confidence was shown in their approach to the tour of England in 1939. Even though the West Indies lost again, the competition was much tighter and they were able to avoid defeat both at Manchester and at The Oval. As was usual in those days, they lost at Lord's, but at least they forced the hosts to bat a second time. This tour not only produced much better West Indian fielding than previously but their bowling was more accurate and better balanced. Bertie Clarke, who spun his leg breaks at almost medium pace, supplemented the speed of Constantine, Hylton, Martindale and Tyrell Johnson. He ended the season with 87 wickets and would certainly have captured more than 100 had the season not been curtailed by the imminence of war. For the first time, too, a West Indian touring side managed to win more first-class matches than it lost.

IMPACT OF THE 'GOODWILL' TOURNAMENTS

The traditional gap between England and the West Indies virtually disappeared during the Second World War. While first-class cricket came to a standstill in England, Barbados and Trinidad arranged a series of 'Goodwill Tournaments' which produced more first-class cricket in the West Indies than the region had ever seen previously. The result was the emergence of a galaxy of young stars, such as Robert Christiani, Wilfred Ferguson, Andy Ganteaume, John Goddard, Gerry Gomez, John Lucas, Jeffrey Stollmeyer, Rupert Tang Choon, Kenny Trestrail, Clyde Walcott, Everton Weekes and Frank Worrell, who were destined to form the nucleus of Caribbean Test XIs for almost a decade after the war was over. When the MCC sent a sub-par squad to the West Indies in 1947/48, the result was a sound thrashing (2-0) in the four Tests and the tourists' failure to win a single first-class match.

Thereafter, England never snubbed the West Indies by sending anything but the strongest combination that its selectors could muster. The team that invaded the Caribbean in 1953/54 was, by every measure, one of the most powerful that England ever sent abroad. It included Leonard Hutton (captain), Trevor Bailey, Denis Compton, Godfrey Evans, Tom Graveney, Jim Laker, Tony Lock, Peter May, Brian Statham, Fred Trueman, Johnnie Wardle and Willie Watson. It was good enough to recover from a 2-0 deficit and draw the series with convincing wins at Georgetown and Kingston. Such was England's dominance during the 1950s, that it lost only three of its nineteen Test series during that decade. It defeated Australia at home in 1953 and 1956 and abroad in the winter of 1954/55, to monopolise the 'Ashes' for six years.

For the West Indies, on the other hand, it was a most topsy-turvy decade. It began with a marvellous win (3-1) over England in England in 1950 and included victories over India at home and abroad, New Zealand twice abroad and Pakistan at home. But, on the debit side, the West Indies lost twice very badly to Australia (4-1 and 3-0) and were beaten by England in 1957 by the convincing margin of 3-0. If the 1951/52 Australian defeat had as much to do with faulty scheduling and incompetent captaincy as with lack of first-class experience, the whole period 1954-60 was one of reconstruction. It witnessed the steady decline of the 'Goodwill' players before the new generation of stars had risen to take their place. Thus the team which toured England in 1957, which seemed so strong on paper, suffered more indignities than their supporters had expected. The majority of the tourists (like Nyron Asgarali, Denis Atkinson,

22

The West Indies cricket team in May 1966. Standing (l-r): B. Butcher, J. Hendriks, M.C. Carew, R.C. Brancker, P.D. Lashley, S. Nurse, J. Solomon. Seated (l-r): R. Kanhai, W. Hall, G. Sobers (captain), C. Hunte and L. Gibbs

Ganteaume, Goddard and the three Ws) were either too old or (like Wesley Hall, Rohan Kanhai, 'Collie' Smith and Garry Sobers) too young. When this new crop of superstars matured, the West Indies were able to ascend the cricketing throne for the first time in 1965.

A LEVEL PLAYING FIELD AT LAST

The playing-field was levelled at long last in the mid-1960s. The arrival of the Shell Shield finally meant that the West Indies could participate in regular, annual first-class seasons like all of their competitors. This was the vital prerequisite to the destruction of Saturday afternoon approaches. It also did much to remove regional barriers since it allowed local audiences to watch other Caribbean players whom they might not otherwise have seen. One of the main causes of parochialism in the old days was ignorance. The Barbadians of the inter-war years, for instance, had accepted Headley as an icon because they heard so regularly of his exceptional deeds. But few of them ever saw the great George in action. Almost incredibly, Headley played only three first-class matches, all of them Tests, at the Kensington Oval in Bridgetown throughout his long career. Prior to 1952, Jamaican cricketers had visited Barbados only once – in 1925, before Headley had embarked on his first-class career. Similarly, a player of Herman Griffith's stature would hardly have been known to Jamaicans. Although he was an active first-class cricketer from 1922 to 1941, he played only once at Sabina Park (in the fourth Test against England in April 1930). The first Barbadian tour to Jamaica did not take place until March/April 1947.

Thus, as late as 1955, when Denis Atkinson was chosen to lead the West Indies against the touring Australians, he was hardly known in Jamaica. He had played at Sabina Park only once before, against England in the fifth Test in 1954. The Jamaicans could consequently afford to pooh-pooh his elevation to the captaincy as they regarded him as nothing more than a white nonentity. Similarly, the Barbadians, who had never seen Easton McMorris in action until his selection in 1959/60 against England, could well feel aggrieved at the omission of their own Cammie Smith, who had just led Barbados to a thrilling ten-wicket victory over the MCC. They were all the more upset when the 'Strokeless Wonder' (as McMorris was promptly dubbed) was unfortunate enough to allow himself be run out off a no-ball before he had scored any runs at all.

It was not only the general public who lacked sufficient information on which to make sound judgements. The selectors also suffered from inadequate knowledge. So few first-class matches were being played up to the 1960s, that most reputations were based on performances in club cricket (seen only by local spectators). It is true that the WICBC tried its best to arrange trial matches prior to important tours. Four games, for instance, were arranged in 1950 to help in the selection of the team to England. The matches produced several heroes and may well have helped to confuse, rather than enlighten, the authorities. Such stars, for instance, as Neville Bonitto, Andy Ganteaume, Frank King, John Lucas, Bruce Pairaudeau, Ken Rickards, Leslie Wight and Gerald Wood, the wicket-keeper, all shone brightly. Eventually, however, they were all overlooked.

In the end, the selectors had to follow their instincts and at least in two cases made very fortunate decisions indeed. Faced with having to choose three spinners from among about four or five promising candidates, they selected Ramadhin, Valentine and C.B. 'Boogles' Williams. The last-named was universally considered the finest of the group and was known to be an excellent fielder and an accomplished batsman in the bargain. He had bowled and batted extremely well against Trinidad in 1949 and was the key bowler in the Barbadian victory against British Guiana in 1950. The expectation was that 'Boogles' would play in the majority of the Tests and he seemed to have earned his pick when, in mid-May, he captured seven good MCC wickets at Lord's in 32 searching overs in a single innings.

But Ferguson, who had bowled so well against England in 1947/48, and had captured 9/130 from 53 overs in one of the trials, also seemed an automatic choice. The selectors finally decided on Valentine, even though that twenty-year-old greenhorn had taken only two wickets for 190 runs in 78.2 overs in his two matches for Jamaica against Trinidad. It was his steadiness of length and his ability to impart extraordinary spin, which seemed to have impressed the authorities most. To his everlasting credit, Gomez, who was Valentine's first victim in first-class cricket, pushed for his inclusion at the expense of Ferguson, his own countryman. But the latter had just cause to feel short-changed in 1950

24

Clive Lloyd smashes a boundary during his brilliant century against England at Bridgetown in March 1981

even though Valentine was destined, in the longer run, to achieve greatness as a result of the selectors' gamble. Ramadhin, in the meantime, had seized his opportunity by taking twelve wickets for Trinidad in the two matches against Jamaica at Port of Spain, where he had disguised his googly most wonderfully.

THE SHELL SHIELD AND ITS IMPACT
With the coming of the Shell Shield, selectorial guessing became less necessary. Although it involved only a limited number of matches each season, the new competition at least ensured that a regular player could expect about three or

four first-class games on an annual basis. This would inevitably take him beyond his native shores and provide him with a regional rather than strictly parochial following. While Jamaican cricketers of the calibre of Hines Johnson, Esmond Kentish, Allan Rae and Ken Rickards could complete their distinguished careers without ever having played before a Barbadian crowd, for instance, such an oddity would hardly be possible nowadays.

Regular regional competition, however, is not a guarantee of permanent success. While it facilitates more intelligent selectorial decisions, it cannot manufacture cricketers of unusual quality. Hence the West Indies, like their opposition, have witnessed peaks and valleys since 1965. The early 1960s saw the flourishing of the genius of Basil Butcher, Lance Gibbs, Charlie Griffith, Wes Hall, Conrad Hunte, Rohan Kanhai, Deryck Murray, Garry Sobers and Joe Solomon. From 1962 to 1967, the West Indian squad was consequently unstoppable. But when this mighty generation faded, it took some years before the new crop of stars matured. From 1968 to 1972, the West Indies failed to win a single Test series. They endured a miserable stretch of twenty Tests without a single victory, even though playing at home in fifteen of these, including ten against India and New Zealand, who were not then looked upon as cricketing giants. Sobers was still feared as the world's greatest cricketer and Kanhai was still capable of sporadic brilliance, but they lacked a supporting cast.

The 1970s were years of constant rebuilding, beginning with the tour of England in 1973 when Kanhai led a squad of youngsters from whom a great deal came to be heard in the years that followed. When Gibbs, Kanhai and Sobers finally departed, the Age of Lloyd began. Lloyd himself suffered much at Australia's hands in 1975/76. But he learned many important lessons in that winter of discontent. The Australians taught him the value of physical fitness, mental preparedness, strategic planning and relentless endeavour. They also demonstrated the effectiveness of a three-pronged pace attack. The sheer and single-minded ruthlessness of the Australians left an indelible impression on the young tourists. By 1976, the West Indies had regrouped. For the next two decades, with very few disappointments along the way, they carried all before them.

IN THE VALLEY OF THE SHADOW OF DEFEAT

These peaks and valleys can actually be charted statistically. The statistics which appear at the end of this book will clearly demonstrate that the individual career records of West Indians in recent years can bear no comparison to those which prospered during the Glory Years. The apparently inexhaustible supply of cricket talent has run dry in the Caribbean and we are still waiting for the worthy successors of Lloyd and Richards, Greenidge and Haynes, Ambrose, Marshall and Walsh.

While the Age of Lloyd and the Age of Richards were years (1975-90) of unexampled success, the whole period since 1995 has been one of acute suffering. The West Indians still perform reasonably well in the Caribbean, but they have continued to flounder miserably abroad. Between 1996 and 2003,

The magnificent Viv Richards in action against England at Trent Bridge in July 1991

The West Indies team looks on during the third Test against Australia in May 2003 at the Kensington Oval in Bridgetown

they played 39 Tests away from home, winning only seven and losing 28. The main cause for these embarrassments has been the batting. Apart from Brian Lara and Richie Richardson, the West Indies have produced no world-class batsman during the last twenty years. Ramnaresh Sarwan has shown signs of immense talent but he is still a year or two away from full maturity. Nor has the present crop of fast bowlers, numerous as it is, maintained the exceptionally high standards set during the previous thirty years. The West Indies are suffering from the simple fact that Mervyn Dillon is their leading speedster. While he is an honest toiler belonging to the category of the good, he cannot yet be elevated to the status of the great. Perhaps the young and promising Jermaine Lawson, who was adjudged the player of the series against Bangladesh in December 2002, may develop into a superior fast bowler within the next few years after he has done some remedial work on his suspect action. The recent emergence of Fidel Edwards and Tino Best provides further cause for guarded optimism.

But there is no reason to despair. Sporting fortunes have always tended to be cyclical. Even with the withdrawal of such sponsors as Shell and Red Stripe, the regional competition has continued and several important infrastructures have been developed in the last ten years. West Indian pessimists must remember that there were no professional cricket coaches, centres or academies in the Caribbean when such stars as Headley, Kanhai, Richards, Sobers and the Three Ws descended upon the land like manna from heaven. Fortunate accidents like these tend to repeat themselves all over the world. By the time other chroniclers emerge in 2028 to write about West Indian Test cricket after 100 years, the prevailing mood may well be much more positive than it is now.

CHAPTER TWO

BARBADOS

NO COUNTRY IN THE WORLD HAS BEEN AS TOTALLY ADDICTED TO the game of cricket as Barbados. Excellence in cricket is such a vital element in the Barbadian ethos and tradition that cricket defeats of Barbadian or West Indian teams are viewed by Barbadians as national disasters. This emphasis on a peculiarly English sport dates back to the 19th century when British soldiers, administrators, priests and educators took cricket to Barbados and made it an almost compulsory feature of the curriculum in the leading secondary schools. Such academic institutions as Codrington College, Combermere School, Harrison College and the Lodge School gave the game a certain respectability that it might otherwise have lacked and their alumni gradually founded a host of cricket clubs all over the island. Before the Victorian age was over, churches and businesses had also become involved in the promotion of cricket as by far the most effective instrument in the process of character-building and socialisation.

Not surprisingly, therefore, Barbados, despite its diminutive size, has always been at the forefront of cricket in the West Indies. The island is very small, even by West Indian standards. It is only 166 square miles in extent and its population is approximately 265,000. To appreciate the magnitude of the Barbadian cricket saga, one has only to consider that Jamaica is 25 times as large and almost nine times as populous; the republic of Trinidad & Tobago is almost twelve times as large and almost five times as populous; and Guyana, with three times the number of inhabitants, is almost five hundred times the size of Barbados. The Barbadians, nevertheless, have consistently dominated the regional tournaments and have won and/or shared the territorial championship no fewer than eighteen times in the 38 years since the inception of annual competition. By way of interesting comparison, Guyana and Jamaica have won the Caribbean title only six times each and the republic of Trinidad & Tobago can boast of only four championships won or shared since 1966.

THE TRADITION ESTABLISHED
This unusual dominance began, ominously, in 1865 when the first inter-colonial match was staged in the West Indies. Barbados defeated British Guiana by 138 runs at Bridgetown by restricting the tourists to scores of 22 & 38. When the first triangular tournament was arranged in the West Indies in 1891, Barbados won that very easily, too. Trinidad, in fact, did not defeat Barbados at all until

1901, in a triangular tournament at Georgetown, and it took Jamaica until 1958 to achieve its very first victory over Barbados. The Barbadians performed so well against English touring teams after 1895 that it became known worldwide that the island was almost invincible at home. When the MCC won an exciting match at Bridgetown by one wicket in 1954, that was the first time in almost 50 years that an English squad had defeated Barbados at the Kensington Oval.

Such were the foundations of that awesome reputation that gave Barbados an honoured place among the so-called 'Big Four' which came to dominate West Indian cricket until the 1970s. The tiny island in the eastern Caribbean had to have its quota of four or more players when West Indian teams were being selected for overseas tours. When, for instance, the West Indies toured England for the first time in 1900 – despite the unavailability of such stars as H.B.G. Austin, Gussie Cox and Hallam Cole – four Barbadians still made the journey: William Bowring, Percy Cox, Percy Goodman and Delmont Hinds. In fact, there were no fewer than six Barbadian natives in the party of fifteen, since Tommie Burton (representing British Guiana) and Joseph 'Float' Woods (representing Trinidad) were also included.

Neither Bowring nor Hinds accomplished a great deal that summer. The former, in fact, might never have made the trip at all, but he was thought to be familiar with English conditions having been educated at Sherborne and Marlborough. As a specialist batsman, his first-class career was undistinguished: 38 runs (av: 4.75) from five matches. Much more disappointing was the performance of 'Fitz Lily' Hinds who had been such a successful player at home. An excellent right-handed all-rounder for the Spartan Cricket Club, he had just won the Challenge Cup Competition for his team almost single-handedly. But he failed to adjust to English conditions and captured only six wickets on the entire tour. Nor did he shine with the bat. He was much more successful in the Caribbean, where, in twelve first-class matches during 1900-1902, he registered 366 runs (av: 20.33), 29 wickets (av: 15.00) and ten catches.

Percy Cox, an attractive right-handed batsman, gave a much better account of himself in 1900, scoring 755 runs (av: 30.20), including a spectacular 142 against Surrey at The Oval. Unfortunately for him, however, the West Indians were not accorded first-class status that season so these runs do not appear in his first-class career record. In nineteen first-class matches during 1896-1906, Cox made 417 runs (av: 13.90), took seventeen wickets (av: 16.29) and held 21 catches. These statistics fail to do justice to the talents of a cricketer who, in January 1900, did most to ensure a Barbadian victory over British Guiana by seven wickets when he top-scored with 70 out of 191 on a very difficult strip and also captured six wickets for 39 runs from twenty overs.

Percy Goodman was the greatest batsman produced by Barbados prior to the advent of the precocious Challenor in 1906. At the highest level available to him at that time, he scored 1,824 runs, including five centuries, at an average of 30.91 per innings. He was also a fine right-arm bowler of medium pace who claimed 88 first-class wickets (av: 13.58) in forty matches during 1891-1913. A brilliant fieldsman, he also held 47 catches. Percy would obviously have left a more significant mark on the international stage had Test cricket come sooner to the West Indies. In 1900, he was everywhere recognised as the best batsman in the Caribbean. During his first tour of England, he played several fine innings, including a splendid 104 not out at Derby. In 1906, Goodman led the tourists with a first-class batting average of 31.94. His aggregate of 607 runs included two superb centuries: 102 not out against Yorkshire and 107 at Northamptonshire's expense. Allowed only 63.2 overs during the tour, he claimed eight wickets for 232 runs. It is noteworthy that Goodman played a key role in all three of the first-class triumphs achieved by the tourists that summer. In addition to the matches against Northamptonshire and Yorkshire, they won the one against Scotland at Edinburgh when Percy (44 not out) guided them to victory by four wickets.

BARBADIANS IN ENGLAND, 1906

When the West Indies returned to England in 1906, and were accorded first-class status there for the first time, Barbadian natives accounted for exactly half of the team of fourteen. The side was led by Austin and included Keith Bancroft, George Challenor, Percy Goodman (again) and Oliver Layne. In addition, Burton went once more as a representative of British Guiana and Archie Cumberbatch replaced Woods as Trinidad's 'professional'. Burton, Cumberbatch and Woods were among the finest fast bowlers ever produced by Barbados but they were excluded from the local Challenge Cup Competition in those days simply because of their class and colour. They never played a single match for their native colony and they had to emigrate from Barbados in order to become eligible for selection to West Indian teams!

Harold Austin looms large in the history of Caribbean sport. He is still universally regarded as the father of West Indian cricket. He captained the team to England in 1906 and did so again, at the age of 46, in 1923. He was also one of the founders of the WICBC in 1927 and served as its president for many years. A product of Harrison College, Austin was an attractive right-handed batsman, a useful right-arm bowler of medium pace off-cutters, an accomplished wicket-keeper and a good fieldsman. By all accounts, he was also a thoughtful and inspiring captain who became a most effective administrator when his playing days were over. In a first-class career that lasted from 1895 to 1928, he scored 2,643 runs (av: 28.42), took fifteen wickets (av: 20.13) and effected 48 dismissals, including three stumpings. Like all of the important pioneers of his generation, however, Austin never had a chance to play Test cricket for the West Indies, but he left an indelible stamp on the game, nevertheless. He personally hand-picked George Challenor (then only eighteen years old) for the English tour of 1906; and in 1923, he insisted upon the selection of Learie Constantine and George Francis despite their inexperience.

Keith Bancroft was one of the finest wicket-keepers ever produced by Barbados and he too would have left a more lasting impact on the game had he emerged at a different time and in a different place. But his first-class career encompassed only fourteen games, including twelve during the tour of 1906 when he scored 266 runs (av: 15.64). A useful right-handed batsman, his finest moment came against Kent at Catford in July when he struck a courageous 53 in a losing cause. Bancroft also accounted for twenty dismissals, including six stumpings, during his first-class career. Oliver Layne was a very promising right-handed all-rounder who recorded 465 runs (av: 23.55) and 34 wickets (av: 24.08) in 1906. Among the tourists, he was one of the most consistent players that summer with both the bat and the ball. His brightest moment came against Essex at Leyton when he scored a valiant 106. He also played two fine innings (63 & 50) against Yorkshire. His best bowling yielded 6/74 in the very first match, against Dr W.G. Grace's XI at Crystal Palace. Layne's career lasted from 1901 to 1913. He played in 27 first-class matches, recording 1,023 runs (av: 22.23), 91 wickets (av: 22.36) and nineteen catches. He would have played much more often, however, had he not been designated a 'professional' and, as such, was ineligible for participation in the inter-colonial matches of those days.

Easily the brightest young star of the 1906 touring team was George Challenor who had impressed Austin with three defiant innings against Trinidad in two low-scoring matches at Port of Spain that January. He made 684 runs (av: 28.50) that summer and achieved his maiden first-class century against a strong Nottinghamshire attack at Trent Bridge. Challenor justified the predictions of Austin and W.G. Grace by developing into one of the finest batsmen in the world during the 1920s. A majestic driver of the ball, this aggressive right-handed opening batsman became the role model for several generations of Caribbean stroke-players. He reached his peak during the tour of England in 1923 when he accumulated 1,556 runs at an average of 51.86 per innings. For almost thirty years, Challenor was one of the bulwarks of Barbadian cricket and was the first of his countrymen to exceed five thousand first-class runs. Test cricket, however, came too late for him. He was almost forty years old when he undertook the tour of England in 1928. He thus had the opportunity to play, in the twilight of his career, in only three Tests. His six Test innings yielded only 101 runs (av: 16.83). In 24 matches that season, he did manage to exceed 1,000 runs again, but he failed to register a single century and averaged only 27.53. Even so, the great George is still everywhere considered the father of modern West Indian batsmanship. It was his superb batting in 1923, as much as any other single factor, which earned the West Indies Test match status in 1928. He was also a very good fieldsman and a useful right-arm medium pace bowler, good enough to capture 54 first-class wickets (av: 23.88) in 95 matches.

BARBADIANS IN ENGLAND, 1923

When Austin led the third West Indian team to England in 1923, it contained no fewer than five Barbadians. Apart from Challenor and the captain himself, the squad included George Francis, Harry Ince and Percy 'Tim' Tarilton. Incredibly, Francis, a practice bowler at the Pickwick nets, had had no previous first-class experience, although he was clearly good enough to have represented Barbados from at least as early as 1920. Austin simply felt that his style was suited to English conditions. The more obvious choice, of course, was Herman Griffith, an alumnus of Combermere. But he was well-known to be much less docile than Francis, who could be relied upon to do exactly as he was told without questioning the captain's judgement.

Austin's intuition proved to be uncannily accurate. Francis combined with Trinidad's George John to form a fearsome combination. He captured 82 wickets that summer at less than sixteen runs apiece. He played a vital role in Surrey's defeat, taking 10/76 and sharing a tenth wicket partnership of 130 runs with Challenor. His 41 on that occasion showed that he was a much better than average lower-order batsman. Unfortunately, however, Francis looked jaded during the tour of 1928, at the age of 31, and failed to reproduce the same form. His 56 wickets that summer cost him 31.96 runs apiece and he was able to garner only six (av: 42.00) in the three Tests. He rebounded to take 6/109 against England at Georgetown in February 1930 when the West Indies secured their first ever Test victory, and he captured eleven Australian wickets (av: 31.81) in five Tests in 1930/31. But by 1933, his first-class career was over. Altogether, George Nathaniel Francis was an excellent right-arm fast bowler, one of the best in the world at his peak. His misfortune was to have emerged at the wrong time. Debarred from inter-colonial competition, he played only 62 first-class matches altogether, scoring 874 runs (av: 12.85) and claiming 223 wickets (av: 23.13). He also held 42 catches. It is a sad reflection on the ethics and morals of his time that Francis, one of the greatest of all Barbadian fast bowlers, should have represented his native colony on only four occasions. Test cricket came too late for him and he took part in only ten Tests for the West Indies, claiming 23 wickets (av: 33.17). He is still remembered as the first in an impressive line of Caribbean fast bowlers in Test cricket.

Neither Ince nor Tarilton got a chance to play Test cricket and neither of them performed with distinction in England in 1923. They were, nevertheless, two of the finest batsmen in the Caribbean during the inter-war years. Ince was a stylish left-handed stroke-player who, while still in his teens, struck a magnificent 167 at Port of Spain in 1913 for a composite West Indian XI against MCC. In fifteen matches for Barbados, he registered 754 runs (av: 47.12) but so disastrously did he bat in England in 1923 that his career average, from 35 first-class games, could finish no higher than 29.39 runs per innings. Older pundits still consider Harry Ince the finest Barbadian left-handed batsman prior to the emergence of Garry Sobers.

33

Tim Tarilton was the most consistent opening batsman in the West Indies for an extremely long time (1905-1930). He established a long-standing record of 1,885 runs (av: 53.85) for Barbados and had the distinction of achieving the first triple-century in Caribbean regional competition. He combined with Challenor to form the greatest pair of Barbadian opening batsmen until the advent of Gordon Greenidge and Desmond Haynes in the late 1970s. But in 1923 (at the age of 38), Tarilton could manufacture only 554 runs (av: 21.30) in England. His only innings of note that season was an unbeaten 109 at Trent Bridge when he and Challenor put on 219 in the second innings without being separated.

BARBADIANS IN ENGLAND IN 1928
In 1928, the West Indians made their fourth trip to England. Once again there was a sizeable contingent of Barbadians among the seventeen cricketers selected: Lawson Bartlett, C.R. 'Snuffie' Browne, Challenor, Francis, Herman Griffith, E.L.G. Hoad and J.M. Neblett. The notorious 'quota' system was still in vogue, but as Browne and Neblett had emigrated to British Guiana, Barbados was considered not to have exceeded its fair share of representatives. Thus, without much rancour, four Barbadian natives could be selected for the first ever Test match involving the West Indies. This contest occurred at Lord's against England in June. Francis had the distinction of bowling the first ball for the West Indies and Challenor of scoring the first run. But though Francis bowled well to take 2/72 from 25 overs and Challenor (29) shared a solid opening stand of 86 with Jamaica's Frank Martin, the West Indies lost their inaugural Test by an innings and 58 runs.

Griffith and 'Snuffie' also participated in this historic match. The former was a great right-arm fast bowler who should definitely have been selected in 1923 when at his peak. Now, at 34, he had lost some of his pace (but not his wits) and bowled intelligently enough on a batsman's paradise to take 2/78 from 29 overs while England were amassing 401. Griffith was a very good fieldsman and a courageous lower-order right-handed batsman who once shared a West Indian record tenth-wicket stand of 138 runs with Teddy Hoad. In the twilight of his career, he played thirteen Tests for the West Indies, recording 44 wickets (av: 28.25), 91 runs (av: 5.05) and four catches. He was the most successful West Indian bowler in that 1928 series with eleven wickets (av: 22.72), including a brilliant 6/103 in the third Test at The Oval.

Griffith, however, was much less effective when he returned to England in 1933 at the age of 39. He played in two Tests without much success (3/92) and seemed a spent force. This was markedly different from his performance in 1929/30 when, in the first ever Test series in the West Indies, he claimed sixteen wickets (av: 31.75) against England. He also headed the West Indian Test averages with fourteen wickets (at 28.07 runs each) during the first West Indian tour of Australia in 1930/31. Had Test cricket come earlier to the West Indies,

George Challenor (left) and Mannie Martindale (right): The finest batsman and fast bowler produced by Barbados before the Second World War

Herman Clarence Griffith would definitely have done much better than he was allowed to do in his late thirties. He pioneered the use of a four-pronged pace attack when he captained Empire in the Barbados Cricket Association competition during the 1930s. He then combined with 'Mannie' Martindale, C.D. 'Pampie' Spooner and E.A.V. 'Foffie' Williams to form the most fearsome quartet of speedsters ever to appear in Barbadian club cricket. Herman had a very sharp cricketing brain and might have proved himself an excellent Test captain had he been given the opportunity.

'Snuffie' Browne was the most dangerous all-rounder produced by the West Indies prior to the emergence of Learie Constantine. He was an attacking right-handed batsman, a brilliant fieldsman and a right-arm bowler of leg-breaks at a brisk medium pace. He bowled 22 quite tidy overs for 53 runs during that Lord's Test in 1928 and then achieved scores of 10 & 44, but failed to save his side from disaster. 'Snuffie' toured England in 1923 and 1928 and eventually played four Tests, scoring 176 runs (av: 25.14) and taking six wickets (av: 48.00). If these statistics look somewhat modest, it has to be borne in mind that he was almost 38 years old when the West Indies played their inaugural Test. Ironically, 'Snuffie' reserved his very best cricket for those games in which he represented British Guiana against his native Barbados during the late 1930s.

Teddy Hoad was selected for the second Test against England at Old Trafford in July 1928. He failed (13 & 4) and gave way to Lawson Bartlett who accordingly made his debut at The Oval in August. Hoad resurfaced to captain the West Indies in the very first Test played on Caribbean soil in January 1930. He was a careful right-handed batsman and a right-arm leg-break and googly bowler. He headed his team's batting average with 765 runs (av: 36.42) in 1928 and exceeded 1,000 runs on his second tour of England in 1933 but his Test record was unimpressive. In four matches at this level, he managed only 98 runs (av: 12.25) and one catch. Hoad, nevertheless, was one of the most difficult batsmen in the Caribbean to dislodge and averaged more than 38 runs per innings from his 63 first-class matches. He also captured 53 wickets (av: 36.28) and held 26 catches in a long career that lasted from 1921 to 1938.

Bartlett was an elegant right-handed batsman who was prevented by injury from doing ample justice to his talents during the 1928 summer. He made a better showing in his tour of Australia in 1930/31 when he captivated the spectators with a stylish 84 at Adelaide in the first Test. But his form declined thereafter and he earned only five Test caps altogether, scoring 131 runs (av: 18.71) and accepting two catches.

BARBADIAN STARS OF THE 1930s

Two Barbadians, J.E.D. Sealy and L.A. Walcott, made their Test debuts during the winter of 1929/30. Both appeared in the Bridgetown Test which also featured E.L.G. Hoad (the captain), 'Snuffie' Browne and Herman Griffith. Derek Sealy, still a student at Combermere, was only seventeen years, 122 days old when the Test began. That remains a West Indian record. It also stood as a world record until 1954. Sealy acquitted himself extremely well with a cultured 58 in the first innings. He was an attractive right-handed batsman, a very good right-arm medium-fast bowler, a brilliant fieldsman and a useful wicket-keeper. He eventually represented the West Indies in eleven Tests, making 478 runs (av: 28.11), capturing three wickets (av: 31.33) and effecting seven dismissals, including one stumping. He toured Australia in 1930/31 and England in 1939 but was surprisingly omitted from the team which visited England in 1933. An almost unplayable bowler on sticky wickets, he once demolished a strong Trinidad XI at Bridgetown taking 8/8 in 55 deliveries.

Leslie A. 'Bessie' Walcott played only one Test, scoring forty runs for once out and claiming one wicket for 32 runs. His first-class career record is not spectacular: 555 runs (av: 30.83), sixteen wickets (av: 29.50), eight catches and one stumping. But he made a most vital contribution to West Indian cricket by serving as an influential cricket master, from 1921 to 1947, first at Harrison College and then at the Lodge School. A competent right-handed all-rounder who could also keep wicket, Walcott was a great source of inspiration to such budding young cricketers as Bartlett, Lionel Birkett, Michael Frederick, John Goddard and Roy Marshall – all of whom were destined to represent the West Indies in Test cricket.

Lionel Birkett enjoyed a very successful Test debut against Australia at

Adelaide in December 1930. He achieved scores of 27 & 64 in a losing cause and shared a defiant opening partnership of 58 with Clifford Roach of Trinidad in the first innings. But the rest of his Test career was disappointing. In four such matches for the West Indies, he scored 136 runs (av: 17.00), claimed one wicket for 71 runs, and took four catches. This seems an unexpectedly small return for a cricketer who once struck a forceful 253 for Trinidad against British Guiana. A right-handed batsman and right-arm bowler of medium pace, Birkett had the rare distinction of representing British Guiana and Trinidad as well as Barbados in first-class cricket.

While five Barbadians (Bartlett, Birkett, Francis, Griffith and Sealy) made the trip to Australia in 1930/31, only three of them, quite surprisingly, were taken to England in 1933: Griffith, Hoad and 'Mannie' Martindale. The ageing Archie Wiles, a fourth Barbadian native, was selected as a representative of Trinidad, whither he had migrated several years earlier. The star of this contingent was the fiery Martindale, then one of the fastest bowlers in the world. 'Mannie' showed his class by taking fourteen wickets (av: 17.92) in that short series in the face of some inept catching and fielding on the part of his colleagues. He ended the season with 103 first-class wickets at less than 21 runs apiece. He took nineteen more wickets in four Tests against England in 1934/35 and ended his career with 37 wickets (av: 21.72) in his ten Tests for the West Indies. Martindale was also a reliable fieldsman and a useful lower-order right-handed batsman who once struck a swashbuckling 134 for Barbados against Trinidad and shared a West Indian record eighth-wicket partnership of 255 runs with E.A.V. 'Foffie' Williams. He was the greatest fast bowler produced by the West Indies before the advent of Wes Hall in the 1950s.

A RARE SLUMP

When England toured the West Indies in 1934/35, Barbados was in the midst of an unusual slump. Only three Barbadians consequently took part in the four Tests: George Carew, Martindale and Derek Sealy. Martindale and Sealy made vital contributions to the first series' victory achieved by the West Indies. The former enhanced his reputation as one of the world's greatest fast bowlers and the latter was unfortunate to enter the nineties twice without achieving a Test century. He top-scored with 92 in the first innings of a winning effort at Port of Spain and shared a crucial stand of 202 runs with George Headley in another winning cause at Kingston. While Headley finished with an unbeaten 270, Sealy was bowled by G.A.E. Paine for 91. That partnership stood as a West Indian record for the third wicket against England until 1950 when Frank Worrell (261) and Everton Weekes (129) added 283 at Trent Bridge.

Carew was an aggressive right-handed opening batsman who began his Test career with a smashing hook off a Ken Farnes bouncer, only to be brilliantly caught just inside the boundary by E.R.T. Holmes for nought. For such audacity he was promptly consigned to oblivion for the next thirteen years. When he reappeared, at Port of Spain in February 1948, he struck a brisk 107 in an entertaining opening partnership of 173 with Trinidad's Andy Ganteaume that stood as a West Indian record for the first wicket against England until Roy Fredericks and Lawrence Rowe achieved 206 at Kingston in 1974. Carew's career statistics are eminently satisfactory: 2,131 runs (av: 34.37) in 39 matches. But as the West Indies came to depend, immediately after the Second World War, more and more upon Jeffrey Stollmeyer and Allan Rae, Carew was eventually restricted to four Tests, in which he scored 170 runs (av: 28.33).

Four Barbadians accompanied Rolph Grant to England in 1939: C.B. Clark, Martindale, Sealy and E.A.V. Williams. Clarke, Martindale and Sealy played in all three Tests while Williams appeared only in one. Martindale, at thirty years old, was but a shadow of his former self; but Sealy showed surprising competence as a reserve wicket-keeper. Bertie Clarke was a resourceful right-arm leg-break bowler who would certainly have exceeded 100 first-class wickets that summer had the campaign not been curtailed because of the imminence of war. In the three Tests, he claimed 6/261 and would have left a more substantial legacy had his Test career not been interrupted by the Second World War.

'Foffie' Williams survived the war to launch a memorable assault on Jim Laker in the latter's Test debut at Bridgetown in January 1948. In the second innings, after Laker (7/103) had wrought much havoc in the first, 'Foffie' began with six, six, four, four off his first four balls from the Surrey spin bowler and reached a dazzling 72 in just over an hour. Williams was an aggressive right-handed batsman, a very good right-arm fast bowler and an excellent fieldsman. He played cricket with such obvious zest that he remained a Barbadian legend until his death, at 83, in 1997. In his four Tests for the West Indies, he recorded 113 runs (av: 18.83), nine wickets (av: 26.77) and two catches.

THE FIRST BARBADIAN CAPTAIN OF DISTINCTION

While most of the cricketing world stood relatively still during the war years, Barbados and Trinidad participated in a number of so-called 'Goodwill Tournaments'. This provided the young players from both islands with greater opportunities than usual to come to the fore. Hence the emergence, in the early 1940s, of John Goddard and the 'Three Terrible Ws', among a host of other Barbadians. Goddard, who made his Test debut in the same match as Laker, was an attacking left-handed batsman, a brilliant fieldsman, and a dangerous right-arm bowler of off-cutters at medium pace. As he was white and wealthy, he was naturally earmarked for the captaincy virtually from the beginning of his Test career. After playing one match under Headley's leadership and another under that of Gerry Gomez, he was appointed captain for his third Test and proceeded to lead the West Indies in their next fifteen Tests. He led them to victory (2-0) against England in the West Indies in 1947/48 and then became the first player to lead the West Indies to a series' triumph (1-0) against India in India in 1948/49 and against England (3-1) in England in 1950.

J.D. Goddard, captain (left), and G.E. Gomez during the tour to England in April 1950

Before the disastrous tour of Australia in 1951/52, Goddard had thus established himself as one of the most successful captains in cricket's history. He won six of eleven matches while losing only once. In Australia, however, Goddard came to grief when he placed too much faith in Sonny Ramadhin and Alfred Valentine and failed to make effective use of his faster bowlers. The West Indies lost that series 1-4. They could just as easily have won it 3-2, however, had they taken some routine catches and shown more patience at the crease. In 1957, too, Goddard had the misfortune to encounter a very powerful England. The West Indies lost that series conclusively (0-3) and could easily have been whitewashed had it not been for some cautious captaincy on Peter May's part on the last day at Birmingham and some courageous batting from 'Collie' Smith on the final day at Trent Bridge. Altogether Goddard captained the West Indies in 22 Tests, winning eight, losing seven, and drawing seven. His own personal statistics were very creditable also: 859 runs (av: 30.67), 33 wickets (av: 31.81) and 22 catches from 27 Tests. In 111 first-class matches during 1936-58, he recorded 3,769 runs (av: 33.35), 146 wickets (av: 26.33) and 95 catches.

Although it has become fashionable in recent years to regard John Goddard as just another one of the old white captains, his contribution to West Indies cricket was enormous. He provided effective leadership during that very important period that followed the Second World War and he continued to serve as a Test selector for several years after his retirement as an active player. Nor should it ever be forgotten that he was one of the best all-rounders of his generation who scored more runs (1,221) and more centuries (4) in the 'Goodwill' games (1941-45) than any other West Indian cricketer.

Clyde Walcott hitting out during the West Indies match against E.W. Swanton's XI at Eastbourne in April 1957

THE FEARSOME 'W FORMATION'

Much of Goddard's success as a Test captain rested on the magnificent batsmanship of the dreaded 'W Formation' which emerged during the war years. Clyde Walcott, Everton Weekes and Frank Worrell, all of whom were eventually knighted for their services to cricket, were three of the finest batsmen in the world during the 1950s. Worrell came to the forefront first, having established a monstrous world record by participating in two separate 500-run partnerships. He also starred against England in 1947/48 with 294 runs (av: 147.00) in three Tests. After a 'cultured' 97 in his debut at Port of Spain, he struck a superb 131 not out at Georgetown. Against England in 1950, he enhanced his reputation by amassing 539 runs (av: 89.83), including a marvellous 261 at Trent Bridge which was then the highest score ever achieved by a West Indian in a Test match on English soil. Worrell eventually played 51 Tests for the West Indies, scoring 3,860 runs (av: 49.48), including nine centuries, taking 69 wickets (av: 38.72), and claiming 43 catches. He was an elegant right-handed batsman, a first-rate left-arm bowler of either spin or pace, and a reliable fieldsman. In a first-class career that involved 208 matches and stretched from 1942 to 1964, he registered 15,025 runs (av: 54.24), 349 wickets (av: 28.98) and 139 catches.

Frank Worrell is best remembered, however, as one of cricket's greatest captains. He led the West Indies in fifteen Tests, winning nine and losing only three. Such was the impression he created upon the Australians in 1960/61 that they instituted the Frank Worrell Trophy for which Australia and the West Indies have been contending ever since. He was the first in a long line of Black captains who moulded the West Indies into a very powerful force in international cricket.

Everton Weekes in action against Cambridge University in June 1950 when he achieved 304 not out, his highest score in first-class cricket

Worrell was not only an inspirational leader, but he was among those pioneers who sought to bring the smaller islands (like Antigua, Dominica and St Vincent) more directly into the mainstream of Caribbean cricket. He also fought fiercely against elitism, racism and regionalism, effectively ensuring the abandonment of the dubious system of 'quotas'. It was Worrell who demonstrated that the West Indian team could be much more than the sum of its individual parts. He insisted on mental alertness as well as physical fitness and thus transformed the West Indies from a loose band of 'Calypso' cricketers into a clinically professional outfit. Worrell thus came to serve, almost inevitably, as the role model for later captains such as Garfield Sobers, Rohan Kanhai, Clive Lloyd and Vivian Richards.

Everton Weekes started rather more slowly than Worrell and was actually dropped for the fourth Test against England at Kingston in 1948. Hastily recalled when George Headley proved unfit, he made the most of his second chance by smashing his way to an innings of 141 which he followed up with four successive centuries at India's expense. His five consecutive Test centuries still constitute an important world record and is one of the oldest of all surviving cricket records. Weekes was a dashing right-handed batsman, a brilliant fieldsman, and an occasional bowler of right-arm leg-breaks. He eventually played in 48 Tests for the West Indies, registering 4,455 runs (av: 58.61) and striking fifteen

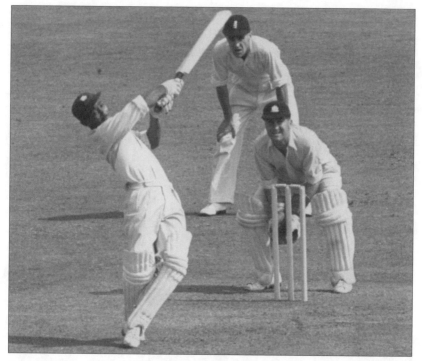

Frank Worrell in action during his excellent innings of 261 against England at Trent Bridge in July 1950

centuries. These stood as West Indian records for some years. He also held 49 Test catches, the most by a West Indian fieldsman until the advent of Sobers. Weekes was a very important cog in the West Indies' Test machine during the 1950s and one of the most popular role models as a professional cricketer. Several younger players, such as Conrad Hunte and Seymour Nurse, deliberately patterned their style and method after his.

Clyde Walcott was an aggressive right-handed batsman, a very good wicket-keeper and a steady right-arm bowler of medium-fast inswingers and off-cutters. He served as the West Indies' No. 1 wicket-keeper from 1948 until his back broke down during the tour of Australia in 1951/52. Although he kept wicket for only his first fifteen Tests, he achieved the remarkable West Indian record of eleven stumpings (which still stands triumphantly after more than fifty years). Altogether, he accounted for 64 dismissals in his 44 Tests and this stood as another record for the West Indies until surpassed by Deryck Murray. Walcott's batting improved significantly after he abandoned the gloves. He enjoyed an astonishing run of fifteen Tests during 1953-55 when he scored 1,982 runs, including ten centuries, at an average of 82.58 per innings. He ended his Test career with 3,798 runs (av: 56.68) and eleven wickets (av: 37.09).

Walcott also shared with Weekes the West Indian record of fifteen Test centuries (until Sobers achieved his sixteenth in 1966). He was one of the very

The versatile Frank Worrell resorting to left-arm spin during the match against Surrey at The Oval in May 1950

best batsmen thus far produced by Barbados, but his contribution to West Indies cricket went far beyond simple arithmetic. He did wonders for the game in British Guiana during the 1950s and 1960s when, as Cricket Organiser and Coach on the Estates of the British Guiana Sugar Producers' Association, he moulded the Guyanese into a powerful cricketing force and helped in the development of such fine players as Basil Butcher, Lance Gibbs, Alvin Kallicharran, Rohan Kanhai, Clive Lloyd, Ivor Mendonca, Joseph Solomon and Charlie Stayers. He then served West Indian cricket in an administrative and managerial capacity for several years. Sir Clyde Walcott also had the distinction of being elected the first non-white president of the International Cricket Council, and was the first president after the decision was made to rotate the presidency and remove it from being an English preserve.

The Three Ws ensured that West Indies cricket generally prospered during the period 1948-64. Serious losses were endured at the hands of England and Australia, it is true, but significant victories were also accomplished against England, India, New Zealand and Pakistan. Indeed, the tour of England in 1950 was a real turning-point in West Indies cricket as it marked the first occasion on which they were able to defeat England in England. The Barbadian contribution to this triumph was immense. Goddard and the Three Ws accounted for twelve wickets and more than 1,200 runs, including four of the six West Indian centuries, in the four Tests that summer. Between them, they also held 24 catches while Walcott effected three stumpings during the series.

OTHER BARBADIAN STARS OF THE 1950s

The Barbadian contingent, in fact, consistently formed the nucleus of West Indian XIs for many years after the Second World War. To India in 1948/49, Goddard took with him Denis Atkinson and George Carew in addition to Walcott and Weekes. The campaign was totally dominated by the two Ws, each of whom exceeded 1,000 runs with ease, with Weekes actually compiling 779 runs (av: 111.28) in the five Tests. Carew, already 38 years old, did not have a particularly good tour. In twelve matches he scored 690 runs (av: 38.33) but saw action in only one Test match, in which he managed only twenty runs in his two innings.

While the tour of the sub-continent marked the end of Carew's active participation in first-class cricket, it was the start of a successful Test career for Atkinson, a promising right-handed all-rounder. A brilliant fieldsman anywhere, he was a steady medium pace bowler and an attacking batsman. He made his Test debut at Delhi in November 1948 and eventually played 22 Tests for the West Indies, making 922 runs (av: 31.79), taking 47 wickets (av: 35.04) and holding eleven catches. Atkinson enjoyed his greatest match in 1955 when, at Bridgetown against Australia, he held the fort with Clairemont Depeiza in an incredible seventh-wicket record partnership of 347 runs. His own contribution to this miracle was a sparkling 219. In the second innings, he saw the West Indies to safety with a further twenty not out. On an unresponsive pitch, which yielded 1,661 runs for 36 wickets, he also returned the remarkable match analysis of 84.2/30/164/7.

It was in this series against the Australians in 1955 that Denis Atkinson was pitchforked into the captaincy of the West Indies at a time when the WICBC frowned on the notion of Black leadership. He handled a delicate situation with great tact and actually lifted his game to a higher notch, scoring 311 runs (av: 44.42) and taking thirteen wickets (av: 35.30) in four Tests. He continued his inspired play against New Zealand in 1955/56, recording 183 runs (av: 36.60) and sixteen wickets (av: 14.56). Against Australia and New Zealand, Atkinson led the West Indies in seven Tests, winning three, losing three, and drawing one.

When John Goddard led the West Indies to England in 1950, five other Barbadians accompanied him. In addition to the Three Ws, the squad included Roy Marshall and C.B. 'Boogles' Williams. Neither of the latter played a Test that summer, but Marshall (who exceeded 1,000 runs) eventually was selected for four Tests against Australia and New Zealand in 1951/52. His Test record is modest: 143 runs (av: 20.42), no wickets and one catch. Roy Marshall, however, proved his worth as a stalwart in county cricket after his emigration to England. He was a dashing, right-handed opening batsman, a useful right-arm off-spinner and a superb fieldsman. He would most certainly have played very often for the West Indies during the 1950s had he not thrown in his lot with Hampshire. He became one of the most consistent batsmen in England during 1955-72.

Completely overshadowed by Sonny Ramadhin and Alfred Valentine, poor 'Boogles' never played in a Test match for the West Indies. He was an accomplished right-handed batsman, a very good right-arm leg-break and googly bowler and a reliable fieldsman. In 1950, he claimed 31 wickets (av: 27.61) and scored 152 runs (av: 10.85). Williams ended his career with 987 runs (av: 29.02), 75 wickets (av: 29.10) and 27 catches in 37 first-class matches. His best bowling performance earned him seven wickets for 55 runs in 32.1 overs against MCC at Lord's in May 1950, and his finest innings was a truly masterful 133 against E.W. Swanton's XI at Bridgetown in March 1956.

When the West Indies toured Australia in 1951/52, six Barbadians made the trip: Goddard (captain), Atkinson, Marshall, Walcott, Weekes and Worrell. When India visited the Caribbean in 1952/53, the Ws accounted for more than 1,500 runs, including six of the eight West Indian centuries, in the five Tests. Weekes established a West Indian record against India by registering 207 in the first Test at Port of Spain. Worrell eclipsed that mark with 237 at Kingston in the fifth. A much longer lasting record was Weekes' aggregate of 716 runs (av: 102.28). No other cricketer has yet scored that many runs in a Test series against India in the Caribbean.

Another Barbadian, Frank King, also made a useful contribution in this series. A fiery right-arm fast bowler, he captured seventeen wickets (av: 28.23) and went on to score 116 runs (av: 8.28), take 29 wickets (av: 39.96) and hold five catches in fourteen Tests. He would have done considerably better had his colleagues been more alert in the field and had the West Indies possessed another fast bowler of real quality to accompany him. King's contribution to the development of cricket in the Caribbean went beyond these modest statistics. As a member of the ground staff at Combermere School, he created an indelible impression on such youngsters as Rawle Brancker, Peter Lashley and Wesley Hall, all of whom were destined to tour England with Sobers in 1966. It was King's classical action that Hall tried so desperately to emulate.

When Len Hutton led England to the West Indies in 1953/54, he found resistance from no fewer than seven Barbadians in that Test series. He had to contend with Atkinson, Michael Frederick, King and Sobers as well as Walcott, Weekes and Worrell. Frederick, a right-handed opening batsman who had emigrated to Jamaica, made 0 & 30 in the first Test and lost his place in the XI. But the three Ws again produced more than 1,500 runs between them, including five centuries, while Atkinson averaged more than forty runs per innings. Although he bowled with great fire and hostility, King claimed only eight wickets (av: 30.87). In the fifth Test, a seventeen-year-old Sobers made a great impression on his debut, claiming 4/75 in an innings of 414 and producing scores of fourteen not out & 26 in a match which the West Indies lost by nine wickets.

Garry Sobers bowling at a match in Arundel on 30 April 1966

THE INCOMPARABLE SOBERS

Garry Sobers was a magnificent left-handed batsman, a versatile left-arm bowler who could produce every conceivable type of delivery, and a fantastic fieldsman, especially close to the wicket. His abundant skills kept the West Indies close to the top of the cricketing world for two decades. His aggregate of 8,032 runs (av: 57.78) in 93 matches made a mockery of all previous West Indian Test records, as did his 26 centuries and 109 catches. Universally considered the greatest all-rounder in the history of the sport, he also captured 235 Test wickets (av: 34.03). Sobers played a key role in the defeat of Pakistan in the West Indies in 1957/58, England in England in 1963, 1966 and 1973, Australia in the West Indies in 1964/65, India in the West Indies in 1961/62 and India in India in 1958/59 and 1966/67. He succeeded Worrell as captain after 1964 and led the West Indies in 39 Tests, winning nine, losing ten, and drawing twenty. If this record looks somewhat modest now, it is really because the West Indies endured a period of slump during 1968-72 when the older stars retired before adequate replacements could be found and too much had therefore to depend on the versatility of the captain himself.

The all-conquering Australians, too, found their stiffest resistance from the Barbadian phalanx when they invaded the Caribbean for the first time in 1955. Barbadians occupied six of the first seven places in the West Indian batting averages and scored eight of the nine West Indian Test centuries. No fewer than eight of them actually participated in the third Test at Georgetown: Atkinson (captain), Depeiza, King, Norman Marshall, Sobers, Walcott, Weekes and Worrell. This proved to be Marshall's lone chance. He was a very steady

46

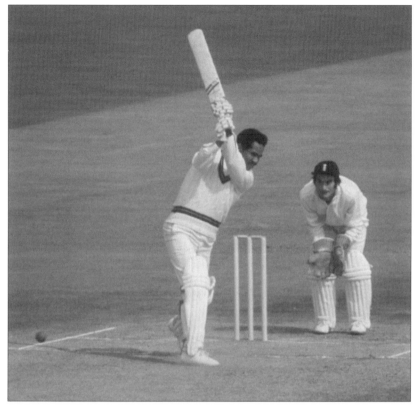

Garry Sobers in action during his marvellous century against England at The Oval in August 1973. It was his 26th (and last) hundred in Test cricket

right-arm bowler of medium pace off-breaks, almost unplayable on a responsive pitch, a hard-hitting right-handed batsman and a useful fieldsman. He scored only eight runs in his two Test innings, but his bowling, as usual, was very accurate. In a losing cause, he returned the remarkable match analysis of 2/63 from 46.3 overs, of which 21 were maidens. It was not for nothing that Roy's elder brother was known throughout Barbados as 'Maiden Marshall'.

Clairemont Depeiza achieved much greater fame. This stylish right-handed batsman was also an accomplished wicket-keeper. He etched his name indelibly in the record books by taking part with Atkinson in a wonderful seventh-wicket stand that yielded 347 runs and saved the West Indies from certain defeat. His share was an attractive 122. Curiously, however, he was discarded after only five Tests, from which he extracted 187 runs (av: 31.16) and eleven dismissals, including four stumpings. 'Deep' would have been a very useful member of the West Indian squad which toured England in 1957 when, for several games, Kanhai was asked to carry the gloves. It is possible that the WICBC considered Barbados to have exhausted its quota of representatives when Goddard took Atkinson, Wes Hall, Sobers and the Three Ws with him that summer.

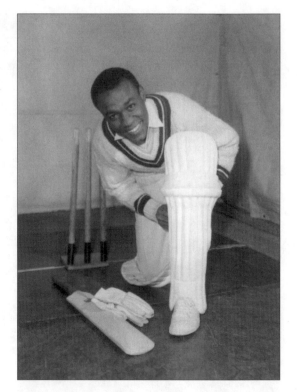

Conrad Hunte padding up for some batting practice at Alf Glover's Cricket School, London, in January 1963. He was the finest opening batsman produced by the West Indies prior to the advent of Gordon Greenidge

HUNTE & HALL

Such a fine right-handed opening batsman as Conrad Hunte, who would clearly have strengthened the team in 1957, thus had to wait until 1957/58 to make his Test debut. He did so in great style by scoring a superb 142 against Pakistan at Bridgetown. In his third Test, at Kingston, he struck a brilliant 260 and shared a mammoth second-wicket stand of 446 with Sobers who established a world record with an unbeaten 365. Their partnership, which fell five runs short of the record that Don Bradman and Bill Ponsford had established in 1934, still stands as the best ever achieved for the West Indies. Hunte scored 622 runs (av: 77.75) in his first Test series and went on to register 3,245 runs (av: 45.06), including eight centuries, and sixteen catches in 44 Tests. He was by far the best opening batsman produced by the West Indies up to his time. Hunte was very successful in his two tours of England in 1963 and 1966 and was a vital member of the West Indies XI until his retirement in 1967. He served as vice-captain both to Worrell and to Sobers during the 1960s and played a pivotal role in the historic tour of Australia in 1960/61. He was also one of the brightest stars in the team which defeated Australia for the very first time in 1964/65, when he scored 550 runs (av: 61.11) in the series.

Eric Atkinson, Denis' younger brother, also made his debut in the Bridgetown Test against Pakistan in January 1958. He bowled extremely well in three Tests in that series, claiming 12/307 from 127 overs. He enjoyed a

Fast bowler, Wes Hall in the practice nets in April 1966. He was the greatest of all West Indian fast bowlers up to his time

great match at Kingston where, on a pitch that yielded 1,406 runs for 23 wickets, he managed to capture 8/78 in 39 overs. Atkinson was a very good right-arm medium-fast bowler, who was among the very first to experiment with what later became known as 'reverse' swing. He was a hard-hitting right-handed batsman and a brilliant fieldsman. He toured India with the West Indies in 1958/59 and ended his Test career with 126 runs (av: 15.75), 25 wickets (av: 23.56) and two catches in eight games.

One outstanding Barbadian star emerged during the West Indian tour of the sub-continent in 1958/59. He was Wesley Winfield Hall, one of the greatest fast bowlers in cricket's history. He had toured England with Goddard in 1957 but had not adjusted properly to English pitches and conditions. Now, at 21 years old, he came into his own, capturing no fewer than 46 wickets in eight Tests (av: 17.76) against India and Pakistan. He proceeded to bowl with sustained hostility and enthusiasm for the next ten years. He made two more tours to England in 1963 and 1966 and another to India in 1966/67. Altogether, in 48 Tests for the West Indies, 'Big Wes' claimed 192 wickets (av: 26.38). This stood for some years as a West Indian record. He was also a safe fieldsman and an aggressive right-handed batsman who scored 818 runs (av: 15.73), including two half-centuries, and held eleven catches. Hall was a great source of inspiration to a whole new generation of fast bowlers who descended upon the Caribbean almost as soon as he himself retired. He continued to make important contributions to West Indies cricket by managing several touring teams and serving the WICB as a Test selector. In 2001 he was elevated to the presidency of the WICB.

Robin Bynoe was one of five Barbadians who toured India and Pakistan in 1958/59. He was a sound right-handed opening batsman and a magnificent fieldsman close to the wicket. His first-class statistics are very good: 3,572 runs (av: 41.05) and 45 catches in 56 matches; but he was allowed only four Tests altogether – even though the West Indies were desperately searching in the early 1960s for a regular opening partner for Hunte. Bynoe certainly ought to have been taken to England in 1963 and 1966, but was inexplicably neglected. His Test record thus makes disappointing reading: 111 runs (av: 18.50), one wicket for five runs, and four catches. It is supremely ironic that Bynoe, who was an excellent batsman against fast bowling but well-known to have been less comfortable against spin, should have been asked to play all of his four Tests against India and Pakistan in two tours there.

BARBADIAN STARS OF THE 1960s
Two Barbadian cricket stars shone brightly during the 1960s: Charles Christopher Griffith and Seymour MacDonald Nurse. The former was a fearsome right-arm fast bowler who made his debut against England at Port of Spain in March 1960 and went on to capture 94 wickets (av: 28.54) in 28 Tests for the West Indies. He was especially dangerous during the tour of England in 1963 when he took 32 wickets (av: 16.21) in five Tests and made a telling contribution to the West Indian triumph by the margin of 3-1. He was much less successful after 1965 when distracted by the constant controversy over the legality of his bowling action. By the late 1960s, he had become a spent force and achieved little in his tour of Australasia in 1968/69. At their peak, Griffith and Hall formed the most effective pair of new-ball bowlers in their era and seemingly paved the way for that long line of tearaway fast bowlers who came to dominate Caribbean cricket for the next thirty years. A sound fieldsman, Griffith took sixteen Test catches. He was also a capable lower-order right-handed batsman who made 530 Test runs (av: 16.56). He became a very useful cricket administrator after his retirement.

Nurse was a stylish right-handed batsman who had to wait in the wings for many years as the West Indies then possessed so many very good middle-order batsmen. But he made excellent use of his chances when they finally arrived. He was already 26 years old when he made his debut against England at Kingston

Seymour Nurse (above) seen here in April 1963, and Charlie Griffith (left) pictured in 1966

in February 1960. He began with scores of 70 & 11, but was still promptly discarded, not to be recalled until the second Test against Australia in 1961. Nurse, nevertheless, scored 2,523 beautiful runs in his 29 Tests for the West Indies. He struck six centuries, including two doubles, and averaged 47.60 per innings. A reliable fieldsman, he also held 21 catches. He made a huge contribution to England's defeat in 1966 when he amassed 501 runs (av: 62.62) and shared a record fifth wicket stand of 265 runs with Sobers at Leeds. His finest results were achieved at New Zealand's expense in 1968/69 when he registered 558 runs (av: 111.60) in the final three Tests of his career. This left many pundits convinced that Nurse retired much too early. He gave valuable service to the Barbados Cricket Association (BCA) as an administrator and a coach after his retirement.

Barbados was still such a powerful force in Caribbean cricket that Worrell took with him to Australia in 1960/61 no fewer than six of his compatriots: Hall, Hunte, 'Peter' Lashley, Nurse, Cammie Smith and Sobers. With the notable exception of Nurse, they all had the good fortune to participate in the memorable tied Test at Brisbane. Lashley was a careful left-handed batsman, a very good fieldsman and a useful right-arm leg-break bowler. He was a prolific scorer for Barbados in regional competition but his Test career was limited to four games in which he recorded 159 runs (av: 22.71), one wicket for one run, and four catches. He then became one of the finest administrators in the history of Barbadian cricket, masterminding the Instant Money Game, a national lottery, which boosted the BCA finances for many years. Smith was a very dangerous right-handed opening batsman and an accomplished wicket-keeper. His Test career, too, was brief: five matches, 222 runs (av: 24.66) and five dismissals. He might perhaps have enjoyed a few more Tests had it not been for the presence of another Barbadian, David Allan. After his retirement as an active player, Smith gave many years of faithful administrative service to the BCA, the WICB and the ICC.

Allan was an excellent wicket-keeper and a capable right-handed batsman. But as he was also competing with Jackie Hendriks of Jamaica and Deryck Murray of Trinidad, his Test career was no more extensive than Smith's: five matches, 75 runs (av: 12.50) and eighteen dismissals, including three stumpings. Allan was the finest wicket-keeper produced by Barbados before the emergence of David Murray in the 1970s. He toured England with the West Indies in 1963 and 1966 but ended up as the reserve wicket-keeper on both occasions, after a splendid debut against India at Bridgetown in March 1962 when he scored an impressive forty not out and accounted for no fewer than five dismissals.

Five other Barbadians represented the West Indies at the Test match level during the 1960s: Richard Edwards, Vanburn Holder, D.A.J. Holford, John Shepherd and A.W. White. 'Prof' Edwards was a lively right-arm fast bowler who played in five Tests towards the end of the decade, scoring 65 runs (av: 9.28) and taking eighteen wickets (av: 34.77). Using Eric Atkinson as his role model, he experimented with 'reverse' swing and made better use of the old ball than many of his contemporaries. He enjoyed one particularly successful match against New Zealand at Wellington in March 1969 when he claimed 7/126 in just under 36 overs. Edwards continued to make useful contributions to Caribbean cricket after his retirement by specialising in the preparation of pitches. His interesting work at the Kensington Oval has resulted in the fact that only one Test match has been left drawn at Bridgetown since 1977.

John Shepherd, a right-handed all-rounder who played most of his cricket for Kent, gained only five Test caps for the West Indies. His contribution to the cause was modest: 77 runs (av: 9.62), nineteen wickets (av: 25.21), and four catches. Tony White, another right-handed all-rounder, had an even more brief Test career. He played two matches against Australia in the West Indies in 1965, registering 71 runs (av: 23.66), three wickets (av: 50.66) and one catch. On the surface, this does not appear very impressive, but White did play a crucial role in the first ever West Indian victory against Australia in the Caribbean. At Kingston, in the first Test, he top-scored with a courageous 57 not out in the first innings when his side was struggling to make 239 on a lively pitch. He then took 3/48 in 29.5 overs to help Hall (9/105) restrict the opponents to scores of 217 & 216.

Much more substantial were the Test careers of Vanburn Holder and David Holford. The latter was a very capable right-handed batsman, a clever right-arm leg-break bowler and a brilliant fieldsman. He made his debut against England at Manchester in 1966 and represented the West Indies in 24 Tests altogether. He scored 768 runs (av: 22.58), claimed 51 wickets (av: 39.39), and held eighteen catches. His greatest moment came at Lord's in 1966 when he conspired with his famous cousin, Sobers, to frustrate England's hopes. Just when it seemed that the West Indies were in full retreat, they added 274 runs for a record unbeaten sixth-wicket partnership. Holford continued to contribute to West Indian cricket, long after his retirement as an active player, by serving as a Test selector. He has also performed admirably in recent years as the intermediary between the WICB and the West Indian Cricket Players' Association.

Holder was a very good right-arm medium-fast bowler, a fine fieldsman and an attacking lower-order right-handed batsman. He made his debut, like John Shepherd, against England at Manchester in 1969 and remained a regular member of the squad until 1976. In forty Tests, he gathered 682 runs (av: 14.20), 109 wickets (av: 33.27), and sixteen catches. Holder was the consummate professional, willing to bowl for long and tidy spells with the old ball or the new without complaint or fanfare. His most successful series occurred in 1974/75 when, in four Tests, he claimed seventeen Indian wickets for 315 runs (av: 18.52). As he was much less flamboyant than most of his colleagues, pundits tend to forget that Holder was a very fine player indeed and that he was only the third Barbadian bowler (following Hall and Sobers) to exceed 100 wickets in Test cricket.

BARBADIAN HEROES OF THE 1970s
Apart from Vanburn Holder, the outstanding Barbadian Test cricketer of the early 1970s was Keith David Boyce, a right-arm fast-medium bowler, a hard-hitting right-handed batsman and a magnificent fieldsman, especially in the deep. Playing 21 Tests for the West Indies, Boyce registered 657 runs (av: 24.33), sixty wickets (av: 30.01) and five catches. He played the leading role in the West Indian triumph over England in 1973, capturing nineteen wickets (av: 15.47) in the three Tests. In the first one at The Oval, he claimed 11/147 in 43.1 overs after hitting a sparkling 72 in the first innings. Boyce also made an enormous contribution to the West Indian triumph in the first (Prudential) World Cup in 1975.

In the 1970s, at a time when the West Indies' selectors were becoming increasingly partial to men of speed, two Barbadian spinners of right-arm off-breaks surfaced: Tony Howard and Albert Padmore. They were naturally restricted to very few Test appearances and even though Padmore toured with West Indian teams to Australia, England and India, he was selected for only two Tests. In frustration, he led a rebel tour to South Africa in 1982 and effectively put an end to his Test career. Howard, even less fortunate, had to be content with a single Test against New Zealand in April 1972. On a featherbed pitch he toiled for 62 overs to take 2/140 before the tourists declared at 543/3. That was the best bowling performance for his side, but he was never chosen again.

An entirely different challenge faced two of the three unrelated Barbadian

Greenidges, Alvin and Geoffrey, at this time. The right-handed opening batsmen had to contend with superior competition in the shape of Roy Fredericks, Gordon Greenidge and Desmond Haynes. Alvin was thus limited to six Tests and Geoffrey to five. The former scored 222 runs (av: 22.20) and the latter 209 (av: 29.85). In different circumstances, they would obviously have accomplished a great deal more.

A similar misfortune befell a pair of extremely good Barbadian right-arm fast bowlers, Sylvester Clarke and Wayne Daniel. They were among the finest and most feared speedsters in the world throughout the period 1975-90 but found themselves eclipsed by such great stars as Colin Croft, Joel Garner, Michael Holding, Malcolm Marshall and Andy Roberts. Clarke was therefore restricted to eleven Tests, 172 runs (av: 15.63), 42 wickets (av: 27.83) and two catches. Daniel also had to be content with ten Tests even though, like Clarke's, his bowling record was eminently satisfactory. He took 36 wickets at 25.57 runs apiece. Clarke and Daniel terrorised English county batsmen during the 1970s and 1980s and were good enough to have represented every other country at that time. The former took 942 first-class wickets at an average cost of 19.52 runs per wicket, and Daniel ended his stellar career with 867 (av: 22.47).

Two other Barbadian Test cricketers of this generation who also felt stifled by the competition and eventually went off to South Africa in 1982, were David Murray (the son of Everton Weekes) and Collis King. The former was a sound right-handed batsman and a very competent wicket-keeper who found himself too often in Deryck Murray's shadow. Operating for years as a reserve wicket-keeper, he played in nineteen Tests, scoring 601 runs (av: 21.46) and accounting for 62 dismissals, including five stumpings. King was a very aggressive right-handed batsman, a steady right-arm medium-fast bowler and a brilliant fieldsman. In his nine Tests for the West Indies he scored 418 runs (av: 32.15), including one century, took three wickets (av: 94.00) and held five catches. In eighteen One-Day Internationals (ODIs), he registered 280 runs (av: 23.33), eleven wickets (av: 48.09), and six catches. King's most memorable contribution to the West Indian cause was made in 1979 when he produced a dazzling 86 off 66 deliveries to lead his side to a convincing victory over England in the World Cup Final at Lord's.

GARNER & MARSHALL

Notwithstanding any of the above, the four greatest cricketers produced by Barbados during the 1970s were Joel Garner, Gordon Greenidge, Desmond Haynes and Malcolm Marshall. Two modern pavilions (the Marshall & Garner Stand and the Greenidge & Haynes Stand) have recently been erected in their honour at the Kensington Oval. All four of them enjoyed lengthy and productive careers and contributed enormously to that golden streak of 29 unbeaten Test series which began in 1980 and did not end until 1995. Garner was a huge right-arm fast bowler, an exceptionally agile fieldsman for a man of his gigantic

The 'Big Bird', Joel Garner, in action during the One Day International against England at Lord's in May 1980. This was not one of his better days, as he failed to take a wicket in his 10.3 overs and the West Indies lost by three wickets

size, and a useful lower-order right-handed batsman. The 'Big Bird' appeared in 58 Tests between 1978 and 1987, claiming 259 wickets (av: 20.97), holding 42 catches, and scoring 672 runs (av: 12.44). He was one of the most accurate and dangerous fast bowlers in the history of the game. He did most, with 31 wickets (av: 16.87), to defeat the Australians in the Caribbean in 1983/84. Against England in England in 1984, he also claimed 29 wickets (av: 18.62) and his 27 wickets against England in the West Indies in 1985/86 cost only 16.14 runs each. Garner was also a major contributor to the West Indian triumph in the 1979 World Cup Final with a return of 5/38 from eleven solid overs. In fact, he was one of the most successful of all bowlers in One-Day Internationals. In 98 ODIs, he claimed 146 wickets (av: 18.84). This remained a West Indian record for some years. After his retirement, Garner continued to serve Caribbean cricket in the capacity of a selector.

Malcolm Marshall, another right-arm fast bowler, was arguably the greatest

September 1983: Malcolm Marshall of the West Indies runs in to bowl during an Asda Challenge Cup match at the Festival in Scarborough, England

of all West Indian bowlers. In 81 Tests, he captured 376 wickets (av: 20.94), including five or more in a single innings on 22 occasions and ten or more in a single match four times. These were all West Indian records when Marshall retired from Test cricket in 1991. Among West Indians, only Curtly Ambrose (405) and Courtney Walsh (519) have so far been able to capture more wickets. Marshall's bowling average, with the solitary exception of Shaun Pollock's, is still the best among all bowlers with more than 200 Test wickets. He was the spearhead of the West Indian attack from 1982 to 1990 and won many a match by the magnificence of his bowling. He was particularly devastating against England in the summer of 1988 when he claimed 35 wickets at less than thirteen runs each. In ODI competition, he was equally effective, taking 157 wickets (av: 26.96) in 136 such games to break the mark that Garner had set. Marshall was also an accomplished right-handed batsman and a very good fielder. He accumulated 1,810 Test runs (av: 18.85), including ten half-centuries, and held 25 catches. Just before his premature death in 1999, he had begun to make a further contribution to Caribbean cricket by serving as a coach.

THE GREENIDGE & HAYNES STAND

It is not at all surprising that the Barbadian officials should have decided, very soon after these two superstars retired, to erect the Greenidge & Haynes Pavilion in Bridgetown. They were, after all, the two most successful opening batsmen ever produced by the West Indies. Greenidge was a particularly violent striker of the ball, especially off the back foot. In 108 Tests, he registered 7,558 runs (av: 44.72) and struck nineteen centuries, including four doubles, a West Indian record (eclipsed so far only by Brian Lara). A brilliant slip fielder, he took 96

Gordon Greenidge batting aggressively in the World Cup semi-final against Pakistan at The Oval in June 1983

catches. Greenidge and Haynes invariably gave the West Indies a solid start, sharing no fewer than sixteen century stands in 89 Tests together. They established the present West Indian record opening partnership when they began with 298 against England at St John's, Antigua, in April 1990. Seven years earlier, on the same sward, they had achieved the West Indian first-wicket record partnership against India with a stand of 296. An unbeaten first-wicket partnership of 250 runs at Georgetown in March 1984 produced another West Indian record, this time against Australia. In addition to these exploits, Greenidge also mustered 5,134 runs (av: 45.03) and 45 catches in 128 ODIs, playing a key role in the World Cup triumphs of 1975 and 1979.

Desmond Haynes represented the West Indies in 116 Tests during 1978-94 and scored 7,487 runs at an average of 42.29 per innings. After launching his career with successive innings of 61, 66 and 55 in his initial two matches

Desmond Haynes, one of the finest opening batsmen of the modern era

against Australia in the West Indies, he proceeded to register eighteen centuries and an additional 36 scores in excess of fifty. Haynes became an even more prolific run-getter in ODI competition, achieving an aggregate of 8,648 runs (av: 41.37) which stood for some years as a world record. His seventeen centuries also served for some time as the best in this version of the game. His 238 appearances in ODIs still constitute a West Indian record as well.

LESSER LIGHTS

Within the past two decades, Barbados has been noticeably less fruitful in the production of West Indian stars. Milton Small, a right-arm fast bowler, had to wait for one of the leading speedsters to become injured in order to gain selection. He thus appeared in only two Tests. In one of them, against England at Lord's in 1984, he made a noteworthy contribution to the West Indian victory by taking 3/40 in twelve hostile overs in the second innings. Thelstone Payne, a very capable left-handed batsman, served for an eternity as a reserve wicket-keeper in the long shadow cast by Jamaica's Jeffrey Dujon. Eventually, he received a single chance, against England at Port of Spain, in March 1986. He scored five runs and effected five dismissals but that was the end of his Test career. Carlisle Best, a brilliant slip fielder and an attractive right-handed opening batsman, was unable to dislodge either Greenidge or Haynes and therefore had to settle for eight Test selections. He scored 342 runs (av: 28.50) and took eight catches. The highlight of his career was a magnificent 164 against England at Bridgetown in April 1990. Receiving more opportunities in ODI competition, he scored 473 runs (av: 24.89) in 24 games.

During the early 1990s, two more very capable Barbadian right-arm fast bowlers, Anderson Cummins and Ezra Moseley, surfaced briefly but could not command regular berths on the West Indies' Test XI. Moseley bowled with great fire and too little luck in two Tests against the Australians in 1990/91. He took six wickets for 261 runs before a series of unfortunate injuries brought a premature end to his first-class career. Cummins eventually appeared in five Tests, capturing eight wickets (av: 42.75) and scoring 98 runs (av: 19.60). He was also a useful lower-order right-handed batsman. Because of his all-round skills, he came to be seen as something of an ODI specialist and was allowed to appear in 63 such matches, recording 459 runs (av: 15.30) and 78 wickets (av: 28.79).

The most promising among the Barbadian Test cricketers who emerged in the early 1990s were Courtney Browne, Sherwin Campbell and A.F.G. Griffith. Browne was an accomplished wicket-keeper and a useful right-handed batsman, but his inconsistency meant that he had to share the gloves with Junior Murray of Grenada and David Williams of Trinidad after Dujon's retirement. Allowed fourteen Tests altogether, he recorded 263 runs (av: 17.53), 63 catches and one stumping. His additional contribution to the West Indian cause amounted, in 28 ODIs, to 187 runs (av: 12.46), forty catches and six stumpings.

The left-handed Adrian Griffith occasionally displayed the temperament

59

and the technique that seemed to suggest that the West Indies had found a satisfactory opening batsman at long last. But he proved unreliable. In fourteen Tests, he scored 638 runs (av: 24.53) and lost his place. Campbell, with whom Griffith established a West Indian record opening partnership of 276 against New Zealand in December 1999, appeared for a while to be a worthy successor to Greenidge and Haynes. But he too lost his form and his confidence and had to be discarded. Even so, his Test record looks creditable enough: 52 matches, 2,882 runs (av: 32.38) and 47 catches. In ninety ODI matches, Campbell registered 2,283 runs (av: 26.24).

The on-going search for a reliable opening batsman led to the selection of the hard-hitting Philo Wallace, but he too disappointed. He struck some heavy blows against England in the Caribbean in 1997/98 but came to considerable grief in South Africa in the very next winter. In seven Tests, Wallace could muster only 279 runs (av: 21.46) and nine catches. His ODI record reads: 33 matches, 701 runs (av: 21.24) and eleven catches.

SLIM PICKINGS OF LATE

It is very disconcerting to reflect that Barbados has not produced a Test player of world class since the retirement of Haynes in 1994. There was some hope, in the mid-1990s, that Roland Holder or Floyd Reifer might step forward to fill the gaping void left by the departure of Gus Logie and Richie Richardson. Reifer established a West Indian record by scoring 756 runs in the 1996/97 Red Stripe Cup season, but, when given his chance, could manufacture only 63 runs (av: 7.87) in four Tests. His ODI record, 31 runs (av: 15.50) in two matches, was equally poor. Holder was a brilliant fieldsman and an attractive right-handed batsman who scored very heavily in first-class cricket at the regional level. During the late 1990s, he was offered eleven Test caps. He produced 380 runs (av: 25.33) and nine catches and was dropped. For some time before that, he had been used primarily as an ODI specialist, scoring 599 runs (av: 23.96) in 37 games.

Seven Barbadian fast bowlers, Tino Best, Pedro Collins, Corey Collymore, Vasbert Drakes, Fidel Edwards, Ottis Gibson and Patterson Thompson, have also been tried in recent years. Drakes, who had been selected for seventeen ODIs during the 1990s, was for a long time ineligible for Test selection as his South African contracts prevented him from appearing often enough in local competition. Suddenly, however, he has been reinstated and earned his very first Test cap, against Bangladesh in December 2002, at the age of 33. In eight Tests so far he has recorded 229 runs (av: 20.81) and 28 wickets (av: 32.25). A useful all-rounder, there is hope that Drakes will buttress the tail which has signally failed to wag for a very long time. A thoughtful and steady bowler, he has already claimed fifty wickets (av: 24.58) in ODI competition.

There is, however, no hope for Thompson, who faded rapidly into oblivion after taking five wickets (av: 43.00) in two Tests. Gibson's case is the same. In fifteen ODIs, he claimed 34 wickets (av: 18.26), but his three wickets in two

Vasbert Drakes celebrates after taking a wicket during day two of the first Test against Australia played at Bourda Oval in Georgetown on 11 April 2003

Test matches cost him a prohibitive 275 runs. Collymore is more promising, but he is too prone to injury and has so far played only in five Tests, taking 24 wickets (av: 23.20). Collins has fared considerably better, capturing 55 wickets (av: 40.32) in nineteen Tests. He bowled so well against India and Bangladesh in 2002 that there was good reason to hope that he could develop into a regular Test player. Recently, however, his place has been challenged by Tino Best and Fidel Edwards. The former played one Test against Australia at Bridgetown in May 2003, and came to considerable grief (0/99); but Edwards justified the selectors' faith in him by becoming the first West Indian to capture five wickets in an innings in each of his first two Tests. So far, in three Tests against Sri Lanka and Zimbabwe, Edwards has claimed fourteen wickets (av: 23.07) and scored 24 runs (av: 8.00). His dogged defence against Zimbabwe at Harare saved West Indies from certain defeat.

The most promising of the new crop of Barbadian cricketers is Ryan Hinds, potentially a useful left-handed all-rounder. He has thus far appeared in four

Tests and scored 162 runs (av: 23.14). This, on the surface, seems to be a fairly ordinary start, but he did look quite composed in two cultured innings against Pakistan at Sharjah in his first Test series. As he once took nine wickets in a single Busta Cup innings, he may also develop into a left-arm spinner of some value. He is only 22 years old and can be expected to reach his peak within the next few years.

FINAL ANALYSIS

If the Barbadian performance has been relatively mediocre since 1990, the overall picture is still very impressive. Between June 1928 and November 2003, no fewer than 69 Barbadians, discounting Michael Frederick, Ralph Legall, James Neblett and Archie Wiles, earned 1,207 Test caps for the West Indies. By way of comparison, 54 Trinidadians, including the Barbadian-born Legall and Wiles, earned 767 caps, and 64 Jamaicans (including Frederick) garnered 846 over the same span.

Nine Barbadians (Keith Boyce, Pedro Collins, Joel Garner, Charlie Griffith, Wes Hall, David Holford, Malcolm Marshall, Garry Sobers and Frank Worrell) claimed fifty or more Test wickets and ten of them (Sherwin Campbell, Gordon Greenidge, Desmond Haynes, Conrad Hunte, Malcolm Marshall, Seymour Nurse, Garry Sobers, Clyde Walcott, Everton Weekes and Frank Worrell) exceeded 1,000 Test runs. Of the eight West Indians with 200 or more Test wickets, three (Garner, Marshall and Sobers) are Barbadians. Nine of the 22 West Indians with more than 2,500 runs in Test cricket were born in Barbados and more than one third (127/369) of all West Indian Test centuries have been achieved by Barbadians. Again excluding Ralph Legall, eight Barbadians (David Allan, Courtney Browne, Clairemont Depeiza, David Murray, Thelstone Payne, Derek Sealy, Cammie Smith and Clyde Walcott) who kept wicket in Test cricket also accounted for 236 dismissals, including 26 stumpings, and two of them (Browne and Murray) share the present West Indian record of nine catches in a single Test. Seven Barbadian captains (Hoad, Goddard, Atkinson, Worrell, Sobers, Greenidge and Haynes) led the West Indies in 89 Tests, achieving thirty wins as against 25 losses, 33 draws and one tie.

Marvellous as it is, this arithmetic of Barbadian cricket still fails to do ample justice to the Barbadian input into the development of the sport in the Caribbean. The administrative and managerial work of such individuals, for instance, as H.B.G. Austin, John Goddard, Wes Hall, David Holford, Conrad Hunte, Jack Kidney, Tom Pierce, Peter Short, Cammie Smith, Clyde Walcott and Laurie Yearwood can never be measured in numerical terms. Nor can the role of such outstanding umpires as David Archer, Lloyd Barker, John Holder, Cortez Jordan and Harold Walcott. It is also impossible to gauge the influence of such authors, commentators and journalists as Dr Hilary Beckles, Tony Cozier, Harold Eastmond, Bruce Hamilton and Donna Symmonds. Suffice it to say that West Indies' cricket has owed more to Barbados over the years than to any other country.

CHAPTER THREE

GUYANA

WHEN THE CRICKET CULT SPREAD LIKE WILDFIRE ACROSS THE Caribbean during the 19th century, one of its earliest victims was Guyana, then known as Demerara. The game prospered there largely because of the support it found from the local aristocracy. The Georgetown Cricket Club, established to serve the interests of the elite, came into being in 1852 and has played a major role in West Indian cricket ever since. It soon established its headquarters at Bourda, which has since become one of the main Caribbean sporting arenas.

It was, in fact, the Demerarans who led the way in promoting inter-colonial cricket in the West Indies during the last third of the 19th century. They undertook the first visit to Barbados in 1865, became Trinidad's very first opponents in 1869, and hosted the first Barbadian touring team in 1871. It was a Demeraran, E.F. Wright, who recorded the first century ever achieved in first-class cricket on Caribbean soil. At Georgetown, in September 1882, he struck an astonishing 123 at Trinidad's expense in a first innings total of 168, which itself was then the highest score ever made by a West Indian XI. Four years later, it was another Demeraran, George N. Wyatt, who did most to facilitate the first tour of a composite West Indian team. In 1886, three Barbadians and six Jamaicans joined four Demerarans in an invasion of Canada and the United States. They played thirteen matches, won six, lost five, and drew two.

After Barbados had won the first two Caribbean triangular tournaments in 1891 and 1893, Demerara won the third convincingly in Georgetown in 1895. It defeated Trinidad by an innings and 217 runs, thanks to the brilliant all-round form of C.H. King, S.W. Sproston and E.F. Wright. King, who opened both the batting and the bowling for his side, scored an impressive 135 to eclipse the record that Wright had set thirteen years before. On this occasion, Demerara erased all previous West Indian records by amassing a total of 444. Twenty-five years would elapse before this record was broken by Barbados with 489 against Trinidad at Bridgetown in February 1920. At Bourda in 1895, King also captured 6/62 against Trinidad and followed that up with 6/70 against Barbados in a match which Demerara won by 175 runs. Wright was the main destroyer of the Barbadians with a match analysis of 10/111. He also enhanced his reputation as one of the best batsmen in the West Indies at the end of the century with scores of 96, 26 and 85 in this tournament, while Stanley Sproston contributed 27, 52 and 24. One of Demerara's stars that year was Walter Evan Goodman, the youngest of the famous brotherhood, who had recently emigrated from Barbados.

The Demerarans showed that their victory was no fluke when they defeated Jamaica twice at Georgetown in 1896. King (10/102) and H.R. Vyfhuis (10/75) were irresistible in the opening encounter, which Demerara won by an innings and 45 runs. In the second match, King again bowled splendidly to take eleven wickets for 92 runs from 65 overs, while the consistent Sproston registered 74 not out and 32 in a low-scoring game which Demerara won by one wicket.

A MEMBER OF THE 'BIG FOUR'

Demerara could not, therefore, be excluded from the itinerary of the earliest English touring teams to the West Indies. Wright bowled and batted well against the English tourists during the 1890s and Sproston distinguished himself with a fine 95 against Lord Hawke's team in 1897. Demerara had staked a strong claim to membership in the so-called 'Big Four' which came to dominate Caribbean cricket for the next seven or eight decades. Demeraran representatives had to be selected when the West Indies undertook their initial tours to England early in the 20th century.

When the West Indian cricketers made their first visit to England in 1900, Demerara supplied three representatives, including the Barbadian-born fast bowler, William Thomas Burton, who had left his native island in frustration because of the racist policy of the sport administration there. The other two were George Learmond and Sproston. Learmond was born in Demerara but had attended Combermere School in Barbados, where he had captained the newly formed Spartan Cricket Club. Ironically, when he made his first-class debut in 1895, he found himself playing at Georgetown against the country of his birth. Learmond, who eventually played for Trinidad also, became the first West Indian cricketer to represent no fewer than three countries. Burton and Learmond also toured England with the second West Indian squad in 1906. The former took 78 wickets in 1900 but did less well in 1906, while the latter never displayed his West Indian form on English soil. Sproston produced a few promising innings in 1900, including an attractive 86 against Hampshire, but generally failed to do justice to his talents.

These results can be seen as a harbinger of what transpired during the first quarter of the 20th century. Demerara, now more generally known as British Guiana, gradually became one of the weak sisters in Caribbean cricket. The triangular tournaments came to be dominated by Barbados and Trinidad between 1897 and 1929. British Guiana lost six consecutive matches to Barbados and did not defeat that island once during the long drought of 1896-1925. When the tide finally turned, it was actually a Barbadian immigrant, C.R. 'Snuffie' Browne, who did the damage. Browne, who scored a swashbuckling 102 at Bourda, then routed the visitors with a match analysis of 74/25/135/13 in October 1925.

British Guiana provided only two native-born representatives to the West Indian squad which toured England under H.B.G. Austin in 1923 and would not have been allowed that many had it not been for the notorious 'quota' system then in vogue. In addition to 'Snuffie', British Guiana contributed Maurius Pacheco Fernandes and C.V. Hunter, a right-handed batsman who never scored more than 66 in any first-class innings, although selected as a specialist in that department. Used mainly as a reserve player in minor matches, Hunter appeared only in two first-class innings that summer. His whole career spanned only seven first-class matches from which he extracted 275 runs (av: 22.91). Many Barbadians were therefore left to lament that such a fine cricketer as 'Johnnie' Browne ('Snuffie's' elder brother) had been left at home. Johnnie might certainly have made a more significant contribution. Barbados, however, already had its full quota of tourists in Austin, George Challenor, George Francis, Harry Ince and 'Tim' Tarilton.

'Maurice' Fernandes, a capable right-handed batsman, did considerably better than Hunter in 1923. He scored 523 runs (av: 34.86), placing second in the West Indian averages behind only Challenor. But he was a total failure when he toured England again in 1928. A stylish stroke-player, Fernandes was the outstanding Guyanese cricketer of the 1920s. He had the double distinction of playing in the very first West Indian Test match at Lord's and of captaining the West Indies in the first Test ever played at Bourda. His team won by 289 runs and he had thus become the first victorious West Indian captain. But this proved to be his last Test. In his four Test innings, he registered 49 runs (av: 12.25). His career record, however, is much more impressive. In 46 first-class matches, Fernandes scored 2,087 runs (av: 28.20) and struck four centuries, including a superb 141 against Barbados at Bourda in September 1929.

In addition to Fernandes, British Guiana sent C.V. Wight to England in 1928. Two Barbadian natives, J.M. Neblett and 'Snuffie' Browne completed Guiana's quota. James Neblett, a left-handed all-rounder, never represented Barbados but played one Test for the West Indies in 1935. Like Fernandes, he performed poorly in 1928, scoring 181 runs (av: 15.08) and taking six wickets (av: 54.16). In his solitary Test, he recorded sixteen runs for once out and claimed one wicket for 75 runs. His career record: twenty matches, 526 runs (av: 18.78) and 29 wickets (av: 41.55) indicates that he was lucky to have been selected and would certainly not have been had he remained at home in Barbados.

Vibart Wight was a consistent right-handed batsman who averaged over thirty runs per innings in a first-class career that involved forty matches during 1925-39. In 1928, he took part in seventeen first-class matches, scoring 343 runs (av: 20.17). He gained selection for the third Test at The Oval and made 23 & 12 not out. In two Tests altogether, he recorded 67 runs (av: 22.33). His statistics may not appear spectacular today, but Wight was certainly one of the most difficult batsmen to dismiss throughout the Caribbean when at his peak.

SOME GUYANESE STARS OF THE 1930s

When England visited the West Indies in 1929/30, British Guiana had regained some of its former lustre, mainly as a result of 'Snuffie's' exploits. It now boasted such promising cricketers as F.I. de Caires, B.McG. Gaskin, C.E.L. Jones, J.S. Mackenzie and Oscar Wight (Vibart's brother). Thanks to these emerging stars, British Guiana managed to win the Triangular Trophy three times during 1934-38. Mackenzie and Wight never gained Test caps, but the other three did. Wight toured Australia with the West Indies in 1930/31 but was not selected for any of the Tests.

A very sound right-handed batsman, Frank de Caires made his Test debut against England at Bridgetown in January 1930. He batted splendidly for 80 & 70, sharing a fine third-wicket partnership of 142 with George Headley in the second innings. He also made a useful 45 in the second innings of the second Test at Port of Spain. He finished that series with 232 runs (av: 38.66) from six innings but never gained Test selection again. When de Caires accompanied the West Indian team to Australia in 1930/31, he suffered the same fate as Oscar Wight. Altogether, in eighteen first-class matches, de Caires made 945 runs (av: 28.63). A competent left-handed all-rounder, Charles Jones played four Tests for the West Indies early in 1930 but could manufacture only 63 runs at nine per innings.

Berkeley Gaskin, a steady right-arm medium-fast bowler, represented the West Indies in only two Tests, scoring seventeen runs (av: 5.66) and taking two wickets (av: 79.00). His career was interrupted by the Second World War and, when almost forty years old, he made his Test debut against England at Bridgetown in January 1948. Gaskin made a greater contribution to Caribbean cricket after his retirement by successfully managing the team which toured England so triumphantly in 1963. The war also impeded the progress of such promising Guyanese players as Henry Peter Bayley, Celso de Freitas, Chatterpaul Persaud and Kenny Wishart. De Freitas and Persaud scored heavily in inter-colonial competition but were never selected to represent the West Indies. Persaud was particularly unfortunate as he achieved innings of 174, 96 and 32 in the tournament of 1937. With Bayley (268) against Barbados that year, he shared a fourth-wicket partnership of 381 that was then the highest ever achieved on British Guiana's behalf. Bayley, an attractive right-handed batsman, established the Guyanese record individual score on that occasion. He toured England with the West Indies in 1939 but failed to find his best form and could not rediscover it when the war was over.

Kenny Wishart's Test career was restricted to a single game. A careful left-handed opening batsman, he performed extremely well against the touring MCC in 1930. He scored 52 & 0 in his great chance at Bourda in the third Test against England in February 1935 but was immediately discarded. He made his greatest contribution as an administrator when he served as British Guiana's representative on the WICBC from 1949 to 1971.

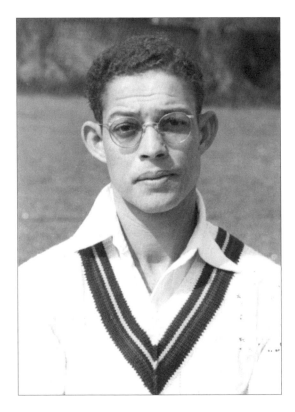

Robert Julian Christiani, seen here in 1950. He was one of the most attractive stroke-players ever to represent the West Indies

One of British Guiana's brightest stars during the 1930s was Cyril Marcel Christiani, still universally regarded as one of the finest wicket-keepers ever seen in the West Indies. In 28 first-class matches, he achieved 64 dismissals, including no fewer than twenty stumpings. He effected seven dismissals during the 1934/35 series against England when he was one of only six West Indians who appeared in all four Tests. He showed some skills also as a batsman, opening on four occasions and scoring a vital 32 not out in the third Test at Georgetown when the West Indies were struggling to achieve a draw. In four Tests he scored 98 runs (av: 19.60) and seemed destined to participate in many more. Sadly, however, Cyril Christiani died of malaria in April 1938 at the tender age of 24. He had toured England in 1933 as a reserve wicket-keeper when only nineteen years old.

ROBERT JULIAN CHRISTIANI

Robert Julian Christiani was Cyril's younger brother. He emerged during the late 1930s as a brilliant right-handed batsman with unlimited potential, but he had to await the coming of peace to demonstrate his abundant skills on an international scale. Prior to the advent of Rohan Kanhai, R.J. Christiani was unquestionably the greatest batsman produced by British Guiana. He announced his arrival with scintillating centuries against Barbados and Trinidad in 1944.

He again put the Barbadians to the sword with a glorious 149 at Bourda in October 1946 when he and J.L. Thomas (117) shared a third-wicket partnership of 250 runs. He was clearly in the top rank of Caribbean batsmen when Test cricket was resumed after the war.

An automatic Test choice, Christiani suffered the misfortune of being dismissed for 99 in the second innings of his debut against England at Bridgetown in January 1948. He then represented the West Indies in nineteen successive Tests before the streak ended in New Zealand early in 1952. Altogether, Christiani played in 22 Tests, scoring 896 runs (av: 26.35), taking three wickets (av: 36.00) and holding nineteen catches. An accomplished wicket-keeper, he also effected two stumpings. In 88 first-class matches during 1938-54, he registered 5,103 runs (av: 40.50), including twelve centuries, eighteen wickets (av: 60.44), 96 catches and twelve stumpings. All of Christiani's batting marks stood as Guyanese records for many years. He was a truly attractive batsman whose statistics fail to convey the quality of his strokes. He was also a brilliant fieldsman and a clever right-arm leg-spinner.

Apart from Christiani and Gaskin, who played six Tests between them in the 1947/48 series against England, British Guiana was also represented by John Trim, the burly right-arm medium-fast bowler, who performed extremely well in the Georgetown Test, claiming 3/44 from 23 very searching overs. Trim, however, was promptly replaced by Hines Johnson when the series shifted to Kingston. Johnson, with the wonderful figures of 10/96, propelled the West Indies to victory but, curiously, was not selected for the 1948/49 tour of India, whereas Trim was. Although performing well again on the sub-continent, Trim was restricted to two Tests in that series, despite bowling the tourists to their lone Test triumph with 7/76 in 43 overs at Madras. Overlooked for the 1950 tour of England, Trim was selected to tour Australia and New Zealand in 1951/52. He bowled superbly at Melbourne, claiming 5/34 in the first innings, but inexplicably was promptly dropped again. Trim thus played in only four Tests altogether and never failed in any of them. Yet, incredibly, he could not command a regular berth on the Test XI at a time when there was a dearth of good speedsters throughout the Caribbean. His eighteen Test wickets cost only 16.16 runs apiece. He was a steady and penetrative bowler whose skills were grossly under-utilised.

GUYANESE HEROES DURING THE 1940s AND 1950s

When the West Indies toured India in 1948/49, their squad included three cricketers from British Guiana: Christiani, Trim and Clifford McWatt. The last-named was a competent wicket-keeper and a hard-hitting left-handed batsman. He was good enough to record 1,673 runs (av: 28.84) and 51 dismissals in 41 first-class matches. He also struck two blistering centuries. He arrived in March 1947 with two fiery innings (56 run out and 123 not out) against Trinidad at Port of Spain. But the selectors did not think that he could compete with Clyde

Walcott for a place in the Test XI. He compelled the selectors to pay more attention to his claims as a wicket-keeper/batsman when he hit a forceful 128 against Trinidad at Port of Spain in October 1953 (after Walcott had surrendered the gloves and become a specialist batsman). In six Tests against England and Australia in 1954 and 1955, McWatt made 202 runs (av: 28.85), caught nine batsmen and stumped another. His best efforts at this level came in his debut against England at Kingston in January 1954 when he scored 54 & 36 not out. He reached 54 again at Bourda in the third Test of that series when he was run out after a courageous stand of 99 with Jamaica's J.K. Holt Jr. Sadly, it was this decision which triggered off the ugly bottle-throwing episode that caused the game to be interrupted for several minutes. McWatt was one of the finest wicket-keepers produced by British Guiana and his statistics suggest that, as in the case of John Trim, the West Indian selectors failed to take full advantage of his talents.

Bruce Hamilton Pairaudeau was another Guyanese star of exceptional promise who rose during the late 1940s. A neat, bespectacled right-handed opening batsman, he first represented British Guiana when he was only fifteen years, eleven months old. Batting at No. 5 against Trinidad at Port of Spain in March 1947, he could muster only nineteen, eight, one and four in his initial tournament. Promoted to his regular position a few months later, however, he scored his maiden century, a stylish 130, against Jamaica at Georgetown. In February 1950 at Bridgetown, he struck a masterful 161 against a very powerful Barbadian attack and would certainly have toured England that year had not Roy Marshall (191) also batted brilliantly.

The presence of Allan Rae, Jeffrey Stollmeyer and Marshall kept Pairaudeau out of the Test XI until 1953, when he finally made his Test debut against India. He scored an attractive century and shared with Everton Weekes a fifth-wicket partnership of 219, then a West Indian record for all Tests. It remains the West Indian record for a fifth-wicket partnership against India. He finished that series with 257 runs (av: 32.12). Against England at Bridgetown in February 1954, he played a superb innings of 71 and shared a splendid fourth-wicket stand of 165 runs with Clyde Walcott after the West Indies had lost three wickets for a paltry 25 runs. This was the critical turning-point in a match which the hosts eventually won. But Pairaudeau was still restricted to only two Tests in that series and his career failed to blossom as everyone expected. Two Tests against England in 1957 brought him only twenty runs (av: 5.00) and his results in New Zealand in 1955/56 were not altogether satisfactory either. In thirteen Tests, he scored 454 runs (av: 21.61) and held six catches. He emigrated to New Zealand in 1958 and played for Northern Districts until 1967. In 89 first-class matches altogether, Pairaudeau recorded 4,930 runs (av: 32.01), including eleven centuries, and 64 catches.

Although it can be argued that Pairaudeau's production was somewhat disappointing, it must be remembered that he played in the days when the selection of West Indian teams was palpably whimsical. Guyanese players like himself, McWatt and Trim were chopped and changed for no apparent reason, thereby undermining their confidence. Even after his fine showing against India in 1952/53, Pairaudeau's place was not secure. He was dropped immediately after his match-saving 71 against England in February 1954 and was not allowed a single Test against the Australians in 1955. McWatt played quite well against England, too, but was replaced by Jamaica's Alfie Binns for the first Test against Australia in the very next series. More laughably, for the first Test against Australia in 1955, Pairaudeau was neglected while the selectors opted for another Guyanese batsman of obviously inferior talent, the left-handed Glendon Gibbs. Gibbs scored 12 & 0 at Kingston and was promptly discarded altogether. McWatt replaced Binns for the second Test against Australia and was then himself replaced by Clairmonte Depeiza for the rest of the series. That proved to be the end of his Test career. When the white Pairaudeau went off to New Zealand in 1955/56, he was chosen mainly as vice-captain to Denis Atkinson at a time when the WICBC firmly believed that Black men were incapable of providing effective leadership.

GLOOMY DAYS FOR BRITISH GUIANA

After its brief upsurge during the 1930s, British Guiana had not performed particularly well in the territorial competitions and this was reflected in the fact that it steadily lost its 'quota' privileges. Between 1928 and 1957 it boasted very few Test players. When the West Indies toured England in 1933, British Guiana's sole representative was Cyril Christiani. Peter Bayley was the only Guyanese player on the team which visited England in 1939. Robert Christiani was the lone Guyanese flag-bearer to England in 1950. He was accompanied by McWatt and Trim during the tour of India in 1948/49 and by Trim alone during the tour of Australia and New Zealand in 1951/52. When the Indians visited the Caribbean in 1952/53, Leslie Wight, a dour left-handed batsman, was given the opportunity to play his solitary Test innings, from which he gleaned 21 runs. Pairaudeau and Wilfred Edun were the only Guyanese members of the team which toured New Zealand in 1955/56. Edun was a powerfully built right-handed all-rounder who eventually played only a handful of first-class matches but is better remembered now for his role as a cricket administrator, a useful member of the Guyana Cricket Board of Control, a national selector and a manager of Guyanese as well as West Indian teams in Georgetown.

Guyanese cricket had lagged behind the rest of the Caribbean mainly because of fierce internal conflicts between the Black, Asian and White communities and because of the blind conservatism of the elitist Georgetown Cricket Club. British Guiana, occupying more than 83,000 square miles, was the largest of the British West Indian colonies and possessed a population in those days in excess of 600,000. There was no valid reason for such a protracted

Basil Butcher, playing in a practice match for Colonel Stevens' XI, cuts a ball from Benaud to the boundary at Eastbourne in April 1963

slump. The turning-point came with the appointment of Clyde Walcott as Cricket Organiser and Coach on the Estates of the British Guiana Sugar Producers' Association in 1954. Walcott did his best to destroy the social and ethnic barriers that had impeded Guyanese cricket. He gave strong encouragement and support to such budding stars as Basil Butcher, Lance Gibbs, Alvin Kallicharran, Rohan Kanhai, Clive Lloyd, Ivan Madray, Ivor Mendonca, Joseph Solomon, Charlie Stayers and Colin Wiltshire.

THE CORNER TURNED

During the Age of Walcott (1954-70), which lasted well into the period of Independence, when British Guiana changed its name, Guyana became a powerful force once again. Signs of improvement were evident almost at once. In a quadrangular tournament at Bourda in 1956, Butcher, Kanhai and Solomon shared five centuries between them in two games against Barbados and Jamaica. It became increasingly difficult to defeat the Guyanese at home. Their Test cricketers also increased dramatically. While only two Guyanese players (Kanhai and Pairaudeau) went with John Goddard to England in 1957, four of them (Butcher, Gibbs, Kanhai and Solomon) made the trip to India and Pakistan under Franz Alexander in 1958/59. By the late 1960s, with the emergence of Stephen Camacho, Lloyd and Roy Fredericks, it was no longer possible to select West Indian teams without considering a large contingent from Guyana. In fact, when Sobers led the West Indies against England at Lord's in 1969, his XI included no fewer than five of them (Butcher, Camacho, Gibbs, Fredericks and Lloyd).

71

Rohan Kanhai in action during his excellent 157 against England at Lord's in August 1973. He was one of the most exciting batsmen that the world has ever seen

ROHAN BHOLALALL KANHAI

The outstanding Guyanese star during the period 1955-75 was the incomparable Rohan Bholalall Kanhai, a simply dazzling right-handed stroke-player, who went on to amass 28,774 runs (av: 49.01), including 83 centuries, in 416 first-class matches for British Guiana, Tasmania, Warwickshire, Western Australia and the West Indies. A magnificent fieldsman and useful wicket-keeper, he also took 318 catches and stumped seven batsmen. Kanhai enjoyed a very successful Test career which yielded 6,227 runs (av: 47.53), including fifteen centuries, and fifty catches in 79 matches. All of these statistics exceeded the old Guyanese standards that Robert Christiani had set. Kanhai was an important member of the great West Indian teams of 1963, 1966 and 1973 which triumphed over England in England. He was the second Guyanese cricketer, following Maurice Fernandes, to serve as captain of the West Indies and was at the helm when they defeated England 2-0 in 1973. Three of his thirteen matches as captain were won, three were lost, and seven were left drawn. After his retirement, Kanhai also served as a successful coach of Jamaican and West Indian teams.

For many years, Kanhai was accompanied by his illustrious compatriots, Butcher and Solomon. Basil Butcher was an excellent right-handed batsman with a wonderful array of wristy strokes. In 44 Tests he scored 3,104 runs (av:

Lance Gibbs (far left), pictured here in 1968, is the greatest bowler ever produced by Guyana. Roy Fredericks (left), seen here also in 1968, was that country's finest opening batsman

43.11), including seven centuries. A reliable fieldsman and useful right-arm leg-break bowler, he held fifteen catches and took five wickets (av: 18.00). Butcher performed extremely well in England in 1963, 1966 and 1969. His splendid 133 at Lord's in 1963 saved the West Indies from almost certain defeat and his memorable 209 at Nottingham in 1966 paved the way for victory. But his finest series was his first, against India in India in 1958/59, when he registered 486 runs at almost seventy per innings.

Joseph Solomon, a sound right-handed batsman, was a more stolid performer than Butcher or Kanhai. He was the sheet anchor while his more flamboyant partners ignited fireworks. The West Indies profited much from his reliable defence and brilliant fielding in a career which encompassed 27 Tests during 1958-65. He patiently gathered 1,326 runs at 34 per innings. He is best remembered for his accurate throw which ran out the last Australian batsman and produced the fantastic tie at Brisbane in December 1960. It is generally, forgotten, however, that Solomon began his first-class career with three successive centuries for British Guiana in 1956. He was the first batsman to accomplish such an unusual feat. In 104 matches altogether, he recorded 5,318 runs at the respectable average of 41.54 per innings.

RICHARD LANCELOT GIBBS

While Butcher, Kanhai and Solomon were accumulating their 23 Test centuries for the West Indies, the Guyanese player who perhaps contributed most to West Indian successes during the period 1960-76 was Richard Lancelot Gibbs, the lanky right-arm off-spinner, who set a long-standing record for slow bowlers with his 309 wickets (av: 29.09) in 79 Tests. No other spin bowler approached this mark until Shane Warne of Australia did so in the late 1990s. Lance Gibbs was a leading star when the West Indies won five consecutive series during 1962-67 and laid claim to the unofficial championship of the cricketing world. He captured 26 English wickets (av: 21.30) in 1963 and 21 more (av: 24.76) in 1966. Against India in 1961/62 he snared 24 Test wickets at a cost of less than 21 runs apiece. Gibbs was not a competent batsman and his Test average was a mere 6.97 runs per innings, but he was a superb fieldsman who held 52 catches in Test cricket and as many as 203 in a first-class career that encompassed 330 games (including 109 for Warwickshire). He was the second West Indian bowler, following Garry Sobers, to exceed 1,000 wickets in first-class cricket.

During the period 1958-62, British Guiana produced three other cricketers whose Test careers proved limited. Ivan Madray, a right-arm leg-break bowler, played twice against Pakistan in 1958, but was sparingly used. He bowled only 35 overs altogether and took no wickets for 108 runs. He was never recalled. Ivor Mendonca was a very capable right-handed batsman and an accomplished wicket-keeper who enjoyed two very successful Tests against India. He scored 78 in his debut at Kingston in March 1962 when he shared with Sobers (153) a West Indian record seventh-wicket partnership of 127. He averaged more than forty runs in his two Test innings and dismissed no fewer than ten batsmen in his two Tests. But that, strangely enough, was that. He had been selected as a substitute for Jackie Hendriks. Illogically, he shared the next four Tests with another newcomer, David Allan of Barbados – although he had done so well in his debut. Charlie Stayers played four Tests against India in that same series, scoring 58 runs (av: 19.33) and taking nine wickets (av: 40.44). He was a right-arm medium-fast bowler with an action which some critics considered doubtful. He was therefore promptly discarded as soon as Charlie Griffith and Lester King emerged.

CLIVE HUBERT LLOYD

Towards the end of the 1960s, another Guyanese colossus came to the fore in the form of Clive Hubert Lloyd, a brilliant all-rounder, who was a hard-hitting left-handed batsman, a magnificent fieldsman anywhere and a right-arm medium-pace bowler. He ought to have been selected to tour England in 1966 but was excluded for obviously political reasons. He made ample amends, however, when his chance came against India at Bombay in December 1966. He struck 82 & 78 not out and was there at the end with his captain, Sobers, when the West Indies won by six wickets. He also gave a dazzling display in the field. This was the beginning of one of the great careers in the history of the game. Lloyd eventually played 490 first-class matches for Guyana, Lancashire and the West Indies, recording 31,232 runs (av: 49.26), including 79 centuries, 114 wickets (av: 36.00) and 377 catches. In 110 Tests, he registered 7,515 runs (av: 46.67), including nineteen centuries, and held ninety catches. In 87 ODIs, he also scored 1,977 runs (av: 39.54), including a magnificent 102 against Australia in the World Cup Final at Lord's in 1975.

More significant, however, was Lloyd's value to the team as an inspirational captain. He led the West Indies in 74 Tests, winning 36 and losing only twelve. No other West Indian cricketer has yet approached this record of leadership. Lloyd was at the helm when the West Indies amazingly won eleven consecutive Tests in one calendar year (1984), including a 5-0 shellacking of England in England. That world record of eleven successive victories remained intact until

Clive Lloyd, an inspirational captain, in action in December 1983

eclipsed by the Australians in 2001. It was Lloyd who pioneered the use of the much-dreaded four-pronged pace attack that was so prominent when the West Indies accomplished the improbable feat of going undefeated in 29 consecutive series during 1980-95. Lloyd served the West Indies briefly in an administrative capacity during the late 1990s in a valiant (but vain) attempt to return to the Glory Days when the West Indies swept all before them with clinical proficiency.

Just as Lloyd was embarking on his incredible career, British Guiana produced two of the finest opening batsmen in the Caribbean: George Stephen Camacho and Roy Clifton Fredericks. Camacho, a grandson of George Learmond, made his Test debut against England at Port of Spain in January 1968. A sound and patient right-handed batsman, he had begun his first-class career with a century against Trinidad at Port of Spain in February 1966. He performed well during the tour of England in 1969 when he headed the West Indian Test averages with 46.75. After eleven Tests during 1968-71, his career was unfortunately cut short by a serious injury during the tour of England in 1973. Altogether, he made 640 runs (av: 29.09) on behalf of the West Indies. After his retirement, Camacho served for many years as the WICBC secretary.

Fredericks, a more dashing left-handed stroke-player, proved to be much more successful. He began his Test career with innings of 76 & 47 against Australia at Melbourne in December 1968 and never really looked back. He became the first West Indian opening batsman to exceed 4,000 runs in Test cricket and finished with 4,334 (av: 42.49), including eight delightful centuries, in his 59 Tests. A brilliant fieldsman, especially close to the wicket, he also took 62 catches. Fredericks exceeded 1,000 runs on each of this three tours to England (1969, 1973 and 1976) and still appeared to be at the top of his form when, in 1978, he suddenly announced his retirement from Test cricket. He had just forged, with Gordon Greenidge of Barbados, one of the most successful opening partnerships that the world had yet known. In twelve ODIs, he contributed a further 311 runs (av: 25.91) to the West Indian cause. Fredericks continued to work on behalf of Caribbean cricket while serving as Guyana's Minister of Sport. He was only 57 years old when he died on 5 September 2000.

Late in the 1960s, another brilliant left-handed batsman was spawned by Guyana. He was Alvin Isaac Kallicharran who made his first-class debut, just before his 18th birthday in March 1967, against the Windward Islands at St George's, Grenada. He began his Test career with 100 not out against New Zealand at Georgetown in April 1972 and followed that with another century (101) at Port of Spain in his second Test. Between 1972 and 1982, he accumulated 4,399 runs (av: 44.43), including twelve centuries, in 66 Tests. He also held 51 catches. During the Packer crisis, when a disagreement occurred between the WICBC and the majority of the regular players (including Lloyd), Kallicharran served as captain for nine Tests. In the absence of their stars, the West Indies won only once, lost twice and achieved six draws with Kallicharran

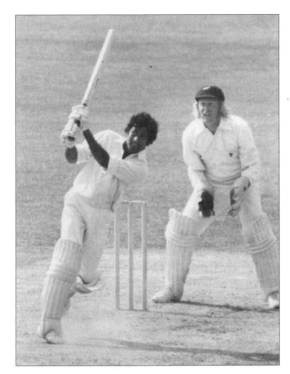

Alvin Kallicharran in action during his splendid innings of 72 against New Zealand in the World Cup semi-final at The Oval in June 1975 when he was chosen "Man of the Match"

at the helm. His Test career ended when he joined the 'rebel' tour of South Africa in 1982, but he continued to play first-class cricket for Orange Free State, Transvaal and Warwickshire until 1990 (when he was 41 years old). His lengthy and stellar career comprised 505 matches which brought 32,650 runs (av: 43.64), including 87 centuries (a Guyanese record). In 31 ODIs, he scored a further 826 runs (av: 34.41). A fine fieldsman anywhere but especially in the deep, Kallicharran took 323 catches altogether. He also claimed 84 wickets (av: 47.97) with his slow right-arm off-breaks. He is the finest left-handed batsman produced by Guyana.

A GUYANESE BOOM

During the 1970s, Guyana was so powerful that most of the West Indian teams of that decade included five of her native sons: Fredericks, Gibbs, Kallicharran, Kanhai and Lloyd. They played together as a solid phalanx, in fact, for eleven consecutive Tests during 1972-74. After Garry Sobers had surrendered the captaincy in 1972, the West Indies also came to be led for the next thirteen years and 96 Tests by three Guyanese (Kanhai, Kallicharran and Lloyd). When Kanhai retired from Test cricket in 1974, his place was promptly taken by another Guyanese, Leonard Baichan, a cautious left-handed opening batsman, whose unwavering concentration took him to an unbeaten 105 in his Test debut against Pakistan at Lahore in February 1975. Baichan began his Test career with partnerships of 66, 30 and 95 with Fredericks, but he was permanently dropped after only three Tests. His record reads: 184 runs (av: 46.00), including one century, and two catches. He was unable to compete for a regular berth on the Test team with such players as Fredericks, Gordon Greenidge and Lawrence Rowe.

The next Guyanese star to emerge was the aggressive right arm-fast bowler, Colin Everton Hunte Croft, who was easily the greatest fast bowler produced by his country. His Test career began against Pakistan at Bridgetown in February 1977 when he captured 7/132 from 46.4 of the most hostile overs. In the first innings of his second match, he took 8/29 which is still the best analysis yet achieved by a West Indian fast bowler in Test cricket. He took 33 wickets in that series and moved rapidly to a total of 125 (av: 23.30) in 27 Tests before touring South Africa with the 'rebels' in 1982. In nineteen ODIs, he captured thirty wickets (av: 20.66). He was a devastatingly fast and accurate bowler who sometimes came perilously close to being charged with intimidatory tactics. One of the most feared bowlers in the world at his peak, Croft became a much mellower cricket broadcaster and journalist after his retirement.

Colin Croft, seen here in action during the tour of England in 1980, was one of the most fearsome of all fast bowlers

The Packer Crisis (1978-79) provided brief opportunities for two Guyanese to play more Test cricket than they would otherwise have done. When Lloyd and Deryck Murray led the 'World Series' cricketers in their famous boycott, the WICBC had to scramble to find suitable replacements. Six newcomers were co-opted for the Georgetown encounter against Australia in March 1978 and a seventh had to be sought for the Test at Port of Spain a few weeks later. This opened the door for Faoud Bacchus, an aggressive right-handed batsman, and Sewdatt Shivnarine, a slow right-arm bowler, who also batted fairly well right-handed.

Bacchus stole the show in his eighth Test match when, according to *Wisden*, he batted with "authority and brilliance" to achieve 250 against India at Kanpur in February 1979. After nineteen matches, he failed to sustain this quality of batsmanship and his Test career ended with 782 runs (av: 26.06). A magnificent fieldsman in the covers, he also accepted seventeen catches. Bacchus removed himself from further consideration when he participated in the 'rebel' tour of South Africa in 1983. Altogether, in 111 first-class matches, he registered 5,944 runs (av: 35.17) and in 29 ODIs he scored 612 runs (av: 26.60).

As a lower-order batsman, Shivnarine was immediately successful, beginning with scores of 53 & 63 against Australia at Bourda. But his bowling (1/167) proved innocuous and he had to be supplanted after only eight Tests. He made 379 runs (av: 29.15), which was impressive enough. But the return of the regulars, after the Board had come to terms with Packer, made it impossible for Shivnarine to retain his place. He played in one ODI, recording twenty not out in his solitary innings and 0/16 in three overs.

A PROTRACTED SLUMP

During the early 1980s, after Bacchus, Croft and Kallicharran had toured South Africa, Guyana, for the first time in many years, found itself with but a single representative, the captain, in the West Indian Test XI. Lloyd remained the sole Guyanese for a long stretch of nine Tests until he was joined by Roger Harper in the match against India at Calcutta in December 1983. Harper was a fine right-handed all-rounder who bowled his off-breaks with commendable accuracy and intelligence. He was also a very aggressive right-handed batsman and one of the greatest fielders ever. He represented the West Indies in 25 Tests but his whole career was hindered by the West Indian determination to abandon spin and place all of their eggs in a fast-bowling basket. Harper thus made a number of tours without playing very many Tests and was often used mainly as an ODI specialist because of his ability to score quickly, to contain opposing batsmen and to save countless runs by his expert fielding. His Test career yielded 46 wickets (av: 28.06), 535 runs (av: 18.44), and 36 catches. In 105 ODIs, he claimed 100 wickets (av: 34.31), made 855 runs (av: 16.13), and held 55 catches. He served as a coach of the West Indies Test team after his retirement.

Clyde Butts, the tall Guyanese right-arm off-spinner who replaced Harper on the West Indies team during the New Zealand tour of the Caribbean in 1984/ 85, was not any more fortunate. Despite consistently bowling well in the Shell Shield (and later Red Stripe) competition, he was selected for only seven Tests altogether and was constantly overlooked after 1988. He retired in frustration in 1994. His contribution to the West Indian cause was 108 runs (av: 15.42), ten wickets (av: 59.50) and two catches.

When both Butts and Harper were excluded from the third Test against New Zealand at Bridgetown in April 1985, this was the first occasion since 1955 that the West Indies team, led now by Viv Richards, entered a Test match without a Guyanese representative. Guyana then remained without representation in West Indies Test cricket for five successive matches until April 1986, when Harper reappeared for the fourth Test against England at Port of Spain. There was little improvement in Guyana's prospects, in fact, until the emergence of Carl Hooper in the late 1980s. 'King Carl', as he is widely known in the Caribbean, made his debut in the second Test against India at Bombay in December 1987.

Hooper was a majestic right-handed batsman of apparently unlimited potential, a heady and steady right-arm off-break bowler and a brilliant fieldsman especially in the slips. He played his strokes with such languid ease and grace that expectations had always been lofty and there was considerable anguish among his many supporters when he failed to achieve exceptional feats. He played in 102 Tests, captaining the West Indies in the last 22. He scored 5,762 runs (av: 36.46), including thirteen centuries, and took 115 catches. His bowling yielded 114 wickets (av: 49.42). In 227 ODIs, he registered 5,761 runs (av: 35.34), 193 wickets (av: 36.05), and 120 catches. These are creditable statistics, of course, but they remain a source of great disappointment to pundits the world over. When, at eighteen years old, Hooper produced a truly splendid 126 against Barbados at Bridgetown in February 1985, knowledgeable Barbadians predicted wonderful things from this batsman who reminded them so much of the young and brilliant 'Tae' Worrell in full flow during the 1940s. Only occasionally, however, did Hooper's genius result in mighty deeds. His inconsistencies might have been considerably more tolerable had the West Indies been able to prosper in spite of them. But his lapses at the crease have too often led to embarrassing middle-order collapses, especially abroad. These failures are reflected in the fact that the teams led by him won only four Tests while losing eleven and drawing seven. Hooper was most unfortunate in playing the greater portion of his career at a time when West Indian cricket had to endure one of its most painful slumps.

A much more reliable player is Shivnarine Chanderpaul, the slim, frail-looking left-handed batsman who made his Test debut against England at Georgetown in March 1994 at the age of nineteen. His batsmanship is based on rock-solid defence and a determination to hold the fort at all costs. He has a number of wristy strokes, but his major aim is survival and he has proven himself

Carl Hooper in action during the ICC Champions Trophy match against South Africa on 13 September 2002 at the SSC Stadium in Colombo, Sri Lanka

to be a veritable sheet-anchor in the midst of otherwise brittle West Indian batting. Still only 29 years old, he has gained selection in 68 Tests and has produced no fewer than 36 scores of fifty runs or more. He has registered 4,260 runs at an average of 43.46 per innings. Chanderpaul is also a right-arm spinner of slow leg-breaks, but his eight wickets thus far have been purchased at a most exorbitant price (725 runs). A fine fieldsman, he has taken 29 catches, some of them truly spectacular. In 137 ODIs, he has recorded 3,963 runs (av: 36.02), fourteen wickets (av: 43.28), and forty catches.

Shivnarine Chanderpaul reaches a century during day one of the first Test against Australia at Bourda Oval in Georgetown on 10 April 2003

The only two other Guyanese to earn Test caps during the 1990s were Reon King, a left-arm fast bowler, and Clayton Lambert, a belligerent left-handed opening batsman, who replaced Gus Logie in the fifth Test against England at Leeds in August 1991. Although he played two attacking innings (39 & 14) in that match, he was not selected again until March 1998 at the age of 36. In five Tests altogether, he scored 284 runs (av: 31.55), including a spirited 104 against England at St John's, Antigua. He also took the wicket of Mark Ramprakash in the dying moments of a game which England won by five wickets to square the series with the West Indies (in 1991) for the first time in seventeen years. In addition, Lambert scored 368 runs (av: 33.45) in eleven ODIs for which his style and method appeared much better suited.

King has played in fourteen Tests so far for the West Indies, performing quite well against New Zealand and Zimbabwe in 1999/2000. He has taken 44 wickets (av: 27.77), scored fifty runs (av: 3.57), and held two catches. His record in 48 ODIs reads: 73 wickets (av: 23.23), 62 runs (av: 6.88), and four catches. Although King is only 28 years old, his prospects do not appear very bright as he has not appeared in any of the recent series against Australia, Bangladesh, India, New Zealand, South Africa, Sri Lanka or Zimbabwe. His batting is feeble and his fielding mediocre. He is also too prone to injury.

THE PRESENT AND THE FUTURE

Within the past few years, Guyana's stock has risen substantially as is reflected in its performances in the regional competitions, especially since the resurrection of Carl Hooper who had retired so very suddenly in 1999. Some interesting new faces have surfaced and Guyana was able to boast as many as six representatives on the West Indian team which invaded Zimbabwe in 2001. Apart from Hooper, as captain, that touring squad included Chanderpaul, King, N.C. McGarrell, Ramnaresh Sarwan and Colin Stuart.

Neil McGarrell is an accomplished left-arm spinner, a brilliant fieldsman and a fairly useful lower-order batsman. He had toiled valiantly for many seasons in regional competition and was already 28 years old when selected to the Test XI for the first time, in April 2001, against South Africa at St John's. He produced 58 very steady overs to take 5/113 in a losing cause, but was promptly dropped. So far, he has played in only four Tests, registering 61 runs (av: 15.25), seventeen wickets (av: 26.64), and two catches. McGarrell has also participated in seventeen ODIs, scoring sixty runs (av: 7.50), taking fifteen wickets (av: 45.40), and holding nine catches. These statistics, however, do not reveal how often his fielding resulted in important run-outs. In one memorable ODI at Port of Spain in April 1998, he personally dismissed three of England's batsmen by hitting the stumps with deadly accurate throws from very difficult angles.

Colin Stuart is a right-arm medium-fast bowler who accompanied the West Indies to Australia in 2000/01 and made his Test debut in the fourth match at Melbourne in December. Since then, like the majority of West Indian fast bowlers in recent years, he has been in and out of the Test XI. He has taken part in six Tests so far, capturing twenty wickets (av: 31.40), making 24 runs (av: 3.42) and taking two catches. In five ODIs, he has claimed eight wickets (av: 25.62), scored three not out in his solitary innings, and held one catch.

The most exciting prospect to emerge in Guyana since Chanderpaul is Ronnie Ramnaresh Sarwan, a potentially brilliant right-handed batsman, a superb fieldsman and a useful right-arm spin bowler, who bids fair to be the Caribbean star of the future. He was only nineteen years old when selected for his first Test, against Pakistan at Bridgetown, in May 2000. So far, he has appeared in 36 such matches, scoring 2,249 runs (av: 38.11), taking three wickets (av: 78.33) and accepting eighteen catches. In 49 ODIs, he has registered 1,551 runs (av: 44.31), two wickets (av: 83.50) and fourteen catches.

There is one other Guyanese who has played Test cricket in the 21st century: Mahendra Nagamootoo, a right-handed all-rounder, who made his debut against England at The Oval in August 2000. In five Tests thus far, he has scored 185 runs (av: 26.42), taken twelve wickets (av: 53.08), and held two catches. In 24 ODIs, Nagamootoo's contribution to the West Indian cause has been 162 runs (av: 13.50), eighteen wickets (av: 55.44), and six catches.

FINAL ANALYSIS

The history of Guyana's cricket may not be as exciting or as miraculous as that of Barbados or the smaller islands, but it contains an epic quality nevertheless. It features 39 individuals (including the Barbadian-born James Neblett) who eventually achieved Test match status and who combined for a total of 876 Test appearances between June 1928 and November 2003. Guyana has produced such superstars as Basil Butcher, Shivnarine Chanderpaul, Colin Croft, Roy Fredericks, Lance Gibbs, Carl Hooper, Alvin Kallicharran, Rohan Kanhai, Clive Lloyd, Ramnaresh Sarwan and Joe Solomon. Whereas only three of its bowlers (Croft, Gibbs and Hooper) have surpassed 100 Test wickets, no fewer than nine of its batsmen have exceeded 1,000 Test runs. Seven among the latter have also scored in excess of 3,000 and three have surpassed 5,000, while Gibbs captured more than 300 Test wickets.

The flat and slow pitches in Guyana have tended to discourage fast bowlers and it is consequently no accident that this country has produced very few speedsters so far. Apart from Colin Croft, Reon King and John Trim, Guyana has provided the West Indies with no fast bowlers of exceptional quality. On the other hand, it has spawned a number of outstanding spinners, led by Lance Gibbs, Roger Harper and Carl Hooper. Others, such as Clyde Butts, 'Rex' Collymore, Neil McGarrell, Ivan Madray and Mahendra Nagamootoo, would obviously also have left a more solid impression on the game had the West Indian selectors been more sympathetic to slow bowlers.

It is also interesting to observe that so many of Guyana's best batsmen have been left-handed: Leonard Baichan, Shivnarine Chanderpaul, Roy

Ramnaresh Sarwan hits out during the ICC Cricket World Cup Pool B match against Canada on 23 February 2003 at Supersport Park in Centurion, South Africa

Fredericks, Glendon Gibbs, Alvin Kallicharran, Clayton Lambert, Clive Lloyd, Clifford McWatt and Kenneth Wishart. Among this group, six were opening batsmen; and yet, somewhat ironically, it is in this department that Guyana has generally been lacking. Apart from Fredericks, Guyana's opening batsmen have not performed exceptionally well in Test cricket. Neither Len Baichan nor Bruce Pairaudeau quite lived up to expectations, and Steve Camacho's career was too quickly curtailed for him to attain superstardom. Little fault, however, can be found with Guyana's middle-order batting over the years. Basil Butcher, Robert Christiani, Carl Hooper, Alvin Kallicharran, Rohan Kanhai, Clive Lloyd, Ronnie Sarwan and Joe Solomon have displayed exceptional skills.

Guyana's production of wicket-keepers has also been somewhat limited.

It has provided the West Indies only with Cyril Christiani, Clifford McWatt and Ivor Mendonca, who combined for twelve Tests altogether. Even though Robert Christiani and Kanhai occasionally wore the gloves, wicket-keeping has remained Guyana's major weakness.

For this there has been ample compensation in the fact that five of Guyana's favourite sons have offered quality leadership to the West Indies in no fewer than 119 Tests so far. Between them, Maurice Fernandes, Carl Hooper, Clive Lloyd, Alvin Kallicharran and Rohan Kanhai have led the West Indies to 45 victories as against only 28 defeats. That alone is a contribution of no mean sort.

Guyana's contribution also includes the administrative and managerial work done over the years by such individuals as Steve Camacho, Wilfred Edun, Berkeley Gaskin, A.C. O'Dowd, Oscar Webber, Vibart Wight and Ken Wishart.

CHAPTER FOUR

TRINIDAD & TOBAGO

SECOND IN SIZE AND POPULATION ONLY TO JAMAICA AMONG THE English-speaking islands in the Caribbean, Trinidad is about 1,864 square miles and contains approximately 1.2 million people. Its multi-ethnic community is a combination of Africans, Indians, Europeans, Chinese and Arabs. It boasts as perfect a 'rainbow coalition' as one can find anywhere. In 1962, it achieved its political independence and has governed itself since 1970 as an independent republic together with the smaller island of Tobago (116 square miles and a population of roughly 50,000). Trinidad had previously been part of the British Empire and Commonwealth since 1802. Before that, it had been owned by the Spanish, Dutch and French governments in turn. The republic of Trinidad & Tobago is thus different in two fundamental respects from other British West Indian countries: its population is more heterogeneous and its European influences are far more diverse. This might help to explain why the peculiarly English game of cricket never prospered as spectacularly there as it did in such other Caribbean islands as Antigua and Barbados. Between June 1928 and November 2003, despite its size and population, the republic of Trinidad & Tobago has produced only 54 cricketers (including the Barbadian-born Ralph Legall and Archie Wiles) who combined for a total of 767 West Indian Test caps between them. In stark contrast, the small island of Barbados has accounted for more than 1,200 caps in Test cricket.

Cricket was taken to Trinidad & Tobago in the 19th century by British sailors, soldiers and traders. Educators and priests also took part in its importation. By the middle of the century, clubs had been established catering mainly to the needs of the small white minority. One of the most famous, Queen's Park Cricket Club, shortly came to dominate the sport in Trinidad. It arrogated to itself the powers and responsibilities of a cricket board of control and, in effect, administered cricket in Trinidad until the establishment in 1956 of the Trinidad & Tobago Cricket Council. It is arguable that this dominance of a small European minority helped to stifle the growth of Trinidadian cricket. The sport found another peculiar difficulty in Trinidad that was absent elsewhere in the Caribbean. The soil apparently created enormous problems for those responsible for wicket-preparation. So, even at the prestigious Queen's Park Oval in Port of Spain, jute-matting pitches had to be used until quite recently.

EARLY DAYS

Even so, because of its physical proximity to Barbados and Demerara, Trinidad appeared as an early participant in Caribbean inter-colonial cricket competition. Four years after Barbados and British Guiana had broken the ice, Trinidad played its inaugural first-class match against British Guiana at Port of Spain in 1869. By the end of the century, Trinidad had become a regular competitor, unlike the more isolated Jamaica. For many years, its representatives were mainly white players, of whom the chief were E. Agostini, A. Cipriani, W. Eccles, E.G. Penalosa, Captain Warburton and Charles Warner. No fewer than three Warners, all presumably related to the future Sir Pelham, represented Trinidad during the 1870s. Even as late as the 1890s, Trinidadian XIs were largely white because the Queen's Park Cricket Club refused to select 'professionals'.

Two of the finest bowlers in the West Indies at the turn of the century were Archie Cumberbatch and Joseph 'Float' Woods. They had emigrated from Barbados because of the racist policies of the Barbados Challenge Cup Committee. In Trinidad, while they were debarred from inter-colonial competition, they were allowed, quite illogically, to play against touring sides from England. In the 1890s, Trinidad consequently performed much better against the English teams led by Robert Slade Lucas, A.B. Priestley and Lord Hawke than it did against Barbados and British Guiana. Cumberbatch and Woods combined to defeat Arthur Priestley's team twice in February 1897, having done the same to Lord Hawke's team in the first colony match in the previous month.

Largely on the strength of its showing against the English visitors, Trinidad was allowed its quota of four players when the West Indian team was selected to tour England in 1900. It supplied Aucher Warner (the captain), Lebrun Constantine, L.S. D'Ade and the Barbadian-born Woods. Neither D'Ade nor Warner accomplished much, but Constantine and Woods were two of the stars of the party. Constantine scored 610 runs (av: 30.50) and Woods claimed 72 wickets (av: 21.54). As the matches were designated as second-class, however, these statistics are not included in their first-class career records.

When the West Indies undertook their second tour of England in 1906, their matches were accorded first-class status for the first time there. In the squad of fourteen, there were five players representing Trinidad: Lebrun Constantine (again), Archie Cumberbatch, A.E. Harragin, George Learmond and S.G. Smith. While Cumberbatch was a Barbadian native, Learmond had just emigrated to Trinidad from British Guiana. Neither of them accomplished very much on this tour. Cumberbatch, who might have been much more formidable in 1900 while at his peak, was now only a shadow of his former self and could claim only 24 wickets at almost thirty runs apiece.

The father of the future Sir Learie Constantine, 'Old Cons' acquitted himself well once more, scoring 776 runs (av: 29.84). His highest score was 92 against Leicestershire in August but his most impressive innings was a defiant 89, in a first innings total of 156, against Dr W.G. Grace's XI in June. Constantine was a hard-hitting right-handed batsman, a useful right-arm bowler of medium pace, an excellent fieldsman (especially in the slips) and a very capable wicket-keeper. Despite his African ancestry, he was one of the bulwarks of Trinidadian cricket for about thirty years (1893-1923). In 56 first-class matches, he recorded 2,433 runs (av: 25.34), 46 wickets (av: 13.73), 95 catches and eighteen stumpings.

Alfred Harragin served as vice-captain of the West Indies in 1906 and enjoyed a reasonably successful tour, scoring 412 runs (av: 31.69) in fourteen first-class innings, finishing second only to Percy Goodman among the tourists. A reliable right-handed batsman and a safe field, he represented Trinidad from 1891 until 1932 and was its captain for several years. With the exception of Pelham Warner, who emigrated to England at the age of fourteen in 1887, Harragin and Lebrun Constantine were the finest batsmen produced by Trinidad before the Second World War.

Trinidad's greatest all-rounder before the emergence of Learie Constantine in the 1920s was Sydney Gordon Smith. He was an aggressive left-handed batsman, an accomplished slow left-arm bowler and a very good fieldsman. In the 1906 tour of England, he registered 751 runs (av: 24.82) and 66 wickets (av: 24.36). After the tour, he remained in England to qualify for Northamptonshire and played for that county from 1907 to 1914. During the Great War, he emigrated to New Zealand and represented Auckland from 1917 until 1926. His career thus encompassed 211 first-class games, from which he gleaned 10,920 runs (av: 31.28), 955 wickets (av: 18.08) and 158 catches. All of these stood as West Indian records for many years. But although Smith played on several composite West Indian and New Zealand XIs, he never participated in an official Test match. Test match status did not come to the West indies until 1928 or to New Zealand before 1929.

THE INTER-WAR YEARS

During the inter-war years, Trinidad's cricket showed remarkable progress as a host of non-white clubs, led by Maple, Shannon and Stingo, began to prosper in the colony. Such fine players as N. Betancourt, A. Cipriani, L.N. Constantine, G.A.R. Dewhurst, G. John, V.S. Pascall, C.A. Roach, Ben Sealy, J.A. Small, E.L. & W.H. St Hill and C.A. Wiles came to the fore. Trinidad thus enjoyed a truly Golden Age during the 1920s and 1930s.

When the West Indies toured England in 1923, Trinidad supplied five members: Learie Constantine, Dewhurst, John, Pascall and Small. Had the quota system not then been in use, the colony might well have been represented also by Wilton St Hill, one of the most graceful right-handed batsmen produced by Trinidad. Had the organisers of the tour been able to afford a larger number of so-called 'professionals', the Stingo wicket-keeper, Piggott (a poor Black player), might also have been preferred to Dewhurst, a distinguished member of the Queen's Park Cricket Club.

Only 22 years old in 1923, Learie Constantine, a hard-hitting right-handed batsman, an aggressive right-arm fast bowler and a brilliant fieldsman anywhere, showed only glimpses of his genius. But when he returned to England with the West Indies in 1928, he achieved the 'double', recording 107 wickets (av: 22.95) and 1,381 runs (av: 34.52) in 26 first-class matches. No other West Indian tourist has yet repeated this feat. Constantine had chequered results on West Indian tours to England in 1933 and Australia in 1930/31, but his 103 wickets in 1939 cost only 17.77 runs each. In eighteen Tests for the West Indies between 1928 and 1939, he scored 635 runs (av: 19.24) and took 58 wickets (av: 30.10). He also held 28 catches. A very dynamic cricketer, he brought a sense of melodrama to everything he did and was one of the most popular professionals ever to appear in the northern leagues in England. His books, *Cricket and I*, *Cricket in the Sun*, and *Cricketers' Carnival*, are still being read with much interest by sociologists of West Indian sport. Constantine lamented the West Indian habit of choosing white captains irrespective of merit and looked forward to the day when the West Indies would be led by a charismatic Black cricketer. His dream was fulfilled when Frank Worrell was appointed captain against Australia in 1960/61 and against England in 1963.

George John was the most successful among the Trinidadian tourists in 1923, although he was almost forty years old and well beyond his prime. He had for years been one of the fastest bowlers in the world and one of the most feared in the Caribbean. He had to be sparingly used in England that summer but still claimed 49 first-class wickets at less than twenty runs apiece. With George Francis of Barbados, John formed a potent opening partnership. It is a pity that Test cricket came too late for him. In 29 first-class matches during 1907-28, he captured 133 wickets (av: 19.24) and was good enough as a hard-hitting lower-order batsman to register one century among his 466 first-class runs. Many pundits still see George John as one of the great pioneers of Caribbean fast bowling.

George Dewhurst accomplished little in 1923. He was a tidy wicket-keeper who finished his first-class career with sixty dismissals, including thirteen stumpings, in 31 games. Victor Pascall, an uncle of Learie Constantine, was a useful left-handed all-rounder who was a regular member of the Trinidad XI during 1905-27. He performed reasonably well with the ball in 1923, capturing 52 wickets (av: 24.28). Like Constantine, Joe Small was a brilliant fieldsman. He was a stylish right-handed batsman and a steady right-arm bowler of medium pace off-cutters. In 1923, he scored 776 runs (av: 31.04) and shone with the ball in 1928 when he took fifty wickets (av: 28.88). Small was one of the leading all-rounders in the Caribbean throughout the 1920s and gained selection to three Test teams, making 79 runs (av: 13.16) and taking three wickets (av: 61.33). Against England at Lord's, in June 1928, he became the first West Indian to register a half-century in Test cricket. In 77 first-class matches between 1909 and 1932, he made 3,063 runs (av: 26.17), captured 165 wickets (av: 27.81), and held 72 catches.

Learie Constantine in action, circa 1930

Four Trinidadians were selected among the sixteen cricketers who toured England in 1928 under Karl Nunes of Jamaica. They were Constantine, Clifford Roach, Small and Wilton St Hill – all of whom had the distinction of participating in the very first Test match played by the West Indies. The match was lost, but Constantine with four wickets and Small with 52 runs in the second innings acquitted themselves nobly. St Hill, 35 years old and already past his best, appeared too impatient all summer and failed to do justice to his enormous skills. He played in three Tests for the West Indies but averaged fewer than twenty runs per innings.

Clifford Roach enjoyed a much more successful Test career. He struck two cultured half-centuries against powerful English teams in 1928 and eventually made 952 runs (av: 30.70) in sixteen Tests. He became the first West Indian to achieve a Test century when he scored 122 against England at Bridgetown in January 1930. In the very next month, at Georgetown, he became the first West Indian to score a double century at this level when he hit a superb 209. Roach was an attractive right-handed batsman, a useful bowler and a fine fieldsman. He exceeded 1,000 runs in both of his tours to England (1928 and 1933). Touring Australia with the West Indies in 1930/31, he scored 637 runs (av: 24.50). Roach was second only to the great George Headley among West Indian batsmen of the 1930s and was the finest

Clifford Roach (left) and Archie Wiles, two of the six Trinidadians who toured England in 1933

of all Trinidadian stroke-players prior to the arrival of Jeffrey Stollmeyer and Gerry Gomez.

When England visited the West Indies in 1929/30, there was no shortage of Trinidadian representation in the four Tests. In fact, the second Test at Port of Spain featured no fewer than eight Trinidadians: Ellis Achong, Nelson Betancourt, Constantine, Mervyn Grell, Errol Hunte, Roach, St Hill and Small. Betancourt captained the first Test ever played in Trinidad and would not have been selected at all had it not been for the dubious policy of choosing a local white player to lead the West Indies in each of the Tests. A useful right-handed batsman, Betancourt made 39 & 13 but he was never selected again and thus suffered the indignity of losing his only Test match as captain.

'Puss' Achong was the first cricketer of Chinese extraction to participate in a Test match. A clever slow left-arm bowler, he left an impact on the game by experimenting with the left-hander's googly which came to be called the 'chinaman' after him. In 38 first-class matches, he scored 503 runs (av: 14.37), took 110 wickets (av: 30.23) and held twenty catches. He also enjoyed a lengthy career in the Lancashire League where he claimed over 1,000 wickets. At the international level, however, he achieved more modest results. In six Tests for the West Indies, Achong recorded only 81 runs (av: 8.10), eight wickets (av: 47.25) and six catches. He toured England with the West Indies in 1933 but found the pitches that summer too unresponsive.

Grell, like Betancourt, never appeared for the West Indies again. A sound right-handed batsman and right-arm bowler of medium pace, he scored 34 runs (av: 17.00) and took 0/17 in five overs in his lone opportunity. Slightly more fortunate was E.A.C. Hunte, a right-handed batsman and a reserve wicket-keeper. He performed splendidly in both roles in the Port of Spain Test in February 1930, scoring 58 & 30. Altogether he made 166 runs (av: 33.20) and held five catches in his three Tests. He was a member of the West Indian squad which toured Australia in 1930/31.

Also in the touring party of 1930/31 was Edwin St Hill, an accurate right-arm medium pace bowler and a useful lower-order right-handed batsman. Like Hunte, he failed to earn a berth on any of the Test teams that winter, but he did play twice against England in the 1929/30 series in the Caribbean. His returns, however, were negligible: eighteen runs (av: 4.50), and three wickets (av: 73.66). Even so, it should be noted that his 47 challenging overs in the Georgetown Test in February 1930 yielded only 87 runs.

THE GOLDEN AGE OF TRINIDADIAN CRICKET

Trinidad was thus powerful enough in those days to boast nine active Test players and to send five of them to Australia with the West Indian tourists in 1930/31. Apart from Constantine, Hunte, Roach and Edwin St Hill, that side also included George Copeland Grant, its captain. 'Jackie' Grant was only 23 years old and had little knowledge of West Indian cricket or even of his team mates, but he was a white and wealthy Cambridge 'blue' and therefore regarded as the most suitable candidate for the captaincy. He thus led the West Indies in twelve Tests during the 1930s. A courageous right-handed batsman and a brilliant fieldsman, especially in the slips and gully, he captained the West Indies with great enthusiasm and enjoyed the distinction of leading them to their first Test series triumph in 1934/35. In his debut against Australia in December 1930, albeit in a losing cause, he became the first batsman to score two unbeaten half-centuries in a Test match. He made 413 runs (av: 25.81) and held ten catches, including some spectacular ones, during his Test career.

Grant was naturally retained as captain against England in 1933. He took with him five other Trinidadians: Achong, Roach, Ben Sealy, Cyril Merry and C.A. Wiles. In addition, it was hoped that Constantine, who was still engaged by Nelson in the Lancashire League, would be able to play in the Test matches. As it was, Constantine was too often unavailable and Jackie's younger brother, Rolph Grant, then a student at Cambridge University, had occasionally to be co-opted. Grant himself exceeded 1,000 first-class runs during the tour, as did Roach, but the Trinidadian contingent, on the whole, did not enjoy a particularly successful campaign.

Much was expected of Benjamin Sealy, a right-handed all-rounder, but his batting was inconsistent and his bowling generally lacked penetration. In 22 first-class matches that season, he claimed only nineteen wickets (av: 38.15). He scored 1,072 runs (av: 39.70) but was selected for only the third Test. He scored 29 & 12 and took 1/10 in five overs in that encounter, but was never selected by the West Indies again. Merry, too, failed to live up to his supporters' expectations. He registered 856 runs (av: 28.53) and thirteen wickets (av: 32.30). In his two Tests that summer, he mustered only 34 runs (av: 8.50), but he amply compensated after his retirement by serving as a cricket administrator and managing the West Indian team which toured Australia in 1951/52. The Barbadian-born Archie Wiles was almost 41 years old when the tour began and should perhaps have been omitted. He played in a solitary Test, scoring only two runs in his two innings.

Rolph Grant was available for Test duty against England in 1934/35, having completed his studies. He played in all four Tests but accomplished little before striking a useful 77 in the fourth match at Kingston when he shared a seventh-wicket partnership with George Headley. He inherited the captaincy from his brother and led the West Indies against England in 1939. Altogether he played in seven Tests, scoring 220 runs (av: 22.00), claiming eleven wickets (av: 32.09) and taking thirteen catches. Grant's brilliant fielding is reported to have often served as a source of inspiration to his players. He was also an attacking right-handed batsman and a right-arm off-break bowler. In 48 first-class matches during 1932-39, he left a fairly creditable all-round record: 1,883 runs (av: 28.53), 79 wickets (av: 25.17), and 66 catches.

Grant took four other Trinidadians with him to England in 1939: Gerry Gomez, Tyrell Johnson and the young Stollmeyer brothers, Jeffrey and Victor. Johnson was a lanky left-arm fast bowler who created a mild sensation when he captured a wicket with his very first ball of the tour. He was allowed but a single Test, the third and last at The Oval, and again made his mark by dismissing Walter Keeton with his first delivery. That proved to be his final Test appearance as the Second World War then intervened. Johnson's modest contribution to the cause was nine runs (not out in his only Test innings), three wickets (av: 43.00), and one catch.

Victor Stollmeyer was an attractive right-handed batsman and a useful right-arm leg-break and googly bowler. He was much hamstrung by illness and injury during the 1939 season and could therefore appear only in thirteen first-class games. Like Johnson, he finally received a Test opportunity in the last match of the series. He scored a delightful 96 but always considered his innings a failure as he blamed himself for the unfortunate running out of Headley when, at 65, that great batsman had appeared on the threshold of another mammoth score. That proved to be Victor's sole Test innings. But he and his brother provided Trinidad with several fine first-wicket partnerships in the 'Goodwill' tournaments arranged in the West Indies during the Second World War and he finished with 2,096 runs (av: 42.77) in a first-class career that involved 33 matches during 1935-46.

GERRY GOMEZ AND JEFFREY STOLLMEYER

If the Second World War meant the end of the Test careers of Rolph Grant, Tyrell Johnson and Victor Stollmeyer, it served only as an interval in those of Gerry Gomez and Jeffrey Stollmeyer. Gomez emerged as the leading West Indian all-rounder when Test cricket resumed. An aggressive right-handed batsman, a very good right-arm medium-pace bowler and an excellent fieldsman, he was one of the major keys to Trinidad's succession of inter-colonial victories at the Queen's Park Oval during the 1940s. He eventually played in 29 Tests in a

Gerry Gomez practising in the nets at Eastbourne on 20 April 1950. The wicket-keeper is Clyde Walcott

career that lasted until 1954. He was one of the stars in the triumphant invasion of India in 1948/49 and of England in 1950. Even in Australia in 1951/52 when his colleagues appeared to be in disarray, Gomez performed with admirable consistency. His Test career yielded 1,243 runs (av: 30.31), 58 wickets (av: 27.41), and eighteen catches. He was the third Trinidadian, following S.G. Smith and Jeffrey Stollmeyer, to surpass 5,000 runs in first-class cricket. He continued to make significant contributions to Caribbean cricket after his retirement as an active player. Gomez was a very influential cricket administrator for many years. He managed the team to Australia in 1960/61 with considerable tact and also had much to do with the improvement of umpiring standards in the region.

Jeffrey Stollmeyer was an elegant right-handed batsman and a dangerous right-arm change bowler of leg-breaks and googlies. He was the finest Trinidadian batsman of his generation and remains the best opening batsman ever produced by that country. One of the bright lights of the 1939 tour of England, he amassed 916 runs (av: 30.53) and would obviously have exceeded 1,000 had the season not been cut short due to the imminence of war. He played in all three Tests, scoring 133 runs (av: 26.60). He was successful again in 1950 when he made 1,334 runs (av: 37.05) and shared many a fine opening stand with Allan Rae. His average in the four Tests that year was 50.83 runs per innings. Stollmeyer and Rae also enjoyed a very profitable tour of India in 1948/49 when they established a long-standing West Indian record first-wicket

Jeffrey Stollmeyer practising in the nets at Fenner's before the match against Cambridge University in May 1950. He made an elegant 83 in the fixture which was dominated by a mammoth partnership of 350 runs between Everton Weekes (304*) and Frank Worrell (160) as the West Indies amassed 730/3

partnership of 239 runs. Stollmeyer was also one of the more successful West Indian batsmen during the tour of Australia and New Zealand in 1951/52. In seven Tests 'Down Under' he made 516 runs (av: 39.69). Altogether, he represented the West Indies in 32 Tests, scoring 2,159 runs (av: 42.33), taking thirteen wickets (av: 39.00), and holding twenty catches. He struck Test centuries against Australia in Australia, India in India and New Zealand in New Zealand. When he retired from first-class cricket in 1957, he had amassed more runs (7,942) than any other Trinidadian apart from Sidney Smith. Stollmeyer led the West Indies in thirteen Tests, winning three, losing four and drawing six. He became a faithful servant of the WICBC after his retirement and managed several West Indian touring teams. He was president of the Board for several years during the 1970s and played a key role in resolving the dispute between the administration and the players during the critical years of Kerry Packer's 'World Series Cricket'.

THE POST-WAR YEARS
Barbados and Trinidad had played so many goodwill tournaments during the war years that they enjoyed a clear advantage over the other Caribbean territories when Test cricket was restarted. They consequently provided the West Indies

Test XI at Bridgetown in January 1948 with no fewer than eight members, including four from Trinidad. Apart from the veterans, Gomez and Stollmeyer, two Trinidadians made their Test debut in that encounter: Wilfred Ferguson and Prior Jones. The former was a wily right-arm leg-spinner and hard-hitting right-handed batsman who justified his selection in all four Tests by capturing 23 wickets (av: 24.65) and scoring 138 runs (av: 34.50). He was selected to tour India in 1948/49 and Australasia in 1951/52 but his Test career came to a screeching halt with the meteoric rise of Sonny Ramadhin in 1950. It ended after eight Tests in which the short, burly all-rounder had scored 200 runs (av: 28.58), taken 34 wickets (av: 34.26), and held eleven catches. A popular cricketer, Ferguson was easily the best spin bowler produced by the West Indies prior to the emergence of Ramadhin and Alfred Valentine.

Prior Jones was one of the fastest bowlers in the Caribbean throughout the 1940s. He was particularly dangerous on the jute-matting pitches of Port of Spain. In his Test debut against England, he captured 4/54 in 25.2 overs of searching pace but, astonishingly, was not called upon again in that series. He toured with West Indian teams to the sub-continent in 1948/49, England in 1950 and Australasia in 1951/52. Although he performed well enough in nine Tests to capture 25 wickets (av: 30.04), his place on the Test XI was never secure. His best performance came against India at Bombay in February 1949 when he took 5/85 in 41 overs.

Two other Trinidadians appeared in the Test series against England in 1947/48. They were Andrew Ganteaume and Lance Pierre. The former was a dapper right-handed opening batsman who scored very consistently in inter-colonial cricket throughout his career. He was selected in February 1948 for the second Test at Port of Spain, as a replacement for the injured Stollmeyer. He scored 112 and shared a record first-wicket stand of 173 with George Carew. Incredibly, however, Ganteaume never played another Test innings. He was completely neglected until 1957 when, long past his prime, he was taken to England at a time when the selection of Jack Holt, Conrad Hunte or Cammie Smith would have made more sense. He naturally achieved only modest results that summer. His tantalisingly brief Test career was a great disappointment for a player of his skills. In fifty first-class matches, Ganteaume accumulated 2,785 runs (av: 34.81). He was also a useful reserve wicket-keeper who effected 37 dismissals, including three stumpings.

The tall and bespectacled Lance Pierre was a fearsome right-arm fast bowler in his prime. He combined with Prior Jones to give Trinidad the best pair of opening bowlers in the West Indies during the war years. But, like Ganteaume, he was allowed a single Test before being permanently discarded. At Georgetown in March 1948, given the chance to bowl only seven overs, he finished with 0/28 and did not bat. He toured England in 1950 but was hampered by nagging injuries throughout the summer and played only in twelve games. He did, however, enjoy a very special day in the field when, at

Liverpool on 5 July, he dismissed eight Lancashire batsmen for 51 runs in nineteen overs. This gave English spectators an indication of what Pierre was really like in his heyday.

When the West Indies toured India, Pakistan and Ceylon in 1948/49, four natives of Trinidad were selected (Ferguson, Gomez, Jones and Stollmeyer). At a time when the infamous quota system was in operation, Trinidad was deemed to have met its quota with the selection of Denis Atkinson, the Barbadian native, who had recently emigrated there. For the tour of England in 1950, six Trinidadians were chosen: Gomez, Jones, Pierre, Ramadhin, Stollmeyer and K.B. Trestrail. Neither Pierre nor Trestrail earned a Test cap that summer and Jones appeared only at Lord's and The Oval without accomplishing a great deal.

In a team that included such great stroke-players as Robert Christiani, Gomez, Clyde Walcott, Everton Weekes and Frank Worrell, Kenny Trestrail's opportunities were naturally limited in 1950. He was a hard-hitting right-handed batsman and a brilliant fieldsman, but he could not crack the Test line-up and appeared in only nineteen first-class matches that summer, scoring 629 runs (av: 27.34). He eventually emigrated to Canada and toured England with a Canadian team in 1954. Trestrail was a good enough player to have represented the West Indies in Test cricket at almost any other time. In 41 first-class matches, he made 2,183 runs (av: 38.29) and struck five centuries. His best effort was a forceful 161 not out against Jamaica at Port of Spain in January 1950.

SONNY RAMADHIN

Gomez and Stollmeyer, of course, performed with their usual competence in England in 1950, but one of the really bright stars of that series was Sonny Ramadhin, who exploded upon the cricket world, literally without warning, at the age of 21. He mesmerised the Jamaican batsmen in two trial matches at Port of Spain in January and February 1950 and proceeded to baffle England's best batsmen throughout the summer. He combined with Alfred Valentine of Jamaica to form one of the most potent spin-bowling duos in cricket's history. With cleverly concealed right-arm off-breaks and googlies, Ramadhin took 26 wickets (av: 23.23) in four Tests against England in 1950 and remained a fixture on the West Indies Test XI throughout that decade. In 43 Tests, he captured 158 wickets (av: 28.98) which served for some years as a West Indian record. Ramadhin and Valentine, with 59 Test wickets between them in 1950, were two of the major contributors to the first West Indian victory in England. They also played a vital role in India's first defeat in the Caribbean in 1952/53. Ramadhin ranks second only to Lance Gibbs of Guyana among West Indian right-arm spinners and still remains the greatest of all slow bowlers ever produced by Trinidad. As a lower-order batsman, he possessed a fairly sound defensive technique, good enough to earn him 361 runs (av: 8.20) in Test cricket. An ordinary fielder, he held nine Test catches.

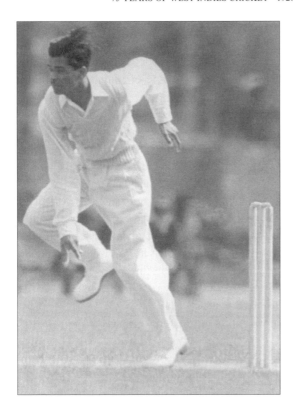

Sonny Ramadhin in action circa 1950 when he baffled England's best batsmen with his ability to bowl leg breaks and off breaks without any discernible change of grip and delivery

At the time when the WICBC was still neglecting the smaller islands, Trinidad was a sufficiently powerful member of the 'Big Four' to secure as many as six places on the squad which toured Australia and New Zealand in 1951/52. Apart from Ferguson, Gomez, Jones, Ramadhin and Stollmeyer (the vice-captain), Trinidad was represented by Simpson Guillen, an accomplished wicket-keeper, who came into his own when Walcott's back broke down. One of the finest 'keepers of his generation, Guillen effected eleven dismissals, including two stumpings, in his five Tests for the West Indies before emigrating to New Zealand and playing three Tests for that country. He was also a capable right-handed batsman, good enough to register 197 for Canterbury against Fiji in 1954 and to average 26 runs per innings in his Tests for the West Indies. He eventually played for New Zealand against the West Indies in 1955/56.

Guillen's departure and Walcott's retirement from wicket-keeping meant that the West Indies had to search for another stumper. They selected Alfred Binns from Jamaica for the first Test against India in 1952/53 before offering the job to Ralph Legall. Although born in Barbados, the latter spent his best years in Trinidad and had emerged as one of Guillen's major rivals. Legall played in four Tests, all against India, scoring fifty runs (av: 10.00) and effecting nine dismissals, including one stumping.

OTHER TRINIDADIAN STARS OF THE 1950s

During the 1950s, four other Trinidadians surfaced briefly in Test cricket: Nyron Asgarali, Lennox Butler, Hammond Furlonge and Jaswick Taylor. Asgarali was a sound right-handed batsman who scored heavily in inter-colonial competitions before being selected, much too late at the age of 37, to tour England in 1957. He exceeded 1,000 runs that summer but his Test career was restricted to two games in which he scored 62 runs (av: 15.50). Butler, a right-arm fast bowler, played one Test against Australia in 1955, took two wickets for 151 runs and was then discarded. Furlonge, a right-handed opening batsman, played one Test against Australia in 1955 and two against New Zealand in 1956. He recorded 99 runs (av: 19.80), including a stubborn 64 at Auckland when the West Indies could make only 145 altogether on the way to their first defeat at New Zealand's hands. Taylor, a right-arm fast-medium bowler, showed considerable promise in his debut against Pakistan at Port of Spain in March 1958 when he captured 5/109 in 36.5 overs in an innings of 496. He was destined, however, shortly to be eclipsed by Roy Gilchrist (Jamaica) and Wesley Hall (Barbados) after taking ten wickets (av: 27.30) in three Test matches.

Ramadhin was the sole Trinidadian in the Test versus Australia at Bridgetown in May 1955 and Furlonge the only one who appeared at Kingston for the fifth match of that series. With the resurgence of British Guiana under the inspired coaching of Clyde Walcott, Trinidad suddenly ceased to be one of the leaders of the 'Big Four'. Had it not been for the persistence of the traditional quota system, the team which John Goddard led to England in 1957 would have been much different. Ramadhin would clearly have been the only Trinidadian representative among the seventeen. As it was, the ageing Asgarali and Ganteaume, at least seven years too late, gained berths. In 1957/58, against Pakistan, Taylor was the sole Trinidadian selected and only in the final Test at Port of Spain. This series marked, at long last, the abandonment of the stifling principle of quotas.

A PAINFUL AND PROLONGED SLUMP

Trinidad's protracted decline was reflected in the fact that only three of its natives (Ramadhin, Willie Rodriguez and Taylor) were selected for the tour of India and Pakistan in 1958/59. Only two (Ramadhin and Charran Singh) participated in the series against England in 1959/60, and Ramadhin was the solitary Trinidadian on the West Indies team which toured Australia in 1960/61. The arrival of Lance Gibbs then meant that no Trinidadian at all played for the West Indies in the final three Tests of that series. Rodriguez, a capable right-handed batsman and a steady right-arm spin bowler, did not make his Test debut until March 1962 against India at Kingston and was restricted to five Tests altogether, scoring 96 runs (av: 13.71), taking seven wickets (av: 53.42), and holding three catches. His greatest contributions to West Indian cricket came in the field of administration and management after his retirement as an active player. Singh, a left-arm spin bowler, played in only two Tests, recording eleven runs (av: 3.66), five wickets (av: 33.20) and two catches.

Three Trinidadians accompanied Worrell to England in 1963: M.C. 'Joey' Carew, Deryck Murray and Rodriguez. Carew, a left-handed opening batsman and right-arm bowler of off-cutters, enjoyed a reasonably successful tour, making 1,060 runs (av: 30.28), but his performance in his first two Tests was disappointing. When he visited England again in 1966, his results were even less satisfactory. Carew did not, in fact, come into his own until the tour of Australia and New Zealand in 1968/69. In seven Tests 'Down Under' that winter he scored 683 runs (av: 48.78) and was one of the pleasant surprises in that campaign. He represented the West Indies in nineteen Tests, making 1,127 runs at an average of 34.15 per innings and claiming eight wickets (av: 54.62). His finest performance came at Brisbane in December 1968 when he scored 68 & 71 not out in a notable West Indian triumph. In a first-class career that involved 129 matches during 1956-74, he registered 7,810 runs (av: 38.47), 108 wickets (av: 29.76) and 83 catches. Carew eventually became a West Indian selector but made his most significant contribution by serving as a mentor to Brian Lara in the latter's adolescence.

The most successful Trinidadian during the tour of England in 1963 was Deryck Murray, an excellent wicket-keeper and a sound right-handed batsman. He was easily the greatest of all Trinidadian wicket-keepers and one of the finest ever to represent the West Indies. He began his Test career with 24 dismissals (including two stumpings) against England and finished with a total of 189, then a West Indian record. For about fifteen years, Murray was one of the steadiest anchors in Caribbean cricket. His reliable batting saved the West Indies in many a crisis, most notably against Pakistan in a memorable World Cup engagement at Birmingham in June 1975. In 62 Tests, he registered 1,993 runs (av: 22.90). In a first-class career that encompassed 367 matches for Cambridge University, Trinidad & Tobago, Warwickshire and the West Indies, he recorded 13,291 runs (av: 28.33), 741 catches and 108 stumpings. These were all Trinidadian records when he retired in 1981 and no other West Indian has yet come close to his 849 dismissals. Murray was also instrumental in establishing the West Indies Players' Association which became a very powerful force, ensuring that the first-class cricketers enjoyed much better contracts and conditions of service.

After the 1963 season, Murray entered Cambridge University and was not available for Test cricket again for a few years. This meant that Trinidad boasted only one representative (Carew) on the West Indian team which toured England under Garry Sobers in 1966. Carew endured a dismal season that year, scoring 720 runs (av: 25.71) and playing in only one Test. His contribution to the cause against England at Lord's was 2 & 0. Not surprisingly, he was excluded from the squad which visited India in 1966/67.

THE DAVIS BROTHERS

Carew's place was filled for a brief spell by another Trinidadian, Bryan Davis, a steady right-handed opening batsman, a useful right-arm leg-break bowler and a brilliant fieldsman. He was selected for four Tests against the Australians in 1964/65 and toured India with Sobers in 1966/67. His Test career produced 245 runs (av: 30.62) and one catch. He failed miserably to adjust to the pitches on the sub-continent where, in seven matches, he could muster only 218 runs (av: 18.16). This brought an end to his Test career. Following his retirement from first-class cricket, Davis continued to make a contribution both with his pen and his voice. He became an influential sports' journalist and cricket commentator.

Bryan's younger brother, Charlie Davis, proved a more successful Test cricketer. His debut against Australia at Melbourne in December 1968 was inauspicious but he was one of the most consistent West Indian batsmen in the early 1970s. After scoring a fine century at Lord's in 1969, he headed the batting averages in 1970/71 with 529 runs (av: 132.25) against India in the Caribbean. He then made 466 runs (av: 58.25) against New Zealand in 1971/72. At Bridgetown in March 1972, he shared a match-saving sixth-wicket partnership of 254 runs with Sobers. This still stands as a West Indian record in Tests against New Zealand. His Test career came to a strangely sudden end in 1973 after only fifteen matches. Davis scored 1,301 runs (av: 54.20) in these games and struck four centuries. He held four catches and took two wickets for 330 runs. His batting average remains one of the highest for the West Indies and has not yet been surpassed by any Trinidadian with more than 1,000 runs in Test cricket. It also seems to suggest that too little use was made of his immense talent. In ninety first-class matches during 1960-76, he registered 5,538 runs at the respectable average of 41.32 per innings.

STARS OF THE 1970s

During the early 1970s, Trinidad produced four promising young spin bowlers in Imtiaz Ali, Inshan Ali, Raphick Jumadeen and Jack Noreiga. A right-arm leg-break and googly bowler, Imtiaz was tried in only one Test (against India in 1975/76) when he took 2/89 from 34 overs. Inshan was a more dangerous slow left-arm bowler who imparted more spin than most but lacked consistent accuracy. He toured England in 1973 and Australia in 1975/76 and bowled reasonably well, but he was allowed only twelve Tests altogether. In these matches, he recorded 172 runs (av: 10.75), 34 wickets (av: 47.67), and seven catches. His finest hour occurred at Port of Spain in April 1972 when he claimed 7/158 from 77.4 searching overs against New Zealand. Jumadeen, another left-arm spinner, also represented the West Indies in twelve Tests, making 84 runs (av: 21.00), taking 29 wickets (av: 39.34) and accepting four catches. But his chances diminished, like those of his compatriots, when the West Indies began to pin their hopes on their faster bowlers. Hence Noreiga, who achieved the distinction of being the only West Indian to capture nine wickets in one Test innings, also found himself discarded after only four Tests. He had taken seventeen wickets (av: 29.00) and two catches and had scored eleven runs (av: 3.66). His 9/95 against India in the first innings at Port of Spain in March 1971 remains the best bowling analysis by a West Indian in Test cricket.

The outstanding Trinidadian all-rounder during the 1970s was Bernard Denis Julien, a dashing right-handed batsman, capable left-arm fast-medium bowler and superb fieldsman. He played in 24 Tests before disqualifying himself permanently by participating in the rebel tour of South Africa in 1982. His Test record was creditable enough: 866 runs (av: 30.92), including two centuries, fifty wickets (av: 37.36) and fourteen catches. It is universally agreed that these statistics do scant justice to his enormous talent. He gave a fine exhibition of exceptional batting skills when, in August 1973 at The Oval, he smashed a glorious century (121) off 127 deliveries. Julien played eighty matches for Kent between 1970 and 1977.

Towards the end of the 1970s, Trinidad finally produced another excellent batsman; but whereas Charlie Davis had departed after an all too brief career, Hilary Angelo Gomes was destined to represent the West Indies in sixty Tests and to provide them with a solid middle-order anchor for about a decade. 'Larry' Gomes was the finest left-handed batsman spawned by his native country before the advent of Brian Lara. With the West Indies, he toured England in 1976 and 1984; Australia in 1979/80, 1981/82, 1984/85 and 1986/87; India in 1978/79 and 1983/84; and Pakistan in 1980/81 and 1986/87. He registered 3,171 Test runs (av: 39.63), including nine centuries, fifteen Test wickets (av: 62.00), and eighteen Test catches. Although he was by no means a swashbuckling batsman, he was still a useful performer in ODIs, scoring 1,415 runs (av: 28.87) and taking 41 wickets with his right-arm off-breaks. Gomes was a quiet, but invaluable member of the teams which Clive Lloyd led from triumph to triumph between 1976 and 1985.

STARS OF THE 1980s

During the early 1980s, only two new Trinidadian Test players came to the fore and one of them, Ranjie Nanan, a right-arm off-break bowler and attacking right-handed batsman, appeared in only one Test. He did so against Pakistan at Faisalabad in December 1980, claiming 4/91 from 36 overs, scoring sixteen runs (av: 8.00) and holding two catches. His contribution to the West Indian victory was substantial. In addition to his steady bowling, which helped to reduce Pakistan to scores of 176 & 145, he shared a record tenth-wicket stand of 44 runs with Sylvester Clarke, the Barbadian fast bowler. Nanan was one of the most consistent all-rounders in Caribbean cricket from 1972 to 1990. During that time, he took more wickets in the regional (Shell Shield) competition than any other player. In 88 first-class matches, he recorded 2,533 runs (av: 21.46), 351 wickets (av: 22.81) and 61 catches. Nanan certainly deserved more than one Test cap.

The dependable Larry Gomes batting against England in the Test match at Barbados in March 1986

Much more fortunate was the diminutive Augustine 'Gus' Logie, an attacking right-handed batsman and a brilliant fielder. He played 52 Tests during 1983-92 and shared with Jeffrey Dujon of Jamaica the enviable distinction of having never taken part in a losing series despite participating in more than fifty Tests. After a somewhat pedestrian start to his Test career, Gus Logie became a vital cog in the Caribbean machine, producing many a match-saving innings when the more famous batsmen had failed. He ended his Test career with 2,470 runs (av: 35.79), including two centuries, and 57 catches. He was also a very important performer in ODIs, scoring 2,809 runs (av: 28.95) and holding 61 catches in 158 such contests.

Late in the 1980s, two extremely good fast bowlers appeared in Trinidad: Ian Bishop and Anthony Gray. The latter was a tall and lanky right-hander who promised to go far, especially after capturing 22 wickets (av: 17.13) in his first five Tests against Pakistan and New Zealand in 1986/87. But, at a time when

Ian Bishop in action during the fourth Test against England at Old Trafford in July 1995

Curtly Ambrose, Malcolm Marshall, Patrick Patterson and Courtney Walsh were still playing, he was soon discarded. Gray was good enough to have represented any other country in those days.

More fortunate, and much more dangerous, was Gray's compatriot, Ian Bishop. The latter succeeded where Gray had failed because he was more accurate with his line and length. Had it not been for serious and recurrent back injuries, he would easily have exceeded 200 Test wickets. As it was, he ended his Test career with 161 (av: 24.27) in 43 matches, thus eclipsing the Trinidadian record of 158 that Ramadhin had set. Bishop is the greatest fast bowler thus far produced by Trinidad and one of the best ever to represent the West Indies. A reliable fielder, he was also a useful lower-order right-handed batsman with 632 Test runs (av: 12.15) and eight catches to his credit. His record in ODIs is also impressive: 405 runs (av: 16.20), 118 wickets (av: 26.50) and twelve catches in 84 games.

TRINIDADIAN TEST CRICKETERS SINCE 1990

Apart from Bishop, the Trinidadian stars of the 1990s have been Marlon Black, Rajendra Dhanraj, Mervyn Dillon, Darren Ganga, Brian Lara, Suruj Ragoonath, Dinanath Ramnarine, Lincoln Roberts, Phil Simmons and David Williams. Dhanraj, Ragoonath and Roberts failed to take advantage of their opportunities. Dhanraj, a right-arm leg-break bowler, was most disappointing in his four Tests against India and England. He took only eight wickets for 595 runs and had to be dropped, despite an outstanding record in regional competition. In two Tests against Australia in March 1999, Ragoonath, a right-handed opening batsman, mustered a paltry thirteen runs (av: 4.33) and had to be discarded. Roberts, a right-handed batsman, played a single Test against Australia in March 1999, made nought in his solitary innings, and was not selected again. He is only the second Tobagonian (following Cyril Merry) to play Test cricket.

If it seems unlikely that Dhanraj, Ragoonath and Roberts will ever be selected to represent the West Indies again, the same is true for Simmons and Williams. The former was a hard-hitting right-handed opening batsman, a steady right-arm bowler of medium pace and an excellent fieldsman. Between 1987 and 1999, he appeared in 26 Tests for the West Indies, scoring 1,002 runs (av: 22.26), taking four wickets (av: 64.25) and holding 26 catches. His technique as an opening batsman was clearly flawed, but the selectors persisted with him because of his reputation as a good team player. Because of his aggressive approach, Simmons was more of an asset in one-day competition. He

Darren Ganga at bat during day three of the first Test against Australia on 11 April 2003 at Bourda Oval in Georgetown

Mervyn Dillon celebrates with team-mates after taking a wicket during day one of the second Test against Australia on 19 April 2003 at Queens Park Oval in Port of Spain

participated in 143 ODIs, recording 3,675 runs (av: 28.93), 83 wickets (av: 34.65), and 55 catches. In one unforgettable display of accurate bowling, he claimed four wickets for three runs in ten overs, including eight maidens, in a day/night match against Pakistan at Sydney in December 1992. This remains one of the most exceptional bowling performances in the history of ODIs.

David Williams, a right-handed wicket-keeper/batsman, moved in and out of the West Indies Test XI during the 1990s, before being palpably eclipsed by Ridley Jacobs at the end of the decade. In eleven Tests, he scored 242 runs (av: 13.44) and effected 42 dismissals, including two stumpings. He also took part in 36 ODIs, recording 147 runs (av: 9.18), 35 catches and ten stumpings. Inconsistency was his major problem.

While Simmons and Williams have obviously come to the end of the line, there is a glimmer of hope for Black, the right-arm fast bowler, who made his Test debut against Australia at Brisbane in November 2000. In six Tests thus far, he has taken twelve wickets and often seems steady enough, but an average of 49.75 runs per wicket is not altogether encouraging.

Ganga and Ramnarine have shown much greater promise but their Test careers have constantly been interrupted by irresolute selectors. Ramnarine, an outstanding right-arm leg-break bowler, has not yet failed in any one Test, but he has been dropped so often that his confidence must surely be undermined. In twelve Tests so far, he has taken 45 wickets (av: 30.73). A stubborn lower-order batsman and a very good fieldsman, he has also scored 106 runs (av: 6.23) and held eight catches. Ganga is a careful right-handed batsman who has so far registered 1,076 runs (av: 25.61) and sixteen catches in 24 Tests. He has been allowed 28 ODIs thus far, scoring 691 runs at an average of 26.57 per innings.

Since the retirement of Courtney Walsh in 2001, Mervyn Dillon has emerged as the leading fast bowler in the West Indies and is one of the best that Trinidad has yet produced. In 35 Tests thus far, he has taken 127 wickets at 31.80 runs apiece. A right-handed lower-order batsman, he has scored 461 runs (av: 7.81). He has also taken sixteen catches. In 93 ODIs, he has claimed 116 wickets (31.41), made 200 runs (av: 7.69), and held eighteen catches.

But by far the brightest star in the Trinidadian firmament since 1990, has been the incomparable Brian Charles Lara, easily the greatest batsman produced thus far by his native republic. An attractive left-handed batsman with a wonderful array of attacking strokes, he has amassed 8,626 runs (av: 51.65) in his first 98 Tests. This easily eclipsed the Trinidadian record of 3,171 established by Larry Gomes. Lara's 22 Test centuries and 63 scores in excess of fifty at that level also constitute Trinidadian records. He broke the West Indian Test record of four double centuries (set by Gordon Greenidge of Barbados between 1974 and 1991) when he struck his fifth against Sri Lanka in 2003. Much more important are the two world records established by Lara in 1994: a Test innings of 375 achieved against England at St John's in April and the incredible 501 not out for Warwickshire against Durham in June. Lara's ability to score at a phenomenally rapid rate has also made him one of the most dangerous batsmen in one-day international competition. In 224 ODIs thus far, he has scored 8,437 runs (av: 43.04). His eighteen centuries in these matches have surpassed the West Indian record (17) that Desmond Haynes had set. A brilliant slip fieldsman, he has taken 131 Test catches and 95 in ODIs. Apart from such wicket-keepers as Jeffrey Dujon (267), Deryck Murray (181) and Ridley Jacobs (173), no West Indian cricketer has taken more Test catches. Still only 34, Lara's chances of surpassing every significant West Indian batting and fielding record are very good.

FINAL ANALYSIS

Trinidad has so far provided the West Indies with ten players (Joey Carew, Charlie Davis, Darren Ganga, Larry Gomes, Gerry Gomez, Brian Lara, Gus Logie, Deryck Murray, Phil Simmons and Jeffrey Stollmeyer) who have exceeded 1,000 runs in Test cricket and six (Ian Bishop, Learie Constantine, Mervyn Dillon, Gomez, Bernard Julien and Sonny Ramadhin) who have exceeded fifty Test wickets. Three of its bowlers (Bishop, Dillon and Ramadhin) have taken more than 100. Seven Trinidadians (Nelson Betancourt, Jackie Grant, Rolph Grant, Gerry Gomez, Brian Lara, Deryck Murray and Jeffrey Stollmeyer) have captained the West Indies in 57 Tests, of which fifteen were won, 26 lost

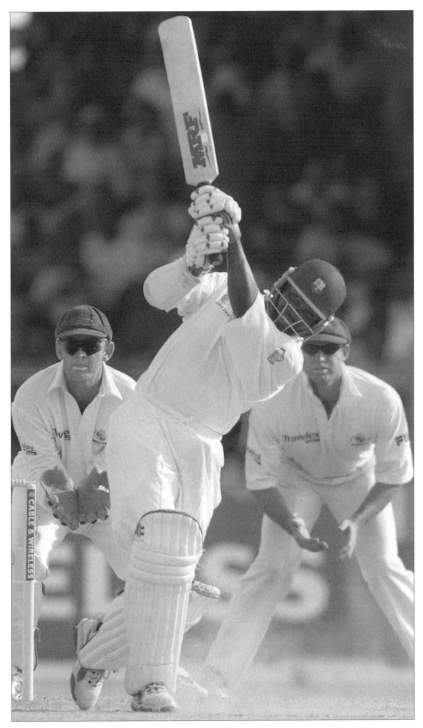

Brian Lara in action during day two of the second Test against Australia on 20 April 2003 at
Queens Park Oval in Port of Spain

and sixteen drawn. This may not appear to be a successful record, but it tells us more about the state of Caribbean cricket at the time when Trinidadians captained the West Indies than about the quality of Trinidadian leadership itself. When the two Grants led the West Indies during the inter-war years, the West Indies had just acquired Test match status and were not yet strong enough to challenge Australia and England on equal terms. When Lara took over the reins from Courtney Walsh in 1996, he found the West Indies mired in a colossal slump, from which they have not yet recovered.

Trinidad's contributions to Caribbean cricket extend far beyond the arithmetic of runs, wickets and victories achieved in Test matches. There have been very important Trinidadian administrators and managers whose work can never be quantified. Such individuals as Harold Burnett, Joey Carew, Sir Errol dos Santos, Gerry Gomez, Sir Kenneth Lindsay Grant, Alloy Lequay, Cyril Merry, Lance Murray and Jeffrey Stollmeyer devoted considerable time and energy to the betterment of the WICBC. Trinidadian umpires like Clyde Cumberbatch, Ralph Gosein and Eric Lee Kow also left an indelible impact. So, too, did Mervyn 'Pee Wee' Wong, one of the best known among all West Indian cricket statisticians.

The Trinidadian contribution to West Indian cricket literature and journalism has also been immense. One of the most important names in the history of cricket sociology is that of the celebrated Trinidadian activist and philosopher, Cyril Lionel Robert James. It was 'Nello' who inspired Caribbean social scientists and historians (like Professors Hilary Beckles, Hubert Devonish, Woodville Marshall, Orlando Patterson, Keith A.P. Sandiford, L.O'B. Thompson and a host of others) to write scholarly books and articles on West Indian cricket. Such Trinidadians as Sir Learie Constantine, Undine Giuseppi, Horace Harragin, Brunell Jones, Trevor McDonald and Jeffrey Stollmeyer have also left a positive imprint on West Indian cricket literature. Nor can we forget the contributions of such cricket journalists and commentators as Bryan Davis, Everard Gordon, Jeff Hackett, 'Sobie' Maharaj, Vinode Mamchan, Valentino Singh, Garth Wattley and Naz Yacoob.

CHAPTER FIVE

JAMAICA

JAMAICA IS THE LARGEST AND MOST POPULOUS OF THE ENGLISH-speaking islands in the Caribbean. It is 4,244 square miles in extent and supports a population of approximately 2.5 million inhabitants. It is by no means as spacious as the republic of Guyana (over 83,000 square miles) on the South American mainland but its population is more than three times as large. In fact, Jamaicans account for almost half the total number of people in the former British West Indies.

It comes, therefore, as something of a disappointment to note that Jamaica has never really been one of the cricketing heavyweights in the Caribbean. Whereas the small island of Antigua with perhaps fewer than 75,000 inhabitants in its 108 square miles can point to such stalwarts as Curtly Ambrose, Eldine Baptiste, Kenny Benjamin, Winston Benjamin, Ridley Jacobs, Vivian Richards, Richie Richardson and Andy Roberts over the past 25 years, Jamaica can only boast of about half-a-dozen cricketers of similar quality over a considerably longer period. Whereas Antigua had generally been ignored by the WICBC prior to the late 1960s, Jamaica had always been a fully-fledged member from the time that the Board was established in 1927.

There are two major reasons for such developments. In the first place, Jamaica never really put as much store on the game of cricket as did the Antiguans and Barbadians. To the Jamaicans, it is true, cricket is of some significance but it has generally ranked a distant second to athletics in their kinetic hierarchy. They are content to produce more brilliant track stars per capita, year after year, than any other community. Such outstanding sprinters as Donald Quarrie and Merlene Ottey, for instance, won numerous medals in international competition. Quarrie alone accumulated more gold medals than all the Barbadians and Antiguans combined and the incredible Ottey won, by everyone's calculation, approximately forty important medals all by herself. This is actually a great deal more than Canada has been able to accomplish with a population of almost thirty million.

THE PROBLEM OF GEOGRAPHY
Secondly, Jamaica is somewhat unfortunately situated. Lying more than 1,200 miles to the northwest of the eastern Caribbean, it was overlooked during that lengthy period (1890-1945) when Barbados, British Guiana and Trinidad were

participating in their triangular tournaments. Early touring teams from England sometimes neglected Jamaica because it was too far away. As late as 1913, for instance, the MCC squad, led by A.W.F. Somerset, regretted that they could not visit Jamaica since that involved a nine-day voyage from the rest of the British West Indies. This meant that while Barbados met British Guiana for the first time in inter-colonial competition in 1865, and Trinidad played British Guiana for the first time in 1869, Jamaica did not take any part in inter-colonial cricket until 1896.

For geographical reasons, then, Jamaica remained beyond the boundary of first-class cricket in the Caribbean for about thirty years. It was first drawn into the fold when George Wyatt of British Guiana was contemplating a West Indian tour of North America in 1886. As it was less expensive to travel to Canada and the United States from Jamaica than from the east, no fewer than seven Jamaican volunteers joined Wyatt's squad of thirteen that year. On the field, the tourists were led by the Jamaican, L.R. Fyfe. He was accompanied by such compatriots as J.M. Burke, W.H. Farquharson, Leo Isaacs, Percy Isaacs, J. Lees and E.N. Marshall. Lees headed the batting averages with 22.40, while Burke (65 wickets at 10.10 runs each) and Farquharson (61 wickets at 9.16) bowled very well. They proved conclusively that Jamaicans were capable of playing the game with no little skill.

Even so, it took another ten years before Jamaicans played their initial first-class matches. In 1896, they travelled to Georgetown and lost twice to Demerara, despite the heroics of A.M. Byng, their leading all-rounder, who captured five wickets and tallied 156 runs in four innings during the tournament. The Jamaicans naturally lost again when they visited Barbados for the first time later that year. They suffered two innings defeats in their first three inter-colonial contests. At home, against Trinidad in 1905, they proceeded to lose four times in a row. They avoided defeat for the first time when they held Barbados to two draws at Bridgetown in 1925. This was a sign of significant progress as Barbados was then regarded as virtually invincible at the Kensington Oval.

A SLOW START

Jamaica, in short, remained a weak sister in Caribbean cricket for a very long time. Thus, in 1900, when the first West Indian team to tour England was selected, it included only two Jamaicans, M.M. Kerr and G.L. Livingstone, neither one of whom, in Christopher Nicole's words, "did anything to justify his selection". In 1906, the three Jamaicans (Dr Joseph Cameron, Charles Stuart Morrison and J.E. Parker) who accompanied H.B.G. Austin's team to England were again "the least distinguished members of the side". Apart from two drawn games against the MCC in 1911, Jamaica had played no first-class cricket for several years prior to 1923 but still had to send its quota of three players again to England in that year. Its representatives were J.K. Holt Sr, R.K. Nunes (the vice-captain) and R.L. Phillips.

Raymond Phillips, a right-arm slow bowler and lower-order right-handed batsman, was injured early in the campaign and played only one first-class match that summer. His whole career involved seven first-class matches in which he took 24 wickets (av: 25.91) and scored 69 runs (av: 17.25). John Kenneth Holt was a useful right-handed all-rounder who could also keep wicket. He achieved very little on that tour but was good enough to register 1,600 runs (av: 27.58), 26 wickets (av: 40.53), 25 catches and one stumping in 36 first-class matches during 1905-30 (at a time when first-class cricket in the Caribbean was most irregular). Holt's greatest contribution to West Indian cricket came in the form of a son, bearing the same name, who played many attractive Test innings during the 1950s.

Of much greater significance than Holt or Phillips was Robert Karl Nunes, son of wealthy white Jamaican parents who sent him to Dulwich for his education. He was a sound left-handed batsman who scored 2,695 runs (av: 31.33) in 61 first-class matches. He captained the West Indies in four of their first seven Tests, scoring 245 runs (av: 30.62) and taking two catches. Nunes was a reserve wicket-keeper, who accounted altogether for 39 dismissals, including eight stumpings during 1924-30. He made two tours to England (1923 and 1928), being captain during the second. He thus had the honour of leading the West Indies in their first Test series. A founder of the Jamaican Cricket Board of Control, he later presided over the WICBC from 1945 to 1952. Karl Nunes, that is to say, made vital contributions to Caribbean cricket both on the field and off it.

During the 1920s, Jamaican cricket received a tremendous boost from entertaining no fewer than four teams from England. Against the MCC in 1925/26, Jamaica achieved two solid draws, thanks to some excellent cricket from Holt, F.R. Martin, C.M. Morales, Nunes, E.A. Rae and O.C. Scott. Lord Tennyson then took teams to Jamaica in two successive winters and gave Nunes the chance in February 1927 to record his highest score (200 not out) in first-class cricket. Rae again played well while L.G. Hylton, a promising right-arm fast bowler, emerged. One year later, Holt distinguished himself with a series of fine scores, while Martin, Morales and Nunes continued to perform splendidly. Ivan Barrow and Nunes did fairly well against Julien Cahn's team in 1928/29. But it was the advent of the great George Headley, during Lord Tennyson's second visit, that dwarfed everything else.

GEORGE ALPHONSO HEADLEY

George Alphonso Headley was the first great cricket star produced by Jamaica. He was one of the finest batsmen in the world throughout the 1930s and is still considered by many to be the most accomplished of all West Indian batsmen. An impeccable technique and an exemplary temperament allowed him to perform with an exceptional consistency for more than two decades. He played 22 Tests for the West Indies, tallying 2,190 runs and averaging 60.83 per

George Alphonso Headley, by far the greatest batsman thus far produced by Jamaica. He averaged almost seventy runs per innings in a first-class career that stretched from 1927 to 1954

innings – the best yet achieved by any West Indian with more than 1,000 Test runs to his credit. He was the first Jamaican to exceed 5,000 runs in first-class cricket and only the second West Indian (following S.G. Smith of Trinidad) to exceed 6,000. He ended his illustrious career in 1954 with 9,921 runs (av: 69.86). His career batting average remains the best by far of any West Indian. A useful right-arm change bowler and a brilliant field, he also recorded 51 wickets (av: 36.11) and 76 catches in 103 first-class matches.

Headley possessed all of the orthodox strokes and was capable of scoring on bad wickets as well as good. He announced his arrival on the international stage with a century in the second innings of his first Test match and proceeded to become the first West Indian to accumulate ten Test hundreds and the first to achieve two double centuries in Test cricket. He struck four double centuries during his two tours of England (1933 and 1939) and accumulated no fewer than 2,320 runs (av: 66.28) during the summer of 1933. That still remains a record for the West Indies during an English tour. In the curtailed campaign of 1939, the great George still had time to score 1,745 runs at an average of 72.70 per innings and would no doubt have exceeded 2,000 again had the season run its natural course. Headley's 33 centuries in first-class cricket remained a West Indian record until surpassed by Clyde Walcott in 1956. His ten centuries in Test cricket stood as the West Indian standard until Walcott and Everton Weekes achieved fifteen in the mid-1950s.

It is difficult to exaggerate Headley's contribution to West Indian cricket. He was the first in a long line of superior Black batsmen to emerge from the Caribbean. He carried the whole weight of the West Indies on his

114

back during his entire career and came therefore to be known simply as 'Atlas'. While he was scoring ten Test centuries against Australia and England in the 1930s, his West Indian colleagues were combining for a grand total of five Test centuries between them. Many English pundits referred to him as the 'Black Bradman' at a time when Jamaicans saw Donald Bradman as the 'White Headley'. His phenomenal batting in 1929/30, when he amassed a record aggregate of 703 runs (av: 87.87), led the West Indies to their first Test victory and their first drawn Test series. On the tour of Australia in 1930/31, he was again the West Indian hero, exceeding 1,000 runs and averaging 44.41 per innings. Naturally, Headley starred once more when the West Indies won their first Test series against England at home in 1934/35. At Kingston, in the fourth Test, he made 270 not out in a total of 535/7 declared to ensure a win. That remained the highest individual score for the West Indies against England until Lawrence Rowe achieved his magnificent 302 at Bridgetown in March 1974. In January 1948, in the twilight of his career, Headley became the first Black captain of a West Indies Test XI. He led them for one match against England at Bridgetown. He was a real source of inspiration to such budding stars as J.K. Holt Jr, Allan Rae, Kenneth Rickards, Jeffrey Stollmeyer and the Three Ws.

The emergence of the great George coincided with the first Golden Age of Jamaican cricket. In the late 1920s, apart from Headley, Holt and Nunes, there appeared a number of highly skilled Jamaican players. They performed so well against the English touring sides that four of them had to be taken to England in 1928. Apart from Nunes (captain), the team included 'Reggie'

Allan Rae, pictured here in 1950 when he made huge contributions to the West Indies' historic triumph in the Test series against England

Martin, Ernest Rae and O.C. Scott. Martin, a very good left-handed opening batsman, was the most successful among them. He headed the Test averages with 29.16 runs per innings and scored 1,370 runs (av: 32.61) during the tour. He accompanied the West Indian team to Australia in 1930/31 and visited England again in 1933. For about a decade, Martin was one of the best batsmen in the Caribbean. In nine Tests, he registered 486 runs (av: 28.58), including a defiant 123 not out against Australia at Sydney in March 1931. That was the highest score achieved by a West Indian against Australia in Australia. It stood as such until Garry Sobers hit 132 at Brisbane in December 1960.

Ernest Rae, a hard-hitting right-handed batsman, did nothing of note in the 1928 tour of England but his overall statistics suggest a player of no mean quality. In 29 first-class matches altogether, he recorded 1,118 runs (av: 30.21). He remained a regular member of the Jamaican XI from 1924 to 1936. He also fathered Allan Rae, the left-handed opening batsman who was destined to make a much more solid impact on Caribbean cricket.

Oscar Scott was a good right-handed all-rounder, capable of scoring useful runs in the lower middle-order and taking vital wickets with his leg-breaks. He took part in only twelve first-class matches in England in 1928, recording 322 runs (av: 20.12), 25 wickets (av: 36.24), and two catches. He was excluded from the first Test at Lord's but played in the second and third, scoring 74 runs (av: 24.66) and taking two wickets for 103 runs. Scott represented the West Indies in eight Tests, making 171 runs (av: 17.10) and taking 22 wickets (av: 42.04). In the 'timeless' Test at Kingston in April 1930, he returned the remarkable match analysis of 105.2/13/374/9. In the first innings, while England were amassing a monumental 849, he bowled 80.2 overs, a long-standing West Indian record which remained unchallenged until Sonny Ramadhin delivered 98 in the second innings against England at Birmingham in May 1957. His contribution to Caribbean cricket included a son, A.P.H. Scott, who represented the West Indies in a Test match against India in 1952/53.

When the West Indies hosted England in 1929/30, no fewer than eight Jamaicans were selected for the fourth Test at Kingston. In addition to Headley, Martin, Nunes and Scott, Ivan Barrow, George Gladstone, Oscar DaCosta and Clarence Passailaigue took part in that extraordinary contest which was left drawn after seven days of inconclusive play. Gladstone and Passailaigue were destined to play no more Test cricket after that, even though they made useful contributions on their debut. Gladstone, a slow left-arm bowler, sent down fifty overs to take one wicket for 189 while the opponents were accumulating 1,121 runs; and he was left unbeaten at twelve in his only Test innings. Passailaigue, an aggressive right-handed batsman, scored 44 and 2 not out. He was most unfortunate to be overlooked afterwards by the selectors since he averaged more than 52 runs per innings in a short but outstanding first-class career that featured a world record sixth-wicket partnership of 487 runs with Headley against Lord Tennyson's XI in 1932. Passailaigue's share was 261 not out. That was the occasion on which Headley (344 not out) also achieved his highest score in first-class cricket. Passailaigue was in such good form in that match that he actually out-scored the great George.

Barrow and DaCosta resurfaced. The former was a neat and cautious right-handed opening batsman who also kept wicket capably. He represented the West Indies in eleven Tests, scoring 276 runs (av: 16.23) and effecting 22 dismissals. His best effort (105) occurred at Old Trafford in July 1933 when he became the first West Indian to achieve a Test century in England. With Headley, he added 200 in 205 minutes, then a West Indian record for the second wicket. Barrow made two tours to England (1933 and 1939) and one to Australia in 1930/31. His finest season was 1933 when he exceeded 1,000 runs (av: 23.77). He was much less successful in 1939, mustering only 304 runs (av: 13.21). Barrow finished his first-class career with 2,551 runs (av: 23.84), 71 catches and 27 stumpings. His 98 dismissals long remained a West Indian record. Even more durable has been the Jamaican third-wicket partnership record of 248 runs which he shared with Headley against Lord Tennyson's XI in 1932. That mark still stands.

DaCosta, a right-handed all-rounder, played in five Tests during 1929-35, contributing 153 runs (av: 19.12), three wickets (av: 58.33) and five catches. He was a member of the West Indian team which toured England in 1933. He scored 1,046 runs (av: 26.82) that summer and ended his career with 1,563 (av: 29.49). When DaCosta died on 1 October 1936, at the tender age of 29, he was the first West Indian Test cricketer to do so.

OTHER JAMAICAN STARS OF THE 1930s

Thanks largely to Headley's brilliance, Jamaica performed so well against visiting teams from England that it could justify the selection of at least four members on West Indian touring teams throughout the 1930s. Barrow, Headley, Martin and Scott travelled to Australia in 1930/31. To England in 1933, the Trinidadian captain, Jackie Grant, was accompanied by five Jamaicans: Barrow, DaCosta, Headley, Martin and Vincent Valentine. In 1939, Rolph Grant took five Jamaicans with him to England: Barrow, John H. Cameron, Headley, Leslie Hylton and Kenneth Weekes.

The son of Dr Joseph Cameron who had toured England with the West Indies in 1906, John H. was a hard-hitting right-handed batsman and a right-arm leg-break bowler who played 105 first-class matches, mainly for Cambridge University and Somerset during 1932-47. For the West Indies in 1939, he took part in seventeen games, scoring 438 runs (av: 20.85) and claiming 31 wickets (av: 21.41). He was much less successful in his two Tests that summer, recording only six runs (av: 2.00) and three wickets (av: 29.33).

Valentine was an aggressive right-handed lower-order batsman and a steady right-arm fast-medium bowler. His selection to tour England in 1933 was a surprise to many, since he had played in only two first-class matches before that and his results had been mediocre. His overall record was undistinguished: 500 runs (av: 17.85) and 49 wickets (av: 40.40) in 24 matches. Not surprisingly, he produced nothing of significance in his two Tests against England that summer: 35 runs (av: 11.66) and one wicket for 104 runs. Had the quota system not been in vogue at that time, Derek Sealy of Barbados would obviously have been selected instead.

Hylton was a powerfully built right-arm fast bowler and an attacking lower-order right-handed batsman who made his Test debut against England at Bridgetown in January 1935. He played against England in all four Tests of that series, scoring 53 runs (av: 13.25) and taking thirteen wickets (av: 19.30). In 1939, he fell somewhat below expectations, taking part in only fifteen first-class matches and capturing only 39 wickets (av: 27.71). In six Tests for the West Indies, Hylton claimed sixteen wickets (av: 26.12). He was one of the best of the early fast bowlers produced by Jamaica.

'Bam Bam' Weekes was an aggressive left-handed batsman and a useful reserve wicket-keeper who might have made a greater impact on the game had his career not been interrupted by the Second World War. He scored a swashbuckling 137 against England in the third Test at The Oval in 1939 and averaged 57.66 in his two Tests that summer. He also struck a forceful 146 against Surrey at the same venue. After the war, he made a confident 84 against Barbados at Kingston but could not compete with the new generation of stroke-players who had emerged during the 'goodwill' tournaments held in the eastern Caribbean. In thirty first-class matches between 1938 and 1948, Weekes scored 1,731 runs (av: 40.25).

Two other Jamaicans, Richard Fuller and George Mudie, represented the West Indies during the 1930s. They both played in the Kingston Test against England in March 1935. Fuller was a right-handed all-rounder who registered a fine 113 not out against MCC at Sabina Park during the tour of 1934/35 to earn selection for the Test which followed. But he managed only one in his solitary Test innings and bowled eight overs of right-arm medium pace for twelve runs without result. He was never selected again.

Mudie, a left-handed all-rounder, was slightly more successful. He scored five and then claimed 3/40 from 29 searching overs, of which twelve were maidens. The West Indies won this match by an innings and 161 runs after Headley scored his unbeaten 270. It was the last Test played in the Caribbean until 1948. Mudie continued to represent Jamaica until 1952 but, like Kenneth Weekes, could not compete with the rising stars recently spawned by Barbados and Trinidad. In nineteen first-class matches altogether, he registered 578 runs (av: 22.23) and 42 wickets (av: 35.45). After the death of John Cameron on 13 February 2000, Mudie reigned for two years (until 8 June 2002) as the longest surviving West Indian Test cricketer.

THE IMMEDIATE POST-WAR YEARS

During the Second World War, while Barbados and Trinidad were participating in their annual 'goodwill' tournaments, Jamaican cricket stood relatively still. It spent an unconscionably long time recovering from this disadvantage. In the first Test against England at Bridgetown in January 1948, Headley, the captain, was the sole Jamaican in the West Indies XI. When injury prevented him from taking any further part in the series, the Jamaicans found themselves without any representation at all at Port of Spain or Georgetown. At Kingston in the final Test, three of them were introduced, mainly to save on passages and accommodations (as was the custom in those days). Thus did Hines Johnson, Esmond Kentish and Kenneth Rickards make their Test debut in front of their home crowd.

Born in 1910, Johnson was a very tall and formidable right-arm fast bowler, a useful lower-order batsman and a reliable fieldsman, whose best years had been lost to the war. Despite his age, he bowled unflaggingly to take 10/96 in 65.5 overs in his first Test and play the major role in the West Indies' victory by eight wickets. He toured England in 1950 with John Goddard's team and took part in two more Tests. Impeded by minor injuries he claimed only 34 first-class wickets (av: 28.05) in seventeen matches that summer. Johnson finished with thirteen Test wickets (av: 18.30) and 38 runs (av: 9.50).

Kentish, another right-arm fast bowler, was allowed only two Tests although he bowled quite well in both. He took 3/106 in 47 overs in 1948 and was discarded until the first Test of the series against England in 1953/54. Selected for the Kingston Test again, he claimed 5/49 in the second innings to bowl West Indies to a convincing victory. But that, amazingly, was the end of his Test career. He ended up with eight Test wickets (av: 22.25). The West Indies might well have made greater use of his abilities.

Rickards was a talented and attractive right-handed batsman who was good enough to have represented most other countries in several Tests in the immediate post-war period. But he had the singular misfortune to emerge at the same time as Robert Christiani, John Goddard, Gerry Gomez, Kenny Trestrail and the Three Ws, who left no space for another batsman in the middle of the West Indian order. Rickards was thus restricted to two Tests, scoring 104 runs (av: 34.66). His best effort was a cultured 67 against England in 1948 when he shared a fifth wicket stand of 116 with Everton Weekes.

Notwithstanding the obvious shift in the Caribbean cricket balance, the normal quota of four Jamaicans had to be selected for the tour of India in 1948/49: F. James Cameron, Headley, Allan Rae and Rickards. An ailing Headley was restricted to four games, including a single Test, and Rickards played only in nine matches and in no Tests at all. He scored 330 runs (av: 36.66) but was completely overshadowed by Christiani, Gomez, Rae, Stollmeyer, Walcott and Weekes.

Jimmy Cameron, who would not have been selected ahead of John Lucas of Barbados or Rupert Tang Choon of Trinidad had it not been for the pernicious quota system, was the younger brother of John H. who had toured England in 1939. A right-handed batsman and right-arm off-break bowler, he played in all five Tests against India, scoring 151 runs (av: 25.16) and capturing three wickets (av: 92.66). His best performance was an attacking 75 not out in the second Test at Bombay. Cameron shortly emigrated to Canada and was lost to West Indian cricket after that.

Much more substantial was the Test career of Allan Fitzroy Rae, the son of E.A. He was a reliable left-handed opening batsman who shared several fine first-wicket partnerships with Jeffrey Stollmeyer. He exceeded 1,000 runs on the tour of India in 1948/49 and did the same in England in 1950. He made a crucial contribution to West Indian triumphs on both of those tours. Against England he registered 377 runs (av: 62.83) and struck two centuries in the four Tests. He ended his Test career with 1,016 runs (av: 46.18), including four centuries. With Stollmeyer at Madras in January 1949, he shared an opening stand of 239 runs which was then a West Indian record. It led to the first West Indian Test victory in India. Rae later became an influential cricket administrator and served as president of the WICBC during the early 1980s. He will long be remembered as the finest opening batsman produced by Jamaica before the advent of Lawrence Rowe.

ALFRED LEWIS VALENTINE

Johnson and Rae were accompanied to England in 1950 by Alfred Lewis Valentine, the greatest spin bowler thus far emanating from Jamaica and by far the finest left-arm spin bowler ever to represent the West Indies. He conspired with Sonny Ramadhin of Trinidad to bewilder England's best batsmen in a most remarkable fashion. In his first four Tests, Valentine captured 33 wickets at less than 21 runs apiece. Against Australia and New Zealand in the tour of 1951/52, he enhanced his reputation by taking 32 more at an average cost of 26.37 runs each. In his first eleven Tests, Valentine had thus, at the age of 21, taken 65 wickets fairly cheaply. He added 28 scalps to his collection when he opposed the touring Indians in 1952/53 and reached his 100th wicket in his nineteenth Test (against England at Georgetown in February 1954) which was then a West Indian record. Valentine ended his career with 139 wickets (av: 30.32) in 36 Tests. In a career that encompassed 125 first-class matches between 1950 and 1965, he recorded 475 wickets (av: 26.21). He also scored 470 runs (av: 5.00) and held 45 catches. Quite simply, he was one of the finest left-arm spin bowlers in the history of cricket.

When the West Indies toured Australia and New Zealand in 1951/52, their squad included three Jamaicans: Rae, Rickards and Valentine. Rickards shortly departed the international scene but Rae and Valentine were joined by a third Jamaican, Alfred Binns, a right-handed batsman and wicket-keeper, who was selected for the first Test against India at Port of Spain in January

Alfred Valentine practising in the nets in June 1950 during his triumphant tour of England

1953. He unfortunately missed a number of chances, however, and was promptly replaced by the Barbadian-born Ralph Legall, then representing Trinidad. Binns was eventually recalled for the Kingston Test against Australia in March 1955 but was promptly dropped again, when he suffered the indignity of a pair of noughts. He then participated in three of the four Tests against New Zealand in 1955/56. His career was thus a chequered one. In his five Tests, Binns recorded 64 runs (av: 9.14) and seventeen dismissals. These statistics do scant justice to the talents of a really competent player who averaged more than 37 runs per innings, scored four centuries and effected 65 dismissals, including seventeen stumpings, in 25 first-class matches during 1950-57.

During the Indian tour of the Caribbean in 1952/53, Jamaica supplied the West Indies with two more Test cricketers: Roy Miller and A.P.H. Scott, each of whom played in a single match. Miller, a right-arm fast bowler, was called up for the fourth Test at Georgetown, was restricted to sixteen overs before suffering an injury, and that was that. Al Scott, Oscar's son, replaced an injured Ramadhin at Kingston in the fifth Test but, on a featherbed pitch, he toiled in vain. His 44 overs of right-arm leg-breaks yielded nine maidens, 140 runs and no wickets.

JAMAICAN STARS OF THE 1950s

One of the brightest Jamaican stars of the 1950s was J.K. Holt Jr, a stylish right-handed stroke-player who made his Test debut against England in January 1954 at Kingston. He created a positive impression at once with an attractive 94. He then produced a dazzling 166 in the second Test at Bridgetown and finished his first series with 432 runs (av: 54.00). He proceeded to play seventeen Tests for the West Indies, scoring 1,066 runs (av: 36.75) and holding eight catches. All of those who witnessed his magnificent innings at the Kensington Oval were left with the impression that Holt was capable of much mightier deeds. He was the sole Jamaican representative in the final two Tests in the series against England in 1953/54.

By the time the Australians arrived in the Caribbean in 1955, a new Jamaican star was rising. O'Neil Gordon Smith promised to be one of the greatest all-rounders ever produced by the West Indies. A clever right-arm off-break bowler, a brilliant fieldsman and an aggressive right-handed batsman, 'Collie' appeared on the threshold of great accomplishments when his life was tragically cut short by a car crash at the age of 26 in September 1959. He began his Test career with a superb century against Australia in his debut and ended it with 1,331 runs (av: 31.69), 48 wickets (av: 33.85), and nine catches in 26 games. During the tour of New Zealand in 1955/56, he captured thirteen wickets (av: 18.53) in the four Tests but did little with the bat. Against England in 1957, however, he headed the West Indian batting averages in the Tests with 396 runs (av: 39.60) after hitting 161 at Birmingham and a match-saving 168 at Nottingham. At home against Pakistan in 1957/58, he registered 283 runs (av: 47.16) and thirteen wickets (av: 38.00). He was again successful during the 1958/59 tour of the sub-continent, scoring 368 runs (av: 28.30) and claiming twelve wickets (av: 27.25) in the eight Tests. Smith was one of the most promising cricketers to come out of Jamaica and there is no telling what he would have accomplished had his career been allowed to run its normal course.

Jamaica produced two fast bowlers of note during the mid-1950s: Tom Dewdney and Roy Gilchrist. Dewdney made his debut against Australia at Bridgetown in May 1955 when he took three early wickets and created a very

A brilliant innings by Collie Smith held up England's chances of victory on the last day of the third Test at Trent Bridge in July 1957

favourable impression. But Australia rallied to amass 668 runs and Dewdney had to be satisfied with a match analysis of 43/9/148/4. He accompanied the West Indies to New Zealand in 1955/56, to England in 1957 and to Australia in 1960/61. He did not distinguish himself in Australia or England but enjoyed one wonderful spell against New Zealand in the fourth Test at Auckland in March 1956 when he took 5/21 in 19.5 devastating overs. Dewdney was a steady and willing performer who captured 21 wickets (av: 38.42) in his nine Tests for the West Indies.

Much faster and far more dangerous was Gilchrist who reached his peak in India in 1958/59 when he captured 26 wickets in four Tests, after having taken 21 against Pakistan in the West Indies during 1957/58. His promising career was unfortunately cut short when he was sent back home from India following a dispute with his captain. Gilchrist was one of the fastest bowlers ever produced by the West Indies. He played in only thirteen Tests but still managed to snare 57 wickets at the reasonable cost of 26.68 runs each. His best match result was 9/73 in 44 overs against India at Calcutta in January 1959. For all too short a period, Gilchrist combined with Wesley Hall to form one of the most fearsome opening pairs in the world. His contributions to West Indian triumphs over India and Pakistan were vital, especially coming so soon after the disastrous series against Australia in 1955 and England in 1957. It is highly likely that had Gilchrist been allowed to participate, the West Indies

'Gerry' Alexander, pictured here in 1957, was Jamaica's finest wicket-keeper/batsman before the advent of Jeffrey Dujon

would have defeated England in the Caribbean in 1959/60 and Australia in Australia in 1960/61.

The captain, who had to make the painful decision to expel Gilchrist from the team in 1959, was Franz Alexander, another Jamaican. He was an excellent wicket-keeper and a very useful right-handed batsman. Alexander made his Test debut against England in 1957 before leading the West Indies to victory over Pakistan in the West Indies in 1957/58 and over India in India in 1958/59. But after losing two consecutive series, to Pakistan abroad in 1959 and England at home in 1959/60, he gave way to Frank Worrell who led the West Indies to Australia in 1960/61. Alexander gave Worrell his whole-hearted support, recording a half-century in each of the five Tests and achieving a superb 108 in the third match at Sydney. He headed the team's batting averages with 484 runs (av: 60.50). In 25 Tests, Alexander scored 961 runs (av: 30.03), caught 85 batsmen and stumped five others. His ninety Test dismissals stood as a West Indian record for many years. He led the West Indies in eighteen Tests, winning seven and losing four.

Three Jamaicans made their Test debut during the period of Alexander's captaincy: Easton McMorris, Reggie Scarlett and Chester Watson. McMorris was a careful right-handed opening batsman, who first played against Pakistan at Port of Spain in February 1958 and returned to the line-up in 1960 after having missed the tour to India and Pakistan. McMorris made two tours to England during the 1960s but failed to find his best form in Test matches there.

Altogether he was selected for thirteen Tests during 1958-66. He made 564 runs (av: 26.85) and struck one century. A prolific gatherer of runs in inter-colonial competition, McMorris seldom gave of his best when the stakes were raised. He consequently left with the reputation of an under-achiever but partially compensated after his retirement by serving for some years as a Test selector.

Neither Scarlett nor Watson quite lived up to their early promise, but it has to be said, in all fairness, that they both faced very stiff competition. Scarlett, a right-arm off-spinner, shortly had to vie for Test selection with the incomparable Lance Gibbs of Guyana; and Watson, a right-arm fast bowler, soon found himself eclipsed by Charles Griffith of Barbados. Scarlett, who ultimately emigrated to England and made a telling contribution to cricket in the north London area, played only three Tests against England at home in 1960, scoring 54 runs (av: 18.00) and taking two wickets (av: 104.50). If his bowling lacked penetration on unresponsive pitches, it was certainly accurate. He delivered 53 maidens among his 134 overs. Watson was slightly more fortunate as he appeared in seven Tests for the West Indies during 1959-61. He finished with nineteen wickets (av: 38.10) and was at his best against England in 1959/60 when he captured sixteen wickets in five Test matches.

HEROES OF THE 1960s AND 1970s

During the 1960s, after Alexander's retirement, Jackie Hendriks of Jamaica emerged as the outstanding wicket-keeper in the Caribbean. There are many pundits who still rate him as the most proficient among all West Indian wicket-keepers. He was also a useful right-handed lower-order batsman, who made 447 runs (av: 18.62) in his twenty Tests. His 47 dismissals included five stumpings. Hendriks' career was a personal triumph over consistent adversity. For two series, he operated as a reserve wicket-keeper in Alexander's shadow. He was injured on the first day of his debut against India at Port of Spain in 1962, but returned to top-score with a defiant and impressive 64 in a low-scoring game which the West Indies eventually won by ten wickets. He played no more in that series and, by the time he had recovered, he found it impossible to replace Deryck Murray who had enjoyed a fantastic series against England in 1963. When he regained his place in 1965, Hendriks promptly suffered another serious injury when struck by one of Garth Mackenzie's deliveries. He resurfaced in 1966 to take part in the triumphant tour of England under Garry Sobers but was able to participate in only three of the five Tests that summer. His only full series was that of 1968/69 against Australia and New Zealand. When his playing career was over, Hendriks continued to render yeoman service to West Indian cricket by acting as manager to several touring teams and chairing the Selection Committee for many years.

Three very good Jamaican batsmen, all right-handed, came to the fore in the early 1970s: Maurice L.C. Foster, Desmond Lewis and Lawrence George Rowe. Foster, who made his Test debut at Old Trafford in 1969, scored very

Jackie Hendriks, seen here in May 1966, is often considered to have been technically the best wicket-keeper ever produced by the West Indies

heavily in Caribbean regional competition but was less prolific in his fourteen Tests which realised only 580 runs (av: 30.52). Even so, he was a polished stroke-player, a useful off-break bowler (who claimed nine Test wickets) and a fine fieldsman. Foster became a popular cricket commentator after his retirement.

Desmond Lewis, who was also an accomplished wicket-keeper, performed extremely well in his three Tests against India in 1970/71, only to be immediately discarded, somewhat inexplicably. With the West Indies struggling at 256/8, he struck an invaluable 81 not out, sharing useful partnerships of 84 and 23 with Lance Gibbs (25) and Jack Noreiga (9). This enabled his side to reach the respectable total of 363. Asked to open in his second Test, he batted well again for 88. Lewis thus left Test cricket with the gaudy batting average of 86.33 runs per innings. He also held eight catches.

Lawrence Rowe made a much greater impact, scoring 214 and 100 not out in his very first Test against New Zealand in February 1972 and producing a truly glorious 302 against England at Bridgetown in 1974. He was the first batsman to score a double century and a century in separate innings of his debut and his match aggregate of 314 remains a world record for a debutante. Unfortunately, however, he showed flashes of such genius very rarely thereafter and curtailed his Test career by taking part in the 'rebel' tour of South Africa in

1982. In thirty Tests for the West Indies, Rowe recorded 2,047 runs (av: 43.55), including seven centuries, and seventeen catches. He was one of the most elegant and commanding stroke-players the world has ever seen. Those who watched him at the crease in the early 1970s are still baffled by his failure to accomplish a great deal more than he eventually did.

A fourth Jamaican batsman, Ronald G.A. Headley, a left-handed opener who played most of his cricket for Worcestershire, was co-opted to represent the West Indies in two Tests during their tour of England in 1973 when the team was depleted by injuries. His contribution to the cause was 62 runs (av: 15.50) and two catches. His Test career naturally ended there, as Gordon Greenidge shortly emerged to partner Roy Fredericks. The son of the great George, Ron sired another international cricketer, Dean Headley, who played for England in the late 1990s. This is a rare example of three successive generations of the same family participating in Test cricket.

Two Jamaican right-arm bowlers, one fast and the other slow, also surfaced at this time: A.G. Barrett and Uton Dowe. The former, a steady leg-spinner, played six Tests in the early 1970s and captured thirteen wickets (av: 46.38) but soon faded from the scene as the West Indian selectors became increasingly partial to men of speed. Dowe was fast and furious enough, but he lacked accuracy and had to be replaced after taking twelve wickets (av: 44.50) in four Tests.

MICHAEL ANTHONY HOLDING

One of the main reasons for Dowe's eclipse was the emergence of his famous countryman, Michael Anthony Holding, one of the greatest fast bowlers in cricket's history. Holding was a member of the original four-pronged pace attack developed by the West Indies during the mid-1970s. He was very successful against India at home and England abroad in 1976 when he took 47 wickets in one calendar year, reaching his peak at The Oval where he captured 14/149 which still remains the best analysis by a West Indian in a Test match. Holding was also a hard-hitting lower-order right-handed batsman and a fine fieldsman. In sixty Tests, he made 910 runs (av: 13.78), claimed 249 wickets (av: 23.68) and held 22 catches. A vital cog in the invincible Caribbean cricket machine during the early 1980s, he made further contributions to the sport by serving as a cricket commentator and writer following his retirement as an active player.

Two very stylish right-handed batsmen shone for Jamaica in regional competition late in the 1970s: Richard Austin and Basil Williams. The former, however, proved a disappointment at the international level. In two Tests against Australia in 1977/78, he could manage only 22 runs (av: 11.00) and two catches. Williams, an opening batsman, was much more productive. Brought into the Test XI when the regular players boycotted the remainder of the series against Australia in 1977/78, he achieved Test centuries against Australia in his debut at Georgetown in April 1978 and against India at Calcutta in December the

Michael Holding in action in the fifth Test against India at Calcutta in December 1983 when he captured 6/88 to help the West Indies win by an innings & 46 runs

same year. But after recording 469 runs (av: 39.08) and five catches in seven Tests, he was superseded by Desmond Haynes of Barbados when the WICBC and Kerry Packer composed their differences.

A third batsman who scored very heavily for Jamaica at this time was Herbert Chang, a careful left-hander, who was finally rewarded for his consistency with a tour to India in 1978/79 when the Packer professionals were on strike. He failed dismally, however, and was not selected again after one solitary Test at Madras. His two Test innings yielded an aggregate of eight runs and an average of 4.00.

JEFFREY DUJON

Throughout the 1980s, Jamaica made only minimal contributions to West Indian batsmanship. Apart from Rowe (until 1982) and the wicket-keeper, Jeffrey Dujon, its sole batting representative was Everton Mattis, a right-handed stylist, who performed reasonably well in Shell Shield competition during 1976-82. After four matches against England in 1980/81, he ended his Test career by touring South Africa in 1982. He had made 145 runs (av: 29.00) and taken three catches for the West Indies.

But Jamaica compensated with quality for what it lacked in quantity during

The acrobatic Jeffrey Dujon displaying his athleticism during the Benson & Hedges World Series match against England in 1987 at Brisbane

that decade. Dujon, who eventually played 81 Tests for the West Indies, was an excellent wicket-keeper who made a number of spectacular catches in support of the four-pronged pace attack first used by Clive Lloyd and later by Viv Richards. Altogether he accounted for 272 dismissals, by far the most by any West Indian cricketer, in a Test career that lasted from 1981 to 1991. Dujon was also an elegant right-handed batsman who scored memorable centuries against Australia, England, India and Pakistan. He never experienced the misfortune of participating in a losing Test series and is the only cricketer who can make that claim after playing for so many years. He made crucial contributions to West Indian triumphs during their golden streak (1980-95) of 29 unbeaten series by recording 3,322 runs (av: 31.94). In addition to being one of the very best wicket-keepers in the history of West Indies cricket, Dujon ranks with Rowe as one of the two finest batsmen produced by Jamaica since George Headley's retirement.

WALSH THE MAGNIFICENT
If Jamaica spawned only a few batsmen of note during the 1970s and 1980s, it can certainly boast of two exceptional fast bowlers during that period. Holding had not yet retired when Courtney Walsh, his most illustrious protege, ascended the stage. He began impressively against Australia in 1984/85 and bowled with great fire and determination until his retirement in 2001. He surpassed all existing standards by capturing 519 Test wickets (av: 24.44), making a mockery of the old record of 434 that India's Kapil Dev had set. For a fast bowler who propelled in excess of 30,000 deliveries at great pace, his durability (132 Tests) was simply phenomenal. He seemed, in fact, to become increasingly dangerous as his career progressed. In his very last series against South Africa, for instance, he claimed 25 wickets at 19.68 runs apiece. On 22 occasions, he took five wickets or more in a single Test innings to equal the West Indian record shared by Curtly Ambrose and Malcolm Marshall. He also captured ten wickets or more in a Test match three times. In 205 ODIs, he snared 227 wickets (av: 30.47), another West Indian record.

Walsh was not renowned as a batsman or a fielder, but he was still good enough to hold 29 Test catches and to score 936 Test runs (av: 7.54). His most productive Test innings was thirty not out against Pakistan at St John's, Antigua, in May 1993 when he shared a tenth wicket partnership of 106 runs with Carl Hooper. This has remained a record for the West Indies. But perhaps his most important effort at the crease was his nought not out against Australia at Bridgetown in April 1999, when he survived long enough to allow Brian Lara to hit the winning runs in a sensational one-wicket triumph. Between 1993 and 1998, Walsh served as captain of the West Indies in 22 Tests, winning six, losing seven, and drawing nine. On the surface, this seems a moderate record of leadership at best, but it is most satisfactory when one considers the state of Caribbean cricket when Walsh succeeded Richie Richardson as captain.

130

Courtney Walsh comes in to bowl in the fourth Test match against Australia on 27 December 2000 at the Melbourne Cricket Ground

One of Walsh's Jamaican colleagues in the West Indian Test XI during 1986-92 was Patrick Patterson, perhaps the world's fastest bowler while at his peak in the late 1980s. With his fearsome right-arm bouncers and yorkers, Patterson claimed 93 wickets (av: 30.90) in 28 Tests. Had his accuracy come close to matching his speed, he would clearly have been a more formidable opponent. The advent of such great pacers as Curtly Ambrose and Ian Bishop led to Patterson's early eclipse after a relatively brief Test career. In 59 ODIs, he also captured ninety wickets (av: 24.51).

After Dujon's retirement, the outstanding Jamaican cricketer apart from Walsh, was Jimmy Adams, an accomplished left-handed batsman, a very capable left-arm spin bowler, a useful wicket-keeper and a brilliant fieldsman. He was easily Jamaica's finest all-rounder since the death of 'Collie' Smith. Adams made his Test debut against South Africa at Bridgetown in April 1992 and played an important role in his team's victory, scoring ninety runs for once out and taking 4/59 in 26.5 overs. He batted extremely well against England in the West Indies in 1993/94 and against India in India in 1994/95, when he made 520 runs (av: 173.33) in three Tests. Towards the end of the decade, however, both his batting and bowling became increasingly ineffective and he lost his place in the Test XI after a dismal tour of Australia in 2000/01. When he replaced Brian Lara as captain, the responsibilities of the position seemed to weigh too heavily upon him.

Even so, the record compiled by Jimmy Adams in international cricket is most creditable. In 54 Tests, he registered 3,012 runs (av: 41.26), 27 wickets (av: 49.48) and 48 catches. Among his six Test centuries, was an unbeaten 208 against New Zealand at the Antigua Recreation Ground in April 1996. But perhaps his finest performance was a valiant innings of 94 against Australia at Kingston in March 1999 when he and Lara (213) participated in a West Indian record fifth wicket partnership of 322, which was the turning-point in a series that had begun most disastrously. Adams' versatility also made him an invaluable performer in one-day cricket. In 127 ODIs, he recorded 2,204 runs (av: 28.62), 43 wickets (av: 34.86), 68 catches and five stumpings. He captained the West Indies in fifteen Tests, winning four, losing eight, and drawing three. He was a studious leader but his teams simply lacked the talent to compete on even terms with a powerful Australia and an emergent England.

THE LATEST GENERATION

Towards the end of the 20th century, Jamaica began to provide the West Indies with an increasing number of Test cricketers. Two of them, Franklyn Rose and Robert Samuels, looked particularly promising during the mid-1990s. The former bowled brilliantly against India in the Caribbean in 1996/97, when he claimed eighteen wickets at less than 23 runs each, but seemed to lack the temperament and the consistency to build on these foundations. In the end, he was discarded after nineteen Tests and 27 ODIs. Rose was a very capable right-

Jimmy Adams pulls a ball from Darren Gough on his way to 98 during the first Test against England at Edgbaston on 16 June 2000. West Indies won by an innings and 93 runs

arm fast bowler, a hard-hitting lower-order batsman and a reliable fieldsman. His Test career yielded 344 runs (av: 13.23), 53 wickets (av: 30.88) and four catches. For the West Indies, in the shorter version of the game, he registered 217 runs (av: 12.05), 29 wickets (av: 36.06), and six catches.

Robert Samuels was treated fairly shabbily by the selectors. He was a sound and courageous left-handed opening batsman, despite the awkwardness of his peculiar stance. He made his Test debut against New Zealand at Bridgetown in April 1996 and while he did not distinguish himself in that game, he scored an impressive 125 in the next. Against a very strong Australian side in 1996/97, he scored 231 runs (av: 33.00) in four Tests, placing third in his team's averages. But, for no apparent reason, he was then dropped permanently from the Test XI while the selectors continued their vain search for more reliable openers. In six Tests, Samuels contributed 372 runs (av: 37.20) and eight catches.

Robert's brother, Marlon Samuels, has enjoyed much better luck thus far. A sound right-handed batsman, useful right-arm medium pace bowler and good fielder, he was flown to Australia as a replacement in December 2000 and thrown to the wolves at once, at the age of nineteen. He acquitted himself well in his first Test series, heading the team's batting average with 172 runs (av: 34.40) and taking three wickets for 185 runs in 60.5 overs. In nineteen Tests thus far, he has made 874 runs (av: 29.13), taken five wickets (av: 110.00), and held nine catches. In 53 ODIs, he has recorded 1,412 runs (av: 32.83), 34 wickets (av: 36.44), and sixteen catches.

The current West Indian opening batsmen, Chris Gayle and Wavell Hinds, are both Jamaican left-handers who like to play attacking strokes. Gayle has so

133

Chris Gayle in action during the second One Day International against Australia at Sabina Park on 18 May 2003

far represented the West Indies in 34 Tests, scoring 1,866 runs (av: 33.32), including two centuries. A useful change bowler and a brilliant fieldsman, he has also captured eleven wickets (av: 45.90) and held 45 catches. In 83 ODIs, he has scored 3,131 runs (av: 40.14), claimed 74 wickets (av: 28.66) and snared 36 catches. Hinds, a very similar player, has appeared so far in 35 Tests. His record reads: 2,083 runs (av: 34.14), nine wickets (av: 28.66), and 29 catches. In 83 ODIs, he has made 2,245 runs (av: 30.75), captured thirteen wickets (av: 26.76), and held 26 catches.

Curiously, the young Jamaican opening batsman who seemed to offer the greatest promise in the early 1990s was Leon Garrick. His career, however, never evolved as his supporters had predicted. In the end, he became just another West Indian 'One Test Wonder'. Against South Africa, in April 2001, when finally given his chance, he cut his very first ball (from Alan Donald) straight to Shaun Pollock in the gully. A score of 27 in the second innings brought his career Test average to 13.50 but could not save him from the axe.

Another Jamaican who is likely to suffer the same fate as Garrick is Gareth Breese, a right-handed all-rounder, who has toiled valiantly in the regional competition for several years. He received an opportunity at long last against India at Chennai in 2002, but could muster only five runs (av: 2.50), two wickets (av: 67.50) and one catch.

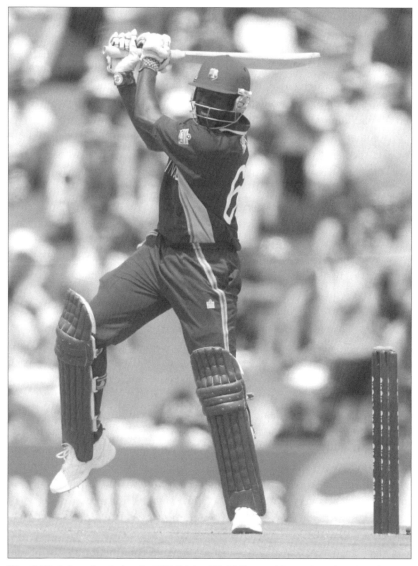

Wavell Hinds in action during the ICC Cricket World Cup Pool B match against Canada on 23 February 2003 at Supersport Park in Centurion, South Africa

One of the most interesting Jamaican 'One Test Wonders' is Ricardo Powell, an aggressive right-handed batsman, who burst upon the scene a few years ago, striking the ball with greater violence than is normal. His quick scoring led to his early promotion to the one-day squad and he has thus far played in seventy ODIs with a fair modicum of success. He has made 1,550 runs at an average of 25.40 runs per innings. But he has so far been selected for a solitary Test, against New Zealand at Hamilton, in December 1999. He could manufacture only 0 & 30 on that occasion and seems to have lost the favour of the Test selectors.

Ricardo's namesake, Darren Powell, has been slightly more fortunate. So far, he has played in four Tests, scoring nineteen runs (av: 3.80) and taking twelve wickets (av: 29.50). He performed fairly well against Bangladesh in December 2002 capturing six wickets for 137 runs in 46 overs with his right-arm medium-fast deliveries. But how often he will be required in the future seems to depend on the availability of such other bowlers as Mervyn Dillon and Adam Sanford.

Another Jamaican who appeared for a while to be regarded mainly as a one-day specialist was the right-arm spinner, Nehemiah Perry, who is also a very capable lower-order batsman. While he was allowed only four Tests at the turn of the century, he has already participated in 21 ODIs. In the latter competitions, he has taken twenty wickets (av: 39.15) and scored 212 runs (av: 26.50). His Test record is less satisfactory. It has so far yielded only 74 runs (av: 12.33) and ten wickets (av: 44.60).

The brightest Jamaican prospect at the moment appears to be Jermaine Lawson, a right-arm fast bowler who played a pivotal role in the West Indies' victory over India in the recent ODI series on the sub-continent. He then bowled brilliantly against Bangladesh, capturing eleven wickets (av: 12.63) in the two Tests there. This included a remarkable analysis of 6/3 in the last innings of the series. Lawson also bowled with great fire against Australia in 2003 and now boasts 29 Test wickets (av: 24.51) in seven matches. But his action is suspect and the ICC has required him to seek remedial help before he can be cleared to bowl in first-class cricket again.

In 2003, three young Jamaicans were introduced to Test cricket with rather disappointing results: Carlton Baugh, David Bernard and Jerome Taylor. In two Tests Baugh, a promising wicket-keeper/batsman, has thus far registered 62 runs (av: 15.50) and three dismissals. Bernard, in his solitary opportunity, scored eleven runs (av: 5.50), and Taylor, a right-arm fast bowler, captured only three wickets very expensively (av: 75.33) in his first three Tests.

FINAL ANALYSIS

It is clear, then, that Jamaica has made a notable contribution to Caribbean cricket even if not commensurate with its size and population. It has provided 63 Test players accounting for 845 Test caps since 1928. Its stars include such superb fast bowlers as Tom Dewdney, Roy Gilchrist, Michael Holding, Hines Johnson, Esmond Kentish, Patrick Patterson, Franklyn Rose and Courtney Walsh and such a brilliant left-arm spinner as Alfred Valentine. Six of these bowlers exceeded fifty wickets in Test cricket and three of them (Holding, Valentine and Walsh) captured in excess of 100. Among them, it is Walsh who holds the world record for the most wickets (519) in a Test career.

Jamaica's batsmen have included Jimmy Adams, Jeffrey Dujon, Chris Gayle, George Headley, Wavell Hinds, Jack Holt, Allan Rae, Lawrence Rowe and Collie Smith – all of whom scored 1,000 runs or more at the highest level.

Jermaine Lawson bowls during day two of the fourth Test against Australia on 10 May 2003 at the Recreation Oval in St John's, Antigua

Headley had the distinction of being the first West Indian to exceed 2,000 runs and achieve ten centuries in Test cricket, while Rowe was one of a few batsmen to register a triple century.

Jamaica has provided the West Indies with a number of valuable wicket-keepers too. Gerry Alexander, Ivan Barrow, Carlton Baugh, Alfie Binns, Dujon, Jackie Hendriks and Desmond Lewis accounted for 459 Test dismissals between them. Twenty-four of their victims were stumped. Dujon's tally of dismissals (272) remains the best by any West Indian in Test cricket. Adams also served as a reserve wicket-keeper. He and Dujon combined for 277 dismissals in ODI competition. Dujon's 183 catches, 21 stumpings and 204 dismissals are all still standing as West Indian ODI records.

Such Jamaicans as Adams, Alexander, George Headley, Karl Nunes and Walsh also served as West Indian Test captains. They did so on sixty occasions, winning seventeen, losing 22, and drawing 21. The most successful was Alexander who led his team to seven wins and only four losses in eighteen Tests. Jamaica has also given the West Indies such able administrators as Hendriks, Cecil Marley, Noel Nethersole, Nunes, Allan Rae and Pat Rousseau whose contributions can never be adequately measured in terms of runs, wickets and wins.

137

Nor can any evaluation of Jamaica's role in the development of Caribbean cricket be complete without some reference to its excellent umpires, led by Stephen Bucknor, Perry Burke, T.A. Ewart, J.R. Gayle, and Douglas Sang Hue, who have set lofty standards for West Indian and other officials; and its very good commentators, journalists and historians, such as C.A. 'Jack' Anderson, Tony Becca, Maurice Foster, Michael Holding, Roy Lawrence, Michael Manley, Jimmy Richards and L.D. 'Strebor' Roberts. Without these Jamaican contributions from beyond the fence, West Indian cricket would have been immeasurably poorer.

CHAPTER SIX

LEEWARD ISLANDS AND WINDWARD ISLANDS

DURING THE 19TH CENTURY, THE CRICKET CULT WAS FIRMLY established in the Caribbean by a formidable array of British administrators, educators, priests and soldiers. It is not altogether clear that the Anglo-Saxons initially intended to use the game as a civilising or imperialising agent, especially since they attempted for a very long time to exclude the local Blacks and Browns from participating in organised competition. The imperialists, however, failed to prevent the non-whites from playing cricket with an enthusiasm that, from the beginning, was almost unbridled. By 1900, consequently, cricket had become a major feature of Caribbean culture.

While considerable attention has thus far been focused on the phenomenal manner in which Barbados adopted the cricket cult, not much has been written on the rise of the sport in the 'smaller islands'. In fact, the game in the Caribbean gradually came to be dominated by the so-called 'Big Four' (Barbados, British Guiana, Jamaica and Trinidad), and the smaller fry tended to be excluded from the deliberations of the WICBC for many years after its inception in 1927. The best players from the Leewards and the Windwards, until very recently, were regrettably ignored. No West Indian cricketer from the smaller islands was selected to represent the West Indies in any Test match prior to the mid-1950s.

The reasons for this neglect are difficult to determine. It is well-known, after all, that a fairly sophisticated brand of cricket was being played in Antigua, Grenada, St Kitts and St Vincent from as long ago as the 1880s. Barbadian XIs and schoolboy teams from Harrison College and the Lodge School visited these islands fairly frequently to play friendly matches late in the 19th century and early in the 20th. When Robert Slade Lucas led the first British cricket team to the West Indies in the winter of 1894/95, his men played several matches against Antigua, St Kitts-Nevis, St Lucia and St Vincent. Lord Hawke's squad in 1896/97, too, opposed teams from Antigua, Grenada, St Kitts, St Lucia and St Vincent. That same winter, Arthur Priestley's men also played against Antigua, St Kitts and St Vincent.

EARLY HEROES

The smaller islands were consequently invited to participate in the enterprise when the decision was taken in 1900 to send a composite West Indian team to England for the first time. Their quota was two players among the fifteen chosen. Thus C.A. Ollivierre of St Vincent and W.H. Mignon of Grenada joined the touring party. Ollivierre proved to be the best cricketer among the tourists in 1900. He created such a positive impression on his hosts that he was encouraged to stay behind and qualify for Derbyshire. Mignon was not consistent enough, but he did bowl quite impressively against Lancashire to capture ten wickets for 117 runs.

Charles Augustus Ollivierre was an attractive right-handed batsman and a very good fieldsman. He led the West Indian tourists in 1900 with 883 runs (av: 32.70), including a brilliant century (159) against Leicestershire when the visitors achieved one of their rare victories. He also made a valiant 94 against Surrey at The Oval and a stylish sixty against Lancashire. For Derbyshire, he eventually played 110 matches between 1901 and 1907, finishing his career with 4,830 runs (av: 23.56) and 109 catches. He remains one of the finest batsmen ever produced by St Vincent.

Ollivierre's younger brother, Richard, was the sole representative from the smaller islands when the West Indies made their second tour of England in 1906. A fine right-handed all-rounder, he was one of the more successful members of the party, heading their bowling averages with 51 wickets (av: 21.56) and scoring 480 runs (av: 20.00). His highest score was 67 against Hampshire and his best bowling performance came at Harrogate in August when he captured 7/23 as Yorkshire could muster only fifty runs in their first innings. R.C. Ollivierre was also a capable reserve wicket-keeper.

Notwithstanding these facts, the 'Big Four' completely ignored the smaller islands throughout the next fifty years. No representative from the Leewards or the Windwards was ever selected for a West Indian tour again until Alphonso Theodore Roberts of St Vincent was taken to New Zealand in 1955/56; and he might not have been considered at all had the circumstances been normal. The West Indies, however, were attempting to rebuild after a humiliating loss (3-0) to the Australians at home in 1955. This was the first time they had ever been defeated in a Test series in the Caribbean. They therefore selected an experimental squad for what they expected to be a relatively easy tour that would provide such greenhorns as Collie Smith and Garry Sobers with much needed experience. Roberts, a very promising eighteen-year-old right-handed batsman was highly recommended by Everton Weekes despite his lack of first-class experience. The West Indian selectors were desperately searching for replacements now that Robert Christiani, Gerry Gomez, Allan Rae and Jeffrey Stollmeyer had retired and Roy Marshall had opted for a county career with Hampshire. John Lucas of Barbados and Kenny Trestrail of Trinidad had also emigrated to Canada.

It may be suggested that, during the long drought of 1906-56, the smaller islands lacked the organisational skills and the financial resources to establish their cricket leagues and associations on a solid footing (even though the Antigua Cricket Association dates back to 1897). There is also the important question of human resources. The population of Antigua and Barbuda combined has never exceeded 75,000; Grenada's was estimated to be approximately 95,000 as late as 1991; Dominica's still lingers around 71,000; and St Vincent & the Grenadines together contain fewer than 115,000 people. These islands also lacked that vital ingredient which the 'Big Four' possessed: a vibrant and aggressive white aristocracy keen to promote cricket at all costs. The small islands continued to play the game with a degree of sophistication but could not arrange the kind of inter-colonial matches that would have provided their outstanding players with the necessary forum to display their skills. Some 'friendly' matches were occasionally arranged between the Leewards and the Windwards but were not accorded first-class status. Even such classics as the Bell Shield and the Cork Cup, for which the smaller islands had been vigorously contending ever since the second decade of the 20th century, seldom attracted much notice elsewhere.

COMBINING THE SMALLER ISLANDS

Almost incredibly, it was not until 1955 that the 'Combined Islands' (as they were then called) played their initial first-class match in the Caribbean. It took place in Port of Spain at the Queen's Park Oval and gave young Alfie Roberts an opportunity to demonstrate his sound technique in a fine innings of 74 when his team could muster only 170 in trying conditions against Lennox Butler and Wilfred Ferguson (both of whom had played previously in Test cricket). This performance clinched his selection for the tour of New Zealand after a single first-class match. This singular lack of first-class opportunities in the Caribbean doomed Roberts, like the rest of his compatriots, to inevitable oblivion after that tour had ended.

The traditional veil of oblivion was occasionally lifted when touring squads played second-class matches in Antigua and Grenada. In 1948, a Combined Leewards-Windwards team, led by the Barbadian-born Frankie Thomas, played a friendly match against British Guiana at Bourda. Sometimes, too, exhibition games were arranged among the smaller islands. This provided such good players as Hubert Anthonyson, Lester Bird, Ferrel Charles, Austin Eddy, Leo Gore, Len Harris, Clement John, Alford Mannix, Frank Mason, Ian Neverson, Mindoo Phillip, A.A. Reid, Malcolm Richards, Rupert Scotland and Sidney Walling an opportunity, albeit infrequently, to exhibit their exceptional talents. But the WICBC took too little notice of them, especially since the Board did not in those days include representatives from the Leewards and the Windwards.

This was all the more unfortunate since, during the middle and late 1950s, the West Indies were in dire need of opening batsmen and opening bowlers. Conrad Hunte, the batsman, and Frank King, the bowler, toiled for years without permanent or satisfactory opening partners, and there are several Caribbean pundits arguing to this day that our record would have been much better had the selectors given a fair chance to Len Harris, a reliable opening batsman and superb slip-fielder, and to Hubert Anthonyson, a fiery fast bowler. The late Tim Hector, a distinguished Antiguan politician, journalist and publisher, always insisted that the West Indies would have been unbeaten in England in 1957 had they used a four-pronged pace attack consisting of Anthonyson, Roy Gilchrist, Wes Hall and Frank Mason. Another knowledgeable Antiguan, Herbert Spencer, who is now a highly respected teacher in Winnipeg, Canada, has argued that Eddie Gilbert, a fine left-handed all-rounder from St Kitts, Eustace Matthew, a very good right-arm off-spinner from Antigua, Mindoo Phillip, the legendary hard-hitting batsman from St Lucia, and A.A. Reid, the excellent wicket-keeper from Dominica, would all clearly have won Test caps for the West Indies had they come from larger islands.

BEGINNING OF THE REVOLUTION
The revolution in West Indian cricket began during the 1950s, when the various islands were agitating for political independence and when support for the federal idea was at its strongest. The establishment of the British West Indian Federation in 1958 focused increasing attention on the smaller islands. Such progressive individuals as C.L.R. James and Frank Worrell began to clamour for the abandonment of the principle of white captaincy and for a much more serious effort to include the Leeward and the Windward islands in Caribbean cricket. The disappointing performance of the West Indian teams after the triumphant tour of England in 1950 inspired a Caribbean-wide protest. Between 1951 and 1957, the West Indies played 31 Tests, winning only eight and losing thirteen, with four of their victories coming at the expense of lowly New Zealand. Their record against Australia read: ten Tests, one victory, seven defeats and two draws. They had failed to win a single Test against Australia at home in 1955 or against England abroad in 1957.

The West Indian public did not attribute these losses to lack of skill. It was universally felt in the Caribbean that the sport was badly administered and that our human resources, limited as they were already, were being too poorly utilised. Hence the move to upgrade the administration of cricket in the smaller islands and to include them with increasing frequency in inter-colonial tournaments. In July 1958, for instance, Jamaica opposed a team from the Leeward Islands at Melbourne Park in Kingston and provided Oscar Williams of Antigua with a chance to register his maiden first-class century. Williams, who had the patience of Job, might have proved a useful foil to Conrad Hunte had he been given the chance. In October 1961, a Combined Islands XI, led by Evelyn Gresham, went down to defeat in Georgetown at the hands of a powerful British Guiana, led then by the great Clyde Walcott. But they did not surrender until after Len Harris and Clem John had enhanced their reputations as quality batsmen and the left-arm spinner, Garnett Brisbane, had rendered yeoman service with the ball.

ANNUAL COMPETITION AT LAST

Thus, when annual territorial competition came at long last to the West Indies in the form of the Shell Shield in 1966, it was impossible to ignore the claims of the smaller islands. Fearing that they would be too feeble to play on their own, the WICBC decided to lump the Leewards and the Windwards together and the Combined Islands became a regular competitor until the early 1980s. They gradually improved to the point where they came within a whisker of winning the competition outright in 1975, when they finally managed to defeat Barbados for the first time. Two years later, when vying again for the title, they were thwarted by a strong Barbados team in Bridgetown. But they would not be denied in 1981 when, under the captaincy of Antigua's Viv Richards, they finally won the Caribbean championship.

By the 1980s, then, cricket in the smaller islands had come of age. The WICBC saw fit to separate the Leewards permanently from the Windwards in 1982 and this seemed somehow to have stimulated an even more rapid development of cricket in these territories. The Leewards have consisted of Antigua, Montserrat, Nevis and St Kitts, while Dominica, Grenada, St Lucia and St Vincent have formed the Windwards. The Windward Islands finished second to Barbados in the Shell Shield competition in 1982 and were second again in 1983, this time to Guyana. The Leewards, who finished fourth in 1983, would obviously have done much better had injury not forced Richards out of action after the first match. Antigua, in fact, began to produce an astonishingly large number of outstanding cricketers, following in the footsteps of the great fast bowler, Andy Roberts. The Leewards, therefore, have been one of the most powerful competitors in Red Stripe competition which took the place of the Shell Shield after 1987. In 1990, with no fewer than six Test players in their midst, they won their first championship convincingly and have won three more titles since then. For the past twenty years, the Leewards have consistently provided stiff competition in these games even when their finest players are absent because of their West Indian commitments abroad. With their aggressive batsmen and excellent fast bowlers, they have also tended to dominate one-day matches. During the 1990s, the Leeward Islands won the Red Stripe trophy (or the President's Cup which replaced it in 1997) as many times (four) as Barbados.

THE MIRACLE THAT IS ANTIGUA

During the 'Wonder Years' (1980-95), when the West Indies were putting all their opponents ruthlessly to the sword, the major contributors to this miracle emanated from the smaller islands. Antigua alone produced such stars as Curtly Ambrose, Eldine Baptiste, Kenny Benjamin, Winston Benjamin, Viv Richards, Richie Richardson and Andy Roberts. Richards and Richardson also served as successful Test captains. The former led the West Indies in fifty Tests, of which 27 were won and only eight lost. He remains the only West Indian captain never to have lost a Test series. Richardson, who had the misfortune to

Viv Richards, the "Master Blaster", who did more perhaps than any other individual to put Antigua on the map

be at the helm when the much ballyhooed streak came to an end against Australia in the Caribbean, led the West Indies in 24 Tests, of which they won eleven and lost only six. Antigua made a contribution of another kind when Roberts served for many years as a Test selector and coach after his retirement as an active first-class player.

The arithmetic of Antigua's contribution to modern Test cricket is almost staggering. Viv Richards, its greatest batsman, accounted for no fewer than 8,540 runs (av: 50.23) and struck 24 centuries between 1974 and 1991. His aggregate exceeded the West Indian record of 8,032 that the immortal Garry Sobers had set during 1953-74. Richards represented the West Indies in more

Andy Roberts, the first great Antiguan cricket star, seen here in action against an Indian XI at Bangalore on 21 December 1983

Tests (121) than anyone had previously done and that number has since been exceeded only by Courtney Walsh (132). With the exception of Clive Lloyd (74), he captained the West Indies more often than anybody else. The West Indies also won more often under him than anyone else except Lloyd, who led them to victory on 36 occasions. Richards also held more Test catches (122) than any previous West Indian fielder, easily surpassing the record of 109 that Sobers had established in his 93 Tests. In addition, Richards was a clever spinner of right-arm off-breaks, which brought him 32 Test wickets (av: 61.37). The mighty Viv was also one of the most brilliant fieldsmen of his generation. Needless to say, his ODI record is fantastic too. In 187 such matches, he recorded 6,721 runs (av:

47.00), 118 wickets (av: 35.83) and 100 catches. His marvellous 189 against England at Old Trafford in 1984 stood for a number of years as the record for such international contests. His teams won 67 of the 105 ODIs in which he was the captain and lost only 36 (with the remaining two producing no result).

Richardson succeeded Richards to the captaincy of the West Indies in 1991. He too was an attacking right-handed batsman, whose average eventually suffered because he took the responsibilities of leadership very seriously indeed. He nevertheless wound up his stellar career in Test cricket with 5,949 runs (av: 44.39) during 1983-95. Like Richards, he was an excellent close-to-the wicket fieldsman and registered ninety catches in his 86 Tests. In 224 ODIs, Richardson made 6,248 runs (av: 33.41) and held 75 catches.

The other Antiguan stars of that period were mainly right-arm fast bowlers. The two unrelated Benjamins shared 153 Test wickets between them at less than 29 runs apiece. Kenny represented the West Indies in 26 Tests while Winston did so in 21. The former claimed 92 wickets (av: 30.27), scored 222 runs (av: 7.92) and took two catches. In 26 ODIs, he made 65 runs (av: 10.83), captured 33 wickets (av: 27.96), and took four catches. Winston was a more accomplished batsman and a more reliable fielder than his namesake. He ended his Test career with 61 wickets (av: 27.01), 470 runs (av: 18.80) and twelve catches. In 85 ODIs, he claimed 100 wickets (av: 30.79), scored 298 runs (av: 7.45) and held sixteen catches.

Far more devastating as fast bowlers were Ambrose and Roberts. The latter was the first Antiguan to gain selection to a West Indian Test team when he made his debut against England at Bridgetown in March 1974. He was arguably the finest fast bowler produced by the West Indies up to his time. Perhaps the most feared bowler in the world during the mid-1970s, he claimed his first 100 Test wickets in the space of two years, 142 days, then the record in terms of time elapsed. In seven Tests against India and Pakistan in 1974/75, he captured 44 wickets, claimed 22 more against Australia in 1975/76, and took 28 against England in 1976. He finished altogether with 202 (av: 25.61) in 47 Tests. He snared 244 wickets in 58 games for Hampshire in the 1970s and ended his first-class career with 856 (av: 20.92) in 220 matches. A hard-hitting right-handed batsman and a reliable fielder, Roberts also contributed 762 runs (av: 14.94) and nine catches to the West Indian cause in Test cricket. With Clive Lloyd against India at Calcutta in December 1983, he shared a record-breaking ninth-wicket stand of 161 when he made his highest score (68) in Test cricket. He also made a notable contribution to the West Indies' triumph in the 1975 Prudential World Cup when a swashbuckling tenth-wicket partnership between himself and Deryck Murray staved off certain elimination at the hands of Pakistan in the semi-final. In 56 ODIs, Roberts recorded 87 wickets (av: 20.35), 231 runs (av: 10.04), and six catches.

Curtly Ambrose thus had a very difficult act to follow when he burst upon the scene towards the end of the 1980s. Accepting the challenge, he out-

Richie Richardson in action against Pakistan in a One Day International at Lahore in November 1991

performed Roberts in every conceivable category with both the ball and the bat. He enjoyed several successful series against Australia and England and finished his career in 2000 with 405 Test wickets (av: 20.99) in 98 matches. His Test average has been bettered so far only by Malcolm Marshall, Joel Garner and Shaun Pollock among all bowlers with more than 200 wickets to their credit. Ambrose became a legend even before he retired and left vivid memories of four remarkable performances that brought victory to his side: a devastatingly accurate spell of 7.4 overs in which the last five English wickets fell for a handful of runs on the final day at Bridgetown in April 1990; a fearsome second-innings assault (6/34 in 24.4 overs) at Bridgetown against South Africa in April 1992; an amazing spell of 7/1 in 32 balls against Australia at Perth in January 1993; and a total demolition of England (6/24) at Port of Spain in March 1994.

147

On 22 occasions he claimed five or more wickets per Test innings, to equal Marshall's West Indian record. He also captured ten wickets in a match in three of his Tests. He did more perhaps than any other bowler to undermine the confidence of England's Graeme Hick, who never quite succeeded in living up to the promise he had shown as the most prolific batsman in modern county cricket.

The magnificence of Ambrose's bowling was one of the major factors in West Indian dominance between 1988 and 1994. Because of his extreme height (6'7") and searing pace, he achieved unusual bounce off the pitch, but it was his deadly accuracy that made him a most formidable opponent. With Courtney Walsh he formed one of the most effective new-ball pairings in the history of Test cricket. Ambrose was also a hard-hitting left-handed lower-order batsman who often provided the West Indian tail with much-needed cement. He scored 1,439 Test runs (av: 12.40), including one half-century. He also took eighteen Test catches. He was only the third West Indian, following Garry Sobers and Malcolm Marshall, to complete the Test double (100 wickets and 1,000 runs). In 176 ODIs, Ambrose recorded 225 wickets (av: 24.12), 639 runs (av: 10.65), and 45 catches. His tally of ODI wickets was a West Indian record until surpassed shortly after his retirement by Walsh (227).

Neither Ambrose nor Roberts, however, can be classified as a genuine all-rounder. Apart, possibly, from Winston Benjamin, Antigua's best all-rounder was Eldine Baptiste, even though he was allowed only ten Test caps during the early 1980s. As a batsman, he averaged 23.30 runs per innings but his value is far better understood by focusing on his superb 87 not out at Birmingham in 1984 when he and Michael Holding added 150 runs in 113 minutes to set a West Indian record for the ninth wicket against England. As a very steady and intelligent right-arm medium-fast stock bowler, Baptiste captured sixteen wickets at just over 35 runs apiece, but he could hope only for limited opportunities in those days when the West Indies possessed exceptional fast bowling depth. He took part in 43 ODIs, tallying 184 runs (av: 15.33), 36 wickets (av: 41.97), and fourteen catches.

Two other Antiguans have represented the West Indies in Test cricket recently: Ridley Jacobs and Dave Joseph. The latter is a hard-hitting right-handed batsman who had scored with fine consistency in territorial competition for some years before being awarded his cap in March 1999 at the age of 29. He began with a belligerent fifty against Australia at Port of Spain but failed to sustain this form during the remainder of that series. He was allowed only four Tests before being discarded. Joseph contributed 141 runs (av: 20.14) and ten catches. His average of 2.5 catches per Test is extraordinary. It is surprising to observe that a fieldsman of his superior skills and a batsman with his reputation for scoring quickly has never been invited to take part in ODI competition.

Jacobs has been much more durable and effective. An excellent wicket-keeper and a very capable left-handed batsman, he has been one of the few bright spots in Caribbean cricket since Richardson's departure. He was the

Curtley Ambrose bowls during his last game, the fifth Test against England at The Oval on 31 August 2000

only West Indian who distinguished himself during the dreadful tour of South Africa in 1998/99, heading his team's batting with 317 runs (av: 45.28). In 53 Tests so far, he has made 2,076 runs (av: 28.05), including two centuries. He has caught 173 batsmen and stumped eight others. Serving as captain in the recent tour of Bangladesh, he led the West Indies to victory in both of their Test matches there. A valuable ODI performer, Jacobs has registered 1,777 runs (av: 23.69), 145 catches and 27 stumpings in 128 such contests. His 27 stumpings have taken him already beyond the West Indian record of 21 set previously by Jeffrey Dujon. Jacobs is one of the best wicket-keeper/batsmen ever produced by the West Indies and it is a pity the selectors kept him waiting so long in the wings. The history of

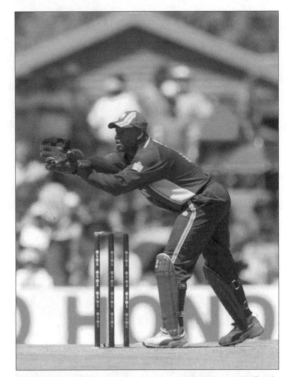

Ridley Jacobs in action during the ICC Cricket World Cup Pool B match against Canada on 23 February 2003 at Supersport Park in Centurion, South Africa

Caribbean cricket might well have been different had he been chosen as Dujon's immediate successor in 1992, when he was at his peak, rather than being unnecessarily held back until 1998 when he was already 31 years old.

To appreciate fully what Antigua has brought to West Indian cricket, since Roberts became in 1974 the first of his countrymen to achieve Test match status, it is necessary only to consider that nine of its native sons have so far made almost 20,000 Test runs (including 42 centuries) at an average of more than 32 per innings. Together they have also captured more than 800 Test wickets at less than 26 runs apiece. In addition, they have held 438 Test catches and effected eight stumpings. For an island of 108 square miles and a limited population, these are incredible statistics indeed. It is safe to say that no community of similar size has been even remotely as successful in the past thirty years.

THE NEVISIANS ARE COMING

The tiny island of Nevis, ordinarily regarded merely as an adjunct to St Kitts, has also played cricket surprisingly well for a community so small. It is just 36 square miles in extent and its population is slightly more than 8,000. It has, nevertheless, provided the West Indies with such Test cricketers as Keith Arthurton, Derek Parry, Elquemedo Willett and Stuart Williams. The most successful among them was Arthurton, a fine left-handed batsman, a useful change bowler and a brilliant fieldsman. Inconsistent form led to his being out of the West Indies' team almost as often as he was in it during the 1990s. In 33

Tests, he scored 1,382 runs (av: 30.71), took one wicket for 183 runs and held 22 catches. He struck fine Test centuries against Australia and England, but eventually lost his form and his confidence. Arthurton proved a more effective all-rounder in one-day competitions. In 105 ODIs, he registered 1,904 runs (av: 26.08), 42 wickets (av: 27.59) and 27 catches.

It was Elquemedo Willett, a left-arm spinner, who led the way for other Nevisians when he made his Test debut against Australia at Bridgetown in March 1973. But the selectors soon began to pin their hopes on the faster bowlers and he was restricted to a total of five Tests although he made tours with the West Indies to England and the sub-continent. His eleven Test wickets came at the relatively high cost of 43.81 runs each. A stubborn lower-order batsman, Willett scored 74 runs (av: 14.80) during his brief Test career.

Derek Parry, a right-arm off-spinner, suffered the same fate as all West Indian slow bowlers after the retirement of Lance Gibbs. He made several tours with West Indian teams but was selected for only twelve Tests. Eventually, in despair, he joined the 'rebels' who toured South Africa in 1982. For the West Indies, Parry took 23 wickets (av: 40.69), scored 381 runs (av: 22.41) and held four catches. A fairly good right-handed batsman, Parry struck a fine and flawless 65 against a strong Australian attack at Port of Spain in April 1978. He actually played the key role in this particular encounter, with an aggregate of 87 runs in

Keith Arthurton in action against Australia in Trinidad in March 1995

a low-scoring game and a match analysis of 6/92 from forty very steady overs. His excellent demonstration of versatility on this occasion allowed the West Indies to recapture the Frank Worrell Trophy which the Australians had tenaciously held since 1969.

The fourth Nevisian to earn selection for the West Indies was Stuart Williams, a dashing right-handed opening batsman and brilliant fieldsman, whose technique and temperament seemed much better suited to one-day internationals. In 31 Tests, he scored 1,183 runs (av: 24.14) and held 27 catches. In 57 ODIs, he made 1,586 runs (av: 32.36) and took eighteen catches. Considering his overall performance, Williams was fortunate to have received as many Test chances as he did. It may consequently be argued that he was as lucky as his spin bowling compatriots were not. But it remains almost a miracle that such a small society as Nevis can boast as many as four Test cricketers.

THE RISE OF ST VINCENT AND THE GRENADINES

St Vincent and the Grenadines occupy an area of about 150 square miles. They are not much bigger, that is to say, than the Isle of Wight. Yet, in the past forty years or so, they have produced as many as six Test cricketers. Their first star, of course, was Charles Ollivierre, a member of that cricketing brotherhood who also included Helon who played for Trinidad whither he had emigrated early in the 20th century. St Vincent gave the West Indies their first small-island Test cricketer in Alfie Roberts; but he was allowed only a single Test, in which he scored 28 runs (av: 14.00), before being discarded. Ian Allen, a right-arm fast bowler, was not much more fortunate. He played two Tests for the West Indies against England in 1991 and ended with five wickets (av: 36.00) and five runs without being dismissed.

The two most successful Vincentian cricketers so far have been Winston Davis and Michael Findlay. The former was a fiery right-arm fast bowler, an attacking lower-order right-handed batsman and a fine fieldsman. He was quite unfortunate to have emerged at the same time as such great rivals as Eldine Baptiste, Sylvester Clarke, Colin Croft, Wayne Daniel, Joel Garner, Michael Holding, Malcolm Marshall and Courtney Walsh. As a result, he was seldom more than a reserve bowler even though he could have represented any other country with great distinction during the 1980s. He thus played only fifteen Tests for the West Indies. His contribution amounted to 45 wickets (av: 32.71), 202 runs (av: 15.53) and ten catches. One of his brightest moments occurred against England at Manchester in July 1984 when he struck a defiant 77 after having been sent in as a night-watchman. With Gordon Greenidge, he shared a vital sixth wicket stand of 170 runs on that occasion. Davis also took part in 35 ODIs, recording 39 wickets (av: 33.38), 28 runs (av: 14.00), and one catch.

Mike Findlay, too, suffered from the severity of the competition. He is easily the greatest wicket-keeper in St Vincent's history. But his rivals for a berth in the West Indian Test squad (1964-78) included such luminaries as

Winston Davis in action against England in Manchester in August 1984

Jackie Hendriks, Desmond Lewis, David Murray and Deryck Murray. He was thus limited to ten Test appearances. He used these opportunities to record 212 runs (av: 16.30) and 21 dismissals, including two stumpings. Findlay made further contributions to Caribbean cricket by serving as a selector after his retirement.

More recently, two other Vincentians have represented the West Indies in Test cricket. Cameron Cuffy and Nixon McLean are both right-arm fast bowlers. Cuffy made his Test debut against India in November 1994 but went through several series before being recalled. He has now appeared in fifteen Tests, taking 43 wickets (av: 33.83), making 58 runs (av: 4.14) and holding five catches. His bowling tends to be steady rather than penetrative and this makes him more valuable in one-day competition. In 41 ODIs so far, he has captured 41 wickets (av: 35.02), scored 62 runs (av: 4.42) and held five catches. Already 34 years old, he is unlikely to play many more Tests, especially since he is now facing stiff competition from such younger fast bowlers as Mervyn Dillon, Pedro Collins, Jermaine Lawson and Adam Sanford.

Nixon McLean made his Test debut in January 1998 against England at Kingston when an underprepared pitch led to the hasty abandonment of the match before he had a chance to bowl a single ball. He took 3/74 in 31 fairly tidy overs in the following Test at Port of Spain; but spent several succeeding series in and out of the line-up. In nineteen Tests so far, he has taken 44 wickets (av: 42.56), scored 368 runs (av: 12.26) and held five catches. His bowling became so unreliable and expensive in his later opportunities that it is highly unlikely he will now, at thirty years old, be able to dislodge any of the younger lions by whom he was replaced. As his aggressiveness as a lower-order right-handed batsman makes him a more suitable candidate for one-day competition, McLean has participated in 45 ODIs, recording 314 runs (av: 12.07), 46 wickets (av: 37.58), and eight catches.

THE DOMINICAN CONTRIBUTION

Apart from England's Philip DeFreitas, Dominica has thus far produced four Test cricketers: Norbert Phillip, Adam Sanford and the two Shillingford cousins, Grayson and Irvine. Phillip, a right-handed all-rounder, who played with commendable consistency in regional competition from 1970 to 1985, became one of the first captains of the Windward Islands after the final separation from the Leewards in 1982. During the Packer crisis, he played nine Tests for the West Indies in the late 1970s, scoring 297 runs (av: 29.70), taking 28 wickets (av: 37.17) and accepting five catches. Phillip, who played some fine cricket for Essex during 1980-85, naturally lost his place in the West Indian Test XI as soon as Kerry Packer and the WICBC reached an amicable agreement.

Grayson Shillingford was an enthusiastic right-arm fast-medium bowler who appeared in seven Test matches between 1969 and 1972. The first Dominican to play at this level for the West Indies, he claimed fifteen wickets (av: 35.80), scored 57 runs (av: 8.14), and held two catches. With the emergence of Keith Boyce and Bernard Julien, however, he could not retain his place in the Test side. Irvine Shillingford was an attractive right-handed batsman who scored heavily in Shell Shield competition from 1962 to 1982. He was selected for only four Tests and then dropped, despite a splendid 120 against Pakistan at Georgetown in March 1977. He registered 218 Test runs (av: 31.14) and one Test catch.

Adam Sanford exploded upon the scene about two years ago, when he captured 41 wickets in his first full Busta Cup season during 2001/02. Although born in Dominica, he represented the Leewards, having emigrated to Antigua to work as a policeman. In seven Tests so far, he has taken twenty wickets (av: 39.70) and scored 35 runs (av: 3.88).

THE ROLE OF GRENADA

More commensurate with their physical stature and population, the remaining Leewards and Windwards have made more modest contributions to Caribbean cricket. Grenada, for example, has supplied only three West Indian representatives, apart from Mignon in 1900. They are Rawl Lewis, Junior Murray and (most recently) Devon Smith. Lewis emerged in the early 1990s as a very promising right-arm leg-break bowler, capable lower-order batsman and fine fieldsman. For the West Indies Board XI against an England XI at St George's in April 1994, he bowled 53 excellent overs to capture 9/146 to play

Junior Murray appeals for a wicket during a World Series match against Australia in Melbourne in January 1993

the leading role in the tourists' defeat. But Lewis failed to live up to expectations. In three Tests he took but a single wicket for 318 runs while scoring only 26 (av: 4.33) and taking no catches at all. His performance in one-day competition was slightly better. In sixteen ODIs, he recorded 157 runs (av: 17.44), twelve wickets (av: 51.16) and five catches.

Junior Murray, an accomplished wicket-keeper and attacking right-handed batsman, has made a much greater impact. In 33 Tests, he has scored 918 runs (av: 22.39) and effected 102 dismissals, including three stumpings. His brightest moment came in Wellington in February 1995 when he struck a scintillating 101 not out from 88 balls against New Zealand. Inconsistency with both the gloves and the bat, however, has led to his being very often dropped in the 1990s and it now appears that he has been completely superseded by Ridley Jacobs. In 55 ODIs, Murray has so far contributed 678 runs (av: 22.60), 46 catches and seven stumpings. Despite his ups and downs, he remains the leading cricketer that has yet come from Grenada.

The young and promising Devon Smith, an aggressive opening batsman, endured a baptism of fire during the 2003 series against Australia. He struck two useful half-centuries in his first four Tests in which he averaged 23.62 runs per innings. But the selectors did not see fit to include him in the series against Sri Lanka and Zimbabwe. Smith's supporters are convinced that he has the potential to become an excellent opener at the Test match level. But he faces keen competition from such rivals as Darren Ganga, Chris Gayle and Wavell Hinds.

FINAL ANALYSIS

St Lucia and St Kitts have yet to provide the West Indies with a cricketing superstar, but the tiny island of Anguilla has just done so. Omari Ahmed Clemente Banks, who made his Test debut against Australia at Bridgetown in May 2003, is the first Anguillian to play cricket at this level. A steady right-arm off-break bowler and useful right-handed batsman, he played a key role in the historic win against the Aussies when his unbeaten 47 took the hosts to their triumphant 418/7 in the fourth innings at the Antigua Recreation Ground. He has justified his selection so far by registering 190 runs (av: 38.00), fourteen wickets (av: 50.07) and two catches in his first five Tests. Banks has also contributed 44 runs (av: 14.66) and four wickets (av: 31.00) to the West Indian cause in three ODIs thus far.

Without the efforts of the Leewards and the Windwards, Caribbean cricket would never have flourished as it has done since the inception of the Shell Shield/Red Stripe/Busta Cup competition. In fact, during the golden streak that is still the wonder of the cricketing world, the West Indies owed a great deal to Ambrose, Richards, Richardson and Roberts. Without them, the West Indies would never have gone unbeaten in 29 successive Test series. Not only did Roberts alter the course of many a Test by his thoughtful bowling and defiant batting in crucial situations, but Ambrose won several Test matches virtually single-handed. The magnificent Richards also dictated the course of most Tests while he was at his peak, and Richardson's sparkling batting and brilliant fielding were often of vital significance.

One is, therefore, left now to wonder what might have been accomplished by the West Indies had more careful thought been given, in days gone by, to the claims of such cricketers as Hubert Anthonyson, Leonard Harris, Alford Mannix, Frank Mason, A.A. Reid and Sidney Walling. Everyone knew that Anthonyson and Mason were two of the most dangerous fast bowlers in the Caribbean during the 1950s, but no effort was made by the WICBC (or within the 'Big Four') to encourage them. Everyone knew that Mannix was a superb all-rounder and Walling one of the most attractive stroke-players in the region during the 1940s and 1950s, but they were not encouraged either.

The history of West Indian cricket, therefore, is one of opportunities lost and resources flagrantly squandered. As it is, however, the Leewards and the Windwards have done more than their fair share since then; and for that the whole cricketing world ought to be profoundly grateful.

CHAPTER SEVEN

WEST INDIAN-BORN CRICKETERS PLAYING FOR OTHER COUNTRIES

IN ADDITION TO THE 253 PLAYERS WHO HAVE REPRESENTED THE West Indies in Test cricket, there are thirteen others born in the Caribbean who performed for other countries. Eleven of them played for England, while one (Simpson Guillen) played for New Zealand and the other (Rabindra Ramnarayan Singh) represented India. Four of these players came from Trinidad, two each from Barbados, Jamaica and St Vincent, and one each from Dominica, Guyana and St Kitts. A fourteenth, Ricardo Ellcock, a Barbadian native, was originally selected to tour the West Indies with England's team in 1989/90 but a serious injury forced him to withdraw. He was replaced by Chris Lewis, a native of Guyana.

'Sammy' Guillen, who emigrated to New Zealand after representing the West Indies in Australia in 1951/52, is the first (and so far, only) cricketer to play for both the West Indies and another country. As the reserve wicket-keeper in the early 1950s, he came into his own when Clyde Walcott was injured 'down under'. Emerging at a time when there was little opportunity for first-class cricket in the Caribbean, he played only six matches for his native Trinidad between 1947 and 1951, but was destined to represent Canterbury on 42 occasions between 1952 and 1961. For the West Indies Guillen played five Tests, including two against New Zealand. In those matches he registered 104 runs (av: 26.00), nine catches and two stumpings. Ironically, his highest Test score was 54 against New Zealand at Christchurch in February 1952. His three Tests for New Zealand were all played against the West Indies. From them, he extracted 98 runs (av: 16.33) and five dismissals. His best Test innings in that series was 41 at Auckland in March 1956. Guillen ended his career with 2,672 runs (av: 26.97), including three centuries, and 145 dismissals, including 34 stumpings, in 66 first-class matches. He was the finest wicket-keeper/batsman produced by Trinidad before the emergence of Deryck Murray and would obviously have represented the West Indies much more often had he not decided to emigrate.

'Robin' Singh was born in Princes Town, Trinidad, on 14 September 1963 and made his first-class cricket debut in 1982/83 when he represented South and Central Trinidad against North and East Trinidad. He emigrated to India shortly afterwards and settled in Madras, where he played extremely well for Tamil Nadu with both the bat and the ball for several years. Singh was an attacking left-handed batsman, a fine right-arm medium pace bowler and a brilliant fieldsman. His consistency as an all-rounder in the Ranji Trophy competition helped Tamil Nadu win its very first national championship in 1988 and earned him a selection on the Indian team which toured the West Indies in 1989. This gave him a chance to perform before his former home crowd in a one-day international at Port of Spain. The tour, however, was not a personal success. He was not selected for any of the Tests and appeared only in four first-class matches without distinguishing himself.

The exciting nature of Singh's all-round cricket earned him the reputation of a one-day specialist and while he made his debut in this version of the game in March 1989, he did not earn a Test cap until October 1998 when he played against Zimbabwe at Harare. On that occasion, he scored 15 & 12, took 0/32 from ten overs, and held five catches. This proved to be his solitary Test appearance. But in 136 ODIs for India between 1989 and 2001, Singh scored 2,336 runs (av: 25.95), took 69 wickets (av: 43.26) and held 38 catches. In 137 first-class matches between 1982 and 2001, he registered 6,997 runs (av: 46.03), including 22 centuries, 172 wickets (av: 35.97), and 109 catches. These statistics suggest that India might well have made more use of Robin Singh's skills.

The Caribbean XI who played Test cricket for England were J.E. Benjamin, R.O. Butcher, N.G. Cowans, P.A.J. DeFreitas, Lord Harris, Chris Lewis, Devon Malcolm, Wilfred Slack, Gladstone Small, P.F. (later Sir Pelham) Warner and Neil Williams.

JOSEPH EMMANUEL BENJAMIN

Joey Benjamin was born in Christ Church, St Kitts, on 2 February 1961. He received his education at Cayon High School in St Kitts and Mount Pleasant School in Highgate, Birmingham. Already sixteen years old when he emigrated with his parents to Britain in 1977, he did not begin to play county cricket until he was 27 years old when offered a contract by Warwickshire in 1988. A right-arm fast-medium bowler, he was capable of swinging the new ball both ways. He was also an attacking right-handed lower-order batsman and a useful fieldsman.

For Warwickshire, Benjamin's best season was 1990 when, in fifteen matches, he took 43 wickets (av: 28.02) and scored 188 runs (av: 26.85). But he was released after having been selected for only three games in 1991. He was immediately signed by Surrey against whom he had taken 6/109 in 41 overs at The Oval in July 1990. He had also scored 28 not out and 41 in that encounter. After claiming 45 wickets (av: 39.55) in 1992, he captured 64 (av: 27.85) in 1993. This included an excellent opening spell of 6/19 in thirteen overs against Nottinghamshire at The Oval in July.

Continuing his steady improvement, Benjamin took eighty wickets (av: 20.72) in 1994. This earned him selection to the Test XI when England met

South Africa in the third Test at The Oval in July that year. He responded by taking 4/42 in the first innings. In the second, he faltered, conceding 38 runs without reward in eleven overs, as Devon Malcolm (9/57) was putting the tourists to flight in a memorable display of hostile fast bowling.

That was the end of Benjamin's Test career. Although he was one of the more successful performers in his debut, he was immediately discarded by the selectors. He thus ended with a Test record of four wickets (av: 20.00), no runs in his solitary innings, and no catches. A consolation prize came by way of a tour to Australia with the England side in 1994/95. Injury, however, restricted him to four first-class matches from which he managed to squeeze only six wickets (av: 56.83) and eleven runs (av: 2.75).

Benjamin continued to play for Surrey until 1999 but with diminishing returns. He ended with a first-class career record of 387 wickets (av: 29.94), 1,161 runs (av: 11.38), and 25 catches in 126 matches. His highest score was 49 against Essex at The Oval in July 1995. He remains the only native of St Kitts ever to have participated in a Test match.

ROLAND ORLANDO BUTCHER

A cousin of Guyana's Basil Butcher, Roland Butcher was born in East Point, St Philip, Barbados, on 14 October 1953. He emigrated with his parents to Britain in 1967 and played for Middlesex from 1974 until 1989. He also represented Barbados in one Shell Shield match in April 1975 when he made 38 & 29 against Jamaica at Montego Bay.

Butcher was an attractive right-handed batsman, a right-arm medium pace bowler and a brilliant fieldsman. After a pedestrian start with Middlesex, he finally began to blossom with a splendid innings of 142 against Gloucestershire at Bristol in August 1978. Another century (106) followed at Leicester in 1979, the year in which he was awarded his county cap. His performance in 1980, when he scored 792 runs (av: 39.60), earned him selection on the English team which toured the West Indies in 1980/81. He enjoyed a reasonably successful tour, scoring 385 runs (av: 35.00) in seven first-class matches. Unfortunately, however, he could not sustain that form in the Tests.

The first Black player ever to represent England in a Test match, Butcher had the good fortune to make his international debut before his home crowd at the Kensington Oval in March 1981. But against the brilliant fast bowling of Colin Croft, Joel Garner, Michael Holding and Andy Roberts, the England side folded and Butcher himself could manage only 17 & 2. In three Tests during that series he mustered 71 runs (av: 14.20). His highest score was 32 in the fifth Test at Kingston. Reliable as usual in the field, he held three catches. This proved to be his career Test record as he was never selected for England again.

Butcher continued to play first-class cricket until 1989, eventually appearing in 277 games for Barbados, England, Middlesex and Tasmania. He registered 12,021 runs (av: 31.22), including seventeen centuries, four wickets (av: 45.50) and 290 catches. An occasional wicket-keeper, he also stumped one batsman. Butcher's best season came in 1982 when he accumulated 1,058 runs (av: 42.32). His highest score was 197 against Yorkshire at Lord's in August 1982 when he and Mike Gatting added 237 runs for the fourth wicket. On that occasion, he also added 156 with Mike Embury (43 not out) before being run out in a desperate effort to reach his double century before the impending declaration. That swashbuckling innings included six sixes and eighteen fours. Butcher retired after receiving his benefit from Middlesex and turned out briefly for Suffolk in the early 1990s.

NORMAN GEORGE COWANS

Norman Cowans was born in Enfield, St Mary, Jamaica, on 17 April 1961 and emigrated to Britain with his parents when he was seven years old. He joined the Middlesex staff in his teens and played for their second XI during the late 1970s before his first-class career began in 1980 with a match against Oxford University. He appeared in only three matches in 1981 but headed the county's averages with eight wickets at less than twenty runs apiece. In 1982, he took 33 wickets (av: 21.84) and began to attract much attention as one of the liveliest right-arm fast bowlers in the country. He had created such a positive impression that the Cricket Writers' Club chose him the 'Young Cricketer of the Year'.

With only 43 first-class wickets to his credit and a mere sixteen first-class games under his belt, Cowans was selected to tour Australia and New Zealand with the English team in 1982/83. He took 26 wickets (av: 28.65) in eight first-class matches and had the enormous satisfaction of bowling England to a sensational victory at Melbourne in the fourth Test of the series. He claimed 6/77 in 26 challenging overs in the second innings. Australia, needing 292 to win, fell short by four runs.

Most observers considered this the start of a stellar Test career, but Cowans proved inconsistent. He was clearly one of the fastest and most dangerous bowlers in England but his accuracy did not always match his speed. He claimed twelve Test wickets (av: 37.25) against New Zealand in 1983, and took an equal number of Test wickets against New Zealand and Pakistan in the winter that followed. But when the West Indies toured England in 1984, he was selected for only one Test. In an innings of 500, Cowans bowled nineteen fruitless overs for 76 runs at Manchester. Nevertheless, he was invited to tour the sub-continent in 1984/85. In five Tests against India, he managed only fourteen wickets (av: 44.78) and that proved to be the end of his disappointing Test career. In nineteen matches for England, he recorded 175 runs (av: 7.95), 51 wickets (av: 39.27), and nine catches. His highest score at this level was 36 against Australia at Perth on his debut in November 1982.

Despite being overlooked by the Test selectors, Cowans continued to bowl impressively for Middlesex, exceeding fifty wickets in each of the next four seasons. He claimed 73 wickets (av: 22.95) in 1985; 71 (av: 18.16) in 1988; and 62 (av: 21.30) in 1989. Thereafter, his production gradually diminished and he was eventually offered a benefit by Middlesex in 1993 and released at the end of the year. Hampshire offered him a contract in 1994 in the hope of rekindling his old fire, but he could manage only 26 wickets (av: 37.92) in twelve matches.

Altogether, between 1980 and 1994, Cowans took part in 239 first-class matches in which he registered 1,605 runs (av: 8.91), 662 wickets (av: 24.86), and 63 catches. His contribution to English cricket included 23 wickets (av: 39.69) in 23 ODIs.

PHILIP ANTHONY JASON DEFREITAS

Born in Scotts Head, Dominica, on 18 February 1966, Philip DeFreitas emigrated with his parents to Britain in 1976 and attended Willesden High School in London before joining the ground staff at Lord's. An aggressive right-handed batsman, a penetrative right-arm fast-medium bowler and brilliant fieldsman, he was signed to a contract by Leicestershire while still in his teens. He embarked on his first-class career in 1985, making 117 runs (av: 13.00) and taking 27 wickets (av: 26.03) in nine matches. DeFreitas was awarded his county cap in the very next year when he captured 94 wickets (av: 23.09) and scored 645 runs (av: 23.03) in his first full season. That performance earned him a place on the English team which toured Australia in 1986/87.

DeFreitas was only twenty years old when he made his Test debut against Australia at Brisbane in November 1986. He began with a confident innings of forty, adding 92 for the eighth wicket with Ian Botham in just over an hour. He then proceeded to take 5/94 in 33 overs as England won comfortably by seven wickets. He could not maintain this form, however, and he finished his first series with 77 runs (av: 19.25) and nine wickets (av: 49.55) in four Tests.

That series seemed to set the pattern for most of DeFreitas' Test career: brilliance interspersed with mediocrity. He thus spent almost as much time out of the Test XI as he did in it. Against the West Indies in 1991, however, he played like a man inspired. In five Tests that summer, he garnered 22 wickets at 20.77 runs each and 134 runs (av: 19.14). In the first encounter, at Leeds in June, he made a key contribution to England's victory with a match analysis if 8/93 in just over 38 challenging overs. He also struck a defiant 55 not out at Trent Bridge in July. DeFreitas was largely responsible for the fact that England were finally able to achieve their first drawn series against the West Indies since 1974. Against Sri Lanka at Lord's in August, he then captured 8/115 in 48 overs to help England rout the visitors. He was duly rewarded with a selection as one of *Wisden's* 'Five Cricketers of the Year' in 1992.

After playing for Leicestershire for four seasons, DeFreitas joined Lancashire in 1989 and continued to perform splendidly on the county circuit even when his Test form was not the best. His versatility gave that county a distinct advantage in the one-day competitions, two of which they were able to win in 1990. Four years later, he joined Derbyshire and played for that county until 1998. DeFreitas enjoyed his finest season in 1994 when, in three Tests against New Zealand, he took 21 wickets (av: 21.47) and scored 134 runs (av: 44.46). He then claimed nine more wickets in three Tests against South Africa. His tour of Australia in 1994/95 was a chequered one (which produced only 141 runs and thirteen expensive wickets in four Tests); and, in 1995, he was selected for only one Test against the West Indies with negligible results. Up to that point, DeFreitas had appeared in 44 Tests, scoring 934 runs (av: 14.82), taking 140 wickets (av: 33.57) and holding fourteen catches. His best innings at this level was a masterful 88 off 95 balls in exactly two hours against Australia at Adelaide in January 1995.

This marked the end of his Test career, but DeFreitas continued to play with fairly satisfactory results not only for Derbyshire but also for Boland in South Africa, whose team he had first joined in 1993/94. So far, in 355 first-class matches, he has made 10,535 runs (av: 22.95), including ten centuries, taken 1,205 wickets (av: 27.66), and held 126 catches. In 103 ODIs for England, his contributions amounted to 690 runs (av: 16.04) and 115 wickets (av: 32.82). Philip DeFreitas must certainly rank as the finest all-rounder thus far produced by Dominica.

LORD HARRIS

George Robert Canning, the fourth Lord Harris, was born in St Anne's, Trinidad, on 3 February 1851. He moved with his parents at an early age to England and actually had his first net at Lord's in 1862 when only eleven years old. He completed his education at Eton and Oxford University and was one of the stars at the latter institution during 1871-74. For Kent he played 157 matches, off and on, during 1871-1911. He rescued that county cricket club from oblivion towards the end of the Victorian age by giving it invaluable leadership both on and off the field. Not only did he serve as its captain during 1871-89, but he was its president in 1875, honorary secretary from 1875 to 1880 and sat on its committee for a great portion of his long life. He also held various posts with the MCC, over which he presided in 1895.

Lord Harris was an attacking right-handed batsman, a brilliant fieldsman and a useful right-arm fast round-arm change bowler. In 224 first-class matches that stretched over a period of forty years, he recorded 9,990 runs (av: 26.85), 75 wickets (av: 25.11) and 190 catches. He would obviously have appeared in many more first-class games had it not been for his other commitments after 1884. He was appointed undersecretary for India and later undersecretary for war in the administrations led by the Marquess of Salisbury. He also spent five years as Governor of Bombay and made a notable contribution to the development of cricket in India. He played four Tests for England, registering

145 runs (av: 29.00) and two catches. He captained England in all of these Tests and was personally responsible for organising the first one ever staged in England, against Australia at The Oval, in September 1880.

Not surprisingly, then, Lord Harris is universally regarded as one of the most important figures in the history of cricket. Not only was he a player of considerable merit but he was one of the game's most influential legislators and administrators, devoting the major portion of his life, as he frequently admitted, to the welfare of Lord's. He did much to eliminate throwing which had reached almost epidemic proportions in the 1890s and he was the one who insisted most vigorously on adherence to the laws and traditions of the sport. One of cricket's leading apostles in the 19th century, he led a team to Canada and the United States in 1872, and another to Australia in 1878/79. Lord Harris also made a useful contribution to cricket literature by publishing his own memoirs, *A Few Short Runs*, and editing the *History of Kent County Cricket* and *Lord's and the MCC*. Such was his devotion to the game that he continued to play good club cricket until well beyond the age of seventy and took part in his final match at Eton at the age of 79. He died in Faversham, Kent, on 24 March 1932, at the age of 81.

CLAIREMONT CHRISTOPHER LEWIS

Chris Lewis was born in Georgetown, Guyana, on 14 February 1968. He emigrated to England with his parents at the age of ten and completed his education at Willesden High School in London. While still in his teens, he was signed to a professional contract by Leicestershire in 1987. His progress was rapid enough to earn him selection to the Young England side for the Youth World Cup in 1988. One year later, although participating in only twelve first-class matches, he captured 45 wickets (av: 21.91) and was selected as a replacement for Ricardo Ellcock when England toured the West Indies in 1989/90. Restricted to only two first-class matches, he never really had a chance on that occasion to distinguish himself before his former home crowds. He was destined to return to the West Indies with the England team in 1993/94. That winter he made a more positive impression, scoring 170 runs (av: 21.25) and taking fourteen wickets (av: 39.50) in the five Tests. He was also one of the most dynamic and effective fieldsmen on either side during that series, saving countless runs by his exceptional athleticism.

Lewis was a potentially dangerous right-arm fast bowler, an attacking right-handed batsman and a brilliant fieldsman, especially in the deep. He left Leicestershire at the end of the 1991 season and threw in his lot with Nottinghamshire, for whom he scored a dazzling 247 against Durham in September 1993 and a belligerent 220 not out against Warwickshire in 1994, when he actually headed the county's batting averages with 881 runs (av: 58.73). Wishing to move closer to his family in London, he joined Surrey in 1996 but returned to Leicestershire in 1997. These constant moves were in keeping with

Lewis' general record of inconsistency at the highest level. Although obviously one of the finest all-rounders in England, he did not always give of his best in Test matches. His record in that department reads: 32 matches, 1,105 runs (av: 23.02), 93 wickets (av: 37.52) and 25 catches. His highest Test score (117) came against India at Madras in February 1993, when he celebrated his 25th birthday by completing his maiden Test century with a straight hit for six off Venkatapathy Raju. His finest bowling performance (6/111 in 35 overs) came against the West Indies at Birmingham in July 1991.

Lewis always gave the impression that he was capable of reaching a higher gear if he were only in the right mood. Occasionally, both his batting and bowling approached heights of brilliance. He was therefore an exciting player to watch in one-day contests, especially at the county level. In 53 ODIs, he mustered 374 runs (av: 14.38), 66 wickets (av: 29.42) and twenty catches. In 189 first-class matches between 1987 and 2000, he registered 7,406 runs (av: 30.73), 543 wickets (av: 29.88) and 154 catches. Lewis was one of the better all-rounders produced by Guyana over the years.

DEVON EUGENE MALCOLM

Devon Malcolm was born in Kingston, Jamaica, on 22 February 1963. He joined his father in England in 1979 and completed his education at Richmond College in Sheffield. Signed to a contract by Derbyshire in 1984 and encouraged by Michael Holding (one of the truly great fast bowlers of all time), he shortly proved himself one of the fastest and most fearsome bowlers in the world. A strong and burly right-arm speedster, Malcolm's accuracy was sometimes lacking, but the velocity of his deliveries could not easily be surpassed. It was his sheer pace which brought him into the England Test XI in 1989. He then played forty Tests for England in a somewhat chequered career.

Malcolm did not distinguish himself in his debut against Australia at Trent Bridge in August 1989, but he performed well enough that season to earn selection on the team which visited the Caribbean in the winter. Bowling before his home crowd at Kingston in February 1990, he contributed greatly to his team's victory in the first Test of the series by removing the dangerous Viv Richards twice fairly cheaply and claiming 4/77 in the West Indies' second innings. He proceeded to take 10/137 in the third Test to be named 'Man of the Match' at Port of Spain in March. He finished with nineteen wickets (av: 30.36) in the four Tests that winter.

During the early 1990s, Malcolm was clearly the fastest bowler in England. He was selected to tour Australia with the senior teams in 1990/91 and 1994/ 95, the sub-continent in 1992/93, the West Indies again in 1993/94 and South Africa in 1995/96. He did not always produce good results, but his superlative speed sometimes affected the outcome in a dramatic and positive fashion. Unfortunately, he was also occasionally impeded by serious injury (as was the case during his second tour of the Caribbean). Against Australia in 1990/91, he was England's most successful bowler in terms of Test wickets taken (16) but they came at the high price of more than 41 runs each. On the whole, except for the Caribbean, he failed to adjust to foreign conditions and did not perform well on the slow pitches in India and Sri Lanka.

Malcolm reached the climax of his career in the summer of 1994, when he claimed 69 first-class wickets (av: 29.20). Having for some time been neglected by the Test selectors, he was reintroduced to face the South Africans at The Oval in the final Test of that series. Incensed at having been struck between the eyes by a bouncer from 'Fanie' de Villiers, he is reported to have told the close fielders "You guys are going to pay for this. You guys are history". He then proceeded in the second innings to destroy South Africa's batting completely in two of the most devastating spells imaginable. Altogether, he sent down 99 thunderbolts to capture 9/57, bowl England to a sensational victory and be crowned 'Man of the Match'. His analysis was a record for England against South Africa and a record for all Tests at The Oval. It was then the sixth best in Test cricket. For his pains, Malcolm was chosen one of *Wisden's* 'Five Cricketers of the Year' in 1995.

Malcolm represented Derbyshire from 1984 to 1997, receiving his county cap in 1989 and his benefit in 1997. He then played for Northamptonshire during 1998-2000, before joining Leicestershire in 2001. In 304 first-class matches between 1984 and 2003, he recorded 1,054 wickets (av: 30.33), 1,985 runs (av: 7.84) and 45 catches. His most fruitful season was 1996 when he claimed 82 wickets (av: 31.67), prompting the Test selectors to bring him back for one last (but futile) fling against the Australians in 1997. His forty Tests yielded 128 wickets (av: 37.09), 236 runs (av: 6.05) and seven catches.

An ordinary fieldsman and a feeble lower-order right-handed batsman, Malcolm was once described by Conrad Hunte in his capacity as Test match referee, as "one of the worst No 11s in the game". These shortcomings militated against his frequent selection for one-day contests. He thus played in only ten ODIs, taking sixteen wickets (av: 25.25), scoring nine runs (av: 3.00) and holding one catch. Even so, he did manage to score 29 in eighteen balls against Australia at Sydney in January 1995 and to register two fifties in his first-class career.

WILFRED NORRIS SLACK

Wilf Slack was born in Troumaca, St Vincent, on 12 December 1954. He emigrated to England in 1966 and learned his cricket at High Wycombe. He batted so well for Buckinghamshire in 1976 that Middlesex offered him a contract in the following year. His first-class career got off to a relatively slow start, but he blossomed in the early 1980s and shared many a fine opening stand with his favourite partner, Graham Barlow. Together, they bettered the old Middlesex county record of 312 for the first wicket by hammering 367 against Kent at Lord's in July 1981. Slack's contribution was 181 not out. In the very next match, against Worcestershire at Lord's, he achieved his career best, a masterful 248 not out. He finished that season with 1,372 runs (av: 47.31) and was awarded his county cap.

Slack was an attractive left-handed opening batsman, a useful right-arm medium pace bowler and a fine fieldsman. He scored runs very consistently for Middlesex throughout the 1980s, exceeding 1,000 runs in eight seasons, and was unlucky to have been selected for only three Tests and two ODIs. In 1985, he enjoyed his best season, scoring 1,900 runs (av: 54.28), including an unbeaten 201 against the Australian tourists at Lord's in August. This was then the Middlesex record in any match against Australia. Even that did not secure Slack a selection in the Test XI, and he only made his debut in March 1986 as a replacement for Mike Gatting who had suffered a broken nose early in England's tour of the Caribbean that winter.

Slack's Test career was not as distinguished as his record for Middlesex. Asked to play against the rampant West Indies who were then carrying all before them, he made only 2 & 0 (run out) in his debut at Port of Spain and was dropped for the next two Tests. Recalled for the fifth Test of the series, he made a patient 52 at Kingston and shared an opening partnership of 127 with Graham Gooch. His final Test was played against India at Leeds in June 1986. He was able to contribute only 0 & 19 to a match that England lost. The selectors concluded, perhaps too hastily, that while Slack was obviously an excellent county player, he was unable to make the necessary adjustments to succeed at the international level. In his three Tests, he recorded 81 runs (av: 13.50) and three catches. In his two ODIs, he made 43 runs (av: 21.50). In 237 first-class games, he recorded 13,950 runs (av: 38.96), including 25 centuries, 21 wickets (av: 32.76) and 174 catches.

Slack was one of the very best batsmen ever produced by St Vincent and it is a pity he was not allowed more chances to prove his worth at the highest level. He played for the Windward Islands in the Shell Shield Competition during 1981-83, scoring 585 runs (av: 36.56) in nine matches. His defiant 97 against the touring Indians at St George's, Grenada, in March 1983 proved to be his highest first-class score in the West Indies. Wilf Slack died suddenly at the age of 34 on 15 January 1989 while batting during a minor tour in Banjul, the capital of The Gambia. A quiet and likeable man, he was mourned throughout England and the Caribbean.

GLADSTONE CLEOPHAS SMALL

Gladstone Small was born in St George, Barbados, on 18 October 1961. He emigrated to England when still young and completed his education at the Hall Green Technical College in Birmingham. A precocious cricketer, he was eagerly signed by Warwickshire, for whom he made his first-class debut in 1980 at the age of eighteen. Small was an accomplished right-arm medium-fast bowler, a reliable fieldsman and a useful lower-order right-handed batsman. He won his county cap after a fine performance in 1982 which produced 63 wickets (av:

30.55) and 309 runs (av: 12.87). He improved on these numbers over the next few years and earned selection for England in two Tests against New Zealand in 1986. The start to his Test career was not particularly spectacular, but he showed enough talent to convince the selectors to send him on the tour of Australia in 1986/87. He did well enough in two Tests to head England's bowling averages with twelve wickets at fifteen runs each. After being hampered by a gimpy knee in the early part of the campaign, he re-emerged in the fourth Test at Melbourne in December to take 7/88 in just over 37 overs to win the 'Man of the Match' award and make a vital contribution to England's victory. On a bouncy pitch on the opening day, he (5/48) and Botham (5/41) virtually settled the result by bundling out the hosts for 141.

Small gained selection on the team which toured the Caribbean in 1989/90. This was the series in which three Caribbean natives (DeFreitas, Malcolm and Small) represented England with fine results even though the tourists lost by two Tests to one. Small took part in all four Tests, finishing second in his team's bowling averages to Angus Fraser with seventeen wickets (av: 29.70). His contribution to England's first Test victory in the Caribbean since 1974 was substantial. At Kingston, where the visitors won the first Test by nine wickets, Small (4/58) and Malcolm (4/77) did all of the major damage in the second innings. In the fourth Test, before his home crowd at the Kensington Oval, he was easily England's best bowler with 8/183 from 55 overs in a losing cause.

Small's Test career, however, did not evolve as his supporters hoped it would. Despite his consistency at the county cricket level and his satisfactory results when offered the opportunity to perform on higher ground, he was confined to seventeen Tests, from which he extracted 55 wickets (av: 34.01), 263 runs (av: 15.47) and nine catches. His highest Test score was a plucky 59 against Australia at The Oval in August 1989 when he and Nick Cook (31) saved England from further embarrassment by adding 73 for the ninth wicket. No other English bowler during the 1980s could match Small's returns in so few chances; but largely because of his steadiness of length and line, his reliability in the field and his ability to score some runs at the tail-end of the batting order, he came to be seen mainly as a one-day cricketer. In 53 ODIs, he registered 98 runs (av: 6.53), 58 wickets (av: 33.48) and seven catches.

It was for Warwickshire that Small played his very best cricket, helping it to three titles in 1994 alone. He represented that county with distinction between 1980 and 1997. His highest innings on its behalf was seventy against Lancashire at Manchester in May 1988. He exceeded fifty wickets in six seasons, his best tally being eighty (av: 20.06) in 1988. His finest bowling performance came against Nottinghamshire at Birmingham in June 1988, when he claimed 7/15 in 11.2 overs to dismiss the visitors for 44 in their second innings and secure victory for his side. Altogether, in 315 first-class matches, Small claimed 852 wickets (av: 28.62), scored 4,409 runs (av: 14.36) and held 95 catches.

SIR PELHAM WARNER

Francis Pelham Warner was born in Port of Spain, Trinidad, on 2 October 1873 but received his early education in Barbados at Harrison College which was then one of the most famous secondary schools in the British Empire. It was there that he first learned the basics of his cricket, representing the school's First XI at the age of thirteen at a time when Harrison College was one of the strongest teams in the island. In 1887, after his father's death, 'Plum' moved with his mother to England and settled there permanently until his death on 30 January 1963 at the ripe age of 89. He completed his education at Rugby and Oxford University, both of which institutions he successfully represented on the cricket field. He was a frail-looking but attractive right-handed batsman who scored runs consistently for Middlesex between 1894 and 1920. In 519 first-class matches, he recorded 29,028 runs (av: 36.28), fifteen wickets (av: 42.40) and 183 catches. He played fifteen Tests for England, finishing with 622 runs (av: 23.92).

Warner was a very fine cricketer but his main contributions to the sport came from his efforts in administrative and managerial capacities. He captained Middlesex from 1908 to 1920 and England in three overseas tours. He also managed the English team during the celebrated 'body line' tour of 1932/33. He served as a Test selector for many years and was often the chairman of the selection committee. For the MCC, Warner was at various times deputy secretary, trustee and president. He was a member of the committee at Lord's for what seems like an eternity. In the end, he was appointed the first Life Vice President of the MCC in 1961. In addition, he was the president of the Middlesex County Cricket Club from 1937 to 1946.

Few individuals, then, have made as great a contribution to cricket as the popular 'Plum' Warner who was eventually knighted in 1937 for his services to the game. He founded, and for a long time edited, *The Cricketer* and was cricket correspondent for the *Morning Post* during 1921-32. Warner also wrote or edited about twenty books which have formed a valuable segment of cricket history and literature. Fittingly, his ashes were scattered at Lord's when he died. He remains one of the best batsmen produced by Trinidad and his aggregate of first-class runs has not yet been exceeded by another Trinidadian.

NEIL FITZGERALD WILLIAMS

Born in Hopewell, St Vincent, on 2 July 1962, Neil Williams emigrated with his family to Britain at the age of thirteen and completed his education at the Acland Burghley Comprehensive School. While playing in the Middlesex County League, he came to the attention of Don Bennett, the county coach, and was signed to a professional contract in 1982. To keep in shape, he played for the Windward Islands in the Shell Shield Competition that winter, recording 134 runs (av: 22.33), seventeen wickets (av: 21.58) and two catches in four matches. In 1983, his first full season for Middlesex, Williams helped that county win the Benson & Hedges Cup and finished with 63 wickets (av: 26.33). He also scored 407 runs (av: 22.61). He then went to Tasmania in the 1983/84 winter to participate in the Sheffield Shield Competition. In seven matches there, he scored 131 runs (av: 13.10), took 22 wickets (av: 38.22) and held four catches.

Williams was a right-arm medium-fast bowler, a hard-hitting lower-order batsman and a useful fieldsman. His all-round play earned him his county cap in 1984. Playing with consistency (rather than brilliance) throughout the 1980s, he remained on the brink of selection to the England Test XI before finally receiving the call to oppose India at The Oval in August 1990. Originally named twelfth man, he was asked to replace an injured Chris Lewis at the last moment. On a batsman's pitch, the visitors amassed 606/9 declared and dealt cavalierly with all the bowlers. Williams toiled for 41 overs to claim 2/148. Sent in as a night watchman with the score at 18/1 late on the second evening, he batted with grim determination for 72 minutes and contributed a valuable 38 in a partnership of 74 with his captain, Graham Gooch. England failed to avert the follow-on, but saved the game by making 477/4 in their second attempt. In the circumstances, Williams had done quite well on his Test debut. But he was never invited to play for England again.

Williams remained with Middlesex until 1994, the year in which he received his benefit. He then played for Essex from 1995 to 1998. He also returned to the West Indies to represent the Windward Islands during 1989-92. In 255 first-class matches altogether, he registered 4,457 runs (av: 18.64), 675 wickets (av: 30.29), and 67 catches. He was a very capable county cricketer who might well have been offered more opportunities to play Test cricket for England, all things considered.

FINAL ANALYSIS

This study of the thirteen Caribbean natives who played Test cricket for other countries provokes a few interesting speculations. In the first place, only one of them would most certainly have played more Test cricket for the West Indies had he not emigrated. Simpson Guillen had performed so well as Clyde Walcott's understudy in Australia and New Zealand in 1951/52 that he might well have carried the gloves until the emergence of Gerry Alexander in 1957. There might have been no need for the West Indian selectors to experiment with Alfie Binns, Clairemont Depeiza, Ralph Legall and Clifford McWatt during the early 1950s. Guillen would most certainly have played for the West Indies against India in 1952/53, even if it can be argued that McWatt would have provided stiffer opposition in 1953/54.

Lord Harris and Pelham Warner were fortunate to have emigrated when they did. This provided them with several opportunities to play first-class and Test cricket at a time when the West Indies had not yet acquired Test match status and when territorial competition was irregular and spasmodic at best.

Had they remained at home, they would certainly have merited selection to any West Indian squads while they were at their peak; but they would inevitably have descended into the shadows of cricket history in the same way that Lebrun Constantine, Percy Goodman and so many others did.

Among the remaining eleven, only DeFreitas (and perhaps Lewis) might have succeeded in cracking the powerful Caribbean line-up during the late 1980s and they might have been able to out-duel the two Benjamins of Antigua for berths in the West Indian Test XI during the early 1990s. Quite possibly, too, Devon Malcolm might have been able to compete with Patrick Patterson for a place between 1988 and 1993. But there would have been no hope for any of the others. Neither Cowans nor Small would have been able to compete and the position would have been even more hopeless for such batsmen as Butcher and Slack. Nor is there any West Indian Test player that Robin Singh could have replaced, even at his peak.

On the whole, then, the talent-drain, such as it was, did not affect the West Indies at all while it profited the individuals who (or whose parents) took the decision to emigrate. The Caribbean immigrants also contributed to English cricket by producing such gifted sons as Dean Headley, David Lawrence, Mark Ramprakash and Alex Tudor who have thus far played several Tests for England.

CHAPTER EIGHT

WORLD RECORDS SET BY WEST INDIANS IN TEST CRICKET

IN THE 75 YEARS SINCE 1928, THE WEST INDIES HAVE SET, EQUALLED and/or broken more than 180 Test cricket records at the impressive rate of more than 2.4 per year. This is a reflection of their phenomenal overall success, notwithstanding the fact that they are currently mired in a deep and protracted slump. The most important of these team and individual records are addressed below in chronological order.

1. SEALY BECOMES THE YOUNGEST TEST PLAYER
On 11 January 1930, Derek Sealy made his debut for the West Indies against England at Bridgetown. He was just seventeen years, 122 days old and was then the youngest player ever to participate in a Test match. He scored 58 & 15 on this occasion and naturally became also the first seventeen-year-old to register a half-century in Test cricket. Sealy's record was not broken until 1 July 1954 when Khalid Hassan, at sixteen years, 352 days old, appeared for Pakistan against England at Nottingham.

2. HEADLEY SETS RECORD AT BRIDGETOWN
In the second innings of his first Test match, George Headley made 176 against England at the Kensington Oval in January 1930. This stood as the highest individual score in a Test innings in Barbados until Clyde Walcott made 220 there against England in February 1954.

3. ROACH SETS RECORD AT GEORGETOWN
Clifford Roach had the distinction of scoring the first West Indian double century in Test cricket when he struck a glorious 209 against England at Bourda in February 1930 to lead the hosts to a first innings total of 471. This remained the highest score achieved by any individual in a Test innings in British Guiana until Glenn Turner of New Zealand made 259 against the West Indies in April 1972.

4. WEST INDIES SET RECORD AT GEORGETOWN
At Bourda in February 1930, the West Indies scored 471 in their first innings against England, thanks to fine centuries from Clifford Roach (209) and George Headley (114). Their total remained the highest innings achieved in any Test in British Guiana until April 1972 when New Zealand, led by Glen Turner's double century, amassed 543/3 declared.

5. HEADLEY SCORES FOUR TEST CENTURIES AT THE AGE OF 20

In February 1930, George Headley became the first batsman to score three Test centuries before his 21st birthday. After scoring 176 in his first Test in January, he achieved separate hundreds (114 & 112) in his third. In his fourth, two months later, he made 223 against England at Kingston. He remained the youngest batsman to register four centuries in Test cricket until India's Sachin Tendulkar scored his fourth (111 against South Africa) in November 1992 at the age of nineteen years, 217 days. Tendulkar, who made his Test debut at sixteen years, 205 days old, scored seven Test centuries before reaching the age of 21. But Headley is still the youngest batsman to accomplish four centuries in his first (or any) Test series. He naturally remains the first cricketer to achieve four centuries in his first four Tests and in only eight innings.

6. HEADLEY BECOMES THE YOUNGEST DOUBLE CENTURION

When George Headley made 223 against England at Kingston on 10 April 1930, he had become, at 20 years, 315 days old, the youngest player to achieve a double century in Test cricket. His score was also the highest ever made against England in a Test match. As such, it lasted only two months before Bradman (254) broke it at Lord's in June. Headley remained the youngest double centurion in Test cricket until Javed Miandad, at nineteen years, 141 days old, scored 206 for Pakistan against New Zealand at Karachi in October 1976.

7. GRANT SCORES TWO HALF-CENTURIES IN A TEST

Jackie Grant, on his debut against Australia at Adelaide in December 1930, became the first batsman to register undefeated fifties in both innings of a Test match. He scored 53* & 71* but failed to save his team from defeat by ten wickets.

8. THREE WEST INDIANS SCORE 90s

Against England at Port of Spain in January 1935, three West Indians established a dubious record by scoring nineties. This was the first such example in Test cricket. Derek Sealy (92) and Learie Constantine (90) failed to reach their century in the first innings, while George Headley was dismissed for 93 in the second.

9. HEADLEY & GRANT SET PARTNERSHIP RECORD AT KINGSTON

In March 1935, George Headley (270*) and Jackie Grant (77) established a long-standing record at Kingston when they added 147 runs in an entertaining seventh-wicket partnership at England's expense. Grant joined Headley at 381/6 and stayed until the score reached 528. The West Indies declared at 535/7 and won the match by an innings & 161 runs. After almost seventy years, this stand still remains a record for the seventh wicket in Tests at Sabina Park.

10. WEST INDIES SET BOWLING RECORD AT KINGSTON

The West Indies set another durable record at Kingston in March 1935 when they dismissed England in their second innings for 103. Mannie Martindale (4/28) and Learie Constantine (3/13) did the damage on a worn pitch. This remained the lowest score in a Test innings at Sabina Park until April 1976 when India mustered only 97 against the West Indies when five of their players were too injured to bat in the second innings.

11. HEADLEY SCORES SEPARATE TEST CENTURIES AT LORD'S

In June 1939, George Headley (106 & 107) became the first batsman to score centuries in both innings of a Test match at Lord's. This was the second occasion on which he had scored separate centuries in a Test, thus equalling a record then held by England's Herbert Sutcliffe. The current record of three instances was set by India's Sunil Gavaskar in January 1979.

12. WEST INDIES DISMISS ENGLAND FOR LOWEST SCORE AT BOURDA

At Georgetown in March 1948, the West Indies bowled out England for 111 runs in their first innings, with John Goddard (the captain) taking 5/31 in 14.2 overs. This was then the lowest score made in a Test innings at Bourda. As such, it stood as a record for the ground until the Australians dismissed the hosts for 109 in April 1973.

13. JOHNSON SETS BOWLING RECORD AT KINGSTON

Playing in his first Test at the age of 37, Hines Johnson produced the wonderful match analysis of 10/96 against England at Kingston in March/April 1948. He claimed 5/41 in 34.5 overs in the first innings and 5/55 in 31 overs in the second, thus playing a key role in the West Indian victory. Johnson's match analysis has not yet been bettered in a Test match in Jamaica.

14. WALCOTT & GOMEZ SET PARTNERSHIP RECORD AT DELHI

Against India in November 1948, Clyde Walcott (152) and Gerry Gomez (101) set a Test partnership record of 267 runs for the fourth wicket at Delhi. They came together at 27/3 and were not separated until the score reached 294. The West Indies proceeded to amass 631 runs in their first Test innings on Indian soil, but their bowlers were not sufficiently penetrative to force a positive result. The Walcott/Gomez record at this venue still stands. It was the most productive Test partnership achieved by two West Indian batsmen up to that time.

15. WEEKES & CHRISTIANI SET PARTNERSHIP RECORD AT DELHI

After Clyde Walcott and Gerry Gomez had softened up the hosts with their record fourth-wicket stand at Delhi in November 1948, Everton Weekes (128) and Robert Christiani (107) added to their misery by sharing a partnership of

118 runs. This has remained the highest seventh-wicket partnership in Tests at Delhi. At 403/6, Christiani joined Weekes who left at 521/7. Christiani and Denis Atkinson then continued the assault on the tired bowlers.

16. CHRISTIANI & ATKINSON SET PARTNERSHIP RECORD AT DELHI

At 524/8, Denis Atkinson arrived to find Robert Christiani in full flight. They added 106 before the ninth wicket fell at 630. Atkinson's share was a hard-hitting 45. Their partnership of 106 is still the best for this wicket in Tests played at Feroz Shah Kotla in Delhi.

17. FOUR CENTURIES IN A TEST INNINGS

At Delhi in November 1948, the West Indies became the second team, equalling England's performance against Australia in 1938, to feature four individual centuries in a Test innings. Clyde Walcott (152), Everton Weekes (128), Robert Christiani (107) and Gerry Gomez (101) starred in a first innings score of 631 against India. This record, which the West Indies shared with England for six years, was surpassed by Australia at Kingston in June 1955 when five batsmen scored centuries in a single Test innings. Neil Harvey (204), Ron Archer (128), Colin McDonald (127), Richie Benaud (121) and Keith Miller (109) made hay as Australia rattled up 758/8 declared against the West Indies.

18. MOST HUNDRED PARTNERSHIPS IN ONE INNINGS

When the West Indies plundered the Indian attack for 631 runs at Delhi in November 1948, they participated in four partnerships that exceeded 100 runs each, thus equalling a record first established by England against Australia at The Oval in August 1938 and duplicated by Pakistan against the West Indies at Bridgetown in March 1958. The West Indian century partnerships were achieved for the fourth wicket (267), the sixth (101), the seventh (118) and the ninth (106).

19. WEST INDIES SET RECORD AT DELHI

The West Indian score of 631 against India at Delhi in November 1948 was then the highest ever made in a Test innings at this venue. As such, it lasted for just over ten years before being eclipsed in February 1959. On this latter occasion, another West Indian team amassed 644/8 declared.

20. WEST INDIES ACHIEVE RECORD SCORE AT BOMBAY

In December 1948, the West Indies made 629/6 declared against India in the second Test of that series. This remains the highest score ever achieved at Brabourne Stadium in a Test innings. On this occasion, six of their batsmen exceeded fifty, which was one short of the record set by England against Australia at Manchester in July 1934. The heroes were Everton Weekes (194), Allan Rae (104), F.J. Cameron (75*), Robert Christiani (74), Clyde Walcott (68) and Jeffrey Stollmeyer (66). But the Indians replied with 273 & 333/3 to secure a draw.

21. WEEKES SETS RECORD AT CALCUTTA

On 31 December 1948, Everton Weekes set a record for a Test innings at Calcutta when he scored 162 against India. This remained the highest individual Test innings achieved on that ground until Rohan Kanhai blasted his way to 256 in January 1959.

22. WEEKES SCORES FIVE SUCCESSIVE CENTURIES

Everton Weekes completed a fantastic record when he scored Test centuries in five consecutive innings. He began with 141 against England at Kingston in March 1948 before registering 128, 194, 162 and 101 against India in the 1948/49 series. This record has now stood triumphantly for more than fifty years and is one of the longest-surviving records in the history of all sport. Weekes came close to extending his string when making ninety in the next innings and would clearly have succeeded had the umpire given him the benefit of the doubt in a controversial run out decision at Madras. The previous record of four consecutive Test centuries had been shared by Jack Fingleton of Australia and Alan Melville of South Africa.

23. RAE & STOLLMEYER SET PARTNERSHIP RECORD AT MADRAS

Opening for the West Indies against India at Madras in January 1949, Allan Rae (109) and Jeffrey Stollmeyer (160) enjoyed a fine stand of 239 runs. This remained a West Indian first-wicket record for a very long time and it is still the highest partnership for the first wicket in Tests at Chepauk in Madras. It paved the way for a huge total (582) and the West Indies earned their very first Test victory on Indian soil.

24. STOLLMEYER ESTABLISHES RECORD SCORE AT MADRAS

It was at Madras in January 1949 that Jeffrey Stollmeyer made his highest score in Test cricket (160). It was then also the highest made in a Test innings at Madras. As such, Stollmeyer's record lasted until January 1980 when Sunil Gavaskar made 166 against Pakistan. The current record for the ground in Test cricket is 236*, also by Gavaskar. He achieved this at the expense of the West Indies in December 1983.

25. WEST INDIES SET RECORD AT MADRAS

The score of 582 made by the West against India at Madras in January 1949 was then the highest total achieved in Test cricket on that ground (Chepauk). The major contributors were Jeffrey Stollmeyer (160), Allan Rae (109), Everton Weekes (90) and Gerry Gomez (50). This record lasted until January 1985 when England scored 652/7 declared against India, thanks to double centuries from Graeme Fowler (201) and Mike Gatting (207).

26. WEST INDIES DISMISS INDIA FOR SMALLEST SCORE AT MADRAS

After compiling 582 runs in their first innings at Madras in January 1949, the West Indies dismissed India for 245 & 144 to win by an innings & 193 runs. The 144 scored by India in their second innings was then the lowest ever mustered in a Test innings at that venue. As such, this record lasted until January 1977 when England bowled out India for 83.

27. WEEKES SCORES SEVEN SUCCESSIVE HALF-CENTURIES

After registering his five consecutive Test centuries, Weekes scored 90 and 56 to complete a phenomenal and unprecedented run of seven consecutive fifties in Test cricket. He almost made it eight in a row, when he fell for 48 in the second innings at Bombay in February 1949. This extraordinary record, which stood unchallenged for more than 52 years, was finally equalled by Andy Flower of Zimbabwe in April 2001. The previous record of six consecutive Test fifties had been shared by Jack Ryder (Australia), 'Patsy' Hendren (England), George Headley (West Indies) and Alan Melville (South Africa).

28. WEEKES ACHIEVES HIGHEST AGGREGATE AGAINST INDIA

In the 1948/49 series, with innings of 128, 194, 162 & 101, 90, 56 & 48, Everton Weekes achieved a Test aggregate of 779 runs (av: 111.28). This is still the most runs ever conceded by India to any individual batsman in a Test series. It broke the old record of 715 (av: 178.15) that Donald Bradman of Australia had set in 1947/48.

29. VALENTINE TAKES FIRST EIGHT WICKETS

Alfred Valentine became the first bowler to take the first available eight wickets at the beginning of his Test career when he made his debut against England at Manchester in June 1950. The two tail-enders fell to Sonny Ramadhin (2/89) and Valentine finished with 8/104 in fifty overs. He was the first bowler to take eight wickets in his first Test innings, and only the second debutante (following Australia's Albert Trott in January 1895) to take eight wickets in an innings in his first Test match. Trott had done so in England's second innings.

30. WORRELL & WEEKES SHARE RECORD PARTNERSHIP AT TRENT BRIDGE

In July 1950, Frank Worrell (261) and Everton Weekes (129) put the English bowlers to the sword in a wonderful display of batsmanship. Coming together at 238/3, they took the score to 521/4 before Worrell was finally caught by Norman Yardley off Alec Bedser. Their stand was worth 283 runs and has remained the best for the third wicket in Tests at Nottingham.

31. WORRELL ACHIEVES RECORD SCORE AT TRENT BRIDGE

Frank Worrell's magnificent 261 at Trent Bridge in July 1950 was then the highest individual Test innings achieved at that venue. It remained the Trent Bridge record until Denis Compton scored 278 for England against Pakistan in July 1954.

32. FEWEST DUCKS IN A TEST CAREER

When Ray Lindwall trapped Clyde Walcott lbw for nought at Brisbane in November 1951, this was the first time that this great West Indian batsman had registered a duck in Test cricket. He never suffered this misfortune again. Walcott ended his career with the fewest ducks among all batsmen with more than seventy Test innings to their credit: 1 in 74 Test innings – a truly remarkable feat.

33. WEST INDIES RESTRICT AUSTRALIA TO SMALLEST TOTAL AT ADELAIDE

On 22 December 1951, the West Indies dismissed Australia for 82 runs in their first innings at Adelaide. This was then the smallest total in a Test innings at that venue, and the record still stands after more than fifty years. The damage was done by Frank Worrell who claimed 6/38 in 12.7 eight-ball overs. The West Indies proceeded to win the match by six wickets on Christmas day.

34. WALCOTT & WORRELL SHARE RECORD PARTNERSHIP AT AUCKLAND

Clyde Walcott (115) and Frank Worrell (100) shared a fruitful partnership against New Zealand at Auckland in February 1952. They came together at 321/4 and carried the score to 510/5, before the West Indies declared at 546/6. The 189 runs added by Walcott and Worrell on that occasion still stands as a record partnership in Tests for the fifth wicket at Auckland.

35. WEEKES & PAIRAUDEAU SET PARTNERSHIP RECORD AT PORT OF SPAIN

In January 1953, Everton Weekes and Bruce Pairaudeau (in his debut) established a record at Port of Spain that still stands after more than fifty years. They shared a fifth-wicket partnership of 219 runs. At 190/4, Pairaudeau joined Weekes who was eventually dismissed for 207 at 409/5. Pairaudeau completed an attractive 115 and the West Indies replied to India's 417 with 438 runs. The match ended in a draw.

36. WEEKES SETS BATTING RECORD AT PORT OF SPAIN

Against India in January 1953, Everton Weekes struck a brilliant 207 in the first Test at Port of Spain when West Indies scored 438 in reply to 417. His score was then the highest ever achieved by any batsman in a Test innings in Trinidad. The previous record was 205*, set by England's 'Patsy' Hendren in February 1930. Weekes' record was destined to be eclipsed by Sunil Gavaskar who made 220 for India against the West Indies in April 1971.

37. WALCOTT SETS RECORD AT BRIDGETOWN

In February 1954, Clyde Walcott played a majestic innings of 220 against England to steer the West Indies to 383 in their first innings. His score was then the highest ever achieved by any batsman in a Test innings in Barbados. The previous best had been 176 by George Headley against England in January 1930. Walcott's record was eventually surpassed by Hanif Mohammad who struck 337 for Pakistan in January 1958.

38. WEEKES & WORRELL SET PARTNERSHIP RECORD IN TRINIDAD

Everton Weekes (206) and Frank Worrell (167) established a partnership record for the third wicket at Port of Spain when they added 338 runs against England in March 1954. Worrell joined Weekes at 92/2 and the latter departed at 430/3, caught by Trevor Bailey off Tony Lock. West Indies compiled the huge score of 681/8 declared, but the high-scoring match petered out in a tame draw. The Weekes/Worrell record at this venue has not yet been broken.

39. WEST INDIES REACH RECORD SCORE AT PORT OF SPAIN

In March 1954, against England at Port of Spain, the West Indies achieved the highest Test innings made at that venue up to that time. They scored 681/8 declared, thanks to centuries from Everton Weekes (206), Frank Worrell (167) and Clyde Walcott (124). Their total still stands as the highest ever made in a single Test innings in Trinidad. The previous mark was 497 by the West Indies against England in February 1948.

40. ATKINSON & DEPEIZA SET SEVENTH-WICKET PARTNERSHIP RECORD

Denis Atkinson and Clairemont Depeiza established a phenomenal record when they added 347 runs for the seventh wicket against Australia at Bridgetown in May 1955. In reply to Australia's 668, the West Indies were perilously perched at 147/6 when these two batsmen came together towards the end of the third evening. They batted throughout the fourth day and took the score to 494 before Depeiza was bowled by Benaud for 122 early on the fifth morning. Atkinson completed a courageous double century (219). The partnership, which still stands as a world record for the seventh wicket in a Test match anywhere, saved the West Indies from certain defeat.

41. ATKINSON IS FIRST TO IMPORTANT 'DOUBLE'

Denis Atkinson did not only set a world record with Depeiza on this occasion. He became the first cricketer to score a double century and take five wickets in an innings of the same Test. On an unresponsive pitch, which yielded 1,661 runs for 36 wickets, Atkinson claimed 5/56 in Australia's second innings after taking 2/108 in the first. In the circumstances, his 7/164 from 84.2 overs was almost as magnificent a feat as was his double century. His unusual double has been duplicated only once. Mushtaq Mohammad of Pakistan scored 201 and took 5/49 against New Zealand at Dunedin in February 1973.

42. WALCOTT SCORES FIVE CENTURIES IN A TEST SERIES

Clyde Walcott established a long-standing world record when he registered five centuries against Australia in the West Indies in 1954/55. His aggregate of 827 runs included innings of 108 & 39, 126 & 110, 8 & 73, 15 & 83, 155 & 110. He was the first (and is still the only) batsman to score more than four centuries in a single Test series.

43. WALCOTT ACHIEVES SEPARATE HUNDREDS TWICE IN ONE SERIES

Clyde Walcott also became the first (and is still the only) batsman to achieve separate hundreds in two Tests during the same series. At Port of Spain in April 1955, he scored 126 & 110 in the second Test of the series against Australia. In the fifth match, at Kingston in June, he made 155 & 110. These centuries were achieved in a losing cause against a powerful attack, spearheaded by Ray Lindwall, Keith Miller, Ron Archer, Richie Benaud and Ian Johnson.

44. WEST INDIES DISMISS NEW ZEALAND FOR SMALLEST SCORE AT DUNEDIN

In February 1956, the West Indies defeated New Zealand by an innings & 71 runs by bundling out the hosts for 74 & 208. The 74 runs New Zealand made in their first innings was the smallest ever reached in a Test innings on that ground. As such, it has remained a record for almost fifty years.

45. WEEKES SETS RECORD AT DUNEDIN

At Dunedin in February 1956, after the West Indies had routed New Zealand for 74, they made 353 in reply. Everton Weekes led the way with 123 which was then the highest score ever achieved in a Test innings at that venue. Weekes' record was first surpassed by Graham Dowling (143) in February 1968. The current mark is held by Bryan Young who made 267* against Sri Lanka in March 1997.

46. SMITH & WORRELL SET PARTNERSHIP RECORD AT BIRMINGHAM

Collie Smith (161) and Frank Worrell (81) added 190 runs in an exciting partnership at Birmingham against England in May/June 1957. This still stands as the record for the sixth wicket in Tests at that venue. They came together at 197/5 and carried the score to 387/6, as the West Indies battled their way to

474 in reply to 186. Smith had the distinction of scoring a century in his first Test against England having already done so in his first Test against Australia in 1955. Peter May (285*) and Colin Cowdrey (154) retaliated with centuries of their own and the match was left drawn.

47. RAMADHIN BOWLS MOST BALLS IN A TEST MATCH
Against England at Birmingham in May/June 1957, Sonny Ramadhin established two very durable world records when he delivered 98 overs in the second innings after having bowled 31 in the first. His 588 balls set a new mark for the number of deliveries in a single Test innings and his 774 did the same for a Test match, surpassing the 766 set by England's Hedley Verity against South Africa at Durban in March 1939. Both records still stand.

48. SMITH & GODDARD SHARE PARTNERSHIP RECORD AT TRENT BRIDGE
At Nottingham in July 1957, the West Indies were trying desperately to save the game when John Goddard, the captain, joined Collie Smith at the crease. Asked to follow on 247 runs in arrears, they were precariously perched in their second innings at 194/6. Goddard (61) stayed defiantly for 220 minutes while Smith (168) scored a truly marvellous century before falling at 348/7. The match was saved and the Smith/Goddard stand of 154 runs remains to this day the record for the seventh wicket in Tests at Trent Bridge.

49. WEEKES SETS BATTING RECORD AT PORT OF SPAIN
When Everton Weekes played his last Test at Port of Spain in March 1958, he scored 51 & 9 against Pakistan to take his Test aggregate at that venue to 1,074 (av: 97.63). This was then the most runs made in a Test career by any batsman at the Queen's Park Oval. Weekes' record was destined to be surpassed by Rohan Kanhai who exceeded 1,200 Test runs there.

50. HUNTE & SOBERS SET PARTNERSHIP RECORD AT KINGSTON
Conrad Hunte and Garry Sobers established a long-lasting record when they shared a second-wicket stand of 446 runs at Pakistan's expense in February/March 1958. This remains the highest score for any Test partnership at Kingston. They came together at 87/1 and were not parted until Hunte (260) was run out at 533. Sobers proceeded to reach 365* and the West Indies declared at 790/3 to win by an innings & 174 runs. Their stand fell just five runs short of equalling the then world record of 451 established for all partnerships in Test cricket by Australia's Don Bradman and Bill Ponsford in 1934. The 446 achieved by Hunte and Sobers remains the most productive of all West Indian Test partnerships.

51. SOBERS SETS WORLD RECORD WITH 365*

Garry Sobers scored 365* against Pakistan at Kingston in February/March 1958 to establish a world record for an individual innings in Test cricket. The previous mark (364) had been set by England's Len Hutton against Australia at The Oval in August 1938. Sobers entered at 87/1 and remained undefeated when the West Indies declared at 790/3 and won the game easily by an innings & 174 runs. He might well have become the first player to exceed 400 runs in a Test innings had the excited spectators not invaded the field and damaged the pitch. This resulted in the loss of the last 45 minutes of play on that day. The West Indies then declared first thing next morning. Sobers' record also naturally eclipsed Andrew Sandham's 325 which had been the highest individual Test score previously achieved at Kingston. Prior to 1958, the highest West Indian individual Test score at Kingston was George Headley's 270* against England in March 1935. Sobers' record remained intact for more than 36 years until eclipsed by another West Indian, Brian Lara, who registered 375 against England at St John's, Antigua, in April 1994. But Sobers' 365* is still the record for Tests played in Jamaica.

52. SOBERS REMAINS THE YOUNGEST TRIPLE CENTURION IN TEST CRICKET

When Garry Sobers scored his 365* against Pakistan at Kingston in February/March 1958, he set two separate records. Not only was it the highest individual Test innings made up to that time, but he also became, at 21 years, 216 days old, the youngest player to achieve a triple hundred in Test cricket. That mark has not yet been surpassed. The previous record, 21 years, 318 days old, had been set by Don Bradman in 1930.

53. MOST RUNS CONCEDED BY PAKISTAN

At Kingston in February/March 1958, the West Indies amassed 790/3 declared in their first innings. This remains the highest score ever conceded by Pakistan in a Test innings. Sobers (365*), Conrad Hunte (260) and Clyde Walcott (88*) were the major contributors.

54. SOBERS ACHIEVES A RECORD AGGREGATE AGAINST PAKISTAN

In the 1957/58 series against Pakistan, Sobers achieved scores of 52, 52 & 80, 365*, 125 & 109*, 14 & 27. This produced a total of 824 runs (av: 137.33), which remains the highest individual aggregate ever conceded by Pakistan in a Test series.

55. SOBERS SETS RECORD AT KANPUR

In December 1958, Garry Sobers struck a superb 198 against India at Kanpur before he was run out. His score was then the highest individual innings achieved in Test cricket on that ground. This record was destined to be eclipsed by Faoud Bacchus (250) in February 1979.

56. HALL SETS BOWLING RECORD AT KANPUR

Some superb batting from Garry Sobers (4 & 198) and some hostile fast bowling from Wesley Hall helped the West Indies defeat India by 203 runs at Kanpur in December 1958. Hall took 6/50 in 28.4 overs, when India fell for 222 in their first innings, and followed that up with 5/76 in 32 overs as India collapsed for 240 in their second. His match analysis of 11/126 was then the best for any bowler in a Test at Kanpur. Hall's record was surpassed exactly one year later by Jasu Patel, who took fourteen wickets for 124 runs against Australia on this ground.

57. KANHAI & BUTCHER SET PARTNERSHIP RECORD AT CALCUTTA

At Calcutta, on 31 December 1958, Basil Butcher joined Rohan Kanhai at 180/ 3. They added 217 for the fourth wicket before being separated on the next day. This remains a Test record for the fourth wicket at Eden Gardens. Kanhai (256) achieved what was then the highest Test score on Indian soil and Butcher (103) achieved his maiden Test century. The West Indies won by an innings & 336 runs, when India collapsed before the hostile bowling of Roy Gilchrist (9/73) and Wesley Hall (6/86). This margin of victory was then a Test record for the venue and the second largest in Test cricket.

58. KANHAI SCORES MOST RUNS IN A TEST INNINGS IN INDIA

Rohan Kanhai made a masterful 256 against India at Calcutta in January 1959. This was then the highest individual score ever recorded in a Test match in India. As such, Kanhai's record lasted until V.V.S. Laxman scored 281 against Australia at Kolkata in March 2001.

59. WEST INDIES SET RECORD FOR INNINGS AT CALCUTTA

Thanks to Rohan Kanhai's double century and excellent support from Basil Butcher (103) and Garry Sobers (106*), the West Indies reached 614/5 against India at Calcutta in January 1959. This was then a record for that venue. It was not surpassed until India scored 633/5 declared against Australia in March 1998. The current record (657/7 declared) was also set by India against Australia in March 2001.

60. HOLT & HUNTE SET PARTNERSHIP RECORD AT DELHI

Against India at Delhi in February 1959, J.K. Holt Jr (123) and Conrad Hunte (92) enjoyed a fine opening partnership which yielded 159 runs and paved the way for a mammoth West Indian first innings total of 644/8 declared. Their stand remains the Test record for the first wicket at Delhi.

61. WEST INDIES SET INNINGS RECORD AT DELHI

In the fifth Test of the series against India at Delhi in February 1959, the West Indies established a record for the venue (Feroz Shah Kotla) by scoring 644/8 declared. The major contributions came from J.K. Holt Jr (123), Collie

Smith (100), Joseph Solomon (100*) and Conrad Hunte (92). The match was left drawn, but the West Indian record for the ground still stands. The previous mark, 631, had been set by the West Indies against India in November 1948.

62. SOBERS & WORRELL BAT THROUGH TWO DAYS' PLAY
Against England at Bridgetown in January 1960, Garry Sobers (226) and Frank Worrell (197*) shared a colossal fourth-wicket partnership of 399 runs. On this occasion, they became the first pair ever to bat throughout two consecutive days of a Test match. They embarked on their stand late on the evening of the third day and were not separated until early on the morning of the sixth (at a time when six days of five hours each was the Caribbean norm).

63. SOBERS & WORRELL SET PARTNERSHIP RECORD AT BRIDGETOWN
In reply to England's first innings score of 482, the West Indies were struggling at 102/3 when Worrell joined Sobers at Bridgetown in January 1960. They took the score to 501 before Sobers was bowled by Fred Trueman for 226. Their partnership of 399 runs remains a record for the fourth wicket in Tests in Barbados. This was then the highest fourth-wicket stand by any country against England and it remains the West Indian record for any wicket against England.

64. WALCOTT SETS BATTING RECORD AT GEORGETOWN
In March 1960, Clyde Walcott played his last Test match at Georgetown and scored nine runs against England in his only innings. This brought his Test aggregate on that ground to 432 runs (av: 54.00) in six matches. This was then the most runs ever made by any individual in Tests played in British Guiana. Walcott's record was surpassed by Garry Sobers who finished with 853 runs (av: 94.77) in seven Tests at Bourda.

65. WALCOTT SETS BATTING RECORD AT KINGSTON
Clyde Walcott played his final Test at Kingston in March 1960, scoring 53 & 22 against England. This took his Test aggregate at that venue to 924 runs (av: 92.40). This was then the record for the number of Test runs scored by any individual in Jamaica. Walcott's record was broken by Garry Sobers who ended his career with 1,354 runs (av: 104.15) at Sabina Park.

66. THE FIRST TIED TEST
At Brisbane in December 1960, the West Indies and Australia combined to achieve the first ever tied Test in cricket's history. Joseph Solomon hit the stumps from a difficult angle to run out Ian Mekiff off the seventh ball of the final over (which saw the collapse of Australia's last three wickets). The West

Indies scored 453 & 284, Australia replying with 505 & 232. This unusual Test result has been duplicated only once thus far. Australia and India played to the second ever Test tie at Madras in September 1986.

67. GIBBS SETS BOWLING RECORD AT BRIDGETOWN

In the second innings against India at Bridgetown in March 1962, Lance Gibbs produced a truly sensational spell on the final day, taking eight wickets for six runs in just over fifteen overs. He finished with an analysis of 53.3/37/38/8. This is still the finest bowling for any one innings in a Test at Bridgetown. Thanks mainly to Gibbs' wizardry, the West Indies won the match by an innings & 30 runs on their way to a 5-0 drubbing of the visitors.

68. WORRELL & HALL SET PARTNERSHIP RECORD AT PORT OF SPAIN

Frank Worrell (73*) and Wesley Hall (50*) set the current Test record for tenth-wicket partnerships at Port of Spain when they added an unbeaten 98 against India in April 1962. Hall joined Worrell (the captain) at 346/9 and the latter declared the innings closed at 444/9 after Hall had achieved his second half-century in Test cricket. The West Indies won this match by seven wickets, with Hall (6/94 in 27 overs) also making a substantial contribution as a bowler.

69. SOBERS IS FIRST TO 4,000 RUNS & 100 WICKETS

When Garry Sobers had Peter Philpott caught for nine by Rohan Kanhai in Australia's second innings at Kingston in March 1965, he became (in his 48th Test) the first player ever to score 4,000 runs and claim 100 wickets in Test cricket.

70. SOBERS & HOLFORD SET PARTNERSHIP RECORD AT LORD'S

Garry Sobers and his cousin, David Holford, saved the West Indies from almost certain defeat when they came together in the second innings at Lord's in June 1966. Trailing England by 86 runs on first innings, the West Indies were 95/5 in their second attempt. Sobers (163*) and Holford (105*) then took the score to 369/5 declared. Their unbeaten partnership of 274 runs remains the best for the sixth wicket in Tests at Lord's.

71. SOBERS BECOMES FIRST TO SCORE 100 AND TAKE FIVE WICKETS IN A TEST MORE THAN ONCE

Against England at Leeds in August 1966, Garry Sobers (174 & 5/41) became the first player to score a century and capture five wickets in a single innings during the same Test on two occasions. He had previously done so (104 & 5/63) against India at Kingston in April 1962. This record was equalled by Pakistan's Mushtaq Mohammad in 1977 and then obliterated by England's Ian Botham who accomplished the feat on five occasions between 1977 and 1984.

72. SOBERS IS FIRST TO ACHIEVE 700 RUNS & 20 WICKETS IN A SERIES

Garry Sobers took England by storm in 1966 when he led the West Indies to a convincing 3-1 triumph in the series. He scored 722 runs (av: 103.14) and captured twenty wickets (av: 27.25) to become the first all-rounder ever to achieve the extraordinary 'double' of 700 runs and twenty wickets in a single series. Amazingly, he also held ten catches.

73. HALL SETS BOWLING RECORD AT KINGSTON

When Wesley Hall played his last Test at Kingston in February 1968, he took 5/66 in thirty overs against England and finished his career with 35 Test wickets (av: 15.25) in six matches at this venue. This was then the highest number of Test wickets taken in Jamaica. The current record is held by Courtney Walsh who claimed 48 (av: 18.68) at Sabina Park.

74. SOBERS IS FIRST TO 6,000 RUNS & 150 WICKETS

At the end of the 1967/68 series against England in the Caribbean, Sobers had become the first player ever to exceed 6,000 runs and 150 wickets in Test cricket. After having participated in 65 Tests, he had registered 6,059 runs (av: 63.77) and 157 wickets (av: 33.92).

75. NURSE SETS RECORD AT CHRISTCHURCH

In March 1969, Seymour Nurse struck a majestic 258 against New Zealand at Christchurch, dominating a West Indian first innings of 417 runs. His score remains a record for any individual in a Test innings at that venue.

76. NOREIGA SETS BOWLING RECORD AT PORT OF SPAIN

Jack Noreiga set the record for the best bowling performance in a Test innings at Port of Spain, when he captured 9/95 in just under fifty overs against India in March 1971. The visitors, however, gained their first victory against the West Indies in their 25th attempt and went on to win the series 1-0. Noreiga's Port of Spain record still stands after more than thirty years.

77. SOBERS IS FIRST TO 7,000 RUNS & 200 WICKETS

When Sobers had Gundappa Viswanath caught by Desmond Lewis for 25 in India's first innings at Bridgetown in April 1971, he had taken his 200th wicket in his 80th Test. This made him the first player in the world to achieve the outstanding double of 7,000 runs and 200 wickets in Test cricket. He was only the second all-rounder (following Australia's Richie Benaud) to exceed 200 Test wickets and 2,000 Test runs.

78. ROWE IS FIRST TO SCORE SINGLE AND DOUBLE CENTURIES ON DEBUT

Lawrence Rowe became the first batsman to register a double century and a single century in his first Test match. Against New Zealand at Kingston in February 1972, he launched his Test career with innings of 214 & 100*. Rowe's match aggregate of 314 remains a record for a batsman on debut, surpassing the 306 that England's R.E. Foster (287 & 19) had achieved against Australia at Sydney in December 1903.

79. SOBERS ACHIEVES RECORD TEST AGGREGATE

At Bridgetown in March 1972, Sobers scored 142 against New Zealand in the second innings of a Test that ended in a draw. When he reached eleven on this occasion, he surpassed the previous world record of 7,459 set by England's Colin Cowdrey. The latter returned to finish his career with 7,624 runs (av: 44.06) but was never able to overtake Sobers.

80. DAVIS & SOBERS SHARE RECORD PARTNERSHIP AT BRIDGETOWN

Charlie Davis (183*) and Garry Sobers (142) took part in an invaluable sixth-wicket partnership which saved the West Indies from possible defeat at the hands of New Zealand at Bridgetown in March 1972. The West Indies trailed by 309 on first innings and were sitting precariously at 171/5 in their second innings when Sobers entered. He departed at 425/6 and the West Indies reached 546/8 to save the game. The 254 runs added by Davis and Sobers has remained a record for the sixth wicket in Tests at Bridgetown.

81. SOBERS SETS BATTING RECORDS AT GEORGETOWN

In April 1972, Garry Sobers played his last Test match at Georgetown against New Zealand and made five runs in his only innings. This was enough to lift his aggregate on that ground to 853 runs (av: 94.77), including five centuries, in seven tests during 1955-72. His number of runs and centuries remain records by an individual in Tests played at Bourda. The previous record of 432 runs (av: 54.00) had been set by Clyde Walcott in six Tests during 1948-60.

82. SOBERS SETS RECORD FOR CONSECUTIVE TESTS

When Garry Sobers played against New Zealand at Port of Spain in April 1972, it marked his 85th consecutive Test appearance. This was then a world record. He had not missed a single Test since April 1955. His record was broken by Gundappa Viswanath who played 87 consecutive Tests for India between March 1971 and February 1983. The current record is 153, set by Australia's Alan Border between March 1979 and March 1994.

83. SOBERS SETS RECORD FOR CONSECUTIVE TESTS AS CAPTAIN

Against New Zealand at Port of Spain in April 1972, Sobers led the West Indies for the 39th consecutive time. This was then a world record, which has since been eclipsed by several captains, including Clive Lloyd of the West Indies.

84. FREDERICKS & ROWE SHARE RECORD PARTNERSHIP AT KINGSTON

Roy Fredericks (94) and Lawrence Rowe (120) began the West Indies' first innings with a stand of 206 runs against England at Kingston in February 1974. This was then a West Indian record for the first wicket in Tests against England. As such it has already been eclipsed. But it remains the highest partnership for the first wicket in all Tests played at Sabina Park. It helped the West Indies score 583 in response to England's 353, but they were then thwarted by Denis Amiss who struck 262 not out at his second attempt.

85. SOBERS SETS RECORD FOR CENTURY PARTNERSHIPS

Garry Sobers and Bernard Julien added 112 for the sixth wicket against England at Kingston in February 1974. They came together at 439/5 and took the score to 551/6 as the West Indies reached 583/9 declared. This was the 43rd century partnership in which Sobers was involved during his distinguished Test career. It established a new record, breaking the mark of 42 that Colin Cowdrey had set. Sobers' record was first broken by England's Geoffrey Boycott (47) and the current mark, held by Australia's Alan Border, is 63.

86. SOBERS SETS BATTING RECORD AT KINGSTON

When Garry Sobers played his last Test at Kingston against England in February 1974, his score of 57 took his career aggregate at this venue to 1,354 (av: 104.15). This remains the highest number of Test runs scored by any individual at Sabina Park. The previous record of 924 (av: 92.40) had been held by Clyde Walcott.

87. SOBERS IS FIRST TO SCORE 8,000 TEST RUNS

Against England at Kingston in February 1974, Sobers scored 57 in a thrilling sixth-wicket stand of 112 runs with Bernard Julien. This innings took him beyond 8,000 runs in Test cricket. He was the first batsman to reach this milestone. At the end of this series, he retired from Test cricket having set a new world record of 8,032 runs (av: 57.78). This mark was bettered by Geoffrey Boycott in December 1981. The current record is 11,174 runs (av: 50.56) in 156 Tests by Alan Border of Australia. But Sobers is still the only cricketer to have achieved the amazing double of 8,000 runs and 200 wickets in Test cricket. As he also held 109 catches, he ended with a Test 'triple' that is very difficult to duplicate.

88. ROWE & KALLICHARRAN SHARE RECORD PARTNERSHIP AT BRIDGETOWN

Lawrence Rowe and Alvin Kallicharran enjoyed an excellent stand against England at Bridgetown in March 1974. Kallicharran entered at 126/1 and departed for 119 at 375/2. The 249 runs they added now constitute a long-standing record. It remains the highest partnership for the second wicket in Tests at Bridgetown. Rowe (302) proceeded to make a superb triple century and the West Indies amassed 596/8 declared, but the match ended in a draw.

89. SOBERS SETS RECORD FOR RUNS MADE AT BRIDGETOWN

When Garry Sobers played his last Test at Bridgetown against England in April 1974, he made nought, thus failing to add to the plethora of runs he had gathered at this venue. He finished his career with 914 Test runs (av: 76.16) at the Kensington Oval. This was then a record for that ground. It was subsequently exceeded by Viv Richards (959) and Desmond Haynes (1,210).

90. GIBBS SETS BOWLING RECORD AT GEORGETOWN

In March 1974, Lance Gibbs played his final Test at Georgetown against England. He took 2/102 in 37 overs to lift his tally of wickets to 28 (av: 20.64) in six Tests at this venue. This remains the record as the highest number of wickets ever captured by any bowler in Tests played in Guyana.

91. GIBBS SETS BOWLING RECORD AT PORT OF SPAIN

Against England in April 1974, Lance Gibbs played his last Test at Port of Spain. He claimed 4/155 in 84.3 very steady overs to take his tally in thirteen Tests at this venue to 52 (av: 31.65). This was then the highest number of Test wickets claimed by any bowler at the Queen's Park Oval. Gibbs' record was destined to be surpassed by Curtly Ambrose who finished with 66 wickets (av: 13.28) in twelve Tests in Trinidad during 1988-2000.

92. KANHAI SETS BATTING RECORD AT PORT OF SPAIN

Rohan Kanhai established the current record for most runs scored by any batsman at Port of Spain when he registered 2 & 7 against England in his last match there in April 1974. This took his Test aggregate in sixteen Tests at the Queen's Park Oval to 1,212 (av: 43.28). The previous mark, 1,074 (av: 97.63), had been set by Everton Weekes in seven Tests at Port of Spain during 1948-58.

93. GREENIDGE & LLOYD SET PARTNERSHIP RECORD AT BANGALORE

Gordon Greenidge (107) in his first Test and Clive Lloyd (163) added 207 for the fourth wicket against India at Bangalore in November 1974. This remains the Test record for the fourth wicket at this venue. At 75/3 in the second innings, Lloyd joined Greenidge who was dismissed at 282/ 4. The West Indies, who had led on first innings by 29, declared at 356/6 and won by 267 runs.

94. LLOYD SETS RECORD AT BANGALORE

Clive Lloyd set a record for the highest individual score in a Test innings at Bangalore when he registered 163 against India in November 1974. This remained a record for that venue until Sunil Gavaskar made 172 against England in December 1981. Sachin Tendulkar lifted the bar slightly when he struck 177 against Australia at Bangalore in March 1998.

95. WEST INDIES DISMISS INDIA FOR SMALLEST SCORE AT BANGALORE

When the West Indies bundled out India for 118 in their second innings at Bangalore in November 1974, this was then a record for the smallest innings at that venue. As such, it was beaten by India in March 1987 when they dismissed Pakistan for 116.

96. LLOYD SETS RECORD AT BOMBAY

In January 1975, Clive Lloyd smashed his way to 242* against India at the new Wankhede Stadium in Bombay, as his team made 604/6 declared and eventually won by 201 runs. Lance Gibbs (9/143) and Vanburn Holder 6/85) were two of the architects of the victory. Lloyd's individual score remains the highest for any cricketer in a Test innings at that venue.

97. WEST INDIES SET RECORD AT BOMBAY

At Bombay against India in January 1975, the West Indies made 604/6 declared, to which Clive Lloyd (242*), Roy Fredericks (104) and Alvin Kallicharran (98) were the major contributors. This total remains a record for a Test innings at Wankhede Stadium.

98. ROWE & KALLICHARRAN SET PARTNERSHIP RECORD AT BRISBANE

At Brisbane in November 1975, Lawrence Rowe (107) and Alvin Kallicharran (101) enjoyed a fruitful partnership that realised 198 runs and remains the record for the fourth wicket in Tests on that ground. In the West Indies' second innings, they came together at 50/3 and took the score to 248/4. Despite their efforts, however, the West Indies lost by eight wickets, thanks to a pair of splendid centuries from the Australian captain, Gregg Chappell (123 & 109*).

99. WEST INDIES SET RECORD AT PERTH

At the W.A.C.A. in Perth in December 1975, the West Indies made 585 against Australia to win by an innings & 87 runs. This was then the highest Test score achieved at that venue, thanks to brilliant centuries by Roy Fredericks (169) and Clive Lloyd (149). This record was broken in November 1986 when England made 592/8 declared against Australia. The current mark is 617/5 declared, established by Australia against Sri Lanka in December 1995.

100. GIBBS SETS NEW BOWLING RECORD

Lance Gibbs eclipsed Fred Trueman's record of 307 Test wickets in January 1976 when he took 5/183 in 58.5 overs in the match at Adelaide against Australia. He ended his career with 309 (av: 29.09) in 79 Tests. Gibbs' record was surpassed in December 1981 by Australia's Dennis Lillee who proceeded to capture 355 (av: 23.92) in seventy Tests.

101. RICHARDS & KALLICHARRAN SHARE PARTNERSHIP RECORD AT BRIDGETOWN

Viv Richards (142) and Alvin Kallicharran (93) shared a fine partnership against India at Bridgetown in March 1976, taking the score from 108/2 to 328/3. Their stand of 220 runs has remained the record for the third wicket in Tests at Bridgetown. It helped the West Indies reach 488/9 declared, which was enough to ensure victory by an innings & 97 runs.

102. WEST INDIES DISMISS INDIA FOR LOWEST SCORE AT KINGSTON

In April 1976, the West Indies defeated India by nine wickets in a contentious match at Kingston. The Indian captain, Bishen Bedi, declared his first innings closed at 306/6 as a protest against intimidatory bowling. In the second attempt, the innings closed at 97/5 with five of the visitors 'absent hurt'. India's score of 97 remains the lowest in a Test innings in Jamaica.

103. FREDERICKS & GREENIDGE SET PARTNERSHIP RECORD AT LEEDS

Roy Fredericks (109) and Gordon Greenidge (115) blazed their way to an opening stand of 192 runs in under three hours when the West Indies met England at Leeds in July 1976. Their partnership remains a record for the first wicket in Test cricket at Headingley. It laid the foundation for a first innings score of 450 and an eventual victory by 55 runs.

104. RICHARDS SCORES MOST RUNS IN A CALENDAR YEAR

In 1976, Viv Richards set an imposing record that has so far stood the test of time. In only eleven Tests, he registered 1,710 runs (av: 90.00) in one calendar year. He began with 44 & 2, 30 & 101, 50 & 98 in the final three Tests in January and February against Australia in Australia. He then scored 142, 130 & 20, 177 & 23 and 64 in four Tests against India in India. Against England in the summer, he achieved innings of 232 & 63, 4 & 135, 66 & 38, and 291 in four Tests, having missed the Lord's encounter due to injury. Richards' record easily eclipsed the previous mark of 1,381 that Australia's Bobby Simpson had established in 1964.

105. WEST INDIES SET INNINGS RECORD AT BANGALORE
When the West Indies made 437 against India at Bangalore in December 1978, that was then the highest score ever made in a Test innings at that venue. This record was surpassed in September 1979 when India reached 457/5 declared against Australia. The current mark for Bangalore is 541/6 declared, achieved by India against Sri Lanka in January 1994.

106. KALLICHARRAN & MURRAY SHARE RECORD PARTNERSHIP AT BOMBAY
Alvin Kallicharran (187) and David Murray (84) enjoyed a splendid partnership against India at Bombay in December 1978. In reply to India's first innings score of 424, the West Indies had reached 150/4 when Murray joined Kallicharran. They took the score to 317. Their partnership of 167 runs was instrumental in taking the West Indies (493) to a first innings lead and has remained a record for the fifth wicket in Tests played at Wankhede Stadium.

107. KALLICHARRAN & PARRY SET PARTNERSHIP RECORD AT MADRAS
At Madras in January 1979, India dismissed the West Indies for the modest total of 255 in their first innings. But even this would have been beyond the reach of the tourists had not Alvin Kallicharran (98), the captain, and Derek Parry (12), an off-spinner, come to the rescue at 68/6. They took the score to 168/7, thus adding exactly 100. Their valiant stand established a partnership record for the seventh wicket at this venue.

108. BACCHUS SETS INNINGS RECORD AT KANPUR
In February 1979, India and the West Indies took part in a high-scoring Test which ended in a draw at Kanpur. Faoud Bacchus was the hero of the match with a score of 250 which still remains the highest individual innings ever achieved in a Test at that venue. The previous record for the ground was held by Garry Sobers who made 198 in December 1958.

109. BACCHUS & MURRAY SHARE PARTNERSHIP RECORD AT KANPUR
In reply to India's first innings total of 644/7 declared, the West Indies were struggling at 268/5 when David Murray joined Faoud Bacchus. They took the score to 428/6 when Bacchus (250) was unfortunately out, hit wicket. Murray resisted for 210 minutes to score a dogged 44 and the West Indies were able to save the follow on. The Bacchus/Murray stand of 150 runs remains the record for the sixth wicket in Test cricket at Kanpur.

110. HAYNES BATS THROUGH BOTH INNINGS OF A TEST
Against New Zealand at Dunedin in February 1980, Desmond Haynes became the first cricketer to bat through both innings of a Test match when he made 55 and was last out in the West Indies' first innings of 140. In the second, he was again the last man out when he made 105 in a score of 212. He survived for 276 minutes in the first innings and 435 in the second. But his defiance failed to save the West Indies from a one-wicket loss.

111. GREENIDGE & KALLICHARRAN SET PARTNERSHIP RECORD AT CHRISTCHURCH
When New Zealand won the toss and asked the West Indies to bat first at Christchurch in February 1980, the visitors were soon in dire straits at 28/3. From this parlous position they were rescued by Gordon Greenidge (91) and Alvin Kallicharran (75) who took the score to 190/4. Their stand of 162 remains a record for the fourth wicket in Tests at Christchurch. But the West Indian tail failed to wag on that occasion and the whole side was soon despatched for 228 runs. The inadequacy of this total was emphasised when New Zealand replied with 460.

112. GREENIDGE & HAYNES SET PARTNERSHIP RECORD AT CHRISTCHURCH
Chasing a deficit of 232 runs, Gordon Greenidge (97) and Desmond Haynes (122) began the second innings for the West Indies against New Zealand at Christchurch in February 1980 with an aggressive opening stand of 225 runs. This has remained the record for the first wicket in Tests at Christchurch.

113. LLOYD ECLIPSES PETER MAY'S RECORD
In December 1980, Lloyd captained the West Indies for the 42nd time when they played against Pakistan at Multan. This surpassed the record of 41 that Peter May had set as England's captain during 1956-60.

114. RICHARDS HITS HIGHEST SCORE AT MULTAN
In the drawn but low-scoring Test between Pakistan and the West Indies at Multan in December 1980, Viv Richards made 120 of his team's 249 in the first innings. This remains the highest individual score achieved in a Test innings at this venue.

115. CROFT SETS BOWLING STANDARD AT ST JOHN'S
In the very first Test played at the Antigua Recreation Ground in St John's, Colin Croft set the standard for bowlers in a Test innings when he claimed 6/74 against England in March 1981. Croft's record remained intact until Courtney Walsh broke it with 6/54 against Australia in May 1995.

116. GOMES & LLOYD EQUAL PORT OF SPAIN RECORD

Larry Gomes (123) and Clive Lloyd (143) equalled a long-standing record at Port of Spain when they added 237 runs in a fourth-wicket partnership against India in March 1983. West Indies started their first innings disastrously, losing their first three wickets for a single run. Gomes and Lloyd then righted the Caribbean ship by taking the score to 238/4 and the West Indies were able to reach 394 in reply to India's 175. Their performance equalled the mark that had been set in February 1930 by England's 'Patsy' Hendren (205*) and Leslie Ames (105) as the highest fourth-wicket partnership achieved in Test cricket in Trinidad.

117. GREENIDGE & HAYNES SET PARTNERSHIP RECORD AT ST JOHN'S

At St John's in April/May 1983, Gordon Greenidge (154) and Desmond Haynes (136) opened the West Indian innings with a stand of 296 runs in reply to India's 457. This was then a Test record for first-wicket partnerships at the Antigua Recreation Ground. As such, it lasted until April 1990 when the same pair made 298 against England.

118. DUJON & LLOYD SET PARTNERSHIP RECORD AT ST JOHN'S

In April/May 1983, Jeffrey Dujon (110) and Clive Lloyd (106) established the current record for sixth-wicket partnerships at the Antigua Recreation Ground when they added 207 runs against India. Their stand began at 334/5 and did not end until the score reached 541/6. But the match ended in a draw.

119. WEST INDIES SET BATTING RECORD AT ST JOHN'S

The West Indies set a record for the ground when they scored 550 against India at St John's in April/May 1983. The chief contributors were Gordon Greenidge (154), Desmond Haynes (136), Jeffrey Dujon (110) and Clive Lloyd (106). This record was surpassed in April 1994 when the West Indies, led by Brian Lara's record Test score of 375*, made 593/5 against England. The current mark now stands at 629/9 by the West Indies against India in May 2002.

120. DUJON & DAVIS SET PARTNERSHIP RECORD AT AHMEDABAD

The West Indies could muster only 281 in their first innings against India at Ahmedabad in November 1983. But their performance contained a significant highlight. Jeffrey Dujon (98) and Winston Davis (3*) frustrated the hosts in a determined partnership of 51 at the end. This has remained a Test record for the tenth wicket at Ahmedabad.

121. MARSHALL & HOLDING SET PARTNERSHIP RECORD AT AHMEDABAD

In the second innings against India at Ahmedabad in November 1983, Michael Holding (58) and Malcolm Marshall (29) came together at 114/7 and pushed the score to 188/8. Their stand of 74 runs has remained a Test record for the eighth wicket on this ground.

122. WEST INDIES DISMISS INDIA FOR LOWEST SCORE AT AHMEDABAD

In November 1983, the West Indies won the first Test of the series against India by restricting the hosts to 241 & 103 at Ahmedabad. Their second innings total (103) remains the smallest ever achieved at this venue. Michael Holding (4/30) and Winston Davis (3/21) wrought the greatest havoc.

123. LLOYD & ROBERTS SET PARTNERSHIP RECORD AT CALCUTTA

Clive Lloyd and Andy Roberts shared an excellent stand of 161 runs against India at Calcutta in December 1983. This remains a record for the ninth wicket in Tests at Eden Gardens. Lloyd (161*) and Roberts (68) played key roles in the West Indian victory. In response to India's 241, the West Indies had scored 213/8 when Roberts joined Lloyd. They took the score to 374/9 and the West Indies reached 377.

124. WEST INDIES DISMISS INDIA FOR LOWEST SCORE AT CALCUTTA

In December 1983, in the fifth Test of the series, the West Indies established another record by bowling out India for ninety runs in their second innings at Calcutta (after Lloyd and Roberts had demoralised them with the bat). This remains the smallest innings ever made in a Test at Eden Gardens. Malcolm Marshall (6/37) and Michael Holding (3/29) were the chief destroyers. The West Indies won by an innings & 46 runs.

125. LOGIE & DUJON SET PARTNERSHIP RECORD AT PORT OF SPAIN

Against Australia in March 1984, Gus Logie (97) and Jeffrey Dujon (130) established the current record of 158 runs for sixth-wicket partnerships at Port of Spain. They came together at 229/5 and took the score to 387/6. The West Indies were able to declare at 468/8 in reply to Australia's 255. But the match petered out in a tame draw.

126. WEST INDIES SET BOWLING RECORD AT BRIDGETOWN

The West Indies defeated Australia by ten wickets at Bridgetown in April 1984 mainly on the strength of some excellent bowling on the last day. They dismissed the visitors for 97 in the second innings, with Malcolm Marshall capturing 5/

42 and Michael Holding 4/24. The Australian score was then the lowest ever made at the Kensington Oval in a Test innings, surpassing the 102 to which the West Indies had been restricted by England in January 1935. This new record was destined to be broken in April 1985.

127. RICHARDS & RICHARDSON SHARE RECORD PARTNERSHIP IN ANTIGUA

Richie Richardson (154) and Viv Richards (178) set a Test partnership record for the Antigua Recreation Ground when they added 308 runs for the third wicket against Australia in April 1984. Coming together at 43/2, they took the score to 351. The West Indies reached 498 and won the match by an innings & 36 runs on the strength of some excellent bowling by Joel Garner (6/97), Michael Holding (4/64) and Malcolm Marshall (4/121).

128. RICHARDS SETS BATTING RECORD AT JOHN'S

When Viv Richards made 178 against Australia in April 1984, that was then the highest individual score achieved in a Test innings at St John's, Antigua. As such, this record lasted until April 1994 when Brian Lara created history by scoring 375 against England. It was also equalled by Carl Hooper who struck 178* against Pakistan in May 1993.

129. WEST INDIES ARE 1ST NOT TO LOSE A SECOND INNINGS WICKET

When the West Indies defeated Australia 3-0 in the Caribbean in 1983/84, they became the first country to go through a five-rubber series without losing a single second innings wicket. In the first Test at Georgetown, they scored 230 & 250/0 in a drawn encounter. At Port of Spain, in another draw, they batted only once for 468/8 declared. They won the third Test at Bridgetown by ten wickets with scores of 509 and 21/0. The fourth, at St John's, Antigua, resulted in victory by an innings & 36 runs after the West Indies made 498 in their lone attempt. At Kingston, in the fifth Test, the West Indies won by ten wickets with scores of 305 & 55/0. In the five Tests altogether, the West Indies lost only 48 wickets.

130. BAPTISTE & HOLDING SHARE RECORD PARTNERSHIP AT BIRMINGHAM

The West Indies defeated England by an innings & 180 runs at Birmingham in June 1984. Their bowlers made a substantial contribution to this result by performing well with both the bat and the ball. After dismissing the hosts for 191, the West Indies amassed 606, thanks to three excellent partnerships, one of which yielded 150 for the ninth wicket. The score stood at 455/8 when Michael Holding joined Eldine Baptiste and the ninth wicket did not fall until Holding was dismissed for 69 at 605. Baptiste was left unbeaten at 87. Their stand remains a record for the ninth wicket in Tests at Edgbaston.

131. WEST INDIES LOSE 2ND INNINGS WICKET FOR 1ST TIME IN SEVEN TESTS

When Desmond Haynes was run out for 17 at 57/1 at Lord's in June 1984, this marked the first time in seven successive Tests that the West Indies had lost a wicket in their second innings. The sequence had started in the first Test of the series against Australia at Georgetown in March 1984. In the sixth match of the streak, they defeated England by an innings & 180 runs at Birmingham. In these seven Tests the West Indies lost only 69 wickets.

132. GREENIDGE & GOMES SET PARTNERSHIP RECORD AT LORD'S

When the West Indies defeated England by nine wickets at Lord's in June 1984, this was largely due to the brilliant batting of Gordon Greenidge (214*) and Larry Gomes (92*) on the final day. They came together at 57/1 and were still undefeated when the match was won at 344/1. Their partnership of 287 runs in 236 minutes has remained a record for the second wicket in Tests at Lord's. Greenidge became the first West Indian to achieve a double century on that ground.

133. GOMES & DUJON SHARE PARTNERSHIP RECORD AT PERTH

Larry Gomes (127) and Jeffrey Dujon (139) batted magnificently on a difficult pitch at Perth in November 1984 to steer the West Indies to a first innings total of 416 after a feeble start. They shared a partnership of 149 which still remains the best for the seventh wicket in a Test match on this ground. Gomes and Dujon first came together at 104/5 but Dujon had to retire hurt at 154/5. He returned to the crease at 186/6 and took the score to 335 before being caught by Wayne Phillips off Terry Alderman. Michael Holding (7/74) Malcolm Marshall (6/93) and Joel Garner (5/76) then dismissed the Aussies for 76 & 228, as the West Indies won convincingly after having lost the toss in conditions very difficult for batting.

134. WEST INDIES SET RECORD WITH ELEVEN TEST WINS IN A ROW

The West Indies became the first team ever to win nine consecutive Tests when they defeated Australia by an innings & 112 runs at Perth in November 1984. This surpassed the old record of eight that Australia had set in 1921. The West Indies proceeded to win both the second Test and the third in this series to establish a new mark of eleven consecutive victories. This record lasted until the Australians completed a marvellous string of sixteen straight wins in 2001.

135. WEST INDIES SET RECORD OF 27 UNBEATEN TESTS

In December 1984, when the fourth Test against Australia at Melbourne was left drawn, the West Indies achieved a world record of 27 consecutive Tests without suffering defeat. This record still stands. The previous record of 26 had been set by England during 1968-71. The amazing West Indian streak ended in January 1985 when they succumbed to Australia (by an innings & 55 runs) in the fifth Test of that series.

136. WEST INDIES DISMISS NEW ZEALAND FOR SMALLEST SCORE AT BRIDGETOWN

In April 1985, the West Indies demolished New Zealand's batting order for 94 runs, then the smallest score ever compiled in a Test innings at Bridgetown. Malcolm Marshall (4/40) and Winston Davis (3/28) were the principal agents of destruction. This Bridgetown record remained intact until March 1997 when India could muster only 81 in their second innings.

137. MARSHALL SETS BOWLING RECORD AT BRIDGETOWN

Malcolm Marshall contributed handsomely to New Zealand's defeat at Bridgetown in April/May 1985 when he claimed 11/120 in the match. New Zealand were restricted to scores of 94 & 248 while the West Indies made 336 & 10/0 to win by ten wickets. Marshall captured 7/80 in 25.3 overs in the second innings. His match analysis remains the best for any bowler in a Test at Barbados. The previous Test record for the Kensington Oval had been 10/195, set by England's G.T.S. Stevens in January 1930.

138. WEST INDIES DEFEAT ENGLAND TEN TIMES IN A ROW

The West Indies won by ten wickets at Port of Spain on 5 April 1986. This marked their ninth consecutive Test victory over England, a new record. The previous mark had been set by Australia during 1920/21. The West Indies proceeded to extend their record to ten when they won the following Test at St John's, Antigua, by 240 runs less than two weeks later.

139. RICHARDS SCORES FASTEST TEST CENTURY

Viv Richards established a record for the fastest Test century in terms of balls received when he smashed his way to 110 in 61 balls against England at the Antigua Recreation Ground in April 1986. He reached his century in 56 balls after only 81 minutes. His sensational innings included seven sixes and six fours and helped to pave the way to another victory over the tourists.

140. WEST INDIES DISMISS PAKISTAN FOR LOWEST SCORE AT LAHORE

The West Indies defeated Pakistan by an innings & 10 runs within three days at Lahore in November 1986 by dismissing the hosts for 131 & 77. Pakistan's second innings total was then the lowest ever made at that venue.

141. WEST INDIES DISMISS INDIA FOR LOWEST SCORE AT DELHI

In November 1987, India collapsed for 75 runs in their first innings against some hostile bowling from Patrick Patterson (5/24) and Winston Davis (3/20). This remains the lowest score ever made in a complete Test innings at Delhi. The West Indies won by five wickets.

142. GREENIDGE & HAYNES SET PARTNERSHIP RECORD AT ST JOHN'S

In April 1990, Gordon Greenidge (149) and Desmond Haynes (167) set the current record for opening partnerships in Tests at the Antigua Recreation Ground when they put on 298 runs against England. This enabled the West Indies to score 446 and emerge victorious by an innings & 32 runs when England could do no better than 260 & 154 against the splendid bowling of Curtly Ambrose (6/101) and Ian Bishop (8/120). The previous record for the first wicket at St John's had been 296 set by Greenidge and Haynes against India in April/May 1983.

143. HAYNES & RICHARDSON SET PARTNERSHIP RECORD AT GEORGETOWN

Desmond Haynes (111) and Richie Richardson (182) established a new record for second-wicket partnerships in Tests at Bourda when they added 297 runs against Australia in March 1991. Coming together at 10/1, they took the score to 307 before being parted. This laid the foundation for a huge score (569) which led to a West Indian victory by ten wickets.

144. WEST INDIES REACH HIGHEST SCORE AT GEORGETOWN

In March 1991, the West Indies amassed 569 runs in reply to Australia's first innings score of 348 and went on to win by ten wickets, thanks to centuries from Desmond Haynes (111) and Richie Richardson (182). Their 569 remains the highest score ever achieved in a Test innings at Georgetown. The previous record had been held by New Zealand who scored 543/3 declared in April 1972.

145. RICHARDS SETS TEST RECORD AT BRIDGETOWN

Viv Richards played his last Test at Bridgetown against Australia in April 1991. He scored 32 & 25 to finish with an aggregate of 959 runs (av: 59.93) at this venue. This was then a record for Test runs scored by any batsman in Barbados, breaking the previous mark of 914 (av: 76.16) that Garry Sobers had established between 1955 and 1974. Richards' record was eventually broken by Desmond Haynes who scored 1,210 Test runs (av: 60.50) at the Kensington Oval between 1978 and 1994.

146. MARSHALL SETS BOWLING RECORD AT BRIDGETOWN
In his last Test at Bridgetown in April 1991, Malcolm Marshall captured six Australian wickets for 95 runs in 33 overs. This took his tally of Test wickets at that venue to 49 (av: 18.59). This was then the record at the Kensington Oval for any bowler in Test cricket. As such, it has been surpassed by Ambrose (52) and Walsh (53).

147. RICHARDS IS UNDEFEATED AT THE FINISH
Viv Richards played his last Test match in August 1991 against England at The Oval. The West Indies lost by five wickets as England drew a rubber against them for the first time in seventeen years. But the draw allowed Richards to leave the game as the only captain ever to lead a team for as many as twelve series, involving fifty matches, without ever losing a Test rubber. Four of these series were played against England and two each against Australia, India, New Zealand and Pakistan.

148. DUJON SETS IMPORTANT RECORD
Jeffrey Dujon also played his final Test against England at The Oval in August 1991. He had made his debut against Australia at Melbourne in December 1981. He was the first cricketer to participate in so many Tests (81), over so many years (10) and in so many series (19), without experiencing a single lost rubber. Dujon played 23 Tests against Australia, 23 against England, nineteen against India, nine against Pakistan, and seven against New Zealand. He finished his career with 272 dismissals and 3,322 runs (av: 31.94), thus making a huge contribution to his teams' successes along the way.

149. LARA & RICHARDSON SET PARTNERSHIP RECORD AT SYDNEY
After Australia declared at 503/9, the West Indians appeared in dire straits at Sydney in January 1993 when they were 31/3 in reply. But Brian Lara (277) joined his captain, Richie Richardson (109), at this stage and took the score all the way to 324 before further damage was done. Their stand of 293 runs remains the best for the third wicket in Tests at this venue. It was the turning-point in a series that the hosts appeared to be dominating. Lara's 277 remains the best by any West Indian in a Test innings in Australia.

150. HAYNES CARRIES BAT FOR THIRD TIME
In April 1993, Desmond Haynes became the first player to carry his bat through three Test innings, when he made 143* against Pakistan at Port of Spain in a total of 382. He had previously carried his bat for 88* (out of 211) against Pakistan at Karachi in November 1986 and 75* (out of 176) against England at The Oval in August 1991. In addition, he was last out twice, after opening the innings, in a Test match against New Zealand in February 1980.

151. WEST INDIES WIN TWELVE TIMES IN A ROW AT BRIDGETOWN

When the West Indies defeated Pakistan at the Kensington Oval by ten wickets on 27 April 1993, they had established an extraordinary record of twelve consecutive wins at that venue. The streak went back to March 1978 when the Australians were beaten by nine wickets. During this period, Australia and England lost at Bridgetown three times each, India and Pakistan twice each, and New Zealand and South Africa once. The streak ended in April 1994 when England won by 208 runs. That marked the first time in 59 years (and only the second time altogether) that the West Indies had ever lost a Test match in Barbados. They have since lost at Bridgetown to Australia in 1995 and 2003 and New Zealand in 2002.

152. HAYNES SETS BATTING RECORD AT ST JOHN'S

Desmond Haynes played his last match at the Antigua Recreation Ground in May 1993 against Pakistan, scoring 23 & 64*. He finished his career with 733 runs (av: 81.44) in 7 Tests in St John's. This was then a Test record aggregate for that venue. The current mark (1,228 runs) is held by Brian Lara.

153. HOOPER & WALSH SET PARTNERSHIP RECORD AT ST JOHN'S

Carl Hooper (178*) and Courtney Walsh (30) established the current record for tenth-wicket partnerships at St John's when they added 106 against Pakistan in May 1993. Walsh entered at 332/9 and survived for 103 minutes before being dismissed at 438. Hooper was so effective in farming the bowling that Walsh had to face only 31 deliveries in 23 overs. But despite his heroics, the match was reduced to a very tame draw because of persistent rain. Hooper's 178* equalled the record for the ground that Richards had established in April 1984.

154. WEST INDIES DISMISS SRI LANKA FOR LOWEST SCORE AT MORATUWA

In December 1993, the West Indies played their inaugural Test in Sri Lanka at the Fernando Stadium at Moratuwa. The game was left drawn, but the score of 190 made by Sri Lanka remains the lowest Test innings at that venue. Winston Benjamin was the most successful bowler with 4/46.

155. WEST INDIES DISMISS ENGLAND FOR LOWEST SCORE AT PORT OF SPAIN

In March 1994, England appeared on the verge of victory when they were left to make only 194 runs to win at Port of Spain. Curtly Ambrose (6/24) and Courtney Walsh (3/16) in 19.3 devastating overs settled the issue as England collapsed for 46. This remains the lowest total ever made in a Test innings in Trinidad. The previous record of 94 had been set by Australia in April 1978.

156. HAYNES SETS RECORD FOR RUNS AT BRIDGETOWN

When Desmond Haynes played his last Test at Bridgetown against England in April 1994, he scored 35 & 15. This gave him an aggregate of 1,210 runs (av: 60.50) in Tests at that venue. This is more than any other batsman has achieved. The previous record Test aggregate at the Kensington Oval was 959 (av: 59.93) set by Viv Richards during 1974-91.

157. LARA & ARTHURTON SET PARTNERSHIP RECORD AT ST JOHN'S

Against England in April 1994, Brian Lara and Keith Arthurton established a record partnership for the fourth wicket in Tests at the Antigua Recreation Ground when they took the score from 191/3 to 374/4 in the West Indies' first innings. Arthurton made 47 while Lara proceeded to register 375, then the highest individual innings in the history of Test cricket. The West Indies declared at 593/5 but the high-scoring match ended in a tame draw.

158. LARA SETS NEW WORLD RECORD

On 18 April 1994, against England at the Antigua Recreation Ground, Brian Lara broke a long-standing record when he surpassed the 365* that Sobers had achieved against Pakistan in 1958. He struck 45 glorious fours in an innings of 375 off 536 balls in 768 minutes. Lara took part in three century partnerships while scoring more runs than any other batsman had ever done in a single Test innings. He added 179 with Jimmy Adams (59) for the third wicket, 183 with Keith Arthurton (47) for the fourth, and 219 with Shivnarine Chanderpaul (75*) for the fifth. The West Indies scored 593/5 declared (then the highest score ever made at St John's), but the match petered out in a tame draw, as England scored 593 as well. Along the way, Lara naturally eclipsed the previous highest individual Test score at the Antigua Recreation Ground that Viv Richards (178) had established in April 1984 and Carl Hooper (178*) had equalled in May 1993. Lara's world record was broken by Australia's Matthew Hayden who scored 380 against Zimbabwe in October 2003.

159. LARA & CHANDERPAUL SET PARTNERSHIP RECORD AT ST JOHN'S

Brian Lara (375) and Shivnarine Chanderpaul (75*) established the current record for fifth-wicket partnerships in Tests at St John's, Antigua, when they added 219 against England in April 1994. Chanderpaul joined Lara at 374/4 and remained unbeaten when the innings was declared closed at 593/5 at the fall of Lara's wicket.

160. WEST INDIES SET INNINGS RECORD AT ST JOHN'S

In April 1994, West Indies compiled 593/5 while Lara was establishing his exciting new world record. This score was then the highest innings total in a

Test match at St John's. It was immediately equalled by England when they were all out for the same total (593) in reply. The West Indies, with 629/9 declared against India, surpassed it in May 2002.

161. WEST INDIES SET RECORD AGAINST NEW ZEALAND
In February 1995, the West Indies registered 606/5 declared against New Zealand at Wellington. This was then the highest score ever conceded by New Zealand in a Test match anywhere. It featured centuries from Jimmy Adams (151), Brian Lara (147) and Junior Murray (101*). Solid contributions were also made by Sherwin Campbell (88), Keith Arthurton (70) and Shivnarine Chanderpaul (61*). With Walsh (13/55) bowling magnificently, the West Indies won by the enormous margin of an innings & 322 runs.

162. WALSH SETS BOWLING RECORD AT WELLINGTON
Against New Zealand in February 1995, Courtney Walsh destroyed the hosts with a brilliant bowling performance which yielded thirteen wickets for 55 runs in 36 challenging overs. This remains the best match analysis by any bowler in a Test at Wellington.

163. WALSH SETS BOWLING RECORD AT ST JOHN'S
Courtney Walsh claimed 6/54 in 21.3 overs against Australia at St John's in May 1995 to set the current Test record for bowling in a single innings at that venue. The Australians were reduced to 216 in their first innings but intermittent rain prevented a positive result. The previous record (6/74) had been set by Colin Croft against England in March 1981.

164. LARA & SAMUELS SHARE PARTNERSHIP RECORD AT PERTH
In February 1997, the West Indies defeated Australia by ten wickets in less than three days' play on a treacherous pitch at Perth. But while other batsmen struggled, Brian Lara (132) and Robert Samuels (76) added 208 for the third wicket in just over three hours. In reply to Australia's 243, they took the score from 43/2 to 251/3, steering the West Indies to a first innings total of 384. The Lara/Samuels stand remains the best for the third wicket in a Test match on this ground.

165. WEST INDIES DISMISS INDIA FOR LOWEST SCORE IN BRIDGETOWN
The old Bridgetown record of 94 made by New Zealand against the West Indies in March 1985 was erased in March 1997 when the West Indies dismissed India for 81 in their second innings to achieve a sensational victory by 38 runs. Ian Bishop (4/22), Franklyn Rose (3/19) and Curtly Ambrose (3/36) were the heroes on the final day after Shivnarine Chanderpaul had scored his maiden Test century (137) in the first innings. The score of 81 is still the lowest ever made in a Test in Barbados.

166. WEST INDIES DISMISS ENGLAND FOR LOWEST SCORE AT ST JOHN'S

In March 1998, the West Indies set the current record at St John's when they routed England for 127, the lowest score thus far compiled in a Test innings at the Antigua Recreation Ground. The major damage was wrought by Curtly Ambrose (3/28) and Dinanath Ramnarine (4/29). The West Indies won by an innings & 32 runs after scoring 500/7 declared, thanks to centuries from Carl Hooper (108*) and Clayton Lambert (104). England's 127 erased the old record of 170 which they had themselves made against the West Indies in April 1986.

167. LARA & ADAMS SET PARTNERSHIP RECORD AT KINGSTON

Brian Lara (213) and Jimmy Adams (94) established a partnership record for the fifth wicket in Tests at Kingston when they added 322 against Australia in March 1999. In reply to 256, the West Indies were 56/4 when Pedro Collins (the night watchman) retired hurt. Lara and Adams remained together until the score reached 378. Their huge stand paved the way for a total of 431 and eventual victory by ten wickets.

168. CAMPBELL & GRIFFITH SET PARTNERSHIP RECORD AT HAMILTON

Sherwin Campbell (170) and Adrian Griffith (114) set the current Test record for opening partnerships in Hamilton when they put on 276 in the first innings against New Zealand in December 1999. But the rest of the batting then inexplicably collapsed twice on an easy pitch and the hosts coasted to a convincing victory by nine wickets.

169. ADAMS & ROSE SET PARTNERSHIP RECORD AT KINGSTON

Jimmy Adams (101*) and Franklyn Rose (69) established a new record for the eighth wicket in Tests at Kingston when they added 147 against Zimbabwe in March 2000. In reply to a first innings total of 308, the West Indies stood at 171/7 when Rose entered. He departed at 318/8 and the hosts were able to reach 339. The West Indies won the Test when the visitors collapsed for 102 in their second innings, thanks to some splendid bowling by Courtney Walsh (3/21) and Rose (2/24).

170. WALSH ESTABLISHES WORLD BOWLING RECORD

Courtney Walsh, in his 114th Test, became the all-time leader among bowlers when he took his 435th Test wicket at Kingston against Zimbabwe on 28 March 2000. His haul of 5/67 in the match enabled him to surpass India's Kapil Dev who had taken 434 in 131 Tests. Walsh eventually extended his lead over the field by finishing his stellar career in 2001 with 519 wickets (av: 24.44) in 132 Tests.

171. AMBROSE SETS BOWLING RECORD AT PORT OF SPAIN
Curtly Ambrose played his last Test at Port of Spain in March 2000, capturing 7/50 against Zimbabwe in 36 devastating overs to clinch a sensational victory for the West Indies by 35 runs. This performance took Ambrose's tally of Test wickets at this venue to 66 at the phenomenal average cost of 13.28 runs apiece. This is the current record for Test wickets claimed in Trinidad, leaving far behind the previous mark of 52 (av: 31.65) that Lance Gibbs had set during 1958-74.

172. AMBROSE SETS BOWLING RECORD AT BRIDGETOWN
Curtly Ambrose played his last Test at Bridgetown in May 2000, claiming 2/107 in 58 overs against Pakistan. This took his tally of Test wickets at Kensington Oval to 52 (av: 27.32). His 52 wickets then served as the career record for Tests in Barbados. Malcolm Marshall, with 49 wickets (av: 18.59) during 1978-91, had held the previous mark. Ambrose's record was destined to be surpassed by Courtney Walsh less than one year later.

173. AMBROSE SETS BOWLING RECORD AT ST JOHN'S
Curtly Ambrose played his last Test at St John's in May 2000. He took 5/89 in 35 overs to play a prominent role in the West Indian victory over Pakistan by one wicket. He finished his career with 48 wickets (av: 19.68) in eleven Tests in Antigua. This is the current record for Test wickets claimed by any individual in that island.

174. WALSH SETS RECORD FOR WICKETS AT BRIDGETOWN
Courtney Walsh played his last Test at Bridgetown in March/April 2001, taking 4/115 in 59 very steady overs against South Africa. This took his tally of Test wickets at Bridgetown to 53 (av: 25.32), thus surpassing the record of 52 that Curtly Ambrose had recently set.

175. WALSH SETS RECORD FOR WICKETS AT KINGSTON
When Courtney Walsh played his last Test at Kingston in April 2001 against South Africa, he claimed 6/93 in forty searching overs. This took his tally of Test wickets captured at Sabina Park to 48 (av: 18.68), a new record. The previous mark had been held by Wesley Hall who took 35 wickets (av: 15.25) in six Tests there between 1960 and 1968.

176. WALSH ESTABLISHES NEW WORLD RECORD
Courtney Walsh retired from Test cricket in 2001 after the series against South Africa in the West Indies. Bowling magnificently, despite his 39 years, he captured more wickets (25) than any one on either side, restricting the opponents to less than twenty runs per wicket and less than two runs per over. This performance was a fitting end to a career that brought him 519 wickets (av: 24.44) in 132 Tests, thus obliterating the previous record of 434 in 131 that India's Kapil Dev had set during 1978-94.

177. WALSH SETS RECORD FOR MOST DELIVERIES

In 132 Test matches between November 1984 and April 2001, Courtney Walsh not only captured more wickets (519) than any other cricketer, but he also delivered more balls (30,019) than any other fast bowler in the history of Test cricket.

178. GANGA & GAYLE SET PARTNERSHIP RECORD AT BULAWAYO

Against Zimbabwe in July 2001, Darren Ganga (89) and Chris Gayle (175) established the current record for opening partnerships at Queens Sports Club, Bulawayo, when they launched the West Indian innings with a first-wicket stand of 214. This laid the foundations for a total of 559/6 declared which was enough to produce victory by an innings & 176 runs. Carl Hooper, the captain, also contributed a sparkling century (149).

179. WEST INDIES SET BATTING RECORD AT BULAWAYO

Splendid centuries by Chris Gayle (175) and Carl Hooper (149) and useful half-centuries from Darren Ganga (89) and Marlon Samuels (58) carried the West Indies to an imposing total of 559/6 declared against Zimbabwe at Bulawayo in July 2001. This is the current record for any Test innings on this ground, surpassing the previous record of 462/9 set by Zimbabwe against Sri Lanka in October 1994.

180. LARA & HOOPER SET PARTNERSHIP RECORD AT GALLE

Brian Lara (178) and Carl Hooper (69) established the current record for fourth-wicket partnerships at Galle in November 2001, when they forged a valuable stand that yielded 153 runs against Sri Lanka. Hooper joined Lara at 240/3 and left at 393/4. The tail did not wag and the West Indies were all out for 448 in their first innings. A total collapse in the second provided Sri Lanka with an easy win by ten wickets. Their great star was Muttiah Muralitharan who captured eleven wickets for 170 runs in 85 overs of venomous spin.

181. WEST INDIES SET NEW BATTING RECORD AT ST JOHN'S

Against India in April 2002, the West Indies amassed the huge total of 629/9 to surpass all previous Test scores achieved in St John's. The main stars on this occasion were Carl Hooper (136), Shivnarine Chanderpaul (136*), Ridley Jacobs (118) Wavell Hinds (65) and Ramnaresh Sarwan (51). The former record for Test matches played at the Antigua Recreation Ground was 593/5 declared that the West Indies had made against England in April 1994.

182. CHANDERPAUL & HOOPER SET PARTNERSHIP RECORD AT BOURDA

In May 2002, Shivnarine Chanderpaul (140) and Carl Hooper (233) set a new fifth-wicket partnership record for Tests in Georgetown, Guyana, when they added 293 runs for the West Indies against India. They came together at 157/4 and took the score to 450/5. But the match, much curtailed by rain, ended in a draw.

183. CHANDERPAUL & SAMUELS SET PARTNERSHIP RECORD AT KOLKATA

Shivnarine Chanderpaul (140) and Marlon Samuels (104) broke all previous records for the sixth wicket at Kolkata when they added 195 in the third Test against India in November 2002. They came together at 255/5 in response to India's 358 and took the score to 450/6. But the high-scoring match ended in a tame draw.

184. LARA SETS CURRENT RECORD FOR RUNS AT ST JOHN'S

Brian Lara scored 68 & 60 against Australia in May 2003 to take his career aggregate at that venue to 1,228 runs (av: 68.22) in eleven Tests. No other batsman has scored so many runs in Test cricket in Antigua. The previous record of 733 (av: 81.44) was established by Desmond Haynes during 1981-93.

185. WEST INDIES SCORE 418/7 TO DEFEAT AUSTRALIA

In the fourth Test of the series, the West Indies, trailing 0-3 in the rubber, established a world record when they defeated Australia at St John's, Antigua, in May 2003 by scoring 418/7 in their second innings. This was the highest score ever made in the fourth innings to win a Test match. The previous record was 406/4 by India against the West Indies at Port of Spain in April 1976. The victory was made possible by some fiery fast bowling by Jermaine Lawson (7/95) and Mervyn Dillon (6/175) and some fine batting by Brian Lara (68 & 60), Ramnaresh Sarwan (24 & 105), Shivnarine Chanderpaul (1 & 104) and Omari Banks (16* & 47*).

APPENDIX to Part I

I. DATES OF BIRTH IN CHRONOLOGICAL ORDER

1. Nelson Betancourt, Trinidad
   4 June 1887 **(23/5)**
2. George Challenor, Barbados
   28 June 1888 **(1/1)**
3. Cyril Browne, Barbados
   8 October 1890 **(9/1)**
4. Archie Wiles, Barbados
   11 August 1892 **(35/14)**
5. Joseph Small, Trinidad
   3 November 1892 **(8/1)**
6. Wilton St Hill, Trinidad
   6 July 1893 **(5/1)**
7. Oscar Scott, Jamaica
   25 August 1893 **(13/2)**
8. Frank Martin, Jamaica
   12 October 1893 **(2/1)**
9. Herman Griffith, Barbados
   1 December 1893 **(11/1)**
10. Leslie Walcott, Barbados
    19 January 1894 **(21/4)**
11. Karl Nunes, Jamaica
    7 June 1894 **(4/1)**
12. E.L.G. Hoad, Barbados
    29 January 1896 **(12/2)**
13. Maurice Fernandes, Guyana
    12 August 1897 **(3/1)**
14. George Francis, Barbados
    11 December 1897 **(10/1)**
15. Benjamin Sealey, Trinidad
    12 August 1899 **(36/15)**
16. Mervyn Grell, Trinidad
    18 December 1899 **(24/5)**
17. George Gladstone, Jamaica
    14 January 1901 **(28/7)**
18. Learie Constantine, Trinidad
    21 September 1901 **(7/1)**
19. James Neblett, Barbados
    13 November 1901 **(41/18)**
20. Vibart Wight, Guyana
    28 July 1902 **(15/3)**
21. Clarence Passailaigue, Jamaica
    4 August 1902 **(29/7)**
22. Charles Jones, Guyana
    3 November 1902 **(25/6)**
23. Ellis Achong, Trinidad
    16 February 1904 **(22/5)**
24. Edwin St Hill, Trinidad
    9 March 1904 **(19/4)**
25. Clifford Roach, Trinidad
    13 March 1904 **(6/1)**
26. Leslie Hylton, Jamaica
    29 March 1905 **(40/16)**
27. Lionel Birkett, Barbados
    14 April 1905 **(30/8)**
28. Errol Hunte, Trinidad
    3 October 1905 **(18/4)**
29. Lawson Bartlett, Barbados
    10 March 1906 **(14/3)**
30. Jackie Grant, Trinidad
    9 May 1907 **(31/8)**
31. Oscar DaCosta, Jamaica
    11 September 1907 **(27/7)**
32. Berkeley Gaskin, Guyana
    21 March 1908 **(55/23)**
33. Vincent Valentine, Jamaica
    4 April 1908 **(34/14)**
34. Kenneth Wishart, Guyana
    28 November 1908 **(42/18)**
35. Frank deCaires, Guyana
    12 May 1909 **(16/4)**
36. George Headley, Jamaica
    30 May 1909 **(17/4)**
37. Mannie Martindale, Barbados
    25 November 1909 **(32/13)**
38. Rolph Grant, Trinidad
    15 December 1909 **(39/16)**

39. George Carew, Barbados
4 June 1910 **(37/16)**
40. Hines Johnson, Jamaica
13 July 1910 **(64/26)**
41. Ivan Barrow, Jamaica
6 January 1911 **(26/7)**
42. Cyril Merry, Trinidad
20 January 1911 **(33/13)**
43. Kenneth Weekes, Jamaica
24 January 1912 **(46/20)**
44. Derek Sealy, Barbados
11 September 1912 **(20/4)**
45. Richard Fuller, Jamaica
30 January 1913 **(43/19)**
46. Cyril Christiani, Guyana
28 October 1913 **(38/16)**
47. John Cameron, Jamaica
8 April 1914 **(45/20)**
48. E.A.V. Williams, Barbados
10 April 1914 **(50/21)**
49. John Trim, Guyana
24 January 1915 **(63/25)**
50. George Mudie, Jamaica
26 November 1915 **(44/19)**
51. Victor Stollmeyer, Trinidad
24 January 1916 **(52/22)**
52. Esmond Kentish, Jamaica
21 November 1916 **(65/26)**
53. Tyrell Johnson, Trinidad
10 January 1917 **(51/22)**
54. Prior Jones, Trinidad
6 June 1917 **(58/23)**
55. Wilred Ferguson, Trinidad
14 December 1917 **(54/23)**
56. Bertie Clarke, Barbados
7 April 1918 **(48/20)**
57. John Goddard, Barbados
21 April 1919 **(56/23)**
58. Gerry Gomez, Trinidad
10 October 1919 **(49/21)**
59. Robert Christiani, Guyana
19 July 1920 **(53/23)**
60. Nyron Asgarali, Trinidad
28 December 1920 **(95/63)**
61. Andy Ganteaume, Trinidad
22 January 1921 **(60/24)**
62. Jeffrey Stollmeyer, Trinidad
11 March 1921 **(47/20)**
63. Lance Pierre, Trinidad
5 June 1921 **(62/25)**
64. Allan Rae, Jamaica
30 September 1922 **(69/27)**

65. Clifford McWatt, Guyana
1 February 1923 **(83/48)**
66. Jimmy Cameron, Jamaica
22 June 1923 **(68/27)**
67. J.K. Holt Jr, Jamaica
12 August 1923 **(82/48)**
68. Kenneth Rickards, Jamaica
23 August 1923 **(66/26)**
69. Norman Marshall, Barbados
27 February 1924 **(89/55)**
70. Frank Worrell, Barbados
1 August 1924 **(61/24)**
71. Simpson Guillen, Trinidad
24 September 1924 **(73/38)**
72. Roy Miller, Jamaica
24 December 1924 **(78/46)**
73. Everton Weekes, Barbados
26 February 1925 **(59/23)**
74. Ralph Legall, Trinidad
1 December 1925 **(77/44)**
75. Glendon Gibbs, Guyana
27 December 1925 **(85/53)**
76. Clyde Walcott, Barbados
17 January 1926 **(58/23)**
77. Denis Atkinson, Barbados
9 August 1926 **(67/27)**
78. Frank King, Barbados
8 December 1926 **(75/43)**
79. Michael Frederick, Barbados
6 May 1927 **(81/48)**
80. Eric Atkinson, Barbados
6 November 1927 **(97/67)**
81. Clairmonte DePeiza, Barbados
10 October 1928 **(88/55)**
82. Franz Alexander, Jamaica
2 November 1928 **(96/65)**
83. Lennox Butler, Trinidad
9 February 1929 **(87/54)**
84. Sonny Ramadhin, Trinidad
1 May 1929 **(70/32)**
85. Leslie Wight, Guyana
28 May 1929 **(79/46)**
86. Alfred Binns, Jamaica
24 July 1929 **(75/43)**
87. Roy Marshall, Barbados
25 April 1930 **(72/36)**
88. Alfred Valentine, Jamaica
29 April 1930 **(71/32)**
89. Joseph Solomon, Guyana
26 August 1930 **(105/73)**
90. Bruce Pairaudeau, Guyana
14 April 1931 **(76/43)**

91. Jaswick Taylor, Trinidad
3 January 1932 **(102/71)**
92. Conrad Hunte, Barbados
9 May 1932 **(98/67)**
93. Collie Smith, Jamaica
5 May 1933 **(86/53)**
94. Cammie Smith, Barbados
29 July 1933 **(113/85)**
95. Basil Butcher, Guyana
3 September 1933 **(103/72)**
96. Tom Dewdney, Jamaica
23 October 1933 **(90/56)**
97. Seymour Nurse, Barbados
10 November 1933 **(110/82)**
98. Jackie Hendriks, Jamaica
21 December 1933 **(114/90)**
99. Hammond Furlonge, Trinidad
19 June 1934 **(91/57)**
100. Willie Rodriguez, Trinidad
25 June 1934 **(117/91)**
101. Roy Gilchrist, Jamaica
28 June 1934 **(93/62)**
102. Ivan Madray, Guyana
2 July 1934 **(101/68)**
103. Ivor Mendonca, Guyana
13 July 1934 **(117/91)**
104. A.P.H. Scott, Jamaica
29 July 1934 **(80/47)**
105. Reggie Scarlett, Jamaica
15 August 1934 **(107/80)**
106. Lance Gibbs, Guyana
29 September 1934 **(99/68)**
107. Easton McMorris, Jamaica
4 April 1935 **(100/68)**
108. Charran Singh, Trinidad
24 November 1935 **(109/81)**
109. Rohan Kanhai, Guyana
26 December 1935 **(94/62)**
110. Jack Noreiga, Trinidad
15 April 1936 **(136/129)**
111. Garfield Sobers, Barbados
28 July 1936 **(84/52)**
112. Peter Lashley, Barbados
11 February 1937 **(112/85)**
113. Charlie Stayers, Guyana
9 June 1937 **(114/90)**
114. Wesley Hall, Barbados
12 September 1937 **(104/72)**
115. Joey Carew, Trinidad
15 September 1937 **(120/95)**
116. Alfie Roberts, St Vincent
18 September 1937 **(92/61)**

117. David Allan, Barbados
5 November 1937 **(118/92)**
118. Chester Watson, Jamaica
1 July 1938 **(108/80)**
119. Tony White, Barbados
20 November 1938 **(122/100)**
120. Charles Griffith, Barbados
14 December 1938 **(111/84)**
121. Lester King, Jamaica
27 February 1939 **(119/94)**
122. Ron Headley, Jamaica
29 June 1939 **(147/144)**
123. David Holford, Barbados
16 April 1940 **(124/105)**
124. Bryan Davis, Trinidad
2 May 1940 **(123/101)**
125. Richard Edwards, Barbados
3 June 1940 **(128/119)**
126. Robin Bynoe, Barbados
23 February 1941 **(106/79)**
127. Roy Fredericks, Guyana
11 November 1942 **(129/119)**
128. Maurice Foster, Jamaica
9 May 1943 **(130/126)**
129. Deryck Murray, Trinidad
20 May 1943 **(121/95)**
130. Keith Boyce, Barbados
11 October 1943 **(137/131)**
131. Mike Findlay, St Vincent
19 October 1943 **(123/127)**
132. John Shepherd, Barbados
9 November 1943 **(132/126)**
133. Charlie Davis, Trinidad
1 January 1944 **(127/119)**
134. Arthur Barrett, Jamaica
4 April 1944 **(135/129)**
135. Irvine Shillingford, Dominica
18 April 1944 **(161/175)**
136. Clive Lloyd, Guyana
31 August 1944 **(125/110)**
137. Grayson Shillingford, Dominica
25 September 1944 **(134/127)**
138. Vanburn Holder, Barbados
8 October 1945 **(131/126)**
139. Steve Camacho, Guyana
15 October 1945 **(126/113)**
140. Desmond Lewis, Jamaica
21 February 1946 **(138/131)**
141. Leonard Baichan, Guyana
12 May 1946 **(152/157)**
142. Tony Howard, Barbados
27 August 1946 **(143/137)**

143. Albert Padmore, Barbados
17 December 1946 **(155/167)**
144. Raphick Jumadeen, Trinidad
12 April 1948 **(145/138)**
145. Geoffrey Greenidge, Barbados
26 May 1948 **(142/137)**
146. Norbert Phillip, Dominica
12 June 1948 **(168/181)**
147. Lawrence Rowe, Jamaica
8 January 1949 **(141/134)**
148. Alvin Kallicharran, Guyana
21 March 1949 **(143/137)**
149. Uton Dowe, Jamaica
29 March 1949 **(140/132)**
150. Inshan Ali, Trinidad
25 September 1949 **(139/132)**
151. Basil Williams, Jamaica
21 November 1949 **(170/181)**
152. Bernard Julien, Trinidad
13 March 1950 **(148/144)**
153. David Murray, Barbados
29 May 1950 **(167/181)**
154. Andy Roberts, Antigua
29 January 1951 **(149/149)**
155. Gordon Greenidge, Barbados
1 May 1951 **(150/152)**
156. Collis King, Barbados
11 June 1951 **(158/171)**
157. Viv Richards, Antigua
7 March 1952 **(151/152)**
158. Sewdatt Shivnarine, Guyana
13 May 1952 **(169/181)**
159. Herbert Chang, Jamaica
22 July 1952 **(173/187)**
160. Joel Garner, Barbados
16 December 1952 **(160/174)**
161. Colin Croft, Guyana
15 March 1953 **(159/174)**
162. Elquemedo Willett, Nevis
1 May 1953 **(146/140)**
163. Ranjie Nanan, Trinidad
29 May 1953 **(174/202)**
164. Larry Gomes, Trinidad
13 July 1953 **(157/169)**
165. Faoud Bacchus, Guyana
31 January 1954 **(171/182)**
166. Michael Holding, Jamaica
16 February 1954 **(153/159)**
167. Imtiaz Ali, Trinidad
28 July 1954 **(154/167)**
168. Richard Austin, Jamaica
5 September 1954 **(162/179)**

169. Sylvester Clarke, Barbados
11 December 1954 **(165/181)**
170. Derick Parry, Nevis
22 December 1954 **(164/179)**
171. Wayne Daniel, Barbados
16 January 1956 **(156/168)**
172. Desmond Haynes, Barbados
15 February 1956 **(163/179)**
173. Jeffrey Dujon, Jamaica
28 May 1956 **(176/209)**
174. Alvin Greenidge, Barbados
20 August 1956 **(166/181)**
175. Thelston Payne, Barbados
13 February 1957 **(187/243)**
176. Everton Mattis, Jamaica
11 April 1957 **(175/205)**
177. Clyde Butts, Guyana
8 July 1957 **(184/239)**
178. Ezra Moseley, Barbados
5 January 1958 **(195/275)**
179. Malcolm Marshall, Barbados
18 April 1958 **(172/185)**
180. Winston Davis, St Vincent
18 September 1958 **(178/216)**
181. Carlisle Best, Barbados
14 May 1959 **(185/242)**
182. Eldene Baptiste, Antigua
12 March 1960 **(179/217)**
183. Augustine Logie, Trinidad
28 September 1960 **(177/212)**
184. Patrick Patterson, Jamaica
15 September 1961 **(186/242)**
185. Richie Richardson, Antigua
12 January 1962 **(180/220)**
186. Clayton Lambert, Guyana
10 February 1962 **(198/290)**
187. Courtney Walsh, Jamaica
30 October 1962 **(183/233)**
188. Roger Harper, Guyana
17 March 1963 **(181/221)**
189. Phil Simmons, Trinidad
18 April 1963 **(191/256)**
190. Tony Gray, Trinidad
23 May 1963 **(188/247)**
191. Curtly Ambrose, Antigua
21 September 1963 **(192/257)**
192. David Williams, Trinidad
4 November 1963 **(201/291)**
193. Milton Small, Barbados
12 February 1964 **(182/224)**
194. Winston Benjamin, Antigua
31 December 1964 **(189/253)**

195. Keith Arthurton, Nevis
21 February 1965 **(193/263)**
196. I.B.A. Allen, St Vincent
6 October 1965 **(197/287)**
197. Anderson Cummins, Barbados
7 May 1966 **(203/296)**
198. Carl Hooper, Guyana
15 December 1966 **(190/254)**
199. Kenny Benjamin, Antigua
8 April 1967 **(200/291)**
200. Ian Bishop, Trinidad
24 October 1967 **(194/270)**
201. Ridley Jacobs, Antigua
26 November 1967 **(222/344)**
202. Roland Holder, Barbados
22 December 1967 **(214/328)**
203. Jimmy Adams, Jamaica
9 January 1968 **(199/291)**
204. Junior Murray, Grenada
20 January 1968 **(202/294)**
205. Suruj Ragoonath, Trinidad
22 March 1968 **(227/349)**
206. Nehemiah Perry, Jamaica
16 June 1968 **(228/350)**
207. Rajendra Dhanraj, Trinidad
6 February 1969 **(207/306)**
208. Ottis Gibson, Barbados
16 March 1969 **(210/316)**
209. Brian Lara, Trinidad
2 May 1969 **(196/280)**
210. Vasbert Drakes, Barbados
5 August 1969 **(246/392)**
211. Stuart Williams, Nevis
12 August 1969 **(205/305)**
212. Dave Joseph, Antigua
15 November 1969 **(226/349)**
213. Cameron Cuffy, St Vincent
8 February 1970 **(206/306)**
214. Philo Wallace, Barbados
2 August 1970 **(219/336)**
215. Sherwin Campbell, Barbados
1 November 1970 **(208/309)**
216. Courtney Browne, Barbados
7 December 1970 **(209/314)**
217. Robert Samuels, Jamaica
13 March 1971 **(211/321)**
218. Patterson Thompson, Barbados
26 September 1971 **(212/321)**
219. Adrian Griffith, Barbados
19 November 1971 **(213/326)**
220. Franklyn Rose, Jamaica
1 February 1972 **(215/328)**

221. Neil McGarrell, Guyana
12 July 1972 **(239/373)**
222. Floyd Reifer, Barbados
23 July 1972 **(217/333)**
223. Nixon McLean, St Vincent
20 July 1973 **(220/338)**
224. Colin Stuart, Guyana
28 September 1973 **(238/368)**
225. Mervyn Dillon, Trinidad
5 June 1974 **(216/329)**
226. Shivnarine Chanderpaul, Guyana
18 August 1974 **(204/302)**
227. Lincoln Roberts, Trinidad
4 September 1974 **(229/350)**
228. Rawl Lewis, Grenada
5 September 1974 **(218/335)**
229. Dinanath Ramnarine, Trinidad
4 June 1975 **(221/340)**
230. Marlon Black, Trinidad
7 June 1975 **(236/365)**
231. Reon King, Guyana
6 October 1975 **(224/348)**
232. Mahendra Nagamootoo, Guyana
9 October 1975 **(235/364)**
233. Gareth Breese, Jamaica
9 January 1976 **(244/390)**
234. Adam Sanford, Leewards
12 July 1976 **(242/382)**
235. Pedro Collins, Barbados
12 August 1976 **(225/349)**
236. Wavell Hinds, Jamaica
7 September 1976 **(233/355)**
237. Leon Garrick, Jamaica
11 November 1976 **(240/374)**
238. Corey Collymore, Barbados
21 December 1977 **(230/352)**
239. Darren Powell, Jamaica
15 April 1978 **(243/387)**
240. Ricardo Powell, Jamaica
16 December 1978 **(231/353)**
241. Darren Ganga, Trinidad
14 January 1979 **(223/346)**
242. Chris Gayle, Jamaica
21 September 1979 **(232/355)**
243. Ramnaresh Sarwan, Guyana
23 June 1980 **(234/358)**
244. Marlon Samuels, Jamaica
5 February 1981 **(237/367)**
245. Ryan Hinds, Barbados
17 February 1981 **(241/380)**
246. David Bernard, Jamaica
19 July 1981 **(249/395)**

247. Tino Best, Barbados
      26 August 1981 **(251/396)**
248. Devon Smith, Grenada
      21 October 1981 **(247/394)**
249. Jermaine Lawson, Jamaica
      13 January 1982 **(245/390)**
250. Fidel Edwards, Barbados
      6 February 1982 **(253/399)**

251. Carlton Baugh, Jamaica
      23 June 1982 **(248/395)**
252. Jerome Taylor, Jamaica
      22 June 1984 **(252/398)**
253. Omari Banks, Anguilla
      17 July 1982 **(250/396)**

NB: The numbers in brackets indicate the order in which each player appeared and the West Indian Test match in which he did so. For example, Vasbert Drakes was the 246th man to be chosen and appeared in the 392nd Test in which the West Indies were involved. Those who took part in the inaugural Test in June 1928 are listed in the batting order of the West Indies' first innings.

II. DATES OF DEATH IN CHRONOLOGICAL ORDER

1.   Oscar DaCosta, Jamaica
     1 October 1936 **(29)**
2.   Cyril Christiani, Guyana
     4 April 1938 **(24)**
3.   George Francis, Barbados
     7 January 1942 **(44)**
4.   George Challenor, Barbados
     30 July 1947 **(59)**
5.   Nelson Betancourt, Trinidad
     12 October 1947 **(60)**
6.   Leslie Hylton, Jamaica
     17 May 1955 **(50)**
7.   Edwin St Hill, Trinidad
     21 May 1957 **(53)**
8.   Wilton St Hill, Trinidad
     1957 **(64)**
9.   Archie Wiles, Barbados
     4 November 1957 **(65)**
10. Joseph Small, Trinidad
     26 April 1958 **(65)**
11. Karl Nunes, Jamaica
     22 July 1958 **(64)**
12. Frank de Caires, Guyana
     2 February 1959 **(49)**
13. James Neblett, Barbados
     28 March 1959 **(57)**
14. Collie Smith, Jamaica
     9 September 1959 **(26)**
15. Charles Jones, Guyana
     10 December 1959 **(57)**
16. John Trim, Guyana
     12 November 1960 **(45)**

17. Wilfred Ferguson, Trinidad
     23 February 1961 **(43)**
18. Oscar Scott, Jamaica
     15 June 1961 **(67)**
19. Benjamin Sealey, Trinidad
     12 September 1963 **(64)**
20. Cyril Browne, Barbados
     12 January 1964 **(73)**
21. Cyril Merry, Trinidad
     19 April 1964 **(53)**
22. Frank Worrell, Barbados
     13 March 1967 **(42)**
23. Errol Hunte, Trinidad
     26 June 1967 **(61)**
24. Frank Martin, Jamaica
     23 November 1967 **(74)**
25. Vibart Wight, Guyana
     4 October 1969 **(67)**
26. Learie Constantine, Trinidad
     1 July 1971 **(69)**
27. Clarence Passailaigue, Jamaica
     7 January 1972 **(69)**
28. Mannie Martindale, Barbados
     17 March 1972 **(62)**
29. Vincent Valentine, Jamaica
     6 July 1972 **(64)**
30. Kenneth Wishart, Guyana
     18 October 1972 **(64)**
31. George Carew, Barbados
     9 December 1974 **(64)**
32. Mervyn Grell, Trinidad
     11 January 1976 **(76)**

33.	Lawson Bartlett, Barbados 21 December 1976 **(70)**	59.	Inshan Ali, Trinidad 24 June 1995 **(45)**
34.	Rolph Grant, Trinidad 18 October 1977 **(67)**	60.	Kenneth Rickards, Jamaica 21 August 1995 **(72)**
35.	George Gladstone, Jamaica 19 May 1978 **(77)**	61.	Clairmonte Depeiza, Barbados 10 November 1995 **(68)**
36.	Jackie Grant, Trinidad 26 October 1978 **(71)**	62.	Alfie Roberts, St Vincent 24 July 1996 **(58)**
37.	Glendon Gibbs, Guyana 21 February 1979 **(53)**	63.	Gerry Gomez, Trinidad 6 August 1996 **(76)**
38.	Ivan Barrow, Jamaica 2 April 1979 **(68)**	64.	Keith Boyce, Barbados 11 October 1996 **(53)**
39.	Berkeley Gaskin, Guyana 2 May 1979 **(71)**	65.	E.A.V. Williams, Barbados 13 April 1997 **(83)**
40.	Herman Griffith, Barbados 18 March 1980 **(86)**	66.	J.K. Holt Jr, Jamaica 2 July 1997 **(73)**
41.	Maurice Fernandes, Guyana 8 May 1981 **(83)**	67.	Clifford McWatt, Guyana 20 July 1997 **(74)**
42.	Derek Sealy, Barbados 3 January 1982 **(69)**	68.	Lionel Birkett, Barbados 16 January 1998 **(92)**
43.	George Headley, Jamaica 30 November 1983 **(74)**	69.	Kenneth Weekes, Jamaica 9 February 1998 **(86)**
44.	Leslie Walcott, Barbados 28 February 1984 **(90)**	70.	Eric Atkinson, Barbados 29 May 1998 **(70)**
45.	Tyrell Johnson, Trinidad 5 April 1985 **(68)**	71.	Lester King, Jamaica 9 July 1998 **(59)**
46.	E.L.G. Hoad, Barbados 5 March 1986 **(90)**	72.	Victor Stollmeyer, Trinidad 21 September 1999 **(83)**
47.	Ellis Achong, Trinidad 30 August 1986 **(82)**	73.	Malcolm Marshall, Barbados 5 November 1999 **(41)**
48.	Richard Fuller, Jamaica 3 May 1987 **(74)**	74.	Jaswick Taylor, Trinidad 13 November 1999 **(67)**
49.	Hines Johnson, Jamaica 24 June 1987 **(77)**	75.	Conrad Hunte, Barbados 3 December 1999 **(67)**
50.	John Goddard, Barbados 26 August 1987 **(68)**	76.	Sylvester Clarke, Barbados 4 December 1999 **(45)**
51.	Clifford Roach, Trinidad 16 April 1988 **(84)**	77.	John Cameron, Jamaica 13 February 2000 **(85)**
52.	Lance Pierre, Trinidad 14 April 1989 **(68)**	78.	Roy Fredericks, Guyana 5 September 2000 **(57)**
53.	Jeffrey Stollmeyer, Trinidad 10 September 1989 **(68)**	79.	Roy Gilchrist, Jamaica 18 July 2001 **(67)**
54.	Frank King, Barbados 23 December 1990 **(64)**	80.	Denis Atkinson, Barbados 9 November 2001 **(75)**
55.	Prior Jones, Trinidad 21 November 1991 **(74)**	81.	George Mudie, Jamaica 8 June 2002 **(86)**
56.	Roy Marshall, Barbados 27 October 1992 **(62)**	82.	Jack Noreiga, Trinidad 8 August 2003 **(67)**
57.	Bertie Clarke, Barbados 14 October 1993 **(75)**	83.	Leslie Wight, Guyana 4 December 2003 **(74)**
58.	Jimmy Cameron, Jamaica 10 June 1994 **(71)**		

III. LONGEVITY OF WEST INDIAN TEST CRICKETERS

1. Lionel Birkett, Barbados (1905-98)
    92 years, 277 days
2. Leslie Walcott, Barbados (1894-1984)
    90 years, 41 days
3. E.L.G. Hoad, Barbados (1896-1986)
    90 years, 35 days
4. Esmond Kentish, Jamaica (1916-)
    87*
5. George Mudie, Jamaica (1915-2002)
    86 years, 195 days
6. Herman Griffith, Barbados (1893-1980)
    86 years, 108 days
7. Kenneth Weekes, Jamaica (1912-98)
    86 years, 16 days
8. John Cameron, Jamaica (1914-2000)
    85 years, 311 days
9. Clifford Roach, Trinidad (1904-88)
    84 years, 36 days
10. Maurice Fernandes, Guyana (1897-1981)
    83 years, 269 days
11. Victor Stollmeyer, Trinidad (1916-99)
    83 years, 240 days
12. Robert Christiani, Guyana (1920-)
    83*
13. Nyron Asgarali, Trinidad (1920-)
    83*
14. E.A.V. Williams, Barbados (1914-97)
    83 years, 3 days
15. Andrew Ganteaume, Trinidad (1921-)
    82*
16. Ellis Achong, Trinidad (1904-86)
    82 years, 194 days
17. Allan Rae, Jamaica (1922-)
    81*

IV. LONGEST SURVIVING WEST INDIAN TEST CRICKETERS IN CHRONOLOGICAL ORDER

1. Nelson Betancourt, Trinidad **(60)**
    From 1928 until 12 October 1947
2. Cyril Browne, Barbados **(73)**
    From 12 October 1947 to 12 January 1964
3. Frank Martin, Jamaica **(74)**
    From 12 Jan 1964 to 23 November 1967
4. Herman Griffith, Barbados **(86)**
    From 23 November 1967 to 18 March 1980
5. Leslie Walcott, Barbados **(90)**
    From 18 March 1980 to 28 February 1984
6. E.L.G. Hoad, Barbados **(90)**
    From 28 February 1984 to 5 March 1986
7. Ellis Achong, Trinidad **(82)**
    From 5 March 1986 to 29 August 1986
8. Clifford Roach, Trinidad **(84)**
    From 29 August 1986 to 18 April 1988
9. Lionel Birkett, Barbados **(92)**
    From 18 April 1988 to 16 January 1998
10. Kenneth Weekes, Jamaica **(86)**
    From 16 January 1998 to 9 February 1998
11. John Cameron, Jamaica **(85)**
    From 9 February 1998 to 13 February 2000
12. George Mudie, Jamaica **(86)**
    From 13 February 2000 to 8 June 2002
13. Esmond Kentish, Jamaica **(86)**
    From 8 June 2002 to ?

NB: Thirteen players have thus far reigned as the longest surviving West Indian Test cricketers. As Nelson Betancourt was born before all the others, he naturally held the crown until his death in 1947. When George Mudie died in 2002, he was succeeded by Esmond Kentish who, as of 31 December 2003, was 86 years old. The current heir to his throne is Robert Christiani.

V. WEST INDIAN TEST CRICKETERS DYING YOUNG

1. Cyril Christiani, Guyana (1913-38)
   24 years, 158 days
2. Collie Smith, Jamaica (1933-59)
   26 years, 127 days
3. Oscar DaCosta, Jamaica (1907-36)
   29 years, 20 days
4. Malcolm Marshall, Barbados (1958-99)
   41 years, 200 days
5. Frank Worrell, Barbados (1924-67)
   42 years, 224 days
6. Wilfred Ferguson, Trinidad (1917-61)
   43 years, 71 days
7. George Francis, Barbados (1897-1942)
   44 years, 36 days
8. Sylvester Clarke, Barbados (1954-99)
   44 years, 358 days

9. Inshan Ali, Trinidad (1949-95)
   45 years, 272 days
10. John Trim, Guyana (1915-60)
    45 years, 323 days
11. Frank de Caires, Guyana (1909-59)
    49 years, 266 days
12. Leslie Hylton, Jamaica (1905-55)
    50 years, 49 days
13. Keith Boyce, Barbados (1943-96)
    53 years, 0 days
14. Glendon Gibbs, Guyana (1925-79)
    53 years, 56 days
15. Edwin St Hill, Trinidad (1904-57)
    53 years, 73 days
16. Cyril Merry, Trinidad (1911-64)
    53 years, 90 days

VI. YOUNGEST WEST INDIAN PLAYERS ON TEST DEBUT

1. Derek Sealy, Barbados
   17 years, 122 days
   (v England, 11 January 1930)
2. Garfield Sobers, Barbados
   17 years, 245 days
   (v England, 30 March 1954)
3. Robin Bynoe, Barbados
   18 years, 31 days
   (v Pakistan, 26 March 1959)
4. Jeffrey Stollmeyer, Trinidad
   18 years, 105 days
   (v England, 24 June 1939)
5. Alfie Roberts, St Vincent
   18 years, 173 days
   (v New Zealand, 9 March 1956)
6. A.P.H. Scott, Jamaica
   18 years, 242 days
   (v India, 28 March 1953)
7. Jerome Taylor, Jamaica
   18 years, 363 days
   (v Sri Lanka, 20 June 2003)
8. Ivan Barrow, Jamaica
   19 years, 87 days
   (v England, 3 April 1930)
9. George Mudie, Jamaica
   19 years, 109 days
   (v England, 14 March 1935)
10. Shivnarine Chanderpaul, Guyana
    19 years, 211 days
    (v England, 17 March 1994)

11. Gerry Gomez, Trinidad
    19 years, 285 days
    (v England, 22 July 1939)
12. Elquemedo Willett, Nevis
    19 years, 312 days
    (v Australia, 9 March 1973)
13. Ramnaresh Sarwan, Guyana
    19 years 312 days
    (v Pakistan, 18 May 2000)
14. Marlon Samuels, Jamaica
    19 years, 314 days
    (v Australia, 15 December 2000)
15. Darren Ganga, Trinidad
    19 years, 346 days
    (v South Africa, 26 December 1998)
16. Deryck Murray, Trinidad
    20 years, 17 days
    (v England, 6 June 1963)
17. Milton Small, Barbados
    20 years, 33 days
    (v Australia, 16 March 1984)
18. Alfred Valentine, Jamaica
    20 years, 40 days
    (v England, 8 June 1950)
19. Wayne Daniel, Barbados
    20 years, 96 days
    (v India, 21 April 1976)

VII. OLDEST WEST INDIAN PLAYERS ON TEST DEBUT

1. Nelson Betancourt, Trinidad
   42 years, 242 days
   (v England, 1 February 1930)
2. Archie Wiles, Barbados
   40 years, 345 days
   (v England, 22 July 1933)
3. George Challenor, Barbados
   39 years, 360 days
   (v England, 23 June 1928)
4. Berkeley Gaskin, Guyana
   39 years, 306 days
   (v England, 21 January 1948)
5. Cyril Browne, Barbados
   37 years, 259 days
   (v England, 23 June 1928)
6. Hines Johnson, Jamaica
   37 years, 258 days
   (v England, 27 March 1948)
7. Nyron Asgarali, Trinidad
   36 years, 174 days
   (v England, 20 June 1957)
8. Leslie Walcott, Barbados
   35 years, 358 days
   (v England, 11 January 1930)

9. Joseph Small, Trinidad
   35 years, 233 days
   (v England, 23 June 1928)
10. Wilton St Hill, Trinidad
    34 years, 353 days
    (v England, 23 June 1928)
11. Tommy Scott, Jamaica
    34 years, 331 days
    (v England, 21 July 1928)
12. Jack Noreiga, Trinidad
    34 years, 309 days
    (v India, 18 February 1971)
13. Frank Martin, Jamaica
    34 years, 255 days
    (v England, 23 June 1928)
14. Herman Griffith, Barbados
    34 years, 205 days
    (v England, 23 June 1928)
15. Karl Nunes, Jamaica
    34 years, 16 days
    (v England, 23 June 1928)
16. Benjamin Sealey, Trinidad
    34 years, 0 days
    (v England, 12 August 1933)

PART II

ACKNOWLEDGEMENTS

TO THE PEOPLE WHO HAVE HELPED ME IN COLLECTING THE FACTS over the years, and there have been many! I would like to say a big "thank you" to you all.

The first people who got me started with copies of score cards in the early days were Robert Brooke and Brian Croudy, without them I don't think there would have been a book. David Gallagher was another person I called upon many times with all types of queries, but the one I have pestered the most, and who has never let me down (or has never failed to come up with the answer) is Philip Bailey (thanks Phil).

I would also like to thank my co-author, Keith Sandiford, who readily agreed to work with me in celebrating 75 years of West Indies Test cricket. Thanks also to Arif Ali for his belief and encouragement, and not forgetting Kash Ali for his total dedication and co-operation. I am most grateful to you all.

Ray Goble

SECTION ONE

INTRODUCTION

The statistics in Section One have been listed in alphabetical order by surname. They comprise all First Class and One Day matches which took place between 23 June 1928 and 30 September 2003. They also include, where appropriate, records prior to 1928.

Each page of statistics has been horizontally separated (by a blank line) into sections.

First Section: Reflects the player's statistics when representing Island cricket

Second Section: Reflects the player's statistics when representing the West Indies XI

Third Section: Reflects the player's statistics when representing teams within other countries in domestic competitions

Players' total career figures for International cricket taken up to 31 July 2003
Players' total career figures for Domestic cricket taken up to 30 September 2003

C A Best and S Shivnarine's O.D. careers figures include matches in ICC Trophy

KEY AND DENOTES

Figures stated for 'Test' and 'O.D.I.' (for example, 40-26), denote that the player in the above example was the 40th player to represent the West Indies in their 26th match.

When 'A' is used in the Third Section of the statistics, it stands for Australia.

An asterisk (*) after scores denotes 'not out'.

Some of the figures stated in 'OV' and 'MD' (Overs and Maidens) are inevitably open to debate regarding their accuracy despite an intensive amount of cross-checking with other sources. The entries for 'Maidens' in Total O.D. Career are blank because the information is not available.

KEY

A	Australia (in 'Venue' column)	RAF	Right Arm Fast
Av	Average	RAFM	Right Arm Fast Medium
B.B.	Best Bowling	RALB	Right Arm Leg Break
CT	Caught	RAM	Right Arm Medium
CT / ST	Caught / Stumped	RAMF	Right Arm Medium Fast
D	Did not bat	RAOB	Right Arm Off Break
D.O.B.	Date of Birth	RAS	Right Arm Slow
E	England	RF	Right Fast
G	Guyana (formerly British Guiana until 26 May 1966)	RFM	Right Fast Medium
HA	Home and/or Away	RHB	Right Hand Bat
H.S.	Highest Score	RLB	Right Leg Break
I	India (in 'Venue' column)	RLS	Right Leg Slow
I	Innings	RM	Right Medium
II	Inter Island	RMF	Right Medium Fast
J	Jamaica	RMLB	Right Medium Leg Break
LAFM	Left Arm Fast Medium	RMOB	Right Medium Off Break
LAS	Left Arm Slow	ROB	Right Off Break
LB	Leg Break	ROS	Right Off Spin
LBG	Leg Break Googly	S	Singapore
LFM	Left Fast Medium	SA	South Africa
LFMS	Left Fast Medium Slow	SLA	Slow Left Arm
LHB	Left Hand Bat	SRA	Slow Right Arm
LM	Left Medium	SRALB	Slow Right Arm Leg Break
LS	Left Slow		
M	Matches	T	Trinidad
M.C.C.	Marylebone Cricket Club	V	Venue
MD	Maidens	W	Wickets
No	Not Out	WI	West Indies
NZ	New Zealand	WK	Wicket-keeper
O.A.L.	Other "A" List matches (O.D. matches only)		
O.D.	One Day		
O.D.I.	One Day International		
O.D.(I.)	One Day International (unofficial)		
OB	Off Break		
OV	Overs		
P	Pakistan		
R	Rhodesia		

STATISTICS

ELLIS EDGAR ACHONG

D.O.B. 16.02.1904 - Belmont, Port of Spain, Trinidad (d. 30.08.1986)

First Class Debut 22.01.1930 - Trinidad v M.C.C.

Test Match Debut 01.02.1930 - West Indies v England

Test 22-5

Teams Played For 3

Trinidad
West Indies
Combined T/B XI

LHB / SLA

SEASON	TEAM	COMPETITION	V	M	I	No	BATTING RUNS	H.S.	Av	100s	50s	CT	BOWLING OV	MD	RUNS	W	Av	B.B.
1930-1935	Trinidad	First Class Matches	II	7	10	4	135	45*	22.50	-	-	6	257-2	66	566	35	16.17	7-73
1930-1935	WEST INDIES	TEST MATCHES	HA	6	11	1	81	22	8.10	-	-	6	153	34	378	8	47.25	2-64
1932-1933	Combined XI	First Class Matches	WI	1	2	2	30	23*	-	-	-	-	24	7	53	1	53.00	1-32
1933//	West Indies	First Class Matches	A	24	32	13	257	25*	13.52	-	-	8	865.3	174	2329	66	35.28	6-138
	Total First Class Career			38	55	20	503	45*	14.37	0	0	20	1299.5	281	3326	110	30.23	7-73

JAMES CLIVE ADAMS

D.O.B.	09.01.1968 - Port Maria, St Mary's, Jamaica
First Class Debut	08.02.1985 - Jamaica v Barbados
Test Match Debut	18.04.1992 - West Indies v South Africa
O.D.I. Debut	17.12.1992 - West Indies v Pakistan
Domestic O.D. Debut	07.03.1985 - Jamaica v Guyana

Test 199-291
O.D.I. 64-242

Teams Played For 12
Jamaica, West Indies
W.I. President's XI, West Indies "B"
W.I. Board XI, West Indies U23 XI
West Indies "A", Nottinghamshire
World XI, Free State, M.C.C., Berkshire

LHB / SLA

SEASON	TEAM	COMPETITION	V	M	I	No	BATTING RUNS	H.S.	Av	100s	50s	CT/ST	BOWLING OV	MD	RUNS	W	Av	B.B.
1985-2001	Jamaica	First Class Matches	==	64	111	16	4188	203*	44.08	11	22	55	380.4	88	882	27	32.66	4-23
1985-2000	Jamaica	Domestic O.D. Matches	==	41	38	5	1270	112	38.48	-	8	22/1	97.5	8	415	20	20.75	3-34
1998-2001	Jamaica	O.A.L. O.D. Matches	A	3	3	2	59	34*	59.00	-	-	3	12.3	1	51	3	17.00	3-8
1992-2001	WEST INDIES	TEST MATCHES	HA	54	90	17	3012	208*	41.26	6	14	48	475.3	99	1336	27	49.48	5-17
1992-2001	West Indies	First Class Matches	HA	30	49	9	1346	114*	33.65	1	8	24	232.1	40	674	17	39.64	3-41
1986-1989	West Indies "B"	First Class Matches	A	5	6	0	134	35	22.33	-	-	5	21	2	76	0	-	-
1988-1991	West Indies U23	First Class Matches	WI	3	5	2	127	58	42.33	-	2	2	5	0	10	1	10.00	1-10
1990-1993	W.I. President's XI	First Class Matches	WI	1	2	1	29	13	9.66	-	-	2	11	1	53	0	-	-
1991//	W.I. Board XI	First Class Matches	WI	1	2	1	41	37	20.50	-	-	1	-	-	-	-	-	-
1992-1999	West Indies "A"	First Class Matches	HA	10	18	3	627	129	41.80	2	3	9	34.2	7	81	1	81.00	1-9
1992-2001-	WEST INDIES	O.D.I. MATCHES	HA	127	105	28	2204	82	28.62	-	14	68/5	309.2	12	1499	43	34.86	5-37
1986-1989	West Indies "B"	O.D.(I.) Matches	A	6	5	2	102	39*	34.00	-	-	2	2	0	16	1	16.00	1-16
1992-1998	West Indies "A"	O.D.(I.) Matches	A	3	3	0	63	42	21.00	-	-	2	8	0	43	0	-	-
1995-2000	West Indies	O.A.L. O.D. Matches	A	9	9	3	251	86*	41.83	-	1	6/1	27	0	162	3	54.00	2-34
1997//	West Indies "A"	O.A.L. O.D. Matches	A	2	1	0	44	44	44.00	-	-	-	14	0	55	0	-	-
1994//	Nottinghamshire	First Class Matches	E	18	32	5	950	144*	35.18	3	2	17	340.5	125	720	23	31.30	4-63
1994//	Nottinghamshire	Nat. West Trophy	E	2	2	0	12	11	6.00	-	-	-	-	-	-	-	-	-
1994//	Nottinghamshire	Benson & Hedges Cup	E	3	3	0	133	86	44.33	-	1	2	3	0	21	0	-	-
1994//	Nottinghamshire	Sunday League	E	15	15	4	674	93*	61.27	-	7	5	49.2	10	199	6	33.16	2-26
1993//	World XI	First Class Matches	E	1	1	0	15	15	15.00	-	-	1	26	1	66	2	33.00	2-53
2001-2003	Free State	First Class Matches	SA	13	20	2	684	124*	38.00	2	2	11	99	30	218	4	54.50	2-41
2001-2003	Free State	Standard Bank Cup	SA	15	14	2	456	64	38.00	-	3	6	62	0	246	7	35.14	2-13
2001//	M.C.C.	First Class Matches	E	1	2	1	81	81*	81.00	-	-	2	6	0	45	1	45.00	1-45
2003	Berkshire	Cheltenham & Gloucester Cup	E	1	1	0	8	8	8.00	-	-	-	6	1	23	0	-	-
	Total First Class Career			202	339	56	11234	208*	39.69	25	54	177	1631.3	402	4161	103	40.39	5-17
	Total O.D. Career			227	199	46	5276	112	34.48	1	34	116/7	591	-	2730	83	32.89	5-37

FRANZ COPELAND MURRAY ALEXANDER

D.O.B. 02.11.1928 - Kingston, Jamaica
First Class Debut 30.04.1952 - Cambridge University v Leicestershire
Test Match Debut 25.07.1957 - West Indies v England

Test 96-65

Teams Played For 4
Jamaica
West Indies
Cambridge University
N.Z. Governor General's XI

RHB / WK

SEASON	TEAM	COMPETITION	V	M	I	No	BATTING RUNS	H.S.	Av	100s	50s	CT/ST	BOWLING OV	MD	RUNS	W	Av	B.B.
1957-1960	Jamaica	First Class Matches	II	7	13	2	297	70	27.00	-	2	16/3	-	-	-	-	-	-
1957-1961	WEST INDIES	TEST MATCHES	HA	25	38	6	961	108	30.03	-	7	85/5	-	-	-	-	-	-
1957-1961	West Indies	First Class Matches	A	32	47	13	947	83	27.85	-	6	77/10	-	-	-	-	-	-
1952-1953	Cambridge University	First Class Matches	E	27	41	8	1011	99	30.63	-	6	39/17	2	0	7	0	-	-
1961//	N.Z. Gov/General's XI	First Class Matches	NZ	1	2	1	22	22	22.00	-	-	0/4	-	-	-	-	-	-
Total First Class Career				92	141	30	3238	108	29.17	1	21	217/39	2	0	7	0	-	-

IMTIAZ ALI

D.O.B. 28.07.1954 - Maraval, Trinidad

First Class Debut 01.04.1972 - East Trinidad v Central Trinidad
Test Match Debut 07.04.1976 - West Indies v India
Domestic O.D. Debut 28.02.1976 - Trinidad v Barbados

Test 154-167

Teams Played For
Trinidad & Tobago
East Trinidad
N/E Trinidad
West Indies
W.I. President's XI

RHB / SRALB

5

SEASON	TEAM	COMPETITION	V	M	I	No	BATTING						BOWLING					
							RUNS	H.S.	Av	100s	50s	CT	OV	MD	RUNS	W	Av	B.B.
1973-1980	Trinidad & Tobago	First Class Matches	II	25	32	7	320	48*	12.80	-	-	10	932.5	230	2591	72	35.95	6-64
1972-1979	East Trinidad	First Class Matches	T	17	24	3	189	28*	9.00	-	-	8	466	109	1206	72	16.75	8-38
1977-1980	N/E Trinidad	First Class Matches	T	2	3	1	27	21	13.50	-	-	4	53.5	14	140	9	15.15	7-66
1976//	Trinidad & Tobago	Domestic O.D. Matches	II	1	1	0	2	2	2.00	-	-	-	10	2	28	1	28.00	1-28
1976//	WEST INDIES	TEST MATCHES	H	1	1	1	1	1*	-	-	-	-	34	10	89	2	44.50	2-37
1973//	W.I. President's XI	First Class Matches	WI	1	2	0	21	16	10.50	-	-	-	27	4	103	2	51.50	2-90
	Total First Class Career			46	62	12	558	48*	11.16	0	0	22	1514	367	4129	157	26.29	8-38
	Total O.D. Career			1	1	0	2	2	2.00	0	0	0	10	2	28	1	28.00	1-28

INSHAN ALI
D.O.B. 25.09.1949 - Preysal Village, Trinidad (d. 24.06.1995)
First Class Debut 15.04.1966 - South Trinidad v North Trinidad
Test Match Debut 01.04.1971 - West Indies v India

Test 139-132   Teams Played For   8   LHB / SLA
Trinidad, South Trinidad
North Trinidad, Central Trinidad
S/C Trinidad, West Indies
W.I. President's XI
World XI

SEASON	TEAM	COMPETITION	V	M	I	No	BATTING RUNS	H.S.	Av	100s	50s	CT	BOWLING OV	MD	RUNS	W	Av	B.B.
1967-1980	Trinidad	First Class Matches	=	43	59	15	692	55	15.72	-	2	17	1549	287	4850	169	28.69	8-58
1966-1970	South Trinidad	First Class Matches	T	4	7	1	34	19	5.66	-	-	-	69.5	7	262	7	37.42	3-89
1967/i	North Trinidad	First Class Matches	T	1	2	1	30	30*	30.00	-	-	-	28	3	97	2	48.50	2-45
1971-1978	Central Trinidad	First Class Matches	T	11	15	1	180	38	12.85	-	-	8	290.4	62	890	42	21.19	6-48
1977-1980	S/C Trinidad	First Class Matches	T	2	3	0	34	22	11.33	-	-	-	62	13	170	8	21.25	3-26
1971-1977	WEST INDIES	TEST MATCHES	HA	12	18	2	172	25	10.75	-	-	7	610.4	137	1621	34	47.67	5-59
1973-1976	West Indies	First Class Matches	A	15	12	1	188	63	17.09	-	1	11	442.1	98	1357	58	23.39	6-36
1968/i	W.I. President's XI	First Class Matches	WI	1	1	0	11	11	11.00	-	-	-	33	6	96	1	96.00	1-80
1973/i	World XI	First Class Match	P	1	1	0	0	0	0.00	-	-	1	47	10	148	7	21.14	5-80
Total First Class Career				90	118	21	1341	63	13.82	0	3	44	3132.2	623	9491	328	28.93	8-58

DAVID WALTER ALLAN

D.O.B. 05.11.1937 - Hastings, Christ Church, Barbados

First Class Debut 21.03.1956 - Barbados v E.W. Swanton's XI

Test Match Debut 23.03.1962 - West Indies v India

Test 118-92

Teams Played For
Barbados
West Indies

RHB / WK 2

SEASON	TEAM	COMPETITION	V	M	I	No	BATTING RUNS	H.S.	Av	100s	50s	CT/ST	BOWLING OV	MD	RUNS	W	Av	B.B.
1956-1966	Barbados	First Class Matches	II	19	22	4	268	45	14.88	-	-	34/5	-	-	-	-	-	-
1962-1966	WEST INDIES	TEST MATCHES	HA	5	7	1	75	40*	12.50	-	-	15/3	-	-	-	-	-	-
1963-1966	West Indies	First Class Matches	A	30	35	7	421	56	15.03	-	2	68/16	-	-	-	-	-	-
		Total First Class Career		54	64	12	764	56	14.69	0	2	117/24	-	-	-	-	-	-

IAN BASIL ALSTON ALLEN

D.O.B. 06.10.1965 - Coults Hill, St Vincent, Windward Island
First Class Debut: 26.01.1989 - Windward Islands v Leeward Islands
Test Match Debut: 20.02.1991 West Indies v England
Domestic O.D. Debut: 08.02.1989 - Windward Islands v Jamaica

Test 197-287

Teams Played For 5
Windward Islands
West Indies
West Indies "B"
West Indies U23
W.I. Board XI

RHB / RAFM

SEASON	TEAM	COMPETITION	V	M	I	No	BATTING RUNS	H.S.	Av	100s	50s	CT	BOWLING OV	MD	RUNS	W	Av	B.B.
1989-1996	Windward Islands	First Class Matches	=	33	55	15	459	36	11.47	-	-	9	835.2	113	2765	77	35.90	7-48
1989-1998	Windward Islands	Domestic O.D. Matches	=	23	14	5	102	26	11.33	-	-	4	175.5	12	751	31	24.22	4-24
WEST INDIES		TEST MATCHES																
1991//	West Indies		A	2	2	2	5	4*	-	-	-	1	47	4	180	5	36.00	2-69
1991//	West Indies	First Class Matches	A	8	3	2	11	8	11.00	-	-	7	170.4	31	631	11	57.36	2-61
1989//	West Indies "B"	First Class Matches	A	1	1	1	2	2*	-	-	-	-	11	0	51	0	-	-
1989//	West Indies U23	First Class Matches	WI	1	1	0	25	25	25.00	-	-	1	19	2	57	1	57.00	1-57
1991//	W.I. Board XI	First Class Matches	WI	1	1	0	4	4	4.00	-	-	-	18	3	51	4	12.75	4-51
1989//	West Indies "B"	O.D.(I.) Matches	A	5	2	1	3	2	3.00	-	-	1	50	3	208	8	26.00	3-27
1991//	West Indies	O.A.L. O.D. Matches	A	1	D	-	-	-	-	-	-	-	10	1	32	0	-	-
		Total First Class Career		46	63	20	506	36	11.76	0	0	18	1101	153	3735	98	38.11	7-48
		Total O.D. Career		29	16	6	105	26	10.50	0	0	5	235.5	16	991	39	25.41	4-24

229

CURTLY ELCONN LYNWALL AMBROSE

D.O.B. 21.09.1963 - Swetes Village, Antigua, Leeward Islands

First Class Debut 12.02.1986 - Leeward Islands v Guyana
Test Match Debut 02.04.1988 - West Indies v Pakistan
O.D.I. Debut 12.03.1988 - West Indies v Pakistan
Domestic O.D. Debut 01.03.1986 - Leeward Islands v Jamaica

Test 192-257
O.D.I. 53-155

Teams Played For
Leeward Islands
West Indies
Northamptonshire
Antigua

LHB / RAF
4

SEASON	TEAM	COMPETITION	V	M	I	No	BATTING						BOWLING					
							RUNS	H.S.	Av	100s	50s	CT	OV	MD	RUNS	W	Av	B.B.
1986-2000	Leeward Islands	First Class Matches	ll	37	49	8	517	49	12.60	-	-	23	1199.2	366	2606	163	15.98	7-66
1986-1999	Leeward Islands	Domestic O.D. Matches	ll	41	21	9	128	18*	10.66	-	-	5	352	35	1127	47	23.97	3-6
1998//	Antigua	Commonwealth Games	S	3	3	2	42	23	42.00	-	-	-	18	2	46	2	23.00	2-29
1988-2000	WEST INDIES	TEST MATCHES	HA	98	145	29	1439	53	12.40	-	1	18	3683.5	1001	8501	405	20.99	8-45
1988-2000	West Indies	First Class Matches	A	26	27	7	392	59	19.60	-	1	9	553.1	163	1389	55	25.25	5-56
1988-2000	West Indies	O.D.I. Matches	HA	176	96	36	639	31*	10.65	-	-	45	1558.5	192	5429	225	24.12	5-17
1991-2000	West Indies	O.A.L. O.D. Matches	A	14	9	3	69	38*	11.50	-	-	1	112	-	406	12	3383	3-16
1989-1996	Northamptonshire	First Class Matches	E	78	96	26	1100	78	15.71	-	2	38	2696.4	732	6552	318	20.60	7-44
1989-1996	Northamptonshire	Nat West Trophy	E	21	8	1	96	48	13.71	-	-	7	232.5	56	513	32	16.03	4-7
1989-96	Northamptonshire	Benson & Hedges Cup	E	15	8	4	81	17*	20.25	-	-	9	151.3	-	478	25	19.12	4-31
1989-96	Northamptonshire	Sunday League	E	59	28	11	227	37	13.35	-	-	14	432.1	-	1558	58	26.86	4-20
Total First Class Career				239	317	70	3448	78	13.95	0	4	88	8133	2262	19048	941	20.24	8-45
Total O.D. Career				329	173	66	1282	48	11.98	0	0	81	2857.2	-	9557	401	23.83	5-17

HAMISH ARBEB GERVAIS ANTHONY

D.O.B. 16.01.1971 - Urlings Village, Antigua, Leeward Islands
First Class Debut 12.01.1990 - Leeward Islands v Guyana
O.D.I. Debut 11.10.1995 - West Indies v Sri Lanka
Domestic O.D. Debut 17.01.1990 - Leeward Islands v Trinidad & Tobago

O.D.I. 74-299

Teams Played For 7
Leeward Islands, West Indies
West Indies U23, W.I. Board XI
Glamorgan, M.C.C.
Antigua

RHB / RAFM

SEASON	TEAM	COMPETITION	V	M	I	No	RUNS	H.S.	Av	100s	50s	CT	OV	MD	RUNS	W	Av	B.B.
1990-1997	Leeward Islands	First Class Matches	II	36	55	5	929	82	18.58	-	5	12	952.5	168	2980	114	26.14	6-22
1990-1999	Leeward Islands	Domestic O.D. Matches	II	38	27	6	233	32	11.09	-	-	8	288.1	20	1292	41	31.51	7-15
1998/i	Antigua	Commonwealth Games	S	2	2	1	30	17	30.00	-	-	2	5	0	34	3	11.33	3-34
1991-1992	West Indies	First Class Matches	A	12	10	3	99	33	14.14	-	-	8	244.3	31	985	28	35.17	3-28
1991-1993	West Indies U23	First Class Matches	WI	2	4	0	55	33	13.75	-	-	-	51.2	10	145	5	29.00	4-75
1991-1996	W.I. Board XI	First Class Matches	WI	3	5	0	64	42	12.80	-	-	1	59.3	10	212	9	23.55	4-53
1995/i	WEST INDIES	O.D.I. MATCHES	A	3	3	0	23	21	7.66	-	-	-	26	0	143	3	47.66	2-47
1991-1992	West Indies	O.A.L. O.D. Matches	A	5	2	0	49	38	24.50	-	-	2	43.5	-	212	4	53.00	2-11
1990-1995	Glamorgan	First Class Matches	E	20	33	1	560	91	17.50	-	2	6	540.3	102	1868	56	33.25	6-77
1995/i	Glamorgan	Nat West Trophy	E	4	2	0	12	8	6.00	-	-	1	32.5	6	111	5	22.20	4-25
1995/i	Glamorgan	Benson & Hedges Cup	E	1	1	0	2	2	2.00	-	-	-	11	-	40	3	13.33	3-40
1995/i	Glamorgan	Sunday League	E	11	8	2	22	7	3.66	-	-	-	75	-	404	11	36.72	3-40
1997/i	M.C.C.	First Class Matches	E	1	1	0	0	0	0.00	-	-	1	42	11	113	10	11.30	6-34
Total First Class Career				74	108	9	1707	91	17.24	-	7	28	1890.4	332	6303	222	28.39	6-22
Total O.D. Career				64	45	9	371	38	10.30	0	0	13	481.5	-	2236	70	31.94	7-15

231

KEITH LLOYD THOMAS ARTHURTON

D.O.B. 21.02.1965 - Jessup, St Thomas, Nevis, Leeward Islands

First Class Debut	24.1.1986 - Leeward Islands v Barbados
Test Match Debut	21.07.1988 - West Indies v England
O.D.I. Debut	22.10.1988 - West Indies v Pakistan
Domestic O.D. Debut	22.01.1986 - Leeward Islands v Barbados

Teams Played For 8
Leeward Islands, West Indies
W.I. President's XI, W.I. Board XI
West Indies U23, World XI
M.C.C. Buckinghamshire

Test 193-263
O.D.I. 55-166

LHB / SLA

SEASON	TEAM	COMPETITION	V	M	I	No	BATTING RUNS	H.S.	Av	100s	50s	CT	BOWLING OV	MD	RUNS	W	Av	B.B.
1986-2000	Leeward Islands	First Class Matches	II	52	84	9	3406	154	45.41	6	24	29	250.1	73	542	16	33.87	2-3
1986-2000	Leeward Islands	Domestic O.D. Matches	II	53	51	9	1688	118	40.19	3	10	15	275.3	21	1052	41	25.65	4-25
1988-95	WEST INDIES	TEST MATCHES	HA	33	50	5	1382	157*	30.71	2	8	22	78.5	14	183	1	183.00	1-17
1988-95	West Indies	First Class Matches	A	30	45	9	1933	146	53.69	7	10	14	113.1	23	348	9	38.66	2-1
1988-99	W.I. President's XI	First Class Matches	WI	7	11	1	466	93	46.60	-	3	1	24.2	2	85	2	42.50	1-6
1988-91	W.I. Board XI	First Class Matches	WI	2	4	0	166	132	41.50	1	-	-	2	0	7	0	-	-
1988//	West Indies U23	First Class Matches	WI	1	2	0	128	124	64.00	1	-	-	8	2	18	3	6.00	3-14
1988-95	WEST INDIES	O.D.I. MATCHES	HA	105	93	20	1904	84	26.08	-	9	27	230.4	4	1159	42	27.59	4-31
1988-95	West Indies	O.A.L. O.D. Matches	A	11	10	1	279	81*	31.00	-	1	2	30.2	2	151	6	25.16	4-26
1993-94	World XI	First Class Matches	E	2	2	0	163	103	81.50	1	1	-	6	5	5	0	-	-
1996-97	M.C.C.	First Class Matches	E	2	2	1	282	200*	282.00	1	1	1	3	1	5	0	-	-
1996//	M.C.C.	O.A.L. O.D. Matches	E	1	1	1	0	0*	-	-	-	-	-	-	-	-	-	-
1997-2000	Buckinghamshire	Nat West Trophy	E	2	2	0	66	48	33.00	-	-	1	20	0	99	7	14.14	4-53
		Total First Class Career		129	200	25	7926	200*	45.29	19	47	68	485.3	120	1193	31	38.48	3-14
		Total O.D. Career		172	157	31	3937	118	31.24	3	20	45	556.3	27	2461	96	25.63	4-25

232

NYRON SULTAN ASGARALI

D.O.B. 28.12.1920 - St. James, Port of Spain, Trinidad
First Class Debut 01.02.1941 - Trinidad v Barbados
Test Match Debut 20.06.1957 - West Indies v England

Test 95-63	4	**RHB / RAM**

Teams Played For
Trinidad
South Trinidad
West Indies
Commonwealth XI

SEASON	TEAM	COMPETITION	V	M	I	No	BATTING RUNS	H.S.	Av	100s	50s	CT	BOWLING OV	MD	RUNS	W	Av	B.B.
1941-1960	Trinidad	First Class Matches	=	23	41	2	1396	141*	35.79	5	3	17	227.3	66	615	15	41.00	3-30
1959-1963	South Trinidad	First Class Matches	T	5	10	0	316	98	31.60	-	2	1	69	13	150	3	50.00	1-7
1957	WEST INDIES	TEST MATCHES	A	2	4	0	62	29	15.50	-	-	-	-	-	-	-	-	-
1957	West Indies	First Class Matches	A	19	33	3	949	130*	31.63	2	3	11	76	24	201	5	40.20	4-72
1956	Commonwealth XI	First Class Matches	E	1	1	0	38	38	38.00	-	-	-	-	-	-	-	-	-
Total First Class Career				50	89	5	2761	141*	32.86	7	8	29	372.3	103	966	23	42.00	4-72

DENIS ST EVAL ATKINSON

D.O.B. 09.08.1926 - Rockley, Christ Church, Barbados (d. 09.01.2001)
First Class Debut 28.09.1946 - Barbados v British Guiana
Test Match Debut 10.11.1948 - West Indies v India

Test 67-27

RHB / RM

Teams Played For
Barbados
Trinidad
West Indies

3

BATTING

SEASON	TEAM	COMPETITION	V	M	I	No	RUNS	H.S.	Av	100s	50s	CT
1946-1961	Barbados	First Class Matches	II	19	31	2	1101	151	37.96	3	6	12
1947-1950	Trinidad	First Class Matches	II	4	4	1	107	83*	35.66	-	1	3
1948-1958	WEST INDIES	TEST MATCHES	HA	22	35	6	922	219	31.79	1	5	11
1948-1952	West Indies	First Class Matches	A	33	45	7	682	101*	17.94	1	2	13
	Total First Class Career			78	115	16	2812	219	28.40	5	14	39

BOWLING

OV	MD	RUNS	W	Av	B.B.
726.2	298	1357	45	30.15	4-58
75	15	205	5	41.00	2-36
862.1	311	1647	47	35.04	7-53
924.3	283	2082	103	20.21	8-58
2588	907	5291	200	26.45	8-58

ERIC ST EVAL ATKINSON

D.O.B. 06.11.1927 - Rockley, Christ Church, Barbados (d. 29.05.1998)

First Class Debut 09.02.1950 - Barbados v British Guiana

Test Match Debut 17.01.1958 - West Indies v Pakistan

Test 97-67

Teams Played For Barbados, West Indies

2

RHB / RM

SEASON	TEAM	COMPETITION	V	M	I	No	BATTING RUNS	H.S.	Av	100s	50s	CT	BOWLING OV	MD	RUNS	W	Av	B.B.
1949-1958	Barbados	First Class Matches	II	12	18	3	453	77	30.20	-	3	6	190.5	34	564	9	62.66	4-70
1958-1959	WEST INDIES	TEST MATCHES	HA	8	9	1	126	37	15.75	-	-	2	272.2	77	589	25	23.56	5-42
1958-1959	West Indies	First Class Matches	A	9	11	2	117	31	13.00	-	-	6	224.4	65	477	27	17.66	6-10
Total First Class Career				29	38	6	696	77	21.75	0	3	14	687.5	176	1630	61	26.72	6-10

RICHARD ARKWRIGHT AUSTIN

D.O.B. 05.09.1954 - Jones Town, Kingston, Jamaica

First Class Debut 21.03.1975 - Jamaica v Trinidad & Tobago
Test Match Debut 03.03.1978 - West Indies v Australia
O.D.I. Debut 22.02.1978 - West Indies v Australia
Domestic O.D. Debut 13.02.1976 - Jamaica v Barbados

Test 162-179
O.D.I. 22-13

Teams Played For
Jamaica
West Indies
W.I. President's XI
West Indies XI

RHB / RM

SEASON	TEAM	COMPETITION	V	M	I	No	RUNS	H.S.	Av	100s	50s	CT	OV	MD	RUNS	W	Av	B.B.
1975-1982	Jamaica	First Class Matches	=	32	54	1	1896	141	35.77	4	13	23	787	186	2096	73	28.71	8-71
1976-1982	Jamaica	Domestic OD Matches	=	14	14	1	336	124*	25.84	1	-	3	114	15	403	20	20.15	5-37
1977-1978	WEST INDIES	TEST MATCHES	H	2	2	0	22	20	11.00	-	-	2	1	0	5	0	-	-
1977-1981	W.I. President's XI	First Class Matches	WI	2	3	0	45	25	15.00	-	-	-	45	10	142	0	-	-
1982-1983	West Indies XI	First Class Matches	A	2	4	0	134	93	33.50	-	1	2	10	1	36	0	-	-
1977-1978	WEST INDIES	O.D.I. MATCHES	H	1	1	0	8	8	8.00	-	-	-	1	0	13	0	-	-
1982-1983	West Indies XI	O.D.(I.) Matches	A	4	4	0	21	11	5.25	-	-	1	12	1	62	1	62.00	1-49
1982-1983	West Indies XI	O.A.L. O.D. Matches	A	3	3	0	20	15	6.66	-	-	4	14	1	57	2	28.50	1-13
		Total First Class Career		38	63	1	2097	141	33.82	4	14	27	843	197	2279	73	31.21	8-71
		Total O.D. Career		22	22	1	385	124*	18.33	1	0	8	141	17	535	23	23.26	5-37

SHEIK FAOUD AHUMUL FASIEL BACCHUS

D.O.B. 31.01.1954 - Campbellville, Georgetown, Demerara, British Guiana
First Class Debut 30.10.1971 - Demerara v Berbice
Test Match Debut 15.04.1978 - West Indies v Australia
O.D.I. Debut 22.02.1978 - West Indies v Australia
Domestic O.D. Debut 16.04.1973 - Guyana v Barbados

Test 171-182
O.D.I. 23-13

Teams Played For 9
Guyana, Demerara
West Indies, West Indies "B"
West Indies XI, Border
Western Province, Implas
USA

RHB / RAM

SEASON	TEAM	COMPETITION	V	M	I	No	RUNS	H.S.	Av	100s	50s	CT	OV	MD	RUNS	W	Av	B.B.
1973-1983	Guyana	First Class Matches	II	37	56	4	2068	154	39.76	4	13	21	7	2	12	0	-	-
1971-1979	Demerara	First Class Matches	G	3	4	0	51	23	12.75	-	-	-	-	-	-	-	-	-
1972-1983	Guyana	Domestic O.D. Matches	II	16	16	2	528	88*	37.71	-	5	1	4	0	29	3	9.66	3-28
1978-1982	WEST INDIES	TEST MATCHES	HA	19	30	0	782	250	26.06	1	17	17	1	0	3	0	-	-
1978-1982	West Indies	First Class Matches	A	26	46	7	1724	164*	42.02	2	12	29	5.1	2	12	0	-	-
1981//	West Indies "B"	First Class Matches	A	3	4	1	69	29	23.00	-	3	3	-	-	-	-	-	-
1983-1984	West Indies XI	First Class Matches	A	7	13	1	432	88	36.00	-	4	3	-	-	-	-	-	-
1978-1983	WEST INDIES	O.D.I. MATCHES	HA	29	26	3	612	80*	26.60	-	3	10	-	-	-	-	-	-
1981//	West Indies "B"	O.D.(I) Matches	A	2	2	0	99	51	49.50	-	1	1	-	-	-	-	-	-
1983-1984	West Indies XI	O.D.(I) Matches	A	1	1	0	2	2	2.00	-	-	1	-	-	-	-	-	-
1979-1980	West Indies	O.A.L. O.D. Matches	A	5	5	2	232	90*	77.33	-	2	2	-	-	-	-	-	-
1984-1985	Western Province	First Class Matches	SA	9	17	0	324	65	19.05	-	3	11	1	0	2	1	2.00	1-2
1985-1986	Border	First Class Matches	SA	7	12	0	494	134	41.16	1	2	4	64.2	10	168	7	24.00	2-18
1984 -1985	Western Province	Nissan Shield	SA	4	4	0	82	42	20.50	-	1	1	-	-	-	-	-	-
1984 -1985	Western Province	Benson & Hedges Cup	SA	4	4	0	262	132	65.50	1	-	-	-	-	-	-	-	-
1985-1986	Border	Nissan Shield	SA	1	1	0	6	6	6.00	-	-	-	8	0	44	3	14.66	3-44
1985-1986	Implas	Benson & Hedges Cup	SA	1	1	0	48	31	12.00	-	2	2	4	0	26	0	-	-
1996-1997	USA	I.C.C. Trophy	A	7	7	2	223	100*	44.60	1	1	3	46	6	155	7	22.14	2-33
		Total First Class Career		111	182	13	5944	250	35.17	8	37	88	78.3	14	197	8	24.62	2-18
		Total O.D. Career		73	70	9	2094	132	34.32	2	13	21	62	6	254	13	19.53	3-28

LEONARD BAICHAN

LHB / RAM

D.O.B. 12.05.1946 - Rose Hall, Berbice, British Guiana
First Class Debut 27.02.1969 - Guyana v Barbados
Test Match Debut 15.02.1975 - West Indies v Pakistan
Domestic O.D. Debut 16.04.1973 - Guyana v Barbados

Test 152-157

Teams Played For
Guyana
Berbice
West Indies
W.I. President's XI

4

SEASON	TEAM	COMPETITION	V	M	I	No	BATTING						BOWLING					
							RUNS	H.S.	Av	100s	50s	CT	OV	MD	RUNS	W	Av	B.B.
1969-1980	Guyana	First Class Matches	II	34	56	5	2136	134	41.88	5	12	17	5	0	26	0	-	-
1972-1982	Berbice	First Class Matches	G	8	12	3	983	216*	109.22	4	5	8	-	-	-	-	-	-
1972-1980	Guyana	Domestic O.D. Matches	II	6	6	0	189	74	31.50	-	2	1	-	-	-	-	-	-
1975//	WEST INDIES	TEST MATCHES	H	3	6	2	184	105*	46.00	1	0	2	-	-	-	-	-	-
1974-1976	West Indies	First Class Matches	A	15	22	2	855	158	42.75	2	4	7	1	0	4	0	-	-
1972-1977	W.I. President's XI	First Class Matches	WI	3	4	1	346	139*	115.33	1	2	1	1	0	4	0	-	-
1975-1976	West Indies	O.A.L. O.D. Matches	A	2	2	1	79	72*	79.00	-	1	1	-	-	-	-	-	-
Total First Class Career				63	100	13	4504	216*	51.77	13	23	35	7	0	34	0	-	-
Total O.D. Career				8	8	1	268	74	38.28	0	3	3	-	-	-	-	-	-

OMARI AHMED CLEMENT BANKS

D.O.B. 17.07.1982 - Road Bay, Anguilla, Leeward Islands
First Class Debut 04.01.2001 - Leeward Islands v Trinidad & Tobago
Test Match Debut 01.05.2003 - West Indies v Australia
O.D.I. Debut 17.05.2003 - West Indies v Autralia
Domestic O.D. Debut 03.10.2001 - Leeward Islands v Trinidad & Tobago

RHB / OB

Test 250-396
O.D.I. 112-461

Teams Played For 4
Leeward Islands
Leicestershire
Carib Cup XI
West Indies

SEASON	TEAM	COMPETITION	V	M	I	No	BATTING RUNS	H.S.	Av	100s	50s	CT	BOWLING OV	MD	RUNS	W	Av	B.B.
2001-2003	Leeward Islands	First Class Matches	II	18	25	4	450	75	21.42	-	3	12	744.4	172	1848	51	36.23	7-70
2001-2002	Leeward Islands	Domestic O.D. Matches	II	7	5	2	101	35*	33.66	-	3	3	62.3	10	192	13	14.76	4-23
2003//	WEST INDIES	TEST MATCHES	HA	4	6	3	171	50*	57.00	-	1	2	165	23	560	9	62.22	3-204
2002-2003	Carib Cup XI	First Class Matches	WI	1	2	0	20	14	10.00	-	-	1	41.5	8	141	3	47.00	3-65
2003//	WEST INDIES	O.D.I. MATCHES	HA	3	3	0	44	29	14.66	-	-	-	25	0	124	4	31.00	2-44
2001//	Leicestershire	First Class Matches	E	1	2	0	4	4	2.00	-	-	-	9	0	38	0	-	-
	Total First Class Career			24	35	7	645	75	23.03	-	4	15	960.3	203	2587	63	41.06	7-70
	Total O.D. Career			10	8	2	145	35*	24.16	0	0	3	87.3	10	316	17	18.58	4-23

ELDINE ASHWORTH EDERLFIELD BAPTISTE

D.O.B. 12.03.1960 – Liberta Village, Antigua, Leeward Islands

First Class Debut	17.06.1981 - Kent v Oxford University
Test Match Debut	21.10.1983 - West Indies v India
O.D.I. Debut	13.10.1983 - West Indies v India
Domestic O.D. Debut	21.06.1981 - Kent v Somerset

Teams Played For
Leeward Islands, Antigua
West Indies, West Indies "B"
W.I. President's XI, Kent
Northamptonshire, Cumberland
World XI, Eastern Province, Kwa-Zulu Natal

Test 179-217
O.D.I. 39-61

RHB / RFM
11

SEASON	TEAM	COMPETITION	V	M	I	No	BATTING RUNS	H.S.	Av	100s	50s	CT	BOWLING OV	MD	RUNS	W	Av	B.B.
1982-1991	Leeward Islands	First Class Matches	=	37	57	5	1324	99	25.46	-	7	24	1058.1	231	2963	132	22.44	6-26
1982-1991	Leeward Islands	Domestic O.D. Matches	=	19	11	2	102	32	11.33	-	-	6	150.3	15	657	27	24.33	5-45
1998//	Antigua	Commonwealth Games	S	3	3	0	29	22	9.66	-	-	-	7	1	36	2	18.00	1-4
1983-1990	WEST INDIES	TEST MATCHES	HA	10	11	1	233	87*	23.30	-	1	2	227	60	563	16	35.18	3-31
1983-1987	West Indies	First Class Matches	A	15	17	4	401	75*	30.84	-	3	4	337.5	79	953	45	21.17	7-70
1986-1987	West Indies "B"	First Class Matches	A	5	6	0	137	55	22.83	-	1	2	156.5	41	408	29	14.06	7-92
1989-1990	W.I. President's XI	First Class Matches	WI	1	2	0	28	19	14.00	-	-	-	60.1	11	133	4	33.25	4-91
1983-1990	WEST INDIES	O.D.I. MATCHES	HA	43	16	4	184	31	15.33	-	-	14	369	30	1511	36	41.97	2-10
1986-1987	West Indies	O.D.(I.) Matches	A	5	3	0	80	38	26.55	-	-	3	38	5	176	9	19.55	4-32
1984//	West Indies	O.A.L. O.D. Matches	A	2	2	0	28	28	14.00	-	-	-	21	-	91	2	45.50	2-35
1981-1987	Kent	First Class Matches	E	87	127	20	3195	136*	29.85	3	15	44	2071.1	470	6209	218	28.48	8-76
1981-1987	Kent	Nat West Trophy	E	12	10	1	78	22	8.66	-	-	6	127	21	424	14	30.28	5-20
1983-1987	Kent	Benson & Hedges Cup	E	19	17	5	200	43*	16.66	-	-	8	175	-	644	22	29.27	5-30
1981-1987	Kent	Sunday League	E	63	52	6	802	60	17.43	-	5	20	413.3	-	1889	73	25.87	4-22
1985//	Kent	O.A.L. O.D. Matches	E	2	D													
1991//	Northamptonshire	First Class Matches	E	18	22	1	589	80	28.04	-	4	9	529.2	122	1443	50	28.86	7-95
1991//	Northamptonshire	Nat West Trophy	E	4	3	1	51	34	25.50	-	-	1	42	4	171	9	19.00	4-27
1991//	Northamptonshire	Benson & Hedges Cup	E	4	3	1	28	15*	14.00	-	-	-	31.1	-	118	1	118.00	1-30
1991//	Northamptonshire	Sunday League & Cup	E	11	11	4	83	15*	11.85	-	-	2	81.1	-	340	6	56.66	2-25
1994//	Cumberland	Nat West Trophy	E	1	1	0	2	2	2.00	-	-	-	12	5	35	0	-	-
1991-1999	Eastern Province	First Class Matches	SA	57	81	12	1822	97	26.40	-	14	28	2138.2	674	4398	205	21.45	5-30
1991-1992	Eastern Province	Nissan Shield	SA	6	4	0	78	36	19.50	-	-	-	60	-	222	8	27.75	3-52
1991-1999	Eastern Province	Benson & Hedges/Total Cup	SA	86	64	17	886	65	18.85	-	4	30	711.3	-	2618	120	21.81	6-13
1993-1994	Eastern Province	O.A.L. O.D. Matches	SA	2	2	0	5	5	2.50	-	-	2	6	1	18	0	-	-
1999-2001	Kwa-Zulu Natal	First Class Matches	SA	14	17	6	321	75*	29.18	-	2	7	341.3	114	738	24	30.75	4-18
1999-2001	Kwa-Zulu Natal	Standard Bank Cup	SA	25	8	2	96	33*	16.00	-	-	6	187	11	716	32	22.37	3-17
2000-2001	Kwa-Zulu Natal	Australian Champions Cup	A	3	1	-	-	-	-	-	-	-	24	1	78	4	19.50	2-40
1994//	World XI	First Class Matches	E	1	1	1	20	20*	-	-	-	-	2	0	15	0	-	-
Total First Class Career				245	341	50	8070	136*	27.73	3	47	120	6922.1	1802	17823	723	24.65	8-76
Total O.D. Career				310	210	43	2732	65	16.35	0	9	98	2455.5	-	9744	365	26.69	6-13

ARTHUR GEORGE BARRETT

D.O.B. 04.04.1944 - Kingston, Jamaica
First Class Debut 08.02.1967 - Jamaica v Trinidad & Tobago
Test Match Debut 18.02.1971 - West Indies v India
Domestic O.D. Debut 13.04.1973 - Jamaica v Guyana

Test 135-129

Teams Played For
Jamaica
West Indies
W.I. President's XI

3

RHB / RALB

SEASON	TEAM	COMPETITION	V	M	I	No	BATTING RUNS	H.S.	Av	100s	50s	CT	BOWLING OV	MD	RUNS	W	Av	B.B.
1967-1981	Jamaica	First Class Matches	=	42	57	10	857	102*	18.23	1	-	50	1491.1	320	3912	134	29.19	7-90
1972-1973	Jamaica	Domestic O.D. Matches	=	1	1	0	9	9	9.00	-	-	1	6.5	0	30	4	7.50	4-30
1971-1975	WEST INDIES	TEST MATCHES	HA	6	7	1	40	19	6.22	-	-	-	268.4	83	603	13	46.38	3-43
1974-1975	West Indies	First Class Matches	A	7	8	2	140	36*	23.33	-	-	2	190	41	535	15	35.66	4-8
1971-1974	W.I. President's XI	First Class Matches	WI	2	3	0	49	37	16.33	-	-	2	86	24	226	7	32.28	4-13
Total First Class Career				57	75	13	1086	102*	17.51	1	0	54	2035.5	468	5276	169	31.21	7-90
Total O.D. Career				1	1	0	9	9	9.00	0	0	1	6.5	0	30	4	7.50	4-30

241

IVANHOE MORDRED BARROW

D.O.B. 06.01.1911 - Beef-Pen, St Thomas, Jamaica (d. 02.04.1979)
First Class Debut 21.02.1929 - Jamaica v Julien Cahns XI
Test Match Debut 03.04.1930 - West Indies v England

Test 26-7

Teams Played For 2
Jamaica
West Indies

RHB / WK

SEASON	TEAM	COMPETITION	V	M	I	No	BATTING RUNS	H.S.	Av	100s	50s	CT/ST	BOWLING OV	MD	RUNS	W	Av	B.B.
1929-1946	Jamaica	First Class Matches	II	15	24	2	920	169	41.81	2	5	15/9	5	0	2	0	-	-
1930-1939	WEST INDIES	TEST MATCHES	HA	11	19	2	276	105	16.23	1	-	17/5	-	-	-	-	-	-
1929-1939	West Indies	First Class Matches	HA	42	70	2	1355	89	19.92	-	5	41/13	4	1	14	0	-	-
		Total First Class Career		68	113	6	2551	169	23.84	3	10	73/27	9	1	34	0	-	-

EDWARD LAWSON BARTLETT

D.O.B. 10.03.1906 - Flint Hall, St Michael, Barbados (d. 21.12.1976)

First Class Debut 19.02.1924 - Barbados v Trinidad

Test Match Debut 11.08.1928 - West Indies v England

Test 14 -3

Teams Played For Barbados / West Indies / Combined B/J XI — 3

RHB

SEASON	TEAM	COMPETITION	V	M	I	No	BATTING RUNS	H.S.	Av	100s	50s	CT	BOWLING OV	MD	RUNS	W	Av	B.B.
1924 -1939	Barbados	First Class Matches	=	18	32	1	770	93*	24.83	-	5	5	-	-	-	-	-	-
1928-1931	WEST INDIES	TEST MATCHES	A	5	8	1	131	84	18.71	-	1	2	-	-	-	-	-	-
1928-1931	West Indies	First Class Matches	A	18	30	1	661	109	22.79	1	2	1	-	-	-	-	-	-
1927-1928	Combined XI	First Class Matches	H	1	2	1	19	11*	19.00	-	-	-	-	-	-	-	-	-
Total First Class Career				42	72	4	1581	109	23.25	1	8	8	-	-	-	-	-	-

CARLTON SEYMOUR BAUGH

RHB / WK / LBG

D.O.B. 23.06.1982 - Meadowland, Kingston, Jamaica

First Class Debut 09.02.2001 - Jamaica v Guyana
Test Match Debut 19.04.2003 - West Indies v Australia
O.D.I. Debut 17.05.2003 - West Indies v Australia

Test 248-395
O.D.I. 113-461

Teams Played For
Jamaica
West Indies
West Indies "B"
Carib Cup XI
W.I. President's XI

SEASON	TEAM	COMPETITION	V	M	I	No	RUNS	H.S.	Av	100s	50s	CT/ST	BOWLING OV	MD	RUNS	W	Av	B.B.
2001-2002	Jamaica	First Class Matches	II	1	1	0	2	2	2.00	-	-	1	5	-	-	-	-	-
2003//	WEST INDIES	TEST MATCHES	HA	2	4	0	62	24	15.50	-	-	2/1	-	-	-	-	-	-
2002-2003	West Indies "B"	First Class Matches	WI	9	16	2	549	100*	39.21	1	5	16	-	-	-	-	-	-
2002-2003	Carib Cup XI	First Class Matches	WI	1	2	1	147	115*	147.00	1	-	1	-	-	-	-	-	-
2003//	WEST INDIES	O.D.I. MATCHES	HA	3	3	1	60	29	30.00	-	-	1	-	-	-	-	-	-
2002-2003	W.I. President's XI	First Class Matches	WI	1	1	0	43	43	43.00	-	-	2/1	-	-	-	-	-	-
Total First Class Career				14	24	3	803	115*	38.73	2	5	22/2	-	-	-	-	-	-
Total O.D. Career				3	3	1	60	29	30.00	0	0	1	-	-	-	-	-	-

JOSEPH EMMANUEL BENJAMIN

D.O.B. 02.02.1961 - Christ Church, St Kitts, Leeward Islands
First Class Debut 24.07.1988 - Warwickshire v Sri Lanka
Test Match Debut 18.08.1994 - England v South Africa
O.D.I. Debut 06.12.1994 - England v Australia
Domestic O.D. Debut 25.06.1986 - Staffordshire v Glamorgan

Teams Played For Warwickshire, Surrey, England, Staffordshire

4   RHB / RAMF

SEASON	TEAM	COMPETITION	V	M	I	No	BATTING RUNS	H.S.	Av	100s	50s	CT	BOWLING OV	MD	RUNS	W	Av	B.B.
1988-1991	Warwickshire	First Class Matches	E	25	22	8	225	41	16.07	-	-	7	659.1	129	2020	64	31.56	5-29
1990//	Warwickshire	Nat West Trophy	E	2	2	2	3	2*	-	-	-	1	14	2	49	0	-	-
1990//	Warwickshire	Benson & Hedges Cup	E	2	1	0	20	20	20.00	-	-	1	22	-	72	3	24.00	2-32
1989-1991	Warwickshire	Sunday League	E	22	6	6	88	24	17.60	-	-	7	153	-	653	20	32.65	3-33
1992-1999	Surrey	First Class Matches	E	96	118	35	925	49	11.14	-	-	17	2984.2	626	9147	313	29.22	6-19
1992-1999	Surrey	Nat West Trophy	E	19	6	3	42	25	14.00	-	-	2	180.5	-	658	21	31.33	4-20
1992-1998	Surrey	Benson & Hedges Cup	E	28	6	5	13	5	13.00	-	-	6	274	-	1103	31	35.58	4-19
1992-1999	Surrey	Sunday League	E	90	37	17	137	16*	6.85	-	-	12	636.3	-	2819	94	29.98	4-44
1994//	ENGLAND	TEST MATCHES	E	1	1	0	0	0	0.00	-	-	-	28	3	80	4	20.00	4-42
1994-1995	England	First Class Matches	A	4	4	0	11	7	2.75	-	-	1	105.5	23	341	6	56.83	2-36
1994-1995	ENGLAND	O.D.I. MATCHES	A	2	1	0	0	0	0.00	-	-	-	12	0	47	1	47.00	1-22
1986-1987	Staffordshire	Nat West Trophy	E	2	2	0	24	19	12.00	-	-	-	23	4	102	3	34.00	2-37
		Total First Class Career		126	145	43	1161	49	11.38	0	0	25	3777.2	781	11588	387	29.94	6-19
		Total O.D. Career		167	66	33	327	25	9.90	0	0	29	1315.2	-	5503	173	31.80	4-19

KENNETH CHARLIE GRIFFITH BENJAMIN

D.O.B. 08.04.1967 - St John's, Antigua, Leeward Islands

First Class Debut 27.01.1989 - Leeward Islands v Windward Islands
Test Match Debut 18.04.1992 - West Indies v South Africa
O.D.I. Debut 04.12.1992 - West Indies v Pakistan
Domestic O.D. Debut 23.02.1989 - Leeward Islands v Guyana

Teams Played For 11
Leeward Islands, West Indies, W.I. President's XI
West Indies U23, West Indies "A"
Antigua, World XI
Worcestershire, Gauteng
Easterns, M.C.C.

Test 200-291
O.D.I. 62-237

RHB / RAF

SEASON	TEAM	COMPETITION	V	M	I	No	BATTING RUNS	H.S.	Av	100s	50s	CT	BOWLING OV	MD	RUNS	W	Av	B.B.
1989-1999	Leeward Islands	First Class Matches	II	38	50	7	479	52*	11.13	-	1	8	1118.3	243	3102	136	22.80	7-51
1989-1998	Leeward Islands	Domestic O.D. Matches	II	34	17	7	85	15	8.50	-	-	4	265	25	1076	49	21.95	4-33
1998//	Antigua	Commonwealth Games	S	3	2	1	6	5*	6.00	-	-	-	12.4	2	69	3	23.00	2-36
1992-1998	WEST INDIES	TEST MATCHES	HA	26	36	8	222	43*	7.92	-	-	2	855.2	158	2785	92	30.27	6-66
1992-1997	West Indies	First Class Matches	A	13	11	5	99	44	16.50	-	-	7	300.3	72	974	40	24.35	5-52
1990-1993	W.I. President's XI	First Class Matches	WI	3	4	2	21	11	10.50	-	-	-	74.2	14	207	10	20.70	3-40
1989//	West Indies U23	First Class Matches	WI	1	1	0	9	9	9.00	-	-	-	25	5	87	1	87.00	1-71
1991-1992	West Indies "A"	First Class Matches	WI	3	4	2	71	25	35.50	-	-	-	109.4	31	239	17	14.05	6-72
1992-1996	WEST INDIES	O.D.I. MATCHES	HA	26	13	7	65	17	10.83	-	-	4	219.5	12	923	33	27.96	3-34
1995-1996	West Indies	O.A.L. O.D. Matches	A	2	1	1	4	4*		-	-	-	15.4	2	48	1	48.00	1-29
1993//	Worcestershire	First Class Matches	E	11	11	3	85	26	10.62	-	-	1	283.5	42	911	37	24.62	6-70
1993//	Worcestershire	Nat West Trophy	E	2	D	-	-	-	-	-	-	1	16	4	49	2	24.50	2-38
1993//	Worcestershire	Benson & Hedges Cup	E	2	1	0	2	2	2.00	-	-	-	22	-	65	4	16.25	2-28
1993//	Worcestershire	Sunday League	E	2	5	1	35	20	8.75	-	-	-	58.1	1	189	11	17.18	3-25
1992-1994	World XI	First Class Matches	E	2	1	1	0	0*	-	-	-	-	27	4	108	3	36.00	3-53
1999-2000	Gauteng	First Class Matches	SA	6	9	2	103	29*	14.71	-	-	3	250	78	594	38	15.63	6-48
1999-2000	Gauteng	Standard Bank Cup	SA	7	2	0	9	8	4.50	-	-	-	57	3	230	7	32.85	3-17
2000-2001	Easterns	First Class Matches	SA	5	9	3	110	48*	18.33	-	-	3	190.4	45	549	29	18.93	6-73
2000-2001	Easterns	Standard Bank Cup	SA	9	5	0	75	22	15.00	-	-	-	75.1	6	283	11	25.73	3-76
1992//	M.C.C.	O.A.L. O.D. Matches	E	1	D	-	-	-	-	-	-	-	19.2	-	40	3	13.33	3-40
Total First Class Career				108	136	33	1199	52*	11.64	0	1	24	3234.5	692	9556	403	23.71	7-51
Total O.D. Career				93	46	17	281	22	9.68	0	0	9	760.3	-	2972	124	23.96	4-33

WINSTON KEITHROY MATTHEW BENJAMIN

RHB / RAF

D.O.B.	31.12.1964 - All Saints, Antigua, Leeward Islands
First Class Debut	08.09.1985 - World XI v D.B. Closes XI
Test Match Debut	25.11.1987 - West Indies v India
O.D.I. Debut	17.10.1986 - West Indies v Pakistan
Domestic O.D. Debut	08.01.1986 - Leeward Islands v Windward Islands

Test 189-253
O.D.I. 49-119

Teams Played For 8
Leeward Islands, West Indies
W.I. President's XI
W.I. Board XI Antigua
Leicestershire, Hampshire
World XI

SEASON	TEAM	COMPETITION	V	M	I	No	RUNS	H.S.	Av	100s	50s	CT	OV	MD	RUNS	W	Av	B.B.
1986-1994	Leeward Islands	First Class Matches	II	29	42	6	755	85	20.97	-	2	10	862.5	186	2314	102	22.68	7-64
1986-1995	Leeward Islands	Domestic O.D. Matches	II	22	14	4	177	30	17.70	-	-	5	175.2	11	606	28	21.64	5-26
1998//	Antigua	Commonwealth Games	S	3	3	0	23	15	7.66	-	-	-	12	1	59	1	59.00	1-35
1987-1995	WEST INDIES	TEST MATCHES	HA	21	26	1	470	85	18.80	0	2	12	615.4	136	1648	61	27.01	4-46
1986-1995	West Indies	First Class Matches	A	22	23	9	426	92	30.42	0	2	12	361.3	76	1030	37	27.83	4-20
1987-1989	W.I. President's XI	First Class Matches	WI	2	1	0	18	18	18.00	-	-	-	48	12	146	5	29.20	2-30
1988-1989	W.I. Board XI	First Class Matches	WI	1	1	-	-	-	-	-	-	1	8	3	11	1	11.00	1-11
1986-1995	WEST INDIES	O.D.I. MATCHES	HA	85	52	12	298	31	7.45	-	-	16	740.2	58	3079	100	30.79	5-22
1987-1995	West Indies	O.A.L. O.D. Matches	A	3	3	0	106	74	35.33	0	2	2	24	-	70	6	11.66	4-10
1986-1993	Leicestershire	First Class Matches	E	84	101	18	1930	101*	23.25	1	13	53	2212.	534	6362	237	26.84	7-54
1986-1993	Leicestershire	Nat West Trophy	E	14	11	2	71	24*	-	-	-	3	146.3	25	475	20	23.75	5-32
1986-1993	Leicestershire	Benson & Hedges Cup	E	16	12	3	170	45	18.88	-	-	3	160.1	-	544	29	18.75	5-17
1986-1993	Leicestershire	Sunday League	E	51	39	8	346	55	11.16	-	1	6	366.5	-	1526	54	28.25	4-19
1990//	Leicestershire	O.A.L. O.D. Matches	E	1	1	1	0	0*	-	-	-	-	11	-	27	1	27.00	1-27
1994-1996	Hampshire	First Class Matches	E	11	18	1	371	117	21.82	1	2	7	350.2	110	786	30	26.20	6-46
1994-1996	Hampshire	Nat West Trophy	E	5	4	0	54	41	13.50	-	-	3	22	3	53	2	26.50	2-24
1986-1993	Hampshire	Benson & Hedges Cup	E	7	5	1	137	58*	34.25	-	1	3	59.4	-	266	10	26.60	3-26
1994-1996	Hampshire	Sunday League	E	15	11	2	343	104*	38.11	1	1	5	68.1	-	295	12	24.58	3-19
1985//	World XI	First Class Matches	E	1	2	1	15	15	15.00	-	-	-	21	5	61	3	20.33	2-31
	Total First Class Career			171	213	36	3985	117	22.51	2	21	95	4479.2	1062	12358	476	25.96	7-54
	Total O.D. Career			222	155	33	1725	104*	14.13	1	4	46	1786	-	7000	263	26.61	5-17

BATTING | BOWLING

DAVID EDDISON BERNARD
D.O.B.   19.07.1981 - Kingston, Jamaica

First Class Debut   05.01.2001 - West Indies "B" v England "A"
Test Match Debut   19.04.2003 - West Indies v Australia
O.D.I. Debut   25.05.2003 - West Indies v Australia
Domestic O.D. Debut   21.09.2000 - Jamaica v South Africa "A"

Test   249-395
O.D.I.   116-465

Teams Played For
Jamaica
West Indies
West Indies "B"
UWI Vice Chancellor's XI
W.I. President's XI

RHB / RMF   5

SEASON	TEAM	COMPETITION	V	M	I	No	BATTING						BOWLING					
							RUNS	H.S.	Av	100s	50s	CT	OV	MD	RUNS	W	Av	B.B.
2002-2003	Jamaica	First Class Matches	II	12	18	2	593	109	37.06	1	2	10	236.4	54	678	31	21.87	5-56
1999-2002	Jamaica	Domestic O.D. Matches	II	4	3	0	76	59	25.33	-	1	-	21	0	99	1	99.00	1-27
2003//	WEST INDIES	TEST MATCHES	HA	1	2	0	11	7	5.50	-	-	-	11	1	61	0	-	-
2001-2002	West Indies "B"	First Class Matches	WI	7	14	0	227	43	16.21	-	-	5	52	13	127	4	31.75	2-7
2002-2003	UWI V/Chancellor's XI	First Class Matches	WI	1	2	0	47	28	23.50	-	-	-	12	0	54	0	-	-
2003//	WEST INDIES	O.D.I. MATCHES	HA	4	2	0	7	7	3.50	-	-	1	4	0	28	1	28.00	1-11
2002-2003	W.I. President's XI	First Class Matches	WI	1	1	0	3	3	3.00	-	-	-	7	2	22	0	-	-
Total First Class Career				22	37	2	881	109	25.17	1	2	15	318.4	70	942	35	26.91	5.56
Total O.D. Career				8	5	0	83	59	16.60	0	1	1	25	0	127	2	63.50	1-11

CARLISLE ALONZA BEST

D.O.B. 14.05.1959 - Richmond Gap, St Michael, Barbados

First Class Debut 28.03.1980 - Barbados v Trinidad & Tobago
Test Match Debut 21.02.1986 - West Indies v England
O.D.I. Debut 04.03.1986 - West Indies v England
Domestic O.D. Debut 22.04.1980 - Barbados v Leeward Islands

Test	185-242	RHB / RAM
O.D.I.	48-116	

Teams Played For 9

Barbados, West Indies
W.I. President's XI, W.I. Board XI
Shell Awards XI, West Indies "B"
West Indies "A", World XI
Western Province

SEASON	TEAM	COMPETITION	V	M	I	No	BATTING RUNS	H.S.	Av	100s	50s	CT	BOWLING OV	MD	RUNS	W	Av	B.B.
1986-1990	WEST INDIES	TEST MATCHES	HA	8	13	1	342	164	28.50	1	1	8	5	0	21	0	-	-
1980-1994	Barbados	First Class Matches	II	58	97	6	3781	179	41.54	10	16	71	205.1	34	570	21	27.14	3-29
1992-1993	Barbados	Domestic O.D. Matches	II	28	27	6	993	137*	47.28	1	8	9	29.5	1	184	5	36.80	2-24
1980-1993	Barbados	O.A.L. O.D. Matches	HA	8	8	0	93	26	11.62	-	-	3	42	0	172	4	43.00	2-42
1991-1992	West Indies	First Class Matches	A	1	2	0	49	37	24.50	-	-	2	-	-	-	-	-	-
1984-1985	Shell Awards XI	First Class Matches	WI	1	2	1	37	28	37.00	-	-	2	-	-	-	-	-	-
1985-1991	W.I. President's XI	First Class Matches	WI	4	8	3	234	104*	46.80	1	1	4	3	0	13	0	-	-
1989-1991	W.I. Board XI	First Class Matches	WI	2	3	0	129	58	43.00	-	1	-	1	0	3	0	-	-
1987/I	West Indies "B"	First Class Matches	WI	5	8	1	245	58*	35.00	-	2	13	25	8	58	1	58.00	1-6
1992/I	West Indies "A"	First Class Matches	WI	3	6	2	150	71	37.50	-	1	4	4	1	9	0	-	-
1992/I	West Indies "A"	O.D.(I.) Matches	WI	5	5	1	151	57	37.75	-	1	1	14	0	70	3	23.33	2-23
1986-1992	WEST INDIES	O.D.I. MATCHES	A	24	23	4	473	100	24.89	1	2	5	3.1	0	12	0	-	-
1991/I	West Indies	O.A.L. O.D. Matches	A	3	3	0	57	30	19.00	-	-	1	-	-	-	-	-	-
1993-1994	Western Province	First Class Matches	SA	7	13	0	333	71	25.61	-	2	3	30.4	5	98	2	49.00	2-80
1993-1994	Western Province	Benson & Hedges Cup	SA	11	10	0	175	57	17.50	-	1	2	24.4	3	133	2	66.50	2-22
1989/I	World XI	First Class Matches	E	1	2	0	139	100	69.50	1	-	-	-	-	-	-	-	-
	Total First Class Career			90	154	14	5439	179	38.25	13	24	107	273.5	48	772	24	32.16	3-29
	Total O.D. Career			79	76	11	1942	137*	29.87	2	12	21	114	4	571	14	40.78	2-22

TINO LA BERTRAM BEST

D.O.B. 26.08.1981 - 3rd Avenue, Richmond Gap, St Michael, Barbados

First Class Debut	25.01.2002 - Barbados v Guyana
Test Match Debut	01.05.2003 - West Indies v Australia
Domestic O.D. Debut	19.06.2002 - West Indies "A" v Sri Lanka

Test 251-396

RHB / RFM

Teams Played For
Barbados
West Indies
West Indies "A"
W.I. President's XI

SEASON	TEAM	COMPETITION	V	M	I	No	BATTING RUNS	H.S.	Av	100s	50s	CT	BOWLING OV	MD	RUNS	W	Av	B.B.
2001-2003	Barbados	First Class Matches	II	14	16	9	57	12*	8.14	-	-	4	299.2	62	1125	56	20.08	5-37
2003//	WEST INDIES	TEST MATCHES	HA	1	2	1	20	20*	20.00	-	-	-	20	1	99	0	-	-
2002//	West Indies "A"	First Class Matches	A	3	1	0	8	8	8.00	-	-	-	69.4	14	249	6	41.50	2-40
2002//	West Indies "A"	O.A.L. O.D. Matches	A	4	2	1	1	1*	1.00	-	-	1	26	2	130	4	32.50	2-29
2002-2003	W.I. President's XI	First Class Matches	WI	1	1	0	18	18	18.00	-	-	-	22	5	62	1	62.00	1-50
		Total First Class Career		19	20	10	103	20*	10.30	0	0	4	411	68	1535	63	24.36	5-37
		Total O.D. Career		4	2	1	1	1*	1.00	0	0	1	26	2	130	4	32.50	2-29

NELSON BETANCOURT

D.O.B. 04.06.‑887 - Port of Spain, Trinidad (d. 12.10.1947)

First Class Debut 14.08.1905 - Trinidad v Jamaica

Test Match Debut 01.02.1903 - West Indies v England

	Test	23-5	Teams Played For	2	RHB
			Trinidad		
			West Indies		

						BATTING						BOWLING				
SEASON	TEAM	COMPETITION	V	M	I	No	RUNS	H.S.	Av	100s	50s	CT	OV	MD	RUNS	W	Av	B.B.
1905-1930	Trinidad	First Class Matches	H	16	28	5	359	71*	15.60	-	1	7	27	4	98	1	98.00	1-65
1930//	WEST INDIES	TEST MATCHES	H	1	2	0	52	39	26.00	-	-	1	-	-	-	-	-	-
1912-1913	West Indies	First Class Matches	H	1	1	0	31	31	31.00	-	-	1	-	-	-	-	-	-
Total First Class Career				18	31	5	442	71*	17.00	0	1	8	27	4	98	1	98.00	1-65

ALFRED PHILLIP BINNS

D.O.B. 24.07.1929 - Kingston, Jamaica
First Class Debut 25.01.1950 - Jamaica v Trinidad
Test Match Debut 21.01.1953 - West Indies v India

Test 74-43

Teams Played For
Jamaica
West Indies

RHB / WK

SEASON	TEAM	COMPETITION	V	M	I	No	BATTING RUNS	H.S.	Av	100s	50s	CT/ST	BOWLING OV	MD	RUNS	W	Av	B.B.
1950:1957	Jamaica	First Class Matches	II	17	30	3	1265	157	46.85	4	4	29/12	2	-	-	-	-	-
1953-1956	WEST INDIES	TEST MATCHES	HA	5	8	1	64	27	9.14	-	-	14/3	-	-	-	-	-	-
1955-1956	West Indies	First Class Matches	A	3	5	0	117	34	23.40	-	-	5/2	-	-	-	-	-	-
	Total First Class Career			25	43	4	1446	157	37.07	4	4	48/17	-	-	-	-	-	-

LIONEL SIDNEY BIRKETT

D.O.B. 14.04.1905 - Strathclyde, St Michael, Barbados (d. 16.01.1998)
First Class Debut 21.01.1925 - Barbados v Jamaica
Test Match Debut 12.12.1930 - West Indies v Australia

Test 30-8

Teams Played For 6   RHB / RAM
Barbados, Trinidad
British Guiana
West Indies
Combined B/J XI
R.S. Grant's XI

SEASON	TEAM	COMPETITION	V	M	I	No	BATTING RUNS	H.S.	Av	100s	50s	CT	BOWLING OV	MD	RUNS	W	Av	B.B.
1925-1929	Barbados	First Class Matches	=	6	7	1	190	62*	31.66	-	1	8	60.3	16	134	7	19.14	2-6
1930.1939	Trinidad	First Class Matches	=	4	6	0	517	253	86.16	2	1	3	48	10	119	0	-	-
1945//	British Guiana	First Class Matches	=	1	2	0	52	34	26.00	-	-	1	5	1	12	0	-	-
1931//	WEST INDIES	TEST MATCHES	A	4	8	0	136	64	17.00	-	1	4	21	1	71	1	17.00	1-16
1930-31//	West Indies	First Class Matches	A	7	12	1	363	128*	33.00	1	-	6	35	1	134	1	134.00	1-101
1928//	Combined B/J XI	First Class Matches	WI	2	4	0	14	14	3.50	-	-	-	7	1	26	0	-	-
1939//	R.S. Grant's XI	First Class Matches	WI	2	3	1	23	14	11.50	-	-	-	5	2	8	0	-	-
Total First Class Career				26	42	3	1295	253	33.20	3	3	22	181.3	32	504	9	56.00	2-6

IAN RAPHAEL BISHOP

D.O.B. 24.10.1967 - Belmont, Port of Spain, Trinidad

First Class Debut	03.04.1987 - Trinidad & Tobago v Guyana
Test Match Debut	25.03.1989 - West Indies v India
O.D.I. Debut	21.05.1988 - West Indies v England
Domestic O.D. Debut	01.04.1987 - Trinidad & Tobago v Guyana

Test 194-270
O.D.I. 54-161

Teams Played For 8
Trinidad & Tobago
West Indies, W.I. President's XI
W.I. Board XI, West Indies U23
West Indies "A", Derbyshire
M.C.C.

RHB / RAF

SEASON	TEAM	COMPETITION	V	M	I	No	BATTING RUNS	H.S.	Av	100s	50s	CT	BOWLING OV	MD	RUNS	W	Av	B.B.
1987-1999	Trinidad & Tobago	First Class Matches	II	38	59	14	769	111	17.08	1	2	19	990.1	151	2987	138	21.64	6-41
1987-1999	Trinidad & Tobago	Domestic O.D. Matches	II	29	15	7	246	39	30.75	-	-	7	211.1	23	904	32	28.25	3-10
1997//	Trinidad & Tobago	O.A.L. O.D. Matches	WI	1	1	0	53	53	53.00	-	1	1	10	0	35	1	35.00	1-35
1989-1998	WEST INDIES	TEST MATCHES	HA	43	63	11	632	48	12.15	-	-	8	1401.1	287	3909	161	24.27	6-40
1988-1997	West Indies	First Class Matches	A	24	24	5	242	35	12.73	-	-	7	538.1	94	1756	60	29.66	6-39
1988-1995	W.I. President's XI	First Class Matches	WI	2	1	1	0	0*	-	-	-	1	45	8	147	2	73.50	1-39
1988//	W.I. Board XI	First Class Matches	WI	1	1	1	6	6*	-	-	-	-	35	2	140	3	46.66	3-100
1988//	West Indies U23	First Class Matches	WI	1	2	1	0	0*	0.00	-	-	1	42.4	9	153	4	38.25	3-52
1998-1999	West Indies "A"	First Class Matches	A	5	4	0	89	39	22.25	-	-	4	147.1	30	411	17	24.17	4-38
1988-1997	WEST INDIES	O.D.I. MATCHES	HA	84	44	19	405	33*	16.20	-	-	12	722	49	3127	118	26.50	2-25
1998-1999	West Indies "A"	O.D.(I.) Matches	A	6	4	0	53	30	13.25	-	-	2	48	2	224	4	56.00	1-20
1998-1997	West Indies	O.A.L. O.D. Matches	A	10	7	2	79	24	15.80	-	-	1	80	-	373	7	53.28	3-21
1989-1992	Derbyshire	First Class Matches	E	45	57	8	901	103*	18.38	1	1	10	1227.3	274	3162	164	19.28	7-34
1992//	Derbyshire	Nat West Trophy	E	2	2	0	6	6	3.00	-	-	-	22	3	61	0	-	-
1992-1993	Derbyshire	Benson & Hedges Cup	E	6	5	1	80	42	20.00	-	-	-	64	-	184	10	18.40	4-30
1989-1992	Derbyshire	Sunday League	E	15	9	4	119	36*	23.80	-	-	-	110.2	-	480	20	24.00	3-18
1990//	Derbyshire	O.A.L. O.D. Matches	E	1	D	-	-	-	-	-	-	-	11	-	44	1	44.00	1-44
1996//	M.C.C.	O.A.L. O.D. Matches	E	1	1	0	6	6	6.00	-	-	-	10	-	42	1	42.00	1-42
Total First Class Career				159	211	41	2639	111	15.52	2	3	50	4425.4	855	12665	549	23.06	7-34
Total O.D. Career				155	88	33	1047	53	19.03	0	1	23	1288.3		5474	194	28.21	5-25

MARLON IAN BLACK   RHB / RAFM

D.O.B. 07.06.1975 - Dow Village, California, Trinidad
First Class Debut 07.01.1994 - Trinidad & Tobago v Windward Islands
Test Match Debut 23.11.2000 - West Indies v Australia
O.D.I. Debut 14.01.2001 - West Indies v Australia
Domestic O.D. Debut 05.01.1994 - Trinidad & Tobago v Windward Islands

Test 236-635
O.D.I. 104-410

Teams Played For 7
Trinidad & Tobago, West Indies
W.I. President's XI
W.I. Board XI
W.I. Select XI
West Indies "A", Carib Cup XI

SEASON	TEAM	COMPETITION	V	M	I	No	BATTING RUNS	H.S.	Av	100s	50s	CT	BOWLING OV	MD	RUNS	W	Av	B.B.
1993-2003	Trinidad & Tobago	First Class Matches	II	26	34	14	146	21*	7.30	-	-	1	688.1	132	2415	97	24.89	6-23
1993-2002	Trinidad & Tobago	Domestic O.D. Matches	II	14	9	5	33	12*	8.25	-	-	3	107	9	371	15	24.73	4-14
2000-2002	WEST INDIES	TEST MATCHES	HA	6	11	3	21	6	2.62	-	-	-	159	27	597	12	49.75	4-83
2000-2001	West Indies	First Class Matches	A	5	6	0	22	11	3.66	-	-	2	137.2	35	455	17	26.76	6-35
1998-2000	W.I. President's XI	First Class Matches	WI	2	4	1	15	7	5.00	-	-	-	44	12	139	4	34.75	4-87
1999-2000	W.I. Board XI	First Class Matches	WI	1	1	1	12	12*	-	-	-	-	25	3	98	2	49.00	2-98
1999-2000	W.I. Select XI	First Class Matches	WI	1	1	1	19	19*	-	-	-	-	8	1	31	0	-	-
1999-2002	West Indies "A"	First Class Matches	HA	6	6	0	34	16	5.66	-	-	3	179.1	47	496	18	27.55	4-32
2000-2002	WEST INDIES	O.D.I. MATCHES	A	5	2	0	4	4	2.00	-	-	-	38	1	196	0	-	-
2002	West Indies "A"	O.A.L. O.D. Matches	A	4	2	2	3	3*	-	-	-	-	28	2	132	3	44.00	1-28
1999-2000	West Indies "A"	O.D.(I.) Matches	H	1	1	0	2	2	2.00	-	-	-	8	4	17	4	4.25	4-17
2000-2001	West Indies	O.A.L. O.D. Matches	A	1	1	0	-	-	-	-	-	-	7	0	31	1	31.00	1-31
2002-2003	Carib Cup XI	First Class Matches	WI	1	1	0	0	0	0.00	-	-	1	22	1	95	1	95.00	1-24
Total First Class Career				48	64	20	269	21*	6.11	-	-	7	1262.4	258	4326	151	28.64	6-23
Total O. D. Career				25	14	7	42	12*	6.00	0	0	3	188	16	747	23	32.47	4-14

KEITH DAVID BOYCE

D.O.B. 11.10.1943 - Castle, St Peter, Barbados (d. 11.10.1996)

First Class Debut	25.02.1965 - Barbados v Cavaliers XI
Test Match Debut	19.03.1971 - West Indies v India
O.D.I. Debut	05.09.1973 - West Indies v England
Domestic O.D. Debut	13.05.1967 - Essex v Kent

Test 137-131
O.D.I. 8-1

Teams Played For
Barbados, West Indies, W.I. President's XI, Essex, M.C.C., World XI, Commonwealth XI, T.N. Pearce's XI

RHB / RAFM

SEASON	TEAM	COMPETITION	V	M	I	No	RUNS	H.S.	Av	100s	50s	CT	OV	MD	RUNS	W	Av	B.B.
							BATTING						BOWLING					
1965-1975	Barbados	First Class Matches	II	22	34	3	795	112	25.64	1	4	17	502.3	85	1506	58	25.96	5-26
1972-1976	Barbados	Domestic O.D. Matches	II	5	5	0	97	80	19.40	-	1	1	32.5	4	127	6	21.16	2-46
1971-1976	WEST INDIES	TEST MATCHES	HA	21	30	3	657	95*	24.33	-	4	5	541.3	99	1801	60	30.01	6-77
1973-1976	West Indies	First Class Matches	A	18	19	2	264	87	15.52	-	1	8	406.5	59	1388	49	28.32	5-45
1971//	W.I. President's XI	First Class Matches	WI	1	1	0	41	41	41.00	-	-	-	34	11	71	2	35.50	2-19
1973-1975	WEST INDIES	O.D.I. MATCHES	HA	8	4	0	57	34	14.25	-	-	-	78.2	4	313	13	24.07	4-50
1973-1975	West Indies	O.A.L. O.D. Matches	A	3	2	0	38	20	19.00	-	-	2	25.5	-	90	6	15.00	3-20
1966-1977	Essex	First Class Matches	E	211	319	18	6848	147*	22.75	3	37	181	5584.3	1058	15704	662	23.72	9-61
1967-1974	Essex	Nat West Trophy	E	13	11	0	185	47	16.81	-	-	4	129	29	316	26	12.15	5-22
1972-1977	Essex	Benson & Hedges Cup	E	26	20	0	341	123	17.05	1	0	7	260.2	44	738	38	19.42	4-18
1969-1977	Essex	Sunday League	E	108	100	6	1677	98	17.84	-	6	30	780.1	-	2720	179	15.19	8-26
1969-1977	Essex	O.A.L. O.D. Matches	E	2	1	0	46	46	46.00	-	-	-						
1970//	M.C.C.	First Class Matches	E	1	2	0	22	18	11.00	-	-	1	15.3	3	48	1	48.00	1-19
1971-1972	T.N. Pearce's XI	First Class Matches	E	2	2	0	29	25	14.50	-	-	-	34.4	5	121	3	40.33	2-23
1967-1968	Commonwealth XI	First Class Matches	A	7	9	1	90	23	11.25	-	-	2	128	26	487	13	37.46	3-53
1973-1974	World XI	First Class Matches	A	2	4	0	54	40	13.50	-	-	1	53	5	198	4	49.50	3-32
Total First Class Career				285	420	27	8800	147*	22.39	4	46	215	7300.3	1351	21324	852	25.02	9-61
Total O.D. Career				165	143	6	2441	123	17.81	1	7	44	1306.3	-	4304	268	16.05	8-26

GARETH ROHAN BREESE

D.O.B. 09.01.1976 - Montego Bay, St. James, Jamaica
First Class Debut 16.02.1996 - Jamaica v Barbados
Test Match Debut 17.10.2002 - West Indies v India
Domestic O.D. Debut 18.10.1996 - Jamaica v Trinidad & Tobago

Test	244-390	Teams Played For	4	RHB / RAOB
		Jamaica		
		West Indies		
		West Indies "A"		
		Busta Cup XI		

							BATTING						BOWLING					
SEASON	TEAM	COMPETITION	V	M	I	No	RUNS	H.S.	Av	100s	50s	CT	OV	MD	RUNS	W	Av	B.B.
1995-2003	Jamaica	First Class Matches	=	37	58	9	1384	124	28.24	1	10	27	1187	342	2593	121	21.42	7-60
1996-2002	Jamaica	Domestic O.D. Matches	=	13	9	2	157	44*	22.42	-	4	4	88	9	314	13	24.15	3-24
1998-2000	Jamaica	O.A.L. O.D. Matches	HA	3	3	0	16	13	5.33	-	-	1	23	0	97	2	48.50	1-25
2002/I	WEST INDIES	TEST MATCHES	A	1	2	0	5	5	2.50	-	-	1	31.2	3	135	2	67.50	2-108
2002/I	West Indies	First Class Matches	A	1	1	1	57	57*	-	-	-	-	31	3	102	2	51.00	2-102
2002/I	West Indies "A"	First Class Matches	A	2	3	1	92	54	46.00	-	1	-	29.5	2	104	3	34.66	1-6
2001-2002	Busta Cup XI	First Class Matches	WI	1	1	0	15	15	15.00	-	1	1	25.1	7	60	3	20.00	2-19
2002/I	West Indies "A"	O.A.L. O.D. Matches	A	3	3	1	44	16	22.00	-	-	2	13	0	78	2	39.00	1-19
	Total First Class Career			42	65	11	1553	124	28.75	1	12	29	1304.2	364	2994	131	22.85	7-60
	Total O.D. Career			19	15	3	217	44*	18.08	0	0	7	124	9	489	17	28.76	3-24

DARRYL BROWN

D.O.B. 18.12.1973 - McBean, Couva, Trinidad

First Class Debut	12.11.1999 - Trinidad & Tobago v India "A"
O.D.I. Debut	16.12.2001 - West Indies v Zimbabwe
Domestic O.D. Debut	12.10.2000 - Trinidad & Tobago v Barbados

O.D.I. 108-436

Teams Played For Trinidad & Tobago, West Indies

RHB / RAM

2

BATTING

SEASON	TEAM	COMPETITION	V	M	I	No	RUNS	H.S.	Av	100s	50s	CT
1999-2001	Trinidad & Tobago	First Class Matches	II	11	19	0	226	47	11.89	-	-	7
2000-2002	Trinidad & Tobago	Domestic O.D. Matches	II	8	7	1	60	19	10.00	-	-	4
2001-2002	WEST INDIES	O.D.I. MATCHES	A	3	2	1	10	9	10.00	-	-	-
		Total First Class Career		11	19	0	226	47	11.89	0	0	7
		Total O.D. Career		11	9	2	70	19	10.00	0	0	4

BOWLING

OV	MD	RUNS	W	Av	B.B.
215.1	34	635	17	37.35	4-80
51.4	3	202	4	50.50	2-28
25	3	124	5	24.80	3-21
215.1	34	635	17	37.35	4-80
76.4	6	326	9	36.22	3-21

BARRINGTON ST. AUBYN BROWNE

D.O.B. 16.09.1967 - New Amsterdam, Berbice, Guyana
First Class Debut 30.10.1987 - Demerara v Berbice
O.D.I. Debut 20.10.1994 - West Indies v India
Domestic O.D. Debut 16.04.1987 - Guyana v Barbados

O.D.I. 69-279

Teams Played For 6
Guyana, Demerara
West Indies, W.I. President's XI
West Indies U23
M.C.C.

RHB / RF

SEASON	TEAM	COMPETITION	V	M	I	No	RUNS	H.S.	Av	100s	50s	CT	OV	MD	RUNS	W	Av	B.B.
1988-1997	Guyana	First Class Matches	II	35	48	17	167	29	5.38	-	-	9	841	150	2879	111	25.93	6-51
1987-1988	Demerara	First Class Matches	G	2	1	1	22	22*	-	-	-	-	14	1	70	1	70.00	1-70
1987-1996	Guyana	Domestic O.D. Matches	II	28	11	6	45	26*	9.00	-	-	3	189.3	27	788	27	29.18	2-9
1994-1995	West Indies	First Class Matches	A	2	2	2	1	1*	-	-	-	-	21	4	96	0	-	-
1987-1988	West Indies U23	First Class Matches	WI	1	2	0	19	19	9.50	-	-	1	42	2	136	3	45.33	2-39
1993-1994	W.I. President's XI	First Class Matches	WI	2	1	-	-	-	-	-	-	-	31	7	119	1	119.00	1-59
1994-1995	WEST INDIES	O.D.I. MATCHES	A	4	3	2	8	8*	8.00	-	-	-	30	0	156	2	78.00	2-50
1996//	M.C.C.	First Class Matches	E	1	D	-	-	-	-	-	-	-	29	7	111	1	111.00	1-55
Total First Class Career				43	53	20	209	29	6.33	0	0	10	978	171	3411	117	29.15	6-51
Total O.D. Career				32	14	8	53	26*	8.83	0	0	3	219.3	27	944	29	32.55	2-9

COURTNEY OSWALD BROWNE

RHB / WK

D.O.B. 07.12.1970 - Lambeth, London, England

First Class Debut	11.01.1991 - Barbados v Guyana
Test Match Debut	29.04.1995 - West Indies v Australia
O.D.I. Debut	11.10.1995 - West Indies v Sri Lanka
Domestic O.D. Debut	09.01.1991 - Barbados v Guyana

Teams Played For
Barbados, West Indies
West Indies U23, W.I. Board XI
West Indies "A", Busta Cup XI
W.I. President's XI

Test 209-314
O.D.I. 75-299

SEASON	TEAM	COMPETITION	V	M	I	No	RUNS	H.S.	Av	100s	50s	CT/ST	OV	MD	RUNS	W	Av	B.B.
													BATTING				BOWLING	
1991-2003	Barbados	First Class Matches	I	73	114	16	2828	161	28.85	3	14	217/26	-	-	-	-	-	-
1991-2002	Barbados	Domestic O.D. Matches	I	54	41	9	780	60*	24.37	-	4	55/13	-	-	-	-	-	-
1992-2000	Barbados	O.A.L. O.D. Matches	HA	9	9	4	178	39*	35.60	-	-	5	-	-	-	-	-	-
1995-2001	WEST INDIES	TEST MATCHES	HA	14	21	6	263	39*	17.53	-	-	63/1	-	-	-	-	-	-
1995-2001	West Indies	First Class Matches	A	18	24	6	768	102*	42.66	2	4	56/10	2	0	16	0	-	-
1993//	West Indies U23	First Class Matches	WI	1	2	0	47	44	23.50	-	-	1	-	-	-	-	-	-
1994-2000	W.I. Board XI	First Class Matches	WI	3	4	0	81	34	20.25	-	-	4/1	-	-	-	-	-	-
1998-2000	West Indies "A"	First Class Matches	HA	8	11	3	263	52*	32.87	-	1	24/4	-	-	-	-	-	-
1995-2001	WEST INDIES	O.D.I. MATCHES	HA	28	19	4	187	26	12.46	-	-	40/6	-	-	-	-	-	-
1998/2000	West Indies "A"	O.D.(L.) Matches	A	7	5	0	73	30	14.60	-	-	6/4	-	-	-	-	-	-
1995-1996	West Indies	O.A.L. O.D. Matches	A	3	2	0	49	26	24.50	-	-	2/2	-	-	-	-	-	-
2000-2001	Busta Cup XI	First Class Matches	WI	1	D	-	-	-	-	-	-	-	-	-	-	-	-	-
1999-2000	W.I. President's XI	First Class Matches	WI	1	2	0	6	6	3.00	-	-	1/1	-	-	-	-	-	-
Total First Class Career				119	178	31	4256	161	28.95	5	19	367/43	2	0	16	0	-	-
Total O.D. Career				101	76	17	1267	60*	21.47	0	4	108/25	-	-	-	-	-	-

CYRIL RUTHERFORD BROWNE

D.O.B. 08.10.1890 - Roberts Tenanty, St Michael, Barbados (d. 12.01.1964)

First Class Debut 13.01.1909 - Barbados v British Guiana

Test Match Debut 23.06.1928 - West Indies v England

	Test	2-1	Teams Played For	3	RHB / RM / LB
			Barbados		
			British Guiana		
			West Indies		

							BATTING						BOWLING				
SEASON	TEAM	COMPETITION	V	M	I	No	RUNS	H.S.	Av	100s	50s	CT	OV	MD	RUNS	W	Av	B.B.
1909-1911	Barbados	First Class Matches	=	7	9	1	73	19	9.12	-	-	10	246.4	59	584	44	13.27	6-60
1922-1939	British Guiana	First Class Matches	=	21	35	1	891	102	26.20	1	6	19	955.3	226	2071	104	19.91	8-58
1928-1930	WEST INDIES	TEST MATCHES	HA	4	8	1	176	70*	25.14	-	1	1	140	38	288	6	48.00	2-72
1910-1928	West Indies	First Class Matches	HA	42	63	8	937	103	17.03	2	3	29	1289.4	284	3285	124	26.48	7-97
		Total First Class Career		74	115	11	2077	103	19.97	3	10	59	2631.5	607	6228	278	22.40	8-58

HENDERSON RICARDO BRYAN

D.O.B. 17.03.1970 - Salmonds, St Lucy, Barbados

First Class Debut 20.01.1995 - Barbados v Guyana
O.D.I. Debut 11.04.1999 - West Indies v Australia
Domestic O.D. Debut 19.02.1995 - Barbados v Jamaica

O.D.I. 92-361

Teams Played For
Barbados
West Indies
Griqualand West

RHB / RAFM

3

SEASON	TEAM	COMPETITION	V	M	I	No	BATTING RUNS	H.S.	Av	100s	50s	CT	BOWLING OV	MD	RUNS	W	Av	B.B.
1995-2001	Barbados	First Class Matches	=	35	52	11	808	76*	19.70	-	2	18	999.2	240	2884	124	23.25	5-38
1995-2002	Barbados	Domestic O.D. Matches	=	24	13	2	107	57	9.72	-	1	9	199.2	14	814	40	20.35	4-31
1998//	Barbados	O.A.L. O.D. Matches	S	3	D	-	-	-	-	-	-	1	20	0	74	3	24.66	3-32
1998-2000	WEST INDIES	O.D.I. MATCHES	HA	15	8	2	43	11	7.16	-	-	4	120.2	6	518	12	43.16	3-36
1997-1998	Griqualand West	First Class Matches	SA	7	13	1	251	71	20.91	-	1	1	223	37	683	23	29.69	6-71
1997-1998	Griqualand West	Seaboad Bowl Series	SA	4	4	0	62	31	15.50	-	-	2	29.5	1	173	5	34.60	3-53
Total First Class Career				42	65	12	1059	76*	19.98	0	3	19	1222	277	3567	147	24.26	6-71
Total O.D. Career				46	25	4	212	57	10.09	0	1	16	369.3	21	1579	60	26.31	4-24

BASIL FITZHERBERT BUTCHER

D.O.B. 03.09.1933 - No 10 Sugar Estate, Port Mourant, Berbice, British Guiana

First Class Debut 29.01.1955 - British Guiana v Barbados
Test Match Debut 28.11.1958 - West Indies v India
Domestic O.D. Debut 13.04.1973 - Guyana v Jamaica

Test 103-72

Teams Played For 7
British Guiana/Guyana
Berbice, West Indies
F.M. Worrell's XI
Commonwealth XI
World XI, Indian President's XI

RHB / RLB

SEASON	TEAM	COMPETITION	V	M	I	No	BATTING RUNS	H.S.	Av	100s	50s	CT	BOWLING OV	MD	RUNS	W	Av	B.B.
1955-1971	Br. Guiana/Guyana	First Class Matches	II	35	55	4	2979	203*	58.41	12	7	13	152.1	33	424	10	42.40	4-30
1959-1971	Berbice	First Class Matches	G	3	4	1	234	131*	78.00	1	1	1	14	3	30	2	15.00	2-30
1972-1973	Guyana	Domestic O.D. Matches	II	1	1	0	8	8	8.00	-	-	-	2	0	10	1	10.00	1-10
1958-1969	WEST INDIES	TEST MATCHES	HA	44	78	6	3104	209*	43.11	7	16	15	42.4	15	90	5	18.00	1-10
1958-1969	West Indies	First Class Matches	HA	74	103	16	4520	172	51.95	10	25	31	114.3	9	500	21	23.80	4-58
1963-1964	F.M. Worrell's XI	First Class Matches	WI	1	2	0	157	108	78.50	1	-	-	-	-	-	-	-	-
1963-69	West Indies	O.A.L. O.D. Matches	A	4	3	1	99	57	49.50	-	1	1	-	-	-	-	-	-
1963-1965	Commonwealth XI	First Class Matches	A	7	10	1	344	95	38.22	-	3	3	24.4	5	108	2	54.00	1-5
1968//	World XI	First Class Matches	E	4	8	1	241	70	34.42	-	2	3	15	1	65	0	-	-
1963//	Indian President's XI	First Class Matches	I	1	2	0	49	37	24.50	-	-	1	-	-	-	-	-	-
Total First Class Career				169	262	29	11628	209*	49.90	31	54	67	363	66	1217	40	30.42	5-34
Total O.D. Career				5	4	1	107	57	35.66	0	1	1	2	0	10	1	10.00	1-10

ROLAND ORLANDO BUTCHER

RHB / RM

D.O.B. 14.10.1953 - East Point, St Philip, Barbados

First Class Debut 22.06.1974 - Middlesex v Yorkshire
Test Match Debut 13.03.1981 - England v West Indies
O.D.I. Debut 22.08.1980 - England v Australia
Domestic O.D. Debut 28.07.1974 - Middlesex v Essex

Teams Played For
Barbados, Middlesex, Tasmania, England, M.C.C., International XI, T.N. Pearce's XI

7

SEASON	TEAM	COMPETITION	V	M	I	No	BATTING RUNS	H.S.	Av	100s	50s	CT/ST	BOWLING OV	MD	RUNS	W	Av	B.B.
1974-1975	Barbados	First Class Matches	II	1	2	0	67	38	34.50	-	-	-	-	-	-	-	-	-
1980-1981	ENGLAND	TEST MATCHES	A	3	5	0	71	32	14.20	-	-	3	-	-	-	-	-	-
1980-1981	England	First Class Matches	A	4	8	2	314	77*	52.33	-	2	4	-	-	-	-	-	-
1974-1990	Middlesex	First Class Matches	E	251	383	38	10935	197	31.69	17	59	265	44.1	9	161	4	40.25	2-37
1980-1981	ENGLAND	O.D.I. Matches	A	3	3	0	58	52	19.33	-	1	-	-	-	-	-	-	-
1975-1990	Middlesex	Nat West Trophy	E	33	29	5	527	65	21.95	-	4	11	2	0	18	1	18.00	1-18
1975-1990	Middlesex	Benson & Hedges Cup	E	43	40	3	811	85	21.91	-	6	8	-	-	-	-	-	-
1974-1990	Middlesex	Sunday League	E	180	162	17	3288	100	22.67	1	15	62	1.2	0	5	0	-	-
1988//	Middlesex	Sunday League Cup	E	1	1	0	14	14	14.00	-	-	-	-	-	-	-	-	-
1981-1987	Middlesex	O.A.L. O.D. Matches	E	4	2	0	112	69	56.00	-	1	2	-	-	-	-	-	-
1976//	T.N. Pearce's XI	First Class Matches	E	1	2	1	54	54*	54.00	-	1	-	-	-	-	-	-	-
1987//	M.C.C.	First Class Matches	E	1	2	0	50	25	25.00	-	-	-	-	-	-	-	-	-
1981-1983	International XI	First Class Matches	A	4	7	0	107	35	15.28	-	-	4/1	3	1	12	0	-	-
1980-1981	England	O.A.L. O.D. Matches	A	3	2	0	53	44	26.50	-	-	-	-	-	-	-	-	-
1981//	International XI	O.A.L. O.D. Matches	A	3	3	0	16	13	5.33	-	-	-	-	-	-	-	-	-
1982-1983	Tasmania	First Class Matches	A	12	19	2	423	53	24.88	-	3	12	4	1	9	0	-	-
1982-1983	Tasmania	MacDonald Cup	A	2	2	0	11	7	5.50	-	-	2	1	0	16	0	-	-
1982-1983	Tasmania	O.A.L. O.D. Matches	A	1	1	0	9	9	9.00	-	-	-	-	-	-	-	-	-
Total First Class Career				277	428	43	12021	197	31.22	17	65	290/1	51.1	11	182	4	45.50	2-37
Total O.D. Career				273	245	25	4899	100	22.26	1	27	83	4.2	0	39	1	39.00	1-18

LENNOX STEPHEN BUTLER

D.O.B.   09.02.1929 - Woodbrook, Port of Spain, Trinidad

First Class Debut   23.02.1949 - Trinidad v Barbados

Test Match Debut   11.04.1955 - West Indies v Australia

	Teams Played For		
Test 87-54	Trinidad	2	RHB / RFM
	West Indies		

SEASON	TEAM	COMPETITION	V	M	I	No	RUNS	H.S.	Av	100s	50s	CT	OV	MD	RUNS	W	Av	B.B.
							BATTING						BOWLING					
1949-1956	Trinidad	First Class Matches	H	10	14	4	145	44	14.50	-	-	2	339.2	110	816	27	30.22	5-89
1954 -1955	WEST INDIES	TEST MATCHES	H	1	1	0	16	16	16.00	-	-	-	40	7	151	2	75.50	2-151
		Total First Class Career		11	15	4	161	44	14.63	0	0	2	379.2	117	967	29	33.24	5-89

CLYDE GODFREY BUTTS

D.O.B. 08.07.1957 - Perseverance, Demerara, British Guiana

First Class Debut 23.01.1981 - Guyana v Trinidad & Tobago
Test Match Debut 06.04.1985 - West Indies v New Zealand
Domestic O.D. Debut 18.01.1984 - Guyana v Jamaica

Test 184-239

RBH / ROS 6

Teams Played For: Guyana, Demerara, West Indies, West Indies "B", W.I. Board XI, Shell Awards XI

SEASON	TEAM	COMPETITION	V	M	I	No	BATTING						BOWLING					
							RUNS	H.S.	Av	100s	50s	CT	OV	MD	RUNS	W	Av	B.B.
1981-1994	Guyana	First Class Matches	II	61	79	12	905	47	13.50	-	-	26	2742.4	709	6142	274	22.41	7-29
1981-1989	Demerara	First Class Matches	G	7	6	1	129	38	25.80	-	-	9	318.1	111	590	30	19.66	7-56
1984-1994	Guyana	Domestic O.D. Matches	II	27	19	8	195	37*	17.72	-	-	7	238	32	670	26	25.76	4-25
1985-1987	WEST INDIES	TEST MATCHES	HA	7	8	1	108	38	18.00	-	-	2	259	70	595	10	59.50	4-73
1986-1987	West Indies	First Class Matches	A	8	7	2	125	57*	25.00	-	1	4	198.4	39	569	18	31.61	4-31
1983-1984	West Indies "B"	First Class Matches	A	2	4	0	109	51	27.25	-	1	1	66	13	226	6	37.66	3-58
1984-1985	Shell Awards XI	First Class Matches	WI	1	1	0	7	7	7.00	-	-	-	61.3	13	126	7	18.00	7-90
1987-1988	W.I. Board XI	First Class Matches	WI	1	1	0	48	48	48.00	-	-	-	67	13	173	3	57.66	2-66
1983-1984	West Indies "B"	O.D.(I.) Matches	A	4	3	1	21	19	10.50	-	-	1	40	2	175	6	29.16	2-48
1987-1988	West Indies	O.A.L. O.D. Matches	A	1	D	-	-	-	-	-	-	-	10	2	26	0	-	-
		Total First Class Career		87	106	16	1431	57*	15.90	0	2	42	3713	968	8421	348	24.19	7-29
		Total O.D. Career		32	22	9	216	37*	16.61	0	0	8	288	36	871	32	27.28	4-25

MICHAEL ROBIN BYNOE

D.O.B. 23.02.1947 - Alleynedale, Black Rock, St. Michael, Barbados

First Class Debut 11.01.1958 - Barbados v Pakistan

Test Match Debut 26.03.1959 - West Indies v Pakistan

Domestic O.D. Debut 14.04.1973 - Barbados v Trinidad

	Test	Teams Played For		RHB / SLA
	106-79	Barbados	2	
		West Indies		

								BATTING						BOWLING					
SEASON	TEAM	COMPETITION	V	M	I	No	RUNS	H.S.	Av	100s	50s	CT	OV	MD	RUNS	W	Av	B.B.
1958-1972	Barbados	First Class Matches	=	37	64	5	2676	190	45.35	6	15	26	40	6	117	2	58.50	2-6
1972-1973	Barbados	Domestic O.D. Matches	=	2	2	0	45	40	22.50	-	-	-	4	0	33	1	33.00	1-33
1969//	Barbados	O.A.L. O.D. Matches	A	1	1	0	37	37	37.00	-	-	-	9	0	62	2	31.00	2-62
1959-1967	WEST INDIES	TEST MATCHES	A	4	6	0	111	48	18.50	-	-	4	5	4	5	1	5.00	1-5
1959-1967	West Indies	First Class Matches	A	15	27	5	785	96*	35.68	-	5	15	36	8	124	6	20.66	2-21
		Total First Class Career		56	97	10	3572	190	41.05	6	20	45	81	18	246	9	27.23	2-6
		Total O.D. Career		3	3	0	82	40	27.33	0	0	0	13	0	95	3	31.66	2-62

GEORGE STEPHEN CAMACHO

D.O.B. 15.10.1945 - Georgetown, British Guiana

First Class Debut	07.04.1965 - British Guiana v Australia
Test Match Debut	19.01.1968 - West Indies v England
Domestic O.D. Debut	13.04.1973 - Guyana v Jamaica

Test 126-113

Teams Played For
British Guiana/Guyana
Demerara
West Indies
W.I. President's XI

RHB / LBG

SEASON	TEAM	COMPETITION	V	M	I	No	BATTING RUNS	H.S.	Av	100s	50s	CT	BOWLING OV	MD	RUNS	W	Av	B.B.
1964-1979	Br. Guiana/Guyana	First Class Matches	II	35	53	4	1758	144	35.87	3	14	16	46	13	100	6	16.66	3-10
1971-1978	Demerara	First Class Matches	G	4	5	0	351	166	70.20	2	0	7	13	2	29	0	-	-
1972-1978	Guyana	Domestic O.D. Matches	II	5	4	1	35	13	11.66	-	-	-	-	-	-	-	-	-
1968-1971	WEST INDIES	TEST MATCHES	HA	11	22	0	640	87	29.09	0	4	4	3	1	12	0	-	-
1968-1973	West Indies	First Class Matches	A	24	41	4	1126	102	30.43	2	5	18	16	2	53	1	53.00	1-2
1968-1971	W.I. President's XI	First Class Matches	WI	2	4	0	204	85	51.00	-	1	2	5	1	22	1	22.00	1-22
1969//	West Indies	O.A.L. O.D. Matches	A	1	1	0	51	51	51.00	-	1	-	-	-	-	-	-	-
Total First Class Career				76	125	8	4079	166	34.86	7	24	47	83	19	216	8	27.00	3-10
Total O.D. Career				6	5	1	86	51	21.50	0	1	0	-	-	-	-	-	-

FRANCIS JAMES CAMERON

D.O.B. 22.06.1923 - Kingston, Jamaica, (d. 10.06.1994)
First Class Debut 03.07.1946 - Jamaica v Trinidad
Test Match Debut 10.11.1948 - West Indies v India

Test 68-27

Teams Played For
Jamaica
West Indies
Canada

3

RHB / ROB

SEASON	TEAM	COMPETITION	V	M	I	No	BATTING RUNS	H.S.	Av	100s	50s	CT	BOWLING OV	MD	RUNS	W	Av	B.B.
1946-1960	Jamaica	First Class Matches	=	3	4	0	94	50	23.50	-	1	-	72.2	11	222	9	24.66	3-56
1948-1949	WEST INDIES	TEST MATCHES	A	5	7	1	151	75*	25.16	-	1	-	131	34	278	3	92.66	2-74
1948-1949	West Indies	First Class Matches	A	9	10	3	179	50	25.27	-	1	7	246.2	51	654	15	43.60	4-52
1954//	Canada	First Class Matches	E	4	6	1	127	39	25.40	-	-	2	66	7	257	2	128.50	2-61
Total First Class Career				21	27	5	551	75*	25.04	0	3	9	515.4	103	1411	29	48.65	4-52

JOHN HEMSLEY CAMERON

D.O.B. 08.04.1914 - Kingston, Jamaica (d. 13.02.2000)

First Class Debut 27.08.1932 - Somerset v Warwickshire
Test Match Debut 24.06.1939 - West Indies v England

Test 45-20

Teams Played For
Jamaica, West Indies
Somerset
Gentlemen's XI
Cambridge University
Combined Universities XI

RHB / OB / LBG
6

SEASON	TEAM	COMPETITION	V	M	I	No	BATTING						BOWLING					
							RUNS	H.S.	Av	100s	50s	CT	OV	MD	RUNS	W	Av	B.B.
1946//	Jamaica	First Class Matches	=	1	1	0	9	9	9.00	-	-	-	19.1	3	44	4	11.00	3-32
1939//	WEST INDIES	TEST MATCHES	A	2	3	0	6	5	2.00	-	-	-	29	6	88	3	29.33	3-66
1939//	West Indies	First Class Matches	A	15	20	2	432	106	21.60	1	1	5	193.6	34	576	28	20.57	6-57
1932-1947	Somerset	First Class Matches	E	48	80	6	1373	113	18.37	3	1	31	555.2	79	1965	45	43.67	6-143
1934-1937	Cambridge University	First Class Matches	E	36	55	3	792	50	15.23	-	1	25	789.1	85	2824	99	28.53	7-73
1938-39//	Combined Universities	First Class Matches	WI	2	4	1	116	62	38.66	-	1	-	36.3	1	120	5	24.00	3-51
1935//	Gentlemen's XI	First Class Matches	E	1	1	-	44	44	44.00	-	-	2	9	1	45	0	-	-
	Total First Class Career			105	164	12	2772	113	18.23	4	4	63	1632.1	209	5662	184	30.77	7-73

SHEWIN LEGAY CAMPBELL

D.O.B. 01.11.1970 - Belleplaine, St Andrew, Barbados
First Class Debut 11.01.1991 - Barbados v Guyana
Test Match Debut 03.02.1995 - West Indies v New Zealand
O.D.I. Debut 23.10.1994 - West Indies v India
Domestic O.D. Debut 10.01.1990 - Barbados v Jamaica

Test	208-309
O.D.I.	70-280

Teams Played For Barbados, West Indies
W.I. Board XI
West Indies "A"
Durham
Busta Cup XI

6   RHB / RAM

SEASON	TEAM	COMPETITION	V	M	I	No	RUNS	H.S.	Av	100s	50s	CT	OV	MD	RUNS	W	Av	B.B.
1991-2003	Barbados	First Class Matches	II	54	98	9	3418	169*	38.40	11	15	66	7	3	15	0	-	-
1990-2001	Barbados	Domestic O.D. Matches	II	36	35	4	868	102	28.00	1	4	20	11.3	1	43	1	43.00	1-1
1992-1998	Barbados	O.A.L. O.D. Matches	HA	7	7	0	229	61	32.71	-	3	1	1	0	2	0	-	-
1995-2002	WEST INDIES	TEST MATCHES	HA	52	93	4	2882	208	32.38	4	18	47	-	-	-	-	-	-
1994-2001	West Indies	First Class Matches	A	28	46	3	2109	172	49.04	9	7	17	20	6	54	0	-	-
1993-1996	W.I. Board XI	First Class Matches	WI	3	6	1	175	81	35.00	-	2	4	-	-	-	-	-	-
1998-1999	West Indies "A"	First Class Matches	HA	5	9	1	134	40	16.75	-	-	6	-	-	-	-	-	-
2000-2001	Busta Cup XI	First Class Matches	WI	1	2	0	141	86	70.50	-	2	2	-	-	-	-	-	-
1994-2001	WEST INDIES	O.D.I. MATCHES	HA	90	87	0	2283	105	26.24	2	14	23	32.4	0	170	8	21.25	4-30
1998-1999	West Indies "A"	O.D.I.(I.) Matches	A	3	3	0	99	60	33.00	-	1	2	-	-	-	-	-	-
1995-2001	West Indies	O.A.L. O.D. Matches	A	7	7	0	52	19	7.42	-	4	4	0.5	0	5	0	-	-
1998//	West Indies "A"	O.A.L. O.D. Matches	A	1	1	0	49	49	49.00	-	-	-	-	-	-	-	-	-
1996//	Durham	First Class Matches	E	16	29	0	1041	118	35.89	1	7	15	16.4	3	60	1	60.00	1-38
1996//	Durham	Nat West Trophy	E	2	2	0	66	39	33.00	-	1	1	1	0	17	0	-	-
1996//	Durham	Benson & Hedges Cup	E	2	2	0	27	27	13.50	-	-	1	-	-	-	-	-	-
1996//	Durham	Sunday League	E	15	15	0	455	77	30.33	-	3	4	5.3	1	34	0	-	-
Total First Class Career				159	283	18	9900	208	37.35	25	51	157	43.4	12	129	1	129.00	1-38
Total O.D. Career				163	159	4	4128	105	26.63	3	25	56	52.3	2	271	9	30.11	4-30

271

GEORGE McDONALD CAREW

D.O.B. 04.06.1970 - Halls Road, St Michael, Barbados (d. 09.12.1974)

First Class Debut 21.09.1934 - Barbados v British Guiana
Test Match Debut 08.01.1935 - West Indies v England

Test 37-16

Teams Played For
Barbados
West Indies

RHB / LS

SEASON	TEAM	COMPETITION	V	M	I	No	BATTING RUNS	H.S.	Av	100s	50s	CT	BOWLING OV	MD	RUNS	W	Av	B.B.
1934-1948	Barbados	First Class Matches	II	23	42	4	1288	100	33.89	1	7	13	119.2	16	485	9	53.88	2-26
1935-1949	WEST INDIES	TEST MATCHES	HA	4	7	1	170	107	28.33	1	-	1	3	2	2	0	-	-
1939-1949	West Indies	First Class Matches	HA	12	20	2	673	100	37.38	1	5	3	47	15	113	4	28.25	2-6
		Total First Class Career		39	69	7	2131	107	34.37	3	12	17	169.2	33	600	13	46.15	2-6

MICHAEL CONRAD CAREW

D.O.B. 15.09.1937 - Woodbrook, Port of Spain, Trinidad
First Class Debut 31.03.1956 - Trinidad v E.W. Swantons XI
Test Match Debut 06.06.1963 - West Indies v England
Domestic O.D. Debut 14.04.1973 - Trinidad & Tobago v Barbados

Test 120-95

Teams Played For 5   LHB / RM / OB
Trinidad & Tobago,
North Trinidad
West Indies
F.M. Worrell's XI
The Rest XI

SEASON	TEAM	COMPETITION	V	M	I	No	BATTING RUNS	H.S.	Av	100s	50s	CT	BOWLING OV	MD	RUNS	W	Av	B.B.
1956-1973	Trinidad & Tobago	First Class Matches	II	40	67	5	2737	164	44.14	6	17	18	450.2	136	1047	49	21.36	5-28
1959-1974	North Trinidad	First Class Matches	T	13	20	0	848	182	42.40	1	6	18	238	77	405	15	27.00	5-33
1972-1973	Trinidad & Tobago	Domestic O.D. Matches	II	1	1	0	35	35	35.00	-	-	-	1	0	12	0	-	-
1963-1972	WEST INDIES	TEST MATCHES	HA	19	36	3	1127	109	34.15	1	2	13	167	46	437	8	54.62	1-11
1963-1969	West Indies	First Class Matches	A	55	94	10	2892	172*	34.42	5	14	34	420.1	117	1229	35	35.11	5-80
1963-1964	F.M. Worrell's XI	First Class Matches	WI	1	2	0	84	47	42.00	-	-	-	11	0	48	1	48.00	1-48
1963-1964	The Rest XI	First Class Matches	WI	1	2	0	122	79	61.00	-	1	-	8	0	49	0	-	-
1966//	West Indies	O.A.L. O.D. Matches	A	1	1	0	78	78	78.00	-	1	-	10	0	60	2	30.00	2-60
	Total First Class Career			129	221	18	7810	182	38.47	13	43	83	1294.3	376	3215	108	29.76	5-28
	Total O.D. Career			2	2	0	113	78	56.50	0	1	0	11	0	72	2	36.00	2-60

GEORGE CHALLENOR

D.O.B. 28.06.1888 - Waterloo, St Michael, Barbados (d. 30.07.1947)
First Class Debut 08.01.1906 - Barbados v British Guiana
Test Match Debut 23.06.1928 - West Indies v England

Test 1-1

Teams Played For
Barbados, West Indies
Gentlemen's XI
M.C.C.
Combined B/J XI
H. Levenson-Gower's XI

RHB / RAM

6

SEASON	TEAM	COMPETITION	V	M	I	No	RUNS	H.S.	Av	100s	50s	CT	OV	MD	RUNS	W	Av	B.B.
1906-1930	Barbados	First Class Matches	II	25	35	2	1724	237*	52.24	8	3	10	343.1	68	992	46	21.56	4-16
1928//	WEST INDIES	TEST MATCHES	A	3	6	0	101	46	16.83	-	-	-	-	-	-	-	-	-
1906-1928	West Indies	First Class Matches	HA	58	102	7	3487	155*	36.70	7	23	14	80.2	19	258	7	36.85	3-71
1928//	Combined B/J XI	First Class Matches	WI	2	4	0	123	65	31.25	-	1	-	-	-	-	-	-	-
1926//	M.C.C.	First Class Matches	E	3	6	0	129	47	21.50	-	-	1	13	4	40	1	40.00	1-15
1926//	Gentlemen's XI	First Class Matches	E	2	3	0	104	56	34.66	-	1	-	-	-	-	-	-	-
1926//	H. Levenson-Gower's XI	First Class Matches	E	2	4	0	154	65	38.50	-	1	-	-	-	-	-	-	-
		Total First Class Career		95	160	9	5822	237*	38.55	15	29	25	436.3	91	1290	54	23.88	4-16

274

SHIVNARINE CHANDERPAUL

D.O.B. 18.08.1974 - Unity Village, Demerara, Guyana
First Class Debut 14.02.1992 - Guyana v Leeward Islands
Test Match Debut 17.03.1994 - West Indies v England
O.D.I. Debut 17.10.1994 - West Indies v India
Domestic O.D. Debut 05.02.1992 - Guyana v Windward Islands

Test 204-302	**Teams Played For**	4
O.D.I. 66-278	Guyana	LHB / LB
	West Indies	
	West Indies U23	
	W.I. President's XI	

SEASON	TEAM	COMPETITION	V	M	I	No	BATTING RUNS	H.S.	Av	100s	50s	CT	BOWLING OV	MD	RUNS	W	Av	B.B.
1992-2003	Guyana	First Class Matches	II	39	62	10	3010	303*	57.88	10	11	38	217.5	43	601	25	24.04	4-48
1992-2002	Guyana	Domestic O.D. Matches	II	52	47	13	1513	112	44.50	1	11	18	146.5	4	677	41	16.51	4-22
1994-2003	WEST INDIES	TEST MATCHES	HA	66	109	15	4155	137*	44.20	8	28	38	240	43	718	8	89.75	1-2
1994-2002	West Indies	First Class Matches	A	37	60	14	2518	216*	54.73	9	22	28	157.4	25	577	16	36.06	3-46
1993//	West Indies U23	First Class Matches	WI	1	2	0	1	1	0.50	-	-	-	33	3	133	1	133.00	1-60
1993-2001	W.I. President's XI	First Class Matches	WI	4	6	2	205	140	51.25	1	-	1	44.5	4	168	4	42.00	3-46
1994-2003	WEST INDIES	O.D.I. MATCHES	HA	132	123	16	3913	150	36.57	3	25	37	118	0	606	14	43.28	3-18
1995-2001	West Indies	O.A.L. O.D. Matches	A	12	11	1	414	91	41.40	-	3	4	5	0	38	0	-	-
		Total First Class Career		147	239	41	9889	303*	49.94	28	48	89	693.2	117	2197	54	40.68	4-48
		Total O.D. Career		196	181	30	5840	150	38.67	4	39	59	269.5	8	1321	55	24.01	4-22

HERBERT SAMUEL CHANG

D.O.B. 22.07.1952 - Kingston, Jamaica

First Class Debut	19.01.1973 - Jamaica v Barbados
Test Match Debut	10.01.1979 - West Indies v India
Domestic O.D. Debut	13.04.1973 - Jamaica v Guyana

Test 173-187

Teams Played For
Jamaica
West Indies
W.I. President's XI
West Indies XI

LHB / RAM

4

SEASON	COMPETITION	TEAM	V	M	I	No	BATTING						BOWLING					
							RUNS	H.S.	Av	100s	50s	CT	OV	MD	RUNS	W	Av	B.B.
1973-1983	First Class Matches	Jamaica	II	48	79	5	2847	155	38.47	5	18	27	5	0	16	0	-	-
1973-1983	Domestic O.D. Matches	Jamaica	II	18	18	0	389	55	21.61	-	1	4	0.4	0	8	0	-	-
1978-1979	TEST MATCHES	WEST INDIES	A	1	2	0	8	6	4.00	-	-	-	-	-	-	-	-	-
1978-1979	First Class Matches	West Indies	A	8	15	0	350	87	23.33	-	2	4	2	0	16	0	-	-
1973-1974	First Class Matches	W.I. President's XI	WI	1	2	0	68	64	34.00	-	1	-	-	-	-	-	-	-
1982-1983	O.D.(I.) Matches	West Indies XI	A	4	4	0	61	33	15.25	-	-	4	-	-	-	-	-	-
1979//	O.A.L. O.D. Matches	West Indies	A	2	1	0	0	0	0.00	-	-	-	-	-	-	-	-	-
1982-1983	O.A.L. O.D. Matches	West Indies XI	A	1	1	0	30	30	30.00	-	-	-	-	-	-	-	-	-
	Total First Class Career			58	98	5	3273	155	35.19	5	21	31	7	0	32	0	-	-
	Total O.D. Career			25	24	0	480	55	20.00	0	1	8	0.4	0	8	0	-	-

CYRIL MARCEL CHRISTIANI

D.O.B. 28.10.1913 - Georgetown, Demerara, British Guiana (d. 04.04.1938)

First Class Debut 22.01.1932 - British Guiana v Trinidad

Test Match Debut 08.01.1935 - West Indies v England

Test	38-16		Teams Played For	3	RHB / WK
			British Guiana		
			West Indies		
			G.C. Grant's XI		

							BATTING							BOWLING				
SEASON	TEAM	COMPETITION	V	M	I	No	RUNS	H.S.	Av	100s	50s	CT/ST	OV	MD	RUNS	W	Av	B.B.
1932-1938	British Guiana	First Class Matches	=	10	16	0	354	79	22.15	-	1	9/15	-	-	-	-	-	-
1934-1935	WEST INDIES	TEST MATCHES	H	4	7	2	98	32*	19.60	-	-	6/1	-	-	-	-	-	-
1933//	West Indies	First Class Matches	A	13	19	1	179	40	9.94	-	-	27/4	1	0	6	0	-	-
1932-1933	G.C. Grant's XI	First Class Matches	H	1	2	1	27	26	27.00	-	-	2	-	-	-	-	-	-
		Total First Class Career		28	44	4	658	79	16.45	0	1	44/20	1	0	6	0	-	-

ROBERT JULIAN CHRISTIANI

D.O.B. 19.07.1920 - Georgetown, Demerara, British Guiana
First Class Debut 25.08.1938 - British Guiana v R.S. Grant's XI
Test Match Debut 21.01.1948 - West Indies v England

Test 53-23

Teams Played For
British Guiana
West Indies

2

RHB / OB / WK

BATTING

SEASON	TEAM	COMPETITION	V	M	I	No	RUNS	H.S.	Av	100s	50s	CT/ST
1938-1954	British Guiana	First Class Matches	II	26	50	2	2178	181	45.37	6	12	37/3
1948-1954	WEST INDIES	TEST MATCHES	HA	22	37	3	896	107	26.35	1	4	19/2
1938-1954	West Indies	First Class Matches	HA	40	55	11	2029	131*	46.11	5	11	40/7
Total First Class Career				88	142	16	5013	181	40.50	12	27	96/12

BOWLING

OV	MD	RUNS	W	Av	B.B.
149.1	14	767	13	59.00	3-31
39	1	108	3	36.00	3-52
55	4	213	2	106.50	1-30
243.1	19	1088	18	60.44	3-31

CARLOS BERTRAM CLARKE

D.O.B. 07.04.1918 - Lakes Folly, Cats Castle, St Michael, Barbados (d. 14.10.1993)

First Class Debut   27.09.1937 - Barbados v British Guiana

Test Match Debut   24.06.1939 - West Indies v England

Test 46-20   Teams Played For: Barbados, West Indies, Northamptonshire, Essex, M.C.C.   5   RHB / LBG

SEASON	TEAM	COMPETITION	V	M	I	No	BATTING RUNS	H.S.	Av	100s	50s	CT	BOWLING OV	MD	RUNS	W	Av	B.B.
1937-1939	Barbados	First Class Matches	II	3	5	2	43	17*	14.33	-	-	-	101.1	19	362	12	30.16	5-62
1939//	WEST INDIES	TEST MATCHES	A	3	4	1	3	2	1.00	-	-	-	57	2	261	6	43.50	3-59
1939//	West Indies	First Class Matches	HA	20	22	10	165	45	13.75	-	-	6	433.3	47	1760	82	21.46	7-75
1946-1949	Northamptonshire	First Class Matches	E	49	81	11	874	86	12.48	-	1	27	1348	201	4638	156	29.73	7-120
1959-1960	Essex	First Class Matches	E	18	27	14	177	39	13.61	-	-	6	437.4	88	1353	58	23.32	7-130
1955-1961	M.C.C.	First Class Matches	E	4	6	2	30	15*	7.50	-	-	3	134.5	23	408	19	21.47	1-28
Total First Class Career				97	145	40	1292	86	12.30	0	1	42	2512.1	380	8782	333	26.37	7-75

SYLVESTER THEOPHILAS CLARKE

D.O.B. 11.12.1954 - Lead Vale, Christ Church, Barbados (d. 04.12.1999)

First Class Debut	19.01.1978 - Barbados v Combined Islands
Test Match Debut	31.03.1978 - West Indies v Australia
O.D.I. Debut	12.04.1978 - West Indies v Australia
Domestic O.D. Debut	13.02.1978 - Barbados v Jamaica

Test 165-181
O.D.I. 27-14

Teams Played For: Barbados, West Indies, West Indies XI, Surrey, Transvaal, Orange Free State, Northern Transvaal

RHB / RAFM
7

SEASON	TEAM	COMPETITION	V	M	I	No	RUNS	H.S.	Av	100s	50s	CT	OV	MD	RUNS	W	Av	B.B.
1978-1982	Barbados	First Class Matches	II	20	22	6	204	36	12.75	-	-	14	628.4	129	1898	68	27.91	6-39
1978-1982	Barbados	Domestic O.D. Matches	II	12	8	2	25	12	4.16	-	-	2	96.3	13	329	17	19.35	3-19
1981//	Barbados	O.A.L. O.D. Matches	WI	1	1	0	5	5	5.00	-	-	-	10	4	14	0	-	-
1978-1982	WEST INDIES	TEST MATCHES	HA	11	16	5	172	35*	15.63	-	-	2	412.5	81	1170	42	27.85	5-126
1978-1982	West Indies	First Class Matches	A	12	12	2	79	22	7.90	-	-	2	280	68	716	48	14.91	5-16
1982-1984	West Indies XI	First Class Matches	A	8	13	4	104	25	11.55	-	-	3	314	88	783	45	17.40	7-34
1978-1982	WEST INDIES	O.D.I. MATCHES	HA	10	8	2	60	20	10.00	-	-	4	87.2	13	245	13	18.84	3-22
1982-1984	West Indies XI	O.D.(I.) Matches	A	8	8	1	75	34	10.71	-	-	2	112.2	19	369	20	18.45	3-23
1979//	West Indies	O.A.L. O.D. Matches	A	2	1	0	2	2	2.00	-	-	-	15	-	34	2	17.00	2-24
1982-1983	West Indies XI	O.A.L. O.D. Matches	A	1	1	0	4	4	4.00	-	-	-	9	1	33	1	33.00	1-33
1979-1988	Surrey	First Class Matches	E	152	155	18	2130	100*	15.54	1	3	101	4463.5	1177	11226	591	18.99	8-62
1980-1988	Surrey	Nat West Trophy	E	25	14	4	168	45*	16.80	-	-	11	258.2	56	634	40	15.85	4-10
1979-1988	Surrey	Benson & Hedges Cup	E	44	27	5	211	39	9-59	-	-	12	435.4	-	1211	70	17.30	5-23
1979-1988	Surrey	Sunday League	E	87	53	16	479	34*	12.94	-	-	22	603.1	-	2446	95	25.74	4-38
1981-1987	Surrey	O.A.L. O.D. Matches	E	3	1	0	2	2	2.00	-	-	1	21	-	79	4	19.75	3-46
1983-1986	Transvaal	First Class Matches	SA	20	22	7	277	78*	18.46	-	1	7	694.5	203	1534	94	16.94	6-19
1983-1986	Transvaal	Nissan & B & H Cup	SA	26	7	1	68	38	11.33	-	-	7	246.1	-	658	48	13.70	5-10
1987-1988	Orange Free State	First Class Matches	SA	7	14	1	201	60	15.46	-	1	8	240.4	58	504	32	15.75	7-48
1987-1988	Orange Free State	Nissan & B & H Cup	SA	12	11	0	139	33	12.63	-	-	4	110.5	-	353	23	15.34	6-31
1988-1990	Northern Transvaal	First Class Matches	SA	8	11	1	102	42*	10.20	-	-	9	234	61	566	22	25.72	5-46
1988-1990	Northern Transvaal	Nissan & B & H Cup	SA	15	6	0	40	18	6.66	-	-	1	140.3	-	428	31	13.80	5-31
Total First Class Career				238	265	44	3269	100*	14.79	1	5	146	7268.5	1865	18397	942	19.52	8-62
Total O.D. Career				250	146	31	1278	45*	11.11	0	0	66	2145.2	-	6833	364	18.77	6-31

280

PEDRO TYRONE COLLINS

D.O.B. 12.08.1976 - Boscobelle, St Peter, Barbados

First Class Debut 23.09.1996 - Barbados v Orange Free State
Test Match Debut 05.03.1999 - West Indies v Australia
O.D.I. Debut 19.10.1999 - West Indies v Pakistan
Domestic O.D. Debut 07.10.1997 - Barbados v Canada

Test 225-349
O.D.I. 97-388

Teams Played For 7
Barbados, West Indies Select XI
West Indies, West Indies U23
W.I. Board XI
West Indies "A"
Busta Cup XI

RHB / LAFM

SEASON	TEAM	COMPETITION	V	M	I	No	BATTING RUNS	H.S.	Av	100s	50s	CT	BOWLING OV	MD	RUNS	W	Av	B.B.
1999-2003	WEST INDIES	TEST MATCHES	HA	19	30	6	165	24	6.87	-	-	2	709.4	130	2218	55	40.32	6-76
1999-2002	West Indies	First Class Matches	A	4	2	0	10	9	5.00	-	-	-	103	25	287	8	35.87	3-43
1997-2000	West Indies "A"	First Class Matches	A	13	16	7	96	22	10.66	-	-	5	349.2	70	1091	44	24.79	4-56
1999//	W.I. Board XI	First Class Matches	WI	1	1	1	21	21*	-	-	-	1	29	6	88	3	29.33	2-45
2001//	Busta Cup	First Class Matches	WI	1	1	0	5	5	5.00	-	-	-	19	2	58	2	29.00	1-12
1999-2003	WEST INDIES	O.D.I. MATCHES	HA	23	7	3	26	10	6.50	-	-	8	205.5	15	946	30	31.53	3-18
1997-1998	West Indies "A"	O.D.I.(I.) Matches	A	3	2	0	17	10	8.50	-	-	-	23	3	112	5	22.40	3-63
1997-1998	West Indies	O.A.L. O.D. Matches	A	1	1	-	-	-	-	-	-	-	8	0	36	2	18.00	2-36
1999-2000	W.I. Select XI	First Class Matches	WI	1	1	0	2	2	2.00	-	-	-	14	3	44	0	-	-
1999-2000	West Indies U23	First Class Matches	WI	1	2	0	0	0	0.00	-	-	-	25	2	82	2	41.00	2-63
1996-2003	Barbados	First Class Matches	=	25	26	7	75	7	3.94	-	-	6	581.3	117	1737	73	23.79	5-56
1997-2002	Barbados	Domestic O.D. Matches	=	19	6	3	64	55*	21.33	-	1	2	164.2	18	676	29	23.31	4-25
		Total First Class Career		65	79	21	374	24	6.44	0	0	14	1830.3	355	5605	187	29.97	6-76
		Total O.D. Career		46	15	6	107	55*	11.88	0	1	10	401.1	36	1770	66	26.81	4-25

COREY DELANO COLLYMORE

D.O.B. 21.12.1977 - Boscobelle, St Peter, Barbados

First Class Debut	29.01.1999 - Barbados v Guyana
Test Match Debut	03.04.1999 - West Indies v Australia
O.D.I. Debut	11.09.1999 - West Indies v India
Domestic O.D. Debut	11.10.2000 - Barbados v Canada

Test 230-352
O.D.I. 99-402

Teams Played For
Barbados, Warwickshire
West Indies
West Indies "A"
W.I. Board XI
UWI Vice Chancellor's XI

6

RHB / RAFM

SEASON	TEAM	COMPETITION	V	M	I	No	BATTING						BOWLING					
							RUNS	H.S.	Av	100s	50s	CT	OV	MD	RUNS	W	Av	B.B.
1999-2003	Barbados	First Class Matches	II	19	19	9	99	20	9.90	-	-	10	562.5	137	1527	76	20.09	6-109
2000-2002	Barbados	Domestic O.D. Matches	II	12	3	2	22	12*	22.00	-	-	2	91.4	7	412	14	29.42	3-57
1999-2003	WEST INDIES	TEST MATCHES	HA	3	4	1	30	13	10.00	-	-	-	104	20	268	15	17.86	7-57
2000-2001	West Indies	First Class Matches	A	8	11	5	31	14	5.16	-	-	2	168.2	50	524	20	26.20	3-18
1999-2000	West Indies "A"	First Class Matches	H	1	2	0	12	12	6.00	-	-	-	24	3	103	1	103.00	1-29
2000-2003	WEST INDIES	O.D.I. MATCHES	HA	42	17	8	56	13*	6.22	-	-	7	356.1	19	1536	49	31.24	5-51
2000-2001	West Indies	O.A.L. O.D. Matches	A	2	D	-	-	-	-	-	-	-	-	-	-	-	-	-
1998-1999	W.I. Board XI	First Class Matches	WI	1	1	0	5	5	5.00	-	-	2	23.1	5	42	3	14.00	2-19
2002-2003	UWI V/Chancellor's XI	First Class Matches	WI	1	2	1	10	10*	10.00	-	-	1	22	8	54	2	27.00	2-54
2003	Warwickshire	First Class Matches	E	5	8	3	25	11*	5.00	-	-	2	138	24	475	8	59.37	3-42
2003	Warwickshire	Sunday League	E	3	D	-	-	-	-	-	-	-	26	2	122	5	24.40	3-26
		Total First Class Career		38	47	19	212	20	7.57	-	-	17	1042.2	247	2993	125	23.94	7-57
		Total O.D. Career		59	20	10	78	13*	7.80	-	-	9	491.5	30	2126	72	29.52	5-51

LEARIE NICHOLAS CONSTANTINE

D.O.B. 21.09.1901 - Diego Martin, Trinidad (d. 01.07.1971)

First Class Debut 19.09.1921 - Trinidad v Barbados

Test Match Debut 23.06.1928 - West Indies v England

Test 4-1   6   RHB / RAF

Teams Played For
Trinidad, Barbados
West Indies
Combined XI
Freelooters (India)
Dominions XI

SEASON	TEAM	COMPETITION	V	M	I	No	BATTING RUNS	H.S.	Av	100s	50s	CT	BOWLING OV	MD	RUNS	W	Av	B.B.
1921-1935	Trinidad	First Class Matches	=	17	32	1	604	133	19.48	1	2	24	400.3	87	1065	55	19.36	8-38
1939//	Barbados	First Class Matches	=	1	2	0	12	11	6.00	-	-	-	19	6	69	4	17.25	4-41
1928-1939	WEST INDIES	TEST MATCHES	HA	18	33	0	635	90	19.24	-	4	28	573.3	125	1746	58	30.10	5-75
1923-1939	West Indies	First Class Matches	HA	78	122	10	3025	130	27.00	4	21	80	1668.1	254	5701	297	19.19	1-45
1927//	Combined T/BG XI	First Class Matches	WI	2	3	0	124	63	41.33	-	1	1	32.3	7	76	9	8.44	5-32
1934-1935	Freelooters	First Class Matches	I	2	3	0	30	17	10.00	-	-	-	58	-	254	15	16.93	6-72
1945//	Dominions XI	First Class Matches	E	1	2	0	45	40	22.50	-	-	-	21	2	80	1	80.00	1-53
Total First Class Career				119	197	11	4475	133	24.05	5	28	133	2772.1	-	8991	439	20.48	8-38

NORMAN GEORGE COWANS

D.O.B. 17.04.1961 - Enfield, St Mary's, Jamaica

First Class Debut	21.06.1980 - Middlesex v Oxford University
Test Match Debut	12.11.1982 - England v Australia
O.D.I. Debut	11.01.1983 - England v Australia
Domestic O.D. Debut	06.09.1981 - Middlesex v Essex

Teams Played For
Middlesex, Hampshire
England
England "B"
M.C.C.
D.B. Closes XI

RHB / RF
6

SEASON	TEAM	COMPETITION	V	M	I	No	RUNS	H.S.	Av	100s	50s	CT	OV	MD	RUNS	W	Av	B.B.
							BATTING						BOWLING					
1982-1985	ENGLAND	TEST MATCHES	HA	19	29	7	175	36	7.95	-	-	9	575.2	112	2003	51	39.27	6-77
1982-1986	England	First Class Matches	A	12	9	1	13	10	1.62	-	-	5	253.4	63	812	32	25.37	4-33
1985-1986	England "B"	First Class Matches	A	3	2	2	2	2*	-	-	-	-	83	22	229	7	32.71	6-50
1982-1985	ENGLAND	O.D.I. MATCHES	HA	23	8	3	13	4*	2-60	-	-	5	213.4	17	913	23	39.69	3-44
1982-1985	England	O.A.L. O.D. Matches	HA	2	D	-	-	-	-	-	-	-	20	-	114	2	57.00	-
1985-1986	England "B"	O.A.L. O.D. Matches	A	4	3	2	2	2*	2.00	-	-	2	31	-	129	4	32.25	-
1980-1993	Middlesex	First Class Matches	E	188	190	49	1307	66	9.26	-	1	46	4096.3	925	12009	532	22.57	6-31
1982-1993	Middlesex	Nat West Trophy	E	32	13	2	45	12*	4.09	-	-	9	321.4	51	1065	48	22.18	4-24
1983-1991	Middlesex	Benson & Hedges Cup	E	33	15	6	50	12	5.55	-	-	6	310.1	-	1027	47	21.85	4-33
1981-1993	Middlesex	Sunday League	E	103	33	12	139	27	6.61	-	-	15	744.1	-	3030	111	27.29	6-9
1988-1990	Middlesex	Sunday League Cup	E	2	1	1	23	23*	-	-	-	-	14	-	40	1	40.00	1-18
1980-1993	Middlesex	O.A.L. O.D. Matches	HA	4	2	1	0	0*	0.00	-	-	1	32	-	163	5	32.60	3-53
1994//	Hampshire	First Class Matches	E	12	15	6	51	19	5.66	-	-	3	349.3	93	986	26	37.92	4-76
1994//	Hampshire	Nat West Trophy	E	2	1	1	6	6*	-	-	-	-	17	2	53	2	26.50	2-21
1994-1995	Hampshire	Benson & Hedges Cup	E	4	D	-	-	-	-	-	-	-	37	-	138	8	17.25	4-36
1994-1995	Hampshire	Sunday League	E	14	4	2	3	2*	1.50	-	-	2	103	-	470	10	47.00	2-21
1994//	Hampshire	O.A.L. O.D. Matches	E	1	D	-	-	-	-	-	-	-	11	-	47	2	23.50	2-47
1984-1990	M.C.C.	First Class Matches	E	4	3	3	57	46*	-	-	-	-	126	23	404	14	28.85	-
1985//	D.B. Closes XI	First Class Matches	E	1	D	-	-	-	-	-	-	-	10	3	18	0	-	-
		Total First Class Career		239	248	68	1605	66	8.91	0	1	63	5494	1241	16461	622	24.86	6-31
		Total O.D. Career		224	80	30	281	27	5.62	0	0	40	1854.4	-	7189	263	27.33	6-9

COLIN EVERTON HUNTE CROFT

D.O.B. 15.03.1959 - Lancaster Village, Demerara, British Guiana

First Class Debut	27.01.1972 - Guyana v Jamaica
Test Match Debut	18.02.1977 - West Indies v Pakistan
O.D.I. Debut	16.03.1977 - West Indies v Pakistan
Domestic O.D. Debut	24.02.1976 - Guyana v Trinidad & Tobago

			Teams Played For	
Test	159-174		Guyana, Demerara	RHB / RF
O.D.I.	20-12		West Indies	6
			W.I. President's XI	
			West Indies XI	
			Lancashire	

SEASON	TEAM	COMPETITION	V	M	I	No	BATTING RUNS	H.S.	Av	100s	50s	CT	BOWLING OV	MD	RUNS	W	Av	B.B.
1972-1982	Guyana	First Class Matches	==	20	27	10	145	27	8.52	-	-	3	591	105	1892	77	24.57	7-64
1975-1981	Demerara	First Class Matches	G	6	6	1	42	15	8.40	-	-	3	183.5	45	525	19	27.63	6-87
1976-1982	Guyana	Domestic O.D. Matches	==	9	4	3	31	17	31.00	-	-	2	75	14	241	10	24.10	3-25
1977-1982	WEST INDIES	TEST MATCHES	HA	27	37	22	158	33	10.53	-	-	8	1027.3	211	2913	125	23.80	8-29
1979-1981	West Indies	First Class Matches	A	15	10	6	61	34	15.25	-	-	3	406.2	74	1234	52	23.73	6-80
1977//	W.I. "President's XI	First Class Matches	WI	1	1	1	4	4*	-	-	-	-	32.2	10	109	10	10.90	6-66
1983-1984	West Indies XI	First Class Matches	A	3	5	4	12	5*	12.00	-	-	-	66	12	250	9	27.77	4-41
1977-1982	WEST INDIES	O.D.I. MATCHES	HA	19	6	4	18	8	9.00	-	-	1	178.2	21	620	30	20.66	6-15
1983-1984	West Indies XI	O.D.(I.) MATCHES	A	4	2	0	24	24	12.00	-	-	-	39	3	170	5	34.00	3-48
1980//	West Indies	O.A.L. O.D. Matches	A	2	-	-	-	-	-	-	-	-	15.4	-	63	3	21.00	2-22
1982-1983	West Indies XI	O.A.L. O.D. Matches	A	3	3	1	37	33	18.50	-	-	3	23	5	77	1	77.00	1-23
1977-1982	Lancashire	First Class Matches	E	49	50	10	433	46*	10.82	-	-	8	1210.3	282	3604	136	26.50	7-54
1977-1982	Lancashire	Nat West Trophy	E	4	3	2	11	5*	11.00	-	-	1	47	7	177	4	44.25	3-53
1977-1982	Lancashire	Benson & Hedges Cup	E	13	6	4	65	26*	32.50	-	-	-	129.5	27	376	27	13.92	6-10
1977-1982	Lancashire	Sunday League	E	27	9	4	45	13	9.00	-	-	10	172.4	-	741	22	33.68	4-29
Total First Class Career				121	136	54	855	46*	10.42	0	0	25	3517.3	739	10527	428	24.59	8-29
Total O.D. Career				81	33	18	231	33	15.40	0	0	17	680.3	-	2465	102	24.16	6-10

CAMEON EUSTACE CUFFY

D.O.B. 08.02.1970 - South Rivers, St Vincent, Windward Islands

First Class Debut	11.01.1991 - Windward Islands v Leeward Islands
Test Match Debut	18.11.1994 - West Indies v India
O.D.I. Debut	17.10.1994 - West Indies v India
Domestic O.D. Debut	16.01.1991 - Windward Islands v Trinidad & Tobago

Test 206-306
O.D.I. 67-278

Teams Played For 9
Windward Islands, West Indies
West Indies U23, W.I. President's XI
W.I. Board XI, WI Select XI
Surrey, West Indies "A"
St Vincent

RHB / RAF

SEASON	TEAM	COMPETITION	V	M	I	No	RUNS	H.S.	Av	100s	50s	CT	OV	MD	RUNS	W	Av	B.B.
1991-2003	Windward Islands	First Class Matches	II	40	63	22	194	15	4.73	-	-	17	1061.4	233	2772	102	23.10	7-80
1991-2001	Windward Islands	Domestic O.D. Matches	II	33	14	8	46	10*	7.66	-	-	10	266	30	885	39	22.69	4-29
2002//	St Vincent	Domestic O.D. Matches	II	2	2	1	34	18*	34.00	-	-	1	18	1	91	1	91.00	1-35
1994-2002	WEST INDIES	TEST MATCHES	HA	15	23	9	58	15	4.14	-	-	5	561	143	1455	43	33.83	4-82
1994-2002	West Indies	First Class Matches	A	3	2	0	0	0	0.00	-	-	1	56	11	163	7	23.28	4-84
1993//	West Indies U23	First Class Matches	WI	1	2	2	6	6*	-	-	-	1	23	3	66	2	33.00	2-23
1994-2000	WI Presidents XI	First Class Matches	WI	4	3	0	50	37	16.66	-	-	-	95.5	19	274	10	27.40	3-35
1996-1997	West Indies "A"	First Class Matches	A	4	4	3	7	6*	7.00	-	-	3	105.2	19	336	18	18.66	7-84
1999-2001	WI Board XI	First Class Matches	WI	2	2	1	0	0	0.00	-	-	-	63	15	139	3	46.33	3-38
1994-2002	WEST INDIES	O.D.I. MATCHES	HA	41	22	8	62	17*	4.42	-	-	5	358.5	41	1436	41	35.02	4-24
1995-1997	West Indies "A"	O.D.(I.) Matches	A	5	4	2	8	4*	4.00	-	-	1	45	3	156	8	19.50	3-27
1999-2000	West Indies Select XI	O.D.(I.) Matches	WI	2	1	1	2	2*	-	-	-	-	17	3	37	2	18.50	1-16
1995-2001	West Indies	O.A.L. O.D. Matches	A	2	1	1	24	24*	-	-	-	-	19	1	59	3	19.66	2-32
1994//	Surrey	First Class Matches	E	12	15	8	42	10	6.00	-	-	1	389.3	107	1082	36	30.05	4-70
1994//	Surrey	Nat West Trophy	E	4	1	1	2	2*	-	-	-	1	42	11	133	6	22.16	4-43
1994//	Surrey	Benson & Hedges Cup	E	3	D	-	-	-	-	-	-	1	27	1	154	0	-	-
1994//	Surrey	Sunday League	E	1	D	-	-	-	-	-	-	-	6	0	43	0	-	-
1994//	Surrey	O.A.L. O.D. Matches	E	1	D	-	-	-	-	-	-	-	11	-	57	2	28.50	2-57
Total First Class Career				81	114	45	357	37	5.17	0	0	27	2355.2	550	6287	239	26.30	7-80
Total O.D. Career				94	45	22	178	24*	7.73	0	0	19	809.5	92	3051	102	29.91	4-24

BATTING | BOWLING

ANDERSON CLEOPHAS CUMMINS

D.O.B. 07.05.1966 - Packers Valley, Christ Church, Barbados

First Class Debut 27.01.1989 - Barbados v Trinidad & Tobago

Test Match Debut 30.01.1993 - West Indies v Australia

O.D.I. Debut 20.11.1991 - West Indies v Pakistan

Domestic O.D. Debut 01.02.1989 - Barbados v Guyana

Test 203-296

O.D.I. 60-215

Teams Played For 7

Barbados, West Indies
W.I. President's XI, W.I. Board XI
West Indies "A"
Durham
Surrey

RHB / RFM

SEASON	TEAM	COMPETITION	V	M	I	No	BATTING RUNS	H.S.	Av	100s	50s	CT	BOWLING OV	MD	RUNS	W	Av	B.B.
1989-1996	Barbados	First Class Matches	II	15	20	2	203	45*	11.27	-	-	4	439.1	71	1421	53	26.81	4-26
1989-1996	Barbados	Domestic O.D. Matches	II	14	9	2	110	43*	15.71	-	1	1	116.3	13	440	20	22.00	5-16
1993-1994	WEST INDIES	TEST MATCHES	HA	5	6	1	98	50	19.60	-	1	1	103	11	342	8	42.75	4-54
1991-1996	West Indies	First Class Matches	A	9	9	2	219	107	31.28	1	-	-	183	25	617	15	41.13	5-60
1991-1994	W.I. Board XI	First Class Matches	WI	2	3	1	21	14	10.50	-	-	-	48.5	5	158	5	31.60	3-82
1993-1995	W.I. President's XI	First Class Matches	WI	2	D	-	-	-	-	-	-	1	38	4	144	2	72.00	2-48
1991-1995	WEST INDIES	O.D.I. MATCHES	HA	63	41	11	459	44*	15.30	-	-	11	523.5	23	2246	78	28.79	5-31
1995//	West Indies "A"	O.D.I.(I.) Matches	H	3	2	0	11	7	5.50	-	-	1	25	2	87	4	21.75	3-41
1991-1995	West Indies	O.A.L. O.D. Matches	A	5	3	2	24	17	24.00	-	1	1	43.3	2	197	7	28.14	3-35
1993-1994	Durham	First Class Matches	E	33	55	4	1131	70	22.17	-	7	8	1025	187	3382	109	31.02	6-64
1993-1994	Durham	Nat West Trophy	E	4	4	2	39	20*	19.50	-	-	-	46	8	154	6	25.66	4-48
1993-1994	Durham	Benson & Hedges Cup	E	2	2	1	24	21	24.00	-	-	-	22	-	73	4	18.25	3-36
1993-1994	Durham	Sunday League	E	31	22	3	438	67	23.05	-	2	5	270.5	-	1253	49	25.87	4-24
1995//	Surrey	O.A.L. O.D. Matches	E	1	1	0	20	20	20.00	-	-	-	11	1	58	0	-	-
Total First Class Career				66	107	10	1672	107	20.14	1	8	15	1836.4	303	6064	192	31.58	6-64
Total O.D. Career				123	84	21	1125	67	17.85	0	2	18	1058.4	-	4508	168	26.83	5-16

287

OSCAR CONSTANTINE DA COSTA

D.O.B. 11.09.1907 - Kingston, Jamaica (d. 01.10.1936)
First Class Debut 21.02.1929 - Jamaica v Julian Cohen's XI
Test Match Debut 03.04.1930 - West Indies v England

Test 27-7

Teams Played For
Jamaica
West Indies
G.C. Grant's XI

3

RHB / RM

SEASON	COMPETITION	TEAM	V	M	I	No	BATTING RUNS	H.S.	Av	100s	50s	CT	BOWLING OV	MD	RUNS	W	Av	B.B.
1929-1935	First Class Matches	Jamaica	II	9	14	4	349	84*	34.90	-	2	9	179.5	27	555	9	61.66	2-51
1930-1935	TEST MATCHES	WEST INDIES	HA	5	9	1	153	39	19.12	-	-	5	62	13	175	3	58.33	1-14
1933//	First Class Matches	West Indies	A	24	39	6	976	105*	29.57	1	6	16	433.1	92	998	30	33.26	4-31
1932-1933	First Class Matches	G.C. Grant's XI	WI	1	2	0	85	70	42.50	-	1	-	13	0	38	2	19.00	2-20
	Total First Class Career			39	64	11	1563	105*	29.49	1	9	30	688	132	1766	44	40.13	4-31

WAYNE WENDELL DANIEL

D.O.B. 16.01.1956 - Brereton Village, St Philip, Barbados
First Class Debut 16.01.1976 - Barbados v Trinidad
Test Match Debut 21.04.1976 - West Indies v India
O.D.I. Debut 22.03.1978 - West Indies v Australia
Domestic O.D. Debut 21.02.1976 - Barbados v Leeward Islands

Test 156-168	**Teams Played For** 5	**RHB / RAF**
O.D.I. 24-13	Barbados	
	West Indies	
	West Indies "B"	
	Middlesex	
	Western Australia	

SEASON	TEAM	COMPETITION	V	M	I	No	BATTING						BOWLING					
							RUNS	H.S.	Av	100s	50s	CT	OV	MD	RUNS	W	Av	B.B.
1976-1985	Barbados	First Class Matches	II	23	28	12	265	53*	16.56	-	1	3	638.1	103	2182	92	23.71	7-33
1976-1985	Barbados	Domestic O.D. Matches	II	9	6	2	43	34	10.75	-	-	1	74	9	275	16	17.18	3-11
1981//	Barbados	O.A.L. O.D. Matches	WI	1	1	1	2	2*	-	-	-	-	10	2	34	2	17.00	2-34
1976-1984	WEST INDIES	TEST MATCHES	HA	10	11	4	46	11	6.57	-	-	4	292.2	61	910	36	25.57	5-39
1976-1983	West Indies	First Class Matches	A	14	9	3	106	30	17.66	-	-	3	310.3	67	931	42	22.16	6-21
1981//	West Indies "B"	First Class Matches	A	3	4	1	68	27	22.66	-	-	1	77.2	20	198	11	18.00	4-38
1978-1984	WEST INDIES	O.D.I. MATCHES	HA	18	5	4	49	16*	49.00	-	-	5	152	17	595	23	25.86	3-27
1981//	West Indies "B"	O.D.I. Matches	A	3	1	0	0	0	0.00	-	-	-	27	4	81	5	16.20	2-26
1984//	West Indies	O.A.L. O.D. Matches	A	1	0	0	0	0	0.00	-	-	-	9	-	32	0	-	-
1977-1988	Middlesex	First Class Matches	E	214	187	86	1043	53*	10.32	-	1	52	5003	1005	15089	685	22.02	9-61
1977-1987	Middlesex	Nat West Trophy	E	34	18	10	42	14	5.25	-	-	7	360	62	1043	70	14.90	6-15
1977-1987	Middlesex	Benson & Hedges Cup	E	50	18	5	73	20*	5.61	-	-	5	434	-	1370	82	16.70	7-12
1977-1987	Middlesex	Sunday League	E	121	40	16	105	14	4.37	-	-	18	831.3	-	3057	163	18.75	5-27
1977-1986	Middlesex	O.A.L. O.D. Matches	E	3	1	1	5	5*	-	-	-	-	11	-	32	1	32.00	1-6
1981-1982	Western Australia	First Class Matches	A	2	2	0	23	21	11.50	-	1	-	63	13	180	1	180.00	1-66
1981-1982	Western Australia	McDonald Cup	A	1	-	-	-	-	-	-	-	-	10.3	-	58	0	-	-
		Total First Class Career		266	241	106	1551	53*	11.48	0	2	63	6384.2	1269	19490	867	22.47	9-61
		Total O.D. Career		241	91	39	319	34	6.13	0	0	36	1919	-	6577	362	18.16	7-12

BRYAN ALAN DAVIS

D.O.B. 02.05.1940 - Belmont, Port of Spain, Trinidad
First Class Debut 02.10.1959 - Trinidad v Jamaica
Test Match Debut 26.03.1965 - West Indies v Australia
Domestic O.D. Debut 24.04.1969 - Glamorgan v Northamptonshire

Test 123-101

RHB / OB

Teams Played For
Trinidad
North Trinidad
West Indies
Glamorgan

SEASON	TEAM	COMPETITION	V	M	I	No	RUNS	H.S.	Av	100s	50s	CT	OV	MD	RUNS	W	Av	B.B.
							BATTING						BOWLING					
1959-1971	Trinidad	First Class Matches	II	32	56	2	2346	176	43.44	3	16	45	2	0	4	0	-	-
1960-1971	North Trinidad	First Class Matches	T	9	14	4	574	188*	57.40	1	3	8	2	0	6	0	-	-
1965//	WEST INDIES	TEST MATCHES	WI	4	8	0	245	68	30.62	-	3	1	-	-	-	-	-	-
1966-67//	West Indies	First Class Matches	A	7	12	0	218	54	18.16	-	2	6	47	7	195	5	39.00	4-79
1968-1970	Glamorgan	First Class Matches	E	60	103	8	2848	103	29.97	1	22	67	74	17	229	4	57.25	1-2
1969-1970	Glamorgan	Nat West Trophy	E	5	5	0	68	44	13.60	-	-	2	1	1	0	0	-	-
1969-1970	Glamorgan	Sunday League	E	29	29	4	852	74	34.08	-	7	8	1	0	13	0	-	-
Total First Class Career				112	193	14	6231	188*	34.81	5	46	127	125	24	434	9	48.22	4-79
Total O.D. Career				34	34	4	920	74	30.66	0	7	10	2	1	13	0	-	-

CHARLES ALLAN DAVIS

D.O.B. 01.01.1944 - Belmont, Port of Spain, Trinidad

First Class Debut 07.04.1961 - Trinidad v E.W. Swanton's XI

Test Match Debut 26.12.1968 - West Indies v Australia

Domestic O.D. Debut 14.04.1973 - Trinidad & Tobago v Barbados

Test 127-119

Teams Played For 4 — Trinidad & Tobago, North Trinidad, West Indies, W.I. President's XI

RHB / RM

SEASON	TEAM	COMPETITION	V	M	I	No	RUNS	H.S.	Av	100s	50s	CT	OV	MD	RUNS	W	Av	B.B.
1961-1973	Trinidad & Tobago	First Class Matches	=	37	65	7	2432	180*	41.93	6	16	23	220	52	521	9	57.88	2-12
1961-1976	North Trinidad	First Class Matches	T	14	20	0	612	162	30.60	2	-	11	195	58	477	23	20.73	5-25
1972-1973	Trinidad & Tobago	Domestic O.D. Matches	=	1	1	0	12	12	12.00	-	-	1	5	0	54	2	27.00	2-54
1968-1973	WEST INDIES	TEST MATCHES	HA	15	29	5	1301	183	54.20	4	4	23	141	32	330	2	165.00	1-27
1968-1969	West Indies	First Class Matches	A	23	37	5	1035	106*	32.34	1	8	4	327	44	1135	29	39.13	7-106
1967-1968	W.I. President's XI	First Class Matches	WI	1	1	1	158	158*	-	1	-	2	7	0	17	0	-	-
1968-1969	West Indies	O.A.L. O.D. Matches	A	1	1	1	0	0*	-	-	-	-						
Total First Class Career				90	152	18	5538	183	41.32	14	28	44	890	186	2480	63	39.36	7-106
Total O.D. Career				2	2	1	12	12	12.00	0	0	1	5	0	54	2	27.00	2-54

WINSTON WALTER DAVIS

D.O.B. 18.09.1958 - Sion Hill, St Vincent, Windward Islands

First Class Debut 11.03.1980 - Windward Islands v Leeward Islands
Test Match Debut 28.04.1983 - West Indies v India
O.D.I. Debut 29.03.1983 - West Indies v India
Domestic O.D. Debut 16.04.1980 - Windward Island v Jamaica

Test 178-216
O.D.I. 38-51

Teams Played For 9
Windward Islands, Combined Islands
West Indies, West Indies "B"
Glamorgan, Northamptonshire
World XI, Tasmania
Wellington

RHB / RAFM

SEASON	TEAM	V	COMPETITION	M	I	No	BATTING					CT	BOWLING					
							RUNS	H.S.	Av	100s	50s		OV	MD	RUNS	W	Av	B.B.
1980-1992	Windward Islands	II	First Class Matches	26	45	9	410	60	11.38	-	1	7	955.3	157	2899	118	24.56	7-57
1980-1981	Combined Islands	II	First Class Matches	7	9	3	85	16*	14.16	-	-	2	151	23	571	12	47.58	3-16
1980-1992	Windward Islands	II	Domestic O.D. Matches	16	11	2	57	18	6.33	-	-	4	142.1	13	576	19	30.31	4-26
1981//	Windward Islands	WI	O.A.L. O.D. Matches	2	2	0	7	7	3.50	-	-	-	18	3	44	2	22.00	2-17
1983-1987	WEST INDIES	HA	TEST MATCHES	15	17	4	202	77	15.33	-	1	10	462.1	54	1472	45	32.71	4-19
1983-1987	West Indies	A	First Class Matches	15	18	6	211	50	17.58	-	1	3	282.4	58	945	32	29.53	5-32
1981//	West Indies "B"	A	First Class Matches	1	1	0	5	5	5.00	-	-	-	22.2	5	51	4	12.75	3-27
1983-1987	WEST INDIES	HA	O.D.I. MATCHES	35	5	3	28	10	14.00	-	-	1	320.3	31	1302	39	33.38	7-51
1981//	West Indies "B"	A	O.D.(I.) Matches	4	2	0	11	6	5.50	-	-	1	34	6	93	3	31.00	2-16
1984//	West Indies	A	O.A.L. O.D. Matches	1	1	1	13	13*	-	-	-	-	10	-	37	0	-	-
1982-1984	Glamorgan	E	First Class Matches	45	51	21	471	50	15.70	-	1	14	1326.2	285	4211	142	29.65	7-70
1982-1984	Glamorgan	E	Nat West Trophy	4	4	2	8	5	4.00	-	-	1	42.5	7	128	4	32.25	3-26
1984//	Glamorgan	E	Benson & Hedges Cup	4	3	0	14	8	4.66	-	-	-	38.2	-	149	9	16.55	5-29
1982-1984	Glamorgan	E	Sunday League	23	4	2	10	5	5.00	-	-	8	156.4	-	649	30	21.63	4-24
1982//	Glamorgan	E	O.A.L. O.D. Matches	1	D	-	-	-	-	-	-	1	4	-	16	0	-	-
1987-1990	Northamptonshire	E	First Class Matches	57	62	13	759	47	15.48	-	-	18	1807.2	286	5776	208	27.76	7-52
1988-1990	Northamptonshire	E	Nat West Trophy	5	2	1	16	14*	16.00	-	-	2	49	5	177	6	29.50	2-45
1987-1990	Northamptonshire	E	Benson & Hedges Cup	13	6	3	50	15*	16.66	-	-	5	125	-	495	13	38.07	3-20
1988-1990	Northamptonshire	E	Sunday League	24	17	3	178	34	12.71	-	-	3	174.3	-	806	21	38.38	4-38
1991//	World XI	E	First Class Matches	1	1	0	54	54*	-	-	1	-	20	5	79	0	-	-
1985-1986	Tasmania	A	First Class Matches	8	14	2	82	21	6.83	-	-	3	287.5	62	768	22	34.90	7-128
1985-1986	Tasmania	A	McDonald Cup	2	D	-	-	-	-	-	-	-	16.2	-	90	1	90.00	1-42
1990-1991	Wellington	NZ	First Class Matches	6	9	2	67	27*	9.57	-	-	-	184.2	35	544	25	21.76	4-43
1990-1991	Wellington	NZ	Shell Cup	7	6	4	43	13*	21.50	-	-	-	55.1	-	200	10	20.00	3-25
Total First Class Career				181	227	61	2346	77	14.13	0	5	57	5499.3	970	17316	608	28.48	7-52
Total O.D. Career				141	63	21	435	34	10.35	0	0	26	1190.3	-	4762	157	30.33	7-51

FRANCIS IGNATIUS DE CAIRES

D.O.B. 12.05.1909 - Georgetown, Demerara, British Guiana, (d. 02.02.1959)

First Class Debut 31.01.1929 - British Guiana v Trinidad

Test Match Debut 11.01.1930 - West Indies v England

	Test	Teams Played For		RHB / RAM
	16-4	British Guiana	2	
		West Indies		

SEASON	TEAM	COMPETITION	V	M	I	No	BATTING RUNS	H.S.	Av	100s	50s	CT	BOWLING OV	MD	RUNS	W	Av	B.B.
1929-1939	British Guiana	First Class Matches	=	11	21	1	548	133	27.40	1	3	4	3	0	19	0	-	-
1929-1930	WEST INDIES	TEST MATCHES	H	3	6	0	232	80	38.66	-	2	1	2	0	9	0	-	-
1930-1931	West Indies	First Class Matches	A	4	7	0	165	76	23.57	-	2	2	6	0	20	1	20.00	1-20
	Total First Class Career			18	34	1	945	133	28.63	1	7	7	11	0	48	1	48.00	1-20

PHILLIP ANTHONY JASON DE FREITAS

D.O.B. 18.02.1966 - Scotts Head, Dominica, Windward Islands

First Class Debut 01.05.1985 - Leicestershire v Oxford University
Test Match Debut 14.11.1986 - England v Australia
O.D.I. Debut 01.01.1987 - England v Australia
Domestic O.D. Debut 04.05.1985 - Leicestershire v Lancashire

Teams Played For Leicestershire, Lancashire, Derbyshire, England, Boland, M.C.C., T.C.C.B. XI

RHB / RFM

7

SEASON	TEAM	COMPETITION	V	M	I	No	BATTING RUNS	H.S.	Av	100s	50s	CT	BOWLING OV	MD	RUNS	W	Av	B.B.
1986-1995	ENGLAND	TEST MATCHES	HA	44	68	5	934	88	14.82	-	4	14	1693.4	367	4700	140	33.57	7-70
1986-1995	England	First Class Matches	A	18	26	6	359	54	17.95	-	1	2	510.1	104	1581	50	31.62	4-44
1986-1996	ENGLAND	O.D.I. MATCHES	HA	103	66	23	690	67	16.04	-	1	26	952	-	3775	115	32.82	4-35
1986-1996	England	O.A.L. O.D. Matches	A	7	5	1	51	21*	12.75	-	-	1	67	11	253	6	42.16	-
1985-2002	Leicestershire	First Class Matches	E	106	145	13	2999	114	22.21	4	15	39	32.58	752	9333	370	25.22	7-44
1986-2002	Leicestershire	Nat West Trophy	E	18	16	1	289	69	19.26	-	1	2	166.3	-	531	22	24.13	5-34
1985-2002	Leicestershire	Benson & Hedges Cup	E	16	11	2	138	57	15.33	-	1	3	136.5	-	434	18	24.11	4-27
1985-2002	Leicestershire	Sunday League	E	85	67	11	926	90	16.53	-	2	14	549.1	-	2427	66	36.77	5-40
1988-1993	Lancashire	First Class Matches	E	76	104	10	2314	102	24.61	2	13	25	2338	499	6916	231	29.93	7-21
1989-1993	Lancashire	Nat West Trophy	E	12	8	2	53	25	8.83	-	-	2	116.2	-	324	18	18.00	5-13
1989-1993	Lancashire	Benson & Hedges Cup	E	28	16	4	303	75*	25.66	-	1	7	283.2	-	961	51	18.84	5-16
1989-1993	Lancashire	Sunday League	E	59	44	10	632	49*	18.58	-	-	7	438.3	-	1919	81	23.69	5-26
1989-1991	Lancashire	Sunday League Cup	E	4	3	0	20	16	6.66	-	-	-	30.2	-	180	2	90.00	1-37
1988-1990	Lancashire	O.A.L. O.D. Matches	E	2	2	0	37	35	18.50	-	-	-	10	2	30	1	30.00	1-30
1994-2000	Derbyshire	First Class Matches	E	97	142	12	3219	123*	24.76	3	14	43	3376.5	781	9697	368	26.35	7-10
1994-2000	Derbyshire	Nat West Trophy	E	18	11	1	184	40	18.40	-	-	5	196.1	-	624	22	28.36	5-28
1994-2000	Derbyshire	Benson & Hedges Trophy	E	23	18	3	317	51*	21.13	-	1	7	172.1	-	648	21	30.85	2-20
1994-2000	Derbyshire	Sunday League	E	83	67	8	1345	72*	22.79	-	6	22	572.1	-	2392	71	33.69	4-9
1987//	M.C.C.	First Class Matches	E	1	1	0	3	3	3.00	-	-	-	32	4	130	9	14.44	-
1986//	T.C.C.B. XI	First Class Matches	E	1	D	-	-	-	-	-	-	1	39	10	98	3	32.66	2-39
1993-1996	Boland	First Class Matches	SA	12	20	1	707	103*	37.21	1	6	2	364	88	884	34	26.00	5-80
1993-1996	Boland	Benson & Hedges Cup	SA	9	8	1	125	30	17.85	-	-	3	78	-	249	13	19.15	3-22
		Total First Class Career		355	506	47	10535	123*	22.95	10	53	126	11557.4	2605	33339	1205	27.66	7-21
		Total O.D. Career		467	339	67	5115	90	18.80	-	13	100	3769	-	14747	534	27.61	5-13

CYRIL CLAIRMONTE DEPEIZA

D.O.B. 10.10.1928 - Mount Standfast, St James, Barbados (d. 10.11.1995)
First Class Debut 24.01.1952 - Barbados v Jamaica
Test Match Debut 26.04.1955 - West Indies v Australia

Test 88-55

Teams Played For 2
Barbados
West Indies

RHB / WK / RAM

SEASON	TEAM	COMPETITION	V	M	I	No	RUNS	H.S.	Av	100s	50s	CT/ST	OV	MD	RUNS	W	Av	B.B.
							BATTING						BOWLING					
1952-1957	Barbados	First Class Matches	11	8	13	3	319	65	31.90	-	3	18/3	-	-	-	-	-	-
1955-1956	WEST INDIES	TEST MATCHES	A	5	8	2	187	122	31.16	1	-	7/4	5	0	15	0	-	-
1955-1956	West Indies	First Class Matches	A	3	3	0	117	66	39.00	-	1	6/2	-	-	-	-	-	-
Total First Class Career				16	24	5	623	122	32.78	1	4	31/9	5	0	15	0	-	-

DAVID THOMAS DEWDNEY

D.O.B. 23.10.1933 - Kingston, Jamaica

First Class Debut 12.02.1955 - Jamaica v Trinidad
Test Match Debut 14.05.1955 - West Indies v Australia

Test 90-56

Teams Played For
Jamaica
West Indies
Commonwealth XI

RHB / RF

3

SEASON	TEAM	COMPETITION	V	M	I	No	BATTING RUNS	H.S.	Av	100s	50s	CT	BOWLING OV	MD	RUNS	W	Av	B.B.
1955-1958	Jamaica	First Class Matches	II	6	7	1	37	13*	6.16	-	-	4	163.2	25	572	18	31.77	7-55
1955-1958	WEST INDIES	TEST MATCHES	HA	9	12	5	17	5*	2.42	-	-	-	273.3	65	807	21	38.42	5-21
1955-1961	West Indies	First Class Matches	A	24	28	12	113	37*	7.06	-	-	2	451.1	73	1408	52	27.07	5-38
1961//	Commonwealth XI	First Class Matches	E	1	2	1	4	3	1.00	-	-	-	16	3	41	1	41.00	1-21
		Total First Class Career		40	49	19	171	37*	5.70	0	0	6	904	166	2828	92	30.73	7-55

RAJINDRA DHANRAJ

D.O.B. 06.02.1969 - Barrackpore, Trinidad
First Class Debut 29.01.1988 - Trinidad & Tobago v Barbados
Test Match Debut 18.11.1994 - West Indies v India
O.D.I. Debut 26.10.1994 - West Indies v India
Domestic O.D. Debut 05.11.1989 - West Indies "B" v Zimbabwe

Test 207-306
O.D.I. 71-281

Teams Played For
Trinidad & Tobago
West Indies
W.I. President's XI
West Indies "B"
West Indies U23

5

RHB / LBG

SEASON	TEAM	COMPETITION	V	M	I	No	RUNS	H.S.	Av	100s	50s	CT	OV	MD	RUNS	W	Av	B.B.
1988-2001	Trinidad & Tobago	First Class Matches	II	49	73	27	428	47	9.30	-	-	19	1729	334	4869	196	24.84	9-97
1990-1998	Trinidad & Tobago	Domestic O.D. Matches	II	32	17	6	80	17*	7.27	-	-	5	217.2	17	842	53	15.88	5-26
1991-1997	Trinidad & Tobago	O.A.L. O.D. Matches	WI	2	1	1	8	8*	-	-	-	2	20	0	105	5	21.00	4-59
1994-1995	WEST INDIES	TEST MATCHES	HA	4	4	0	17	9	4.25	-	-	1	181.1	32	595	8	74.37	2-49
1994-1995	West Indies	First Class Matches	A	17	15	4	90	22	8.18	-	-	5	505	92	1680	71	23.66	6-50
1988-1991	West Indies U23	First Class Matches	WI	3	5	2	9	6	3.00	-	-	-	99	13	327	4	81.75	2-18
1989/I	West Indies "B"	First Class Matches	A	3	3	2	5	3*	5.00	-	-	4	125.5	22	316	13	24.30	6-79
1994-1995	W.I. President's XI	First Class Matches	WI	2	1	1	1	1*	-	-	-	-	61.5	6	208	3	69.33	2-70
1994/I	WEST INDIES	O.D.I. MATCHES	HA	6	2	1	8	8	8.00	-	-	1	44	2	170	10	17.00	4-26
1989/I	West Indies "B"	O.D.(I.) Matches	A	1	1	-	1	1*	-	-	-	-	10	0	39	3	13.00	3-39
1995/I	West Indies	O.A.L. O.D. Matches	A	3	2	1	1	1*	1.00	-	-	1	21	2	95	8	11.87	4-25
Total First Class Career				78	101	36	550	47	8.46	0	0	29	2696.4	499	7995	295	27.10	9-97
Total O.D. Career				44	23	10	98	17*	7.59	0	0	9	312.2	21	1251	79	15.83	5-26

297

MERVYN DILLON

D.O.B. 05.06.1974 - Mission Village, Toco, Trinidad

First Class Debut	24.01.1997 - Trinidad & Tobago v Windward Islands
Test Match Debut	14.03.1997 - West Indies v India
O.D.I. Debut	03.11.1997 - West Indies v South Africa
Domestic O.D. Debut	04.10.1996 - Trinidad & Tobago v Leeward Islands

Test 216-329
O.D.I. 86-300

Teams Played For
Trinidad & Tobago
West Indies
West Indies "A"
W.I. Select XI
Busta Cup XI

RHB / RAFM
5

SEASON	TEAM	COMPETITION	V	M	I	No	RUNS	H.S.	Av	100s	50s	CT	OV	MD	RUNS	W	Av	B.B.
							BATTING						BOWLING					
1997-2003	Trinidad & Tobago	First Class Matches	II	24	37	9	226	24	8.07	-	-	7	654.4	126	2087	84	24.84	6-46
1996-2002	Trinidad & Tobago	Domestic O.D. Matches	II	23	15	3	135	41	11.25	-	-	9	172	16	574	31	18.51	4-22
1997//	Trinidad & Tobago	O.A.L. O.D. Matches	WI	1	1	1	4	4*	-	-	-	-	9	0	30	1	30.00	1-30
1997-2003	WEST INDIES	TEST MATCHES	HA	34	60	2	415	43	7.15	-	-	16	1296.4	236	3965	123	32.23	5-71
1997-2002	West Indies	First Class Matches	A	13	14	3	103	44	9.36	-	-	7	307.2	69	912	27	33.77	4-48
1997-2002	WEST INDIES	O.D.I. MATCHES	HA	89	44	19	195	21*	7.80	-	-	18	770.3	57	3507	114	30.76	5-51
1999-2000	W.I. Select XI	O.D.(I.) Matches	WI	2	2	0	7	6	3.50	-	-	-	17	0	72	1	72.00	1-33
1999-2000	West Indies "A"	O.D.(I.) Matches	H	2	2	0	10	8	5.00	-	-	1	16	3	47	1	47.00	1-27
1997-2000	West Indies	O.A.L. O.D. Matches	A	3	1	0	6	6	6.00	-	-	1	24	2	110	0	-	-
2000-2001	Busta Cup XI	First Class Matches	WI	1	2	0	4	2	2.00	-	1	1	29	11	58	1	58.00	1-31
1999-2000	West Indies "A"	First Class Matches	H	2	3	0	53	52	17.66	-	-	-	83	27	167	14	11.92	6-40
		Total First Class Career		74	116	14	801	52	7.85	0	1	31	2370.4	469	7189	249	28.05	6-40
		Total O.D. Career		120	65	23	357	41	8.50	0	0	28	1008.3	78	4340	148	29.32	5-51

UTON GEORGE DOWE

D.O.B. 29.03.1949 - St Mary's, Jamaica
First Class Debut 07.02.1970 - Jamaica v Cavaliers XI
Test Match Debut 01.04.1971 - West Indies v India
Domestic O.D. Debut 13.04.1973 - Jamaica v Guyana

Test 140-132   **Teams Played For** 2   RHB / RF
Jamaica
West Indies

SEASON	TEAM	COMPETITION	V	M	I	No	BATTING RUNS	H.S.	Av	100s	50s	CT	BOWLING OV	MD	RUNS	W	Av	B.B.
1970-1977	Jamaica	First Class Matches	I	23	24	7	120	25*	7.05	-	-	6	694.1	138	2169	85	25.51	7-19
1973-1977	Jamaica	Domestic O.D. Matches	II	3	2	2	11	6*	-	-	-	-	26.3	3	128	4	32.00	2-39
1971-1973	WEST INDIES	TEST MATCHES	H	4	3	2	8	5*	8.00	-	-	3	169	30	534	12	44.50	4-69
		Total First Class Career		27	27	9	128	25*	7.11	0	0	9	863.1	168	2703	97	27.86	7-19
		Total O.D. Career		3	2	2	11	6*	-	0	0	0	26.3	3	128	4	32.00	2-39

VASBERT CONNIEL DRAKES

D.O.B. 05.08.1969 - Springhead, St Andrew, Barbados

First Class Debut	07.02.1992 - Barbados v Leeward Islands
Test Match Debut	08.12.2002.West Indies v Bangladesh
O.D.I. Debut	08.03.1995 - West Indies v Australia
Domestic O.D. Debut	19.02.1992 - Barbados v Guyana

Test 246-932
O.D.I. 72-291

Teams Played For 9
Barbados, West Indies
West Indies U23, W.I. Board XI
Sussex, Nottinghamshire
Warwickshire, Leicestershire
Border

RHB / RF

SEASON	TEAM	COMPETITION	V	M	I	No	RUNS	H.S.	Av	100s	50s	CT	OV	MD	RUNS	W	Av	B.B.
1992-2003	Barbados	First Class Matches	II	27	38	8	971	180*	32.36	2	2	8	741.5	124	2488	92	2.04	7-47
1992-2002	Barbados	Domestic O.D. Matches	II	23	13	3	219	46*	21.90	-	-	5	184.2	19	686	28	24.50	3-15
1992-1998	Barbados	O.A.L. O.D. Matches	HA	11	10	5	108	27*	21.60	-	-	1	81.2	9	283	9	31.44	4-26
2002-2003	WEST INDIES	TEST MATCHES	HA	7	11	2	194	30	21.55	-	-	1	234.1	37	751	23	32.65	5-93
1995//	West Indies	First Class Matches	A	6	9	1	118	48*	14.75	-	-	2	106.1	7	400	16	25.00	5-20
1995//	W.I. Board XI	First Class Matches	WI	1	2	0	8	7	4.00	-	-	-	14	2	53	1	53.00	1-53
1995-2003	WEST INDIES	O.D.I. MATCHES	HA	30	14	5	82	25	9.11	-	-	5	242.2	17	1158	47	24.63	5-33
1995-2003	West Indies	O.A.L. O.D. Matches	A	2	2	1	1	1*	1.00	-	-	-	16	1	83	2	41.50	1-41
1992-1993	West Indies U23	First Class Matches	WI	1	2	0	51	34	25.50	-	-	-	21	0	90	2	45.00	2-44
1996-1997	Sussex	First Class Matches	E	25	45	4	870	145*	21.21	2	4	8	754.3	139	2718	81	33.55	5-47
1996-1997	Sussex	Nat West Trophy	E	7	4	1	104	35	34.66	-	1	-	73.3	-	250	15	16.66	4-62
1996-1997	Sussex	Benson & Hedges Cup	E	8	6	1	130	58	26.00	-	1	-	66	-	289	11	26.27	5-19
1996-1997	Sussex	Sunday League	E	23	20	4	213	37	13.31	-	-	2	160.2	-	862	24	35.91	4-50
1999//	Nottinghamshire	First Class Matches	E	17	30	3	427	80	15.81	-	2	5	586.2	131	1794	80	22.42	6-39
1999//	Nottinghamshire	Nat West Trophy	E	1	1	0	7	7	7.00	-	-	-	10	-	47	3	15.66	3-47
1999//	Nottinghamshire	Sunday League	E	15	12	2	181	40	18.70	-	-	4	112.4	-	511	24	21.29	5-31
2001//	Warwickshire	First Class Matches	E	14	13	3	209	50	20.90	-	1	1	505.2	107	1537	42	36.59	5-37
2001//	Warwickshire	Cheltenham & Gloucs Trophy	E	4	1	0	7	7	7.00	-	-	-	38.3	5	145	3	48.33	2-31
2001//	Warwickshire	Benson & Hedges Cup	E	6	4	1	13	9	4.33	-	-	-	56.2	14	164	7	23.42	3-25
2001//	Warwickshire	Sunday League	E	8	4	2	64	43	32.00	-	-	1	70.4	11	279	9	31.00	3-35
1996-2002	Border	First Class Matches	SA	53	86	7	1581	98	20.01	-	7	27	1883	442	4997	243	20.56	8-59
1996-2002	Border	B & H/Standard Bank Cup	SA	61	45	5	538	104	13.45	4	-	15	487.4	-	1942	83	23.39	4-16
2003//	Leicestershire	First Class Matches	E	5	7	1	57	18	9.50	-	-	1	143.1	33	463	11	42.09	3-58
2003//	Leicestershire	National Sunday League	E	7	6	2	74	43*	18.50	-	-	2	52	3	244	4	61.00	1-22
	Total First Class Career			156	243	29	4486	180*	20.96	4	16	52	4989.3	1027	15290	591	25.87	8-59
	Total O.D. Career			206	142	32	1741	104	15.82	1	1	36	1650.4	142	6943	269	25.81	5-19

BATTING / BOWLING

PETER JEFFREY LEROY DUJON

RHB / RAM / WK

D.O.B.	28.05.1956 - Kingston, Jamaica
First Class Debut	21.03.1975 - Jamaica v Trinidad & Tobago
Test Match Debut	26.12.1981 - West Indies v Australia
O.D.I. Debut	05.12.1981 - West Indies v Pakistan
Domestic O.D. Debut	22.02.1976 - Jamaica v Barbados

		Teams Played For	
Test	176-209	Jamaica	5
O.D.I.	36-38	West Indies	
		W.I. President's XI	
		West Indies "B"	
		World XI	

SEASON	TEAM	COMPETITION	V	M	I	No	BATTING RUNS	H.S.	Av	100s	50s	CT/ST	BOWLING OV	MD	RUNS	W	Av	B.B.
1975-1993	Jamaica	First Class Matches	II	70	114	18	3927	163*	40.90	8	23	108/13	2	1	1	0	-	-
1976-1993	Jamaica	Domestic O.D. Matches	II	34	33	5	650	97	23.21	-	6	33/6	-	-	-	-	-	-
1984//	Jamaica	O.A.L. O.D. Matches	WI	1	D	-	-	-	-	-	-	-	-	-	-	-	-	-
1981-1991	WEST INDIES	TEST MATCHES	HA	81	115	11	3322	139	31.94	5	16	267/5	-	-	-	-	-	-
1981-1991	West Indies	First Class Matches	A	42	56	16	2194	151*	54.85	7	10	61/4	10	3	44	1	44.00	1-43
1981//	West Indies "B"	First Class Matches	A	3	6	0	124	60	20.66	-	1	8	-	-	-	-	-	-
1981//	W.I. President's XI	First Class Matches	WI	1	2	1	106	105*	106.00	1	-	-	-	-	-	-	-	-
1981-1991	WEST INDIES	O.D.I. MATCHES	HA	169	120	36	1945	82*	23.15	-	6	183/21	-	-	-	-	-	-
1981//	West Indies "B"	O.D.(I.) Matches	A	4	4	0	37	20	9.25	-	-	3	-	-	-	-	-	-
1984-1988	West Indies	O.A.L. O.D. Matches	A	4	4	2	73	27	36.50	-	-	-	-	-	-	-	-	-
1987-1989	World XI	First Class Matches	E	3	5	2	90	42*	30.00	-	-	3	-	-	-	-	-	-
Total First Class Career				200	298	48	9763	163*	39.05	21	50	447/22	12	4	45	1	45.00	1-43
Total O.D. Career				212	161	43	2705	97	22.92	0	12	219/27	-	-	-	-	-	-

FIDEL HENDERSON EDWARDS

D.O.B. 06.02.1982 - Gays Village, St Peter, Barbados

First Class Debut 01.02.2002 - Barbados v Windward Islands

Test Match Debut 27.06.2003 - West Indies v Sri Lanka

Test 353-399

Teams Played For
Barbados
West Indies

RHB / RF

SEASON	TEAM	COMPETITION	V	M	I	No	RUNS	H.S.	Av	100s	50s	CT	OV	MD	RUNS	W	Av	B.B.
							BATTING						**BOWLING**					
2001-2002	Barbados	First Class Matches	=	1	2	0	9	9	9.00	-	-	1	16	3	53	1	53.00	1-22
2002-2003	West Indies	Test Matches	H	1	1	1	5	5*	-	-	-	-	30.4	3	90	6	15.00	5-36
		Total First Class Career		2	3	1	14	9	7.00	0	0	1	46.4	6	143	7	20.42	5-36

2

302

RICHARD MARTIN EDWARDS

D.O.B.	03.06.1940 - Garden Gap, Worthing, Christ Church, Barbados
First Class Debut	21.10.1961 - Barbados v British Guiana
Test Match Debut	26.12.1968 - West Indies v Australia

RHB / RF

Test	128-119	Teams Played For	4
		Barbados	
		West Indies	
		W.I. President's XI	
		N.Z. Governor's XI	

SEASON	TEAM	COMPETITION	V	M	I	No	BATTING						BOWLING					
							RUNS	H.S.	Av	100s	50s	CT	OV	MD	RUNS	W	Av	B.B.
1961-1970	Barbados	First Class Matches	II	20	23	6	199	31	11.70	-	-	11	443.5	96	1395	42	33.21	6-45
1968-1969	WEST INDIES	TEST MATCHES	A	5	8	1	65	22	9.28	-	-	-	163.7	25	626	18	34.77	5-84
1968-1969	West Indies	First Class Matches	A	8	9	2	77	28*	11.00	-	-	1	152.7	19	655	14	46.78	4-13
1967-1968	W.I. President's XI	First Class Matches	WI	1	1	0	13	13	13.00	-	-	1	24	6	83	1	83.00	1-73
1968-1969	N.Z. Governor's XI	First Class Matches	NZ	1	2	1	35	34	35.00	-	-	2	16	1	72	3	24.00	2-53
Total First Class Career				35	43	10	389	34	11.78	0	0	15	800.3	147	2831	78	36.29	6-45

WILFRED F. FERGUSON

D.O.B. 14.12.1917 - Longdenville, Caroni, Trinidad (d. 23.02.1961)
First Class Debut 20.02.1943 - Trinidad v Barbados
Test Match Debut 21.01.1948 - West Indies v England

Test 54-23

Teams Played For
Trinidad
West Indies

RHB / RLS

2

SEASON	TEAM	COMPETITION	V	M	I	No	BATTING RUNS	H.S.	Av	100s	50s	CT	BOWLING OV	MD	RUNS	W	Av	B.B.
1943-1956	Trinidad	First Class Matches	=	25	37	5	769	90	24.03	-	4	22	764.4	94	2834	90	31.48	7-73
1948-1954	WEST INDIES	TEST MATCHES	HA	8	10	3	200	75	28.58	-	2	11	428	83	1165	34	34.26	6-92
1948-1952	West Indies	First Class Matches	A	16	18	5	256	52	19.69	-	1	15	364.1	51	1207	41	29.43	6-45
		Total First Class Career		49	65	13	1225	90	23.55	0	7	48	1556.5	228	5206	165	31.55	7-73

MAURIUS PACHECO FERNANDES

D.O.B. 12.08.1897 - Georgetown, Demerara, British Guiana (d. 08.05.1981)

First Class Debut 23.09.1922 - British Guiana v Trinidad

Test Match Debut 23.06.1928 - West Indies v England

Test	3-1		**Teams Played For**	British Guiana		**2**	**RHB**
				West Indies			

BATTING / BOWLING

SEASON	TEAM	COMPETITION	V	M	I	No	RUNS	H.S.	Av	100s	50s	CT	OV	MD	RUNS	W	Av	B.B.
1922-1932	British Guiana	First Class Matches	H	13	24	0	939	141	39.12	3	4	5	53.3	0	183	5	36.60	2-29
1928-1930	WEST INDIES	TEST MATCHES	HA	2	4	0	49	22	12.25	-	-	-	-	-	-	-	-	-
1923-1928	West Indies	First Class Matches	HA	31	51	5	1099	110	23.89	1	5	25	-	-	-	-	-	-
Total First Class Career				46	79	5	2087	141	28.20	4	9	30	53.3	0	183	5	36.60	2-29

THADDEUS MICHAEL FINDLAY

D.O.B. 19.10.1943 - Trouamaca, St Vincent, Windward Islands

First Class Debut 22.05.1965 - Windward Islands v Australia
Test Match Debut 26.06.1969 - West Indies v England
Domestic O.D. Debut 21.02.1976 - Windward Islands v Trinidad & Tobago

Test 123-127

Teams Played For: Windward Islands, Combined Islands, West Indies, W.I. President's XI

RHB / WK

SEASON	TEAM	COMPETITION	V	M	I	No	BATTING RUNS	H.S.	Av	100s	50s	CT/ST	BOWLING OV	MD	RUNS	W	Av	B.B.
1965-1978	Windward Islands	First Class Matches	II	26	45	5	1118	90	27.95	-	10	51/11	-	-	-	-	-	-
1970-1978	Combined Islands	First Class Matches	II	36	60	6	951	68*	21.61	-	2	66/16	-	-	-	-	-	-
1976-1977	Windward Islands	Domestic O.D. Matches	II	6	5	0	53	28	7.57	-	-	1	-	-	-	-	-	-
1972//	Windward Islands	O.A.L. O.D. Matches	WI	1	1	1	9	9*	-	-	-	1	-	-	-	-	-	-
1973-1974	Combined Islands	O.A.L. O.D. Matches	WI	1	1	0	3	3	3.00	-	-	0/1	-	-	-	-	-	-
1969-1973	WEST INDIES	TEST MATCHES	HA	10	16	3	212	44*	16.30	-	-	19/2	-	-	-	-	-	-
1968-1976	West Indies	First Class Matches	A	36	47	10	624	59	16.86	-	2	71/14	-	-	-	-	-	-
1972-1977	W.I. President's XI	First Class Matches	WI	2	2	1	22	19	22.00	-	-	2	-	-	-	-	-	-
1976//	West Indies	O.A.L. O.D Matches	A	1	1	1	6	6*	-	-	-	-	1	0	4	0	-	-
	Total First Class Career			110	170	25	2927	90	20.18	0	14	209/43	-	-	-	-	-	-
	Total O.D. Career			9	8	2	71	28	11.83	0	0	2/1	1	0	4	0	-	-

MAURICE LINTON CHURCHILL FOSTER

D.O.B. 09.05.1943 - Retreat, St Mary's, Jamaica

First Class Debut 09.01.1964 - Jamaica v Cavaliers XI
Test Match Debut 12.06.1969 - West Indies v England
O.D.I. Debut 05.09.1973 - West Indies v England
Domestic O.D. Debut 13.04.1973 - Jamaica v Guyana

Test 130-126
O.D.I 3-1

Teams Played For: Jamaica, West Indies, W.I. President's XI — 3

RHB / OB

SEASON	TEAM	COMPETITION	V	M	I	No	BATTING RUNS	H.S.	Av	100s	50s	CT	BOWLING OV	MD	RUNS	W	Av	B.B.
1964-1978	Jamaica	First Class Matches	=	68	109	9	4845	234	48.45	15	23	27	1512.3	561	2835	101	28.06	5-65
1972-1978	Jamaica	Domestic O.D. Matches	=	6	6	1	118	49	23.60	-	-	4	55.3	3	166	12	13.83	5-24
1969-1978	WEST INDIES	TEST MATCHES	HA	14	24	5	580	125	30.52	1	1	3	296	106	600	9	66.66	2-41
1969-1973	West Indies	First Class Matches	A	27	36	11	1208	127	48.32	1	11	6	169.4	53	430	14	30.71	3-28
1968-1974	W.I. President's XI	First Class Matches	WI	3	6	1	98	48	19.60	-	-	1	88.4	23	191	8	23.87	4-59
1973//	WEST INDIES	O.D.I. MATCHES	A	2	1	0	25	25	25.00	-	-	-	5	0	22	2	11.00	2-22
1969//	West Indies	O.A.L. O.D. Matches	A	1	1	0	8	8	8.00	-	-	-						
Total First Class Career				112	175	26	6731	234	45.17	17	35	37	2066.5	743	4056	132	30.72	2-65
Total O.D. Career				9	8	14	151	49	21.57	0	0	4	60.3	3	188	14	13.42	5-24

307

GEORGE NATHANIEL FRANCIS

D.O.B. 11.12.1897 - Trent, St James, Barbados (d. 07.01.1942)

First Class Debut 23.05.1923 - West Indies v Sussex
Test Match Debut 23.06.1928 - West Indies v England

Test 10-1 RHB / RF

Teams Played For
Barbados
West Indies
Combined B/J XI
C.A. Merry's XI

							BATTING						BOWLING					
SEASON	TEAM	COMPETITION	V	M	I	No	RUNS	H.S.	Av	100s	50s	CT	OV	MD	RUNS	W	Av	B.B.
1924-1930	Barbados	First Class Matches	II	5	3	0	98	47	32.66	-	-	2	170.1	29	452	28	16.14	7-50
1928-1933	WEST INDIES	TEST MATCHES	HA	10	18	4	81	19*	5.78	-	-	7	269.5	54	763	23	33.17	4-40
1923-1931	West Indies	First Class Matches	A	44	64	19	591	61	13.13	-	1	32	1316.3	262	3695	160	23.09	6-33
1927-1928	Combined B/J XI	First Class Matches	WI	2	4	0	83	37	20.75	-	-	1	46	9	194	6	32.33	4-110
1932-1933	C.A. Merry's XI	First Class Matches	WI	1	2	0	21	18	10.50	-	-	-	17	3	55	6	9.16	5-38
Total First Class Career				62	91	23	874	61	12.85	0	1	42	1819.3	357	5159	223	23.13	7-50

MICHAEL CAMPBELL FREDERICK

D.O.B. 06.05.1927 - Mile and a Quarter, St Peter, Barbados

First Class Debut 02.10.1944 - Barbados v British Guiana

Test Match Debut 15.01.1954 - West Indies v England

	Test	Teams Played For		
	81-48	Barbados	4	RHB / RM
		Jamaica		
		West Indies		
		Derbyshire		

							BATTING						BOWLING					
SEASON	TEAM	COMPETITION	V	M	I	No	RUNS	H.S.	Av	100s	50s	CT	OV	MD	RUNS	W	Av	B.B.
1944-1945	Barbados	First Class Matches	=	1	1	0	8	8	8.00	-	-	-	-	-	-	-	-	-
1953-1954	Jamaica	First Class Matches	=	2	4	0	158	60	39.50	-	2	2	-	-	-	-	-	-
1953-1954	WEST INDIES	TEST MATCHES	H	1	2	0	30	30	15.00	-	-	-	-	-	-	-	-	-
1949//	Derbyshire	First Class Matches	E	2	3	0	98	84	32.67	-	1	1	-	-	-	-	-	-
		Total First Class Career		6	10	0	294	84	29.40	0	3	3	-	-	-	-	-	-

ROY CLIFTON FREDERICKS

D.O.B. 11.11.1942 - Blairmont, Berbice, British Guiana (d. 05.09.2000)

First Class Debut	05.03.1964 - British Guiana v Jamaica
Test Match Debut	26.12.1968 - West Indies v Australia
O.D.I. Debut	05.09.1973 - West Indies v England
Domestic O.D. Debut	25.04.1971 - Glamorgan v Essex

Teams Played For 8
British Guiana/Guyana, Berbice
Demerara, West Indies
W.I. President's XI, Glamorgan
Cavaliers XI
N.Z. Governor's XI

Test 129-119
O.D.I. 2-1

LHB / SLA

SEASON	TEAM	COMPETITION	V	M	I	No	BATTING RUNS	H.S.	Av	100s	50s	CT	BOWLING OV	MD	RUNS	W	Av	B.B.
1964-1983	Br. Guiana/Guyana	First Class Matches	II	47	79	8	4532	250	63.83	15	22	34	234.2	45	793	19	41.73	4-36
1972//	Berbice	First Class Matches	G	1	2	0	80	62	40.00	-	1	-	28	4	108	7	15.42	4-48
1979//	Demerara	First Class Matches	G	1	D	-	-	-	-	-	-	-	-	-	-	-	-	-
1977-1983	Guyana	Domestic O.D. Matches	II	6	6	0	187	119	31.16	1	0	1	13	2	45	1	45.00	1-27
1968-1977	WEST INDIES	TEST MATCHES	HA	59	109	7	4334	169	42.49	8	26	62	189.1	41	548	7	78.28	1-12
1968-1976	West Indies	First Class Matches	A	66	113	40	4194	202	40.71	10	17	53	191.2	35	694	20	34.70	3-10
1968-1974	W.I. President's XI	First Class Matches	WI	2	4	1	94	64*	31.33	-	1	3	8	1	28	0	-	-
1973-1976	WEST INDIES	O.D.I. MATCHES	HA	12	12	0	311	105	25.91	1	1	4	1.4	0	10	2	5.00	2-10
1969-1976	West Indies	O.A.L. O.D. Matches	A	5	5	0	99	54	19.80	-	1	4	8.1	1	26	3	8.66	3-5
1971-1973	Glamorgan	First Class Matches	E	45	80	8	2991	228*	41.54	7	12	21	207.1	45	667	20	33.35	3-37
1972//	Glamorgan	Nat West Trophy	E	3	3	0	114	82	38.00	-	1	2	-	-	-	-	-	-
1972-1973	Glamorgan	Benson & Hedges Cup	E	10	10	0	195	87	19.50	-	1	6	2	0	10	0	-	-
1971-1973	Glamorgan	Sunday League	E	32	32	0	738	84	23.06	-	5	16	4.5	0	25	1	25.00	1-17
1969//	Cavaliers XI	First Class Matches	E	1	2	0	83	43	41.50	-	-	2	-	-	-	-	-	-
1968-1969	N.Z. Governor's XI	First Class Matches	NZ	1	2	0	76	62	38.00	-	1	2	1.7	0	8	2	4.00	2-8
Total First Class Career				223	391	34	16384	250	45.89	40	80	177	859.5	171	2846	75	37.94	4-36
Total O.D. Career				68	68	0	1644	119	24.17	2	9	33	29.4	3	116	7	16.57	3-5

RICHARD LIVINGSTON FULLER

D.O.B. 30.01.1913 - St Anns Bay, St Ann, Jamaica (d. 03.05.1987)

First Class Debut 05.03.1935 - Jamaica v M.C.C.

Test Match Debut 14.03.1935 - West Indies v England

Test 43-19

Teams Played For Jamaica, West Indies

2

RHB / RFM

SEASON	TEAM	COMPETITION	V	M	I	No	RUNS	H.S.	Av	100s	50s	CT	OV	MD	RUNS	W	Av	B.B.
							BATTING						**BOWLING**					
1935-1947	Jamaica	First Class Matches	E	7	12	3	279	113*	31.00	1	-	5	142.2	17	512	12	42.66	4-69
1934-1935	WEST INDIES	TEST MATCHES	E	1	1	0	1	1	1.00	-	-	-	8	2	12	0	-	-
Total First Class Career				8	13	3	280	113*	28.00	1	0	5	150.2	19	524	12	43.66	4-69

HAMMOND ALAN FURLONGE

D.O.B. 19.06.1934 - Fyzabad Village, Trinidad
First Class Debut 05.02.1955 - Trinidad v Jamaica
Test Match Debut 11.06.1955 - West Indies v Australia

Test 91-57

Teams Played For 3
Trinidad
North Trinidad
West Indies

RHB

SEASON	TEAM	COMPETITION	V	M	I	No	RUNS	H.S.	Av	100s	50s	CT	OV	MD	RUNS	W	Av	B.B.
							BATTING						**BOWLING**					
1955-1962	Trinidad	First Class Matches	J	8	15	1	516	150*	36.85	2	1	3	6	0	30	0	-	-
1960-1961	North Trinidad	First Class Matches	T	2	3	0	87	38	29.00	-	-	1	-	-	-	-	-	-
1955-1956	WEST INDIES	TEST MATCHES	HA	3	5	0	99	64	19.80	-	1	-	-	-	-	-	-	-
1955-1956	West Indies	First Class Matches	A	3	4	1	106	65	35.33	-	1	3	-	-	-	-	-	-
Total First Class Career				16	27	2	808	150*	32.33	2	3	7	6	0	30	0	-	-

RICHARD SIMEON GABRIEL

D.O.B. 05.06.1952 - Point Fortin, Trinidad

First Class Debut 17.01.1969 - Trinidad & Tobago v Windward Islands
O.D.I. Debut 08.01.1984 - West Indies v Australia
Domestic O.D. Debut 12.03.1977 - Trinidad & Tobago v Windward Islands

O.D.I. 42-66

RHB / OB

Teams Played For 7
Trinidad & Tobago, North Trinidad
South Trinidad, East Trinidad
N/E Trinidad
West Indies
W.I. President's XI

SEASON	TEAM	COMPETITION	V	M	I	No	BATTING RUNS	H.S.	Av	100s	50s	CT	BOWLING OV	MD	RUNS	W	Av	B.B.
1969-1986	Trinidad & Tobago	First Class Matches	=	59	103	6	3127	129	32.33	4	14	51	11.3	2	32	1	32.00	1-7
1970-1979	North Trinidad	First Class Matches	T	9	14	1	375	95	28.84	-	3	6	7	1	16	3	5.33	3-15
1971-1972	South Trinidad	First Class Matches	T	2	4	0	60	28	15.00	-	1	-	-	-	-	-	-	-
1973-1976	East Trinidad	First Class Matches	T	8	15	0	177	32	11.80	-	-	7	2	1	1	0	-	-
1977-1985	N/E Trinidad	First Class Matches	T	4	6	0	189	103	31.50	1	1	1	1.1	0	5	0	-	-
1977-1986	Trinidad & Tobago	Domestic O.D. Matches	=	21	20	1	528	108*	27.78	1	2	6	2.2	0	14	1	14.00	1-8
1973-1981	W.I. President's XI	First Class Matches	WI	2	4	0	46	22	11.50	-	-	4	-	-	-	-	-	-
1983-1984	WEST INDIES	O.D.I. MATCHES	A	11	11	0	167	41	15.18	-	1	1	-	-	-	-	-	-
1984//	West Indies	O.A.L. O.D. Matches	A	1	1	0	2	2	2.00	-	-	-	-	-	-	-	-	-
		Total First Class Career		84	146	7	3974	129	28.58	5	18	70	21.4	4	54	4	13.50	3-15
		Total O.D. Career		33	32	1	697	108*	22.48	1	2	7	2.2	0	14	1	14.00	1-8

DARREN GANGA

D.O.B. 14.01.1979 - Barrackpore, Trinidad

First Class Debut	21.02.19973 - Trinidad & Tobago v Guyana
Test Match Debut	26.12.1998 - West Indies v South Africa
O.D.I. Debut	02.02.1999 - West Indies v South Africa
Domestic O.D. Debut	04.10.1997 - Trinidad & Tobago v Bermuda

Teams Played For 8
Trinidad & Tobago, West Indies
West Indies "A", W.I. Board XI
W.I. President's XI, W.I. Select XI
West Indies U23
Busta Cup XI

Test 223-346
O.D.I. 91-358

RHB / ROS

SEASON	TEAM	V	COMPETITION	M	I	No	BATTING						BOWLING					
							RUNS	H.S.	Av	100s	50s	CT	OV	MD	RUNS	W	Av	B.B.
1997-2003	Trinidad & Tobago	TT	First Class Matches	26	50	5	1790	151*	39.77	4	8	25	14.5	2	43	0	-	-
1997-2002	Trinidad & Tobago	TT	Domestic O.D. Matches	18	18	2	376	62	23.50	-	2	3	48	5	187	5	37.40	2-20
1997//	Trinidad & Tobago	WI	O.A.L. O.D. Matches	1	1	0	4	4	4.00	-	-	1	-	-	-	-	-	-
1998-2003	WEST INDIES	HA	TEST MATCHES	22	38	0	956	117	25.15	2	3	13	5	0	10	0	-	-
1998-2002	West Indies	A	First Class Matches	15	22	1	664	105	31.61	2	4	6	18	4	61	1	61.00	1-7
1999-2003	W.I. President's XI	WI	First Class Matches	3	5	0	157	54	31.40	-	1	1	0.3	0	7	7	7.00	1-7
1999-2002	West Indies "A"	HA	First Class Matches	8	13	3	482	139*	48.20	2	2	7	3	1	4	0	-	-
1999-2000	W.I. Select XI	WI	First Class Matches	1	1	0	24	24	24.00	-	-	-	-	-	-	-	-	-
2000-2001	W.I. Board XI	WI	First Class Matches	2	3	1	133	57	66.50	-	1	4	-	-	-	-	-	-
2001-2002	Busta Cup XI	WI	First Class Matches	2	3	1	120	80	60.00	-	1	1	1	0	1	0	-	-
1999-2002	WEST INDIES	HA	O.D.I. MATCHES	28	27	1	691	71	26.57	-	8	8	0.1	0	4	0	-	-
2001//	West Indies	A	O.A.L. O.D. Matches	2	2	0	108	101	54.00	1	-	-	-	-	-	-	-	-
2002//	West Indies "A"	A	O.A.L. O.D. Matches	5	5	1	105	57*	26.25	-	1	-	-	-	-	-	-	-
1999-2000	West Indies U23	WI	First Class Matches	1	2	0	9	5	4-50	-	-	-	-	-	-	-	-	-
Total First Class Career				80	137	11	4335	151*	34.40	10	20	57	42.2	7	126	2	63.00	1-7
Total O.D. Career				54	53	4	1284	101	26.20	1	11	12	48.1	5	191	5	38.20	2-20

ANDREW GORDON GANTEAUME

D.O.B. 22.01.1921 - Belmont, Port of Spain, Trinidad

First Class Debut 08.02.1941 - Trinidad v Barbados

Test Match Debut 11.02.1948 - West Indies v England

Test	Teams Played For		RHB / WK
60-24	Trinidad	2	
	West Indies		

SEASON	TEAM	COMPETITION	V	M	I	No	BATTING						BOWLING					
							RUNS	H.S.	Av	100s	50s	CT/ST	OV	MD	RUNS	W	Av	B.B.
1941-1963	Trinidad	First Class Matches	=	30	52	2	1873	159	37.46	4	10	23/3	5	0	31	0	-	-
1947-1948	WEST INDIES	TEST MATCHES	H	1	1	0	112	112	112.00	1	-	-	-	-	-	-	-	-
1957/l	West Indies	First Class Matches	A	19	32	3	800	92	27.58	-	7	11	3	0	20	0	-	-
		Total First Class Career		50	85	5	2785	159	34.81	5	17	34/3	8	0	51	0	-	-

JOEL GARNER

D.O.B. 16.12.1952 - Enterprise, Christ Church, Barbados

First Class Debut	30.01.1976 - Barbados v Combined Islands
Test Match Debut	18.02.1977 - West Indies v Pakistan
O.D.I. Debut	16.03.1977 - West Indies v Pakistan
Domestic O.D. Debut	26.01.1977 - Barbados v Pakistan

Test 160-174
O.D.I. 21-12

Teams Played For
Barbados, West Indies
W.I. President's XI
Somerset
South Australia
M.C.C.

6

RHB / RF

SEASON	TEAM	COMPETITION	V	M	I	No	BATTING						BOWLING					
							RUNS	H.S.	Av	100s	50s	CT	OV	MD	RUNS	W	Av	B.B.
1976-1988	Barbados	First Class Matches	II	29	36	7	656	67	22.62	-	4	20	868.5	185	2491	136	18.31	6-28
1977-1988	Barbados	Domestic O.D. Matches	II	19	8	2	37	19	6.16	-	-	8	163.2	31	449	35	12.82	5-32
1981//	Barbados	O.A.L. O.D. Matches	WI	1	1	0	9	9	9.00	-	-	-	10	0	38	2	19.00	2-38
1977-1986	WEST INDIES	TEST MATCHES	HA	58	68	14	672	60	12.44	-	1	42	2195.5	576	5433	259	20.97	6-56
1979-1986	West Indies	First Class Matches	A	24	21	5	318	104	19.87	1	0	16	495	141	1226	86	14.25	5-19
1977//	W.I. President's XI	First Class Matches	WI	1	1	0	10	10	10.00	-	-	1	31	10	86	7	12.28	4-40
1977-1986	WEST INDIES	O.D.I. MATCHES	HA	98	41	15	239	37	9.19	-	-	30	888.2	141	2752	146	18.84	5-31
1980-1987	West Indies	O.A.L. O.D. Matches	A	7	5	1	20	13	5.00	-	-	3	59	-	184	6	30.66	2-16
1977-1985	Somerset	First Class Matches	E	94	92	27	1170	90	18.00	-	3	47	2635	750	6121	338	18.10	8-31
1977-1985	Somerset	Nat West Trophy	E	26	13	4	121	38*	13.44	-	-	5	277.3	75	683	65	10.50	6-29
1978-1986	Somerset	Benson & Hedges Cup	E	21	10	5	70	17	14.00	-	-	4	209.4	-	521	40	13.02	5-14
1979-1986	Somerset	Sunday League	E	81	53	19	512	59*	15.05	-	1	21	592	-	1918	101	18.99	5-27
1992//	M.C.C.	O.A.L. O.D. Matches	E	1	0	-	-	-	-	-	-	-	8	-	17	2	8.50	2-17
1982-1983	South Australia	First Class Matches	A	8	13	1	138	22	11.50	-	-	3	403.1	131	976	55	17.74	7-78
1982-1983	South Australia	MacDonald Cup	A	2	2	0	15	8	7.50	-	-	-	19	-	36	0	-	-
		Total First Class Career		214	231	54	2964	104	16.74	1	8	129	6628.5	1793	16333	881	18.53	8-31
		Total O.D. Career		256	133	46	1023	59*	11.75	0	1	71	2226.5	-	6598	397	16.61	6-29

LEON VIVIAN GARRICK

D.O.B. 11.11.1976 - St.Ann, Jamaica
First Class Debut 24.01.1997 - Jamaica v Leeward Islands
Test Match Debut 19.04.2001 - West Indies v South Africa
O.D.I. Debut 28.04.2001 - West Indies v South Africa
Domestic O.D. Debut 12.10.1996 - Jamaica v Canada

Test 240-374
O.D.I. 106-418

Teams Played For 4
Jamaica
West Indies
West Indies "A"
W.I. Board XI

RHB / RM / WK

SEASON	TEAM	COMPETITION	V	M	I	No	BATTING RUNS	H.S.	Av	100s	50s	CT	BOWLING OV	MD	RUNS	W	Av	B.B.
1996-2003	Jamaica	First Class Matches	II	46	83	5	2701	200*	34.62	6	12	51	2	2	0	0	-	-
1996-2002	Jamaica	Domestic O.D. Matches	II	20	20	4	447	74	27.93	-	3	6	-	-	-	-	-	-
2000-2001	Jamaica	O.A.L. O.D. Matches	WI	4	4	0	65	25	16.25	-	-	1	0.4	-	6	0	-	-
2001//	WEST INDIES	TEST MATCHES	H	1	2	0	27	27	13.50	-	-	2	-	-	-	-	-	-
2000-2001	West Indies	First Class Matches	A	3	4	0	99	71	24.75	-	1	-	-	-	-	-	-	-
1997-1998	West Indies "A"	First Class Matches	HA	6	11	0	231	82	21.00	-	1	4	0.2	0	4	1	4.00	1-4
2001//	W.I. Board XI	First Class Matches	WI	1	2	0	33	28	16.50	-	2	-	-	-	-	-	-	-
2000-2001	WEST INDIES	O.D.I. MATCHES	HA	3	3	0	99	76	33.00	-	1	-	-	-	-	-	-	-
1997-1998	West Indies "A"	O.D.(I.) Matches	H	2	2	0	4	2	2.00	-	-	-	-	-	-	-	-	-
1997//	West Indies "A"	O.A.L. O.D. Matches	A	1	1	0	48	48	48.00	-	-	-	-	-	-	-	-	-
Total First Class Career				57	102	5	3121	200*	32.17	6	14	59	2.2	2	4	1	4.00	1-4
Total O.D. Career				30	30	4	663	76	25.50	0	4	7	0.4	0	6	0	-	-

BERKELEY BERTRAM McGARRELL GASKIN

D.O.B. 21.03.1908 - Georgetown, Demerara, British Guiana (d. 01.05.1979)

First Class Debut 31.01.1929 - British Guiana v Trinidad
Test Match Debut 21.01.1948 - West Indies v England

Test 55-23

Teams Played For
British Guiana
West Indies

2

RHB / RM

SEASON	TEAM	COMPETITION	V	M	I	No	BATTING RUNS	H.S.	Av	100s	50s	CT	BOWLING OV	MD	RUNS	W	Av	B.B.
1929-1954	British Guiana	First Class Matches	II	38	64	13	764	64	14.98	-	2	16	1572.1	377	4186	136	30.77	7-58
1947-1948	WEST INDIES	TEST MATCHES	H	2	3	0	17	10	5.66	-	-	1	79	24	158	2	79.00	1-15
1938-1939	West Indies	First Class Matches	H	1	1	0	1	1	1.00	-	-	2	18	1	50	0	-	-
		Total First Class Career		41	68	13	782	64	14.21	0	2	19	1669.1	402	4394	138	31.84	7-58

CHRISTOPHER HENRY GAYLE

D.O.B. 21.09.1979 - Kingston, Jamaica

First Class Debut 21.10.1998 - Jamaica v West Indies "A"

Test Match Debut 16.03.2000 - West Indies v Zimbabwe

O.D.I. Debut 11.09.1999 - West Indies v India

Domestic O.D. Debut 07.10.1998 - Jamaica v USA

Test 232-355
O.D.I. 96-377

Teams Played For 5
Jamaica
West Indies
West Indies "A"
W.I. Board XI
UWI Vice Chancellor's XI

LHB / OB

SEASON	TEAM	COMPETITION	V	M	I	No	BATTING RUNS	H.S.	Av	100s	50s	CT	BOWLING OV	MD	RUNS	W	Av	B.B.
1998-2003	Jamaica	First Class Matches	II	27	52	6	2047	208*	44.50	5	10	22	363.2	106	703	20	35.15	3-73
1998-2002	Jamaica	Domestic O.D. Matches	II	16	16	3	668	122	51.38	2	3	6	117	7	353	19	18.57	4-24
2000-2003	WEST INDIES	TEST MATCHES	HA	32	54	2	1792	204	34.46	2	11	43	183.1	37	444	11	40.36	3-25
2000-2002	West Indies	First Class Matches	A	14	23	3	1384	259*	69.20	5	6	22	64	8	201	5	40.20	4-86
1998-2002	West Indies "A"	First Class Matches	HA	9	16	2	454	94	32.42	-	3	10	129	16	376	7	53.71	2-30
1999/I	W.I. Board XI	First Class Matches	WI	1	2	1	22	11*	22.00	-	-	-	-	-	-	-	-	-
1999-2003	WEST INDIES	O.D.I. MATCHES	HA	78	76	1	2746	152	36.61	5	18	36	436	18	2033	67	30.34	5-46
1998-2000	West Indies "A"	O.D.I.(I.) Matches	A	5	5	1	196	70*	49.00	-	1	1	20	0	100	5	20.00	3-46
2002/II	West Indies "A"	O.A.L. O.D. Matches	A	2	2	0	132	83	66.00	-	1	1	11	1	51	2	25.50	2-11
2000-2001	West Indies	O.A.L. O.D. Matches	A	4	4	0	155	76	38.75	-	1	-	-	-	-	-	-	-
2002-2003	UWI V/Chancellor's XI	First Class Matches	WI	1	2	0	129	129	64.50	1	-	1	13	1	47	1	47.00	1-7
	Total First Class Career			84	149	14	5828	259*	43.17	13	29	82	752-3	168	1771	44	40.25	4-86
	Total O.D. Career			105	103	5	3897	152	39.76	7	24	45	3504	26	2537	93	27.27	5-46

GLENDON LIONEL GIBBS

D.O.B. 27.12.1925 - Georgetown, Demerara, British Guiana (d. 21.02.1979)

First Class Debut 09.02.1950 - British Guiana v Barbados

Test Match Debut 26.03.1955 - West Indies v Australia

Test 85-53

Teams Played For
British Guiana
West Indies

LHB / SLA

SEASON	TEAM	COMPETITION	V	M	I	No	BATTING RUNS	H.S.	Av	100s	50s	CT	BOWLING OV	MD	RUNS	W	Av	B.B.
1950-1963	British Guiana	First Class Matches	II	27	48	3	1718	216	38.17	5	6	14	357.5	41	1223	23	53.17	6-80
1954-1955	WEST INDIES	TEST MATCHES	H	1	2	0	12	12	6.00	-	-	1	4	1	7	0	-	-
	Total First Class Career			28	50	3	1730	216	36.80	5	6	15	361.5	42	1230	23	53.47	6-80

LANCELOT RICHARD GIBBS

D.O.B. 29.09.1934 - Georgetown, Demerara, British Guiana   RHB / OB

First Class Debut	17.02.1954 - British Guiana v M.C.C.
Test Match Debut	05.02.1958 - West Indies v Pakistan
O.D.I. Debut	05.09.1973 - West Indies v England
Domestic O.D. Debut	25.2.1968 - Warwickshire v Yorkshire

Test 99-68
O.D.I. 11-1

Teams Played For 8
British Guiana/Guyana, Demerara
West Indies, C.C. Hunte's XI
Warwickshire, South Australia
Commonwealth XI
World XI

SEASON	TEAM	COMPETITION	V	M	I	No	BATTING RUNS	H.S.	Av	100s	50s	CT	BOWLING OV	MD	RUNS	W	Av	B.B.
1954-1975	Br. Guiana/Guyana	First Class Matches	=	39	45	19	263	31	10.11	-	-	18	1828.5	538	3589	127	28.26	6-27
1972-1973	Demerara	First Class Matches	G	1	2	0	7	6	3.50	-	-	-	69.3	30	129	10	12.90	5-49
1958-1976	WEST INDIES	TEST MATCHES	HA	79	109	39	488	25	6.97	-	-	52	4206.5	1313	8989	309	29.09	8-38
1958-1976	West Indies	First Class Matches	A	81	69	28	458	43	11.17	-	-	39	2050.2	582	5127	192	26.70	5-22
1963//	C.C. Hunte's XI	First Class Matches	WI	1	2	0	20	12	10.00	-	1	-	28	2	116	3	38.66	2-70
1963-1969	West Indies	O.A.L. O.D Matches	A	3	1	1	1	1*	-	-	-	2	22	2	51	2	25.50	2-27
1973-1975	WEST INDIES	O.D.I. MATCHES	HA	3	1	1	0	0*	-	-	-	-	26	4	59	2	29.50	1-12
1967-1973	Warwickshire	First Class Matches	E	109	96	48	370	24	7.70	-	-	80	3610.5	1123	8281	338	24.50	8-37
1968-1973	Warwickshire	Nat West Trophy	E	12	5	4	20	6*	20.00	-	-	7	134	22	396	14	28.28	5-38
1972-1973	Warwickshire	Benson & Hedges Cup	E	9	3	1	5	4	2.50	-	-	2	98	-	294	13	22.61	3-18
1969-1973	Warwickshire	Sunday League	E	26	15	5	27	8*	2.70	-	-	9	191.2	-	778	33	23.58	3-28
1965-1973	World XI	First Class Matches	A	11	13	10	19	5	6.33	-	-	6	361.2	97	879	24	36.62	4-62
1964-1965	Commonwealth XI	First Class Matches	I	1	2	0	16	12	8.00	-	-	1	39	9	136	3	45.33	2-47
1969-1970	South Australia	First Class Matches	A	8	14	6	88	21*	11.00	-	-	6	254.4	74	632	18	35.11	4-84
1969-1970	South Australia	MacDonald Cup	A	1	D	-	-	-	-	-	-	-	10.3	0	39	0	-	-
Total First Class Career				330	352	150	1729	43	8.55	0	0	203	12449.2	3768	27878	1024	27.22	8-37
Total O.D. Career				54	25	12	53	8*	4.07	0	0	20	481.5	-	1617	64	25.26	5-38

OTTIS DELROY GIBSON

D.O.B. 16.03.1969 - Sion Hill, St Peter, Barbados

First Class Debut	01.02.1991 - Barbados v Windward Islands
Test Match Debut	22.06.1995 - West Indies v England
O.D.I. Debut	28.05.1995 - West Indies v England
Domestic O.D. Debut	19.02.1992 - Barbados v Guyana

Test 210-316
O.D.I. 73-298

Teams Played For: Barbados, W.I. Board XI, W.I. President's XI, West Indies, West Indies "A", Glamorgan, Border, Griqualand West, Gauteng, Staffordshire

RHB / RF   10

SEASON	TEAM	COMPETITION	V	M	I	No	BATTING RUNS	H.S.	Av	100s	50s	CT	BOWLING OV	MD	RUNS	W	Av	B.B.
1991-1998	Barbados	First Class Matches	II	34	48	6	620	49	14.76	-	-	20	1028.5	165	3385	139	24.35	7-78
1992-1998	Barbados	Domestic O.D. Matches	II	23	17	5	213	41*	17.75	-	-	10	194.2	15	814	37	23.00	5-25
1992-1998	Barbados	O.A.L. O.D. Matches	HA	4	4	3	65	37*	65.00	-	-	1	34	5	116	7	16.57	3-38
1995-1999	WEST INDIES	TEST MATCHES	HA	2	4	0	93	37	23.25	-	-	-	78.4	9	275	3	91.66	2-81
1995-1996	West Indies	First Class Matches	A	11	12	2	261	101*	26.10	1	-	5	234.4	42	914	32	28.56	4-32
1993//	W.I. President's XI	First Class Matches	WI	1	D	-	-	-	-	-	-	-	15	0	69	0	-	-
1994-1995	West Indies "A"	First Class Matches	WI	2	2	0	55	55	27.50	-	1	1	52.4	11	132	8	16.50	4-45
1992-1998	West Indies "A"	First Class Matches	HA	7	11	1	180	41	18.00	-	1	1	192.1	38	578	20	28.90	5-85
1995-1996	WEST INDIES	O.D.I. MATCHES	HA	15	11	1	141	52	14.10	-	1	3	123.1	8	621	34	18.26	5-40
1996-1998	West Indies "A"	O.D.(I.) Matches	A	5	5	0	57	38	11.40	-	-	1	38.4	1	193	5	38.60	3-32
1995-1996	West Indies	O.A.L. O.D. Matches	A	5	4	0	99	57	24.75	-	1	2	42	3	208	5	41.60	3-25
1996-1997	West Indies "A"	O.A.L. O.D. Matches	A	3	2	1	9	6*	9.00	-	-	3	29	3	110	8	13.75	5-28
1994-1996	Glamorgan	First Class Matches	E	29	46	7	1159	97	29.71	-	10	13	833.4	141	3209	80	40.11	6-64
1994-1996	Glamorgan	Nat West Trophy	E	3	3	0	68	44	22.66	-	-	1	27	3	116	5	23.20	3-34
1994-1996	Glamorgan	Benson & Hedges Cup	E	4	3	0	105	68	52.50	-	1	-	33.4	-	176	3	58.66	2-50
1994-1996	Glamorgan	Sunday League	E	29	24	8	362	47*	22.62	-	-	8	169.3	-	785	22	35.68	2-18
2001	Staffordshire	Nat West Trophy	E	3	3	1	143	102*	71.50	1	-	-	25	2	97	3	32.33	2-49
1992-1995	Border	First Class Matches	SA	14	26	4	515	83*	23.40	-	3	3	521.5	88	1560	67	23.28	7-55
1992//	Border	Nissan Cup	SA	2	1	0	17	17	17.00	-	-	-	21.4	4	62	7	8.85	5-19
1992-1995	Border	Benson & Hedges Cup	SA	17	11	1	233	41	23.30	-	-	3	154.1	13	656	28	23.42	4-35
1998-2000	Griqualand West	First Class Matches	SA	14	22	2	545	62	27.25	-	2	5	488.5	87	1509	60	25.15	7-141
1998-2000	Griqualand West	Benson & Hedges Cup	SA	23	21	5	384	76	24.00	-	1	6	190.3	17	856	33	25.93	4-19
2000-2001	Gauteng	First Class Matches	SA	5	8	1	143	52	20.42	-	1	2	162.3	41	443	16	27.68	6-53
2000-2001	Gauteng	Standard Bank Cup	SA	10	10	1	133	30	14.77	-	-	1	86	3	453	9	50.33	3-44
1993-1994	Border	O.A.L. O.D. Matches	SA	1	D	-	-	-	-	-	-	-	9.3	0	79	4	19.75	4-79
Total First Class Career				119	179	23	3571	101*	22.89	1	17	50	3609	622	12074	425	28.40	7-55
Total O.D. Career				147	118	26	2029	102*	22.05	1	4	39	1178.2	-	5342	210	25.43	5-19

ROY GILCHRIST

D.O.B. 28.06.1934 - Seaforth, St Thomas, Jamaica (d. 18.07.2001)

First Class Debut 11.10.1956 - Jamaica v British Guiana

Test Match Debut 30.05.1957 - West Indies v England

RHB / RF

Test 93-62   6

Teams Played For
Jamaica, West Indies
Hyderabad
South Zone
Chidambarams XI
Chief Minister's XI

SEASON	TEAM	COMPETITION	V	M	I	No	BATTING RUNS	H.S.	Av	100s	50s	CT	BOWLING OV	MD	RUNS	W	Av	B.B.
1956-1962	Jamaica	First Class Matches	≡	5	8	1	60	16	8.57	-	-	1	211.2	37	774	16	48.37	5-110
1957-1958	WEST INDIES	TEST MATCHES	HA	13	14	3	60	12	5.45	-	-	4	537.5	124	1521	57	26.68	6-55
1957-1958	West Indies	First Class Matches	A	18	14	6	106	43*	13.25	-	-	4	430.3	79	1255	72	17.43	6-16
1962-1963	Hyderabad	First Class Matches	-	1	1	0	0	0	0.00	-	-	-	54.3	9	235	9	26.11	5-124
1962-1963	South Zone	First Class Matches	-	2	2	0	0	0	0.00	-	-	-	49	4	259	5	51.80	3-116
1962-1963	Chidambarams XI	First Class Matches	-	1	1	0	7	7	7.00	-	-	1	22	2	69	3	23.00	2-29
1962-1963	Chief Minister's XI	First Class Matches	-	2	3	0	25	16	8.33	-	-	-	41	4	229	5	45.80	3-82
	Total First Class Career			42	43	10	258	43*	7.81	0	0	10	1346.1	259	4342	167	26.00	6-16

GEORGE GLADSTONE

D.O.B. 14.01.1901 - Kingston, Jamaica (d. 19.05.1978)

First Class Debut 28.03.1930 - Jamaica v M.C.C.
Test Match Debut 03.04.1930 - West Indies v England

Teams Played For
Jamaica
West Indies

Test 28-7

LHB / SLA

SEASON	TEAM	COMPETITION	V	M	I	No	BATTING RUNS	H.S.	Av	100s	50s	CT	BOWLING OV	MD	RUNS	W	Av	B.B.
1929-1930	Jamaica	First Class Matches	=	1	1	1	14	14*	-	-	-	1	75.3	12	252	9	28.00	6-142
1929-1930	WEST INDIES	TEST MATCHES	H	1	1	1	12	12*	-	-	-	-	50	5	189	1	189.00	1-139
		Total First Class Career		2	2	2	26	14*	-	0	0	1	125.3	17	441	10	44.10	6-142

JOHN DOUGLAS CLAUDE GODDARD

D.O.B. 21.04.1919 - Fontabelle, St Michael, Barbados (d. 26.08.1987)

First Class Debut 16.01.1937 - Barbados v Trinidad

Test Match Debut 21.01.1948 - West Indies v England

Test 56-23

Teams Played For
Barbados
West Indies
R.S. Grant's XI
M.C.C.

4

LHB / RMOB

SEASON	TEAM	COMPETITION	V	M	I	No	BATTING						BOWLING					
							RUNS	H.S.	Av	100s	50s	CT	OV	MD	RUNS	W	Av	B.B.
1937-1958	Barbados	First Class Matches	II	32	53	13	2102	218*	52.55	5	12	27	503.3	118	1376	51	26.98	5-43
1948-1957	WEST INDIES	TEST MATCHES	HA	27	39	11	859	83*	30.67	-	4	22	457.5	148	1050	33	31.81	5-31
1948-1957	West Indies	First Class Matches	A	49	49	8	767	77	18.70	-	1	43	610	186	1389	62	22.40	5-20
1939//	R.S. Grant's XI	First Class Matches	WI	2	2	0	32	22	16.00	-	-	1	9	3	15	0	-	-
1957//	M.C.C.	First Class Matches	E	1	2	0	9	5	4.50	-	-	1	5	1	15	0	-	-
Total First Class Career				111	145	32	3769	218*	33.35	5	17	94	1585.2	456	3845	146	26.33	5-20

HILARY ANGELO GOMES

D.O.B. 13.07.1953 - Arima, Trinidad

First Class Debut	03.03.1972 - Trinidad & Tobago v New Zealand
Test Match Debut	03.06.1976 - West Indies v England
O.D.I. Debut	12.04.1978 - West Indies v Australia
Domestic O.D. Debut	20.05.1973 - Middlesex v Lancashire

Test 157-169
O.D.I. 28-14

Teams Played For 6
Trinidad & Tobago, East Trinidad
N/E Trinidad
West Indies
W.I. President's XI
Middlesex

LHB / RM / OB

SEASON	TEAM	COMPETITION	V	M	I	No	BATTING RUNS	H.S.	Av	100s	50s	CT	BOWLING OV	MD	RUNS	W	Av	B.B.
1972-1988	Trinidad & Tobago	First Class Matches	=	55	97	9	3819	171*	43.39	8	22	27	385.2	99	1034	23	44.95	3-30
1973-1978	East Trinidad	First Class Matches	T	11	21	1	737	123	36.85	2	4	8	77.5	23	178	7	25.42	2-18
1980//	N/E Trinidad	First Class Matches	T	1	2	0	40	32	20.00	-	-	1	11	1	43	0	-	-
1976-1988	Trinidad & Tobago	Domestic O.D. Matches	=	23	23	4	644	103*	33.89	1	2	9	134	20	428	17	25.17	3-5
1976-1986	WEST INDIES	TEST MATCHES	HA	60	91	11	3171	143	39.63	9	13	18	400.1	79	930	15	62.00	2-20
1976-1986	West Indies	First Class Matches	A	61	95	20	4012	200*	53.49	13	17	10	423.5	103	1100	39	28.20	4-30
1977//	W.I. President's XI	First Class Matches	WI	1	1	0	4	4	4.00	-	-	2						
1978-1987	WEST INDIES	O.D.I. MATCHES	HA	83	64	15	1415	101	28.87	1	6	14	224	10	1045	41	25.48	4-31
1976-1987	West Indies	O.A.L. O.D. Matches	A	8	8	0	206	87	25.75	-	1	2	15	-	89	2	44.50	2-2
1973-1976	Middlesex	First Class Matches	E	42	63	9	1199	93*	22.20	-	7	11	334.5	80	923	23	40.13	4-22
1973-1975	Middlesex	Nat West Trophy	E	6	4	0	91	44	22.75	-	-	2	47	9	149	5	29.80	2-48
1973-1975	Middlesex	Benson & Hedges Cup	E	8	8	0	234	78	29.25	-	2	3	51.5	-	172	3	57.33	1-22
1973-1976	Middlesex	Sunday League	E	28	25	5	525	58	26.25	-	2	4	119.2	-	510	16	31.87	3-16
		Total First Class Career		231	370	50	12982	200*	40.56	32	63	77	1633	385	4208	107	39.32	4-22
		Total O.D. Career		156	132	24	3115	103*	28.84	2	13	34	591.1	-	2393	84	28.48	4-31

GERALD ETHRIDGE GOMEZ

RHB / RM

D.O.B. 10.10.1919 - Woodbrook, Port of Spain, Trinidad (d. 06.08.1996)
First Class Debut 04.10.1937 - Trinidad v British Guiana
Test Match Debut 22.07.1939 - West Indies v England

Test 49-21

Teams Played For
Trinidad
West Indies
R.S. Grant's XI
M.C.C.

4

SEASON	TEAM	COMPETITION	V	M	I	No	BATTING RUNS	H.S.	Av	100s	50s	CT	BOWLING OV	MD	RUNS	W	Av	B.B.
1937-1956	Trinidad	First Class Matches	II	36	55	9	2993	216*	65.06	10	9	24	406.4	109	1023	22	46.50	3-58
1939-1954	WEST INDIES	TEST MATCHES	HA	29	46	5	1243	101	30.31	1	8	18	838	289	1590	58	27.41	7-55
1939-1952	West Indies	First Class Matches	A	58	76	12	2239	149	34.98	2	11	49	1152.5	364	2383	117	20.36	9-24
1939//	R.S. Grant's XI	First Class Matches	WI	2	3	1	227	119	113.50	1	1	1	7	1	23	1	23.00	1-12
1957//	M.C.C.	First Class Matches	E	1	2	0	62	31	31.00	-	-	-	15	5	33	2	16.50	2-9
Total First Class Career				126	182	27	6764	216*	43.63	14	29	92	2419.3	768	5052	200	25.26	9-24

GEORGE COPELAND GRANT

D.O.B. 09.05.1907 - Port of Spain, Trinidad (d. 26.10.1978)

First Class Debut 13.06.1928 - Cambridge University v Northamptonshire
Test Match Debut 12.12.1930 - West Indies v Australia

Test 31-8

Teams Played For
Trinidad
West Indies
G.C. Grant's XI
Cambridge University
Rhodesia

RHB / RFM

5

SEASON	TEAM	COMPETITION	V	M	I	No	BATTING						BOWLING					
							RUNS	H.S.	Av	100s	50s	CT	OV	MD	RUNS	W	Av	B.B.
1934-1935	Trinidad	First Class Matches	||	4	8	1	208	80	29.71	-	1	7	4	0	8	0	-	-
1930-1935	WEST INDIES	TEST MATCHES	HA	12	22	6	413	71*	25.81	-	3	10	4	0	18	0	-	-
1930-1933	West Indies	First Class Matches	A	33	54	7	1577	115	33.55	3	6	29	43	1	234	9	26.00	3-24
1933//	G.C. Grant's XI	First Class Matches	WI	1	2	0	6	6	3.00	-		1						
1928-1930	Cambridge University	First Class Matches	E	26	41	9	1412	100	37.15	1	6	17	180	22	634	7	90.57	2-33
1931-1932	Rhodesia	First Class Matches	SA	5	9	0	215	68	23.88	-	1	7	25	2	75	3	25.00	2-5
		Total First Class Career		81	136	17	3831	115	32.19	4	17	71	256	25	969	19	51.00	3-24

ROLPH STEWART GRANT

D.O.B. 15.12.1909 - Port of Spain, Trinidad (d. 18.10.1977)
First Class Debut 04.05.1932 - Cambridge University v Kent
Test Match Debut 08.01.1935 - West Indies v England

Test 39-16

Teams Played For
Trinidad
West Indies
R.S. Grant's XI
Cambridge University

4

RHB / OB

SEASON	TEAM	COMPETITION	V	M	I	No	BATTING RUNS	H.S.	Av	100s	50s	CT	BOWLING OV	MD	RUNS	W	Av	B.B.
1934-1939	Trinidad	First Class Matches	ll	9	13	0	450	152	34.61	1	2	12	218	79	421	20	21.05	3-37
1935-1939	WEST INDIES	TEST MATCHES	HA	7	11	1	220	77	22.00	-	1	13	153.2	32	353	11	32.09	3-68
1933-1939	West Indies	First Class Matches	A	20	30	5	786	95	31.44	-	4	23	194.3	32	582	26	22.76	441
1939//	R.S. Grant's XI	First Class Matches	WI	2	3	0	197	70	65.66	-	3	3	45	11	140	5	28.00	3-28
1932-1933	Cambridge University	First Class Matches	E	10	17	2	230	29	15.33	-	-	15	189	53	483	17	28.41	4-101
		Total First Class Career		48	74	8	1883	152	28.53	1	10	66	799.5	207	1989	79	25.17	4-41

RHB / RF

ANTHONY HOLLIS GRAY

D.O.B. 23.05.1963 - Santa Cruz, Port of Spain, Trinidad

First Class Debut	05.01.1984 - North Trinidad v South Trinidad
Test Match Debut	24.10.1986 - West Indies v Pakistan
O.D.I. Debut	15.11.1985 - West Indies v Pakistan
Domestic O.D. Debut	26.01.1984 - Trinidad & Tobago v Guyana

Teams Played For 13
Trinidad & Tobago, N/E Trinidad, West Indies "B"
West Indies, North Trinidad, Surrey
W.I. Board XI, W.I. President's XI, Implas
Shell Awards XI, West Indies U23
Western Transvaal, West Indies "A"

Test 188-247
O.D.I. 46-108

SEASON	TEAM	COMPETITION	V	M	I	No	BATTING			100s	50s	CT	BOWLING					
							RUNS	H.S.	Av				OV	MD	RUNS	W	Av	B.B.
1984-1995	Trinidad & Tobago	First Class Matches	I	45	68	8	1058	69	17.63	-	3	18	1178.2	199	3736	146	25.58	6-78
1984//	North Trinidad	First Class Matches	T	1	2	0	28	21	14.00	-	-	1	20	0	94	1	94.00	1-71
1985//	N/E Trinidad	First Class Matches	T	1	1	0	9	9	9.00	-	-	1	27	6	65	2	32.50	2-48
1984-1996	Trinidad & Tobago	Domestic O.D. Matches	I	26	19	5	183	23*	13.07	-	-	7	201.5	25	751	33	22.75	4-54
1986-1987	WEST INDIES	TEST MATCHES	HA	5	8	2	48	12*	8.00	-	-	6	148	37	377	22	17.13	4-39
1986-1987	West Indies	First Class Matches	A	3	1	0	1	1	1.00	-	-	-	72	16	211	12	17.58	4-22
1985//	West Indies U23	First Class Matches	WI	1	1	0	7	7	7.00	-	-	-	29	10	65	3	21.66	2-36
1985-1991	W.I. President's XI	First Class Matches	WI	4	5	0	85	58	17.00	-	1	3	139	15	453	10	45.30	3-85
1988-1989	W.I. Board XI	First Class Matches	WI	2	1	0	15	15	15.00	-	-	1	55.1	12	154	5	30.80	3-31
1989//	West Indies "B"	First Class Matches	A	3	3	0	30	14	10.00	-	-	1	81.3	22	162	18	9.00	7-30
1992//	West Indies "A"	First Class Matches	WI	3	4	0	83	50	20.75	-	1	5	93	12	260	8	32.50	2-36
1985//	Shell Awards XI	First Class Matches	WI	1	1	0	9	9	9.00	-	-	2	33.2	6	88	6	14.66	5-55
1985-1991	WEST INDIES	O.D.I. MATCHES	HA	25	11	5	51	10*	8.50	-	-	3	211.4	16	835	44	18.97	6-50
1989//	West Indies "B"	O.D.(I.) Matches	A	5	2	1	30	24*	30.00	-	-	2	45	7	135	3	45.00	2-36
1987//	West Indies	O.A.L. O.D. Matches	A	2	1	1	1	1*	-	-	-	-	18	0	107	0	-	-
1985-1990	Surrey	First Class Matches	E	48	34	6	245	35	9.42	-	-	18	1423.3	283	4234	199	21.27	8-40
1985-1986	Surrey	Nat West Trophy	E	2	1	0	3	3	3.00	-	-	-	23	3	89	5	17.80	3-23
1986-1990	Surrey	Benson & Hedges	E	3	D	-	-	-	-	-	-	-	32	-	105	0	-	-
1985-1988	Surrey	Sunday League	E	24	11	6	115	24*	23.00	-	-	3	173	-	768	39	19.69	4-21
1986-1990	Surrey	O.A.L. O.D. Matches	E	2	D	-	-	-	-	-	-	-	20	-	87	2	43.50	2-35
1993-1994	Western Transvaal	First Class Matches	SA	5	7	0	84	36	12.00	-	-	1	122.3	30	384	19	20.21	4-83
1993-1994	Implas	Benson & Hedges Cup	SA	2	2	1	28	20*	28.00	-	-	-	20	4	75	2	37.50	2-51
Total First Class Career				122	136	16	1702	69	14.18	0	5	57	3424.4	611	10283	451	22.80	8-40
Total O.D. Career				91	47	19	411	24*	14.67	0	0	15	744.3	-	2952	128	23.06	6-50

ALVIN ETHELBERT GREENIDGE

D.O.B. 20.08.1956 - Bath Village, Christ Church, Barbados

First Class Debut 14.03.1978 - Barbados v Trinidad & Tobago
Test Match Debut 31.03.1978 - West Indies v Australia
O.D.I. Debut 12.04.1978 - West Indies v Australia
Domestic O.D. Debut 13.02.1978 - Barbados v Jamaica

Test	166-181	Teams Played For	3	RHB / RM
O.D.I.	29-14	Barbados		
		West Indies		
		West Indies XI		

SEASON	TEAM	COMPETITION	V	M	I	No	BATTING RUNS	H.S.	Av	100s	50s	CT	BOWLING OV	MD	RUNS	W	Av	B.B.
1975-1982	Barbados	First Class Matches	=	24	38	4	1455	172	42.79	4	6	18	28.4	2	99	3	33.00	2-52
1978-1982	Barbados	Domestic O.D. Matches	=	13	13	3	334	75*	33.40	-	2	2	-	-	-	-	-	-
1981//	Barbados	O.A.L. O.D. Matches	WI	1	1	0	9	9	9.00	-	-	-	-	-	-	-	-	-
1978-1979	WEST INDIES	TEST MATCHES	HA	6	10	0	222	69	22.20	-	2	5	-	-	-	-	-	-
1978-1979	West Indies	First Class Matches	A	10	17	0	317	48	18.64	-	-	5	17.4	3	47	2	23.50	1-60
1982-1984	West Indies XI	First Class Matches	A	8	16	1	325	48	21.66	-	-	4	1	0	1	0	-	-
1978//	WEST INDIES	O.D.I. MATCHES	H	1	1	0	23	23	23.00	-	-	-	-	-	-	-	-	-
1982-1984	West Indies XI	O.D.(I.) Matches	A	9	9	0	188	68	20.88	-	1	1	-	-	-	-	-	-
1979//	West Indies	O.A.L. O.D. Matches	A	3	3	0	46	36	15.33	-	-	3	10	0	37	1	37.00	1-37
1982-1983	West Indies XI	O.A.L. O.D. Matches	A	2	2	0	10	10	5.00	-	-	1	-	-	-	-	-	-
Total First Class Career				48	81	5	2319	172	30.51	4	8	32	47.2	5	147	5	29.40	2-52
Total O.D. Career				29	29	3	610	75*	23.46	0	3	7	10	0	37	1	37.00	1-37

CUTHBERT GORDON GREENIDGE

D.O.B. 01.05.1951 - Black Bess, St Peter, Barbados

First Class Debut	05.08.1970 - Hampshire v Sussex
Test Match Debut	22.11.1974 - West Indies v India
O.D.I. Debut	11.06.1975 - West Indies v Pakistan
Domestic O.D. Debut	16.08.1970 - Hampshire v Glamorgan

Test	150-152
O.D.I.	16-4

Teams Played For: Barbados, West Indies, W.I. President's XI, M.C.C., Hampshire, D.H. Robins XI, World XI, Scotland

RHB / RM / OB — 8

SEASON	TEAM	COMPETITION	V	M	I	No	RUNS	H.S.	Av	100s	50s	CT	OV	MD	RUNS	W	Av	B.B.
1973-1991	Barbados	First Class Matches	II	49	81	6	3547	237	47.29	9	17	38	6	0	31	0	-	-
1972-1991	Barbados	Domestic O.D. Matches	II	21	21	1	744	81	37.20	-	5	10	2	0	11	0	-	-
1981//	Barbados	O.A.L. O.D. Matches	WI	1	1	0	1	1	1.00	-	-	-	-	-	-	-	-	-
		TEST MATCHES																
1974-1990	WEST INDIES	Test Matches	HA	108	185	16	7558	226	44.72	19	34	96	4	3	4	0	-	-
1974-1991	West Indies	First Class Matches	A	84	138	17	5761	213	47.61	14	31	63	17.2	7	18	2	9.00	1-7
1973-1974	W.I. President's XI	First Class Matches	WI	2	4	0	108	37	27.00	-	-	1	7.3	2	39	0	-	-
1975-1991	WEST INDIES	O.D.I. Matches	HA	128	127	13	5134	133*	45.03	11	31	45	10	0	45	1	45.00	1-21
1975-1988	West Indies	O.A.L. O.D. Matches	A	10	10	2	537	186*	67.12	2	3	6	1	0	4	0	-	-
1970-1987	Hampshire	First Class Matches	E	275	472	35	19840	259	58.27	48	100	315	124	29	387	16	24.18	5-49
1970-1987	Hampshire	Nat West Trophy	E	33	33	1	1284	177	40.12	4	7	21	1.5	0	5	0	-	-
1970-1987	Hampshire	Benson & Hedges Cup	E	58	58	3	2157	173*	39.21	5	13	20	12.5	1	57	0	-	-
1970-1987	Hampshire	Sunday League	E	182	180	12	6344	172*	37.76	11	34	67	18	1	89	1	89.00	1-36
1986//	Hampshire	O.A.L. O.D. Matches	E	1	1	1	16	16*	15.40	-	-	1	-	-	-	-	-	-
1989-1992	World XI	First Class Matches	E	3	5	0	77	25	15.40	-	-	2	-	-	-	-	-	-
1974//	D.H. Robins XI	First Class Matches	E	1	2	1	289	273*	289.00	1	0	1	-	-	-	-	-	-
1987//	M.C.C.	First Class Matches	E	1	2	0	174	122	87.00	1	1	0	-	-	-	-	-	-
1990//	Scotland	Nat West Trophy	E	1	1	0	15	15	15.00	-	-	-	-	-	-	-	-	-
1990//	Scotland	Benson & Hedges Cup	E	4	4	0	117	50	29.25	-	1	1	-	-	-	-	-	-
1992//	M.C.C.	O.A.L. O.D. Matches	E	1	D	-	-	-	-	-	-	-	-	-	-	-	-	-
		Total First Class Career		523	889	75	37354	273*	45.88	92	183	516	158.5	41	479	18	26.61	5-49
		Total O.D. Career		440	436	33	16349	186*	40.56	33	94	171	35.4	2	211	2	105.50	1-21

GEOFFREY ALAN GREENIDGE

D.O.B. 26.05.1948 - Fontabelle, St Michael, Barbados

First Class Debut 09.02.1967 - Barbados v Leeward Islands
Test Match Debut 06.04.1972 - West Indies v New Zealand
Domestic O.D. Debut 18.05.1969 - Sussex v Surrey

Test 142-137

Teams Played For Barbados, West Indies, W.I. President's XI, Sussex, D.H. Robins XI, International XI

6   RHB / LBG

SEASON	TEAM	COMPETITION	V	M	I	No	RUNS	H.S.	Av	100s	50s	CT	OV	MD	RUNS	W	Av	B.B.
1967-1976	Barbados	First Class Matches	II	22	37	3	1237	205	36.38	3	8	8	88.2	13	398	8	49.75	7-124
1972-1973	Barbados	Domestic O.D. Matches	II	2	2	0	51	48	25.50	-	-	3	-	-	-	-	-	-
1972-1973	WEST INDIES	TEST MATCHES	H	5	9	2	209	50	29.85	-	1	3	26	4	75	0	-	-
1968//	W.I. President's XI	First Class Matches	WI	1	1	0	28	28	28.00	-	-	-	9	1	31	0	-	-
1968-1975	Sussex	First Class Matches	E	152	283	16	7629	172	28.57	13	38	84	98.3	10	444	5	88.80	2-62
1970-1975	Sussex	Nat. West Trophy	E	13	13	0	320	76	24.61	-	3	9	-	-	-	-	-	-
1972-1974	Sussex	Benson & Hedges Cup	E	12	12	0	172	56	14.33	-	1	-	-	-	-	-	-	-
1969-1975	Sussex	Sunday League	E	79	72	6	1310	82	19.85	-	7	19	1	0	6	1	6.00	1-6
1972//	Sussex	O.A.L. O.D. Matches	E	1	1	1	26	26*	-	-	-	-	-	-	-	-	-	-
1974-1975	D.H. Robins XI	First Class Matches	SA	1	-	-	-	-	-	-	-	-	-	-	-	-	-	-
1975-1976	International XI	First Class Matches	R	1	2	1	9	7*	9.00	-	-	-	-	-	-	-	-	-
Total First Class Career				182	332	22	9112	205	29.39	16	45	95	221.5	28	948	13	72.92	7-124
Total O.D. Career				107	100	7	1879	82	20.20	0	11	32	1	0	6	1	6.00	1-6

MERVYN GEORGE GRELL

D.O.B. 18.12.1899 - Cocorite, Trinidad (d. 11.01.1976)

First Class Debut 22.01.1930 - Trinidad V M.C.C.

Test Match Debut 01.02.1930 - West Indies v England

Test 24-5

Teams Played For
Trinidad
West Indies

RHB / RM 2

SEASON	TEAM	COMPETITION	V	M	I	No	BATTING						CT	BOWLING						
							RUNS	H.S.	Av	100s	50s			OV	MD	RUNS	W	Av	B.B.
1930-1938	Trinidad	First Class Matches	=	9	17	2	455	74*	30.33	-	4	2		55	4	155	5	31.00	2-14
1929-1930	WEST INDIES	TEST MATCHES	H	1	2	0	34	21	17.00	-	-	1		5	1	17	0	-	-
		Total First Class Career		10	19	2	489	74*	28.76	-	4	3		60	5	172	5	34.40	2-14

ADRIAN FRANK GORDON GRIFFITH

D.O.B. 19.11.1971 - Holders Hill, St James, Barbados

First Class Debut	19.02.1993 - Barbados v Guyana
Test Match Debut	25.01.1997 - West Indies v Australia
O.D.I. Debut	08.12.1996 - West Indies v Australia
Domestic O.D. Debut	17.02.1993 - Barbados v Guyana

Test	213-326	Teams Played For	6	LHB / RM
O.D.I.	80-325	Barbados, West Indies		
		West Indies U23		
		W.I. Board XI		
		West Indies "A"		
		W.I. Select XI		

SEASON	TEAM	COMPETITION	V	M	I	No	BATTING RUNS	H.S.	Av	100s	50s	CT	BOWLING OV	MD	RUNS	W	Av	B.B.
1993-2001	Barbados	First Class Matches	=	45	82	5	2590	186	33.63	5	13	39	5	0	29	0	-	-
1993-2002	Barbados	Domestic O.D. Matches	=	33	33	2	745	66	24.03	-	3	10	-	-	-	-	-	-
1993-1998	Barbados	O.A.L. O.D. Matches	=	9	9	0	229	66	25.44	-	2	-	-	-	-	-	-	-
1997-2000	WEST INDIES	TEST MATCHES	HA	14	27	1	638	114	24.53	1	4	5	-	-	-	-	-	-
1996-2000	West Indies	First Class Matches	A	11	19	2	435	130	25.58	1	1	4	1	0	7	0	-	-
1993//	West Indies U23	First Class Matches	WI	1	2	0	49	29	24.50	-	-	1	-	-	-	-	-	-
1996-1999	W.I. Board XI	First Class Matches	WI	2	3	1	46	38*	23.00	-	-	3	-	-	-	-	-	-
1998-1999	West Indies "A"	First Class Matches	HA	6	11	0	286	93	26.00	-	2	7	-	-	-	-	-	-
1998-1999	West Indies "A"	O.D.(I.) Matches	A	6	6	0	160	91	26.66	-	1	2	-	-	-	-	-	-
1999-2000	W.I. Select XI	O.A.L. O.D. Matches	WI	2	2	0	8	6	4.00	-	-	4	-	-	-	-	-	-
1999-2000	West Indies	O.A.L. O.D Matches	A	4	4	0	50	26	12.50	-	-	3	-	-	-	-	-	-
1996-2000	WEST INDIES	O.D.I. MATCHES	HA	9	8	1	99	47	14.14	-	-	5	-	-	-	-	-	-
	Total First Class Career			79	144	9	4044	186	29.95	7	20	59	6	0	36	0	-	-
	Total O. D. Career			63	62	3	1291	66	21.88	0	6	24	-	-	-	-	-	-

CHARLES CHRISTOPHER GRIFFITH

D.O.B. 14.12.1938 - Pie Corner, St Lucy, Barbados

First Class Debut 30.12.1959 - Barbados v M.C.C.
Test Match Debut 25.03.1960 - West Indies v England
Domestic O.D. Debut 31-7-1966 West Indies v Surrey

Test 111-84

Teams Played For
Barbados, West Indies
Commonwealth XI
F.M. Worrell's XI
World XI
Indian President's XI

6

RHB / RF

SEASON	TEAM	COMPETITION	V	M	I	No	BATTING						BOWLING					
							RUNS	H.S.	Av	100s	50s	CT	OV	MD	RUNS	W	Av	B.B.
1959-1967	Barbados	First Class Matches	II	18	18	5	161	38	12.38	-	-	7	531.4	114	1509	69	21.86	5-50
1960-1969	WEST INDIES	TEST MATCHES	HA	28	42	10	530	54	16.56	0	1	16	884.1	177	2683	94	28.54	6-36
1963-1969	West Indies	First Class Matches	A	42	49	15	557	70	16.38	0	2	11	864	228	2352	150	15.68	8-23
1964//	F.M. Worrell's XI	First Class Matches	WI	1	1	1	23	23*	-	-	-	1	22	0	91	3	30.33	2-76
1966//	West Indies	O.A.L. O.D. Matches	A	2	D	-	-	-	-	-	-	1	12	0	52	3	17.33	3-26
1963-1964	Commonwealth XI	First Class Matches	P	5	6	0	180	98	30.00	0	1	2	159.4	37	434	15	28.93	4-49
1963-1964	Indian President's XI	First Class Matches	I	1	2	1	13	8*	13.00	-	-	2	21	3	77	0	-	-
1965//	World XI	First Class Matches	E	1	1	0	38	38	38.00	-	-	-	11.3	3	26	1	26.00	1-26
		Total First Class Career		96	119	32	1502	98	17.26	0	4	39	2494	562	7172	332	21.60	8-23
		Total O.D. Career		2	D	-	-	-	-	0	0	1	12	0	52	3	17.33	3-26

336

HERMAN CLARENCE GRIFFITH

D.O.B. 01.12.1893 - Arima, St Andrew, Trinidad (d. 18.03.1980)
First Class Debut 21.09.1921 - Barbados v Trinidad
Test Match Debut 23.06.1928 - West Indies v England

Test 11-1
Teams Played For Barbados, West Indies, Combined B/J XI — 3
RHB / RF

SEASON	TEAM	COMPETITION	V	M	I	No	BATTING RUNS	H.S.	Av	100s	50s	CT	BOWLING OV	MD	RUNS	W	Av	B.B.
1921-1941	Barbados	First Class Matches	=	18	23	3	328	60	16.40	-	1	11	613.2	105	1826	87	20.98	7-38
1928-1933	WEST INDIES	TEST MATCHES	HA	13	23	5	91	18	5.05	-	-	4	443.5	89	1243	44	28.25	6-103
1928-1933	West Indies	First Class Matches	A	47	61	19	770	84	18.33	-	3	20	1351	258	4130	123	33.57	4-46
1927-1928	Combined B/J XI	First Class Matches	WI	1	1	1	15	15*	-	-	-	1	25	3	95	4	23.75	4-81
Total First Class Career				79	108	28	1204	84	15.05	0	4	36	2433.1	455	7294	258	28.27	7-38

SIMPSON CLAIRMONTE GUILLEN

D.O.B. 24.09.1924 - Port of Spain, Trinidad

First Class Debut 04.02.1948 - Trinidad v M.C.C.

Test Match Debut 22.12.1951 - West Indies v Australia

Teams Played For Trinidad, West Indies, Canterbury, New Zealand

Test 73-38

RHB / WK 4

SEASON	TEAM	COMPETITION	V	M	I	No	BATTING RUNS	H.S.	Av	100s	50s	CT/ST	BOWLING OV	MD	RUNS	W	Av	B.B.
1948-1951	Trinidad	First Class Matches	II	6	10	0	105	29	10.50	-	-	11/5	-	-	-	-	-	-
1951-1952	WEST INDIES	TEST MATCHES	HA	5	6	2	104	54	26.00	-	1	9/2	-	-	-	-	-	-
1951-1952	West Indies	First Class Matches	A	6	8	2	64	23	10.66	-	-	15/8	-	-	-	-	-	-
1955-56//	NEW ZEALAND	TEST MATCHES	NZ	3	6	0	98	41	16.33	-	-	4/1	-	-	-	-	-	-
1954-1957	New Zealand	First Class Matches	NZ	4	6	1	115	54*	23.00	-	1	3	-	-	-	-	-	-
1952-1961	Canterbury	First Class Matches	NZ	42	73	5	2186	197	32.14	3	12	69/18	20	9	49	1	49.00	1-1
		Total First Class Career		66	109	10	2672	197	26.98	3	14	111/34	20	9	49	1	49.00	1-1

WESLEY WINFIELD HALL

D.O.B. 12.09.1937 - Glebe Land, Station Hill, St Michael, Barbados
First Class Debut 21.03.1956 - Barbados v E.W. Swantons XI
Test Match Debut 28.11.1958 - West Indies v India
Domestic O.D. Debut 12.09.1963 - West Indies v Sussex

Test 104-72   **Teams Played For**   9   **RHB / RF**

Barbados, Trinidad
West Indies, Jamaican XI
F.M. Worrell's XI, Commonwealth XI
World XI, Queensland
Indian President's XI

SEASON	TEAM	COMPETITION	V	M	I	No	BATTING RUNS	H.S.	Av	100s	50s	CT	BOWLING OV	MD	RUNS	W	Av	B.B.
1956-1971	Barbados	First Class Matches	ll	13	18	4	258	88	18.42	-	2	6	382	68	1238	41	30.19	6-75
1967-1970	Trinidad	First Class Matches	ll	9	11	1	77	25	7.70	-	-	1	181	26	623	23	27.08	4-51
1965//	Jamaican XI	First Class Matches	J	1	2	1	26	16	26.00	-	-	1	23	2	87	5	17.40	4-46
1958-1969	WEST INDIES	TEST MATCHES	HA	48	66	14	818	50*	15.73	-	2	11	1657.7	312	5066	192	26.38	7-69
1957-1969	West Indies	First Class Matches	HA	74	80	12	980	102*	14.41	1	1	28	1493.3	334	4690	199	23.56	7-51
1964//	F.M. Worrell's XI	First Class Matches	WI	1	1	0	27	27	27.00	-	-	1	14	1	62	1	62.00	1-35
1963-1966	West Indies	O.A.L. O.D. Matches	A	2	1	0	0	0	0.00	-	-	-	18	2	71	3	23.66	2-53
1961-1963	Queensland	First Class Matches	A	17	26	3	409	50	17.78	-	1	9	421	58	1998	76	26.28	7-76
1965-1968	World XI	First Class Matches	E	4	5	2	27	10	9.00	-	-	-	77	5	286	5	57.20	3-68
1961-1963	Commonwealth XI	First Class Matches	A	2	4	1	16	6	5.33	-	-	-	32	1	111	2	55.50	1-36
1963//	Indian President's XI	First Class Matches	I	1	2	0	35	19	17.50	-	-	1	24	2	112	2	56.00	2-53
Total First Class Career				170	215	38	2673	102*	15.10	1	6	58	4305.2	809	14273	546	26.14	7-51
Total O.D. Career				2	1	0	0	0	0.00	0	0	0	18	2	71	3	23.66	2-53

ROGER ANDREW HARPER

D.O.B. 17.03.1963 - Georgetown, Demerara, British Guiana

First Class Debut 20.10.1979 - Demerara v Berbice
Test Match Debut 10.12.1983 - West Indies v India
O.D.I. Debut 13.10.1983 - West Indies v India
Domestic O.D. Debut 28.03.1980 - Guyana v Jamaica

Test 181-221
O.D.I. 40-61

Teams Played For 10
Guyana, Demerara
West Indies, W.I. Board XI
W.I. President's XI, West Indies U23
West Indies "A", Northamptonshire
D.B. Closes XI, World XI

RHB / OB

| | | | | | | | BATTING | | | | | | BOWLING | | | | | |
SEASON	TEAM	COMPETITION	V	M	I	No	RUNS	H.S.	Av	100s	50s	CT	OV	MD	RUNS	W	Av	B.B.
1980-1996	Guyana	First Class Matches	II	57	89	6	2844	202	34.26	5	14	98	2080	505	4568	206	22.17	6-24
1979-1989	Demerara	First Class Matches	G	5	6	2	142	61	35.50	-	1	6	133	25	370	16	23.12	5-72
1980-1996	Guyana	Domestic O.D. Matches	II	48	41	9	760	53	23.75	-	1	27	390.2	33	1199	53	22.62	5-37
1983-1993	WEST INDIES	TEST MATCHES	HA	25	32	3	535	74	18.44	-	3	36	602.3	183	1291	46	28.06	6-57
1983-1995	West Indies	First Class Matches	A	42	52	13	1740	217*	44.61	2	11	46	1123.3	288	2752	106	25.96	6-85
1981-1988	W.I. President's XI	First Class Matches	WI	2	2	0	30	30	10.00	-	-	4	118	22	321	11	29.18	5-142
1988-19889	W.I. Board XI	First Class Matches	WI	2	2	1	10	10*	10.00	-	-	1	64	8	172	3	57.33	2-117
1985//	West Indies U23	First Class Matches	WI	1	1	0	20	20	20.00	-	-	-	23	7	64	0	-	-
1996//	West Indies "A"	First Class Matches	A	3	4	1	109	51	36.33	-	1	5	113.1	32	205	17	12.05	5-61
1983-1996	WEST INDIES	O.D.I. MATCHES	HA	105	73	20	855	45*	16.13	-	-	55	862.3	47	3431	100	34.31	4-40
1996//	West Indies "A"	O.D.(I.) Matches	A	3	3	1	51	30	25.30	-	-	1	26	3	84	3	28.00	3-27
1984-1987	West Indies	O.A.L. O.D. Matches	A	5	5	2	66	46*	22.00	-	-	3	49	-	181	2	90.50	1-30
1996//	West Indies "A"	O.A.L. O.D. Matches	A	1	1	1	38	38*	-	-	-	3	10	0	28	0	-	-
1985-1987	Northamptonshire	First Class Matches	E	54	63	14	1834	234	37.42	3	5	58	1776	512	4188	137	30.56	5-28
1985-1987	Northamptonshire	Nat West Trophy	E	3	3	1	5	4*	2.50	-	-	1	32	7	109	4	27.25	3-40
1985-1986	Northamptonshire	Benson & Hedges Cup	E	8	5	0	118	56	23.60	-	1	5	76	-	217	7	31.00	3-48
1985-1987	Northamptonshire	Sunday League	E	40	33	9	668	65*	27.83	-	3	24	276	-	1186	40	29.65	4-17
1986//	Northamptonshire	O.A.L. O.D. Matches	E	1	1	1	69	69*	-	-	1	1	12	-	31	1	31.00	1-31
1983-1984	D.B. Closes XI	First Class Matches	E	2	2	0	12	7	6.00	-	-	-	40	11	125	5	25.00	3-36
1985-1994	World XI	First Class Matches	E	7	9	3	204	76*	34.00	-	1	8	231.3	48	670	20	33.50	6-71
Total First Class Career				200	263	43	7480	234	34.00	10	36	262	6304.1	1641	14726	567	25.97	6-24
Total O.D. Career				214	165	44	2630	69*	21.73	0	6	120	1733.5	-	6466	210	30.79	5-37

LORD GEORGE ROBERT CANNING HARRIS

D.O.B. 03.02.1851 - St.Anns, Trinidad (d. 24.03.1932)
First Class Debut 11.08.1870 - Kent v M.C.C.
Test Match Debut 02.01.1879 - England v Australia

RHB / RFM

Teams Played For 12
Kent, England, Oxford University
M.C.C., Zingari, Gentlemen's XI
The South XI, Combined K/G XI
The Smokers XI, Past/Present Oxford XI
Lord Londesborough XI, Gentlemen of Kent XI

SEASON	TEAM	COMPETITION	V	M	I	No	BATTING						BOWLING					
							RUNS	H.S.	Av	100s	50s	CT	OV	MD	RUNS	W	Av	B.B.
1879-1884	ENGLAND	TEST MATCHES	HA	4	6	1	145	52	29.00	-	1	2	8	1	29	0	-	-
1878-1884	England XI	First Class Matches	HA	5	9	0	240	67	26.66	-	1	3	14	6	24	1	24.00	1-24
1870-1911	Kent	First Class Matches	E	157	278	17	7842	176	36.04	10	45	155	751	224	1523	64	23.79	5-57
1871-1874	Oxford University	First Class Matches	E	16	28	3	464	67*	18.56	-	2	8	25	5	59	4	14.75	3-13
1875-1886	Gentlemen's XI	First Class Matches	E	16	28	1	446	85	16.51	-	1	12	4	1	4	0	-	-
1871-1895	M.C.C.	First Class Matches	E	8	14	0	213	107	15.21	1	1	3	-	-	-	-	-	-
1873-1884	The South XI	First Class Matches	E	7	13	1	210	69	17.50	-	1	5	5	0	9	0	-	-
1874-1876	Combined K/G XI	First Class Matches	E	3	5	0	162	45	32.40	-	-	4	9	6	18	2	9.00	2-18
1882-1888	Zingari	First Class Matches	E	4	7	0	109	47	15.27	-	-	-	20	4	40	3	13.33	2-28
1884//	The Smokers XI	First Class Matches	E	1	2	0	5	5	2.50	-	-	2	-	-	-	-	-	-
1888//	Past/Present Oxford XI	First Class Matches	E	1	2	0	64	52	32.00	-	1	-	-	-	-	-	-	-
1888/	Lord Londesborough XI	First Class Matches	E	1	2	0	16	16	8.00	-	-	-	-	-	-	-	-	-
1880//	Gentlemen of Kent XI	First Class Matches	E	1	1	0	74	74	74.00	-	1	-	28	11	52	1	52.00	1-52
Total First Class Career				224	395	23	9990	176	26.85	11	54	190	864	258	1758	75	23.44	5-57

DESMOND LEO HAYNES

D.O.B. 15.02.1956 - Holders Hall, St James, Barbados

First Class Debut	07.01.1977 - Barbados v Jamaica
Test Match Debut	03.03.1978 - West Indies v Australia
O.D.I. Debut	22.02.1978 - West Indies v Australia
Domestic O.D. Debut	26.01.1977 - Barbados v Guyana

Teams Played For: Barbados, West Indies, West Indies "B", Middlesex, Western Province, Scotland, D.B. Closes XI, World XI, Wills XI

Test 163-179   **O.D.I.** 25-13

RHB / LBG   9

SEASON	TEAM	COMPETITION	V	M	I	No	RUNS	H.S.	Av	100s	50s	CT	OV	MD	RUNS	W	Av	B.B.
1977-1995	Barbados	First Class Matches	II	63	107	10	4843	246	49.92	13	21	31	16	7	28	1	28.00	1-2
1977-1994	Barbados	Domestic O.D. Matches	II	35	35	3	1049	121*	32.78	1	8	16	7	1	45	0	-	-
1978-1994	WEST INDIES	TEST MATCHES	HA	116	202	25	7487	184	42.49	18	39	65	3	0	8	1	8.00	1-2
1979-1994	West Indies	First Class Matches	A	73	119	15	4788	158	46.03	6	35	37	7.4	0	36	1	36.00	1-6
1981//	West Indies "B"	First Class Matches	A	3	6	1	169	69	33.80	-	1	3	1	1	0	0	-	-
1978-1994	WEST INDIES	O.D.I. MATCHES	HA	238	237	28	8648	152*	41.37	17	57	59	5	0	24	0	-	-
1981//	West Indies "B"	O.D.(I.) Matches	A	4	4	0	193	122	48.25	1	-	1	13	1	52	1	52.00	1-44
1980-1992	West Indies	O.A.L. O.D. Matches	A	16	16	2	759	101	54.21	1	7	3	-	-	-	-	-	-
1989-1994	Middlesex	First Class Matches	E	95	162	18	7071	255*	49.10	21	31	48	52.4	13	192	4	48.00	1-4
1989-1994	Middlesex	Nat West Trophy	E	14	14	3	838	149*	76.18	2	7	2	22	3	66	1	66.00	1-41
1989-1994	Middlesex	Benson & Hedges Cup	E	12	12	1	701	131	63.72	1	7	5	14	-	78	2	39.00	1-21
1989-1994	Middlesex	Sunday League	E	68	66	6	2445	142*	40.75	3	20	23	51	0	287	3	95.66	1-17
1994//	Middlesex	Sunday League Cup	E	2	2	0	121	72	60.50	-	1	-	3	0	16	1	16.00	1-16
1983//	Scotland	Benson & Hedges Cup	E	3	3	0	72	44	24.00	-	-	2	18	-	32	1	32.00	1-9
1982-1984	D.B. Closes XI	First Class Matches	E	2	2	0	115	111	57.50	1	-	3	-	-	-	-	-	-
1987-1988	World XI	First Class Matches	E	3	6	1	217	130	43.40	1	-	4/1	1	0	4	1	4.00	1-4
1994-1997	Western Province	First Class Matches	SA	21	35	2	1340	202*	40.60	1	10	11	8	3	11	0	-	-
1994-1997	Western Province	Benson & Hedges	SA	26	26	0	896	106	34.46	3	3	5	-	-	-	-	-	-
1994-1995	Wills XI	Wills Trophy	I	2	2	1	51	30	51.00	-	-	2	-	-	-	-	-	-
		Total First Class Career		376	639	72	26030	255*	49.50	61	137	202/1	89.2	24	279	8	34.87	1-2
		Total O.D. Career		420	417	44	15773	152*	42.28	29	110	118	133	-	600	9	66.66	1-9

BATTING   **BOWLING**

ROBERT CHRISTOPHER HAYNES

D.O.B. 02.11.1964 - Kingston, Jamaica

First Class Debut 05.03.1982 - Jamaica v Guyana

O.D.I. Debut 17.10.1989 - West Indies v Pakistan

Domestic O.D. Debut 22.01.1985 - Jamaica v Trinidad & Tobago

O.D.I. 56-186

Teams Played For 3
Jamaica
West Indies
W.I. President's XI

LHB / LBG

SEASON	TEAM	COMPETITION	V	M	I	No	BATTING RUNS	H.S.	Av	100s	50s	CT	BOWLING OV	MD	RUNS	W	Av	B.B.
1982-1995	Jamaica	First Class Matches	=	59	94	3	1966	98	21.60	-	10	53	2195.5	502	5801	197	29.44	6-53
1985-1996	Jamaica	Domestic O.D. Matches	=	40	35	5	546	83	18.20	-	1	16	345.3	14	1197	56	21.37	4-22
1982-1990	West Indies	First Class Matches	A	3	4	0	49	20	12.25	-	-	1	71.2	12	253	9	28.11	4-106
1989-1991	W.I. President's XI	First Class Matches	WI	3	6	1	151	46	30.20	-	-	1	168.5	36	273	15	18.20	6-96
1989-1991	WEST INDIES	O.D.I. MATCHES	HA	8	6	1	26	18	5.20	-	-	5	45	1	224	5	44.80	2-36
1991//	West Indies	O.A.L. O.D. Matches	A	4	3	1	2	2*	1.00	-	-	1	30	2	110	3	36.66	1-30
		Total First Class Career		65	104	4	2166	98	21.66	-	10	55	2436	550	6327	221	28.62	6-53
		Total O.D. Career		52	44	7	574	83	15.51	0	1	22	420.3	17	1531	64	23.92	4-22

343

GEORGE ALPHONSO HEADLEY

D.O.B. 30.05.1909 - Colon, Panama (d. 30.11.1983)
First Class Debut 09.02.1928 - Jamaica v L.H. Tennyson's XI
Test Match Debut 11.01.1930 - West Indies v England

Test 17-4

RHB / OB

Teams Played For
Jamaica
West Indies
Combined J/BG XI
Commonwealth XI
L. Parkinson's XI

BATTING

SEASON	TEAM	COMPETITION	V	M	I	No	RUNS	H.S.	Av	100s	50s	CT
1928-1954	Jamaica	First Class Matches	II	27	39	9	2848	344*	94.93	9	15	30
1930-1954	WEST INDIES	TEST MATCHES	HA	22	40	4	2190	270*	60.83	10	5	14
1929-1949	West Indies	First Class Matches	HA	49	77	9	4437	234*	65.25	13	21	31
1933//	Combined J/BG XI	First Class Matches	WI	1	2	0	51	30	25.50	-	-	-
1951-1954	Commonwealth XI	First Class Matches	E	3	4	0	243	98	60.75	-	3	1
1935//	L. Parkinson's XI	First Class Matches	E	1	2	0	152	134	76.00	1	-	-
Total First Class Career				103	164	22	9921	344*	69.86	33	44	76

BOWLING

OV	MD	RUNS	W	Av	B.B.
5					
270.3	49	767	23	33.34	5-33
65	7	230	0	-	-
292.2	51	808	27	29.92	4-27
-	-	-	-	-	-
-	-	-	-	-	-
8	0	37	1	37.00	1-37
635.5	107	1842	51	36.11	5-33

RONALD GEORGE ALPHONSO HEADLEY

D.O.B. 29.06.1939 - Mountain View, Vineyard Town, Kingston, Jamaica
First Class Debut 28.06.1958 - Worcestershire v Cambridge University
Test Match Debut 26.07.1973 - West Indies v England
O.D.I. Debut 07.09.1973 - West Indies v England
Domestic O.D. Debut 22.05.1963 - Worcestershire v Surrey

Test 147-144   **O.D.I.** 12-2

Teams Played For
Jamaica, West Indies
Worcestershire
Commonwealth XI
Cavaliers XI
Derbyshire

6   LHB / LB

SEASON	TEAM	COMPETITION	V	M	I	No	RUNS	H.S.	Av	100s	50s	CT	OV	MD	RUNS	W	Av	B.B.
1966-1974	Jamaica	First Class Matches	II	9	13	0	489	86	37.61	-	4	7	2	0	10	0	-	-
1973/I	WEST INDIES	TEST MATCHES	E	2	4	0	62	42	15.50	-	-	2	-	-	-	-	-	-
1973/I	West Indies	First Class Matches	E	5	9	0	230	62	25.55	-	2	3	-	-	-	-	-	-
1973/I	West Indies	O.D.I. Matches	E	1	1	0	19	19	19.00	-	-	-	-	-	-	-	-	-
1958-1974	Worcestershire	First Class Matches	E	403	725	60	20712	187	31.14	32	109	343	198.2	52	568	12	47.33	4-40
1963-1974	Worcestershire	Nat West Trophy	E	24	24	1	575	83	25.00	-	4	6	-	-	-	-	-	-
1972-1974	Worcestershire	Benson & Hedges Cup	E	15	15	0	491	132	32.73	1	3	9	-	-	-	-	-	-
1969-1974	Worcestershire	Sunday League	E	81	79	9	2379	112*	33.99	1	14	26	-	-	-	-	-	-
1975-1976	Derbyshire	Nat West Trophy	E	6	6	0	191	58	31.83	-	1	2	-	-	-	-	-	-
1975-1976	Derbyshire	Benson & Hedges Cup	E	6	6	0	208	94	34.66	-	2	2	-	-	-	-	-	-
1975-1976	Derbyshire	Sunday League	E	28	28	2	894	95	34.38	-	6	13	-	-	-	-	-	-
1975-1976	Derbyshire	O.A.L. O.D. Matches	E	1	1	0	31	31	31.00	-	-	-	-	-	-	-	-	-
1971/I	Worcestershire	First Class Matches	A	2	3	0	22	12	7.33	-	-	1	-	-	-	-	-	-
1961-1971	Commonwealth XI	First Class Matches	A	2	4	0	62	31	15.50	-	-	1	-	-	-	-	-	-
1965/I	Cavaliers XI	First Class Matches	WI	2	4	1	180	76	60.00	-	2	1	5	1	10	0	-	-
Total First Class Career				423	758	61	21695	187	31.12	32	117	356	205.2	53	588	12	49.00	4-40
Total O.D. Career				162	160	12	4788	132	32.35	2	30	58	-	-	-	-	-	-

JOHN LESLIE HENDRIKS

D.O.B. 21.12.1933 - St Andrew, Kingston, Jamaica

First Class Debut 08.02.1954 - Jamaica v M.C.C.
Test Match Debut 16.02.1962 - West Indies v India
Domestic O.D. Debut 31.07.1966 West Indies v Surrey

Test 114-90

Teams Played For
Jamaica
West Indies
NZ Governor's XI

RHB / WK / RS

SEASON	TEAM	COMPETITION	V	M	I	No	RUNS	H.S.	Av	100s	50s	CT/ST	OV	MD	RUNS	W	Av	B.B.
							BATTING						BOWLING					
1954-1967	Jamaica	First Class Matches	II	22	35	5	492	73*	16.40	-	2	36/19	3	-	-	-	-	-
1962-1969	WEST INDIES	TEST MATCHES	HA	20	32	8	447	64	18.62	-	2	42/5	-	-	-	-	-	-
1958-1969	West Indies	First Class Matches	A	40	44	9	628	82	17.94	-	5	61/26	7	1	49	0	-	-
1966-1969	West Indies	O.A.L. O.D. Matches	A	3	D	-	-	-	-	-	-	0/2	-	-	-	-	-	-
1968-1969	NZ Governor's XI	First Class Matches	NZ	1	2	1	1	1*	1.00	-	-	1	1	0	12	0	-	-
		Total First Class Career		83	113	23	1568	82	17.42	0	9	140/50	8	1	61	0	-	-
		Total O.D. Career		3	D	-	-	-	-	-	-	0/2	-	-	-	-	-	-

RYAN O'NEAL HINDS

D.O.B. 17.02.1981 - Kings Village, Holders Hill, St. James, Barbados
First Class Debut 15.01.1999 - Barbados v Windward Islands
Test Match Debut 31.01.2002 - West Indies v Pakistan
O.D.I. Debut 16.12.2001 - West Indies v Zimbabwe
Domestic O.D. Debut 08.10.1998 - Barbados v Leeward Islands

LHB / SLA

Test	241-380	**Teams Played For**	8
O.D.I.	109-436	Barbados, West Indies	
		West Indies U23, W.I. Board XI	
		West Indies "A", W.I. President's XI	
		W.I. Select XI	
		Busta Cup XI	

SEASON	TEAM	COMPETITION	V	M	I	No	RUNS	H.S.	Av	100s	50s	CT	OV	MD	RUNS	W	Av	B.B.
1998-2003	Barbados	First Class Matches	II	26	45	7	1252	166	32.94	1	6	22	358	97	819	40	20.47	9-68
1998-2002	Barbados	Domestic O.D. Matches	II	19	16	2	502	81	35.85	-	4	7	124	13	447	21	21.28	4-32
1998-2000	Barbados	O.A.L. O.D. Matches	WI	3	1	0	1	1	1.00	-	-	1	17	3	70	1	70.00	1-19
2002//	WEST INDIES	TEST MATCHES	HA	4	8	1	162	62	23.14	-	1	-	36	5	119	0	-	-
2002//	West Indies	First Class Matches	A	2	2	1	93	74*	93.00	-	1	-	4	1	3	1	3.00	1-3
1998-2001	W.I. Board XI	First Class Matches	WI	3	4	0	65	31	16.25	-	-	1	58.1	11	149	8	18.62	4-23
1999-2002	West Indies "A"	First Class Matches	HA	8	13	2	422	75	38.36	-	5	3	142.1	31	409	11	37.18	3-54
1999-2000	West Indies U23	First Class Matches	WI	1	2	0	6	5	3.00	-	-	1	2	0	13	0	-	-
1999-2000	W.I. Select XI	First Class Matches	WI	1	1	0	15	15	15.00	-	-	-	4	0	10	0	-	-
2003//	W.I. President's XI	First Class Matches	WI	1	1	0	83	83	83.00	-	1	-	25	8	30	1	30.00	1-30
2001-2002	WEST INDIES	O.D.I. MATCHES	HA	11	8	3	93	18*	18.60	-	-	2	57.1	0	317	6	52.83	2-19
1999-2000	West Indies "A"	O.D.(I.) Matches	H	4	4	0	24	15	6.00	-	-	1	19	2	87	3	49.00	2-40
2000-2002	Busta Cup XI	First Class Matches	WI	2	2	1	37	27*	37.00	-	2	2	43	8	96	4	24.00	3-48
2002//	West Indies	O.A.L. O.D. Matches	A	2	1	0	68	68	68.00	-	1	3	7	0	46	6	7.66	6-46
Total First Class Career				48	78	12	2135	166	32.34	1	14	29	672.2	161	1648	65	25.35	9-68
Total O.D. Career				39	30	5	688	81	27.52	0	5	14	124.1	18	967	37	26.13	6-46

WAVELL WAYNE HINDS

D.O.B. 07.09.1976 - Kingston Jamaica

First Class Debut 10.04.1996 - Jamaica v Lancashire
Test Match Debut 16.03.2000 - West Indies v Zimbabwe
O.D.I. Debut 05.09.1999 - West Indies v India
Domestic O.D. Debut 04.10.1997 - Jamaica v Windward Islands

Teams Played For
Jamaica
West Indies
West Indies "A"
W.I. Board XI
Busta Cup XI

Test 233-355
O.D.I. 95-374

LHB / RM

5

SEASON	TEAM	COMPETITION	V	M	I	No	RUNS	H.S.	Av	100s	50s	CT	OV	MD	RUNS	W	Av	B.B.
							BATTING						BOWLING					
1996-2003	Jamaica	First Class Matches	II	29	52	2	1454	127	29.08	4	6	8	71.4	22	152	6	25.33	3-9
1997-2002	Jamaica	Domestic O.D. Matches	II	27	24	4	575	103	28.75	1	2	11	1.3	0	6	1	6.00	1-6
1998-2001	Jamaica	O.A.L. O.D. Matches	HA	4	4	0	39	17	9.75	-	-	-	8	1	23	1	23.00	1-14
2000-2003	WEST INDIES	TEST MATCHES	HA	33	58	1	1871	165	32.82	4	10	28	56.3	10	180	6	30.00	2-23
1999-2002	West Indies	First Class Matches	A	15	23	2	1056	150	50.28	6	6	12	39.5	9	124	4	31.00	3-32
1999//	W.I. Board XI	First Class Matches	WI	1	2	0	17	17	8.50	-	-	-	2	0	13	0	-	-
1999-2003	WEST INDIES	O.D.I. MATCHES	HA	78	74	5	2047	125*	29.66	3	12	25	54.5	0	284	11	25.81	3-25
1997-1999	West Indies "A"	First Class Matches	HA	11	21	1	683	115	34.15	2	3	2	7	1	15	0	-	-
1997-1998	West Indies "A"	O.D.(I.) Matches	A	9	9	0	280	80	31.11	-	2	-	1	0	5	0	-	-
1997-1998	West Indies "A"	O.A.L. O.D. Matches	A	2	1	0	71	71	71.00	-	1	-	6	1	24	3	8.00	3-24
1999-2001	West Indies	O.A.L. O.D. Matches	A	4	4	0	123	55	30.75	-	1	1	6	0	36	2	18.00	2-15
2001-2002	Busta Cup XI	First Class Matches	WI	1	1	0	175	175	175.00	1	-	-	2	0	6	0	-	-
		Total First Class Career		90	157	6	5256	175	34.80	15	25	50	179	42	490	16	30.62	3-9
		Total O.D. Career		124	116	9	3135	125*	29.29	4	18	37	77.2	1	378	18	21.00	3-24

EDWARD LISLE GOLDSWORTHY HOAD

D.O.B. 29.01.1896 - Richmond, St Michael, Barbados (d. 05.03.1986)
First Class Debut 28.09.1922 - Barbados v Trinidad
Test Match Debut 21.07.1928 - West Indies v England

Test 12-2

Teams Played For
Barbados
West Indies
Combined B/J XI

3

RHB / LBG

SEASON	TEAM	COMPETITION	V	M	I	No	RUNS	H.S.	Av	100s	50s	CT	OV	MD	RUNS	W	Av	B.B.
							BATTING						**BOWLING**					
1922-1938	Barbados	First Class Matches	II	20	31	5	1583	174*	60.88	5	8	15	482.4	55	1452	46	31.56	5-84
1928-1933	WEST INDIES	TEST MATCHES	HA	4	8	0	98	36	12.25	-	-	1	-	-	-	-	-	-
1926-1933	West Indies	First Class Matches	HA	37	63	8	1774	149*	32.25	3	6	9	73	3	399	6	66.50	2-63
1927-1982	Combined B/J XI	First Class Matches	WI	1	1	0	47	47	47.00	-	-	-	14	1	56	1	56.00	1-31
Total First Class Career				62	103	13	3502	174*	38.91	8	14	25	569.4	59	1907	53	35.98	5-84

ROLAND IRWIN CHRISTOPHER HOLDER

RHB / RM   7

D.O.B. 22.12.1967 - Port of Spain, Trinidad

First Class Debut 10.01.1986 - Barbados v Trinidad & Tobago
Test Match Debut 06.03.1997 - West Indies v India
O.D.I. Debut 03.11.1993 - West Indies v Sri Lanka
Domestic O.D. Debut 15.01.1986 - Barbados v Windward Islands

Teams Played For
Barbados, West Indies
W.I. President's XI, W.I. Board XI
West Indies U23
West Indies "A"
West Indies "B"

Test 214-328
O.D.I. 65-262

SEASON	TEAM	COMPETITION	V	M	I	No	BATTING RUNS	H.S.	Av	100s	50s	CT	BOWLING OV	MD	RUNS	W	Av	B.B.
1986-2001	Barbados	First Class Matches	II	70	120	12	4245	162*	39.30	13	17	45	-	-	-	-	-	-
1986-2000	Barbados	Domestic O.D. Matches	II	47	41	6	1159	111	33.11	1	7	16	2	2	0	0	-	-
1992-1998	Barbados	O.A.L. O.D. Matches	HA	9	8	0	116	41	14.50	-	-	2	-	-	-	-	-	-
1997-1999	WEST INDIES	TEST MATCHES	HA	11	17	2	380	91	25.33	-	2	9	-	-	-	-	-	-
1993-1998	West Indies	First Class Matches	A	8	13	3	235	71*	23.50	-	2	3	-	-	-	-	-	-
1991-1995	W.I. President's XI	First Class Matches	WI	3	4	0	177	144	42.25	1	1	-	-	-	-	-	-	-
1994//	W.I. Board XI	First Class Matches	WI	1	1	0	116	116	116.00	1	-	-	-	-	-	-	-	-
1988//	West Indies U23	First Class Matches	WI	1	2	0	35	25	17.50	-	-	-	-	-	-	-	-	-
1992-1998	West Indies "A"	First Class Matches	H	4	5	0	362	183	72.40	1	2	2	-	-	-	-	-	-
2002//	West Indies "B"	First Class Matches	WI	7	13	1	395	112*	32.91	1	2	6	-	-	-	-	-	-
1993-1998	WEST INDIES	O.D.I. MATACHES	HA	37	31	6	599	65	23.96	-	2	8	-	-	-	-	-	-
1995//	West Indies "A"	O.D.(I.) Matches	WI	3	3	1	86	45*	43.00	-	-	1	-	-	-	-	-	-
1995-1997	West Indies	O.A.L. O.D. Matches	A	5	5	1	114	80*	28.50	-	1	-	0.1	0	1	0	-	-
Total First Class Career				105	175	18	5945	183	37.86	17	25	66	-	-	-	-	-	-
Total O.D. Career				101	88	14	2074	111	28.02	1	10	27	2.1	2	1	0	-	-

VANBURN ALONZO HOLDER

D.O.B. 08.10.1945 - Deans Village, St Michael, Barbados
First Class Debut 22.02.1967 - Barbados v Trinidad & Tobago
Test Match Debut 12.06.1969 - West Indies v England
O.D.I. Debut 05.09.1973 - West Indies v England
Domestic O.D. Debut 04.05.1968 - Worcestershire v Durham

Test 131-126

O.D.I. 10-1

Teams Played For
Barbados, West Indies
Worcestershire
World XI
Orange Free State
Minor Counties

6

RHB / RFM

SEASON	TEAM	COMPETITION	V	M	I	No	BATTING RUNS	H.S.	Av	100s	50s	CT	BOWLING OV	MD	RUNS	W	Av	B.B.
1967-1978	Barbados	First Class Matches	II	43	57	11	742	122	16.13	1	1	17	1282.3	328	3140	134	23.43	7-44
1972-1978	Barbados	Domestic O.D. Matches	II	10	6	4	10	4	4.00	-	-	4	72	10	221	10	22.10	3-28
1969-1978	WEST INDIES	TEST MATCHES	HA	40	59	11	682	42	14.20	-	-	16	1460.3	367	3627	109	33.27	6-28
1969-1978	West Indies	First Class Matches	A	45	38	7	504	89	16.25	-	2	7	1037.1	265	2775	116	23.92	6-55
1973-1976	WEST INDIES	O.D.I. MATCHES	A	12	6	1	64	30	12.80	-	-	6	113.3	9	454	19	23.99	5-50
1969-1979	West Indies	O.A.L. O.D. Matches	A	7	3	1	16	9	8.00	-	-	1	39.4	-	159	7	22.71	3-8
1968-1980	Worcestershire	First Class Matches	E	181	196	51	1553	52	10.71	-	1	57	5316.5	1146	13530	586	23.08	7-40
1968-1980	Worcestershire	Nat West Trophy	E	18	14	5	79	25*	8.77	-	-	2	197.3	34	604	22	27.45	3-14
1972-1979	Worcestershire	Benson & Hedges Cup	E	25	17	8	67	17*	7.44	-	-	5	238.4	37	691	37	18.67	5-12
1969-1980	Worcestershire	Sunday League	E	120	61	15	323	35*	7.02	-	-	26	864.5	-	2970	176	16.87	6-33
1971//	Worcestershire	O.A.L. O.D. Matches	E	1	-	-	-	-	-	-	-	-	6	-	20	2	10.00	2-20
1981//	Minor Counties	Benson & Hedges Cup	E	2	2	1	28	22*	28.00	-	-	1	12	-	78	2	39.00	1-32
1985-1986	Orange Free State	First Class Matches	SA	2	4	0	34	28	8.50	-	-	1	33	3	117	2	58.50	1-58
1985-1986	Orange Free State	Nissan Cup	SA	1	-	-	-	-	-	-	-	1	16	-	31	1	31.00	1-31
1973-1974	World XI	First Class Matches	P	2	4	1	78	30	26.00	-	-	1	42.1	12	111	3	37.00	1-27
Total First Class Career				313	358	81	3593	122	12.97	1	4	99	9172.1	2121	23300	950	24.52	7-40
Total O.D. Career				196	109	35	587	35*	7.93	0	0	46	1560.1	-	5228	276	18.94	6-33

MICHAEL ANTHONY HOLDING

D.O.B. 16.02.1954 - Half-way Tree, Kingston, Jamaica
First Class Debut 19.01.1973 - Jamaica v Barbados
Test Match Debut 28.11.1975 - West Indies v Australia
O.D.I. Debut 26.08.1976 - West Indies v England
Domestic O.D. Debut 28.03.1976 - Jamaica v Guyana

Teams Played For
Jamaica, West Indies
W.I. President's XI, Lancashire
Derbyshire, Tasmania
Canterbury
International XI

Test 153-159
O.D.I. 18-9

RHB / RF

8

SEASON	TEAM	COMPETITION	V	M	I	No	BATTING RUNS	H.S.	Av	100s	50s	CT	BOWLING OV	MD	RUNS	W	Av	B.B.
1973-1989	Jamaica	First Class Matches	II	34	47	5	454	34	10.80	-	-	29	743.4	138	2323	90	25.81	5-96
1976-1988	Jamaica	Domestic O.D. Matches	II	11	9	0	31	9	3.44			1	100	15	346	17	20.35	4-32
1975-1986	WEST INDIES	TEST MATCHES	HA	60	76	10	910	73	13.78	-	6	22	2066.4	458	5898	249	23.68	8-92
1975-1986	West Indies	First Class Matches	A	35	35	6	488	62	16.82		2	20	808.3	202	2142	101	21.20	6-60
1973-1974	W.I. President's XI	First Class Matches	WI	4	4	1	7	5	2.33			1	25	3	73	3	73.00	1-9
1976-1986	WEST INDIES	O.D.I. MATCHES	HA	102	42	11	282	64	9.09		2	30	912.1	99	3034	142	21.36	5-26
1975-1980	West Indies	O.A.L. O.D. Matches	A	6	4	0	14	13	3.50			3	43.3	-	137	5	27.40	2-21
1981//	Lancashire	First Class Matches	E	7	8	2	66	32	11.00			2	271.1	75	715	40	17.87	6-74
1981//	Lancashire	Nat West Trophy	E	2	1	1	12	12*	-			-	24	3	71	3	23.66	3-35
1981//	Lancashire	Benson & Hedges Cup	E	2	1	0	1	1	1.00			1	22	-	49	3	16.33	2-21
1981//	Lancashire	Sunday League	E	2	1	0	1	0	0.00			-	12	-	45	2	22.50	2-31
1981//	Lancashire	O.A.L. O.D. Matches	E	1	D	-	-	-	-			-	7	-	18	1	18.00	1-18
1983-1989	Derbyshire	First Class Matches	E	66	87	12	1295	80	17.26		5	39	1840.3	385	5504	224	24.57	7-97
1983-1989	Derbyshire	Nat West Trophy	E	12	9	0	96	32	10.66			6	126.4	27	306	23	13.30	8-21
1983-1989	Derbyshire	Benson & Hedges Cup	E	24	16	4	278	69	23.16		1	9	229	-	719	32	22.46	5-31
1983-1989	Derbyshire	Sunday League	E	75	60	6	788	58	14.59		4	24	531.5	-	2103	98	21.45	4-18
1984//	Derbyshire	O.A.L. O.D. Matches	E	1	1	0	6	6	6.00			-	1	0	1	1	1.00	1-1
1982-1983	Tasmania	First Class Matches	A	9	11	2	187	47*	20.77			3	371.4	93	946	36	26.27	7-59
1982-1983	Tasmania	MacDonald Cup	A	2	2	1	0	0*	0.00			-	19.1	0	47	2	23.50	-
1982-1983	Tasmania	O.A.L. O.D. Matches	A	1	1	0	19	19	19.00			-	9	-	16	2	8.00	2-16
1987-1988	Canterbury	First Class Matches	NZ	7	11	4	62	31	8.85			9	258.5	90	488	29	16.82	7-52
1987-1988	Canterbury	Shell Cup	NZ	5	4	2	25	18*	12.50			1	47	-	129	8	16.12	2-21
1987-1988	Canterbury	O.A.L. O.D. Matches	NZ	1	1	0	0	0	0.00			-	10	-	31	2	15.50	2-31
1981-1982	International XI	First Class Matches	P	2	4	1	131	67	43.66		1	-	46.1	11	144	8	18.00	6-49
1981-1982	International XI	O.A.L. O.D Matches	P	2	1	0	23	23	23.00			5	15	-	22	2	11.00	1-7
		Total First Class Career		222	283	43	3600	80	15.00	0	14	125	6432.1	1455	18233	778	23.43	8-92
		Total O.D. Career		249	153	25	1575	69	12.30	0	7	81	2110.2	-	7074	343	20.62	8-21

DAVID ANTHONY JEROME HOLFORD

D.O.B. 16.04.1940 - Upper Collymore Rock, St Michael, Barbados
First Class Debut 26.01.1961 - Barbados v Trinidad
Test Match Debut 02.06.1966 - West Indies v England
Domestic O.D. Debut 14.04.1973 - Barbados v Trinidad & Tobago

Test	Teams Played For		RHB / LBG
124-105	Barbados / Trinidad / North Trinidad / West Indies	4	

SEASON	TEAM	COMPETITION	V	M	I	No	BATTING RUNS	H.S.	Av	100s	50s	CT	BOWLING OV	MD	RUNS	W	Av	B.B.
1961-1979	Barbados	First Class Matches	=	46	68	13	1993	111	36.23	1	12	46	1374.2	313	3683	130	28.33	6-61
1963//	Trinidad	First Class Matches	=	1	2	0	22	14	11.00	-	-	1	17	0	82	0	-	-
1963//	North Trinidad	First Class Matches	T	1	1	0	9	9	9.00	-	-	-	-	-	-	-	-	-
1972-1979	Barbados	Domestic O.D. Matches	=	10	8	1	124	46	17.71	-	-	3	45	2	199	7	28.42	3-29
1969//	Barbados	O.A.L. O.D. Matches	A	1	1	0	0	0	0.00	-	-	-	-	-	-	-	-	-
1966-1977	WEST INDIES	TEST MATCHES	HA	24	39	5	768	105*	22.58	1	3	18	757	164	2009	51	39.39	5-23
1966-1969	West Indies	First Class Matches	A	27	39	9	1029	107*	34.30	1	5	18	675.2	135	2321	72	32.23	8-52
1966//	West Indies	O.A.L. O.D. Matches	A	2	1	1	11	11*	-	-	-	1	10	2	51	1	51.00	1-51
Total First Class Career				99	149	27	3821	111	31.31	3	20	83	2823.4	612	8095	253	31.99	8-52
Total O.D. Career				13	10	2	135	46	16.87	0	0	4	55	4	250	8	31.25	3-29

JOHN KENNETH CONSTANTINE HOLT

D.O.B. 12.08.1923 - Kingston, Jamaica (d. 02.07.1997)

First Class Debut 26.06.1946 - Jamaica v Trinidad
Test Match Debut 15.01.1954 - West Indies v England

Test 82-48

Teams Played For
Jamaica
West Indies
Commonwealth XI

RHB / OB

3

SEASON	TEAM	COMPETITION	V	M	I	No	BATTING RUNS	H.S.	Av	100s	50s	CT/ST	BOWLING OV	MD	RUNS	W	Av	B.B.
1946-1962	Jamaica	First Class Matches	II	26	45	4	1736	172	42.34	4	9	18/1	53	9	153	4	38.25	1-2
1954-1958	WEST INDIES	TEST MATCHES	HA	17	31	2	1066	166	36.75	2	5	8	5	2	20	1	20.00	1-20
1958-1959	West Indies	First Class Matches	A	11	15	3	618	105	51.50	2	3	1	1	0	4	0	-	-
1949-1950	Commonwealth XI	First Class Matches	I	17	24	3	838	162	39.90	1	5	3	-	-	-	-	-	-
		Total First Class Career		71	115	12	4258	172	41.33	9	22	30/1	59	11	177	5	35.40	1-2

CARL LLEWELLYN HOOPER

D.O.B. 15.12.1966 - Georgetown, Demerara, Guyana
First Class Debut 08.10.1983 - Demerara v Berbice
Test Match Debut 11.12.1987 - West Indies v India
O.D.I. Debut 18.03.1987 - West Indies v New Zealand
Domestic O.D. Debut 30.01.1985 - Guyana v Barbados

Test	190-254
O.D.I.	50-138

Teams Played For 11
Guyana, Demerara, Lancashire
West Indies, West Indies U23
W.I. President's XI, W.I. Board XI
West Indies "B", West Indies "A"
Shell Awards XI, Kent

RHB / OB

SEASON	TEAM	COMPETITION	V	M	I	No	BATTING RUNS	H.S.	Av	100s	50s	CT	BOWLING OV	MD	RUNS	W	Av	B.B.
1983-1988	Demerara	First Class Matches	G	3	5	1	78	32	19.50	-	-	2	60.4	11	163	13	12.53	5-71
1985-2003	Guyana	First Class Matches	II	45	66	8	3372	222	58.13	13	12	43	1162.2	270	2742	93	29.48	5-48
1985-2002	Guyana	Domestic O.D. Matches	II	54	47	14	1769	104	53.60	1	13	27	417.1	24	1482	57	26.00	3-23
1987-2002	WEST INDIES	TEST MATCHES	HA	102	173	15	5762	233	36.43	13	27	115	2299	525	5635	114	49.42	5-26
1986-2002	West Indies	First Class Matches	A	62	91	12	4517	196	57.17	12	23	41	1175.4	225	3396	104	32.65	5-33
1985/	West Indies U23	First Class Matches	WI	1	1	0	37	37	37.00	-	-	1	31	4	94	5	18.80	5-35
1985/	W.I. President's XI	First Class Matches	WI	3	3	0	74	67	24.66	-	1	2	100.1	15	300	7	42.85	4-72
1985-1994	West Indies "B"	First Class Matches	A	8	9	1	366	88	45.75	-	3	11	100	26	252	11	22.90	3-10
1986-1989	WI Board XI	First Class Matches	WI	1	1	1	54	54*	-	-	1	2						
1989/	West Indies "A"	First Class Matches	WI	1	2	0	112	102	56.00	1	-	2	43	10	93	9	10.33	5-53
1999/	West Indies "A"	First Class Matches	WI	1	1	0	36	36	36.00	-	-	2	5.2	0	24	0	-	
1985/	Shell Awards XI	First Class Matches	WI	1	1	0	36	36	36.00	-	-	-						
1986-2003	WEST INDIES	O.D.I. MATCHES	HA	227	206	43	5762	113*	35.34	7	29	120	1595.3	53	6958	193	36.05	4-34
1986-1989	West Indies "B"	O.D.I.(I.) Matches	A	10	7	0	176	84	25.14	-	1	6	95.5	3	367	12	30.58	3-22
1987-2001	West Indies	O.A.L. O.D. Matches	A	19	18	3	527	110	35.13	1	2	10	136	7	537	18	29.83	4-173
1992-1998	Kent	First Class Matches	E	85	142	9	6714	236*	50.48	22	30	121	2167.5	520	5389	154	34.99	7-93
1992-1998	Kent	Nat West Trophy	E	13	12	1	461	136*	41.90	1	1	8	129.5	-	472	7	67.42	2-12
1992-1998	Kent	Benson & Hedges Cup	E	17	17	0	617	98	36.29	-	6	8	150	-	529	16	33.06	3-28
1992-1998	Kent	Sunday League	E	82	76	10	3065	145	46.34	5	23	43	554.1	-	2344	68	34.47	5-41
1994/	Kent	O.A.L. O.D. Matches	E	1	1	0	15	15	15.00	-	-	-	9.5	0	48	0	-	-
2003/	Lancashire	First Class Matches	E	14	20	2	1219	201	67.72	6	3	15	366.2	86	912	30	30.40	6-51
2003/	Lancashire	Cheltenham & Gloucester Cup	E	3	3	0	73	61	24.33	-	1	2	20	0	82	2	41.00	2-29
2003/	Lancashire	National Sunday League	E	16	14	6	597	88*	74.62	-	7	13	90.1	2	379	14	27.07	3-18
Total First Class Career				326	514	49	22341	236*	48.04	67	100	356	7510	1692	19000	540	35.18	7-93
Total O.D. Career				442	401	77	12061	145	40.31	15	83	237	3198.2	118	13198	387	34.10	5-41

ANTHONY BOURNE HOWARD

D.O.B. 27.08.1946 - Lower Collymore Rock, St Michael, Barbados
First Class Debut 18.02.1966 - Barbados v British Guiana
Test Match Debut 06.04.1972 - West Indies v New Zealand

Test 143-137

Teams Played For
West Indies
Barbados

RHB / RM

2

BATTING

SEASON	TEAM	COMPETITION	V	M	I	No	RUNS	H.S.	Av	100s	50s	CT
1966-1975	Barbados	First Class Matches	=	30	38	7	310	42*	10.00	-	-	10
1971-1972	WEST INDIES	TEST MATCHES	H	1	D	-	-	-	-	-	-	-
		Total First Class Career		31	38	7	310	42*	10.00	0	0	10

BOWLING

OV	MD	RUNS	W	Av	B.B.
889	217	2181	83	26.27	5-46
62	16	140	2	70.00	2-140
951	233	2321	85	27.30	5-46

CONRAD CLEOPHAS HUNTE

D.O.B. 09.05.1932 - Shorey Village, St Andrew, Barbados (d. 03.12.1999)
First Class Debut 21.02.1951 - Barbados v Trinidad
Test Match Debut 17.01.1958 - West Indies v Pakistan

Test 98-67

RHB / RM

Teams Played For 7
Barbados, Jamaican XI
West Indies, C.C. Hunte's XI
Commonwealth XI
World XI
Indian Prime Minister's XI

SEASON	TEAM	COMPETITION	V	M	I	No	RUNS	H.S.	Av	100s	50s	CT/ST	OV	MD	RUNS	W	Av	B.B.
1951-1967	Barbados	First Class Matches	II	27	43	4	2004	263	51.38	3	14	12/1	26	1	89	0	-	-
1964-1965	Jamaican XI	First Class Matches	WI	1	2	0	90	78	45.00	-	1	-	-	-	-	-	-	-
1958-1967	WEST INDIES	TEST MATCHES	HA	44	78	6	3245	260	45.06	8	13	16	45	11	110	2	55.00	1-17
1956-1967	West Indies	First Class Matches	HA	54	89	8	3301	206	40.75	5	22	33	125.1	26	329	12	27.41	3-5
1964//	C.C. Hunte's XI	First Class Matches	WI	1	2	0	38	33	19.00	-	-	1	7	0	33	0	33.00	1-26
1963-1966	West Indies	O.A.L. O.D. Matches	A	3	3	0	12	11	4.00	-	-	3	19.1	2	61	6	10.16	4-38
1956-1961	Commonwealth XI	First Class Matches	E	2	3	1	83	43	41.50	-	-	2	16	2	63	1	63.00	1-63
1963-1967	World XI	First Class Matches	E	2	3	0	104	63	34.66	-	1	1	-	-	-	-	-	-
1963-1964	Indian PM's XI	First Class Matches	I	1	2	0	51	30	25.50	-	-	3	5	1	20	1	20.00	1-20
Total First Class Career				132	222	19	8916	263	43.92	16	51	68/1	224.1	41	644	17	37.88	3-5
Total O.D. Career				3	3	0	12	11	4.00	0	0	3	19.1	2	61	6	10.16	4-38

ERROL ASHTON CLAIRMORE HUNTE

D.O.B. 03.10.1905 - Port of Spain, Trinidad (d. 26.06.1967)

First Class Debut 31.01.1929 - Trinidad v British Guiana

Test Match Debut 11.01.1930 - West Indies v England

Test 18-4

Teams Played For
Trinidad
West Indies

RHB / WK

2

SEASON	TEAM	COMPETITION	V	M	I	No	BATTING RUNS	H.S.	Av	100s	50s	CT/ST	BOWLING OV	MD	RUNS	W	Av	B.B.
1929-1934	Trinidad	First Class Matches	II	7	13	2	171	56	15.54	-	1	18/5	-	-	-	-	-	-
1929-1930	WEST INDIES	TEST MATCHES	H	3	6	1	166	58	33.20	-	2	5	-	-	-	-	-	-
1930-1931	West Indies	First Class Matches	A	5	9	2	135	29	19.28	-	-	6/2	-	-	-	-	-	-
		Total First Class Career		15	28	5	472	58	20.52	0	3	29/7	-	-	-	-	-	-

RYAN O'NEIL HURLEY

O.D.I. 115-464   Teams Played For   2   RHB / OB
Barbados
West Indies

D.O.B. 13.09.1975 - Springhead, St Andrew, Barbados
First Class Debut 16.02.1996 - Barbados v Jamaica
O.D.I. Debut 24.05.2003 - West Indies v Australia
Domestic O.D. Debut 04.10.1996 - Barbados v Guyana

SEASON	TEAM	COMPETITION	V	M	I	No	BATTING RUNS	H.S.	Av	100s	50s	CT	BOWLING OV	MD	RUNS	W	Av	B.B.
1996-2003	Barbados	First Class Matches	=	21	30	2	771	122	27.53	2	2	10	457.5	106	1192	43	27.72	5-66
1996-2001	Barbados	Domestic O.D. Matches	=	13	11	1	117	24	11.70	-	-	5	126	15	391	11	35.54	3-34
2000/I	Barbados	O.A.L. O.D. Matches	WI	1	1	0	7	7	7.00	-	-	-	5	2	9	0	-	-
2003/I	WEST INDIES	O.D.I. MATCHES	H	4	1	0	0	0	0.00	-	-	4	25	1	111	2	55.50	1-25
		Total First Class Career		21	30	2	771	122	27.53	2	2	10	457.5	106	1192	43	27.72	5-66
		Total O.D. Career		18	13	1	124	24	10.33	0	0	9	156	18	511	13	39.30	3-34

LESLIE GEORGE HYLTON

D.O.B. 29.03.1905 - Kingston, Jamaica (d. 17.05.1955)

First Class Debut 19.02.1927 - Jamaica v Lord Tennyson's XI
Test Match Debut 08.01.1935 - West Indies v England

Test 40-16

Teams Played For
Jamaica
West Indies
G.C. Grant's XI
Combined J/B XI

RHB / RFM

4

BATTING

SEASON	TEAM	COMPETITION	V	M	I	No	RUNS	H.S.	Av	100s	50s	CT
1927-1939	Jamaica	First Class Matches	=	18	25	4	552	80	26.28	-	4	19
1935-1939	WEST INDIES	TEST MATCHES	HA	6	8	2	70	19	11.66	-	-	1
1939//	West Indies	First Class Matches	A	13	16	3	198	55	15.23	-	1	10
1932-1933	G.C. Grant's XI	First Class Matches	WI	1	2	0	2	2	1.00	-	-	-
1927-1928	Combined J/B XI	First Class Matches	WI	2	3	0	21	10	7.00	-	-	1
	Total First Class Career			40	54	9	843	80	18.73	0	5	31

BOWLING

OV	MD	RUNS	W	Av	B.B.
551.2	89	1591	61	26.08	5-24
144.5	31	418	16	26.12	4-27
253	23	914	36	25.38	5-35
40.3	7	75	4	18.75	3-30
20	1	77	3	25.66	3-77
1009.4	151	3075	120	25.62	5-24

RIDLEY DETAMORE JACOBS

D.O.B. 26.11.1967 - Swetes Village, Antigua, Leeward Islands
First Class Debut 24.01.1992 - Leeward Islands v Windward Islands
Test Match Debut 26.11.1998 - West Indies v South Africa
O.D.I. Debut 26.03.1996 - West Indies v New Zealand
Domestic O.D. Debut 29.01.1992 - Leeward Islands

Test 222-344
O.D.I. 76-318

Teams Played For 7
Leeward Islands, West Indies "A"
Antigua, Busta Cup XI
West Indies
W.I. Board XI
W.I. President's XI

LHB / WK

SEASON	TEAM	COMPETITION	V	M	I	No	BATTING RUNS	H.S.	Av	100s	50s	CT/ST	BOWLING OV	MD	RUNS	W	Av	B.B.
1992-2003	Leeward Islands	First Class Matches	II	54	85	18	2622	119*	39.13	5	17	170/13	-	-	-	-	-	-
1992-2001	Leeward Islands	Domestic O.D. Matches	II	50	41	9	850	85	26.26	-	5	65/6	-	-	-	-	-	-
1998//	Antigua	O.A.L. O.D. Matches	A	3	3	1	74	43*	37.00	-	2	-	-	-	-	-	-	-
2002-2002	Antigua	Domestic O.D. Matches	II	5	5	2	131	76*	43.66	-	1	4/2	-	-	-	-	-	-
1998-2003	WEST INDIES	TEST MATCHES	HA	51	88	17	2000	118	28.16	2	11	167/8	-	-	-	-	-	-
1998-2003	West Indies	First Class Matches	A	16	22	6	661	131	41.31	1	3	28/5	1	-	0	0	-	-
1993-1995	W.I. President's XI	First Class Matches	WI	2	2	2	135	100*	-	-	-	3/2	-	-	-	-	-	-
1994//	W.I. Board XI	First Class Matches	WI	1	1	0	41	41	41.00	-	-	2	-	-	-	-	-	-
1996-2003	West Indies "A"	First Class Matches	HA	1	1	1	100	100*	-	1	-	3	-	-	-	-	-	-
1996-2003	WEST INDIES	O.D.I. MATCHES	HA	125	101	26	1752	80*	23.36	-	9	142/26	-	-	-	-	-	-
1995-1997	West Indies "A"	O.D.(I.) Matches	HA	6	5	1	86	52	21.50	-	1	9/2	-	-	-	-	-	-
1998-2001	West Indies	O.A.L. O.D. Matches	A	5	4	2	56	20	28.00	-	-	4/2	-	-	-	-	-	-
1996//	West Indies "A"	O.A.L. O.D. Matches	A	1	1	0	1	1	1.00	-	-	-	-	-	-	-	-	-
2002//	Busta Cup XI	First Class Matches	WI	1	1	1	55	55*	-	-	-	-	-	-	00	-	-	-
Total First Class Career				126	200	45	5614	131	36.21	10	32	373/28	1	-	00	-	-	-
				195	160	41	2950	85	24.78	0	16	226/38	-	1	-	-	-	-

361

RHB / RFM

KERRY CLIFFORD BRYAN JEREMY

D.O.B. 06.02.1980 - Antigua, Leeward Islands

First Class Debut 29.01.1999 - Leeward Islands v Windward Islands
O.D.I. Debut 04.10.2000 - West Indies v Sri Lanka
Domestic O.D. Debut 23.09.2000 - West Indies "A" v South Africa

O.D.I. 102-407

Teams Played For 9
Leeward Islands, West Indies U23
Antigua, West Indies "A"
West Indies, Busta Cup XI
W.I. Board XI, Shell Academy XI
W.I. Select XI

SEASON	TEAM	COMPETITION	V	M	I	No	BATTING RUNS	H.S.	Av	100s	50s	CT	BOWLING OV	MD	RUNS	W	Av	B.B.
1998-2003	Leeward Islands	First Class Matches	II	27	39	15	212	70*	8.83	-	1	16	874.3	214	2312	108	21.40	6-33
2000-2001	Leeward Islands	Domestic O.D. Matches	II	6	3	2	9	5*	9.00	-	-	1	55	8	180	12	15.00	6-42
2001-2002	Antigua	Domestic O.D. Matches	II	7	4	1	27	27	9.00	-	-	2	49.1	4	210	5	42.00	2-22
1999-2000	W.I. Board XI	First Class Matches	WI	1	1	0	6	6	6.00	-	-	-	31.4	6	94	6	15.66	6-81
1999-2000	W.I. Select XI	First Class Matches	WI	1	1	0	9	9	9.00	-	-	-	14	3	40	2	20.00	2-40
1999-2000	West Indies U23	First Class Matches	WI	1	2	1	8	7*	8.00	-	-	-	24.1	5	68	4	17.00	3-46
1999-2000	West Indies "A"	First Class Matches	H	1	1	1	6	6*	-	-	-	1	19	6	42	0	-	-
2000-2001	West Indies	First Class Matches	A	2	2	1	16	9	16.00	-	-	-	41	8	127	3	42.33	2-42
2001-2002	Busta Cup XI	First Class Matches	WI	2	3	1	24	9	12.00	-	-	2	39	8	117	3	39.00	1-6
2000-2001	WEST INDIES	O.D.I. MATCHES	HA	6	4	2	17	8*	8.50	-	-	-	32	1	163	4	40.75	2-42
1999-2000	West Indies "A"	O.D(I.) Matches	H	2	2	1	5	4	5.00	-	-	-	13	1	65	1	65.00	1-36
2000-2001	West Indies	O.A.L. O.D. Matches	A	2	0	-	-	-	-	-	-	1	7	0	48	0	-	-
2002-2003	Shell Academy	O.A.L. O.D. Matches	WI	1	1	1	18	18*	-	-	-	-	9	0	48	0	-	-
Total First Class Career				35	49	19	281	70*	9.36	-	1	19	1043.2	250	2800	126	22.22	6-33
Total O.D. Career				24	14	7	76	27	10.85	0	0	4	165.1	14	714	22	32.45	6-42

HOPHNIE HOBAH HINES JOHNSON

D.O.B. 13.07.1910 - Kingston, Jamaica (d. 24.06.1987)

First Class Debut 09.03.1935 - Jamaica v M.C.C.

Test Match Debut 27.03.1948 - West Indies v England

	Test	64-26		Teams Played For		2			RHB / RF
				Jamaica					
				West Indies					

| | | | | | | | BATTING | | | | | | BOWLING | | | | | |
SEASON	TEAM	COMPETITION	V	M	I	No	RUNS	H.S.	Av	100s	50s	CT	OV	MD	RUNS	W	Av	B.B.
1935-1951	Jamaica	First Class Matches	II	10	13	8	124	39*	24.80	-	-	8	209.1	34	539	24	22.45	5-33
1948-1950	WEST INDIES	TEST MATCHES	HA	3	4	0	38	22	9.50	-	-		131.3	37	238	13	18.30	5-41
1950//	West Indies	First Class Matches	A	15	13	4	124	39*	17.11	-	-	5	370.1	89	812	31	26.19	5-33
		Total First Class Career		28	30	12	346	39*	17.55	0	0	13	710.5	160	1589	68	23.36	5-23

TYRELL FABIAN JOHNSON

D.O.B.   10.01.1917 - Tunapuna, Trinidad (d. 05.04.1985)

First Class Debut   29.01.1936 - Trinidad v Barbados

Test Match Debut   19.08.1939 - West Indies v England

Test   51-22

Teams Played For: Trinidad, West Indies

LHB / LF   2

SEASON	TEAM	COMPETITION	V	M	I	No	BATTING RUNS	H.S.	Av	100s	50s	CT	BOWLING OV	MD	RUNS	W	Av	B.B.
1936-1939	Trinidad	First Class Matches	II	8	11	7	60	27	15.00	-	-	4	224.1	64	489	27	18.11	4-15
1939//	WEST INDIES	TEST MATCHES	A	1	1	1	9	9*	-	-	-	1	30	3	129	3	43.00	2-53
1938-1939	West Indies	First Class Matches	HA	9	9	3	21	12	3.50	-	-	3	150.1	28	457	20	22.85	6-41
		Total First Class Career		18	21	11	90	27	9.00	0	0	8	404.2	95	1075	50	21.50	6-41

CHARLES ERNEST LLEWELLYN JONES

D.O.B. 03.11.1902 - Georgetown, Demerara, British Guiana (d. 10.12.1959)

First Class Debut 01.10.1925 - British Guiana v Barbados

Test Match Debut 21.02.1930 - West Indies v England

Test 25-6

Teams Played For
British Guiana
Barbados XI
West Indies
Combined T/BG XI
R.S. Grant's XI

5

RHB / SLA / WK

SEASON	TEAM	COMPETITION	V	M	I	No	BATTING RUNS	H.S.	Av	100s	50s	CT	BOWLING OV	MD	RUNS	W	Av	B.B.
1925-1939	British Guiana	First Class Matches	II	19	34	3	801	89*	25.83	-	5	16	330.1	64	864	19	45.47	3-19
1928//	Barbados XI	First Class Matches	II	1	1	0	0	0	0.00	-	-	-	21	0	93	0	-	-
1930-1935	WEST INDIES	TEST MATCHES	WI	4	7	0	63	19	9.00	-	-	3	17	11	11	0	-	-
1928//	Combined T/BG XI	First Class Matches	WI	2	2	0	39	34	19.50	-	-	3	37	11	91	5	18.20	2-18
1939//	R.S. Grant's XI	First Class Matches	WI	1	1	0	14	14	14.00	-	-	-	-	-	-	-	-	-
	Total First Class Career			27	45	3	917	89*	21.83	0	5	22	405.1	86	1059	24	44.12	3-19

PRIOR ERSKINE WAVERLY JONES

D.O.B. 06.06.1917 - Princes Town, Trinidad (d. 21.11.1991)
First Class Debut 08.02.1941 - Trinidad v Barbados
Test Match Debut 21.02.1948 - West Indies v England

Test 57-23

Teams Played For
Trinidad
West Indies

RHB / RF
2

BATTING

SEASON	TEAM	COMPETITION	V	M	I	No	RUNS	H.S.	Av	100s	50s	CT
1941-1951	Trinidad	First Class Matches	H	22	31	5	517	60*	19.88	-	1	8
1948-1954	WEST INDIES	TEST MATCHES	HA	9	11	2	47	10*	5.22	-	-	4
1948-1952	West Indies	First Class Matches	A	30	29	9	211	46	10.55	-	-	21
Total First Class Career				61	71	16	775	60*	14.09	0	1	33

BOWLING

OV	MD	RUNS	W	Av	B.B.
566.4	79	1918	69	27.79	6-66
296.2	64	751	25	30.04	5-85
727	167	1862	75	24.82	7-29
1590	310	4531	169	26.81	7-29

DAVID ROISTON EMMANUEL JOSEPH

D.O.B. 15.11.1969 - Antigua, Leeward Islands
First Class Debut 18.01.1991 - Leeward Islands v Barbados
Test Match Debut 05.03.1999 - West Indies v Australia
Domestic O.D. Debut 16.01.1991 - Leeward Islands v Barbados

Test 226-349   6   RHB

Teams Played For
Leeward Islands, West Indies
W.I. President's XI
W.I. Board XI
West Indies "A"
Antigua

SEASON	TEAM	COMPETITION	V	M	I	No	RUNS	H.S.	Av	100s	50s	CT	OV	MD	RUNS	W	Av	B.B.
1991-2002	Leeward Islands	First Class Matches	II	46	74	6	2097	131	30.83	6	11	45	-	-	-	-	-	-
1991-2001	Leeward Islands	Domestic O.D. Matches	II	37	32	6	759	94	29.19	-	4	13	0.3	0	1	0	-	-
1998//	Antigua	O.A.L. O.D. Matches	S	3	3	0	49	21	16.33	-	-	-	-	-	-	-	-	-
2001-2002	Antigua	Domestic O.D. Matches	II	3	3	0	81	74	27.00	-	1	-	-	-	-	-	-	-
1999//	WEST INDIES	TEST MATCHES	H	4	7	0	141	50	20.14	-	1	10	-	-	-	-	-	-
1995-1999	W.I. President's XI	First Class Matches	WI	3	4	0	190	83	47.50	-	2	2	-	-	-	-	-	-
1995//	W.I. Board XI	First Class Matches	WI	1	2	0	9	8	4.50	-	-	1	-	-	-	-	-	-
1996-1997	West Indies "A"	First Class Matches	A	4	5	0	150	93	30.00	-	1	5	-	-	-	-	-	-
1995-1997	West Indies "A"	O.D.(I) Matches	HA	6	6	1	110	58	22.00	-	1	1	-	-	-	-	-	-
1996//	West Indies "A"	O.A.L. O.D. Matches	A	1	1	0	65	65	65.00	-	-	-	-	-	-	-	-	-
		Total First Class Career		58	92	6	2587	131	30.08	6	15	63	-	-	-	-	-	-
		Total O.D. Career		50	45	7	1064	94	28.00	0	7	14	0.3	0	1	0	-	-

SYLVESTER CLEOFOSTER JOSEPH

D.O.B. 05.09.1978 - New Winthorpes, Antigua, Leeward Islands

First Class Debut 24.01.1997 - Leeward Islands v Jamaica
O.D.I. Debut 19.04.2000 - West Indies v Pakistan
Domestic O.D. Debut 12.10.1996 - Leeward Islands v Trinidad & Tobago

O.D.I. 98-398

Teams Played For 9
Leeward Islands, Antigua
West Indies, West Indies "A"
W.I. President's XI, W.I. Select XI
Busta Cup XI, Carib Cup XI
West Indies U23

RHB / OB

SEASON	TEAM	COMPETITION	V	M	I	No	BATTING RUNS	H.S.	Av	100s	50s	CT	BOWLING OV	MD	RUNS	W	Av	B.B.
1997-2003	Leeward Islands	First Class Matches	II	33	58	4	1348	211*	24.96	1	5	32	28	9	59	4	14.75	2-13
1996-2001	Leeward Islands	Domestic O.D. Matches	II	23	23	5	770	100*	42.77	1	7	5	3	0	36	1	36.00	1-9
2001-2002	Antigua	Domestic O.D. Matches	II	7	7	0	158	83	22.57	-	1	4	-	-	-	-	-	-
1998//	Antigua	Commonwealth Games	S	3	3	0	70	41	23.22	-	-	4	-	-	-	-	-	-
1999-2000	West Indies "A"	First Class Matches	H	5	9	1	122	58	15.25	-	1	3	-	-	-	-	-	-
1999-2000	W.I. President's XI	First Class Matches	WI	1	2	0	151	100	75.50	1	1	2	-	-	-	-	-	-
1999-2000	West Indies U23	First Class Matches	WI	1	2	0	68	45	34.00	-	-	2	16	3	60	0	-	-
1999-2001	WEST INDIES	O.D.I. MATCHES	HA	4	4	0	57	28	14.25	-	-	1	-	-	-	-	-	-
1999-2000	West Indies "A"	O.D.(I.) Matches	H	4	4	0	68	46	17.00	-	-	5	-	-	-	-	-	-
1999-2000	W.I. Select XI	O.D. Matches	WI	2	2	0	3	2	1.50	-	-	1	-	-	-	-	-	-
2000-2001	West Indies	O.A.L. O.D. Matches	A	1	1	0	13	13	13.00	-	-	-	-	-	-	-	-	-
2001//	Busta Cup XI	First Class Matches	WI	1	2	0	14	8	7.00	-	-	2	5	1	18	0	-	-
2002-2003	Carib Cup XI	First Class Matches	WI	1	2	0	8	6	4.00	-	-	2	-	-	-	-	-	-
Total First Class Career				42	75	5	1711	211*	24.44	2	7	43	49	13	137	4	34.25	2-13
Total O.D. Career				44	44	5	1139	100*	29.20	1	8	20	3	0	36	1	36.00	1-9

BERNARD DENIS JULIEN

D.O.B. 13.03.1950 - Carenage Village, Trinidad

First Class Debut	19.04.1968 - North Trinidad v South Trinidad	
Test Match Debut	26.07.1973 - West Indies v England	
O.D.I. Debut	05.09.1973 - West Indies v England	
Domestic O.D. Debut	14.04.1973 - Trinidad v Barbados	

Test 148-144   **O.D.I.** 7-1

Teams Played For
Trinidad, North Trinidad
N/E Trinidad, West Indies
W.I. President's XI
West Indies XI
Kent

7   RHB / LFM

SEASON	TEAM	COMPETITION	V	M	I	No	RUNS	H.S.	Av	100s	50s	CT	OV	MD	RUNS	W	Av	B.B.
1969-1982	Trinidad	First Class Matches	II	41	60	7	1229	82*	23.18	-	6	36	1070.1	200	3212	111	28.93	9-97
1968-1977	North Trinidad	First Class Matches	T	5	7	1	194	68*	32.33	-	3	4	170.5	48	430	21	20.47	7-63
1980//	N/E Trinidad	First Class Matches	T	1	2	0	4	4	2.00	-	-	2	17	5	48	1	48.00	1-20
1973-1982	Trinidad	Domestic O.D. Matches	II	12	11	3	126	29*	15.75	-	-	2	93.3	12	354	14	25.28	3-39
1973-1977	WEST INDIES	TEST MATCHES	HA	24	34	6	866	121	30.92	2	3	14	719.4	192	1868	50	37.36	5-57
1973-1976	West Indies	First Class Matches	A	38	51	6	1230	127	27.33	1	5	20	810.1	169	2629	93	28.26	7-78
1971-1973	W.I. President's XI	First Class Matches	WI	3	4	0	93	59	23.25	-	1	1	91.4	26	213	5	42.60	2-41
1983-1984	West Indies XI	First Class Matches	SA	3	6	1	119	33*	23.80	-	-	2	59	11	215	4	53.75	2-76
1973-1977	WEST INDIES	O.D.I. MATCHES	HA	12	8	2	86	26*	14.33	-	-	4	129.4	21	463	18	25.72	4-20
1982-1983	West Indies XI	O.D.(I.) Matches	SA	3	3	0	3	2	1.00	-	-	-	29	9	67	5	13.40	3-17
1973-1976	West Indies	O.A.L. O.D. Matches	A	3	2	1	137	104	68.50	1	1	1	20	0	65	3	21.66	3-16
1982-1983	West Indies XI	O.A.L. O.D. Matches	SA	2	2	0	6	3	3.00	-	-	2	18	0	63	1	63.00	1-29
1970-1977	Kent	First Class Matches	E	80	109	15	2057	98	21.88	-	9	47	1808.1	438	5256	198	26.54	7-66
1971-1977	Kent	Nat West Trophy	E	8	8	0	75	35	9.37	-	-	1	64.4	8	186	15	12.40	5-25
1972-1977	Kent	Benson & Hedges Cup	E	17	17	2	255	44	17.00	-	-	4	180.1	-	589	34	17.32	5-21
1971-1977	Kent	Sunday League	E	57	43	8	762	87	21.77	-	-	14	366	-	1552	60	25.86	4-28
1972//	Kent	O.A.L. O.D. Matches	E	1	1	0	0	0	0.00	-	-	-	6	-	23	3	7.66	3-23
		Total First Class Career		195	273	36	5792	127	24.43	3	27	126	4746.4	1089	13871	483	28.71	9-97
		Total O.D. Career		115	95	16	1450	104	18.35	1	3	28	904.2	-	3362	153	21.97	5-21

BATTING / **BOWLING**

RAPHICK RASIF JUMADEEN

D.O.B. 12.04.1948 - Harmony Hall, Gasparillo, Trinidad

First Class Debut 14.04.1967 - South Trinidad v North Trinidad
Test Match Debut 20.04.1972 - West Indies v New Zealand
Domestic O.D. Debut 14.04.1973 - Trinidad v Barbados

Test 145-138

Teams Played For
Trinidad & Tobago
South Trinidad
S/C Trinidad
West Indies
W.I. President's XI

RHB / SLA

5

SEASON	TEAM	COMPETITION	V	M	I	No	BATTING RUNS	H.S.	Av	100s	50s	CT	BOWLING OV	MD	RUNS	W	Av	B.B.
1971-1981	Trinidad & Tobago	First Class Matches	II	44	56	22	265	40	7.79	-	-	21	2043.1	609	4532	152	29.81	6-31
1967-1978	South Trinidad	First Class Matches	T	15	23	5	102	12	5.66	-	-	1	653.5	202	1400	86	16.27	6-30
1977-1980	S/C Trinidad	First Class Matches	T	2	3	2	18	10	18.00	-	-	3	64.2	17	169	7	24.14	4-112
1973-1981	Trinidad & Tobago	Domestic O.D. Matches	II	16	8	4	18	4	4.50	-	-	2	146.4	32	401	20	20.05	3-5
1972-1979	WEST INDIES	TEST MATCHES	HA	12	14	10	84	56	21.00	-	1	4	523.2	140	1141	29	39.34	4-72
1976-1979	West Indies	First Class Matches	A	25	22	9	135	52	10.38	-	1	16	793	184	2328	72	32.33	6-40
1972//	W.I. President's XI	First Class Matches	WI	1	1	0	0	0	0.00	-	-		40	9	116	1	116.00	1-116
1976//	West Indies	O.A.L. O.D. Matches	A	1	D	-	-	-	-	-	-	1	8	0	40	1	40.00	1-40
		Total First Class Career		99	119	48	604	56	8-50	0	2	45	4117.4	1161	9686	347	27.91	6-30
		Total O.D. Career		17	8	4	18	4	4.50	0	0	3	154.4	32	441	21	21.00	3-5

ALVIN ISAAC KALLICHARRAN

D.O.B. 21.03.1949 - Paidama, Port Mourant, Berbice, British Guiana
First Class Debut 15.03.1967 - Guyana v Windward Islands
Test Match Debut 06.04.1972 - West Indies v New Zealand
O.D.I. Debut 05.09.1973 - West Indies v England
Domestic O.D. Debut 13.04.1973 - Guyana v Jamaica

Test	144-137		Teams Played For	11	LHB / SRA
O.D.I.	5-1		Guyana, Berbice, West Indies		
			W.I. President's XI, West Indies XI		
			Warwickshire, Queensland		
			World XI, Transvaal		
			Orange Free State, Implas		

SEASON	TEAM	COMPETITION	V	M	I	No	BATTING RUNS	H.S.	Av	100s	50s	CT	BOWLING OV	MD	RUNS	W	Av	B.B.
1967-1981	Guyana	First Class Matches	II	37	58	4	2552	197	47.25	6	17	28	80.5	6	286	3	95.33	1-1
1972-1973	Berbice	First Class Matches	G	2	3	0	6	4	2.00	-	-	-	1	0	4	0	-	-
1972-1978	Guyana	Domestic O.D. Matches	II	4	4	0	97	53	24.25	-	1	2	-	-	-	-	-	-
1972-1980	WEST INDIES	TEST MATCHES	HA	66	109	10	4399	187	44.43	12	21	51	66.4	14	158	4	39.50	2-16
1973-1980	West Indies	First Class Matches	HA	59	92	8	3599	151	42.84	7	20	36	65.3	7	238	7	34.00	1-1
1971-1977	W.I. President's XI	First Class Matches	WI	3	4	1	248	134	82.66	1	2	-	10	0	25	0	-	-
1982-1984	West Indies XI	First Class Matches	A	10	19	1	625	103	34.72	1	4	6	14.3	3	62	4	15.50	4-26
1973-1981	WEST INDIES	O.D.I. MATCHES	HA	31	28	4	826	78	34.41	-	6	8	17.3	3	64	3	21.33	2-10
1982-1984	West Indies XI	O.D.(I.) Matches	A	12	12	1	237	80	21.54	-	2	4	-	-	-	-	-	-
1973-1980	West Indies	O.A.L. O.D. Matches	A	10	12	1	332	101	41.50	1	2	1	9	0	42	1	42.00	1-20
1982-1983	West Indies XI	O.A.L. O.D. Matches	A	2	2	0	65	65	32.50	-	1	-	1	0	3	0	-	-
1971-1990	Warwickshire	First Class Matches	E	285	472	57	18158	243*	43.75	52	78	174	652.2	97	2352	49	48.00	4-48
1972-1990	Warwickshire	Nat West Trophy	E	31	30	3	1372	206	50.81	3	7	12	92.4	9	319	14	22.78	6-32
1972-1990	Warwickshire	Benson & Hedges Cup	E	68	64	7	2392	122*	41.96	4	17	16	22	0	111	0	-	-
1972-1990	Warwickshire	Sunday League	E	188	178	19	5039	104	31.69	5	31	32	165.1	14	914	14	65.28	3-32
1981-1986	Warwickshire	O.A.L. O.D. Matches	E	2	2	0	20	13	10.00	-	-	-	-	-	-	-	-	-
1981-1984	Transvaal	First Class Matches	SA	17	27	2	1236	151	49.44	4	8	8	81	14	311	11	28.27	5-45
1981-1984	Transvaal	Nissan Shield	SA	10	10	1	531	136	53.10	2	3	2	29	0	133	5	26.60	2-21
1981-1984	Transvaal	Benson & Hedges Cup	SA	9	9	1	198	85	24.75	-	1	3	9	0	64	0	-	-
1984-1988	Orange Free State	First Class Matches	SA	17	32	2	1248	110	41.60	2	12	10	198.2	35	574	6	95.66	3-63
1984-1988	Orange Free State	Nissan Shield	SA	8	8	0	137	40	17.12	-	3	-	31	0	142	4	35.50	3-43
1987-1988	Orange Free State	Benson & Hedges Cup	SA	5	5	0	73	38	14.60	-	1	1	6	0	31	1	31.00	1-18
1984-1987	Implas	Benson & Hedges Cup	SA	3	3	0	17	8	5.66	-	-	2	-	-	-	-	-	-
1973-1974	World XI	First Class Matches	P	2	4	0	177	103	44.25	1	1	1	2.4	0	20	0	-	-
1977-1978	Queensland	First Class Matches	A	7	14	1	402	129*	30.92	1	2	9	-	-	-	-	-	-
Total First Class Career				505	834	86	32650	243*	43.64	87	160	323	1170.5	179	4030	84	47.97	5-45
Total O.D. Career				383	363	36	11336	206	34.66	15	71	86	382.2	-	1823	42	43.40	6-32

ROHAN BHOLALALL KANHAI

D.O.B. 26.12.1935 - Port Mourant, Berbice, British Guiana

First Class Debut	05.05.1955 - British Guiana v Barbados
Test Match Debut	30.05.1957 - West Indies v England
O.D.I. Debut	05.09.1973 - West Indies v England
Domestic O.D. Debut	25.05.1968 - Warwickshire v Yorkshire

Test 94-62
O.D.I. 1-1

Teams Played For 13
British Guiana, Guyana, Trinidad & Tobago
Indian President's XI, West Indies, Western Australia
Berbice, Tasmania, Warwickshire, World XI
International XI, Commonwealth XI
A.E. Gilligan's XI, C.C. Hunte's XI

RHB / RM

SEASON	TEAM	COMPETITION	V	M	I	No	BATTING RUNS	H.S.	Av	100s	50s	CT/ST	BOWLING OV	MD	RUNS	W	Av	B.B.
1955-1974	Br. Guiana/Guyana	First Class Matches	II	30	46	4	2385	195	56.78	7	12	29	54.1	11	171	4	42.75	2-57
1959-1960	Berbice	First Class Matches	G	1	1	0	13	13	13.00	-	-	-	-	-	-	-	-	-
1965//	Trinidad & Tobago	First Class Matches	II	1	2	0	86	52	43.00	-	1	-	-	-	-	-	-	-
1972-1973	Guyana	Domestic O.D. Matches	II	2	2	0	92	82	46.00	-	1	1	1	0	8	0	-	-
1957-1974	WEST INDIES	TEST MATCHES	HA	79	137	6	6227	256	47.53	15	28	50	30.1	8	85	0	-	-
1956-1973	West Indies	First Class Matches	A	88	133	15	5198	252	44.05	14	24	54/7	36.2	2	226	4	56.50	2-54
1964//	C.C. Hunte's XI	First Class Matches	WI	1	2	0	37	28	18.50	-	-	1	5	1	21	0	-	-
1973-1975	WEST INDIES	O.D.I. MATCHES	HA	7	5	2	164	55	54.66	-	2	4	-	-	-	-	-	-
1963-1973	West Indies	O.A.L. O.D. Matches	A	4	4	0	45	21	11.25	-	-	0/1	0.3	0	5	0	-	-
1968-1977	Warwickshire	First Class Matches	E	173	272	47	11615	253	51.62	35	43	155	56.2	7	211	4	52.75	2-33
1968-1977	Warwickshire	Nat West Trophy	E	20	20	3	739	126	43.47	1	5	13	-	-	-	-	-	-
1972-1977	Warwickshire	Benson & Hedges Cup	E	31	30	13	1073	119*	63.11	2	4	16	2	1	2	1	2.00	1-2
1969-1977	Warwickshire	Sunday League	E	91	87	11	2631	120	34.62	4	14	36	2	0	15	1	15.00	1-15
1960//	A.E.R. Gilligan's XI	First Class Matches	E	1	2	0	64	62	32.00	-	1	3	7	0	21	0	-	-
1961-1962	Western Australia	First Class Matches	A	8	14	1	533	135	41.00	2	2	3	5.4	1	39	1	39.00	1-27
1969-1970	Tasmania	First Class Matches	A	2	2	2	308	200*	-	2	-	5	19	4	78	1	78.00	1-61
1960-1964	Commonwealth XI	First Class Matches	A	9	15	1	726	161	51.85	3	2	7	19	2	86	2	43.00	2-5
1965-1973	World XI	First Class Matches	A	19	35	6	1364	121*	47.03	5	6	10	6	0	39	1	39.00	1-32
1963//	Indian President's XI	First Class Matches	I	1	2	0	83	43	41.50	-	-	-	-	-	-	-	-	-
1981//	International XI	First Class Matches	P	3	6	0	135	54	22.50	1	1	2	3	0	17	0	-	-
1971//	World XI	O.A.L. O.D. Matches	A	2	2	0	18	13	9.00	-	-	-	-	-	-	-	-	-
1981//	International XI	O.A.L. O.D. Matches	A	2	1	0	7	7	7.00	-	-	-	-	-	-	-	-	-
	Total First Class Career			416	669	82	28774	256	49.01	83	120	319/7	243.4	36	1009	18	56.05	2-5
	Total O.D. Career			159	151	29	4769	126	39.09	7	26	70/1	4.3	1	17	1	17.00	1-2

ESMOND SEYMOUR MAURICE KENTISH

D.O.B. 21.11.1916 - Cornwall Mountain, Westmoreland, Jamaica

First Class Debut 06.10.1947 - Jamaica v British Guiana

Test Match Debut 27.03.1948 - West Indies v England

					Test	65-26		Teams Played For	3						RHB / RFM
								Jamaica						
								West Indies						
								Oxford University						

						BATTING							**BOWLING**					
SEASON	**TEAM**	**COMPETITION**	**V**	**M**	**I**	**No**	**RUNS**	**H.S.**	**Av**	**100s**	**50s**	**CT**	**OV**	**MD**	**RUNS**	**W**	**Av**	**B.B.**
1947-1957	Jamaica	First Class Matches	=	11	14	10	90	15*	22.50	-	-	2	261.2	38	772	26	29.69	5-36
1948-1954	WEST INDIES	TEST MATCHES	H	2	2	1	1	1*	1.00	-	-	1	90	31	178	8	22.55	5-49
1956//	Oxford University	First Class Matches	E	14	13	10	18	6*	6.00	-	-	3	362.3	77	1134	44	25.77	5-49
		Total First Class Career		27	29	21	109	15*	13.62	0	0	6	713.5	146	2084	78	26.71	5-36

COLLIS LLEWELLYN KING

D.O.B. 11.06.1951 - Fairview, Christ Church, Barbados

First Class Debut	06.01.1973 - Barbados v Combined Islands
Test Match Debut	08.07.1976 - West Indies v England
O.D.I. Debut	26.08.1976 - West Indies v England
Domestic O.D. Debut	21.02.1976 - Barbados v Leeward Islands

Test 158-171
O.D.I. 19-9

Teams Played For 9
Barbados, West Indies
W.I. President's XI, West Indies XI
Glamorgan, Worcestershire
International XI, Natal
D.B. Closes XI

RHB / RM

SEASON	TEAM	COMPETITION	V	M	I	No	BATTING RUNS	H.S.	Av	100s	50s	CT	BOWLING OV	MD	RUNS	W	Av	B.B.
1973-1982	Barbados	First Class Matches	I	35	55	6	2173	156	44.34	4	14	34	428.4	93	1130	46	24.56	5-91
1976-1982	Barbados	Domestic O.D. Matches	I	15	14	3	253	58*	23.00	-	1	8	110	11	427	12	35.58	3-15
1981//	Barbados	O.A.L. O.D. Matches	WI	1	1	0	43	43	43.00	-	-	-	10	2	37	2	18.50	2-37
1976-1980	WEST INDIES	TEST MATCHES	HA	9	16	3	418	100*	32.15	1	2	5	97	24	282	3	94.00	1-30
1976-1980	West Indies	First Class Matches	A	31	49	12	1559	163	42.13	6	4	29	489.4	130	1316	42	31.33	4-93
1977//	W.I. President's XI	First Class Matches	WI	1	1	0	2	2	2.00	-	-	1	1	0	1	0	-	-
1976-1980	WEST INDIES	O.D.I. MATCHES	HA	18	14	2	280	86	23.33	-	1	6	124	7	529	11	48.09	4-23
1982-1984	West Indies	O.D.(I.) Matches	A	12	10	2	221	63*	27.62	-	2	6	95	6	403	9	44.77	2-26
1976-1980	West Indies XI	O.A.L. O.D. Matches	A	8	6	1	48	17	9.60	-	-	2	69	-	237	10	23.70	3-48
1982-1983	West Indies XI	O.A.L. O.D. Matches	A	2	2	1	150	79*	150.00	-	2	1	7	2	23	2	11.50	2-14
1982-1984	West Indies XI	First Class Matches	A	9	17	2	622	101	41.46	1	4	4	60	11	223	5	44.60	3-30
1977//	Glamorgan	First Class Matches	E	16	27	1	811	78	31.19	-	6	13	259.1	58	730	20	36.50	4-31
1977//	Glamorgan	Nat West Trophy	E	4	4	0	93	55	23.25	-	1	-	34.2	7	117	5	23.40	2-31
1977//	Glamorgan	Benson & Hedges Cup	E	3	3	0	29	14	9.66	-	-	-	22	-	84	1	84.00	1-32
1977//	Glamorgan	Sunday League	E	14	14	0	269	66	19.21	-	2	5	80	2	364	11	33.09	2-17
1983//	Worcestershire	First Class Matches	E	2	3	0	158	123	52.66	1	-	1	15	0	39	1	39.00	1-26
1985//	Worcestershire	Nat West Trophy	E	1	1	0	11	11	11.00	-	-	-	8	-	36	1	36.00	1-36
1983-1984	Worcestershire	Benson & Hedges Cup	E	4	4	0	138	61	34.50	-	2	-	21	1	61	1	138.00	1-18
1983-1984	Worcestershire	Sunday League	E	6	6	1	317	127	63.40	2	-	7	23	-	138	0	-	-
1982-1986	D.B. Closes XI	First Class Matches	E	3	5	0	97	48	19.40	-	-	2	11	1	68	0	-	-
1984-1987	Natal	First Class Matches	SA	18	27	1	885	154	34.03	1	4	9	165	35	529	9	58.77	3-27
1983-1988	Natal	Nissan Shield	SA	19	16	2	484	76	34.57	-	5	7	118.5	18	455	8	56.87	3-27
1983-1990	Natal	Benson & Hedges Cup	SA	26	25	3	298	47	13.54	-	-	3	195.5	-	757	33	22.93	3-21
1981//	International XI	First Class Matches	P	1	2	2	45	34	22.50	-	-	-	20	4	62	2	31.00	2-53
1981//	International XI	O.A.L. O.D. Matches	P	3	2	1	104	55*	104.00	-	1	-	8	-	57	2	28.50	1-11
Total First Class Career				125	202	25	6770	163	38.24	14	34	98	1546.3	358	4380	128	34.21	5-91
Total O.D. Career				136	122	16	2738	127	25.83	2	17	41	926	-	3725	108	34.49	4-23

FRANK MCDONALD KING

D.O.B. 08.12.1926 - Delamere Land, Brighton, St. Michael, Barbados (d. 23.12.1990)

First Class Debut 09.01.1948 - Barbados v M.C.C.

Test Match Debut 21.01.1953 - West Indies v India

Test 75-43

Teams Played For
Barbados
Trinidad
West Indies

3

RHB / RF

SEASON	TEAM	COMPETITION	V	M	I	No	BATTING RUNS	H.S.	Av	100s	50s	CT	BOWLING OV	MD	RUNS	W	Av	B.B.
1948-1957	Barbados	First Class Matches	=	12	11	3	78	30*	9.75	-	-	9	353.4	76	1050	49	21.42	5-35
1950-1951	Trinidad	First Class Matches	II	2	2	2	4	4*	-	-	-	-	47	4	202	3	67.33	2-24
1953-1956	WEST INDIES	TEST MATCHES	HA	14	17	3	116	21	8.28	-	-	5	478.1	140	1159	29	39.96	5-74
1955-1956	West Indies	First Class Matches	A	3	4	0	39	17	9.75	-	-	3	68	14	177	9	19.66	3-30
Total First Class Career				31	34	8	237	30*	9.11	0	0	17	946.5	234	2588	90	28.75	5-35

LESTER ANTHONY KING

D.O.B. 27.02.1939 - St Catherine, Jamaica (d. 09.07.1998)

First Class Debut 13.10.1961 - Jamaica v Barbados
Test Match Debut 13.04.1962 - West Indies v India
Domestic O.D. Debut 12.09.1963 - West Indies v Sussex

Test 119-94

Teams Played For 10
Jamaica, West Indies
C.C. Hunte's XI, The Rest XI
Bengal East Zone
Chidambarams XI, Chief Minister's XI
Bombay Governor's XI, NZ Governor's XI

RHB / RF

SEASON	TEAM	COMPETITION	V	M	I	No	BATTING RUNS	H.S.	Av	100s	50s	CT	BOWLING OV	MD	RUNS	W	Av	B.B.
1961-1968	Jamaica	First Class Matches	II	16	23	3	551	89	27.55	-	6	14	475.1	89	1426	35	40.74	4-129
1962-1968	WEST INDIES	TEST MATCHES	WI	2	4	0	41	20	10.25	-	-	2	79.2	19	154	9	17.11	5-46
1963-1969	West Indies	First Class Matches	A	35	44	16	607	46*	21.67	-	-	17	820.3	157	2284	75	30.45	5-47
1964//	C.C. Hunte's XI	First Class Matches	WI	1	2	0	18	10	9.00	-	-	1	12	3	25	1	-	-
1964//	The Rest XI	First Class Matches	WI	1	2	0	28	15	14.00	-	-	2	10	1	40	2	20.00	2-17
1963//	West Indies	O.A.L. O.D. Matches	A	1	1	0	8	8	8.00	-	-	-	12	2	35	3	11.66	3-35
1962-63//	Bengal	First Class Matches	I	2	4	0	68	32	17.00	-	-	-	36	1	192	6	32.00	5-146
1962-63//	East Zone	First Class Matches	I	1	2	0	4	4	2.00	-	-	-	9	1	57	0	-	-
1962-63//	Chidambarams XI	First Class Matches	I	1	2	0	52	35	26.00	-	-	1	36.6	6	114	7	16.28	4-53
1962-63//	Chief Minister's XI	First Class Matches	I	1	D	-	-	-	-	-	-	-	11	2	44	1	44.00	1-44
1962-63//	Bombay Governor's XI	First Class Matches	I	1	2	0	14	14	7.00	-	-	-	22	3	92	5	18.40	3-25
1968-69//	NZ Governor's XI	First Class Matches	NZ	1	2	0	21	42	10.50	-	-	1	9	0	35	2	17.50	2-18
	Total First Class Career			62	87	19	1404	89	20.64	0	6	38	1521	282	4463	142	31.42	5-46
	Total O.D. Career			1	1	0	8	8	8.00	0	0	0	12	2	35	3	11.66	3-25

REON DANE KING

D.O.B. 06.10.1975 - Georgetown, Demerara, Guyana
First Class Debut 26.01.1996 - Guyana v Jamaica
Test Match Debut 05.01.1999 - West Indies v South Africa
O.D.I. Debut 31.10.1998 - West Indies v India
Domestic O.D. Debut 18.02.1995 - Guyana v Leeward Islands

Test 224-348
O.D.I. 89-352

Teams Played For
Guyana, West Indies
W.I. President's XI
W.I. Board XI
West Indies "A"
M.C.C.

6   RHB / RFM

SEASON	TEAM	COMPETITION	V	M	I	No	RUNS	H.S.	Av	100s	50s	CT	OV	MD	RUNS	W	Av	B.B.
							BATTING						BOWLING					
1996-2003	Guyana	First Class Matches	=	32	41	13	218	30	7.78	-	-	5	980.4	226	2919	115	25.38	7-82
1995-2002	Guyana	Domestic O.D. Matches	=	31	9	5	27	13*	6.75	-	-	5	227.1	24	974	35	27.82	3-27
1999-2001	WEST INDIES	TEST MATCHES	HA	14	19	5	50	12*	3.57	-	-	2	414.1	96	1222	44	27.77	5-51
1999-2002	West Indies	First Class Matches	A	11	9	4	56	21	11.20	-	-	-	264.4	82	662	32	20.68	3-22
1996-2001	W.I. Board XI	First Class Matches	WI	2	3	0	8	6	2.66	-	-	1	57	12	160	3	53.33	1-32
1999//	W.I. President's XI	First Class Matches	WI	1	2	1	0	0*	-	-	-	-	25	3	75	5	15.00	5-75
1997-2002	West Indies "A"	First Class Matches	A	10	14	8	33	9	5.50	-	-	1	334.2	77	974	36	27.05	5-63
1998-2001	WEST INDIES	O.D.I. MATCHES	HA	48	22	13	62	12*	6.88	-	-	4	413.5	41	1696	73	23.23	4-25
1998-1999	West Indies "A"	O.D.(I.) Matches	A	6	1	1	5	5*	-	-	-	1	52.1	9	189	12	15.75	3-17
2000-2001	West Indies	O.A.L. O.D. Matches	A	3	1	1	1	1*	-	-	-	1	21	6	101	3	33.66	2-29
1998-2002	West Indies "A"	O.A.L. O.D. Matches	A	3	1	1	3	3*	-	-	-	1	27	0	133	5	26.60	2-36
1999//	M.C.C.	First Class Matches	E	1	D	-	-	-	-	-	-	-	35	9	24	6	14.00	4-41
		Total First Class Career		71	88	31	365	30	6.40	-	-	9	2110.5	505	6096	241	25.29	7-82
		Total O.D. Career		91	34	21	106	13*	8.15	-	-	11	741.1	80	3093	128	24.16	4-25

CLAYTON BENJAMIN LAMBERT

D.O.B. 10.02.1962 - Islington Village, New Amsterdam, Berbice, British Guiana

First Class Debut 08.10.1983 - Berbice v Demerara
Test Match Debut 08.08.1991 - West Indies v England
O.D.I. Debut 15.03.1990 - West Indies v England
Domestic O.D. Debut 30.01.1985 - Guyana v Barbados

Test 198-290
O.D.I. 58-198

Teams Played For 9
Guyana, Berbice
West Indies, W.I. President's XI
W.I. Board XI, West Indies "B"
West Indies "A", Northern Transvaal
World XI

LHB / OB

SEASON	TEAM	COMPETITION	V	M	I	No	RUNS	H.S.	Av	100s	50s	CT	OV	MD	RUNS	W	Av	B.B.
1984-1999	Guyana	First Class Matches	II	61	108	12	4681	263*	48.76	14	22	88	14.3	0	64	1	64.00	1-21
1983-1988	Berbice	First Class Matches	G	6	8	0	288	104	36.00	1	1	7	8	3	10	0	-	-
1985-1998	Guyana	Domestic O.D. Matches	II	39	39	4	1330	151	38.00	2	8	24	15	0	68	2	34.00	2-30
1991-1999	WEST INDIES	TEST MATCHES	HA	5	9	0	284	104	31.55	1	1	8	1.4	0	5	1	5.00	1-4
1991-1999	West Indies	First Class Matches	HA	11	19	2	741	116	43.58	1	6	11	32	8	98	3	32.66	2-33
1988-1991	W.I. Board XI	First Class Matches	WI	3	5	0	154	72	30.80	-	1	1	-	-	-	-	-	-
1989-1990	W.I. President's XI	First Class Matches	WI	1	2	0	12	12	6.00	-	-	1	-	-	-	-	-	-
1989-90//	West Indies "B"	First Class Matches	A	2	2	0	247	219	123.50	1	-	4	-	-	-	-	-	-
1992//	West Indies "A"	First Class Matches	WI	3	6	0	157	83	26.16	-	1	7	-	-	-	-	-	-
1990-1998	WEST INDIES	O.D.I. MATCHES	HA	11	11	0	368	119	33.45	4	2	-	2	0	8	0	-	-
1989-90//	West Indies "B"	O.D.(I.) Matches	A	5	5	1	165	105	41.25	1	-	1	-	-	-	-	-	-
1993-1996	Northern Transvaal	First Class Matches	SA	25	49	3	1802	214	39.17	4	5	30	-	-	-	-	-	-
1993-1996	Northern Transvaal	Benson & Hedges Cup	SA	24	24	0	421	76	17.54	-	1	12	-	-	-	-	-	-
1993//	World XI	First Class Matches	E	1	1	0	9	9	9.00	-	-	-	3	0	11	0	-	-
Total First Class Career				118	209	17	8375	263*	43.61	22	37	157	59.1	11	188	5	37.60	2-33
Total O.D. Career				79	79	5	2284	151	30.86	4	11	37	17	0	76	2	38.00	2-30

BRIAN CHARLES LARA

D.O.B. 02.05.1969 - Contoro Village, Santa Cruz, Trinidad
First Class Debut 22.01.1988 - Trinidad & Tobago v Leeward Islands
Test Match Debut 06.12.1990 - West Indies v Pakistan
O.D.I. Debut 09.11.1990 - West Indies v Pakistan
Domestic O.D. Debut 27.01.1990 - Trinidad & Tobago v Barbados

Test	196-280	
O.D.I.	59-200	

Teams Played For 8
Trinidad & Tobago, West Indies, West Indies "B"
West Indies, Warwickshire
W.I. President's XI, Northern Transvaal
West Indies U23
W.I. Board XI

LHB / LBG

SEASON	TEAM	COMPETITION	V	M	I	No	RUNS	H.S.	Av	100s	50s	CT	OV	MD	RUNS	W	Av	B.B.
							BATTING						**BOWLING**					
1988-2003	Trinidad & Tobago	First Class Matches	=	40	68	1	3361	206	50.16	9	16	69	15.5	1	71	2	35.50	1-14
1988-2002	Trinidad & Tobago	Domestic O.D. Matches	=	49	44	6	1880	129	49.47	5	12	22	6.4	1	30	0	-	-
1991-1997	Trinidad & Tobago	O.A.L. O.D. Matches	WI	2	2	0	112	91	56.00	-	1	1	-	-	-	-	-	-
1990-2003	WEST INDIES	TEST MATCHES	HA	96	168	5	8404	375	51.55	21	41	128	10	1	28	0	-	-
1990-2002	West Indies	First Class Matches	A	40	60	1	2259	231	38.28	4	13	38	32.5	2	156	2	78.00	1-1
1988-1991	West Indies U23	First Class Matches	WI	3	5	0	225	182	45.00	1	-	5	-	-	-	-	-	-
1989//	West Indies "B"	First Class Matches	A	3	3	0	187	145	62.33	1	-	5	-	-	-	-	-	-
1989-1990	W.I. President's XI	First Class Matches	WI	2	4	0	184	134	46.00	1	-	1	-	-	-	-	-	-
1989-1991	W.I. Board XI	First Class Matches	WI	2	2	0	92	56	46.00	-	1	-	-	-	-	-	-	-
1990-2003	WEST INDIES	O.D.I. MATCHES	HA	219	214	23	8233	169	43.10	17	52	93	8.1	0	61	4	15.25	2-5
1989//	West Indies "B"	O.D.(I.) Matches	A	5	4	0	136	55	34.00	-	1	6	2.5	0	22	0	-	-
1991-2001	West Indies	O.A.L. O.D. Matches	A	17	17	0	321	51	18.88	-	1	9	4	0	36	1	36.00	1-36
1994-1998	Warwickshire	First Class Matches	E	30	51	2	3099	501*	63.24	12	6	26	26	1	156	0	-	-
1994-1998	Warwickshire	Nat West Trophy	E	8	8	0	305	133	38.12	1	1	4	-	-	-	-	-	-
1994-1998	Warwickshire	Benson & Hedges Cup	E	8	8	0	354	101	50.57	1	1	1	-	-	-	-	-	-
1994-1998	Warwickshire	Sunday League	E	28	27	1	649	75	24.96	-	5	11	-	-	-	-	-	-
1992-1993	Northern Transvaal	Benson & Hedges Cup	SA	3	3	0	102	48	34.00	-	-	-	-	-	-	-	-	-
Total First Class Career				216	361	9	17811	501*	50.59	49	77	272	84.4	5	411	4	102.75	1-1
Total O.D. Career				339	327	31	12092	169	40.85	24	74	147	21.4	1	149	5	29.80	2-5

PATRICK DOUGLAS LASHLEY

D.O.B. 11.02.1937 - St Matthias Gap, Christ Church, Barbados

First Class Debut 11.02.1958 - Barbados v Pakistan
Test Match Debut 09.12.1960 - West Indies v Australia
Domestic O.D. Debut 14.04.1973 - Barbados v Trinidad & Tobago

Test 112-85

Teams Played For
Barbados
West Indies

LHB / RM

2

SEASON	TEAM	COMPETITION	V	M	I	No	BATTING RUNS	H.S.	Av	100s	50s	CT	BOWLING OV	MD	RUNS	W	Av	B.B.
1958-1975	Barbados	First Class Matches	=	58	93	11	3994	204	48.70	8	25	45	184.2	49	551	13	42.38	2-10
1972-1973	Barbados	Domestic O.D. Matches	=	2	1	0	32	32	32.00	-	-	1	9	0	48	3	16.00	2-32
1960-1966	WEST INDIES	TEST MATCHES	A	4	7	0	159	49	22.71	-	-	4	3	2	1	1	1.00	1-1
1960-1966	West Indies	First Class Matches	A	23	32	2	779	78	25.96	-	7	17	159.2	38	406	13	31.23	3-15
1966//	West Indies	O.A.L. O.D. Matches	A	1	1	1	75	75*	-	-	1	-	10	3	39	1	39.00	1-39
		Total First Class Career		85	132	13	4932	204	41.44	8	32	66	345.4	89	958	27	35.48	3-15
		Total O.D. Career		3	2	1	107	75*	107.00	0	1	1	19	3	87	4	21.75	2-32

380

JERMAINE JAY CHARLES LAWSON

D.O.B. 13.01.1982 - Spanish Town, St Catherine, Jamaica
First Class Debut 05.01.2001 - West Indies "B" v England "A"
Test Match Debut 17.10.2002 - West Indies v India
O.D.I. Debut 11.12.2001 - West Indies v Sri Lanka
Domestic O.D. Debut 02.10.2001 - Jamaica v Northern Windwards

Test	245-390		Teams Played For		4		RHB / RF
O.D.I.	107-434		Jamaica				
			West Indies				
			West Indies "B"				
			West Indies "A"				

SEASON	TEAM	COMPETITION	V	M	I	No	RUNS	H.S.	Av	100s	50s	CT	OV	MD	RUNS	W	Av	B.B.
2001-2003	Jamaica	First Class Matches	II	10	11	2	66	17	7.33	-	-	6	231.4	51	658	22	29.90	4-28
2001-2002	Jamaica	Domestic O.D. Matches	II	10	4	2	8	6	4.00	-	-	1	79	11	264	11	24.00	3-11
2002-2003	WEST INDIES	TEST MATCHES	A	7	10	1	34	14	3.77	-	-	1	209.1	38	715	29	24.66	7-78
2002/I	West Indies	First Class Matches	A	1	-	-	-	-	-	-	-	-	13	2	57	2	28.50	2-57
2000-2001	West Indies "B"	First Class Matches	WI	5	9	4	75	25	15.00	-	-	2	136.4	21	450	14	32.14	4-79
2002/I	West Indies "A"	First Class Matches	A	4	4	0	37	17	9.25	-	-	-	123.4	19	480	18	26.66	6-76
2001-2003	WEST INDIES	O.D.I. MATCHES	A	6	1	0	3	3	3.00	-	-	-	45	2	217	9	24.11	4-57
2002/I	West Indies "A"	O.A.L. O.D. Matches	A	2	0	0	0	0	0.00	-	-	1	25.1	1	92	10	9.20	4-24
Total First Class Career			II	27	34	7	212	25	7.85	0	0	9	714.1	131	2360	85	27.76	7-78
Total O.D. Career			II	20	7	2	11	6	2.20	0	0	2	149.1	14	573	30	19.10	4-24

RALPH ARCHIBALD LEGALL

D.O.B. 01.12.1925 - Bridgetown, St Michael, Barbados

First Class Debut 15.03.1947 - Trinidad v British Guyana

Test Match Debut 07.02.1953 - West Indies v India

Test 77-44

Teams Played For
Trinidad
West Indies

RHB / WK

2

SEASON	TEAM	COMPETITION	V	M	I	No	BATTING RUNS	H.S.	Av	100s	50s	CT/ST	BOWLING OV	MD	RUNS	W	Av	B.B.
1947-1958	Trinidad	First Class Matches	II	12	19	2	435	68	25.58	-	2	24/9	-	-	-	-	-	-
1952-1953	WEST INDIES	TEST MATCHES	H	4	5	0	50	23	10.00	-	-	8/1	-	-	-	-	-	-
		Total First Class Career		16	24	2	485	68	22.04	0	2	32/10	-	-	-	-	-	-

CHRISTOPHER CLAIRMONTE LEWIS

D.O.B. 14.02.1968 - Georgetown, Demerara, Guyana

First Class Debut	13.06.1987 - Leicestershire v Worcestershire
Test Match Debut	05.07.1990 - England v New Zealand
O.D.I. Debut	14.02.1990 - England v West Indies
Domestic O.D. Debut	07.06.1987 - Leicestershire v Worcestershire

Teams Played For 4 RHB / RFM

Leicestershire
Nottinghamshire
Surrey
England

SEASON	TEAM	COMPETITION	V	M	I	No	BATTING RUNS	H.S.	Av	100s	50s	CT	BOWLING OV	MD	RUNS	W	Av	B.B.
1990-1996	ENGLAND	TEST MATCHES	HA	32	51	3	1105	117	23.02	1	4	25	1142	219	3490	93	37.52	6-111
1989-1994	England	First Class Matches	A	11	13	2	270	73	24.54	-	8	20	253.2	47	773	20	38.65	3-21
1989-1998	ENGLAND	O.D.I. MATCHES	HA	53	40	14	374	33	14.38	-	-	20	437.3	-	1942	66	29.42	4-30
1987-2000	Leicestershire	First Class Matches	E	87	119	16	2843	189	27.60	3	13	62	1903.2	442	6463	241	26.81	6-22
1987-2000	Leicestershire	Nat West Trophy	E	16	11	0	230	53	20.90	-	1	9	135.4	-	458	19	24.10	5-19
1987-2000	Leicestershire	Benson & Hedges Cup	E	24	19	8	249	55*	22.63	-	1	11	212.3	-	873	31	28.16	4-40
1988-2000	Leicestershire	Sunday League	E	81	73	17	1427	116*	25.48	1	4	26	480.5	-	1978	78	25.35	4-13
1987-2000	Leicestershire	O.A.L. O.D. Matches	E	5	5	0	121	65	24.20	-	2	4	27	2	133	1	133.00	-
1990-1999	Leicestershire	First Class Matches	E	37	58	10	2256	247	47.00	5	11	36	1255	263	3552	127	27.96	6-90
1992-1994	Nottinghamshire	Nat West Trophy	E	6	6	0	89	89	25.83	-	1	5	51	3	189	6	31.50	3-24
1992-1994	Nottinghamshire	Benson & Hedges Cup	E	10	6	1	160	48*	32.00	-	-	2	86	-	328	17	19.29	5-46
1992-1995	Nottinghamshire	Sunday League	E	29	25	3	557	75	25.31	-	6	6	218.1	-	1011	31	32.61	4-45
1992-1995	Nottinghamshire	First Class Matches	E	22	34	3	932	94	30.06	-	5	23	780	164	1947	62	31.40	5-25
1996-1997	Surrey	Nat West Trophy	E	4	4	2	67	45*	33.50	-	-	2	42	-	153	8	19.12	3-33
1996-1997	Surrey	Benson & Hedges	E	12	8	4	174	35*	43.50	-	-	5	104	-	412	21	19.61	3-29
1996-1997	Surrey	Sunday League	E	20	16	6	350	68*	35.00	-	2	12	125.4	-	508	27	18.81	4-21
1990-1996	England	O.A.L. O.D. Matches	A	5	3	1	62	26	31.00	-	-	2	45	4	196	7	28.00	-
	Total First Class Career			189	275	34	7406	247	30.73	9	34	154	5334	1135	16225	543	29.88	6-22
	Total O.D. Career			265	216	56	3926	116*	24.53	1	14	104	1965.2	-	8181	312	26.22	5-19

DESMOND MICHAEL LEWIS

D.O.B. 21.02.1946 - Kingston, Jamaica

First Class Debut	25.07.1970 - Jamaica v Glamorgan
Test Match Debut	19.03.1971 - West Indies v India
Domestic O.D. Debut	13.04.1973 - Jamaica v Guyana

Test 138-131

Teams Played For
Jamaica
West Indies

RHB / WK

SEASON	TEAM	COMPETITION	V	M	I	No	BATTING RUNS	H.S.	Av	100s	50s	CT/ST	BOWLING OV	MD	RUNS	W	Av	B.B.
1970-1976	Jamaica	First Class Matches	=	33	51	3	1364	96	28.41	-	9	59/11	2	-	-	-	-	-
1972-1973	Jamaica	Domestic O.D. Matches	=	2	2	0	81	53	40.50	-	1	4/1	-	-	-	-	-	-
1970-1971	WEST INDIES	TEST MATCHES	H	3	5	2	259	88	86.33	-	3	8	-	-	-	-	-	-
		Total First Class Career		36	56	5	1623	96	31.82	0	12	67/11	-	-	-	-	-	-
		Total O.D. Career		2	2	0	81	53	40.50	0	1	4/1	-	-	-	-	-	-

RAWL NICHOLAS LEWIS

Test 218-335 | **O.D.I.** 85-340 | **RHB / LBG**

D.O.B. 05.09.1974 - Union Village, St Andrews, Grenada, Windward Islands

First Class Debut 31.01.1992 - Windward Islands v Barbados

Test Match Debut 17.11.1997 - West Indies v Pakistan

O.D.I. Debut 03.11.1997 - West Indies v South Africa

Domestic O.D. Debut 03.03.1993 - Windward Islands v Leeward Islands

Teams Played For 6

Windward Islands, Southern Windwards
West Indies
W.I. President's XI
W.I. Board XI
West Indies "A"

							BATTING						BOWLING					
SEASON	**TEAM**	**COMPETITION**	**V**	**M**	**I**	**No**	**RUNS**	**H.S.**	**Av**	**100s**	**50s**	**CT**	**OV**	**MD**	**RUNS**	**W**	**Av**	**B.B.**
1992-2003	Windward Islands	First Class Matches	II	59	107	19	1924	117*	21.86	1	7	49	1482.2	241	4411	117	37.70	7-66
1993-2002	Windward Islands	Domestic O.D. Matches	II	33	28	5	329	67	14.30	-	1	10	214.4	20	923	33	27.96	3-10
2001-2002	Southern Windwards	Domestic O.D. Matches	II	3	3	0	99	55	33.00	-	1	2	25	0	155	4	38.75	2-70
1997-1999	WEST INDIES	TEST MATCHES	HA	3	6	0	26	12	4.33	-	-	-	97.3	16	318	1	318.00	1-67
1998-1999	West Indies	First Class Matches	A	4	6	1	180	59	36.00	-	1	2	142.3	29	436	13	33.53	4-45
1993-1994	W.I. Board XI	First Class Matches	WI	1	1	1	15	15*	-	-	-	1	53	13	146	9	16.22	5-95
1996-2000	W.I. President's XI	First Class Matches	WI	3	5	0	70	62	14.00	-	1	2	67.2	9	253	5	50.60	2-79
1996-2000	West Indies "A"	First Class Matches	HA	9	10	0	161	64	16.10	-	1	6	329	64	994	33	30.12	4-23
1997-1999	WEST INDIES	O.D.I. MATCHES	HA	16	12	3	157	49	17.44	-	-	5	119.1	2	614	12	51.16	2-40
1998-2000	West Indies "A"	O.D.(I.) Matches	HA	5	4	1	41	16	13.66	-	-	2	39.1	2	149	11	13.54	4-31
1997//	West Indies	O.A.L. O.D. Matches	A	1	1	0	5	5	5.00	-	-	-	9	0	45	2	22-50	2-45
		Total First Class Career		79	135	21	2376	117*	20.84	1	10	60	2171.4	372	6558	178	36.84	7-66
		Total O.D. Career		58	48	9	631	67	16.17	0	2	19	407	24	1886	62	30.41	4-31

CLIVE HUBERT LLOYD

D.O.B. 31.08.1944 - Queenstown, Georgetown, Demerara, British Guiana

First Class Debut	05.03.1964 - British Guiana v Jamaica
Test Match Debut	13.12.1966 - West Indies v India
O.D.I. Debut	05.09.1973 - West Indies v England
Domestic O.D. Debut	13.04.1973 - Guyana v Jamaica

Test 125-110
O.D.I. 4-1

Teams Played For 6
British Guiana/Guyana, West Indies
W.I. President's XI
Lancashire
World XI
NZ Governor's XI

LHB / RMLB

SEASON	TEAM	COMPETITION	V	M	I	No	BATTING RUNS	H.S.	Av	100s	50s	CT	BOWLING OV	MD	RUNS	W	Av	B.B.
1964-1983	Br. Guiana/Guyana	First Class Matches	||	42	64	10	3476	194	64.37	14	17	33	229.4	53	486	12	40.50	3-34
1973-1983	Guyana	Domestic O.D. Matches	||	8	8	0	229	71	28.62	-	1	9	17	0	95	2	47.50	1-40
1966-1985	WEST INDIES	TEST MATCHES	HA	110	175	14	7515	242*	46.67	19	39	90	273	75	622	10	62.20	2-13
1966-1985	West Indies	First Class Matches	A	100	131	27	6277	502*	60.35	14	38	79	248.5	46	816	24	34.00	3-32
1972-1973	W.I. President's XI	First Class Matches	WI	1	2	0	85	59	42.50	-	1	-	-	-	-	-	-	-
1973-1985	WEST INDIES	O.D.I. MATCHES	HA	87	69	19	1977	102	39.54	1	11	39	59.4	7	210	8	26.25	2-4
1969-1984	West Indies	O.A.L. O.D. Matches	A	8	6	1	187	79*	37.40	-	2	4	12	-	72	1	72.00	1-47
1968-1986	Lancashire	First Class Matches	E	219	326	42	12764	217*	44.94	30	71	162	709.2	176	1809	55	32.89	4-48
1969-1986	Lancashire	Nat West Trophy	E	42	41	6	1920	126	54.85	3	13	9	92.3	16	320	12	26.66	3-39
1972-1986	Lancashire	Benson & Hedges Cup	E	48	45	6	1338	124	34.30	2	9	13	83.3	-	302	12	25.16	3-23
1969-1986	Lancashire	Sunday League	E	178	171	40	5198	134*	39.67	6	32	72	221	-	935	36	25.97	4-33
1969-1986	Lancashire	O.A.L. O.D. Matches	E	4	2	0	66	58	33.00	-	1	-	4	-	24	0	-	-
1967-1973	World XI	First Class Matches	A	17	30	3	1039	114*	38.48	2	5	12	125	26	371	13	28.53	3-34
1968-1969	NZ Governor's XI	First Class	NZ	1	2	0	76	71	38.00	-	1	1	1	1	0	0	-	-
1971//	World XI	O.A.L. O.D. Matches	A	1	1	0	0	0	0.00	-	-	-	-	-	-	-	-	-
		Total First Class Career		490	730	96	31232	242*	49.26	79	172	377	1586.5	377	4104	114	36.00	4-48
		Total O.D. Career		376	343	72	10915	134*	40.27	12	69	146	489.4	-	1958	71	27.57	4-33

AUGUSTINE LAWRENCE LOGIE

D.O.B. 28.09.1960 - Sobo Village, La Brea, Trinidad
First Class Debut 06.01.1978 - South Trinidad v Central Trinidad
Test Match Debut 23.02.1983 - West Indies v India
O.D.I. Debut 19.12.1981 - West Indies v Pakistan
Domestic O.D. Debut 28.04.1979 - Trinidad & Tobago v Barbados

Test 177-212
O.D.I. 37-39

Teams Played For 6
Trinidad & Tobago, South Trinidad
S/C Trinidad
West Indies
West Indies "B"
W.I. President's XI

RHB / OB

SEASON	TEAM	COMPETITION	V	M	I	No	BATTING RUNS	H.S.	Av	100s	50s	CT/ST	BOWLING OV	MD	RUNS	W	Av	B.B.
1979-1992	Trinidad & Tobago	First Class Matches	=	39	69	6	2220	171	35.23	5	10	17/1	9	0	34	0	-	-
1978-1979	South Trinidad	First Class Matches	T	7	10	2	193	57	24.12	0	3	17	17	3	35	2	17.50	1-2
1979-1980	S/C Trinidad	First Class Matches	T	2	4	0	182	114	45.50	1	0	4	26	5	26	0	-	-
1979-1992	Trinidad & Tobago	Domestic O.D. Matches	=	22	22	2	585	107*	29.25	1	2	10	8	0	37	2	18.50	2-1
1983-1991	WEST INDIES	TEST MATCHES	HA	52	78	9	2470	130	35.79	2	16	57	1.1	1	4	0	-	-
1982-1993	West Indies	First Class Matches	A	53	76	7	2464	141	35.71	5	12	24	10	1	29	1	29.00	1-29
1990//	W.I. President's XI	First Class Matches	WI	1	2	0	66	40	33.00	-	-	-	-	-	-	-	-	-
1981-1982	West Indies "B"	First Class Matches	A	3	5	1	87	29	21.75	-	1	1	-	-	-	-	-	-
1981-1993	WEST INDIES	O.D.I. MATCHES	HA	158	133	36	2809	109*	28.95	1	14	60	4	0	18	0	-	-
1981-1982	West Indies "B"	O.D.(I) Matches	HA	4	4	0	137	73	34.25	-	1	4	-	-	-	-	-	-
1984-1992	West Indies	O.A.L. O.D. Matches	A	5	5	2	75	27	25.00	-	-	1	-	-	-	-	-	-
Total First Class Career				157	244	25	7682	171	35.07	13	40	106/1	48.1	10	128	3	42.66	1-2
Total O.D. Career				189	164	40	3606	109*	29.08	2	17	75	12	0	55	2	27.50	2-1

MONTE ALAN LYNCH

D.O.B. 21.05.1958 - Plaisance Village, Demerara, British Guiana

First Class Debut 30.07.1977 - Surrey v Northamptonshire
O.D.I. Debut 19.05.1988 - England v West Indies
Domestic O.D. Debut 07.02.1977 - Surrey v Leicestershire

O.D.I. 99-154

Teams Played For
Guyana, Demerara
West Indies XI, Surrey
Gloucestershire
England
International XI

RHB / OB

7

SEASON	TEAM	COMPETITION	V	M	I	No	BATTING RUNS	H.S.	Av	100s	50s	CT	BOWLING OV	MD	RUNS	W	Av	B.B.
1982-1983	Guyana	First Class Matches	=	5	9	1	169	75	21.12	-	1	4	13	3	32	0	-	-
1982-1983	Demerara	First Class Matches	G	1	1	0	52	52	52.00	-	1	3	-	-	-	-	-	-
1982-1983	Guyana	Domestic O.D. Matches	=	3	3	0	169	129	56.33	1	-	-	12	0	47	5	9.40	3-41
1983-1984	West Indies XI	First Class Matches	A	6	11	0	308	105	28.00	1	1	1	-	-	-	-	-	-
1983-1984	West Indies XI	O.D.(I.) Matches	A	4	4	0	68	25	17.00	-	-	2	-	-	-	-	-	-
1988//	ENGLAND	O.D.I. MATCHES	E	3	3	0	8	6	2-66	-	-	1	-	-	-	-	-	-
1977-1994	Surrey	First Class Matches	E	304	491	59	15674	172*	36.28	33	76	314	321.5	60	1251	24	52.12	3-6
1979-1993	Surrey	Nat West Trophy	E	37	32	5	779	129	28.85	1	3	18	47	8	168	6	28.00	2-28
1979-1993	Surrey	Benson & Hedges Cup	E	57	52	3	1312	112*	26.77	2	7	26	22	-	121	0	-	-
1977-1994	Surrey	Sunday League	E	209	191	26	4675	136	28.33	2	29	74	24.5	-	182	7	26.00	2-2
1981-1987	Surrey	O.A.L. O.D. Matches	E	5	3	1	64	34	32.00	-	-	1	-	-	-	-	-	-
1995-1997	Gloucestershire	First Class Matches	E	40	67	4	2044	114	32.44	5	10	44	2	0	3	0	-	-
1995-1997	Gloucestershire	Nat West Trophy	E	6	6	1	209	100	41.80	1	1	2	3.4	-	11	1	11.00	1-11
1995-1997	Gloucestershire	Benson & Hedges Cup	E	11	11	1	209	87	20.90	-	1	8	-	-	-	-	-	-
1995-1997	Gloucestershire	Sunday League	E	39	37	1	918	88*	27.00	-	5	11	3	0	23	1	23.00	1-22
1996//	Gloucestershire	O.A.L. O.D. Matches	E	1	1	0	52	52	52.00	-	1	1	-	-	-	-	-	-
1981-1982	International XI	First Class Matches	P	3	6	0	78	44	13.00	-	-	1	30	6	112	2	56.00	1-15
1981-1982	International XI	O.A.L. O.D. Matches	P	3	3	0	20	15	6.66	-	-	2	9	40	0	-	-	-
Total First Class Career				359	585	64	18325	172*	35.17	39	88	367	365.5	69	1398	26	53.76	3-6
Total O.D. Career				378	346	40	8483	136	27.72	7	47	146	121.3	-	592	20	29.60	3-41

IVAN SAMUEL MADRAY
D.O.B.   02.07.1934 - Port Mourant, Berbice, British Guiana
First Class Debut   20.04.1955 - British Guiana v Australia
Test Match Debut   05.02.1958 - West Indies v Pakistan
Domestic O.D. Debut   05.05.1966 - Lincolnshire v Hampshire

Test 101-68

Teams Played For
British Guiana
West Indies
Lincolnshire

3

RHB / LBG

SEASON	TEAM	COMPETITION	V	M	I	No	BATTING RUNS	H.S.	Av	100s	50s	CT	BOWLING OV	MD	RUNS	W	Av	B.B.
1955-1958	British Guiana	First Class Matches	A	4	5	0	70	28	14.00	-	-	3	182.2	25	514	16	32.12	4-61
1957-1958	WEST INDIES	TEST MATCHES	P	2	3	0	3	2	1.00	-	-	2	35	6	108	0	-	-
1966-1967	Lincolnshire	Gillette Cup	E	2	2	0	59	58	29.50	-	1	-	3	0	19	0	-	-
Total First Class Career				6	8	0	73	28	9.12	-	-	5	217.2	31	622	16	38.87	4-61
Total O.D. Career				2	2	0	59	58	29.50	-	1	-	3	0	19	0	-	-

DEVON EUGENE MALCOLM

D.O.B.	22.02.1963 - Kingston, Jamaica
First Class Debut	14.07.1984 - Derbyshire v Surrey
Test Match Debut	10.08.1989 - England v Australia
O.D.I. Debut	25.05.1990 - England v New Zealand
Domestic O.D. Debut	06.07.1986 - Derbyshire v Kent

Teams Played For
Derbyshire
Northamptonshire
Leicestershire
England
England "A"

RHB / RF 5

SEASON	TEAM	COMPETITION	V	M	I	No	BATTING RUNS	H.S.	Av	100s	50s	CT	BOWLING OV	MD	RUNS	W	Av	B.B.
1989-1997	ENGLAND	TEST MATCHES	HA	40	58	19	236	29	6.05	-	-	7	1413.2	252	4748	128	37.09	9-57
1989-1996	England	First Class Matches	A	20	22	4	141	48*	7.83	-	-	63	645.1	106	2239	78	28.70	7-74
1990-1994	ENGLAND	O.D.I. MATCHES	HA	10	5	2	9	4	3.00	-	-	1	87.4	-	404	16	25.25	3-40
1990-1996	England	O.A.L. O.D. Matches	A	2	2	0	4	2	2.00	-	-	-	16	1	55	3	18.33	-
1991-1992	England "A"	First Class Matches	HA	4	2	1	1	1*	1.00	-	-	-	88	8	355	8	44.37	4-68
1991-1992	England "A"	O.A.L. O.D. Matches	A	1	0	-				-	-	-	6	0	30	1	30.00	1-30
1984-1997	Derbyshire	First Class Matches	E	168	195	62	1146	51	8.61	-	1	20	4613.5	754	16905	579	29.19	6-23
1987-1997	Derbyshire	Nat West Trophy	E	21	10	4	29	10*	3.22	-	-	1	217.5	-	847	33	25.66	7-35
1988-1997	Derbyshire	Benson & Hedges Cup	E	32	17	4	88	15	6.76	-	-	3	299.5	-	1320	50	26.40	5-27
1986-1997	Derbyshire	Sunday League	E	64	25	10	134	42	8.93	-	-	7	471.1	-	2428	87	27.90	4-21
1990//	Derbyshire	Sunday League Cup	E	2	0	-				-	-	-	16	-	86	4	21.50	3-41
1993//	Derbyshire	O.A.L. O.D. Matches	E	1	0	-				-	-	-						
1998-2000	Northamptonshire	First Class Matches	E	36	42	12	170	42	5.66	-	-	7	1003.2	184	3598	119	30.23	6-39
1998-2000	Northamptonshire	Nat West Trophy	E	6	3	1	2	1	0.66	-	-	-	50	-	188	5	37.60	2-55
1998-2000	Northamptonshire	Benson & Hedges Cup	E	6	4	2	22	16	11.00	-	-	2	60	-	227	5	45.40	2-50
1998-2000	Northamptonshire	Sunday League	E	22	11	2	19	6	2.11	-	-	3	145	-	668	24	27.83	3-16
1998//	Northamptonshire	O.A.L. O.D. Matches	E	2	0	-				-	-	-	19	2	100	1	100.00	-
2001-2003	Leicestershire	First Class Matches	E	36	47	15	291	50	9.09	-	1	5	1117	195	4128	142	29.07	8-63
2001-2002	Leicestershire	Cheltenham & Gloucester Cup	E	3	1	0	0	0	0.00	-	-	3	25	4	82	5	16.40	3-24
2001-2002	Leicestershire	Benson & Hedges Cup	E	5	2	0	4	4	2.00	-	-	1	32.3	1	168	7	24.00	3-13
2001-2002	Leicestershire	Sunday League	E	8	2	1	2	2*	2.00	-	-	-	51	4	273	8	34.12	3-34
Total First Class Career				304	366	113	1985	51	7.84	0	2	45	8880.4	1499	31973	1054	30.33	9-57
Total O.D. Career				185	82	22	313	42	5.21	0	0	21	1497	99	6876	249	27.61	7-35

MALCOLM DENZIL MARSHALL

D.O.B. 18.04.1958 - Dearns Village, Station Hill, St Michael, Barbados (d. 05.11.1999)

First Class Debut 17.02.1978 - Barbados v Jamaica
Test Match Debut 15.02.1978 - West Indies v India
O.D.I. Debut 28.05.1980 - West Indies v England
Domestic O.D. Debut 13.02.1978 - Barbados v Jamaica

Test 172-185
O.D.I. 33-29

Teams Played For 9
Barbados, West Indies
West Indies U26, World XI
W.I. President's XI, Hampshire
Scotland, Natal, M.C.C.

RHB / RF

SEASON	TEAM	COMPETITION	V	M	I	No	BATTING RUNS	H.S.	Av	100s	50s	CT	BOWLING OV	MD	RUNS	W	Av	B.B.
1978-1991	Barbados	First Class Matches	II	37	49	7	1270	89	30.23	-	9	21	1152.4	254	3146	180	17.47	6-38
1978-1991	Barbados	Domestic O.D. Matches	II	16	11	0	73	24	6.63	-	-	5	126.4	20	394	33	11.93	5-17
1978-1991	WEST INDIES	TEST MATCHES	HA	81	107	11	1810	92	18.85	-	10	25	2930.4	612	7876	376	20.94	7-22
1978-1991	West Indies	First Class Matches	A	46	49	9	953	76	23.82	-	5	11	971.1	237	5290	155	16.70	7-56
1981//	West Indies U26	First Class Matches	A	3	4	0	175	109	43.75	1	-	-	80.4	18	192	7	27.42	4-39
1979-1983	W.I. President's XI	First Class Matches	WI	1	2	0	58	31	29.00	-	-	-	43	14	102	4	25.50	3-48
1980-1992	WEST INDIES	O.D.I. MATCHES	HA	136	83	19	955	66	14.92	-	2	15	1195.5	122	4233	157	26.96	4-78
1981//	West Indies U26	O.D.(I.) Matches	A	3	3	0	11	8	3.66	-	-	1	28	8	62	5	12.40	3-11
1979-1991	West Indies	O.A.L. O.D. Matches	A	17	8	3	85	43	17.00	-	-	2	153	-	440	24	18.33	4-27
1979-1993	Hampshire	First Class Matches	E	210	269	37	5847	117	25.20	5	26	76	6277	1727	15401	826	18.64	8-71
1979-1993	Hampshire	Nat West Trophy	E	31	21	9	348	77	29.00	-	2	3	328	54	895	34	26.32	4-15
1979-1993	Hampshire	Benson & Hedges Cup	E	41	30	2	387	34	13.82	-	-	7	384.1	73	1143	53	21.56	4-20
1979-1993	Hampshire	Sunday League	E	142	95	22	1338	59	18.32	-	1	29	1059.4	90	3835	150	25.56	5-13
1986-1990	Hampshire	O.A.L. O.D. Matches	E	2	-	-	-	-	-	-	-	-	22	-	75	2	37.50	2-27
1995//	Scotland	Nat West Trophy	E	1	1	0	45	45	45.00	-	-	-	9	-	32	0	-	-
1995//	Scotland	Benson & Hedges Cup	E	4	4	0	40	36	10.00	-	-	1	34	3	125	3	41.66	2-35
1987//	M.C.C.	First Class Matches	E	1	-	-	-	-	-	-	-	1	22.3	3	63	4	15.75	3-53
1994//	World XI	First Class Matches	E	1	-	-	-	-	-	-	-	-	16	2	60	3	20.00	3-60
1992-1996	Natal	First Class Matches	SA	28	36	9	891	120*	33.00	1	4	11	973.4	309	2118	96	22.06	6-45
1992-1993	Natal	Total Power Series Cup	SA	4	3	0	37	30	12.33	-	-	-	38.5	11	74	8	9.25	4-21
1992-1996	Natal	Benson & Hedges Cup	SA	41	27	5	484	64*	22.00	-	-	3	330.5	45	1015	52	19.51	4-15
1992-1996	Natal	O.A.L. O.D. Matches	SA	3	-	-	-	-	-	-	-	-	20	-	46	3	15.33	2-16
		Total First Class Career		408	516	73	11004	120*	24.83	7	54	145	12467.2	3176	31548	1651	19.10	8-71
		Total O.D. Career		441	286	60	3803	77	16.82	0	8	68	3730	-	12369	524	23.60	5-13

NORMAN EDGAR MARSHALL

D.O.B. 27.02.1924 - Welchman Hall Plantation, St Thomas, Barbados

First Class Debut 08.02.1941 - Barbados v Trinidad

Test Match Debut 26.04.1955 - West Indies v Australia

Test 89-55

Teams Played For 4   **RHB / OB**
Barbados
Trinidad
North Trinidad
West Indies

SEASON	TEAM	COMPETITION	V	M	I	No	BATTING RUNS	H.S.	Av	100s	50s	CT	BOWLING OV	MD	RUNS	W	Av	B.B.
1941-1956	Barbados	First Class Matches	II	27	40	6	1125	134	33.08	2	3	5	999.5	333	2426	70	34.65	6-117
1954-1955	Trinidad	First Class Matches	II	4	6	0	138	66	23.00	-	1	1	223.2	114	335	18	18.61	6-49
1958-1959	North Trinidad	First Class Matches	T	1	2	0	66	57	33.00	-	1	-	8	1	32	0	-	-
1954-1955	WEST INDIES	TEST MATCHES	H	1	2	0	8	8	4.00	-	-	-	46.3	22	62	2	31.00	1-22
		Total First Class Career		33	50	6	1337	134	30.38	2	5	6	1277.4	470	2855	90	31.72	6-49

ROY EDWIN MARSHALL

D.O.B. 25.04.1930 - Farmers Plantation, St Thomas, Barbados (d. 27.10.1992)

First Class Debut 26.01.1946 - Barbados v Trinidad
Test Match Debut 09.11.1951 - West Indies v Australia
Domestic O.D. Debut 22.05.1963 - Hampshire v Derbyshire

Test 72-36 **Teams Played For** 13 **RHB / OB**

Barbados, West Indies, Hampshire, World XI
Commonwealth XI, The South XI, International XI
The Players XI, M.C.C.
Duke of Norfolk XI, Rest of League XI
Cavaliers XI, T.N. Pearce's XI

SEASON	TEAM	COMPETITION	v	M	I	No	BATTING RUNS	H.S.	Av	100s	50s	CT	BOWLING OV	MD	RUNS	W	Av	B.B.
1946-1953	Barbados	First Class Matches	II	8	12	0	695	191	57.91	3	2	6	196	58	501	16	31.31	3-25
1951-1952	WEST INDIES	TEST MATCHES	A	4	7	0	143	30	20.42	-	-	6	7	2	15	0	-	-
1950-1964	West Indies	First Class Matches	A	31	47	2	1687	188	37.48	5	4	23	208.4	54	602	15	40.13	4-70
1953-1972	Hampshire	First Class Matches	E	504	890	49	30303	228*	36.03	60	161	232	1165.4	363	2403	99	24.27	6-36
1963-1972	Hampshire	Nat West Trophy	E	23	23	1	832	140	37.81	2	3	6	-	-	-	-	-	-
1972//	Hampshire	Benson & Hedges Cup	E	4	4	0	51	34	12.75	-	-	1	-	-	-	-	-	-
1969-1972	Hampshire	Sunday League	E	48	47	5	1307	96	31.12	-	9	9	-	-	-	-	-	-
1953-1963	Commonwealth XI	First Class Matches	A	26	42	5	1193	90	32.24	-	7	18	362	97	947	29	32.65	4-56
1959-1963	M.C.C.	First Class Matches	E	3	5	0	135	85	27.00	-	3	3	-	-	-	-	-	-
1954-1957	The South XI	First Class Matches	E	3	6	0	232	72	38.66	-	1	3	27	1	114	2	57.00	2-59
1958-1970	The Players XI	First Class Matches	E	4	8	2	243	76	40.50	-	1	1	9	2	36	2	18.00	1-12
1958-1960	T.N. Pearce's XI	First Class Matches	E	3	6	0	264	78	44.00	-	3	-	20	7	44	2	22.00	2-10
1957//	Rest of League XI	First Class Matches	E	1	2	0	55	55	27.50	-	1	-	-	-	-	-	-	-
1968//	World XI	First Class Matches	E	2	2	0	29	24	14.50	-	-	1	-	-	-	-	-	-
1956-57//	Duke of Norfolk XI	First Class Matches	WI	3	6	0	273	97	45.50	-	2	-	9	0	32	1	32.00	1-32
1963-1965	Cavaliers XI	First Class Matches	WI	5	10	0	171	38	17.70	-	1	1	73.2	9	281	5	56.20	2-31
1961-62//	International XI	First Class Matches	A	6	10	1	302	76	33.55	-	2	3	40	11	117	5	23.40	2-27
Total First Class Career				602	1053	59	35725	228*	35.94	68	185	293	2087.4	604	5092	176	28.93	6-36
Total O.D. Career				75	74	6	2190	140	32.20	2	12	16	-	-	-	-	-	-

393

FRANK REGINALD MARTIN

D.O.B. 12.10.1893 - Kingston, Jamaica (d. 23.11.1967)
First Class Debut 21.01.1925 - Jamaica v Barbados
Test Match Debut 23.06.1928 - West Indies v England

Test 2-1

Teams Played For
Jamaica
West Indies

LHB / SLA

TEAM		
Jamaica		
WEST INDIES	West Indies	

SEASON	TEAM	COMPETITION	V	M	I	No	BATTING RUNS	H.S.	Av	100s	50s	CT	BOWLING OV	MD	RUNS	W	Av	B.B.
1925-1930	Jamaica	First Class Matches	II	15	25	7	1262	204*	70.11	4	5	7	392	94	845	17	49.70	4-67
1928-1931	West Indies	TEST MATCHES	HA	9	18	1	486	123*	28.58	1	-	2	224.2	27	619	8	77.37	3-91
1928-1933	West Indies	First Class Matches	HA	41	65	5	1841	165	30.68	1	11	10	648.4	145	1685	49	34.38	5-90
		Total First Class Career		65	108	13	3589	204*	37.77	6	16	19	1265	266	3149	74	42.55	5-90

EMANUEL ALFRED MARTINDALE

D.O.B. 25.11.1909 - St Lucy, Barbados (d. 17.03.1972)
First Class Debut 24.09.1929 - Barbados v British Guiana
Test Match Debut 24.06.1933 - West Indies v England

Test 32-13

Teams Played For
Barbados
West Indies
C.A. Merry's XI

3

RHB / RF

SEASON	TEAM	COMPETITION	V	M	I	No	BATTING RUNS	H.S.	Av	100s	50s	CT	BOWLING OV	MD	RUNS	W	Av	B.B.
1929-1936	Barbados	First Class Matches	II	9	15	2	355	134	27.30	1	-	8	333.4	52	1149	30	38.30	5-106
1933-1939	WEST INDIES	TEST MATCHES	HA	10	14	3	58	22	5.27	-	-	5	243.7	40	804	37	21.72	5-22
1933-1939	West Indies	First Class Matches	A	39	53	15	489	39	12.86	-	-	16	919.5	133	3183	131	24.29	8-32
1932-1933	C.A. Merry's XI	First Class Matches	WI	1	2	0	70	42	35.00	-	-	-	28	8	69	5	13.80	3-54
Total First Class Career				59	84	20	972	134	15.18	1	0	29	1525.4	233	5205	203	25.64	8-32

EVERTON HUGH MATTIS

D.O.B. 11.04.1957 - Kingston, Jamaica

First Class Debut	28.01.1977 - Jamaica v Combined Islands
Test Match Debut	13.02.1981 - West Indies v England
O.D.I. Debut	04.02.1981 - West Indies v England
Domestic O.D. Debut	25.01.1977 - Jamaica v Windward Islands

Test 175-205   **O.D.I.** 35-34

Teams Played For
Jamaica
West Indies
W.I. President's XI
West Indies U26
West Indies XI

RHB / OB
5

SEASON	TEAM	COMPETITION	V	M	I	No	BATTING RUNS	H.S.	Av	100s	50s	CT	BOWLING OV	MD	RUNS	W	Av	B.B.
1977-1982	Jamaica	First Class Matches	II	23	40	3	1490	132	40.27	2	10	14	42.4	14	70	8	8.75	4-22
1977-1982	Jamaica	Domestic O.D. Matches	II	14	13	0	228	67	17.53	-	1	6	4	0	13	2	6.50	1-4
1981//	WEST INDIES	TEST MATCHES	H	4	5	0	145	71	29.00	-	1	3	6	1	14	0	-	-
1981//	W.I. President's XI	First Class Matches	WI	1	2	0	87	46	43.50	-	-	1	-	-	-	-	-	-
1981//	West Indies U26	First Class Matches	A	3	4	0	118	106	29.50	1	-	4	2	0	5	0	-	-
1982-1984	West Indies XI	First Class Matches	A	7	14	0	224	51	16.00	-	1	3	0.4	0	0	1	-	1-0
1981//	WEST INDIES	O.D.I. MATCHES	H	2	2	0	86	62	43.00	-	1	2	-	-	-	-	-	-
1981//	West Indies U26	O.D.(I.) Matches	A	3	3	0	42	32	14.00	-	-	1	18	1	93	2	46.50	2-46
1982-1984	West Indies XI	O.D.(I.) Matches	A	5	4	0	48	24	12.00	-	-	-	-	-	-	-	-	-
1982-1983	West Indies	O.A.L. O.D. Matches	A	3	3	0	38	16	12.66	-	-	-	-	-	-	-	-	-
		Total First Class Career		38	65	3	2064	132	33.29	3	12	25	51.2	16	89	9	9.88	4-22
		Total O.D. Career		27	25	0	442	67	17.68	0	2	9	22	1	106	4	26.50	2-46

NEIL CHRISTOPHER McGARRELL

D.O.B. 12.07.1972 - Georgetown, Demerara, Guyana

First Class Debut 26.01.1996 - Guyana v Jamaica
Test Match Debut 06.04.2001 - West Indies v South Africa
O.D.I. Debut 08.04.1998 - West Indies v England
Domestic O.D. Debut 28.10.1995 - Guyana v Trinidad & Tobago

Test	239-373	Teams Played For	3		RHB / SLA
O.D.I.	88-350	Guyana			
		West Indies			
		West Indies "A"			

SEASON	TEAM	COMPETITION	V	M	I	No	BATTING RUNS	H.S.	Av	100s	50s	CT	BOWLING OV	MD	RUNS	W	Av	B.B.
1996-2003	Guyana	First Class Matches	=	53	72	8	1322	88	20.65	-	7	64	2311.1	710	4845	192	25.23	7-71
1995-2002	Guyana	Domestic O.D. Matches	=	38	21	10	270	28*	24.54	-	-	13	292.1	36	988	36	27.44	5-20
1999//	Guyana	O.A.L. O.D. Matches	WI	1	1	0	5	5	5.00	-	-	-	10	0	28	4	7.00	4-28
2001-2002	WEST INDIES	TEST MATCHES	HA	4	6	2	61	33	15.25	-	-	2	202	65	453	17	26.64	4-72
1998-1999	West Indies "A"	First Class Matches	HA	4	5	2	148	54*	49.33	-	1	1	82.4	18	207	4	51.75	2-57
2001-2002	West Indies	First Class Matches	A	5	6	1	87	51	17.40	-	1	5	182	29	507	20	25.35	5-42
1992-2002	WEST INDIES	O.D.I. MATCHES	HA	17	10	2	60	19	7.50	-	-	9	143.1	2	681	15	45.40	3-32
1998-1999	West Indies "A"	O.D.(I.) Matches	A	6	4	1	40	24	16.00	-	-	2	56.1	3	224	6	37.33	2-28
2001//	West Indies	O.A.L. O.D. Matches	A	1	-	-	-	-	-	-	-	-	9	1	38	0	-	-
1998//	West Indies "A"	O.A.L. O.D. Matches	A	1	-	-	-	-	-	-	-	-	45	2	45	2	22.50	2-45
Total First Class Career				66	89	13	1618	88	21.28	0	9	72	2778.3	822	6012	233	25.80	7-71
Total O.D. Career				64	36	13	383	28*	16.65	0	0	24	518.3	43	2004	63	31.80	5-20

NIXON ALEXEI McNAMARA McLEAN

LHB / RF

D.O.B. 20.07.1973 - Stubbs Village, St Vincent, Windward Islands

First Class Debut	26.02.1993 - Windward Islands v Jamaica	
Test Match Debut	29.01.1998 - West Indies v England	
O.D.I. Debut	06.12.1996 - West Indies v Australia	
Domestic O.D. Debut	24.02.1993 - Windward Islands v Jamaica	

Test 220-338 **O.D.I.** 78-324

Teams Played For 9
Windward Islands, West Indies
W.I. President's XI, West Indies "A"
W.I. Select XI, Hampshire
St Vincent, Somerset
Kwa-Zulu Natal

SEASON	TEAM	COMPETITION	V	M	I	No	BATTING						BOWLING					
							RUNS	H.S.	Av	100s	50s	CT	OV	MD	RUNS	W	Av	B.B.
1993-2000	Windward Islands	First Class Matches	II	18	32	9	376	52	16.34	-	1	3	447.1	93	1247	41	30.41	5-37
1993-2000	Windward Islands	Domestic O.D. Matches	II	28	21	5	203	41*	12.68	-	-	8	185.2	13	814	34	23.94	5-35
2002//	St Vincent	Domestic O.D. Matches	II	4	4	0	51	21	12.75	-	-	-	62.4	2	173	8	21.62	4-26
1998-2001	WEST INDIES	TEST MATCHES	HA	19	32	2	368	46	12.26	-	-	5	549.5	85	1873	44	42.56	3-53
1996-2001	West Indies	First Class Matches	A	14	24	2	213	46	9.68	-	-	-	363.1	75	1149	54	21.27	7-28
1996-1999	W.I. President's XI	First Class Matches	WI	2	3	1	63	49*	31.50	-	-	1	41.4	5	195	11	17.72	4-32
1997-2000	West Indies "A"	First Class Matches	HA	9	14	1	188	39	14.46	-	-	2	256.3	46	792	28	28.28	6-28
1996-2003	WEST INDIES	O.D.I. MATCHES	HA	45	34	8	314	50*	12.07	-	1	8	353.2	18	1729	46	37.58	3-21
1997-2000	West Indies "A"	O.D.(I.) Matches	WI	5	5	2	31	13	10.33	-	-	-	32	1	141	4	35.25	2-41
1999-2000	W.I. Select XI	O.D.(I.) Matches	WI	2	2	0	31	24	15.50	-	-	-	16.3	0	66	7	9.42	5-26
1996//	West Indies	O.A.L. O.D. Matches	A	3	3	3	4	2*	-	-	-	-	20	2	110	2	55.00	1-37
1997//	West Indies "A"	O.A.L. O.D. Matches	A	1	D	-	-	-	.	-	-	-	-	-	45	2	22.50	2-45
1998-1999	Hampshire	First Class Matches	E	30	41	5	494	70	13.72	-	1	11	989.5	210	3064	108	28.37	6-101
1998-1999	Hampshire	Nat West Trophy	E	6	6	3	112	36	37.33	-	-	-	51.1	-	177	9	19.66	3-27
1998-1999	Hampshire	Benson & Hedges Cup	E	5	4	1	35	28*	11.66	-	-	2	45.1	-	230	2	115.00	1-32
1998-1999	Hampshire	Sunday League	E	31	24	3	280	32	13.33	-	-	3	207	-	1016	40	25.40	3-27
2001-2003	Kwa-Zulu Natal	First Class Matches	SA	12	20	3	208	30	12.23	-	-	10	368	99	1082	60	18.03	6-84
2001-2003	Kwa-Zulu Natal	Standard Bank Cup	SA	14	6	2	68	24	17.00	-	-	5	109	12	350	24	14.58	4-15
2003//	Somerset	First Class Matches	E	17	23	4	318	76	16.73	-	1	2	551.3	115	1872	65	28.80	5-43
2003//	Somerset	Cheltenham & Glouster Cup	E	2	1	0	6	6	6.00	-	-	-	20	3	57	2	28.50	1-28
2003//	Somerset	National Sunday League	E	12	9	4	133	28	26.60	-	-	2	87.3	3	468	21	22.28	3-51
Total First Class Career				121	189	27	2228	76	13.75	0	3	34	3567.4	728	11274	411	27.43	7-28
Total O.D. Career				158	120	31	1268	50*	14.24	0	1	28	1162.4	69	5376	201	26.74	5-26

EASTON DUDLEY ASHTON ST. JOHN McMORRIS

D.O.B. 04.04.1935 - St Andrew, Kingston Jamaica

First Class Debut 11.10.1956 - Jamaica v British Guiana
Test Match Debut 05.02.1958 - West Indies v Pakistan
Domestic O.D. Debut 12.09.1963 - West Indies v Sussex

Test 100-68

Teams Played For 4
Jamaica
West Indies
The Rest XI
F.M. Worrell's XI

RHB / OB

SEASON	TEAM	COMPETITION	V	M	I	No	RUNS	H.S.	Av	100s	50s	CT	OV	MD	RUNS	W	Av	B.B.
1956-1972	Jamaica	First Class Matches	=	50	86	10	3800	218	50.00	13	14	21	12	5	37	0	-	-
1958-1966	WEST INDIES	TEST MATCHES	HA	13	21	0	564	125	26.85	1	3	5	-	-	-	-	-	-
1963-1966	West Indies	First Class Matches	A	30	47	8	1450	190*	37.17	4	5	6	3	0	26	0	-	-
1963-1964	The Rest XI	First Class Matches	WI	1	2	0	59	37	29.50	-	1	1	4	0	44	0	-	-
1963-1964	F.M. Worrell's XI	First Class Matches	WI	1	2	0	33	22	16.50	-	-	3	-	-	-	-	-	-
1963//	West Indies	O.A.L. O.D. Matches	E	1	1	0	4	4	4.00	-	-	1	-	-	-	-	-	-
Total First Class Career				95	158	18	5906	218	42.18	18	22	36	19	5	107	0	-	-
Total O.D. Career				1	1	0	4	4	4.00	0	0	1	-	-	-	-	-	-

CLIFFORD AUBREY McWATT

D.O.B. 01.02.1923 - Georgetown, Demerara, British Guiana

First Class Debut 11.03.1944 - British Guiana v Trinidad
Test Match Debut 15.01.1954 - West Indies v England

Test 83-48

Teams Played For
British Guiana
West Indies

LHB / WK

BATTING

SEASON	TEAM	COMPETITION	V	M	I	No	RUNS	H.S.	Av	100s	50s	CT/ST
1944-1957	British Guiana	First Class Matches	II	24	44	4	1185	128	29.62	2	4	23/3
1954-1955	West Indies	Test Matches	HA	6	9	2	202	54	28.85	-	2	9/1
1948-1949	West Indies	First Class Matches	A	11	12	1	286	51	26.00	-	1	13/2
		Total First Class Career		41	65	7	1673	128	28.84	2	7	45/6

BOWLING

OV	MD	RUNS	W	Av	B.B.
17	1	89	1	89.00	1-17
4	2	16	1	16.00	1-16
-	-	-	-	-	-
21	3	105	2	52.50	1-16

IVOR LEON MENDONCA

D.O.B.   13.07.1934 - Bartica, Essequibo, British Guiana

First Class Debut   24.01.1959 - British Guiana v Barbados

Test Match Debut   07.03.1962 - West Indies v India

							Test	116-91		Teams Played For		2				RHB / WK
										British Guiana						
										West Indies						

							BATTING							BOWLING				
SEASON	TEAM	COMPETITION	V	M	I	No	RUNS	H.S.	Av	100s	50s	CT/ST	OV	MD	RUNS	W	Av	B.B.
1959-1962	British Guiana	First Class Matches	H	8	14	3	326	74	29.63	-	2	17/3	-	-	-	-	-	-
1961-1962	WEST INDIES	TEST MATCHES	H	2	2	0	81	78	40.50	-	1	8/2	-	-	-	-	-	-
		Total First Class Career		10	16	3	407	78	31.30	0	3	25/5	-	-	-	-	-	-

CYRIL ARTHUR MERRY

D.O.B. 20.01.1911 - Scarborough, Tobago (d. 19.04.1964)

First Class Debut 22.01.1930 - Trinidad v M.C.C.

Test Match Debut 24.06.1938 - West Indies v England

Test 33-13

Teams Played For
Trinidad
West Indies
C.A. Merry's XI

3

RHB / RM

BATTING

SEASON	TEAM	COMPETITION	V	M	I	No	RUNS	H.S.	Av	100s	50s	CT
1930-1939	Trinidad	First Class Matches	II	15	28	3	661	88	26.44	-	1	17
1933//	WEST INDIES	TEST MATCHES	A	2	4	0	34	13	8.50	-	-	1
1933//	West Indies	First Class Matches	A	19	30	4	822	146	31.61	1	3	14
1932-1933	C.A. Merry's XI	First Class Matches	WI	1	2	0	30	30	15.00	-	-	1
Total First Class Career				37	64	7	1547	146	27.14	1	4	33

BOWLING

OV	MD	RUNS	W	Av	B.B.
134	32	307	18	17.05	3-13
-	-	-	-	-	-
150	25	420	13	32.30	2-5
5.1	1	19	2	9.50	1-9
289.1	58	746	33	22.60	3-13

ROY C. MILLER

D.O.B. 24.12.1924 - Kingston, Jamaica
First Class Debut 10.03.1951 - Jamaica v British Guiana
Test Match Debut 11.03.1953 - West Indies v India

Test	78-46	Teams Played For: Jamaica, West Indies — 2
		RHB / RFM

SEASON	TEAM	COMPETITION	V	M	I	No	BATTING						BOWLING					
							RUNS	H.S.	Av	100s	50s	CT	OV	MD	RUNS	W	Av	B.B.
1951-1954	Jamaica	First Class Matches	II	7	10	2	208	86	26.00	-	1	2	213	38	607	14	43.35	3-65
1952-1953	WEST INDIES	TEST MATCHES	H	1	1	0	23	23	23.00	-	-	-	16	8	28	0	-	-
Total First Class Career				8	11	2	231	86	25.66	0	1	2	229	46	635	14	45.35	3-65

RUNAKO SHAKUR MORTON

D.O.B. 22.07.1978 - Rawlins Village, Gingerland, Nevis, Leeward Islands

First Class Debut 23.05.1997 - Leeward Islands v Trinidad & Tobago
O.D.I. Debut 15.02.2002 - West Indies v Pakistan
Domestic O.D. Debut 05.10.1997 - Leeward Islands v Barbados

O.D.I. 110-439

Teams Played For 6
Leeward Islands, West Indies
West Indies U23
West Indies "A"
Busta Cup XI
W.I. Select XI

RHB / OB

SEASON	TEAM	COMPETITION	V	M	I	No	RUNS	H.S.	Av	100s	50s	CT	OV	MD	RUNS	W	Av	B.B.
1997-2002	Leeward Islands	First Class Matches	II	25	41	2	1366	110	35.02	3	10	34	36.3	6	118	3	39.33	3-17
1997-2002	Leeward Islands	Domestic O.D. Matches	II	23	22	6	381	56	23.81	-	1	12	12	0	86	2	43.00	2-35
1999-2000	West Indies U23	First Class Matches	WI	1	2	0	9	8	4.50	-	-	-	-	-	-	-	-	-
1999-2002	West Indies "A"	First Class Matches	HA	7	12	2	328	79	32.80	-	3	6	2	0	15	1	15.00	1-15
2001-2002	Busta Cup XI	First Class Matches	WI	1	1	0	33	33	33.00	-	-	1	5	0	20	0	-	-
2001-2002	WEST INDIES	O.D.I. MATCHES	A	2	2	0	19	16	9.50	-	-	1	-	-	-	-	-	-
2002//	West Indies "A"	O.A.L. O.D. Matches	A	5	5	1	220	126	55.00	1	-	1	-	-	-	-	-	-
1999-2000	W.I. Select XI	O.D.(I.) Matches	H	2	2	0	59	34	29.50	-	-	1	-	-	-	-	-	-
1999-2000	West Indies "A"	O.D.(I.) Matches	H	2	2	0	29	15	14.50	-	-	1	-	-	-	-	-	-
		Total First Class Career		34	56	4	1736	110	33.38	3	13	41	43.3	6	153	4	38.25	3-17
		Total O.D. Career		34	33	7	708	126	27.23	1	1	16	12	0	86	2	43.00	2-35

BATTING

BOWLING

EZRA ALPHONSA MOSELEY

D.O.B. 05.01.1958 - Walronds Village, Christ Church, Barbados

First Class Debut 30.04.1980 - Glamorgan v Essex
Test Match Debut 23.03.1990 - West Indies v England
O.D.I. Debut 14.02.1990 - West Indies v England
Domestic O.D. Debut 10.05.1980 - Glamorgan v Gloucester

Test 195-275
O.D.I. 57-194

Teams Played For 8
Barbados, West Indies
W.I. Board XI, West Indies XI
Glamorgan, Eastern Province
Northern Transvaal
World XI

RHB / RFM

SEASON	TEAM	COMPETITION	V	M	I	No	BATTING RUNS	H.S.	Av	100s	50s	CT	BOWLING OV	MD	RUNS	W	Av	B.B.
1982-1991	Barbados	First Class Matches	=	14	18	3	339	70*	22.60	-	1	8	445.2	71	1382	56	24.67	6-52
1982-1992	Barbados	Domestic O.D. Matches	=	10	6	1	48	25*	9.60	-	-	5	82.2	8	311	7	44.62	2-34
1990//	WEST INDIES	TEST MATCHES	H	2	4	0	35	26	8.75	-	-	1	87	13	261	6	43.50	2-70
1990//	West Indies	First Class Matches	A	1	1	0	13	13	13.00	-	-	-	20.1	3	57	3	19.00	3-57
1991//	W.I. Board XI	First Class Matches	WI	1	2	1	25	14*	25.00	-	-	-	17	5	37	1	37.00	1-37
1982-1984	West Indies XI	First Class Matches	A	7	11	1	197	35	19.70	-	-	2	207.5	38	709	28	25.32	4-36
1990-1991	WEST INDIES	O.D.I. MATCHES	A	9	6	2	7	2*	1.75	-	-	-	55	2	278	7	39.71	2-44
1982-1984	West Indies XI	O.D.(I.) Matches	HA	11	8	4	121	63*	30.25	-	1	1	108.5	7	457	19	24.05	4-27
1982-1983	West Indies XI	O.A.L. O.D. Matches	A	3	3	0	9	8	3.00	-	-	1	25.4	5	81	5	16.20	4-23
1980-1986	Glamorgan	First Class Matches	E	35	43	10	655	70*	19.85	-	3	7	910.1	195	2729	114	23.94	6-23
1981-1986	Glamorgan	Nat West Trophy	E	3	2	0	6	4	3.00	-	-	2	30.2	8	70	4	17.50	2-19
1980-1986	Glamorgan	Benson & Hedges Cup	E	9	8	3	51	25	10.20	-	-	-	70	-	207	8	25.87	4-8
1980-1986	Glamorgan	Sunday League	E	17	9	3	50	20	8.33	-	-	1	107.4	-	389	23	16.91	4-22
1980//	Glamorgan	O.A.L. O.D. Matches	E	1	-	-	-	-	-	-	-	-	6.5	2	28	2	14.00	2-28
1980//	World XI	O.A.L. O.D. Matches	E	1	-	-	-	-	-	-	-	-	21	3	58	1	58.00	1-36
1984-1985	Eastern Province	First Class Matches	SA	9	12	2	115	40	11.50	-	-	2	291.3	90	665	34	19.55	5-48
1984-1985	Eastern Province	Nissan Shield	SA	1	1	0	16	16	16.00	-	-	-	12	-	32	2	16.00	2-32
1984-1985	Eastern Province	Benson & Hedges Cup	SA	7	6	1	64	15	12.80	-	-	3	58.4	-	219	15	14.60	4-41
1991-1992	Northern Transvaal	First Class Matches	SA	6	9	1	52	27	6.50	-	-	1	244.2	56	608	36	16.88	6-66
1991-1992	Northern Transvaal	Nissan Shield	SA	6	2	0	6	3	3.00	-	-	-	61	-	191	10	19.10	4-12
1991-1992	Northern Transvaal	Benson & Hedges Cup	SA	6	4	0	11	7	2.75	-	-	-	45.3	-	203	4	50.75	3-40
		Total First Class Career		76	100	18	1431	70*	17.45	0	4	21	2444.2	474	6506	279	23.31	6-23
		Total O.D. Career		83	55	14	389	63*	9.48	0	1	13	662.5	-	2466	106	23.26	4-8

GEORGE HORATIO MUDIE

D.O.B. 26.11.1915 - Spanish Town, St Catherine, Jamaica (d. 08.06.2002)

First Class Debut 27.02.1932 - Jamaica v L.H. Tennyson's XI
Test Match Debut 14.03.1935 - West Indies v England

Test 44-19

Teams Played For
Jamaica
West Indies
G.C. Grant's XI

3

RHB / SLA

SEASON	COMPETITION	TEAM	V	M	I	No	RUNS	H.S.	Av	100s	50s	CT	OV	MD	RUNS	W	Av	B.B.
							BATTING						**BOWLING**					
1932-1952	First Class Matches	Jamaica	II	17	28	5	565	94	24.56	-	4	11	499.3	71	1366	36	37.94	5-32
1934-1935	TEST MATCHES	WEST INDIES	H	1	1	0	5	5	5.00	-	-	-	29	12	40	3	13.33	2-23
1932-1933	First Class Matches	G.C. Grant's XI	WI	1	2	0	8	7	4.00	-	-	-	36	11	83	3	27.66	2-50
Total First Class Career				19	31	5	578	94	22.23	0	4	11	564.3	94	1489	42	35.45	5-32

DAVID ANTHONY MURRAY

D.O.B. 29.05.1950 - Murrays Gap, Westbury Road, St Michael, Barbados
First Class Debut 22.01.1971 - Barbados v Combined Islands
Test Match Debut 31.03.1978 - West Indies v Australia
O.D.I. Debut 07.09.1973 - West Indies v England
Domestic O.D. Debut 13.04.1973 - Barbados v Trinidad & Tobago

Test	167-181				4
O.D.I.	13-2		**Teams Played For**		RHB / WK
			Barbados		
			West Indies		
			W.I. President's XI		
			West Indies XI		

SEASON	TEAM	COMPETITION	V	M	I	No	RUNS	H.S.	Av	100s	50s	CT/ST	OV	MD	RUNS	W	Av	B.B.
							BATTING						BOWLING					
1971-1982	Barbados	First Class Matches	II	42	68	12	2136	143	38.14	4	12	104/10	-	-	-	-	-	-
1972-1982	Barbados	Domestic O.D. Matches	II	17	13	3	322	78	32.22	-	3	17/3	-	-	-	-	-	-
1981//	Barbados	O.A.L. O.D. Matches	WI	1	1	0	8	8	8.00	-	-	2	-	-	-	-	-	-
1973-1982	WEST INDIES	TEST MATCHES	HA	19	31	3	601	84	21.46	-	3	57/5	-	-	-	-	-	-
1973-1982	West Indies	First Class Matches	A	40	54	12	1340	206*	31.90	3	4	91/15	2	0	11	0	-	-
1973-1974	W.I. President's XI	First Class Matches	WI	2	4	0	81	28	20.25	-	-	2/1	-	-	-	-	-	-
1982-1984	West Indies	First Class Matches	A	11	19	3	345	43	21.56	-	-	39	-	-	-	-	-	-
1973-1982	WEST INDIES	O.D.I. MATCHES	HA	10	7	2	45	35	9.00	-	-	16	-	-	-	-	-	-
1982-1982	West Indies XI	O.D.(I.) Matches	WI	12	10	5	129	32*	25.80	-	-	23	-	-	-	-	-	-
1973-1980	West Indies	O.A.L. O.D. Matches	A	9	5	0	105	61	21.00	-	1	8	1.2	0	13	0	-	-
1982-1983	West Indies XI	O.A.L. O.D. Matches	A	1	1	1	18	18*	-	-	-	2	-	-	-	-	-	-
Total First Class Career				114	176	30	4503	206*	30.84	7	19	293/31	2	0	11	0	-	-
Total O.D. Career				50	37	11	627	78	24.11	0	4	68/3	1.2	0	13	0	-	-

DERYCK LANCE MURRAY

D.O.B. 20.05.1943 - Port of Spain, Trinidad

First Class Debut	07.04.1961 - Trinidad v E.W. Swantons XI
Test Match Debut	06.06.1963 - West Indies v England
O.D.I. Debut	05.09.1973 - West Indies v England
Domestic O.D. Debut	23.04.1967 - Nottinghamshire v Durham

Test 121-95
O.D.I. 9-1

Teams Played For 12
Trinidad & Tobago, N/E Trinidad, Warwickshire
West Indies, North Trinidad, World XI
Nottinghamshire, F.M. Worrell's XI
Cambridge University, W.I. President's XI
A.E.R. Gilligan's XI, M.C.C.

RHB / WK / LB

SEASON	TEAM	COMPETITION	V	M	I	No	BATTING RUNS	H.S.	Av	100s	50s	CT/ST	BOWLING OV	MD	RUNS	W	Av	B.B.
1961-1981	Trinidad & Tobago	First Class Matches	II	43	67	8	1902	148	32.23	3	11	64/30	5.4	0	39	1	39.00	1-13
1961-1977	North Trinidad	First Class Matches	T	4	6	2	98	43*	24.50	-	-	9	-	-	-	-	-	-
1977-1980	N/E Trinidad	First Class Matches	T	2	3	0	24	13	8.00	-	-	3/1	-	-	-	-	-	-
1972-1981	Trinidad & Tobago	Domestic O.D. Matches	II	13	11	2	152	36	16.88	-	-	20/3	-	-	-	-	-	-
1963-1980	WEST INDIES	TEST MATCHES	HA	62	96	9	1993	91	22.90	-	11	181/8	-	-	-	-	-	-
1963-1980	West Indies	First Class Matches	A	67	89	24	1869	103	28.75	1	10	124/28	25.4	4	114	2	57.00	2-50
1968//	W.I. President's XI	First Class Matches	WI	1	1	0	63	63	63.00	-	1	2	-	-	-	-	-	-
1964//	F.M. Worrell's XI	First Class Matches	WI	1	2	2	108	102*	-	1	-	4	-	-	-	-	-	-
1973-1980	WEST INDIES	O.D.I. MATCHES	HA	26	17	5	294	61*	24.50	-	2	37/1	-	-	-	-	-	-
1963-1981	West Indies	O.A.L. O.D. Matches	A	9	5	2	116	46*	38.66	-	-	3/2	-	-	-	-	-	-
1965-1966	Cambridge University	First Class Matches	E	24	45	2	1248	133	29.02	2	8	33/5	12	3	66	1	66.00	1-46
1966-1969	Nottinghamshire	First Class Matches	E	97	148	24	3873	166*	31.23	3	22	158/15	14	2	65	1	65.00	1-2
1967-1969	Nottinghamshire	Nat West Trophy	E	8	7	0	151	53	21.57	-	1	17/2	-	-	-	-	-	-
1969//	Nottinghamshire	Sunday League	E	15	13	2	200	58*	18.18	-	1	17	-	-	-	-	-	-
1972-1975	Warwickshire	First Class Matches	E	58	87	12	1773	78	23.64	-	5	136/15	25	8	83	0	-	-
1972-1975	Warwickshire	Nat West Trophy	E	7	6	2	137	72	34.25	-	1	10	-	-	-	-	-	-
1972-1975	Warwickshire	Benson & Hedges Cup	E	20	15	5	303	82	30.30	-	1	18/2	-	-	-	-	-	-
1972-1975	Warwickshire	Sunday League	E	47	38	12	585	65*	22.50	-	1	39/4	-	-	-	-	-	-
1966-1970	World XI	First Class Matches	E	5	8	1	283	95	40.42	-	2	20/2	-	-	-	-	-	-
1964//	M.C.C.	First Class Matches	E	2	2	1	57	52	57.00	-	1	6/2	-	-	-	-	-	-
1966//	A.E.R. Gilligan's XI	First Class Matches	E	1	D	-	-	-	-	-	-	0/2	-	-	-	-	-	-
Total First Class Career				367	554	85	13291	166*	28.33	10	71	740/108	82.2	17	367	5	73.40	2-50
Total O.D. Career				145	112	30	1938	82	23.63	0	7	164/14	-	-	-	-	-	-

JUNIOR RANDOLPH MURRAY

D.O.B. 20.01.1968 - River Road Village, St George, Grenada, Windward Islands
First Class Debut 21.03.1987 - Windward Islands v Barbados
Test Match Debut 02.01.1993 - West Indies v Australia
O.D.I. Debut 04.12.1992 - West Indies v Pakistan
Domestic O.D. Debut 27.01.1988 - Windward Islands v Leeward Islands

RHB / WK

Test	202-294	
O.D.I.	63-237	

Teams Played For 8
Windward Islands, Southern Windward
West Indies, W.I. President's XI
West Indies U23, West Indies "A"
West Indies "B"
W.I. Select XI

SEASON	TEAM	COMPETITION	V	M	I	No	RUNS	H.S.	Av	100s	50s	CT/ST	OV	MD	RUNS	W	Av	B.B.
1986-2003	Windward Islands	First Class Matches	I	75	141	13	4249	218	33.19	8	19	148/19	-	-	-	-	-	-
1987-2001	Windward Islands	Domestic O.D. Matches	I	38	33	6	606	100*	22.44	-	1	22/12	-	-	-	-	-	-
2001-2002	Southern Windwards	Domestic O.D. Matches	I	3	3	0	47	25	15.66	-	-	2/3	-	-	-	-	-	-

SEASON	TEAM	COMPETITION	V	M	I	No	RUNS	H.S.	Av	100s	50s	CT/ST	OV	MD	RUNS	W	Av	B.B.
1993-2002	WEST INDIES	TEST MATCHES	HA	33	45	4	918	101*	22.39	1	3	99/3	-	-	-	-	-	-
1992-1999	West Indies	First Class Matches	A	16	23	7	680	141*	42.50	2	1	25/3	-	-	-	-	-	-
1988-1991	West Indies U23	First Class Matches	WI	3	5	0	17	14	3.40	-	-	4/1	-	-	-	-	-	-
1996/i	W.I. President's XI	First Class Matches	WI	1	1	0	23	23	23.00	-	-	3	-	-	-	-	-	-
1992/i	West Indies "A"	First Class Matches	H	3	4	1	117	47*	39.00	-	-	11/0	-	-	-	-	-	-
1992-1998	WEST INDIES	O.D.I. MATCHES	HA	55	36	6	678	86	22.60	-	5	46/7	-	-	-	-	-	-
1989/i	West Indies "B"	O.D.(I.) MATCHES	A	1	D	-	-	-	-	-	-	-	-	-	-	-	-	-
1999/i	W.I. Select XI	O.D.I.(I.) Matches	WI	2	2	0	25	25	12.50	-	-	3	-	-	-	-	-	-
1992-1996	West Indies	O.A.L. O.D. Matches	A	5	5	0	87	31	17.40	-	-	4/3	-	-	-	-	-	-
	Total First Class Career			131	219	25	6004	218	30.94	11	23	290/26	-	-	-	-	-	-
	Total O.D. Career			104	79	12	1443	100*	21.53	1	5	77/25	-	-	-	-	-	-

MAHENDRA VEREEN NAGAMOOTOO

D.O.B. 09.10.1975 - Whim Village, Berbice, Guyana

First Class Debut	27.01.1995 - Guyana v Trinidad & Tobago
Test Match Debut	31.08.2000 - West Indies v England
O.D.I. Debut	16.07.2000 - West Indies v Zimbabwe
Domestic O.D. Debut	26.11.1995 - Guyana v Trinidad & Tobago

Test 235-364
O.D.I. 100-405

Teams Played For
Guyana
West Indies
West Indies "A"
W.I. Board XI
W.I. Select XI

LHB / LBG

5

SEASON	TEAM	COMPETITION	V	M	I	No	BATTING RUNS	H.S.	Av	100s	50s	CT	BOWLING OV	MD	RUNS	W	Av	B.B.
1995-2003	Guyana	First Class Matches	II	57	87	10	1241	68	16.11	-	3	48	2417.2	531	6318	239	26.43	7-76
1995-2002	Guyana	Domestic O.D. Matches	II	38	16	4	190	63	15.83	-	1	17	371.2	46	1099	61	18.01	5-23
1999//	Guyana	O.A.L. O.D. Matches	WI	1	1	0	7	7	7.00	-	-	-	10	0	33	0	-	-
2000-2002	WEST INDIES	TEST MATCHES	HA	5	8	1	185	68	26.42	-	1	2	249	70	637	12	53.08	3-119
2000-2002	West Indies	First Class Matches	A	11	18	4	440	100	31.42	1	-	3	337	85	902	21	42.95	4-12
2000//	West Indies "A"	First Class Matches	HA	1	2	0	65	59	32.50	-	1	2	28	5	84	3	28.00	2-18
1996//	W.I. Board XI	First Class Matches	WI	1	2	0	59	38	29.50	-	-	-	33	3	102	3	34.00	2-42
2000-2002	WEST INDIES	O.D.I. MATCHES	HA	24	18	6	162	33	13.50	-	-	6	198.1	4	998	18	55.44	4-32
1996-1999	West Indies "A"	O.D.(I.) Matches	HA	5	4	3	16	11*	16.00	-	-	2	33	0	125	6	20.83	4-31
2000//	W.I. Select XI	O.D.(I.) Matches	WI	1	1	1	32	32*	-	-	-	-	7	0	29	1	29.00	1-29
1996//	West Indies "A"	O.A.L. O.D. Matches	A	1	D	-	-	-	-	-	-	-	10	3	30	2	15.00	2-30
2000-2001	West Indies	O.A.L. O.D. Matches	A	4	3	1	50	43	25.00	-	-	-	39	3	166	7	23.71	4-49
Total First Class Career				75	117	15	1990	100	19.50	1	5	55	3064.2	694	8043	278	28.93	7-76
Total O.D. Career				74	43	15	457	63	16.32	0	1	25	614.3	56	2480	96	25.83	5-23

RANGIE NANAN

D.O.B. 29.05.1953 - Prysal Village, Trinidad
First Class Debut 19.01.1973 - Central Trinidad v East Trinidad
Test Match Debut 08.12.1980 - West Indies v Pakistan
Domestic O.D. Debut 18.01.1977 - Trinidad & Tobago v Jamaica

Test 174-202

Teams Played For
Trinidad & Tobago
Central Trinidad
S/C Trinidad
West Indies

4

RHB / OB

SEASON	TEAM	COMPETITION	V	M	I	No	BATTING RUNS	H.S.	Av	100s	50s	CT	BOWLING OV	MD	RUNS	W	Av	B.B.
1973-1991	Trinidad & Tobago	First Class Matches	II	72	112	17	2102	125	22.12	1	7	34	3230.1	912	6994	272	25.71	7-109
1973-1979	Central Trinidad	First Class Matches	T	13	17	0	237	49	13.94	-	-	16	392.2	112	794	57	13.92	6-15
1976-1985	S/C Trinidad	First Class Matches	T	5	8	1	197	75*	28.14	-	2	8	155.1	34	378	19	19.89	4-63
1977-1991	Trinidad & Tobago	Domestic O.D. Matches	II	34	23	3	198	39	9.90	-	-	12	282.3	32	904	44	20.54	4-36
1991//	Trinidad & Tobago	O.A.L. O.D. Matches	WI	1	1	0	3	3	3.00	-	-	-	10	0	44	1	44.00	1-44
1980//	WEST INDIES	TEST MATCHES	A	1	2	0	16	8	8.00	-	-	2	36	7	91	4	22.75	2-37
1980//	West Indies	First Class Matches	A	3	4	0	55	32	13.75	-	-	1	74	18	200	14	14.28	6-48
Total First Class Career				94	143	18	2607	125	20.85	1	9	61	3887.4	1083	8457	366	23.10	7-109
Total O.D. Career				35	24	3	201	39	9.57	0	0	12	292.3	32	948	45	21.06	4-36

411

JAMES MONTAGUE NEBLETT

D.O.B. 13.11.1901 - Taylors Land, St Michael, Barbados (d. 28.03.1959)
First Class Debut 09.02.1926 - British Guiana v M.C.C.
Test Match Debut 14.02.1935 - West Indies v England

Test 41-18

Teams Played For
British Guiana
Barbados XI
Combined J/B XI
West Indies

RHB / LBG

4

SEASON	TEAM	COMPETITION	V	M	I	No	BATTING RUNS	H.S.	Av	100s	50s	CT	BOWLING OV	MD	RUNS	W	Av	B.B.
1926-1939	British Guiana	First Class Matches	=	7	11	1	201	36	20.10	-	-	6	170.5	34	472	12	39.33	3-39
1927-1928	Barbados XI	First Class Matches	=	1	2	1	30	23*	30.00	-	-	-	37	7	114	4	28.50	4-82
1934-1935	WEST INDIES	TEST MATCHES	H	1	2	1	16	11*	16.00	-	-	-	36	11	75	1	75.00	1-44
1926-1928	West Indies	First Class Matches	HA	9	14	1	181	61	13.92	-	1	9	131	24	429	9	47.66	2-22
1927-1928	Combined J/B XI	First Class Matches	WI	2	4	1	98	59	32.66	-	1	1	37	6	115	3	38.33	2-64
		Total First Class Career		20	33	5	526	61	18.78	0	2	16	407.5	82	1205	29	41.55	4-82

412

JACK MOLLISON NOREIGA

D.O.B. 15.04.1936 - St. Joseph, Trinidad
First Class Debut 09.02.1962 - Trinidad v India
Test Match Debut 18.02.1971 - West Indies v India

Test	136-129	Teams Played For	4	RHB / OB
		Trinidad & Tobago		
		North Trinidad		
		East Trinidad		
		West Indies		

| | | | | | | | BATTING | | | | | | BOWLING | | | | | |
SEASON	TEAM	COMPETITION	V	M	I	No	RUNS	H.S.	Av	100s	50s	CT	OV	MD	RUNS	W	Av	B.B.
1962-1972	Trinidad & Tobago	First Class Matches	=	9	10	3	42	13	6.00	-	-	-	381.5	98	922	25	36.88	6-67
1962-1969	North Trinidad	First Class Matches	T	2	3	0	15	9	5.00	-	-	1	90	40	164	9	18.22	3-32
1971-1975	East Trinidad	First Class Matches	T	6	10	3	113	25	16.14	-	-	1	185.4	49	439	17	25.82	4-64
1970-1971	WEST INDIES	TEST MATCHES	H	4	5	2	11	9	3.66	-	-	2	220.2	47	493	17	29.00	9-95
	Total First Class Career			21	28	8	181	25	9.05	0	0	4	877.5	187	2018	68	29.67	9-95

ROBERT KARL NUNES

D.O.B. 07.06.1894 - Kingston, Jamaica (d. 22.07.1958)

First Class Debut 19.05.1923 - West Indies v Cambridge University

Test Match Debut 23.06.1928 - West Indies v England

Test 4-1

Teams Played For
Jamaica
West Indies

LHB / WK

TEAM									
Jamaica									2

BATTING

SEASON	COMPETITION	V	M	I	No	RUNS	H.S.	Av	100s	50s	CT/ST
1925-1932	First Class Matches	II	18	28	3	1263	200*	50.52	5	3	15/8
1928-1930	TEST MATCHES	HA	4	8	0	245	92	30.62	-	2	2
1923-1930	First Class Matches	HA	39	58	5	1187	127*	22.39	1	6	14
	Total First Class Career		61	94	8	2695	200*	31.33	6	11	31/8

BOWLING

	OV	MD	RUNS	W	Av	B.B.
	26	2	83	3	27.66	2-49
	-	-	-	-	-	-
	-	-	-	-	-	-
	26	2	83	3	27.66	2-49

SEYMOUR MACDONALD NURSE

D.O.B. 10.11.1933 - Jack-My-Nanny Gap, Black Rock, St Michael, Barbados
First Class Debut 19.07.1958 - Barbados v Jamaica
Test Match Debut 17.02.1960 - West Indies v England
Domestic O.D. Debut 14.04.1973 - Barbados v Trinidad & Tobago

Test 110-82

Teams Played For
Barbados, West Indies
C.C. Hunte's XI, The Rest XI
World XI, Commonwealth XI
Indian Prime Minister's XI
E.W. Swanton's XI

8   RHB / OB

SEASON	TEAM	COMPETITION	V	M	I	No	BATTING RUNS	H.S.	Av	100s	50s	CT	BOWLING OV	MD	RUNS	W	Av	B.B.
1958-1972	Barbados	First Class Matches	=	41	66	7	3049	213	51.67	10	12	42	15	2	51	2	25.50	1-0
1972-1973	Barbados	Domestic O.D. Matches	=	2	2	0	35	21	17.50	-	1	1	-	-	-	-	-	-
1969	Barbados	O.A.L. O.D. Matches	A	1	1	0	36	36	36.00	-	-	1	-	-	-	-	-	-
WEST INDIES	**TEST MATCHES**																	
1960-1969	West Indies	First Class Matches	HA	29	51	1	2523	258	47.60	6	10	21	7	4	7	0	-	-
1960-1969	West Indies	First Class Matches	A	55	89	6	2850	155	34.33	6	13	45	25.5	5	109	6	18.16	3-36
1964//	C.C. Hunte's XI	First Class Matches	WI	1	1	1	65	65*	-	-	1	-	4	0	44	0	-	-
1964//	The Rest XI	First Class Matches	WI	1	2	0	27	20	13.50	-	1	1	10	0	85	2	42.50	2-41
1963-1966	West Indies	O.A.L. O.D. Matches	A	3	3	1	175	102*	87.50	1	1	-	6	0	41	2	20.50	1-19
1967-1968	World XI	First Class Matches	E	11	11	1	275	121	27.50	1	2	2	3	2	0	0	-	-
1963-1964	Commonwealth XI	First Class Matches	P	6	11	2	369	126*	14.00	1	4	4	23	3	91	2	45.50	1-6
1963-1964	Indian PM's XI	First Class Matches	I	1	1	0	90	78	45.00	-	1	-	-	-	-	-	-	-
1963-1964	E.W. Swanton's XI	First Class Matches	I	1	2	1	241	135*	241.00	2	-	-	-	-	-	-	-	-
Total First Class Career				141	235	19	9489	258	43.93	26	40	116	87.5	16	389	12	32.41	3-36
Total O.D. Career				6	6	1	246	102*	49.20	1	1	2	6	0	41	2	20.50	1-19

ALBERT LEROY PADMORE

D.O.B. 17.12.1946 - Halls Village, St James, Barbados

First Class Debut 19.01.1973 - Barbados v Jamaica
Test Match Debut 07.04.1976 - West Indies v India
Domestic O.D. Debut 26.01.1977 - Barbados v Guyana

Test 155-167

Teams Played For
Barbados
West Indies
W.I. President's XI
West Indies XI

4

RHB / OB

SEASON	TEAM	COMPETITION	V	M	I	No	BATTING RUNS	H.S.	Av	100s	50s	CT	BOWLING OV	MD	RUNS	W	Av	B.B.
1973-1982	Barbados	First Class Matches	=	34	36	12	369	79	15.37	-	2	16	1030.4	263	2441	82	29.76	5-42
1977-1982	Barbados	Domestic O.D. Matches	=	13	8	2	35	23	5.83	-	-	4	97.4	6	308	16	19.27	3-24
1981//	Barbados	O.A.L. O.D. Matches	WI	1	1	0	13	13	13.00	-	-	-	9	1	58	0	-	-
1976//	WEST INDIES	TEST MATCHES	H	2	2	1	8	8*	8.00	-	-	-	79	23	135	1	135.00	1-36
1974-1976	West Indies	First Class Matches	A	28	23	8	160	30	10.66	-	-	10	877.4	243	2741	102	26.87	6-69
1974//	W.I. President's XI	First Class Matches	WI	1	2	0	7	7	3.50	-	-	1	61.3	10	186	3	62.00	2-149
1983-1984	West Indies XI	First Class Matches	A	3	3	2	18	9*	18.00	-	-	2	108	20	277	5	55.40	3-103
1975//	West Indies	O.A.L. O.D. Matches	A	2	1	1	4	4*	-	-	-	1	18.4	0	78	2	39.00	2-33
1983-1984	West Indies XI	O.D.(I.) Matches	A	1	D	-	-	-	-	-	-	-	9.4	0	55	1	55.00	1-55
1982-1983	West Indies XI	O.A.L. O.D. Matches	A	1	1	1	7	7*	-	-	-	-	10	1	19	1	19.00	1-19
Total First Class Career				68	66	23	562	79	13.06	0	2	29	2156.5	559	5780	193	29.94	6-69
Total O.D. Career				18	11	4	59	23	8.42	0	0	5	145	8	518	20	25.90	3-24

BRUCE HAMILTON PAIRAUDEAU

D.O.B. 14.04.1931 - Georgetown, Demerara, British Guiana
First Class Debut 15.03.1947 - British Guiana v Trinidad
Test Match Debut 21.01.1953 - West Indies v India

Test 76-43

Teams Played For
British Guiana
West Indies
Commonwealth XI
Northern Districts

4

RHB / LBG

SEASON	TEAM	COMPETITION	V	M	I	No	BATTING RUNS	H.S.	Av	100s	50s	CT	BOWLING OV	MD	RUNS	W	Av	B.B.
1947-1958	British Guiana	First Class Matches	II	18	32	2	1403	161	46.76	6	3	16	5	0	47	0	-	-
1953-1957	WEST INDIES	TEST MATCHES	HA	13	21	-	454	115	21.61	1	3	6	1	0	3	0	-	-
1955-1957	West Indies	First Class Matches	A	18	32	-	947	163	29.59	3	3	9	-	-	-	-	-	-
1958-1967	North Districts	First Class Matches	NZ	39	73	3	2106	102	30.08	1	16	33	5.4	0	32	0	-	-
1950//	Commonwealth XI	First Class Matches	E	1	1	-	20	20	20.00	-	-	-	-	-	-	-	-	-
Total First Class Career				89	159	5	4930	163	32.01	11	25	64	11.4	0	82	0	-	-

DERICK RECALDO PARRY

D.O.B. 22.12.1954 - Cotton Ground, Nevis, Leeward Islands

First Class Debut	05.01.1976 – Leeward Islands v Windward Islands
Test Match Debut	03.03.1978 - West Indies v Australia
O.D.I. Debut	12.04.1978 - West Indies v Australia
Domestic O.D. Debut	18.01.1977 - Leeward Islands v Guyana

Test 164-179   O.D.I. 30-14

Teams Played For
Leeward Islands
Combined Islands
West Indies
West Indies XI
Cambridgeshire

RHB / OB   5

SEASON	TEAM	COMPETITION	V	M	I	No	BATTING RUNS	H.S.	Av	100s	50s	CT	BOWLING OV	MD	RUNS	W	Av	B.B.
1976-1982	Leeward Islands	First Class Matches	=	12	22	3	393	85	20.68	-	1	12	442.5	92	1309	39	33.56	5-57
1977-1981	Combined Islands	First Class Matches	=	20	29	2	812	96	30.07	-	6	23	948.3	249	2272	92	24.69	9-76
1977-1982	Leeward Islands	Domestic O.D. Matches	=	14	10	3	138	32	19.71	-	-	4	129	21	346	18	19.22	4-5
1978-1980	WEST INDIES	TEST MATCHES	HA	12	20	3	381	65	22.41	-	3	4	318.1	65	936	23	40.69	5-15
1978-1980	West Indies	First Class Matches	A	26	35	13	677	72	30.77	-	2	6	721.3	166	2128	77	27.63	5-48
1982-1984	West Indies XI	First Class Matches	A	7	13	3	289	63	28.90	-	2	5	233	50	623	20	31.15	5-117
1978-1980	WEST INDIES	O.D.I. MATCHES	HA	6	5	1	61	32	15.25	-	-	8	55	2	259	11	23.54	3-47
1982-1983	West Indies XI	O.D.(I.) Matches	A	3	3	0	4	4	1.33	-	-	-	21	4	71	2	35.50	2-38
1979-1980	West Indies	O.A.L. O.D. Matches	A	7	6	3	59	17	19.66	-	-	2	38	-	178	8	22.25	5-34
1982-1983	West Indies XI	O.A.L. O.D. Matches	A	2	2	0	4	2	2.00	-	-	-	10	1	43	0	-	-
1982-1986	Cambridgeshire	Nat West Trophy	E	3	3	0	70	43	23.33	-	-	-	36	2	121	0	-	-
		Total First Class Career		77	119	24	2552	96	26.86	0	14	50	2664	622	7268	251	28.95	9-76
		Total O.D. Career		35	29	7	336	43	15.27	0	0	14	289	-	1018	39	26.10	5-34

CLARENCE CHARLES PASSAILAIGUE

D.O.B. 04.08.1901 - Kingston, Jamaica (d. 07.01.1972)
First Class Debut 28.03.1930 - Jamaica v M.C.C.
Test Match Debut 03.04.1930 - West Indies v England

Test 29-7

Teams Played For 3
Jamaica
West Indies
G.C. Grant's XI

RHB / RM

SEASON	TEAM	COMPETITION	V	M	I	No	RUNS	H.S.	Av	100s	50s	CT	OV	MD	RUNS	W	Av	B.B.
1930-1939	Jamaica	First Class Matches	II	10	14	2	733	261*	61.08	2	2	8	8	1	41	1	41.00	1-22
1929-1930	WEST INDIES	TEST MATCHES	H	1	2	1	46	44	46.00	-	-	3	2	0	15	0	-	-
1932-1933	G.C. Grant's XI	First Class Matches	WI	1	2	0	9	9	4.50	-	-	-	-	-	-	-	-	-
Total First Class Career				12	18	3	788	261*	52.53	2	2	11	10	1	56	1	56.00	1-22

BATTING · **BOWLING**

BELFOUR PATRICK PATTERSON

D.O.B. 15.09.1961 - Happy Grove, Williamsfield, Portland, Jamaica

First Class Debut 11.02.1983 - Jamaica v Leeward Islands
Test Match Debut 21.02.1986 - West Indies v England
O.D.I. Debut 18.02.1986 - West Indies v England
Domestic O.D. Debut 19.01.1983 - Jamaica v Trinidad & Tobago

Test 186-242
O.D.I. 47-115

Teams Played For
Jamaica, West Indies
W.I. President's XI
W.I. Board XI
Lancashire
Tasmania

RHB / RF
6

SEASON	TEAM	COMPETITION	V	M	I	No	BATTING						BOWLING					
							RUNS	H.S.	Av	100s	50s	CT	OV	MD	RUNS	W	Av	B.B.
1983-1992	Jamaica	First Class Matches	II	23	33	10	106	19	4.60	-	-	7	554.2	91	1836	83	22.12	7-24
1983-1998	Jamaica	Domestic O.D. Matches	II	18	5	2	29	16	9.66	-	-	4	158.4	23	546	30	18.20	4-13
1984//	Jamaica	O.A.L. O.D. Matches	WI	1	D	-	-	-	-	-	-	-	5	0	26	0	-	-
1986-1993	WEST INDIES	TEST MATCHES	HA	28	38	16	145	21*	6.59	-	-	5	804.5	108	2874	93	30.90	5-24
1986-1993	West Indies	First Class Matches	A	27	19	4	130	23*	8.66	-	-	7	540	111	1751	65	26.93	5-39
1990-1991	W.I. President's XI	First Class Matches	WI	2	4	2	23	11	11.50	-	-	-	74.5	16	200	8	25.00	4-62
1988-1989	W.I. Board XI	First Class Matches	WI	1	D	-	-	-	-	-	-	-	19	3	47	5	9.40	5-47
1986-1993	WEST INDIES	O.D.I. MATCHES	HA	59	20	15	44	13*	8.80	-	-	9	508.2	37	2206	90	24.51	6-29
1988-1991	West Indies	O.A.L. O.D. Matches	A	5	2	2	6	5*	-	-	-	-	40	-	169	6	28.16	4-35
1984-1990	Lancashire	First Class Matches	E	70	61	24	187	29	5.05	-	-	12	1689.3	280	5496	202	27.20	7-49
1984-1987	Lancashire	Nat West Trophy	E	2	2	1	4	4	4.00	-	-	-	24	1	120	1	120.00	1-69
1985-1990	Lancashire	Benson & Hedges Cup	E	7	2	2	18	15*	-	-	-	1	62.1	-	181	7	25.85	3-31
1985-1990	Lancashire	Sunday League	E	5	2	2	5	3*	-	-	-	1	30.2	-	153	5	30.60	3-25
1990//	Lancashire	O.A.L. O.D. Matches	E	1	D	-	-	-	-	-	-	-	4	-	23	1	23.00	1-23
1984-1985	Tasmania	First Class Matches	A	10	9	2	27	12	3.85	-	-	1	376	51	1359	37	36.72	5-67
1984-1985	Tasmania	MacDonald Cup	A	2	2	1	0	0*	0.00	-	-	-	21.4	-	72	4	18.00	-
Total First Class Career				161	164	58	618	29	5.83	0	0	32	4058.4	660	13563	493	27.51	7-24
Total O.D. Career				100	35	25	106	16	10.60	0	0	15	854.1	-	3496	144	24.27	6-29

420

THELSTON RODNEY O'NEAL PAYNE

D.O.B. 13.02.1957 - Foul Bay, St Philip, Barbados
First Class Debut 16.03.1979 - Barbados v Jamaica
Test Match Debut 07.03.1986 - West Indies v England
O.D.I. Debut 19.04.1984 - West Indies v Australia
Domestic O.D. Debut 23.03.1979 - Barbados v Leeward Islands

Test 187-243
O.D.I. 44-81

Teams Played For 4
Barbados
West Indies
West Indies "B"
W.I. President's XI

LHB / WK

SEASON	TEAM	COMPETITION	V	M	I	No	RUNS	H.S.	Av	100s	50s	CT/st	OV	MD	RUNS	W	Av	B.B.
1979-1990	Barbados	First Class Matches	=	49	79	10	2862	140	14.47	6	21	74/7	-	-	-	-	-	-
1979-1990	Barbados	Domestic O.D. Matches	=	25	24	5	565	100*	29.73	1	2	18/1	-	-	-	-	-	-
1986//	WEST INDIES	TEST MATCHES	H	1	1	0	5	5	5.00	-	-	5	-	-	-	-	-	-
1984-1986	West Indies	First Class Matches	A	14	18	4	409	60*	29.21	-	3	18/1	-	-	-	-	-	-
1981-1988	W.I. President's XI	First Class Matches	WI	3	6	0	71	56	11.83	-	1	5	-	-	-	-	-	-
1983-1994	West Indies "B"	First Class Matches	A	1	2	0	44	28	22.00	-	-	1	-	-	-	-	-	-
1984-1986	WEST INDIES	O.D.I. MATCHES	HA	7	4	0	126	60	31.50	-	1	6	-	-	-	-	-	-
1983-1984	West Indies "B"	O.D.(I.) Matches	A	4	4	1	58	28	19.33	-	-	5/1	-	-	-	-	-	-
1984-1987	West Indies	O.A.L. O.D. Matches	A	2	2	1	46	38	46.00	-	-	1/1	-	-	-	-	-	-
Total First Class Career				68	106	14	3391	140	36.85	6	25	103/8	-	-	-	-	-	-
Total O.D. Career				38	34	7	795	100*	29.44	1	3	30/3	-	-	-	-	-	-

421

NEHEMIAH ODOLPHUS PERRY

D.O.B. 16.06.1968 - St Andrew, Kingston, Jamaica

First Class Debut	28.03.1987 - Jamaica v Lancashire
Test Match Debut	13.03.1999 - West Indies v Australia
O.D.I. Debut	11.04.1999 - West Indies v Australia
Domestic O.D. Debut	06.02.1992 - Jamaica v Trinidad & Tobago

Test 228-350
O.D.I. 93-361

Teams Played For
Jamaica, West Indies
West Indies "B", W.I. Board XI
W.I. President's XI, West Indies "A"
West Indies U23
W.I. Select XI

8

RHB / OB

							BATTING						BOWLING					
SEASON	TEAM	COMPETITION	V	M	I	No	RUNS	H.S.	Av	100s	50s	CT	OV	MD	RUNS	W	Av	B.B.
1987-2003	Jamaica	First Class Matches	II	77	117	14	2156	160	20.93	1	11	47	2517.3	669	5699	242	23.54	8-45
1992-2000	Jamaica	Domestic O.D. Matches	II	34	22	4	290	56	16.11	-	1	16	278	37	937	29	32.31	4-45
1998//	Jamaica	O.A.L. O.D. Matches	S	3	2	0	7	6	3.50	-	-	1	30	6	67	1	67.00	1-17
1999-2000	WEST INDIES	TEST MATCHES	HA	4	7	1	74	26	12.33	-	-	1	134	24	446	10	44.60	5-70
1999-2000	West Indies	First Class Matches	A	3	2	0	37	25	18.50	-	-	1	73.3	18	184	9	20.44	5-84
1989-1991	West Indies U23	First Class Matches	WI	3	5	0	37	22	7.40	-	-	1	127.5	24	364	10	36.40	3-51
1989//	West Indies "B"	First Class Matches	A	3	3	0	18	15	6.00	-	-	2	71	24	146	4	36.50	3-61
1989-1994	W.I. President's XI	First Class Matches	WI	2	2	0	38	32	19.00	-	1	2	78	13	219	5	43.80	3-91
1995//	W.I. Board XI	First Class Matches	WI	1	2	1	75	57	75.00	-	1	-	17	0	81	0	-	-
1992//	West Indies "A"	First Class Matches	WI	2	2	0	8	7	4.00	-	-	4	61.1	22	137	10	13.70	5-47
1999-2000	WEST INDIES	O.D.I. MATCHES	HA	21	16	8	212	52*	26.50	-	1	4	157.4	2	783	20	39.15	3-45
1989//	West Indies "B"	O.D.(I.) Matches	A	4	1	0	1	1	1.00	-	-	1	39	1	173	3	57.66	1-31
1999-2000	W.I. Select XI	O.D.(I.) Matches	WI	1	1	0	0	0	0.00	-	-	-	10	0	33	0	-	-
Total First Class Career				95	140	16	2443	160	19.70	1	12	54	3080	796	7276	290	25.08	8-45
Total O.D. Career				63	42	12	510	56	17.00	0	2	22	514.4	46	1993	53	37.60	4-45

NORBERT PHILLIP

D.O.B.	12.06.1948 - Bioche Village, Dominica, Windward Islands
First Class Debut	07.04.1970 - Windward Islands v Glamorgan
Test Match Debut	31.03.1978 - West Indies v Australia
O.D.I. Debut	12.04.1978 - West Indies v Australia
Domestic O.D. Debut	19.02.1976 - Windward Islands v Guyana

Test	168-181	Teams Played For	5
O.D.I.	31-14	Windward Islands	
		Combined Islands	
		West Indies	
		W.I. President's XI	
		Essex	

RHB / RFM

SEASON	TEAM	COMPETITION	V	BATTING									BOWLING					
				M	I	No	RUNS	H.S.	Av	100s	50s	CT	OV	MD	RUNS	W	Av	B.B.
1970-1985	Windward Islands	First Class Matches	=	39	60	4	1626	96	29.03	-	11	12	948.1	178	2736	114	24.00	7-33
1971-1980	Combined Islands	First Class Matches	=	31	50	6	1143	99	25.97	-	10	12	825.4	191	2238	106	21.11	5-43
1976-1985	Windward Islands	Domestic O.D. Matches	=	17	15	1	428	71	30.57	-	3	2	136	11	493	20	24.65	3-40
1972//	Windward Islands	O.A.L. O.D. Matches	WI	1	1	0	11	11	11.00	-	-	-	8	1	34	1	34.00	1-34
1973-1974	Combined Islands	O.A.L. O.D. Matches	WI	1	1	0	7	7	7.00	-	-	1	10	0	41	3	13.66	3-41
1978-1979	WEST INDIES	TEST MATCHES	HA	9	15	5	297	47	29.70	-	-	5	303.2	46	1041	28	37.17	4-48
1978-1979	West Indies	First Class Matches	A	5	5	0	90	47	18.00	-	-	-	99.3	27	273	14	19.50	5-34
1973-1977	W.I. President's XI	First Class Matches	WI	2	3	0	73	35	24.33	-	1	-	29.1	3	106	3	35.33	2-61
1978//	WEST INDIES	O.D.I. MATCHES	H	1	1	0	0	0	0.00	-	-	-	7	0	22	1	22.00	1-22
1979//	West Indies	O.A.L. O.D. Matches	A	3	2	0	23	17	11.50	-	-	-	25	-	81	3	27.00	2-30
1978-1985	Essex	First Class Matches	E	144	201	22	3784	134	21.13	1	18	45	3477.1	644	10638	423	25.14	6-4
1978-1984	Essex	Nat West Trophy	E	15	15	2	201	45	15.46	-	-	2	129	16	473	21	22.52	4-26
1978-1985	Essex	Benson & Hedges Cup	E	32	20	7	232	33*	17.84	-	2	2	306.4	-	1113	44	25.29	4-32
1978-1985	Essex	Sunday League	E	111	98	19	1515	95	19.17	-	6	20	719	-	2879	134	21.48	6-13
1978-1984	Essex	O.A.L. O.D. Matches	E	1	1	0	33	33	33.00	-	-	-	5	-	25	0	-	-
	Total First Class Career			230	334	37	7013	134	23.61	1	39	75	5683	1089	17032	688	24.75	7-33
	Total O.D. Career			182	154	29	2450	95	19.60	0	9	27	1345.4	-	5161	227	22.73	6-13

LANCELOT RICHARD PIERRE

D.O.B. 05.06.1921 - Woodbrook, Port of Spain, Trinidad (d. 14.04.1989)
First Class Debut 01.02.1941 - Trinidad v Barbados
Test Match Debut 03.03.1948 - West Indies v England

Test 62-25

Teams Played For
Trinidad
West Indies

RHB / RFM
2

SEASON	TEAM	COMPETITION	V	M	I	No	BATTING RUNS	H.S.	Av	100s	50s	CT	BOWLING OV	MD	RUNS	W	Av	B.B.
1941-1950	Trinidad	First Class Matches	=	22	28	13	129	23	8.60	-	-	9	492.1	54	1937	78	24.83	6-47
1947-1948	WEST INDIES	TEST MATCHES	H	1	0	-	-	-	-	-	-	-	7	0	28	0	-	-
1950//	West Indies	First Class Matches	A	12	7	1	2	1	0.33	-	-	5	204	39	557	24	23.20	8-51
		Total First Class Career		35	35	14	131	23	6.23	0	0	14	703.1	93	2522	102	24.72	8-51

DAREN BRENT-LYLE POWELL

D.O.B. 15.04.1978 - Malvern, St Elizabeth, Jamaica
First Class Debut 19.01.2001 - Jamaica v Leeward Islands
Test Match Debut 21.06.2002 - West Indies v New Zealand
O.D.I. Debut 03.12.2002 - West Indies v Bangladesh
Domestic O.D. Debut 15.08.2002 - Jamaica v Leeward Islands

		RHB / RFM
Test 243-387	**Teams Played For**	5
O.D.I. 111-460	Jamaica	
	West Indies	
	West Indies "A"	
	Busta Cup XI	
	W.I. President's XI	

SEASON	TEAM	COMPETITION	V	M	I	No	BATTING RUNS	H.S.	Av	100s	50s	CT	BOWLING OV	MD	RUNS	W	Av	B.B.
2001-2003	Jamaica	First Class Matches	II	19	22	5	232	38	13.64	-	-	5	429.2	94	1328	52	25.53	5-28
2002/I	Jamaica	Domestic O.D. Matches	II	6	2	0	4	3	2.00	-	-	-	47.1	8	179	13	13.76	5-23
2001-2003	WEST INDIES	TEST MATCHES	HA	4	5	0	19	16	3.80	-	-	1	128.2	27	354	12	29.50	3-36
2001-2002	West Indies	First Class Matches	A	1	1	0	0	0	0.00	-	-	2	18	1	85	0	-	-
2002/I	Busta Cup XI	First Class Matches	WI	1	1	0	0	0	0.00	-	-	1	25	6	48	1	48.00	1-16
2002/I	West Indies "A"	First Class Matches	A	3	3	1	19	11	9.50	-	-	2	81	19	303	10	30.30	3-55
2002-2003	WEST INDIES	O.D.I. MATCHES	A	2	D	-	-	-	-	-	-	-	19	2	71	1	71.00	1-34
2002/I	West Indies "A"	O.A.L. O.D. Matches	A	2	1	0	2	2	2.00	-	-	-	20	2	81	2	40.50	2-36
2002-2003	W.I. President's XI	First Class Matches	WI	1	1	0	0	0	0.00	-	-	-	27	6	78	1	78.00	1-50
Total First Class Career				29	33	6	270	38	10.00	0	0	12	708.4	153	2196	76	28.89	5-28
Total O.D. Career				10	3	0	6	3	2.00	0	0	0	86.1	12	331	16	20.68	5-23

RICARDO LLOYD POWELL

D.O.B. 16.12.1978 - St Elizabeth, Jamaica

First Class Debut	09.01.1998 - Jamaica v Barbados
Test Match Debut	16.12.1999 - West Indies v New Zealand
O.D.I. Debut	05.09.1999 - West Indies v India
Domestic O.D. Debut	04.10.1997 - Jamaica v Windward Islands

Test 231-353
O.D.I. 94-368

Teams Played For 6
Jamaica, UWI Vice Chancellor's XI
West Indies
West Indies "A"
W.I. Board XI
W.I. Select XI

RHB / OB

							BATTING						BOWLING					
SEASON	TEAM	COMPETITION	V	M	I	No	RUNS	H.S.	Av	100s	50s	CT	OV	MD	RUNS	W	Av	B.B.
1998-2003	Jamaica	First Class Matches	II	20	34	2	857	114*	26.78	1	4	16	180.2	57	385	10	38.50	3-75
1999-2002	Jamaica	Domestic O.D. Matches	II	14	12	5	171	29*	24.42	-	-	7	44.3	1	198	11	18.00	3-27
2001//	Jamaica	O.A.L. O.D. Matches	WI	1	1	0	52	52	52.00	-	1	1	8	0	22	0	-	-
1999-2000	WEST INDIES	TEST MATCHES	HA	1	2	0	30	30	15.00	-	-	1	5	2	13	0	-	-
1999-2000	West Indies	First Class Matches	A	3	4	0	133	86	33.25	-	1	3	1	0	4	0	-	-
1999-2000	West Indies "A"	First Class Matches	H	3	5	0	59	43	11.80	-	-	1	1	0	3	0	-	-
1999-2001	W.I. Board XI	First Class Matches	WI	2	2	0	47	47	23.50	-	-		21	1	62	0	-	-
1999-2003	WEST INDIES	O.D.I. MATCHES	HA	74	68	10	1515	124	26.12	1	6	33	36.3	3	230	6	38.33	2-5
2001//	West Indies	O.A.L. O.D. Matches	A	1	1	0	0	0	0.00	-	-	2					-	-
1999-2000	W.I. Select XI	O.D.(I.) Matches	WI	2	2	0	13	13	6.50	-	-	1	3	0	22	0	-	-
2002-2003	UWI V/Chancellor's XI	First Class Matches	WI	1	2	0	21	14	10.50	-	-	1	17.3	1	84	2	42.00	2-66
		Total First Class Career		30	49	2	1147	114*	24.40	1	5	22	225.5	61	551	12	45.91	3-75
		Total O.D. Career		92	84	15	1751	124	25.37	1	7	44	92	4	472	17	27.70	3-27

MILTON ROBERT PYDANNA

D.O.B. 27.01.1950 - New Amsterdam, Berbice, British Guiana
First Class Debut 29.01.1971 - Guyana v Barbados
O.D.I. Debut 21.11.1980 - West Indies v Pakistan
Domestic O.D. Debut 13.04.1973 - Guyana v Jamaica

O.D.I. 34-31

Teams Played For 3
Guyana
Berbice
West Indies

RHB / WK

							BATTING						BOWLING					
SEASON	TEAM	COMPETITION	V	M	I	No	RUNS	H.S.	Av	100s	50s	CT/ST	OV	MD	RUNS	W	Av	B.B.
1971-1988	Guyana	First Class Matches	=	63	94	13	1475	117*	18.20	1	5	111/26	1	0	17	0	-	-
1971-1987	Berbice	First Class Matches	G	15	23	1	517	127	23.50	1	2	36/9	-	-	-	-	-	-
1972-1988	Guyana	Domestic O.D. Matches	=	24	21	6	218	29	14.53	-	-	19/10	-	-	-	-	-	-
1980-1983	West Indies	First Class Matches	A	7	10	2	231	59	28.87	-	2	5/1	-	-	-	-	-	-
1980-1983	WEST INDIES	O.D.I. MATCHES	A	3	1	1	2	2*	-	-	-	2/1	-	-	-	-	-	-
Total First Class Career				85	127	16	2223	127	22.02	2	9	152/36	1	0	17	0	-	-
Total O.D. Career				27	22	7	220	29	14.66	0	0	21/11	-	-	-	-	-	-

427

ALLAN FITZROY RAE

D.O.B. 30.09.1922 - Rollington Town, Kingston, Jamaica

First Class Debut 22.03.1947 - Jamaica v Barbados
Test Match Debut 10.11.1948 - West Indies v India

Test 69-27

Teams Played For
Jamaica
West Indies

LHB

SEASON	TEAM	COMPETITION	V	M	I	No	BATTING RUNS	H.S.	Av	100s	50s	CT	BOWLING OV	MD	RUNS	W	Av	B.B.
1947-1960	Jamaica	First Class Matches	H	21	38	2	1464	142	40.66	5	6	14	1.4	0	8	0	-	-
1948-1953	WEST INDIES	TEST MATCHES	HA	15	24	2	1016	109	46.18	4	4	10	-	-	-	-	-	-
1948-1956	West Indies	First Class Matches	HA	44	66	3	2318	179	36.79	8	5	18	2	0	18	0	-	-
	Total First Class Career			80	128	7	4798	179	39.65	17	15	42	3.4	0	26	0	-	-

2

SURUJ RAGOONATH

D.O.B. 22.03.1968 - Charlieville, Chaguanas, Trinidad
First Class Debut 10.02.1989 - Trinidad & Tobago v Leeward Islands
Test Match Debut 05.03.1999 - West Indies v Australia
Domestic O.D. Debut 16.01.1991 - Trinidad & Tobago v Windward Islands

Test 227-349   **Teams Played For**   5   RHB / OB

Teams Played For: Trinidad & Tobago, West Indies, W.I. President's XI, W.I. Board XI, West Indies "A"

SEASON	TEAM	COMPETITION	V	M	I	No	RUNS	H.S.	Av	100s	50s	CT	OV	MD	RUNS	W	Av	B.B.
1989-2001	Trinidad & Tobago	First Class Matches	II	58	103	5	2859	128	29.17	2	21	33	1.5	0	6	0	-	-
1991-2000	Trinidad & Tobago	Domestic O.D. Matches	II	40	38	1	833	75	28.24	-	5	6	-	-	-	-	-	-
1991-1997	Trinidad & Tobago	O.A.L. O.D. Matches	WI	2	2	1	116	110*	58.00	1	-	1	-	-	-	-	-	-
1999-2000	WEST INDIES	TEST MATCHES	H	2	4	1	13	9	4.33	-	-	-	-	-	-	-	-	-
1995//	W.I. Board XI	First Class Matches	WI	1	2	1	67	46	67.00	-	-	-	-	-	-	-	-	-
1999//	W.I. President's XI	First Class Matches	WI	1	2	0	61	53	30.50	-	1	1	-	-	-	-	-	-
1997-1998	West Indies "A"	First Class Matches	A	4	8	0	261	77	32.62	-	2	2	6	1	10	0	-	-
1995-1998	West Indies "A"	O.D.(I.) Matches	HA	5	5	0	82	49	16.40	-	1	1	2.3	1	17	0	-	-
1997//	West Indies "A"	O.A.L. O.D. Matches	A	1	1	1	14	14*	-	-	-	-	-	-	-	-	-	-
Total First Class Career				66	119	7	3261	128	29.11	2	24	36	7.5	1	16	0	-	-
Total O.D. Career				48	46	3	1045	110*	24.30	1	5	8	2.3	1	17	0	-	-

SONNY RAMADHIN

D.O.B. 01.05.1929 - St Charles Village, Trinidad

First Class Debut: 25.01.1950 - Trinidad v Jamaica
Test Match Debut: 08.06.1950 - West Indies v England
Domestic O.D. Debut: 27.05.1964 - Lancashire v Kent

Test 70-32

Teams Played For
Trinidad, West Indies
Lancashire, Commonwealth XI
International XI, E.W. Swanton's XI
M.C.C., Lincolnshire

RHB / OB
8

SEASON	TEAM	COMPETITION	V	M	I	No	BATTING RUNS	H.S.	Av	100s	50s	CT	BOWLING OV	MD	RUNS	W	Av	B.B.
1950-1953	Trinidad	First Class Matches	II	3	2	1	12	12*	12.00	-	-	1	142.5	41	315	14	22.50	5-39
1950-1961	WEST INDIES	TEST MATCHES	HA	43	58	14	361	44	8.20	-	-	9	2233.3	813	4579	158	28.98	7-49
1950-1961	West Indies	First Class Matches	HA	58	47	16	260	28	8.38	-	-	9	2168.5	783	4333	312	13.88	8-15
1964-1965	Lancashire	First Class Matches	E	33	40	19	151	13	7.19	-	-	5	1049.1	334	2267	97	23.27	8-121
1964	Lancashire	Nat West Trophy	E	3	0	-	-	-	-	-	-	-	25.3	2	101	3	33.66	2-51
1961//	M.C.C.	First Class Matches	E	1	2	0	47	41	23.50	-	-	-	76	25	169	8	21.12	4-69
1971//	Lincolnshire	Nat West Trophy	E	2	1	0	0	0	0.00	-	-	-	24	5	89	1	89.00	1-21
1950-1956	Commonwealth XI	First Class Matches	HA	39	34	12	229	27*	10.40	-	-	12	1351.4	428	2907	148	19.64	6-23
1961-62//	International XI	First Class Matches	A	6	7	2	24	8	4.80	-	-	2	256.1	73	715	21	34.04	4-98
1963-64//	E.W. Swanton's XI	First Class Matches	I	1	1	1	8	8*	-	-	-	-	25	8	60	0	-	-
Total First Class Career				184	191	65	1092	44	8.66	0	0	38	7302.5	2505	15345	758	20.24	8-15
Total O.D. Career				5	1	0	0	0	0.00	0	0	0	49.3	7	190	4	47.50	2-51

DINANATH RAMNARINE

LHB / LBG

D.O.B. 04.06.1975 - Charlieville, Chaguanas, Trinidad
First Class Debut 07.01.1994 - Trinidad & Tobago v Windward Islands
Test Match Debut 27.02.1998 - West Indies v England
O.D.I. Debut 06.06.1997 - West Indies v Sri Lanka
Domestic O.D. Debut 05.01.1994 - Trinidad & Tobago v Windward Islands

Test 221-340
O.D.I. 83-338

Teams Played For 6
Trinidad & Tobago, West Indies
W.I. Board XI
West Indies "A"
Busta Cup XI
W.I. Select XI

SEASON	TEAM	COMPETITION	V	M	I	No	RUNS	H.S.	Av	100s	50s	CT	OV	MD	RUNS	W	Av	B.B.
1994-2003	Trinidad & Tobago	First Class Matches	=	40	65	14	521	43	10.23	-	-	30	1507.3	361	3803	160	23.76	6-54
1994-2002	Trinidad & Tobago	Domestic O.D. Matches	=	33	20	4	91	14	5.68	-	-	7	264.5	24	960	53	18.11	4-23
1998-2002	WEST INDIES	TEST MATCHES	HA	12	21	4	106	35*	6.23	-	-	8	582.3	169	1383	45	30.73	5-78
1998-2002	West Indies	First Class Matches	A	4	3	2	43	28	43.00	-	-	1	125.3	37	371	17	21.82	4-54
1995//	W.I. Board XI	First Class Matches	WI	1	1	1	5	5*	-	-	-	-	23	4	49	0	-	-
1997-2000	West Indies "A"	First Class Matches	HA	9	14	2	82	38	6.83	-	-	4	324.1	88	749	25	29.96	3-25
2001-2002	Busta Cup XI	First Class Matches	WI	1	1	0	15	15	15.00	-	-	-	33	9	68	4	17.00	4-49
1996-2001	WEST INDIES	O.D.I. MATCHES	WI	4	3	0	5	2	1.66	-	-	-	33.2	3	164	3	54.66	1-48
1997-2000	West Indies "A"	O.D.(I.) Matches	HA	5	4	2	13	13	6.50	-	-	-	41	2	162	2	81.00	2-39
1997//	West Indies "A"	O.A.L. O.D. Matches	A	2	1	1	1	1*	-	-	-	-	-	-	73	1	73.00	1-56
1999-2000	W.I. Select XI	First Class Matches	WI	1	1	0	1	1	1.00	-	-	-	20	8	30	1	30.00	1-30
Total First Class Career				68	106	23	773	43	9.31	0	0	43	2615.4	676	6453	252	25.60	6-54
Total O.D. Career				44	28	7	110	14	5.23	0	0	7	359.1	30	1359	59	23.03	4-23

FLOYD LAMONTE REIFER

D.O.B.   23.07.1972 - Parish Land, St George, Barbados

First Class Debut	24.02.1992 - Barbados v Trinidad & Tobago
Test Match Debut	13.06.1997 - West Indies v Sri Lanka
O.D.I. Debut	06.06.1997 - West Indies v Sri Lanka
Domestic O.D. Debut	19.03.1992 - Barbados v Guyana

Test 217-333
O.D.I. 84-338

Teams Played For
Barbados
West Indies
W.I. President's XI
West Indies "A"
Shell Academy XI

LHB / RM
5

| | | | | | | | BATTING | | | | | | BOWLING | | | | | |
SEASON	TEAM	COMPETITION	V	M	I	No	RUNS	H.S.	Av	100s	50s	CT	OV	MD	RUNS	W	Av	B.B.
1992-2003	Barbados	First Class Matches	II	63	108	15	3657	200	39.32	6	22	47	20	2	71	1	71.05	1-19
1992-2002	Barbados	Domestic O.D. Matches	II	49	47	8	1421	104*	36.43	1	7	14	31	1	162	3	54.00	1-6
1992-1998	Barbados	O.A.L. O.D. Matches	HA	10	10	1	148	38*	16.44	-	-	2	4	0	12	0	-	-
1997-1999	WEST INDIES	TEST MATCHES	HA	4	8	0	63	29	7.87	-	-	4	-	-	-	-	-	-
1998-1999	West Indies	First Class Matches	A	3	5	1	77	36	19.25	-	-	3	3	1	18	0	-	-
1996//	W.I. President's XI	First Class Matches	WI	1	1	0	130	130	130.00	1	-	-	-	-	-	-	-	-
1994-1999	West Indies "A"	First Class Matches	HA	12	19	1	425	96	23.61	-	4	9	19	0	67	0	-	-
1996-1999	WEST INDIES	O.D.I. MATCHES	HA	2	2	0	31	22	15.50	-	-	1	-	-	-	-	-	-
1994-1999	West Indies "A"	O.D.(I.) Matches	HA	10	9	1	256	69	36.57	-	4	5	4.5	0	31	0	-	-
1996-1997	West Indies "A"	O.A.L. O.D. Matches	A	3	2	0	18	18	9.00	-	-	1	2	0	12	0	-	-
2002-2003	Shell Academy XI	O.A.L. O.D. Matches	WI	1	1	0	4	4	4.00	-	-	1	-	-	-	-	-	-
Total First Class Career				83	141	17	4352	200	35.09	7	26	13	47	3	156	1	156.00	1-19
Total O.D. Career				75	71	10	1878	104*	30.78	1	11	24	41.5	1	217	3	72.33	1-6

ISSAC VIVIAN ALEXANDER RICHARDS

D.O.B. 07.03.1952 - St. John's, Antigua, Leeward Islands
First Class Debut 15.01.1972 - Leeward Islands v Windward Islands
Test Match Debut 22.11.1974 - West Indies v India
O.D.I. Debut 07.06.1975 - West Indies v Sri Lanka
Domestic O.D. Debut 27.04.1974 - Somerset v Glamorgan

Test 151-152
O.D.I. 14-3

Teams Played For 8
Leeward Islands, Combined Islands
West Indies, W.I. President's XI
Somerset, Glamorgan
Queensland, International XI

RHB / RM / OB

SEASON	TEAM	COMPETITION	V	M	I	No	BATTING RUNS	H.S.	Av	100s	50s	CT/ST	BOWLING OV	MD	RUNS	W	Av	B.B.
1972-1991	Leeward Islands	First Class Matches	II	28	41	4	1669	167	45.10	4	9	36	452.2	112	1006	29	34.68	4-55
1972-1981	Combined Islands	First Class Matches	II	26	49	2	1661	168*	35.34	5	9	18	331.1	97	763	20	38.15	3-30
1973-1974	Combined Islands	O.A.L. O.D. Matches	WI	1	1	0	8	8.00	-	-	-	-	7	0	25	0	-	-
1976-1991	Leeward Islands	Domestic O.D. Matches	II	20	18	0	552	77	30.66	-	5	11	133	10	529	17	31.11	4-18
1974-1991	WEST INDIES	TEST MATCHES	HA	121	182	12	8540	291	50.23	24	45	122	856	203	1964	32	61.37	2-17
1974-1991	West Indies	First Class Matches	A	85	116	16	5867	176	58.67	23	26	75/1	503.5	112	1326	36	36.83	5-88
1973-1974	W.I. President's XI	First Class Matches	WI	1	2	0	23	18	11.50	-	-	-	10	1	30	0	-	-
1975-1991	WEST INDIES	O.D.I. MATCHES	HA	187	167	24	6721	189*	47.00	11	45	101	940.4	26	4228	118	35.83	6-41
1975-1988	West Indies	O.A.L. O.D. Matches	A	12	11	2	394	122	43.77	1	2	2	42.5	-	166	7	23.71	3-37
1974-1986	Somerset	First Class Matches	E	191	313	18	14698	322	49.82	47	57	164	1495.3	371	4239	96	44.15	4-36
1974-1986	Somerset	Nat West Trophy	E	31	31	3	1209	139*	43.17	3	6	16	135.1	15	478	16	29.37	3-15
1974-1986	Somerset	Benson & Hedges Cup	E	43	39	6	1335	132*	42.27	1	10	19	67.4	-	225	7	32.14	1-9
1974-1986	Somerset	Sunday League	E	144	139	16	4745	126*	38.57	7	31	62	387	-	1758	70	25.11	6-24
1990-1993	Glamorgan	First Class Matches	E	49	83	11	3382	224*	46.97	10	14	43	233	46	695	9	77.33	3-22
1990-1993	Glamorgan	Nat West Trophy	E	10	10	3	485	162*	69.28	2	1	3	80.2	-	343	7	49.00	2-31
1990-1993	Glamorgan	Benson & Hedges Cup	E	10	10	0	192	48	19.20	-	1	6	85	-	311	11	28.27	3-38
1990-1993	Glamorgan	Sunday League	E	40	38	7	1244	109*	40.12	1	8	18	157	-	809	37	21.86	3-12
1990//	Glamorgan	O.A.L. O.D. Matches	E	1	D	-	-	-	-	-	-	-	-	-	-	-	-	-
1976-1977	Queensland	First Class Matches	A	5	8	0	349	143	43.62	1	2	4	4	-	0	0	-	-
1976-1977	Queensland	Gillette Cup	A	2	2	0	50	50	25.00	-	1	1	-	-	-	-	-	-
1975//	International XI	First Class Matches	E	1	2	0	23	20	11.50	-	-	2	2	-	6	1	6.00	1-6
Total First Class Career				507	796	63	36212	322	49.40	114	162	464/1	3887.5	943	10070	223	45.15	5-88
Total O.D. Career				501	466	61	16995	189*	41.96	26	109	239	2035.4	-	8872	290	30.59	6-24

RICHARD BENJAMIN RICHARDSON

D.O.B. 12.01.1962 - Five Islands Village, Antigua, Leeward Islands

First Class Debut	20.03.1982 - Leeward Islands v Barbados
Test Match Debut	24.11.1983 - West Indies v India
O.D.I. Debut	17.12.1983 - West Indies v India
Domestic O.D. Debut	18.03.1982 - Leeward Islands v Barbados

Teams Played For 11
Leeward Islands, W.I. President's XI, M.C.C.
Windward Islands, West Indies
West Indies U23, Antigua
Yorkshire, West Indies "B"
World XI, Northern Transvaal

RHB / RM

Test 180-220
O.D.I. 41-65

SEASON	TEAM	COMPETITION	V	M	I	No	RUNS	H.S.	Av	100s	50s	CT	OV	MD	RUNS	W	Av	B.B.
1982-1996	Leeward Islands	First Class Matches	II	41	69	5	2894	176	45.21	10	10	38	37	6	89	5	17.80	5-40
1998//	Windward Islands	First Class Matches	II	4	8	1	198	62*	28.28	-	1	1	7.2	0	18	0	-	-
1982-1996	Leeward Islands	Domestic O.D. Matches	II	29	27	0	648	84	24.00	-	4	8	5	0	39	1	39.00	1-25
1998//	Antigua	O.A.L. O.D. Matches	S	3	3	0	20	13	6.66	-	-	1	-	-	-	-	-	-
1983-1995	WEST INDIES	TEST MATCHES	HA	86	146	12	5949	194	44.39	16	27	90	11	2	18	0	-	-
1983-1995	West Indies	First Class Matches	A	63	98	11	3662	147	42.09	10	15	49	26	4	108	0	-	-
1985//	West Indies U23	First Class Matches	WI	1	1	0	1	1	1.00	-	-	1	-	-	-	-	-	-
1991//	W.I. President's XI	First Class Matches	WI	1	2	0	22	14	11.00	-	-	1	-	-	-	-	-	-
2000-2001	West Indies "B"	First Class Matches	WI	7	13	1	216	49*	18.00	-	-	3	59.5	8	174	6	29.00	2-4
1983-1995	WEST INDIES	O.D.I. MATCHES	HA	224	271	30	6248	122	33.41	5	44	74	9.2	0	46	1	46.00	1-4
1984-1995	West Indies	O.A.L. O.D. MATCHES	A	17	17	1	335	84	20.93	-	2	1	-	-	-	-	-	-
1993-1994	Yorkshire	First Class Matches	E	23	39	1	1310	112	34.47	1	11	18	7	0	23	1	23.00	1-5
1993-1994	Yorkshire	Nat West Trophy	E	5	5	0	194	90	38.80	-	2	-	-	-	-	-	-	-
1993-1994	Yorkshire	Benson & Hedges Cup	E	2	2	0	59	52	29.50	-	1	-	-	-	-	-	-	-
1993-1994	Yorkshire	Sunday League	E	21	21	6	740	103	49.33	1	5	5	-	-	-	-	-	-
1990-1998	World XI	First Class Matches	E	2	3	0	112	65	37.33	-	1	1	-	-	-	-	-	-
1996-1997	Northern Transvaal	First Class Matches	SA	6	11	0	254	69	23.09	-	3	5	4	0	11	1	11.00	1-11
1996-1997	Northern Transvaal	Benson & Hedges Cup	SA	11	11	0	194	55	17.63	-	1	2	-	-	-	-	-	-
192//	M.C.C.	O.A.L. O.D. Matches	E	1	1	0	20	20	20.00	-	-	1	-	-	-	-	-	-
Total First Class Career				234	390	31	14618	194	40.71	37	62	207	152.1	20	441	13	33.92	5-40
Total O.D. Career				313	304	37	8458	122	31.67	6	59	92	14	0	85	2	42.50	1-4

BATTING

BOWLING

KENNETH ROY RICKARDS

D.O.B. 23.08.1923 - Rollington Town, Kingston, Jamaica (d. 21.08.1995)

First Class Debut 26.06.1946 - Jamaica v Trinidad

Test Match Debut 27.03.1948 - West Indies v England

	Test	Teams Played For		RHB / LB
	66-26	Jamaica	4	
		West Indies		
		Commonwealth XI		
		Essex		

SEASON	TEAM	COMPETITION	V	M	I	No	BATTING RUNS	H.S.	Av	100s	50s	CT	BOWLING OV	MD	RUNS	W	Av	B.B.
1946-1959	Jamaica	First Class Matches	II	17	31	5	1265	195	48.65	2	9	2	26	1	113	1	113.00	1-66
1948-1952	West Indies	First Class Matches	A	15	20	1	538	99	28.31	-	4	8	2	0	15	0	-	-
1948-1952	WEST INDIES	TEST MATCHES	HA	2	3	0	104	67	34.66	-	1	-	-	-	-	-	-	-
1952//	Commonwealth XI	First Class Matches	E	2	4	1	133	69	44.33	-	1	-	-	-	-	-	-	-
1953//	Essex	First Class Matches	E	1	2	0	25	13	12.50	-	-	-	-	-	-	-	-	-
	Total First Class Career			37	60	7	2065	195	38.96	2	15	10	28	1	128	1	128.00	1-66

CLIFFORD ARCHIBALD ROACH

D.O.B. 13.03.1904 - Port of Spain, Trinidad (d. 16.04.1988)

First Class Debut 14.02.1924 - Trinidad v British Guiana
Test Match Debut 23.06.1928 - West Indies v England

Test 6-1

RHB / LB

Teams Played For 4
Trinidad
West Indies
Combined T/BG XI
C.A. Merry's XI

SEASON	TEAM	COMPETITION	V	M	I	No	RUNS	H.S.	Av	100s	50s	CT	OV	MD	RUNS	W	Av	B.B.
							BATTING						**BOWLING**					
1924-1938	Trinidad	First Class Matches	II	19	36	0	1035	128	28.75	1	4	8	33	10	83	0	-	-
1928-1935	WEST INDIES	TEST MATCHES	HA	16	32	1	952	209	30.70	2	6	5	37	5	103	2	51.50	1-18
1928-1933	West Indies	First Class Matches	HA	60	105	3	2713	180	26.59	2	14	28	85	10	326	3	108.66	1-20
1928//	Combined T/BG XI	First Class Matches	WI	2	2	0	98	84	49.00	-	1	2	4	0	14	0	-	-
1933//	C.A. Merry's XI	First Class Matches	WI	1	2	0	53	33	26.50	-	-	-	-	-	-	-	-	-
	Total First Class Career			98	177	4	4851	209	28.04	5	25	43	159	25	256	5	105.20	1-18

ALPHONSO THEODORE ROBERTS

D.O.B. 18.09.1937 - Kingstown, St Vincent, Windward Islands (d. 24.07.1996)

First Class Debut 20.01.1956 - West Indies v Auckland

Test Match Debut 09.03.1956 - West Indies v New Zealand

						Test	92-61			**Teams Played For**		3							**RHB**
										Trinidad									
										Windward Islands									
										West Indies									

						BATTING							BOWLING					
SEASON	**TEAM**	**COMPETITION**	**V**	**M**	**I**	**No**	**RUNS**	**H.S.**	**Av**	**100s**	**50s**	**CT**	**OV**	**MD**	**RUNS**	**W**	**Av**	**B.B.**
1956-1957	Trinidad	First Class Matches	=	1	2	0	15	15	7.50	-	-	-	-	-	-	-	-	-
1959-1960	Windward Islands	First Class Matches	=	1	2	0	1	1	0.50	-	-	1	-	-	-	-	-	-
1955-1956	WEST INDIES	TEST MATCHES	A	1	2	0	28	28	14.00	-	-	2	-	-	-	-	-	-
1955-1956	West Indies	First Class Matches	A	4	6	1	109	45	21.80	-	-	2	-	-	-	-	-	-
	Total First Class Career			7	12	1	153	45	13.90	0	0	3	-	-	-	-	-	-

ANDERSON MONTGOMERY EVERTON ROBERTS

D.O.B. 29.01.1951 - Urlings Village, Antigua, Leeward Islands

Teams Played For 7
Leeward Islands, Combined Islands
West Indies, W.I. President's XI
Hampshire
Leicestershire
New South Wales

RHB / RF

Test 149-149
O.D.I. 15-3

First Class Debut 16.01.1970 - Leeward Islands v Windward Islands
Test Match Debut 06.03.1975 - West Indies v England
O.D.I. Debut 07.06.1975 - West Indies v Sri Lanka
Domestic O.D. Debut 27.04.1974 - Hampshire v Gloucestershire

SEASON	TEAM	COMPETITION	V	M	I	No	BATTING						BOWLING					
							RUNS	H.S.	Av	100s	50s	CT	OV	MD	RUNS	W	Av	B.B.
1970-1984	Leeward Islands	First Class Matches	II	25	36	7	347	54	11.96	-	1	8	752.5	186	1970	104	18.94	8-62
1971-1981	Combined Islands	First Class Matches	II	26	44	8	483	63	13.41	-	2	10	737.4	166	2017	107	18.85	7-30
1973-1974	Combined Islands	O.A.L. O.D. Matches	WI	1	D	-	-	-	-	-	-	-	10	1	27	2	13.50	2-27
1976-1984	Leeward Islands	Domestic O.D. Matches	II	17	9	4	98	39*	19.60	-	-	7	133.5	27	412	21	19.61	3-16
1974-1983	WEST INDIES	TEST MATCHES	HA	47	62	11	762	68	14.94	-	3	9	1778.5	382	5174	202	25.61	7-54
1974-1983	West Indies	First Class Matches	A	33	28	6	386	56*	17.54	-	1	6	780.3	163	2197	86	25.54	4-18
1974//	W.I. President's XI	First Class Matches	WI	1	2	2	48	48*	-	-	-	-	34	8	91	2	45.50	2-59
1975-1984	WEST INDIES	O.D.I. MATCHES	HA	56	32	9	231	37*	10.04	-	-	6	520.3	76	1771	87	20.35	5-22
1975-1980	West Indies	O.A.L. O.D. Matches	A	7	1	0	8	8	8.00	-	-	-	59	-	179	10	17.90	4-20
1973-1978	Hampshire	First Class Matches	E	58	65	23	583	39	13.88	-	-	11	1784.1	526	4076	244	16.70	8-47
1974-1978	Hampshire	Nat West Trophy	E	8	5	1	41	15	10.25	-	-	-	81.5	23	170	14	12.14	3-17
1974-1978	Hampshire	Benson & Hedges Cup	E	18	9	3	87	29	14.50	-	-	-	173.1	38	383	31	12.35	4-12
1974-1978	Hampshire	Sunday League	E	44	25	16	225	49*	25.00	-	-	10	301.5	38	867	59	14.69	5-13
1981-1984	Leicestershire	First Class Matches	E	36	52	9	895	89	20.81	-	3	8	1103.5	283	3067	141	21.75	8-56
1981-1984	Leicestershire	Nat West Trophy	E	8	7	1	108	46	18.00	-	-	2	68.1	9	264	6	44.00	2-39
1981-1984	Leicestershire	Benson & Hedges Cup	E	10	8	1	79	29	11.28	-	-	3	97.4	-	293	10	29.30	2-25
1981-1984	Leicestershire	Sunday League	E	25	16	3	202	59*	15.53	-	1	5	190.1	-	719	34	21.14	4-27
1981//	Leicestershire	O.A.L. O.D. Matches	E	1	1	0	12	12	12.00	-	-	-	-	-	-	-	-	-
1976-1977	New South Wales	First Class Matches	A	2	2	1	12	8	12.00	-	-	-	32.3	5	87	3	29.00	2-56
Total First Class Career				228	291	67	3516	89	15.69	0	10	52	7004.2	1719	18679	889	21.01	8-47
Total O.D. Career				195	113	38	1091	59*	14.54	0	1	33	1634.4	-	5085	274	18.55	5-13

LINCOLN ABRAHAM ROBERTS

D.O.B. 04.09.1974 - Accord, Tobago

First Class Debut 26.01.1996 - Trinidad & Tobago v Barbados
Test Match Debut 13.03.1999 - West Indies v Australia
Domestic O.D. Debut 28.10.1995 - Trinidad & Tobago v Guyana

Test 229-350   RHB / RM

Teams Played For
Trinidad & Tobago
West Indies
West Indies "A"
W.I. President's XI
Herefordshire

Test 5

SEASON	TEAM	COMPETITION	V	M	I	No	RUNS	H.S.	Av	100s	50s	CT	OV	MD	RUNS	W	Av	B.B.
1995-2002	Trinidad & Tobago	First Class Matches	=	48	82	3	2157	220	27.30	5	7	24	53	9	152	3	50.66	3-45
1995-2002	Trinidad & Tobago	Domestic O.D. Matches	=	27	23	2	509	55	24.23	-	2	6	10	0	78	0	-	-
1999//	WEST INDIES	TEST MATCHES	H	1	1	0	0	0	0.00	-	-	-	-	-	-	-	-	-
1998-1999	W.I. President's XI	First Class Matches	WI	1	2	0	38	38	19.00	-	-	-	-	-	-	-	-	-
1999-2000	West Indies "A"	First Class Matches	H	1	2	0	84	74	42.00	-	1	-	-	-	-	-	-	-
1999-2000	West Indies	O.D.(I.) Matches	H	2	2	0	40	27	-	-	-	-	-	-	-	-	-	-
2002//	Herefordshire	Cheltenham & Glouster Cup	E	1	1	0	10	10	10.00	-	-	-	6	1	36	2	18.00	2-36
	Total First Class Career			51	87	3	2279	220	27.13	5	8	24	53	9	152	3	50.66	3-45
	Total O.D. Career			30	26	2	559	55	23.29	0	2	6	16	1	114	2	57.00	2-36

BATTING   BOWLING

WILLIAM VINCENTE RODRIGUEZ

D.O.B. 25.06.1934 - St Clair, Port of Spain, Trinidad

First Class Debut 16.10.1953 - Trinidad v British Guiana
Test Match Debut 07.03.1962 - West Indies v India
Domestic O.D. Debut 19.09.1966 West Indies v Sussex

Test 117-91

RHB / LBG

Teams Played For
Trinidad
North Trinidad
West Indies
C.C. Hunte's XI

4

SEASON	TEAM	COMPETITION	V	M	I	No	BATTING RUNS	H.S.	Av	100s	50s	CT	BOWLING OV	MD	RUNS	W	Av	B.B.
1953-1970	Trinidad	First Class Matches	=	30	50	9	1127	105	27.48	1	4	8	578.5	118	1803	73	24.69	6-30
1961-1968	North Trinidad	First Class Matches	T	6	8	0	145	42	18.12	-	-	6	108	19	379	15	25.26	3-31
1962-1968	WEST INDIES	TEST MATCHES	HA	5	7	0	96	50	13.71	-	1	3	95.3	10	374	7	53.42	3-51
1958-1964	West Indies	First Class Matches	HA	22	31	6	613	93	24.53	-	4	19	168.4	19	700	23	30.34	7-90
1963-1964	C.C. Hunte's XI	First Class Matches	WI	1	2	0	80	43	40.00	-	-	-	16	0	86	1	86.00	1-46
1963//	West Indies	O.A.L. O.D. Matches	A	1	1	0	6	6	6.00	-	-	-	-	-	-	-	-	-
		Total First Class Career		64	98	15	2061	105	24.83	1	9	36	967	166	3342	119	28.08	7-90
		Total O.D. Career		1	1	0	6	6	6.00	0	0	0	-	-	-	-	-	-

440

FRANKLYN ALBERT ROSE

D.O.B. 01.02.1972 - Chalkley Hill, St Anns Bay, St Ann, Jamaica

First Class Debut 05.02.1993 - Jamaica v Barbados
Test Match Debut 06.03.1997 - West Indies v India
O.D.I. Debut 26.04.1997 - West Indies v India
Domestic O.D. Debut 03.02.1993 - Jamaica v Barbados

Test	215-328
O.D.I.	28-334

Teams Played For 7   RHB / RF
Jamaica, West Indies
West Indies U23
West Indies "A"
Northamptonshire
Gauteng
Surrey

SEASON	TEAM	COMPETITION	V	M	I	No	BATTING RUNS	H.S.	Av	100s	50s	CT	BOWLING OV	MD	RUNS	W	Av	B.B.
1993-2003	Jamaica	First Class Matches	=	43	60	14	728	96	15.82	-	1	15	1039.5	186	3476	145	23.97	6-63
1993-2001	Jamaica	Domestic O.D. Matches	=	30	18	5	129	37	3.48	-	-	8	222.1	31	863	31	28.76	4-16
2001/	Jamaica	O.A.L. O.D. Matches	WI	1	1	0	3	3	3.00	-	-	-	8	1	20	1	20.00	1-20
1997-2000	WEST INDIES	TEST MATCHES	HA	19	28	2	344	69	13.23	-	1	4	520.4	102	1637	53	30.88	7-84
1997-2000	West Indies	First Class Matches	A	10	11	2	106	41	11.77	-	-	1	223.1	43	695	24	28.95	4-63
1993/	West Indies U23	First Class Matches	WI	1	2	0	3	3	1.50	-	-	-	25	7	105	2	52.50	1-46
1999/	West Indies "A"	First Class Matches	HA	1	2	1	1	1	1.00	-	-	2	23	2	78	2	39.00	2-41
1997-2000	WEST INDIES	O.D.I. MATCHES	HA	27	23	5	271	30	12.05	-	-	6	221	13	1046	29	36.06	5-23
1998/	Northamptonshire	First Class Matches	E	14	17	2	133	21	8.86	-	-	-	373.2	59	1367	50	27.34	7-39
1998/	Northamptonshire	Nat West Trophy	E	1	1	0	19	19	19.00	-	-	1	12	3	43	3	14.33	3-43
1998/	Northamptonshire	Benson & Hedges Cup	E	5	5	0	20	15	4.00	-	-	1	45.1	-	204	12	17.00	5-14
1998/	Northamptonshire	Sunday League	E	13	4	1	13	9*	4.33	-	-	2	87.1	-	380	15	25.33	2-19
2000-2001	Gauteng	First Class Matches	SA	5	8	0	74	39	9.25	-	-	2	145.5	32	390	17	22.94	6-48
2003/	Surrey	First Class Matches	E	1	2	0	37	36	18.50	-	-	3	28	8	101	3	33.66	3-101
2003/	Surrey	National Sunday League	E	2	1	0	1	1	1.00	-	-	-	17	1	78	2	39.00	1-33
	Total First Class Career			94	130	21	1426	96	13.08	0	2	24	2379	439	7849	296	26.51	7-39
	Total O.D. Career			79	53	11	402	37	7.73	0	0	18	612.3	60	2634	92	28.63	5-14

441

LAWRENCE GEORGE ROWE

RHB / LFM

D.O.B.	08.01.1949 - Whitfield Town, Kingston, Jamaica
First Class Debut	25.01.1969 - Jamaica v Windward Islands
Test Match Debut	16.02.1972 - West Indies v New Zealand
O.D.I. Debut	20.12.1975 - West Indies v Australia
Domestic O.D. Debut	05.05.1974 - Derbyshire v Essex

Test 141-134
O.D.I. 17-8

6

Teams Played For
Jamaica, West Indies
W.I. President's XI
West Indies XI
Derbyshire
The Cavaliers XI

SEASON	TEAM	COMPETITION	V	M	I	No	RUNS	H.S.	Av	100s	50s	CT	OV	MD	RUNS	W	Av	B.B.
1969-1982	Jamaica	First Class Matches	II	53	89	6	3487	227	42.01	8	17	57	26	5	74	1	74.00	1-19
1980-1982	Jamaica	Domestic O.D. Matches	II	7	7	0	179	71	25.57	-	2	3	5	0	30	1	30.00	1-22
1972-1979	WEST IDIES	TEST MATCHES	HA	30	49	2	2047	302	43.55	7	7	17	14	3	44	0	-	-
1973-1982	West Indies	First Class Matches	A	38	57	3	1685	152	31.20	2	7	22	3	0	22	0	-	-
1971//	W.I. President's XI	First Class Matches	WI	1	2	0	50	27	25.00	-	-	-	-	-	-	-	-	-
1982-1984	West Indies XI	First Class Matches	A	9	16	0	418	157	26.12	1	-	6	-	-	-	-	-	-
1975-1980	WEST INDIES	O.D.I. MATCHES	HA	11	8	0	136	60	17.00	-	1	2	-	-	-	-	-	-
1982-1984	West Indies XI	O.D.(I.) Matches	A	11	11	2	377	87	41.88	-	2	2	-	-	-	-	-	-
1975-1980	West Indies	O.A.L. O.D. Matches	A	4	3	0	67	33	22.33	-	1	5	1	0	0	1	-	1-0
1982-1983	West Indies XI	O.A.L. O.D. Matches	A	2	2	0	107	66	53.50	-	1	-	-	-	-	-	-	-
1974//	Derbyshire	First Class Matches	E	17	30	1	1059	94	36.51	-	7	15	27.4	7	84	1	84.00	1-22
1974//	Derbyshire	Nat West Trophy	E	1	1	0	20	20	20.00	-	-	-	-	-	-	-	-	-
1974//	Derbyshire	Benson & Hedges Cup	E	3	3	1	23	10	7.66	-	-	3	-	-	-	-	-	-
1974//	Derbyshire	Sunday League	E	13	13	0	491	72	37.77	-	4	3	-	-	-	-	-	-
1969//	The Cavaliers XI	First Class Matches	E	1	2	0	9	8	4.50	-	-	1	-	-	-	-	-	-
Total First Class Career				149	245	12	8755	302	37.57	18	38	118	70.4	15	224	2	112.00	1-19
Total O.D. Career				52	48	2	1400	87	30.43	0	10	18	6	0	30	2	15.00	1-0

BATTING / BOWLING

MARLON NATHANIEL SAMUELS

D.O.B. 05.02.1981 - Kingston, Jamaica

First Class Debut	16.05.1997 - Jamaica v Trinidad & Tobago	
Test Match Debut	15.12.2000 - West Indies v Australia	**Test** 237-367
O.D.I. Debut	11.01.2001 - West Indies v Australia	**O.D.I.** 103-407
Domestic O.D. Debut	11.10.2000 - Jamaica v USA	

Teams Played For 5 RHB / OB
Jamaica
West Indies
West Indies U23
West Indies "A"
W.I. Select XI

SEASON	TEAM	COMPETITION	V	M	I	No	BATTING						BOWLING					
							RUNS	H.S.	Av	100s	50s	CT	OV	MD	RUNS	W	Av	B.B.
1996-2003	Jamaica	First Class Matches	=	7	13	1	258	79	21.50	-	1	3	31	9	60	1	60.00	1-18
2000-2002	Jamaica	Domestic O.D. Matches	II	15	12	2	387	59*	38.70	-	4	1	58	13	194	8	24.25	2-20

SEASON	TEAM	COMPETITION	V	M	I	No	RUNS	H.S.	Av	100s	50s	CT	OV	MD	RUNS	W	Av	B.B.
2000-2003	WEST INDIES	TEST MATCHES	HA	19	33	3	874	104	29.13	1	6	9	175	27	550	5	110.00	2-49
2000-2002	West Indies	First Class Matches	A	7	8	0	233	84	29.12	-	3	2	61.3	10	184	3	61.33	3-100
1999-2000	West Indies U23	First Class Matches	WI	1	2	0	63	61	31.50	-	1	2	24	3	60	2	30.00	1-28
1999-2000	West Indies "A"	First Class Matches	H	3	5	1	68	31	17.00	-	-	1	54	18	104	3	34.66	2-65
1999-2000	W.I. Select XI	First Class Matches	WI	1	1	0	59	59	59.00	-	1	-	3	1	9	0	-	-
2000-2003	WEST INDIES	O.D.I. MATCHES	HA	50	48	7	1345	108*	32.80	1	10	16	239	6	1184	34	34.82	3-25
1999-2000	West Indies "A"	O.D.I.(I.) Matches	H	2	2	0	43	31	21.50	-	-	-	1.1	0	11	0	-	-
2000-2001	West Indies	O.A.L. O.D. Matches	A	4	4	1	73	45	24.33	-	-	2	20.3	0	79	6	13.16	3-30

				M	I	No	RUNS	H.S.	Av	100s	50s	CT	OV	MD	RUNS	W	Av	B.B.
Total First Class Career				38	62	5	1555	104	27.28	1	12	17	348.3	68	967	14	69.07	3-100
Total O.D. Career				71	66	10	1848	108*	33.00	1	14	19	318.4	19	1468	48	30.58	3-25

ROBERT GEORGE SAMUELS

D.O.B. 13.03.1971 - Kingston, Jamaica

First Class Debut	22.04.1989 - Jamaica v India
Test Match Debut	19.04.1996 - West Indies v New Zealand
O.D.I. Debut	06.12.1996 - West Indies v Australia
Domestic O.D. Debut	09.01.1991 - Jamaica v Trinidad & Tobago

Test 211-321
O.D.I. 79-324

Teams Played For
Jamaica, West Indies
W.I. President's XI
West Indies U23
W.I. Board XI
West Indies "A"

LHB 6

SEASON	TEAM	COMPETITION	V	M	I	No	RUNS	H.S.	Av	100s	50s	CT	OV	MD	RUNS	W	Av	B.B.
1989-2003	Jamaica	First Class Matches	JI	82	144	12	4201	159	31.82	4	26	67	1	1	-	-	-	-
1991-2002	Jamaica	Domestic O.D. Matches	JI	53	47	6	1195	103	29.14	1	7	17	-	-	0	0	-	-
1998-2001	Jamaica	O.A.L. O.D. Matches	HA	5	5	0	62	19	12.40	-	-	3	-	-	-	-	-	-
1996-1997	WEST INDIES	TEST MATCHES	HA	6	12	2	372	125	37.20	1	1	8	-	-	-	-	-	-
1996-1997	West Indies	First Class Matches	A	3	6	0	141	96	23.50	-	1	2	-	-	-	-	-	-
1992-1993	West Indies U23	First Class Matches	WI	1	2	0	72	49	36.00	-	-	-	-	-	-	-	-	-
1992-1998	West Indies "A"	First Class Matches	HA	10	20	2	413	76	22.94	-	4	9	-	-	-	-	-	-
1994-1996	W.I. President's XI	First Class Matches	WI	3	4	0	204	124	51.00	1	1	1	-	-	-	-	-	-
1994-1995	W.I. Board XI	First Class Matches	WI	1	2	0	126	95	63.00	-	1	-	-	-	-	-	-	-
1996-1997	WEST INDIES	O.D.I. MATCHES	A	8	5	2	54	36*	18.00	-	-	-	-	-	-	-	-	-
1995-1998	West Indies "A"	O.D.(I.) Matches	HA	3	3	-	36	19	12.00	-	-	-	-	-	-	-	-	-
1997-1998	West Indies "A"	O.A.L. O.D. MATCHES	A	2	2	0	15	13	7.50	-	-	2	-	-	-	-	-	-
1996-1997	West Indies	O.A.L. O.D. MATCHES	A	1	1	0	0	0	0.00	-	-	-	-	-	-	-	-	-
		Total First Class Career		106	190	16	5529	159	31.77	6	34	87	-	1	-	-	-	-
		Total O.D. Career		72	63	8	1362	103	51.76	1	7	22	1	1	0	0	-	-

BATTING / **BOWLING**

444

ADAM SANFORD

D.O.B. 12.07.1976 - Dominica, Windward Islands
First Class Debut 23.05.1997 - Windward Islands v Guyana
Test Match Debut 11.04.2002 - West Indies v India
Domestic O.D. Debut 14.08.2002 - Antigua v Canada

Test 242-382

Teams Played For
Windward Islands
Leeward Islands
West Indies
Antigua
Carib Cup XI

5

RHB / RFM

SEASON	TEAM	COMPETITION	V	M	I	No	BATTING						BOWLING					
							RUNS	H.S.	Av	100s	50s	CT	OV	MD	RUNS	W	Av	B.B.
1996-1997	Windward Islands	First Class Matches	=	1	1	1	30	30*	-	-	-	-	25	9	55	2	27.50	1-5
2001-2003	Leeward Islands	First Class Matches	=	15	19	3	107	20	6.68	-	-	9	562.4	106	1781	69	25.81	6-43
2002-2003	Antigua	Domestic O.D. Matches	=	2	2	1	16	16*	16.00	-	-	-	9	0	44	0	-	-
2002//	WEST INDIES	TEST MATCHES	H	7	10	1	35	12	3.88	-	-	-	234.1	52	794	20	39.70	3-20
2002-2003	Carib Cup XI	First Class Matches	WI	1	1	0	0	0	0.00	-	-	-	29	3	99	3	33.00	3-28
	Total First Class Career			24	31	5	172	30*	6.61	-	-	9	850.5	170	2729	94	29.03	6-43
	Total O.D. Career			2	2	1	16	16*	16.00	0	0	0	9	0	44	0	-	-

RAMNARESH RONNIE SARWAN

D.O.B. 23.06.1980 - Wakenaam Island, Essequibo, Guyana

First Class Debut	23.02.1996 - Guyana v Barbados
Test Match Debut	19.05.2000 - West Indies v Pakistan
O.D.I. Debut	20.07.2000 - West Indies v England
Domestic O.D. Debut	19.06.1996 - Guyana v Trinidad & Tobago

Teams Played For
Guyana, W.I. Select XI
West Indies
W.I. President's XI
W.I. Board XI
West Indies "A"

Test 234-358
O.D.I. 101-406

RHB / LB

SEASON	TEAM	COMPETITION	V	M	I	No	BATTING RUNS	H.S.	Av	100s	50s	CT	BOWLING OV	MD	RUNS	W	Av	B.B.
1996-2002	Guyana	First Class Matches	II	34	55	5	1548	122	30.96	2	11	22	111	20	275	11	25.00	6-62
1996-2002	Guyana	Domestic O.D. Matches	II	20	19	2	439	80	25.82	-	1	7	31.4	2	95	10	9.50	5-10
1999//	Guyana	O.A.L. O.D. Matches	WI	1	1	0	10	10	10.00	-	-	-	5	0	16	0	-	-
2000-2003	WEST INDIES	TEST MATCHES	HA	34	60	5	2127	119	38.67	2	16	18	276	5	151	3	50.33	2-1
2000-2002	West Indies	First Class Matches	A	16	24	2	764	140*	34.72	2	3	10	15	6	23	2	11.50	1-0
1997-2000	West Indies "A"	First Class Matches	HA	12	21	3	616	102	34.22	1	3	8	28	6	117	2	58.50	1-39
2000//	W.I. President's XI	First Class Matches	WI	1	2	0	211	111	105.20	2	-	1	2	0	6	0	-	-
2000//	W.I. Board XI	First Class Matches	WI	1	1	0	5	5	5.00	-	-	1	2	0	9	0	-	-
2000-2003	WEST INDIES	O.D.I. MATCHES	HA	44	42	11	1491	102*	48.09	1	7	12	132	1	135	2	67.50	1-32
2000-2001	West Indies	O.A.L. O.D. Matches	A	2	2	1	110	94	55.00	-	1	1	-	-	-	-	-	-
1997-1999	West Indies "A"	O.D.(I.) Matches	HA	6	6	1	111	48	22.20	-	-	3	4	1	21	2	10.50	1-8
1999-2000	W.I. Select XI	O.D.(I.) Matches	WI	2	2	0	73	47	36.50	-	-	1	-	-	-	-	-	-
1997//	West Indies "A"	O.A.L. O.D. Matches	A	1	1	0	16	16	16.00	-	-	-	-	-	-	-	-	-
Total First Class Career				98	163	15	5271	140*	35.61	9	33	59	1224	37	581	18	32.27	6-62
Total O.D. Career				76	73	14	2250	102*	38.13	1	9	24	376	4	267	14	19.07	5-10

REGINALD OSMOND SCARLETT

D.O.B.   15.08.1934 - Port Maria, St Mary, Jamaica

First Class Debut   17.01.1952 - Jamaica v Barbados

Test Match Debut   06.01.1960 - West Indies v England

Test   107-80

Teams Played For   Jamaica, West Indies   2

RHB / OB

SEASON	TEAM	COMPETITION	V	M	I	No	BATTING RUNS	H.S.	Av	100s	50s	CT	BOWLING OV	MD	RUNS	W	Av	B.B.
1952-1960	Jamaica	First Class Matches	II	14	23	6	423	72*	24.88	-	2	4	515.5	118	1429	46	31.06	5-69
1959-1960	WEST INDIES	TEST MATCHES	H	3	4	1	54	29*	18.00	-	-	2	134	53	209	2	104.50	1-46
Total First Class Career				17	27	7	477	72*	23.85	0	2	6	649.5	171	1638	48	34.12	5-69

ALFRED HOMER PATRICK SCOTT

D.O.B. 29.07.1934 - Spanish Town, St Catherine, Jamaica

First Class Debut 09.10.1952 - Jamaica v British Guiana

Test Match Debut 28.03.1953 - West Indies v India

Test 80-47

Teams Played For
Jamaica
West Indies

LHB / LB

BATTING

SEASON	TEAM	COMPETITION	V	M	I	No	RUNS	H.S.	Av	100s	50s	CT
1952-1954	Jamaica	First Class Matches	II	4	4	2	33	17*	16.50	-	-	3
1952-1953	WEST INDIES	TEST MATCHES	H	1	1	0	5	5	5.00	-	-	-
		Total First Class Career		5	5	2	38	17*	12.66	0	0	3

BOWLING

OV	MD	RUNS	W	Av	B.B.
155.1	26	454	18	25.22	4-46
44	9	140	0	-	-
199.1	35	594	18	33.00	4-46

2

OSCAR CHARLES SCOTT

D.O.B. 14.08.1893 - Franklyn Town, Kingston, Jamaica (d. 15.06.1961)
First Class Debut 03.04.1911 - Jamaica v M.C.C.
Test Match Debut 21.07.1928 - West Indies v England

	Test 13-2	Teams Played For	2	RHB / LBG
		Jamaica		
		West Indies		

SEASON	TEAM	COMPETITION	V	M	I	No	BATTING RUNS	H.S.	Av	100s	50s	CT	BOWLING OV	MD	RUNS	W	Av	B.B.
1911-1935	Jamaica	First Class Matches	II	19	25	3	715	94	32.50	-	6	10	878.4	128	2781	105	26.48	8-67
1928-1931	WEST INDIES	TEST MATCHES	HA	8	13	3	171	35	17.10	-	-	-	234.1	18	925	22	42.04	5-26
1928-1931	West Indies	First Class Matches	HA	18	28	6	431	75	19.59	-	3	4	433.3	31	1850	55	33.63	5-61
Total First Class Career				45	66	12	1317	94	24.38	0	9	14	1546.1	177	5556	182	30.52	8-67

BENJAMIN JAMES SEALEY

D.O.B. 12.08.1899 - St Joseph, Trinidad (d. 12.09.1963)

First Class Debut 14.02.1924 - Trinidad v British Guiana

Test Match Debut 12.08.1933 - West Indies v England

Test 36-15

Teams Played For Trinidad, West Indies, Combined T/BG XI, C.A. Merry's XI, R.S. Grant's XI, Barbados XI

RHB / RM 6

SEASON	TEAM	COMPETITION	V	M	I	No	BATTING RUNS	H.S.	Av	100s	50s	CT	BOWLING OV	MD	RUNS	W	Av	B.B.
1924-1941	Trinidad	First Class Matches	II	23	42	5	908	116	24.54	1	4	12	439.2	141	851	48	17.72	5-22
1928//	Barbados XI	First Class Matches	WI	1	1	0	5	5	5.00	-	-	2	29	2	147	3	49.00	2-113
1933//	WEST INDIES	TEST MATCHES	A	1	2	0	41	29	20.50	-	-	-	5	1	10	1	10.00	1-10
1933//	West Indies	First Class Matches	A	21	32	7	1031	106*	41.24	3	5	8	261	45	715	18	39.72	3-36
1928//	Combined T/BG XI	First Class Matches	WI	2	2	0	54	47	27.00	-	-	-	-	-	-	-	-	-
1933//	C.A Merry's XI	First Class Matches	WI	1	2	0	37	37	18.50	-	-	-	16	1	66	4	16.50	4-37
1939//	R.S. Grant's XI	First Class Matches	WI	2	3	0	39	24	13.00	-	-	-	90	16	237	4	59.25	1-31
	Total First Class Career			51	84	12	2115	116	29.37	4	9	22	840.2	206	2026	78	25.97	5-22

JAMES EDWARD DEREK SEALY

D.O.B. 11.09.1912 - Collymore Rock, St Michael, Barbados (d. 03.01.1982)
First Class Debut 05.02.1929 - Barbados v Trinidad
Test Match Debut 11.01.1930 - West Indies v England

Test 20-4

Teams Played For 5

Barbados
Trinidad
West Indies
C.A. Merry's XI
R.S. Grant's XI

RHB / WK / RM

SEASON	TEAM	COMPETITION	V	M	I	No	RUNS	H.S.	Av	100s	50s	CT/ST	OV	MD	RUNS	W	Av	B.B.
1929-1943	Barbados	First Class Matches	=	22	41	0	1135	107	27.68	2	5	15	278.3	45	771	33	23.36	8-8
1936-1949	Trinidad	First Class Matches	=	17	28	2	753	123	28.96	2	2	18/8	168.2	18	625	19	32.89	5-33
1930-1939	WEST INDIES	TEST MATCHES	HA	11	19	2	478	92	28.11	-	3	6/1	25	4	94	3	31.33	2-7
1930-1939	West Indies	First Class Matches	A	27	41	4	1168	181	31.56	2	6	23/2	70	6	272	7	38.85	1-4
1933//	C.A. Merry's XI	First Class Matches	WI	1	2	0	16	15	8.00	-	-	2/2	-	-	-	-	-	-
1939//	R.S. Grant's XI	First Class Matches	WI	2	3	0	281	141	93.66	2	-	3	11	1	40	1	40.00	1-24
Total First Class Career				80	134	8	3831	181	30.40	8	16	67/13	553.1	74	1802	63	28.60	8-8

451

KEITH FITZPATRICK SEMPLE

D.O.B. 21.08.1970 - Georgetown, Demerara, Guyana

First Class Debut	19.07.1990 - Guyana v Barbados
O.D.I. Debut	22.01.1999 - West Indies v South Africa
Domestic O.D. Debut	03.02.1993 - Guyana v Windward Islands

O.D.I. 90-354   **RHB / RM**

Teams Played For
Guyana, West Indies
W.I. President's XI
W.I. Board XI
West Indies "A"
W.I. Select XI

SEASON	TEAM	COMPETITION	V	M	I	No	RUNS	H.S.	Av	100s	50s	CT	OV	MD	RUNS	W	Av	B.B.
1990-2002	Guyana	First Class Matches	=	47	77	5	1805	142	25.06	1	14	52	72	14	166	0	-	-
1993-2001	Guyana	Domestic O.D. Matches	=	42	37	6	865	79	27.90	-	6	11	110	6	383	6	63.83	3-13
1994//	W.I. President's XI	First Class Matches	WI	1	2	1	105	76	105.00	-	1	2	-	-	-	-	-	-
1995-2000	W.I. Board XI	First Class Matches	WI	2	3	0	43	39	14.33	-	-	2	13	3	45	1	45.00	1-8
1998-1999	West Indies "A"	First Class Matches	HA	5	8	1	300	141	42.85	1	1	4	52.3	12	135	5	27.00	2-34
1999//	WEST INDIES	O.D.I. MATCHES	HA	7	6	0	64	23	10.66	-	-	3	22	0	121	3	40.33	2-35
1998//	West Indies "A"	O.D.(L.) Matches	A	4	4	1	97	69*	32.33	-	1	-	32	1	97	2	48.50	2-18
1998//	West Indies "A"	O.A.L. O.D. Matches	A	1	1	0	69	69	69.00	-	1	-	-	-	-	-	-	-
1999-2000	W.I. Select XI	First Class Matches	WI	1	1	0	58	58	58.00	-	1	-	-	-	-	-	-	-
		Total First Class Career		56	91	7	2311	142	27.51	2	17	60	137.3	29	346	6	57.66	2-34
		Total O.D. Career		54	48	7	1095	79	26.70	0	8	14	164	7	601	11	54.63	3-13

452

JOHN NEIL SHEPHERD

D.O.B. 09.11.1943 - Belleplaine, St Andrew, Barbados
First Class Debut 25.02.1965 - Barbados v Cavaliers XI
Test Match Debut 12.06.1969 - West Indies v England
Domestic O.D. Debut 13.05.1967 - Kent v Essex

Test 132-126

Teams Played For Barbados, West Indies, Kent, Gloucestershire, D.H. Robins XI, Eastern Province, International Wanderers XI, Rhodesia

8   RHB / RM

SEASON	TEAM	COMPETITION	V	M	I	No	RUNS	H.S.	Av	100s	50s	CT	OV	MD	RUNS	W	Av	B.B.
1965-1971	Barbados	First Class Matches	II	10	17	1	357	73	22.31	-	2	12	225.2	59	592	19	31.15	4-40
1969-1971	WEST INDIES	TEST MATCHES	HA	5	8	0	77	32	9.62	-	-	4	240.5	70	479	19	25.21	5-104
1969//	West Indies	First Class Matches	A	10	11	2	121	22	11.00	-	-	5	191.4	56	537	17	31.58	8-40
1969//	West Indies	O.A.L. O.D. Matches	A	1	1	1	7	7*	-	-	-	-	-	-	-	-	-	-
1966-1981	Kent	First Class Matches	E	303	431	74	9401	170	26.33	8	49	212	8813.2	2390	22106	832	26.56	8-83
1967-1981	Kent	Nat West Trophy	E	33	27	2	468	101	18.72	1	1	7	360.4	67	1094	47	23.27	4-23
1972-1981	Kent	Benson & Hedges Cup	E	50	42	6	658	96	18.27	-	2	18	469.1	-	1516	76	19.94	4-25
1969-1972	Kent	Sunday League	E	165	135	35	2428	94	24.28	-	9	46	1109.5	-	4114	207	19.87	4-17
1967-1972	Kent	O.A.L. O.D. Matches	E	2	2	0	1	1	0.50	-	-	3	12	-	56	2	28.00	1-18
1982-1987	Gloucestershire	First Class Matches	E	71	109	22	2506	168	28.80	2	15	44	2360.5	607	6431	204	31.52	6-75
1982-1984	Gloucestershire	Nat West Trophy	E	7	5	1	49	25*	12.25	-	-	-	83	13	294	13	22.61	4-20
1982-1985	Gloucestershire	Benson & Hedges Cup	E	17	10	1	103	47	11.44	-	-	2	160	-	600	26	23.07	3-25
1982-1987	Gloucestershire	Sunday League	E	45	39	13	525	52*	20.19	-	1	9	334.2	-	1618	60	26.96	6-52
1985//	Gloucestershire	O.A.L. O.D. Matches	E	1	-	-	-	-	-	-	-	-	-	-	-	-	-	-
1973-1975	D.H. Robins XI	First Class Matches	HA	13	17	4	435	53	33.46	-	2	8	368.5	81	1080	31	34.83	4-54
1974-1976	International XI	First Class Matches	SA	8	15	3	273	71*	22.75	-	2	6	258.3	54	652	29	22.48	4-37
1975-1976	Rhodesia	First Class Matches	SA	3	5	0	189	65	37.80	-	1	1	85	22	191	6	31.83	3-57
1974-1975	D.H. Robins XI	O.A.L. O.D. Matches	SA	1	1	0	10	10	10.00	-	-	-	8	-	31	1	31.00	1-31
1974-1975	International XI	O.A.L. O.D. Matches	SA	3	3	1	80	49	40.00	-	-	-	27	-	75	4	18.75	2-20
1975-1976	Eastern Province	Gillette Cup	SA	1	1	0	8	8	8.00	-	-	1	16	-	31	0	-	-
Total First Class Career				423	613	106	13359	170	26.34	10	72	292	12544.2	3339	32068	1157	27.71	8-40
Total O.D. Career				326	266	60	4337	101	21.05	1	13	86	2580	-	9429	436	21.62	6-52

International Wanderers XI
Rhodesia

453

GRAYSON CLEOPHAS SHILLINGFORD

D.O.B. 25.09.1944 - Macoucherie, Dominica, Windward Islands

First Class Debut 08.03.1968 - Windward Islands v M.C.C.
Test Match Debut 26.06.1969 - West Indies v England
Domestic O.D. Debut 21.02.1976 - Windward Islands v Trinidad & Tobago

Test 134-127

Teams Played For
Windward Islands
Combined Islands
West Indies
W.I. President's XI

LHB / RFM

4

SEASON	TEAM	COMPETITION	V	M	I	No	BATTING						BOWLING					
							RUNS	H.S.	Av	100s	50s	CT	OV	MD	RUNS	W	Av	B.B.
1968-1979	Windward Islands	First Class Matches	II	22	33	7	270	35	10.38	-	-	6	487.1	85	1433	52	27.55	5-79
1970-1979	Combined Islands	First Class Matches	II	31	51	15	377	42	10.47	-	-	12	807.3	138	2475	95	26.05	6-49
1976-1979	Windward Islands	Domestic O.D. Matches	II	6	4	0	70	32	17.50	-	-	1	50	12	132	4	33.00	1-18
1972//	Windward Islands	O.A.L. O.D. Matches	WI	1	1	0	9	9	9.00	-	-	-	9	2	23	1	23.00	1-23
1973-1974	Combined Islands	O.A.L. O.D. Matches	WI	1	D	-	-	-	-	-	-	-	6	2	7	0	-	-
1969-1972	WEST INDIES	TEST MATCHES	HA	7	8	1	57	25	8.14	-	-	2	196.5	38	537	15	35.80	3-63
1969-1973	West Indies	First Class Matches	A	20	13	5	86	35*	10.75	-	-	2	386.3	75	1229	52	23.63	6-63
1971//	W.I. President's XI	First Class Matches	WI	1	1	0	1	1	1.00	-	-	-	30	5	86	3	28.66	3-41
1973//	West Indies	O.A.L. O.D. Matches	A	1	1	1	3	3*	-	-	-	1	8	1	33	0	-	-
		Total First Class Career		81	106	28	791	42	10.14	0	0	22	1908	341	5760	217	26.54	6-49
		Total O.D. Career		9	6	1	82	32	16.40	0	0	2	73	17	195	5	39.00	1-18

IRVINE THEODORE SHILLINGFORD

D.O.B. 18.04.1944 - Dublanc, Dominica, Windward Islands
First Class Debut 06.10.1961 - Combined Islands v British Guiana
Test Match Debut 04.03.1977 - West Indies v Pakistan
O.D.I. Debut 22.02.1978 - West Indies v Australia
Domestic O.D. Debut 19.02.1976 - Windward Islands v Guyana

Test	161-175
O.D.I.	26-13

Teams Played For 4
Windward Islands
Combined Islands
West Indies
W.I. President's XI

RHB / RM

SEASON	TEAM	COMPETITION	V	M	I	No	BATTING RUNS	H.S.	Av	100s	50s	CT	BOWLING OV	MD	RUNS	W	Av	B.B.
1965-1982	Windward Islands	First Class Matches	=	37	65	3	2250	238	36.29	3	11	39	20	6	46	1	46.00	1-15
1961-1981	Combined Islands	First Class Matches	=	49	83	5	2788	120	35.74	6	16	54	12	2	30	0	-	-
1976-1982	Windward Islands	Domestic O.D. Matches	=	15	14	2	197	36	16.41	-	-	7	2.5	0	18	0	-	-
1972-1981	Combined Islands	O.A.L. O.D. Matches	WI	3	3	0	93	36	31.00	-	-	1	-	-	-	-	-	-
1977-1978	WEST INDIES	TEST MATCHES	HA	4	7	0	218	120	31.14	1	1	1	-	-	-	-	-	-
1972-1977	W.I. President's XI	First Class Matches	WI	2	2	0	193	124	96.50	1	1	-	2	0	9	0	-	-
1978/I	WEST INDIES	O.D.I. MATCHES	WI	2	2	0	30	24	15.00	-	-	2	-	-	-	-	-	-
Total First Class Career				92	157	8	5449	238	36.57	11	28	94	34	8	85	1	85.00	1-15
Total O.D. Career				20	19	2	320	36	18.82	0	0	10	2.5	0	18	0	-	-

SEWDATT SHIVNARINE

D.O.B. 13.05.1952 - Albion, Berbice, British Guiana

First Class Debut	27.02.1971 - Guyana v Jamaica
Test Match Debut	31.03.1978 - West Indies v Australia
O.D.I. Debut	12.04.1978 - West Indies v Australia
Domestic O.D. Debut	18.01.1977 - Guyana v Leeward Islands

Test 169-181
O.D.I. 32-14

Teams Played For
Guyana
Berbice
West Indies
USA

RHB / LAS

SEASON	TEAM	COMPETITION	V	M	I	No	BATTING RUNS	H.S.	Av	100s	50s	CT	BOWLING OV	MD	RUNS	W	Av	B.B.
1971-1981	Guyana	First Class Matches	II	27	41	1	1004	101	25.10	1	7	18	671.5	176	1727	51	33.86	4-29
1971-1979	Berbice	First Class Matches	G	7	11	5	338	82	56.33	-	2	7	158	36	364	10	36.40	3-63
1976-1981	Guyana	Domestic O.D. Matches	II	9	8	0	187	46	15.87	-	-	6	63.1	10	246	7	35.14	2-25
1978-1979	WEST INDIES	TEST MATCHES	HA	8	14	1	379	63	29.15	-	4	6	56	10	167	1	167.00	1-13
1978-1979	West Indies	First Class Matches	A	7	12	4	461	131*	57.62	2	1	5	63	10	191	5	38.20	2-35
1978//	WEST INDIES	O.D.I. MATCHES	H	1	1	1	20	20*	-	-	-	-	3	0	16	0	-	-
1979//	West Indies	O.A.L. O.D. Matches	A	3	3	0	59	23	19.66	-	-	-	8	1	26	2	13.00	2-26
1986-1994	USA	I.C.C. Trophy	A	15	14	3	463	70*	42.09	-	2	8	46.4	6	162	3	54.00	1-36
Total First Class Career				49	78	11	2182	131*	32.56	3	14	36	948.5	232	2449	67	36.55	4-29
Total O.D. Career				28	26	4	669	70*	30.40	0	2	14	120.5	17	450	12	37.50	2-25

PHILIP VERANT SIMMONS

D.O.B. 18.04.1963 - Arima, Trinidad
First Class Debut 07.01.1983 - N/E Trinidad v S/C Trinidad
Test Match Debut 11.01.1988 - West Indies v India
O.D.I. Debut 16.10.1987 - West Indies v Pakistan
Domestic O.D. Debut 19.01.1983 - Trinidad & Tobago v Jamaica

Test 191-256
O.D.I. 51-143

RHB / RM

Teams Played For 14
Trinidad & Tobago, West Indies, Durham
W.I. Board XI, N/E Trinidad, Border
West Indies "B", West Indies U23, Easterns
Leicestershire, W.I. President's XI, M.C. Wales
World XI, West Indies "A"

SEASON	TEAM	COMPETITION	V	M	I	No	BATTING RUNS	H.S.	Av	100s	50s	CT	BOWLING OV	MD	RUNS	W	Av	B.B.
1983-2001	Trinidad & Tobago	First Class Matches	=	76	137	5	4739	202	35.90	5	36	85	856.5	184	2437	70	34.81	5-24
1983-1985	N/E Trinidad	First Class Matches	T	3	5	0	184	71	36.80	-	2	3	1	0	9	0	-	-
1983-1998	Trinidad & Tobago	Domestic O.D. Matches	=	45	41	4	1176	125	31.78	1	10	27	224.5	20	941	34	27.67	5-36
1991//	Trinidad & Tobago	O.A.L. O.D. Matches	WI	1	1	0	0	0	0.00	-	-	-	10	1	35	2	17.50	2-35
1988-1997	WEST INDIES	TEST MATCHES	HA	26	47	2	1002	110	22.26	1	4	26	104	27	257	4	64.25	2-34
1987-1997	West Indies	First Class Matches	A	24	38	4	1820	139*	53.52	7	8	20	175	40	591	11	53.72	2-34
1985-1991	W.I. President's XI	First Class Matches	WI	4	7	1	264	116*	44.00	1	1	1	24	7	57	2	28.50	2-57
1988-1994	W.I. Board XI	First Class Matches	WI	4	7	1	255	122	42.50	1	-	2	15	1	43	0	-	-
1984-1985	West Indies U23	First Class Matches	WI	1	1	0	1	1	1.00	-	-	-	-	-	-	-	-	-
1983-1986	West Indies "B"	First Class Matches	A	6	10	1	200	107	22.22	1	-	8	24	5	70	3	23.33	2-53
1987-1999	WEST INDIES	O.D.(I.) MATCHES	HA	143	138	11	3675	122	28.93	5	18	55	646.4	38	2876	83	34.65	4-3
1983-1986	West Indies "B"	O.D.(I.) Matches	A	8	8	1	341	166*	48.71	1	1	7	41	7	213	4	53.25	2-31
1994-1995	West Indies "A"	O.D.(I.) Matches	H	8	8	1	83	60	11.86	-	1	2	24	2	93	4	23.25	3-30
1988-1997	West Indies	O.A.L. O.D. Matches	A	5	5	0	84	55	16.80	-	1	1	27	-	141	3	47.00	2-28
1994-1998	Leicestershire	First Class Matches	E	51	73	2	2661	261	37.47	6	12	81	836.2	212	2281	109	20.92	7-49
1994-1998	Leicestershire	Nat West Trophy	E	8	8	2	363	107*	60.50	1	2	7	62	-	289	8	36.12	3-31
1994-1998	Leicestershire	Benson & Hedges Cup	E	12	12	4	412	89	51.50	-	3	7	85.1	11	467	11	42.45	5-33
1994-1998	Leicestershire	Sunday League	E	49	49	2	1938	140	41.23	4	12	23	264.5	-	1344	44	30.54	5-37
1994//	Leicestershire	O.A.L. O.D. Matches	E	3	3	0	3	3	3.00	-	-	1	4	-	18	0	-	-
1992-1993	World XI	First Class Matches	E	2	2	0	69	46	34.50	-	-	3	18	2	71	1	71.00	1-43
1989-1990	Durham	Nat West Trophy	E	2	2	0	47	33	23.50	-	-	4	16	2	16	0	-	-
2000-2002	M.C. Wales	Cheltenham & Gloucs Trophy	E	9	9	2	226	82	32.28	-	4	10	78	20	353	11	32.09	3-34
1996-2000	M.C. Wales	First Class Matches	SA	10	18	1	487	122	28.64	2	2	4	143.1	38	373	15	24.86	3-27
1996-2000	Easterns	Standard Bank Cup	SA	17	16	1	427	87	28.46	-	3	3	101.1	7	479	7	68.42	2-37
1999-2000	Easterns	O.A.L. O.D. Matches	SA	1	1	0	29	29	29.00	-	-	1	-	-	-	-	-	-
1992-1993	Border	Benson & Hedges Cup	SA	2	2	0	85	44	42.50	-	1	-	18	-	61	3	20.33	2-32
Total First Class Career				207	345	17	11682	261	35.61	24	65	241	2199.2	525	6138	214	28.68	7-49
Total O.D. Career				306	296	27	8929	166*	33.19	12	54	137	1598.4	-	7381	215	34.33	5-33

CHARRAN KAMKARAN SINGH

D.O.B. 27.11.1935 - San Juan, Trinidad

First Class Debut 02.10.1959 - Trinidad v Jamaica
Test Match Debut 28.01.1960 - West Indies v England

Test 109-81

Teams Played For
Trinidad
North Trinidad
West Indies

RHB / SLA

3

SEASON	TEAM	COMPETITION	V	M	I	No	BATTING						BOWLING					
							RUNS	H.S.	Av	100s	50s	CT	OV	MD	RUNS	W	Av	B.B.
1960-1962	Trinidad	First Class Matches	=	7	10	3	82	29*	11.71	-	-	5	393	136	858	37	23.18	7-38
1960-1961	North Trinidad	First Class Matches	T	2	2	0	9	9	4.50	-	-		80	32	125	6	20.83	4-41
1959-1960	WEST INDIES	TEST MATCHES	H	2	3	0	11	11	3.66	-	-	2	84.2	35	166	5	33.20	2-28
		Total First Class Career		11	15	3	102	29*	8.50	0	0	7	557.2	203	1149	48	23.93	7-38

RABINDRA 'ROBIN' RAMANARAYAN SINGH

LHB / RMF

D.O.B. 14.09.1963 - Princes Town, Trinidad
First Class Debut 07.01.1983 - S/C Trinidad v N/E Trinidad
Test Match Debut 07.10.1998 - India v Zimbabwe
O.D.I. Debut 11.03.1989 - India v West Indies
Domestic O.D. Debut 26.01.1983 - Trinidad & Tobago v Windward Islands

Teams Played For 11
S/C Trinidad, India, Wills XI
Tamil Nadu, Trinidad & Tobago
India "A", South Zone
Board President's XI, India "B"
India Seniors XI, Rest of India XI

SEASON	TEAM	COMPETITION	V	M	I	No	RUNS	H.S.	Av	100s	50s	CT	OV	MD	RUNS	W	Av	B.B.
1982-1983	S/C Trinidad	First Class Matches	T	1	2	0	13	13	6.50	-	-	1	10	0	45	0	-	-
1982-1984	Trinidad & Tobago	Domestic O.D. Matches	II	2	2	1	6	5*	6.00	-	-	1	20	3	86	0	-	-
1998-1999	INDIA	TEST MATCHES	A	1	2	0	27	15	13.50	-	-	5	10	4	32	0	-	-
1988-1997	India	First Class Matches	A	7	11	3	213	53	26.62	-	1	1	76	12	263	1	263.00	1-15
1987-1996	Board President's XI	First Class Matches		2	3	0	65	50	21.66	-	1	1	13	2	56	0	-	-
1985-2002	Tamil Nadu	First Class Matches		100	120	22	4958	183*	50.59	16	22	81	1474	-	4372	141	31.00	7-54
1988-2002	South Zone	First Class Matches		25	40	3	1721	141	46.51	6	9	21	420.4	-	1358	30	45.26	4-30
1997-1998	Rest of India XI	First Class Matches		1	2	0	0	0	0.00	-	-	-	28	6	62	0	-	-
1989-2002	INDIA	O.D.I. MATCHES	HA	136	113	23	2336	100	25.95	1	9	33	622.2	28	2985	69	43.26	5-22
1987-1988	Board President's XI	Wills Trophy O.D.		3	3	3	32	25*	-	-	-	-	23	1	122	3	40.66	2-35
1997-2000	India	NKP Challenge Trophy O.D.		7	5	2	120	37*	24.00	-	-	1	25	1	140	4	35.00	2-22
1994-1997	India Seniors XI	NKP Challenge Trophy O.D.		5	5	0	157	91	31.40	-	1	5	47	2	194	4	48.50	2-46
1998-1999	India "A"	NKP Challenge Trophy O.D.		5	2	0	20	14	10.00	-	-	-	23	2	76	2	38.00	2-17
2000-2001	India	NKP Challenge Trophy O.D.	A	3	2	1	94	64	94.00	-	1	-	3	0	35	0	-	-
1996-1998	India "B"	NKP Challenge Trophy O.D.	A	2	2	1	33	33	33.00	-	-	-	-	-	-	-	-	-
1992-1996	India	O.A.L. O.D. Matches		2	2	0	33	16	16.50	-	-	-	17	1	72	1	72.00	1-49
1988-2001	Wills XI	Wills Trophy O.D.		4	2	1	23	16	23.00	-	-	3	30	2	133	5	26.60	2-36
1989-1998	South Zone	Deodhar Trophy O.D.		23	22	5	506	67	29.76	-	4	-	171.1	5	806	24	33.58	3-33
1998-2002	Tamil Nadu	Wills Trophy O.D.		4	4	0	94	40	23.50	-	-	-	29	2	133	3	44.33	2-32
1998-2002	Tamil Nadu	Ranji O.D. Trophy		35	29	5	533	63	22.20	-	4	13	231	11	1018	33	30.84	3-25
1988-1990	Tamil Nadu	O.A.L. O.D. Matches		1	3	0	110	69	36.66	-	1	1	15	0	70	2	35.00	2-48
Total First Class Career				137	180	28	6997	183*	46.03	22	33	109	2031.4	-	6188	172	35.97	7-54
Total O.D. Career				229	196	41	4064	100	26.21	1	20	57	1257.2	57	5870	150	39.13	5-22

459

WILFRED NORRIS SLACK

D.O.B. 12.12.1954 - Troumaca, St Vincent, Windward Islands (d. 15.01.1989)

First Class Debut	15.06.1977 - Middlesex v Cambridge University
Test Match Debut	07.03.1986 - England v West Indies
O.D.I. Debut	04.03.1986 - England v West Indies
Domestic O.D. Debut	14.05.1980 - Middlesex v Hampshire

Teams Played For
Windward Islands
Middlesex
England
England "B"
International XI

LHB / RM

SEASON	TEAM	V	COMPETITION	M	I	No	RUNS	H.S.	Av	100s	50s	CT	OV	MD	RUNS	W	Av	B.B.
1981-1983	Windward Islands	II	First Class Matches	9	17	1	585	97	36.56	-	3	13	15.1	4	41	2	20.50	2-15
1981-1983	Windward Islands	II	Domestic O.D. Matches	6	6	0	198	63	33.00	-	1	3	26.2	2	114	3	38.00	2-10
1985-1986	ENGLAND	HA	TEST MATCHES	3	6	0	81	52	13.50	-	1	3	-	-	-	-	-	-
1985-1987	England	A	First Class Matches	7	13	1	256	89	21.33	-	1	6	-	-	-	-	-	-
1985-1986	England "B"	A	First Class Matches	6	10	0	431	96	43.10	-	4	-	8	1	15	0	-	-
1985-1986	ENGLAND	A	O.D.I. MATCHES	2	2	0	43	34	21.50	-	-	-	-	-	-	-	-	-
1985-1986	England "B"	A	O.A.L. O.D. Matches	3	3	1	144	122*	72.00	1	-	1	-	-	-	-	-	-
1977-1988	Middlesex	E	First Class Matches	210	348	38	12565	248*	40.53	25	66	148	230	59	632	19	33.26	3-17
1980-1988	Middlesex	E	Nat West Trophy	26	26	1	827	98	33.08	-	7	4	84	6	317	8	39.62	3-37
1980-1988	Middlesex	E	Benson & Hedges Cup	37	36	4	895	110	27.96	1	5	6	7	-	34	0	-	-
1978-1988	Middlesex	E	Sunday League	103	95	13	2353	101*	28.69	1	16	22	176.2	-	878	34	25.82	5-32
1988//	Middlesex	E	Sunday League Cup	1	1	0	7	7	7.00	-	-	-	-	-	-	-	-	-
1980-1987	Middlesex	HA	O.A.L. O.D. Matches	4	3	1	151	84	75.50	-	2	-	-	-	-	-	-	-
1981-1982	International XI	P	First Class Matches	2	4	0	32	17	8.00	-	-	4	-	-	-	-	-	-
1981-1982	International XI	P	O.A.L. O.D. Matches	1	1	0	21	21	21.00	-	-	-	0.4	0	9	0	-	-
Total First Class Career				237	398	40	13950	248*	38.96	25	75	174	253.1	64	688	21	32.76	3-17
Total O.D. Career				183	173	20	4693	122*	30.32	3	31	36	294.2	-	1352	45	30.04	5-32

GLADSTONE CLEOPHAS SMALL

6   RHB / RFM

D.O.B. 18.10.1961 - Brighton, St George, Barbados

First Class Debut 22.03.1980 - D.H. Robins XI v Northern District
Test Match Debut 07.08.1986 - England v New Zealand
O.D.I. Debut 01.01.1987 - England v Australia
Domestic O.D. Debut 04.05.1980 - Warwickshire v Hampshire

Teams Played For
Warwickshire, England
M.C.C.
D.H. Robins XI
South Australia
International XI

SEASON	TEAM	COMPETITION	V	M	I	No	BATTING RUNS	H.S.	Av	100s	50s	CT	BOWLING OV	MD	RUNS	W	Av	B.B.
1986-1991	ENGLAND	TEST MATCHES	HA	17	24	7	263	59	15.47	-	1	9	654.3	154	1871	55	34.01	5-48
1986-1991	England	First Class Matches	A	12	16	4	170	37*	14.16	-	-	7	348	87	935	37	25.27	5-81
1986-1992	ENGLAND	O.D.I. MATCHES	HA	53	24	9	98	18*	6.53	-	-	7	465.3	-	1942	58	33.48	4-31
1987-1991	England	O.A.L. O.D. Matches	A	2	1	0	6	6	6.00	-	-	-	20	2	60	2	30.00	-
1980-1997	Warwickshire	First Class Matches	E	272	344	81	3757	70	14.28	-	6	77	6805	1503	20053	717	27.96	7-15
1980-1998	Warwickshire	Nat West Trophy	E	50	30	9	256	33	12.19	-	-	9	488.3	-	1550	54	28.70	3-22
1980-1998	Warwickshire	Benson & Hedges Cup	E	68	40	12	210	22	7.50	-	-	11	627.2	-	2194	81	27.08	5-23
1980-1999	Warwickshire	Sunday League	E	208	90	32	461	40*	7.94	-	-	45	1432	-	6342	261	24.29	5-18
1986-1991	Warwickshire	O.A.L. O.D. Matches	E	4	2	1	21	21*	21.00	-	-	1	4	7	0	-	-	-
1979-1980	D.H. Robins XI	First Class Matches	NZ	1	-	-	-	-	-	-	-	-	16	5	50	0	-	-
1981-1982	International XI	First Class Matches	P	2	4	2	54	21*	27.00	-	-	-	47	8	161	4	40.25	3-83
1988//	M.C.C.	First Class Matches	E	1	1	1	21	21*	-	-	-	-	26	5	78	0	-	-
1981-1982	International XI	O.A.L. O.D. Matches	P	3	2	0	3	3	1.50	-	-	1	16	-	63	3	21.00	3-18
1985-1986	South Australia	First Class Matches	A	10	15	2	144	33	11.07	-	-	2	415.4	74	1244	39	31.89	7-42
1985-1986	South Australia	MacDonalds Cup	A	2	2	2	17	16*	-	-	-	-	18.4	-	72	3	24.00	3-42
		Total First Class Career		315	404	97	4409	70	14.36	-	7	95	8312.1	1836	24392	852	28.62	7-15
		Total O.D. Career		390	191	65	1072	40*	8.50	0	0	74	3072.2	-	12230	462	26.47	5-18

JOSEPH A. SMALL

D.O.B. 03.11.1892 - Princes Town, Trinidad (d. 26.04.1958)

First Class Debut 11.11.1909 - Trinidad v W.C. Shepherds XI
Test Match Debut 23.06.1928 - West Indies v England

Test 8-1

Teams Played For
Trinidad
West Indies
Combined T/BG XI   3

RHB / RM

BATTING

SEASON	TEAM	COMPETITION	V	M	I	No	RUNS	H.S.	Av	100s	50s	CT	OV	MD	RUNS	W	Av	B.B.
1909-1932	Trinidad	First Class Matches	=	28	50	3	1366	133	29.06	3	6	28	807.1	220	1790	74	24.18	7-49
1928-1930	WEST INDIES	TEST MATCHES	HA	3	6	0	79	52	13.16	-	1	3	61	11	184	3	61.33	2-67
1913-1929	West Indies	First Class Matches	HA	44	69	7	1510	106*	24.35	1	9	40	890.4	161	2501	83	30.13	7-77
1927-1928	Combined T/BG XI	First Class Matches	WI	2	3	1	108	45*	54.00	-	-	1	52	15	114	5	22.80	3-8
Total First Class Career				77	128	11	3063	133	26.17	4	16	72	1810.5	407	4589	165	27.81	7-49

BOWLING

MILTON ASTER SMALL

D.O.B. 12.02.1964 - Blades Point, St Philip, Barbados

First Class Debut 20.01.1984 - Barbados v Trinidad & Tobago

Test Match Debut 16.03.1984 - West Indies v Australia

O.D.I. Debut 29.02.1984 - West Indies v Australia

Domestic O.D. Debut 08.02.1984 - Barbados v Leeward Islands

Test	182-224	Teams Played For	2	RHB / RFM
O.D.I.	43-79	Barbados		
		West Indies		

							BATTING						BOWLING					
SEASON	TEAM	COMPETITION	V	M	I	No	RUNS	H.S.	Av	100s	50s	CT	OV	MD	RUNS	W	Av	B.B.
1984-1992	Barbados	First Class Matches	=	12	14	3	45	15	4.09	-	-	4	383.5	54	1185	42	28.21	6-55
1984-1989	Barbados	Domestic O.D. Matches	=	5	3	1	9	7	4.50	-	-	-	39	8	110	6	18.33	4-24
1983-1984	WEST INDIES	TEST MATCHES	A	2	1	1	3	3*	-	-	-	-	45	7	153	4	38.25	3-40
1983-1984	West Indies	First Class Matches	A	4	2	1	3	2*	3.00	-	-	1	79	15	243	10	24.30	4-52
1983-1984	WEST INDIES	O.D.I. MATCHES	A	2	D	-	-	-	-	-	-	1	14	0	54	1	54.00	1-22
1983-1984	West Indies	O.A.L. O.D. Matches	A	1	D	-	-	-	-	-	-	-	11	1	48	1	48.00	1-48
Total First Class Career				18	17	5	51	15	4.25	0	0	5	507.5	76	1581	56	28.23	6-55
Total O.D. Career				8	3	1	9	7	4.50	0	0	1	64	9	212	8	26.50	4-24

CAMERON WILBERFORCE SMITH

D.O.B. 29.07.1933 - Upper Dayrells Road, St Michael, Barbados
First Class Debut 29.09.1951 - Barbados v British Guiana
Test Match Debut 09.12.1960 - West Indies v Australia

Test 113-85

Teams Played For
Barbados
West Indies
Commonwealth XI
NZ Governor General's XI

RHB / WK
4

SEASON	TEAM	COMPETITION	V	M	I	No	BATTING						BOWLING					
							RUNS	H.S.	Av	100s	50s	CT/ST	OV	MD	RUNS	W	Av	B.B.
1951-1963	Barbados	First Class Matches	II	20	32	2	1434	140	47.80	5	6	22	25	2	73	1	73.00	1-8
1960-1962	WEST INDIES	TEST MATCHES	HA	5	10	1	222	55	24.66	-	1	4/1	-	-	-	-	-	-
1960-1964	West Indies	First Class Matches	A	10	18	0	494	68	27.44	-	2	4/2	-	-	-	-	-	-
1960-1964	NZ Gov. General's XI	First Class Matches	NZ	1	2	0	53	35	26.50	-	-	1/1	7	0	24	2	12.00	2-24
1964-1965	Commonwealth XI	First Class Matches	I	1	2	0	74	68	37.00	-	1	-	-	-	-	-	-	-
		Total First Class Career		37	64	3	2277	140	37.32	5	10	31/4	32	2	97	3	32.33	2-24

464

DEVON SHELDON SMITH

D.O.B. 21.10.1981 - Hermitage, St Patrick, Grenada
First Class Debut 14.01.1999 - Windward Islands v Barbados
Test Match Debut 10.04.2003 - West Indies v Australia
O.D.I. Debut 17.05.2003 - West Indies v Australia
Domestic O.D. Debut 28.10.1999 - Windward Islands v Guyana

Test 247-394
O.D.I. 114-461

LHB / OB

Teams Played For 7
Windward Islands, Southern Windwards
West Indies, W.I. President's XI
West Indies "A"
Busta Cup XI
Carib Cup XI

SEASON	TEAM	COMPETITION	V	M	I	No	RUNS	H.S.	Av	100s	50s	CT	OV	MD	RUNS	W	Av	B.B.
1999-2003	Windward Islands	First Class Matches	=	31	59	2	1953	143	34.26	2	13	30	1	0	1	0	-	-
1999-2000	Windward Islands	Domestic O.D. Matches	=	8	8	0	89	31	11.12	-	-	3	-	-	-	-	-	-
2001-2002	Southern Windwards	Domestic O.D. Matches	=	3	3	0	83	48	27.66	-	-	-	-	-	-	-	-	-
2003//	WEST INDIES	TEST MATCHES	HA	4	8	0	189	62	23.62	-	2	2	-	-	-	-	-	-
1999-2002	West Indies "A"	First Class Matches	HA	7	12	0	502	181	41.83	1	4	4	-	-	-	-	-	-
2002//	Busta Cup XI	First Class Matches	WI	1	1	0	91	91	91.00	-	1	-	-	-	-	-	-	-
2003//	Carib Cup XI	First Class Matches	WI	1	2	0	37	37	18.50	-	-	-	-	-	-	-	-	-
2003//	WEST INDIES	O.D.I. MATCHES	HA	3	3	0	36	26	12.00	-	-	1	-	-	-	-	-	-
2002//	West Indies "A"	O.A.L. O.D. Matches	A	5	5	0	35	25	7.00	-	-	1	-	-	-	-	-	-
2002-2003	W.I. President's XI	First Class Matches	WI	1	1	0	8	8	8.00	-	-	1	-	-	-	-	-	-
Total First Class Career				45	83	2	2780	181	34.32	3	18	37	1	0	1	0	-	-
Total O.D. Career				19	19	0	243	48	12.78	0	0	5	-	-	-	-	-	-

BATTING | **BOWLING**

O'NEIL GORDON SMITH
D.O.B. 05.05.1933 - Denham Town, Kingston, Jamaica (d. 09.09.1959)
First Class Debut 05.02.1955 - Jamaica v Trinidad
Test Match Debut 26.03.1956 - West Indies v Australia

Test 86-53

Teams Played For
Jamaica
West Indies
Commonwealth XI

3

RHB / OB

SEASON	TEAM	COMPETITION	V	M	I	No	BATTING RUNS	H.S.	Av	100s	50s	CT	BOWLING OV	MD	RUNS	W	Av	B.B.
1955-1958	Jamaica	First Class Matches	ll	8	14	1	873	169	67.15	4	3	7	335.5	73	859	26	33.03	4-84
1956-1959	WEST INDIES	TEST MATCHES	HA	26	42	0	1331	168	31.69	4	6	9	738.3	229	1625	48	33.85	5-90
1955-1959	West Indies	First Class Matches	HA	35	54	11	1798	140*	41.81	2	11	22	515.3	187	1203	46	26.15	5-63
1958//	Commonwealth XI	First Class Matches	E	1	2	0	29	17	14.50	-	-	1	21	5	67	1	67.00	1-53
		Total First Class Career		70	112	12	4031	169	40.31	10	20	39	1610.5	494	3754	121	31.02	5-63

GARFIELD ST. AUBRUN SOBERS

D.O.B. 28.07.1936 - Chelsea Road, Bayland, St. Michael, Barbados
First Class Debut 31.01.1953 - Barbados v India
Test Match Debut 30.03.1954 - West Indies v England
O.D.I. Debut 05.09.1973 - West Indies v England
Domestic O.D. Debut 27.04.1968 - Nottinghamshire v Lancashire

Test	84-52	Teams Played For	12	LHB / LFMS
O.D.I.	6-1			

Barbados, Jamaican XI, West Indies, M.C.C.,
C.C. Hunte's XI, Cavaliers XI
Commonwealth XI, Nottinghamshire
E.W. Swanton's XI, World XI
South Australia, A.E.R. Gilligan's XI

SEASON	TEAM	COMPETITION	V	M	I	No	BATTING						BOWLING					
							RUNS	H.S.	Av	100s	50s	CT	OV	MD	RUNS	W	Av	B.B.
1953-1974	Barbados	First Class Matches	I=	30	40	9	2355	204	75.96	8	8	22	925.3	293	2133	71	30.04	6-56
1965-1966	Jamaican XI	First Class Matches	WI	2	3	0	267	129	89.00	2	-	2	78.4	19	205	7	29.28	3-41
1972-1973	Barbados	Domestic O.D. Matches	I=	2	2	0	32	19	16.00	-	-	-	12.3	1	44	4	11.00	2-16
1954-1974	WEST INDIES	TEST MATCHES	HA	93	160	21	8032	365*	57.78	26	30	109	3432.3	974	7999	235	34.03	6-73
1955-1969	West Indies	First Class Matches	A	94	134	24	5567	219*	50.60	14	25	108	1988.4	506	5430	226	24.02	9-49
1963-1964	C.C. Hunte's XI	First Class Matches	WI	1	2	0	118	107	59.00	1	-	-	27	1	135	5	27.00	4-86
1973/I	WEST INDIES	O.D.I. MATCHES	WI	1	1	0	0	0	0.00	-	-	1	10.3	3	31	1	31.00	1-31
1963-1966	West Indies	O.A.L. O.D. Matches	A	3	2	1	92	64	46.00	-	1	3	29	5	79	1	79.00	1-13
1968-1974	Nottinghamshire	First Class Matches	E	107	174	30	7041	160	48.69	18	39	110	2852.4	777	7202	281	25.62	7-69
1968-1974	Nottinghamshire	Nat West Trophy	E	12	12	6	676	96*	112.66	-	8	2	135.2	42	342	24	14.25	4-11
1972-1974	Nottinghamshire	Benson & Hedges Cup	E	12	11	2	326	97*	36.22	-	2	7	124	-	340	11	30.90	2-17
1969-1974	Nottinghamshire	Sunday League	E	62	62	11	1549	116*	30.37	1	7	28	413.2	-	1545	68	22.72	5-43
1958-1964	Commonwealth XI	First Class Matches	A	4	8	0	456	102	57.00	1	4	6	87	12	295	12	24.58	4-69
1965-1972	World XI	First Class Matches	A	19	31	5	1250	254	48.07	4	3	20	540.6	141	1364	50	17.28	6-21
1958-1959	A.E.R. Gilligan's XI	First Class Matches	E	2	3	0	194	75	64.66	-	2	1	13	2	63	2	31.50	-
1961-1962	M.C.C.	First Class Matches	I-	3	5	1	154	103	38.50	1	1	1	100	27	283	8	35.37	3-9
1963-1964	E.W. Swanton's XI	First Class Matches	E	1	1	0	130	123	130.00	1	-	-	46	9	141	9	15.66	6-63
1970/I	Cavaliers XI	First Class Matches	WI	2	2	0	123	35	21.50	-	2	2	49	16	126	2	63.00	2-77
1961-1964	South Australia	First Class Matches	A	26	45	2	2707	251	62.95	10	26	117	1006.6	117	3565	137	26.05	7-110
1971/I	World XI	O.A.L. O.D. Matches	A	2	2	1	44	44*	44.00	-	-	-	8	-	12	0	-	-
Total First Class Career				383	609	93	28314	365*	54.87	86	121	407	11147.5	2894	28941	1043	27.74	9-49
Total O.D. Career				94	92	21	2719	116*	38.29	1	18	41	732.4	-	2393	109	21.95	5-43

JOSEPH STANISLAUS SOLOMON

D.O.B. 26.08.1930 - Port Mourant, Berbice, British Guiana

First Class Debut	11.10.1956 - British Guiana v Jamaica	
Test Match Debut	12.12.1958 - West Indies v India	
Domestic O.D. Debut	13.04.1973 - Guyana v Jamaica	

Test 105-73

Teams Played For
British Guiana/Guyana
Berbice
West Indies
C.C. Hunte's XI

RHB / LB

4

SEASON	TEAM	COMPETITION	V	M	I	No	BATTING RUNS	H.S.	Av	100s	50s	CT	BOWLING OV	MD	RUNS	W	Av	B.B.
1956-1969	Br. Guiana / Guyana	First Class Matches	=	23	34	6	1905	179	68.03	9	4	13	181	38	472	14	33.71	4-28
1959-1960	Berbice	First Class Matches	G	2	3	1	334	201*	167.00	1	2	2	27	0	131	1	131.00	1-83
1972-1973	Guyana	Domestic O.D. Matches	=	1	1	0	1	1	1.00	-	-	-	2	0	9	1	9.00	1-9
1958-1965	WEST INDIES	TEST MATCHES	HA	27	46	7	1326	100*	34.00	1	9	13	116	39	268	4	67.00	1-20
1958-1966	West Indies	First Class Matches	A	51	71	14	1648	104*	28.91	1	11	18	259.5	41	943	31	30.41	4-34
1964//	C.C. Hunte's XI	First Class Matches	WI	1	2	0	105	74	52.50	-	1	-	21	0	136	1	136.00	1-61
1966//	West Indies	O.A.L. O.D. Matches	A	1	D	-	-	-	-	-	-	1	-	-	-	-	-	-
		Total First Class Career		104	156	28	5318	201*	41.54	12	27	46	604.5	118	1950	51	38.23	4-28
		Total O.D. Career		2	1	0	1	1	1.00	0	0	1	2	0	9	1	9.00	1-9

SVEN CONRAD STAYERS

D.O.B. 09.06.1937 - Georgetown, Demerara, British Guiana

First Class Debut 06.03.1958 - British Guiana v Pakistan

Test Match Debut 16.02.1962 - West Indies v India

Test 115-90   RHB / RFM

Teams Played For 5
British Guiana
West Indies
Bombay
West Zone
Indian Chief Minister's XI

SEASON	TEAM	COMPETITION	V	M	I	No	BATTING RUNS	H.S.	Av	100s	50s	CT	BOWLING OV	MD	RUNS	W	Av	B.B.
1958-1962	British Guiana	First Class Matches	=	9	13	2	336	120	30.54	1	1	3	308.1	41	1090	45	24.22	6-63
1962//	WEST INDIES	TEST MATCHES	H	4	4	1	58	35*	19.33	-	-	-	106	20	364	9	40.44	3-65
1962-1963	Bombay	First Class Matches	-	2	1	0	53	53	53.00	-	1	-	53	8	215	11	19.54	6-36
1962-1963	West Zone	First Class Matches	-	1	1	0	22	22	22.00	-	-	-	13	2	66	3	22.00	2-42
1962-1963	Indian C/Minister's XI	First Class Matches	-	1	2	1	16	12	16.00	-	-	-	7	0	40	0	-	-
Total First Class Career				17	21	4	485	120	28.52	1	2	3	488.1	71	1775	68	26.10	6-36

EDWIN LLOYD ST. HILL

D.O.B. 09.03.1904 - Port of Spain, Trinidad (d. 21.05.1957)

First Class Debut 14.02.1924 - Trinidad v British Guiana
Test Match Debut 11.01.1930 - West Indies v England

Test 19-4

Teams Played For
Trinidad
West Indies

RHB / RM

2

SEASON	TEAM	COMPETITION	V	M	I	No	BATTING RUNS	H.S.	Av	100s	50s	CT	BOWLING OV	MD	RUNS	W	Av	B.B.
1924-1930	Trinidad	First Class Matches	‖	11	19	5	240	67	17.14	-	1	9	524.1	143	1134	45	25.20	6-117
1929-1930	WEST INDIES	TEST MATCHES	H	2	4	0	18	12	4.50	-	-	-	93	29	221	3	73.66	2-110
1930-1931	West Indies	First Class Matches	A	4	6	1	16	9	3.20	-	-	2	151.1	10	477	16	29.81	4-57
		Total First Class Career		17	29	6	274	67	11.91	0	1	11	768.2	182	1832	64	28.62	6-117

470

WILTON H. ST. HILL
D.O.B. 06.07.1893 - Port of Spain, Trinidad (d. 1957)
First Class Debut 12.01.1912 - Trinidad v British Guiana
Test Match Debut 23.06.1928 - West Indies v England

RHB / RM

Test 5-1

Teams Played For 3
Trinidad
West Indies
Combined T/BG XI

SEASON	TEAM	COMPETITION	V	M	I	No	BATTING RUNS	H.S.	Av	100s	50s	CT	BOWLING OV	MD	RUNS	W	Av	B.B.
1912-1930	Trinidad	First Class Matches	=	22	39	2	1158	105	31.29	4	4	8	46.3	8	167	3	55.66	2-29
1928-1930	WEST INDIES	TEST MATCHES	HA	3	6	0	117	38	19.50	-	-	1	2	0	9	0	-	-
1926-1928	West Indies	First Class Matches	HA	16	27	1	464	72	17.84	-	3	4	10	0	33	2	16.50	2-14
1927-1928	Combined T/BG XI	First Class Matches	WI	2	2	0	189	144	94.50	1	-	1	-	-	-	-	-	-
Total First Class Career				43	74	3	1928	144	27.15	5	7	14	58.3	8	209	5	41.80	2-14

JEFFREY BAXTER STOLLMEYER

D.O.B. 11.03.1921 - Santa Cruz, Trinidad (d. 10.09.1989)

First Class Debut 13.08.1938 - R.S. Grant's XI v British Guiana

Test Match Debut 24.06.1939 - West Indies v England

Test 47-20

Teams Played For
Trinidad
West Indies
R.S. Grant's XI

RHB / LBG

3

SEASON	TEAM	COMPETITION	V	M	I	No	BATTING RUNS	H.S.	Av	100s	50s	CT	BOWLING OV	MD	RUNS	W	Av	B.B.
1938-1957	Trinidad	First Class Matches	II	32	54	5	2903	324	59.24	6	12	62	242.5	20	1041	23	45.26	3-26
1939-1955	WEST INDIES	TEST MATCHES	HA	32	56	5	2159	160	42.33	4	12	20	165	30	507	13	39.00	3-32
1939-1952	West Indies	First Class Matches	A	52	83	6	2762	244*	35.87	3	14	11	216	21	865	18	48.05	3-40
1938-1939	R.S. Grants XI	First Class Matches	WI	1	1	0	118	118	118.00	1	-	-	20	2	69	1	69.00	1-69
	Total First Class Career			117	194	16	7942	324	44.61	14	38	93	643.5	73	2482	55	45.12	3-26

472

VICTOR HUMPHREY STOLLMEYER

D.O.B. 24.01.1916 - Santa Cruz, Trinidad (d. 21.09.1999)

First Class Debut 05.02.1936 - Trinidad v British Guiana

Test Match Debut 19.08.1939 - West Indies v England

					Test	52-22	Teams Played For	2			RHB / LBG
							Trinidad				
							West Indies				

							BATTING							BOWLING				
SEASON	TEAM	COMPETITION	V	M	I	No	RUNS	H.S.	Av	100s	50s	CT	OV	MD	RUNS	W	Av	B.B.
1936-1946	Trinidad	First Class Matches	=	20	36	5	1554	139	50.12	4	10	13	124.1	4	579	14	41.35	3-38
1939//	WEST INDIES	TEST MATCHES	A	1	1	0	96	96	96.00	-	1	-	-	-	-	-	-	-
1939//	West Indies	First Class Matches	A	12	21	4	446	73*	26.23	-	2	3	6	1	33	1	33.00	1-8
		Total First Class Career		33	58	9	2096	139	42.77	4	13	16	130.1	5	612	15	40.80	3-38

473

COLIN ELLSWORTH LAURIE STUART

D.O.B. 28.09.1973 - Georgetown, Demerara, Guyana

First Class Debut	13.01.1995 - Guyana v Leeward Islands
Test Match Debut	26.12.2000 - West Indies v Australia
O.D.I. Debut	17.01.2001 - West Indies v Australia
Domestic O.D. Debut	11.10.2000 - Guyana v Cayman Islands

Test 238-368
O.D.I. 105-411

Teams Played For
Guyana
West Indies
West Indies "A"
W.I. Board XI

RHB / RFM
4

SEASON	TEAM	COMPETITION	V	M	I	No	BATTING RUNS	H.S.	Av	100s	50s	CT	BOWLING OV	MD	RUNS	W	Av	B.B.
1994-2003	Guyana	First Class Matches	II	36	51	18	251	33	7.60	-	-	13	853.2	151	2836	81	35.01	4-55
2000-2002	Guyana	Domestic O.D. Matches	II	11	5	1	20	14	5.00	-	-	1	66	3	301	6	50.16	2-37
1999-	Guyana	O.A.L. O.D. Matches	G	1	1	0	2	2	2.00	-	-	-	10	2	20	3	6.66	3-20
2000-2001	WEST INDIES	TEST MATCHES	A	6	9	2	24	12*	3.42	-	-	2	186	37	628	20	31.40	3-33
2000-2001	West Indies	First Class Matches	A	6	6	2	50	15*	12.50	-	-	1	154.4	35	535	21	25.47	5-58
1995-2001	W.I. Board XI	First Class Matches	WI	2	3	1	14	11	-	-	-	1	50.3	3	183	10	18.30	4-57
1999-2000	West Indies "A"	First Class Matches	A	2	2	1	13	13	13.00	-	-	1	63.5	16	152	12	12.66	4-42
2001//	WEST INDIES	O.D.I. MATCHES	A	5	1	1	3	3*	-	-	-	1	43	3	205	8	25.62	5-44
1999-2000	West Indies "A"	O.D.(I.) Matches	H	3	1	0	6	6	6.00	-	-	-	21	1	94	6	15.66	3-33
Total First Class Career				52	71	24	352	33	7.48	0	0	18	1308.3	242	4334	144	30.09	5-58
Total O.D. Career				20	8	2	31	14	5.16	0	0	2	140	9	620	23	26.95	5-44

JASWICK OSSIE TAYLOR

D.O.B. 03.01.1932 - Arousa, Trinidad (d. 13.11.1999)
First Class Debut 09.10.1953 - Trinidad v British Guiana
Test Match Debut 26.03.1958 - West Indies v Pakistan

Test 102-71

Teams Played For
Trinidad
West Indies

2

RHB / RFM

SEASON	TEAM	COMPETITION	V	M	I	No	BATTING						BOWLING					
							RUNS	H.S.	Av	100s	50s	CT	OV	MD	RUNS	W	Av	B.B.
1953-1960	Trinidad	First Class Matches	II	7	10	5	22	12	4.40	-	-	2	182.5	30	561	10	56.10	1-7
1958-1959	WEST INDIES	TEST MATCHES	HA	3	5	3	4	4*	2.00	-	-	-	112	33	273	10	27.30	5-109
1958-1959	West Indies	First Class Matches	A	8	6	2	36	18	9.00	-	-	2	185	59	477	30	15.90	5-36
		Total First Class Career		18	21	10	62	18	5.63	0	0	4	479.5	122	1311	50	26.22	5-36

JEROME EVERTON TAYLOR

D.O.B. 22.06.1984 - St Elizabeth, Jamaica

First Class Debut	07.02.2003 - Jamaica v Windward Islands
Test Match Debut	20.06.2003 - West Indies v Sri Lanka
O.D.I. Debut	11.06.2003 - West Indies v Sri Lanka
Domestic O.D. Debut	04.06.2003 - Shell Academy XI v Sri Lanka

Test 252-398
O.D.I. 117-470

Teams Played For
Jamaica
West Indies
Shell Academy XI
W.I. President's XI

RHB / RFM
4

SEASON	TEAM	COMPETITION	V	M	I	No	BATTING RUNS	H.S.	Av	100s	50s	CT	BOWLING OV	MD	RUNS	W	Av	B.B.
2002-2003	Jamaica	First Class Matches	II	6	8	3	11	10*	2.00	-	-	1	146	25	423	21	20.14	8-59
2002-2003	WEST INDIES	Test Matches	H	2	2	1	10	9*	10.00	-	-	-	54	6	194	2	97.00	2-38
2002-2003	Shell Academy XI	O.A.L. O.D. Matches	WI	1	1	1	7	7*	-	-	-	1	10	2	39	1	39.00	1-39
2002-2003	WEST INDIES	O.D.I. MATCHES	H	1	D	-	-	-	-	-	-	-	10	0	39	2	19.50	2-39
2002-2003	WI President's XI	First Class Matches	WI	1	1	0	10	10	10.00	-	-	-	10	4	22	2	11.00	2-22
		Total First Class Career		9	11	4	31	11	4.42	0	0	1	210	35	639	25	25.56	8-59
		Total O.D. Career		2	1	1	7	7*	-	-	-	1	20	2	78	3	26.00	2-39

PATTERSON IAN THOMPSON

D.O.B. 26.09.1971 - Pine Gardens, St Michael, Barbados
First Class Debut 27.01.1995 - Barbados v Leeward Islands
Test Match Debut 19.04.1996 - West Indies v New Zealand
O.D.I. Debut 10.01.1997 - West Indies v Pakistan
Domestic O.D. Debut 04.10.1996 - Barbados v Guyana

Test 212-321 **O.D.I.** 81-329 **Teams Played For** Barbados, West Indies 2 RHB / RFM

SEASON	TEAM	COMPETITION	V	M	I	No	BATTING						BOWLING					
							RUNS	H.S.	Av	100s	50s	CT	OV	MD	RUNS	W	Av	B.B.
1995-1999	Barbados	First Class Matches	=	24	30	12	79	15	4.38	-	-	7	518.2	79	1877	61	30.77	5-105
1996-1999	Barbados	Domestic O.D. Matches	=	8	4	2	6	3*	3.00	-	-	5	64	2	291	7	41.57	2-36
1996-1997	WEST INDIES	TEST MATCHES	HA	2	3	1	17	10*	8.50	-	-	-	38	1	215	5	43.00	2-58
1996-1997	West Indies	First Class Matches	A	3	3	0	1	1	0.33	-	-	-	69	10	291	4	72.75	2-42
1997//	WEST INDIES	O.D.I. MATCHES	A	2	1	0	2	2	2.00	-	-	-	19	2	110	2	55.00	1-46
1997//	West Indies	O.A.L. O.D. Matches	A	1	D	-	-	-	-	-	-	-	1.2	0	17	0	-	-
Total First Class Career				29	36	13	97	15	4.21	0	0	7	625.2	90	2383	70	34.04	5-105
Total O.D. Career				11	5	2	8	3*	2.66	0	0	5	84.2	4	418	9	46.44	2-36

JOHN TRIM

D.O.B. 24.01.1915 - Skeldon, Berbice, British Guiana (d. 12.11.1960)
First Class Debut 11.03.1944 - British Guiana v Trinidad
Test Match Debut 03.03.1948 - West Indies v England

Test 63-25

Teams Played For
British Guiana
West Indies

2

RHB / RFM

SEASON	TEAM	COMPETITION	V	M	I	No	BATTING RUNS	H.S.	Av	100s	50s	CT	BOWLING OV	MD	RUNS	W	Av	B.B.
1944-1953	British Guiana	First Class Matches	II	15	27	7	277	78*	13.85	-	1	9	388	45	1614	37	42.62	5-36
1948-1952	WEST INDIES	TEST MATCHES	HA	4	5	1	21	12	5.25	-	-	2	125	28	291	18	16.16	5-34
1948-1952	West Indies	First Class Matches	A	15	11	2	88	16	9.77	-	-	6	361.4	71	976	40	24.40	7-80
		Total First Class Career		34	43	10	386	78*	11.69	0	1	17	874.4	144	2881	95	30.32	7-80

CARL McARTHUR TUCKET

D.O.B. 18.05.1970 - Government Road, Charlestown, Nevis, Leeward Island
First Class Debut 27.01.1995 - Leeward Islands v Barbados
O.D.I. Debut 08.04.1998 - West Indies v England
Domestic O.D. Debut 04.10.1996 - Leeward Islands v Trinidad & Tobago

O.D.I. 87-350   **Teams Played For** 3   **RHB / RFM**
Leeward Islands
West Indies
West Indies "A"

SEASON	TEAM	COMPETITION	V	M	I	No	RUNS	H.S.	Av	100s	50s	CT	OV	MD	RUNS	W	Av	B.B.
1995-2001	Leeward Islands	First Class Matches	=	29	47	9	1055	84	27.76	-	7	13	482.2	135	1168	55	21.23	4-16
1996-2002	Leeward Islands	Domestic O.D. Matches	=	21	12	3	144	39	16.00	-	-	10	96	9	388	10	38.80	2-24
1998-1999	West Indies "A"	First Class Matches	HA	5	6	1	123	54	24.60	-	1	2	126	39	290	18	16.11	6-25
1998//	WEST INDIES	O.D.I. MATCHES	H	1	D	-	-	-	-	-	-	-	8	0	41	2	20.50	2-41
1998-1999	West Indies "A"	O.D.(I) Matches	HA	4	2	1	17	13	17.00	-	-	1	37	7	122	1	122.00	1-40
		Total First Class Career		34	53	10	1178	84	27.39	0	8	15	608.2	174	1458	73	19.97	6-25
		Total O.D. Career		26	14	4	161	39	16.10	0	0	11	141	16	551	13	42.38	2-24

479

ALFRED LEWIS VALENTINE

D.O.B. 28.04.1930 - Kingston, Jamaica

First Class Debut 25.01.1950 - Jamaica v Trinidad

Test Match Debut 08.06.1950 - West Indies v England

Test 71-32

RHB / SLA

5

Teams Played For
Jamaica
West Indies
F.M. Worrell's XI
The Rest XI
Commonwealth XI

SEASON	TEAM	COMPETITION	V	M	I	No	BATTING						BOWLING					
							RUNS	H.S.	Av	100s	50s	CT	OV	MD	RUNS	W	Av	B.B.
1950-1965	Jamaica	First Class Matches	II	26	36	6	223	24	7.43	-	-	11	1129.4	269	3078	89	34.58	8-78
1950-1963	WEST INDIES	TEST MATCHES	HA	36	51	21	141	14	4.70	-	-	13	2029.5	789	4215	139	30.32	8-104
1950-1963	West Indies	First Class Matches	A	59	50	17	80	9*	2.42	-	-	20	2085	664	4814	236	20.39	8-26
1964//	F.M. Worrell's XI	First Class Matches	WI	1	D	-	-	-	-	-	-	1	-	-	-	-	-	-
1964//	The Rest XI	First Class Matches	WI	1	2	2	25	24*	-	-	-	-	21.2	6	119	6	19.83	5-72
1952-1953	Commonwealth XI	First Class Matches	E	2	3	2	1	1	1.00	-	-	-	100.1	33	225	5	45.00	2-23
	Total First Class Career			125	142	48	470	24*	5.00	0	0	45	5366	1762	12451	475	26.21	8-26

VINCENT ADOLPHUS VALENTINE

D.O.B. 04.04.1908 - Buff Bay, Portland, Jamaica (d. 06.07.1972)
First Class Debut 20.02.1932 - Jamaica v L.H. Tennyson's XI
Test Match Debut 22.07.1933 - West Indies v England

Test 34-14

Teams Played For 3
Jamaica
West Indies
G.C. Grant's XI

RHB / RM

SEASON	TEAM	COMPETITION	V	M	I	No	BATTING						BOWLING					
							RUNS	H.S.	Av	100s	50s	CT	OV	MD	RUNS	W	Av	B.B.
1933-1939	Jamaica	First Class Matches	II	4	4	0	104	36	26.00	-	-	-	154.2	36	372	12	31.00	4-119
1933//	WEST INDIES	TEST MATCHES	A	2	4	1	35	19*	11.66	-	-	-	48	14	104	1	104.00	1-55
1933//	West Indies	First Class Matches	A	17	23	3	356	59*	17.80	-	1	11	539	112	1437	35	41.05	4-83
1932-1933	G.C. Grant's XI	First Class Matches	WI	1	2	1	5	3	5.00	-	-	-	25	5	67	1	67.00	1-35
Total First Class Career				24	33	5	500	59*	17.85	0	1	11	766.2	167	1980	49	40.40	4-83

481

CLYDE LEOPOLD WALCOTT

D.O.B. 17.01.1926 - New Orleans, St Michael, Barbados

First Class Debut 17.01.1942 - Barbados v Trinidad
Test Match Debut 21.01.1948 - West Indies v England

Test 58-23

Teams Played For 6
Barbados, British Guiana
West Indies
F.M. Worrell's XI
The Rest XI
Commonwealth XI

RHB / RM / WK

SEASON	TEAM	COMPETITION	V	M	I	No	BATTING						BOWLING					
							RUNS	H.S.	Av	100s	50s	CT/ST	OV	MD	RUNS	W	Av	B.B.
1942-1956	Barbados	First Class Matches	II	25	43	3	2328	314*	58.20	7	11	22/4	176.5	58	409	16	25.56	4-26
1955-1964	British Guiana	First Class Matches	II	16	25	4	911	108	43.38	1	8	22	67.3	18	159	0	-	-
1948-1960	WEST INDIES	TEST MATCHES	HA	44	74	7	3798	220	56.68	15	14	53/11	199	72	408	11	37.09	3-50
1948-1957	West Indies	First Class Matches	HA	56	86	14	4355	186	60.48	15	20	72/18	99	30	190	3	63.66	1-8
1964//	F.M. Worrell's XI	First Class Matches	WI	1	2	0	146	105	73.00	1	-	-	20.1	4	61	5	12.20	5-41
1964//	The Rest XI	First Class Matches	WI	1	2	0	99	82	49.50	-	1	1	8	2	29	0	-	-
1953-1954	Commonwealth XI	First Class Matches	E	3	6	1	183	115	36.60	1	-	4	4	0	13	0	-	-
		Total First Class Career		146	238	29	11820	314*	56.55	40	54	174/33	574.3	184	1269	35	36.25	5-41

LESLIE ARTHUR WALCOTT

D.O.B. 19.01.1894 - Fontabelle, St Michael, Barbados (d. 27.02.1984)

First Class Debut 01.10.1925 - Barbados v British Guiana

Test Match Debut 11.01.1930 - West Indies v England

Teams Played For Barbados, West Indies

RHB / OB / WK

				BATTING						BOWLING				
SEASON	TEAM	COMPETITION	V	M	I	No	RUNS	H.S.	Av	100s	50s	CT/ST	OV	MD	RUNS	W	Av	B.B.

SEASON	TEAM	COMPETITION	V	M	I	No	RUNS	H.S.	Av	100s	50s	CT/ST	OV	MD	RUNS	W	Av	B.B.
1925-1936	Barbados	First Class Matches	II	11	19	2	515	73*	30.29	-	5	8/1	122	14	440	15	29.33	3-30
1929-1930	WEST INDIES	TEST MATCHES	H	1	2	1	40	24	40.00	-	-	-	8	1	32	1	32.00	1-17
		Total First Class Career		12	21	3	555	73*	30.83	0	5	8/1	130	15	472	16	29.50	3-30

Test 21-4   **2**

483

PHILO ALPHONSO WALLACE

RHB / RM

D.O.B.	02.08.1970 - Haynesville, St James, Barbados
First Class Debut	12.01.1990 - Barbados v Jamaica
Test Match Debut	29.11.1997 - West Indies v Pakistan
O.D.I. Debut	20.11.1991 - West Indies v Pakistan
Domestic O.D. Debut	10.1.1990 - Barbados v Jamaica

Test - 219-336
O.D.I. - 61-215

Teams Played For: Barbados, West Indies; W.I. President's XI; West Indies U23; W.I. Board XI, West Indies "A"; UWI Vice Chancellor's XI

7

SEASON	TEAM	COMPETITION	V	M	I	No	RUNS	H.S.	Av	100s	50s	CT	OV	MD	RUNS	W	Av	B.B.
1990-2003	Barbados	First Class Matches	I	83	150	6	5274	140	36.62	9	32	55	-	-	-	-	-	-
1990-2002	Barbados	Domestic O.D. Matches	I	54	53	3	1590	104*	31.80	1	11	11	-	-	-	-	-	-
1992-2000	Barbados	O.A.L. O.D. Matches	HA	11	11	0	426	92	38.72	-	4	3	-	-	-	-	-	-
1997-1999	WEST INDIES	TEST MATCHES	HA	7	13	0	279	92	21.46	-	2	9	-	-	-	-	-	-
1991-1999	West Indies	First Class Matches	A	6	10	0	407	142	40.70	1	2	9	-	-	-	-	-	-
1991-1993	West Indies U23	First Class Matches	WI	2	4	0	115	52	28.75	-	1	1	-	-	-	-	-	-
1994-2000	W.I. Board XI	First Class Matches	WI	2	3	0	74	40	24.66	-	-	5	-	-	-	-	-	-
1995-2000	W.I. President's XI	First Class Matches	WI	2	3	0	57	34	19.00	-	-	2	-	-	-	-	-	-
1996-1997	West Indies "A"	First Class Matches	HA	4	6	1	407	125	81.40	2	2	5	-	-	-	-	-	-
1991-2000	WEST INDIES	O.D.I. MATCHES	HA	33	33	0	701	103	21.24	1	2	11	-	-	-	-	-	-
1995-1997	West Indies "A"	O.D.(I.) Matches	HA	5	5	0	136	48	27.20	-	-	1	-	-	-	-	-	-
1996//	West Indies "A"	O.A.L. O.D. Matches	A	1	1	0	10	10	10.00	-	-	-	-	-	-	-	-	-
1991//	West Indies	O.A.L. O.D. Matches	A	4	4	1	40	40*	13.33	-	-	1	-	-	-	-	-	-
2002-2003	UWI V/Chancellor's XI	First Class Matches	WI	1	2	0	57	53	28.50	-	1	1	-	-	-	-	-	-
	Total First Class Career			107	191	7	6670	142	36.25	12	40	87	-	-	-	-	-	-
	Total O.D. Career			108	107	4	2903	104*	28.18	2	17	27	-	-	-	-	-	-

BATTING — BOWLING

COURTNEY ANDREW WALSH

D.O.B. 30.10.1962 - Molynes Road, Kingston, Jamaica
First Class Debut 12.03.1982 - Jamaica v Leeward Islands
Test Match Debut 09.11.1985 - West Indies v Australia
O.D.I. Debut 10.01.1985 - West Indies v Sri Lanka
Domestic O.D. Debut 02.03.1982 - Jamaica v Guyana

Test	183-233	Teams Played For	8	RHB / RF
O.D.I.	45-87	Jamaica, West Indies		
		W.I. President's XI, West Indies "B"		
		West Indies "A", West Indies U23		
		Gloucestershire, World XI		

SEASON	TEAM	COMPETITION	V	M	I	No	BATTING RUNS	H.S.	Av	100s	50s	CT	BOWLING OV	MD	RUNS	W	Av	B.B.
1982-2001	Jamaica	First Class Matches	II	64	95	25	712	34*	10.17	-	-	27	1970.5	414	5441	279	19.50	8-92
1982-1999	Jamaica	Domestic O.D. Matches	II	48	24	6	129	32*	7.16	-	-	10	404.5	54	1402	64	21.90	5-27
1984//	Jamaica	O.A.L. O.D. Matches	WI	1	D	-	-	-	-	-	-	-	4	0	19	0	-	-
1985-2001	WEST INDIES	TEST MATCHES	HA	132	185	61	936	30*	7.54	-	-	29	5003.1	1144	12688	519	24.44	7-37
1984-2001	West Indies	First Class Matches	A	40	29	11	183	50	10.16	-	1	7	1029.4	192	2874	109	26.36	6-119
1983-1984	West Indies "B"	First Class Matches	A	2	4	0	26	12	6.50	-	-	-	80	22	222	11	20.18	5-40
1984-1985	West Indies U23	First Class Matches	WI	1	1	1	10	10*	-	-	-	-	27	7	94	0	-	-
1984-1985	W.I. President's XI	First Class Matches	WI	1	1	0	13	13	13.00	-	-	-	33	1	141	6	23.50	4-61
1991-1992	West Indies "A"	First Class Matches	H	3	4	2	46	20*	23.00	-	-	-	114	34	207	10	20.70	3-41
1985-2000	WEST INDIES	O.D.I. MATCHES	HA	205	79	33	321	30	6.97	-	-	27	1803.4	185	6918	227	30.47	5-1
1984-2000	West Indies	O.A.L. O.D. Matches	A	7	1	0	1	1	1.00	-	-	1	59	-	216	10	21.60	3-30
1983-1984	West Indies "B"	O.D.(I.) Matches	A	4	2	2	16	15*	-	-	-	1	39	3	184	7	26.28	3-44
1984-1998	Gloucestershire	First Class Matches	E	184	237	58	2581	66	14.41	-	7	53	6027.2	1386	17390	869	20.01	9-72
1985-1998	Gloucestershire	Nat West Trophy	E	23	15	3	153	37	12.75	-	3	3	242	-	769	45	17.08	6-21
1985-1998	Gloucestershire	Benson & Hedges Cup	E	27	17	6	130	28	11.81	-	-	2	265.2	22	985	31	31.77	3-36
1984-1998	Gloucestershire	Sunday League	E	123	75	14	552	38	9.04	-	-	24	828	-	3358	167	20.10	5-23
1985-1990	Gloucestershire	O.A.L. O.D. Matches	E	2	1	1	2	2*	-	-	-	-	1	0	3	0	-	-
1987//	World XI	First Class Matches	E	2	2	0	23	21	11.50	-	-	1	53.1	13	176	4	44.00	2-20
Total First Class Career				429	558	158	4530	66	11.32	0	8	117	14338.1	3213	39233	1807	21.71	9-72
Total O.D. Career				440	214	65	1304	38	8.75	0	0	68	3646.5	-	13854	551	25.14	6-21

PELHAM FRANCIS WARNER

D.O.B. 02.10.1873 - The Hall, Port of Spain, Trinidad (d. 30.01.1963)

First Class Debut 07.06.1894 - M.C.C. v Oxford University

Test Match Debut 14.02.1899 - England v South Africa

Teams Played For 12
Middlesex, Oxford University, A.J. Webbes XI
M.C.C., England, Lord Londesborough XI
Rest of England XI, Lord Hawkes XI
P.F. Warner's XI, Gentlemen's XI
C.I. Thorntons XI, The South XI

RHB / RAS

SEASON	TEAM	COMPETITION	V	M	I	No	BATTING RUNS	H.S.	Av	100s	50s	CT	BOWLING OV	MD	RUNS	W	Av	B.B.
1899-1912	ENGLAND	TEST MATCHES	HA	15	28	2	622	132*	23.92	1	3	3	-	-	-	-	-	-
1908-1912	England XI	First Class Matches	H	2	3	0	22	16	7.33	-	-	2	-	-	-	-	-	-
1894-1920	Middlesex	First Class Matches	E	346	571	50	19507	197*	37.44	46	96	123	57.5	13	198	4	49.50	1-4
1894-1896	Oxford University	First Class Matches	E	18	32	0	966	90	30.18	-	8	13	5	2	18	0	-	-
1894-1929	M.C.C.	First Class Matches	E	62	106	12	3516	204	37.40	6	19	15	48	7	143	3	47.66	2-26
1897-1919	Gentlemen's XI	First Class Matches	E	26	51	1	1386	97	27.72	-	11	10	22	4	92	1	92.00	1-63
1896-1903	Lord Hawkes XI	First Class Matches	HA	20	33	5	1185	211	42.32	3	2	8	64.5	17	151	6	25.16	2-31
1897-1920	P.F. Warner's XI	First Class Matches	HA	8	16	2	344	60*	24.57	-	3	2	-	-	-	-	-	-
1901-1913	Rest of England XI	First Class Matches	E	11	16	1	976	244	65.06	4	3	4	3.1	1	13	1	13.00	1-12
1900-1908	The South XI	First Class Matches	E	4	7	2	210	88	42.00	-	2	1	3	1	10	0	-	-
1897-1900	A.J. Webbes XI	First Class Matches	E	3	5	0	87	51	17.40	-	1	1	1	0	3	0	-	-
1899-1903	C.I. Thorntons XI	First Class Matches	E	3	5	0	107	40	21.40	-	-		0.4	0	8	0	-	-
1910//	Lord Londesbor. XI	First Class Matches	E	1	2	0	100	60	50.00	-	1	1	-	-	-	-	-	-
Total First Class Career				519	875	75	29028	244	36.28	60	149	183	205.3	45	636	15	42.40	2-26

CHESTER DONALD WATSON

D.O.B. 01.07.1938 - Negril, Westmoreland, Jamaica

First Class Debut 05.07.1958 - Jamaica v Leeward Islands

Test Match Debut 06.01.1960 - West Indies v England

	Test	108-80		RHB / RF
	Teams Played For	7		
	Jamaica, West Indies			
	Commonwealth XI, Cavaliers XI			
	New Delhi, West Zone			
	Indian Governor's XI			

							BATTING						BOWLING				
SEASON	**TEAM**	**COMPETITION**	**V**	**M**	**I**	**No**	**RUNS**	**H.S.**	**Av**	**100s**	**50s**	**CT**	**OV**	**MD**	**RUNS**	**W**	**Av**	**B.B.**
1958-1962	Jamaica	First Class Matches	=	7	7	1	25	9	4.16	-	-	4	230.1	51	667	22	30.31	6-33
1960-1962	WEST INDIES	TEST MATCHES	HA	7	6	1	12	5	2.40	-	-	1	236	19	724	19	38.10	4-62
1960//	West Indies	First Class Matches	A	6	7	4	48	16	16.00	-	-	4	105	9	364	11	33.09	4-30
1962-1964	Commonwealth XI	First Class Matches	A	6	5	4	6	3*	1.50	-	-	2	164.1	38	490	12	40.83	3-103
1962-63//	New Delhi	First Class Matches	-	1	2	0	57	50	28.50	-	1	1	24	1	97	4	24.25	4-75
1962-63//	West Zone	First Class Matches	-	2	2	0	23	12	11.50	-	-	2	43	6	154	7	22.00	4-41
1962-63//	Indian Governor's XI	First Class Matches	-	2	4	1	27	12	9.00	-	-	-	35	6	175	3	58.33	-
1962-63//	Cavaliers XI	First Class Matches	-	1	1	0	0	0	0.00	-	-	-	22.5	5	55	7	7.85	4-28
		Total First Class Career		32	34	8	198	50	7.61	0	1	14	860.1	163	2726	85	32.07	6-33

EVERTON DE COURCY WEEKES

D.O.B. 26.02.1925 - Westbury, St Michael, Barbados
First Class Debut 24.02.1945 - Barbados v Trinidad
Test Match Debut 21.01.1948 - West Indies v England

Test 59-23

Teams Played For
Barbados, West Indies
F.M. Worrell's XI, The Rest XI
Commonwealth XI
E.W. Swanton's XI
International XI

7

RHB / LB

SEASON	TEAM	COMPETITION	V	M	I	No	BATTING						BOWLING					
							RUNS	H.S.	Av	100s	50s	CT/ST	OV	MD	RUNS	W	Av	B.B.
1945-1964	Barbados	First Class Matches	II	32	53	6	2518	253	53.57	8	11	16	90.3	11	297	7	42.42	4-38
1948-1958	WEST INDIES	TEST MATCHES	HA	48	81	5	4455	207	58.61	15	19	49	20.2	3	77	1	77.00	1-8
1948-1957	West Indies	First Class Matches	HA	57	83	11	4343	304*	60.31	12	22	44/1	40	2	163	4	40.75	2-25
1964//	F.M. Worrell's XI	First Class Matches	WI	1	2	0	31	27*	31.00	-	-	1	14	0	96	2	48.00	2-96
1964//	The Rest XI	First Class Matches	WI	1	2	0	60	41	30.00	-	-	1	5	0	38	0	-	-
1961//	E.W. Swanton's XI	First Class Matches	WI	4	6	0	211	63	35.16	-	1	3	16	2	60	3	20.00	2-26
1961-62//	International XI	First Class Matches	A	7	11	1	231	55	23.10	-	1	8	-	-	-	-	-	-
1951-1953	Commonwealth XI	First Class Matches	E	2	3	0	161	117	53.66	1	-	3	-	-	-	-	-	-
Total First Class Career				152	241	24	12010	304*	55.34	36	54	125/1	185.5	18	731	17	43.00	4-38

488

KENNETH HUNNELL WEEKES

D.O.B. 24.01.1912 - Boston, Massachusetts, USA (d. 09.02.1998)

First Class Debut 10.08.1938 - Jamaica v Cambridge University

Test Match Debut 24.06.1939 - West Indies v England

Test	48-20	Teams Played For	2	LHB / LB
		Jamaica		
		West Indies		

							BATTING						BOWLING					
SEASON	TEAM	COMPETITION	V	M	I	No	RUNS	H.S.	Av	100s	50s	CT/ST	OV	MD	RUNS	W	Av	B.B.
1938-1948	Jamaica	First Class Matches		11	19	3	928	106	58.00	2	7	15/1	145.4	14	464	12	38.66	3-84
1939/I	WEST INDIES	TEST MATCHES	A	2	3	0	173	137	57.66	1	-	-	-	-	-	-	-	-
1939/I	West Indies	First Class Matches	A	17	25	1	630	146	26.25	1	5	6	-	-	-	-	-	-
	Total First Class Career			30	47	4	1731	146	40.25	4	12	21/1	145.4	14	464	12	38.66	3-84

ANTHONY WILBUR WHITE

D.O.B. 20.11.1938 - Brighton, St Michael, Barbados

First Class Debut 19.07.1958 - Barbados v Jamaica
Test Match Debut 03.03.1965 - West Indies v Australia

Test 122-100

Teams Played For
Barbados
West Indies
F.M. Worrell's XI
The Rest XI

RHB / OB

SEASON	TEAM	COMPETITION	V	M	I	No	BATTING RUNS	H.S.	Av	100s	50s	CT	BOWLING OV	MD	RUNS	W	Av	B.B.
1958-1966	Barbados	First Class Matches	=	18	25	3	584	75	26.54	-	6	22	738.2	247	1656	60	27.60	6-80
1964-1965	WEST INDIES	TEST MATCHES	H	2	4	1	71	57*	23.66	-	1	1	81.5	27	152	3	50.66	2-34
1963//	West Indies	First Class Matches	A	9	14	3	228	68*	20.72	-	1	8	286	83	647	28	23.10	4-48
1963-1964	F.M. Worrell's XI	First Class Matches	WI	1	1	0	42	42	42.00	-	-	-	37	1	133	2	66.50	2-107
1963-1964	The Rest XI	First Class Matches	WI	1	2	0	71	71	35.50	-	1	1	22	4	77	2	38.50	1-28
		Total First Class Career		31	46	7	996	75	25.53	0	9	32	1165.1	362	2665	95	28.05	6-80

CLAUDE VIBART WIGHT

D.O.B. 28.07.1902 - Georgetown, Demerara, British Guiana (d. 04.10.1969)

First Class Debut 01.10.1925 - British Guiana v Barbados

Test Match Debut 11.08.1928 - West Indies v England

Test 15-3

Teams Played For 3
British Guiana
West Indies
Combined T/BG XI

RHB / OB

SEASON	TEAM	COMPETITION	V	M	I	No	BATTING RUNS	H.S.	Av	100s	50s	CT	BOWLING OV	MD	RUNS	W	Av	B.B.
1925-1939	British Guiana	First Class Matches	=	18	29	1	942	130	33.64	2	3	5	50	7	203	3	67.66	1-18
1928-1930	WEST INDIES	TEST MATCHES	HA	2	4	1	67	23	22.33	-	-	-	5	1	6	0	-	-
1926-1928	West Indies	First Class Matches	HA	18	26	9	517	119*	57.44	1	-	13	-	-	-	-	-	-
1927-1928	Combined T/BG XI	First Class Matches	WI	2	2	0	21	11	10.50	-	-	2	-	-	-	-	-	-
Total First Class Career				40	61	11	1547	130	30.94	3	3	20	55	8	209	3	69.66	1-18

GEORGE LESLIE WIGHT

D.O.B. 28.05.1929 - Georgetown, Demerara, British Guiana

First Class Debut 09.02.1950 - British Guiana v Barbados

Test Match Debut 11.03.1953 - West Indies v India

Test 79-46

Teams Played For
British Guiana
West Indies

RHB

BATTING

SEASON	TEAM	COMPETITION	V	M	I	No	RUNS	H.S.	Av	100s	50s	CT
1950-1953	British Guiana	First Class Matches	II	11	20	2	1239	262*	68.83	4	6	12
1952-1953	WEST INDIES	TEST MATCHES	H	1	1	0	21	21	21.00	-	-	-
		Total First Class Career		12	21	2	1260	262*	66.31	4	6	12

BOWLING

	OV	MD	RUNS	W	Av	B.B.
	-	-	-	-	-	-
	-	-	-	-	-	-
	-	-	-	-	-	-

2

CHARLES ARCHIBALD WILES

D.O.B. 11.08.1892 - Bridgetown, St Michael, Barbados (d. 04.11.1957)
First Class Debut 06.02.1920 - Trinidad v Barbados
Test Match Debut 22.07.1933 - West Indies v England

Test 35-14

Teams Played For 5
Trinidad
Barbados XI
West Indies
Combined T/BG XI
C.A. Merry's XI

RHB

SEASON	TEAM	COMPETITION	V	M	I	No	BATTING RUNS	H.S.	Av	100s	50s	CT	BOWLING OV	MD	RUNS	W	Av	B.B.
1920-1936	Trinidad	First Class Matches	=	20	37	3	1092	192	32.11	2	3	5	-	-	-	-	-	-
1928//	Barbados XI	First Class Matches	WI	1	2	1	57	34	57.00	-	-	-	-	-	-	-	-	-
1933//	WEST INDIES	TEST MATCHES	A	1	2	0	2	2	1.00	-	-	-	-	-	-	-	-	-
1926-1933	West Indies	First Class Matches	HA	13	24	1	521	75	22.65	-	3	5	-	-	-	-	-	-
1928//	Combined T/BG XI	First Class Matches	WI	2	2	0	16	13	8.00	-	-	1	-	-	-	-	-	-
1933//	C.A. Merry's XI	First Class Matches	WI	1	2	0	78	43	39.00	-	-	-	-	-	-	-	-	-
Total First Class Career				38	69	5	1766	192	27.59	2	6	7	-	-	-	-	-	-

ELQUEMEDO TONITO WILLETT

D.O.B. 01.05.1958 - Charlestown, Nevis, Leeward Islands

First Class Debut	14.01.1971 - Leeward Islands v Windward Islands
Test Match Debut	09.03.1973 - West Indies v Australia
Domestic O.D. Debut	21.02.1976 - Leeward Islands v Barbados

Test 146-140

Teams Played For
Leeward Islands
Combined Islands
West Indies
W.I. President's XI

LHB / SLA
4

SEASON	TEAM	COMPETITION	V	M	I	No	BATTING						BOWLING					
							RUNS	H.S.	Av	100s	50s	CT	OV	MD	RUNS	W	Av	B.B.
1971-1989	Leeward Islands	First Class Matches	LI	41	54	23	398	40	12.83	-	-	27	1626.1	434	3609	151	23.90	6-47
1971-1980	Combined Islands	First Class Matches	LI	33	53	13	421	47	10.52	-	-	29	1205.5	302	2687	73	36.80	6-40
1976-1988	Leeward Islands	Domestic O.D. Matches	LI	11	4	1	13	10*	4.33	-	-	5	84	8	292	10	29.20	3-37
1973-1974	Combined Islands	O.A.L. O.D. Matches	WI	1	D	-	-	-	-	-	-	-	7	0	20	0	-	-
1973-1975	WEST INDIES	TEST MATCHES	HA	5	8	3	74	26	14.80	-	-	-	221	78	482	11	43.81	3-33
1973-1975	West Indies	First Class Matches	A	18	14	6	187	56	31.16	-	1	9	439.4	125	1222	44	27.77	8-73
1973//	W.I. President's XI	First Class Matches	WI	1	2	1	20	17*	20.00	-	-	1	49	15	132	7	18.85	5-111
1973//	West Indies	O.A.L. O.D. Matches	A	1	1	1	1	1*	-	-	-	-	8	0	54	1	54.00	1-54
		Total First Class Career		98	131	46	1100	56	12.94	0	1	66	3541.4	954	8132	286	28.43	8-73
		Total O.D. Career		13	5	2	14	10*	4.66	0	0	5	99	8	376	11	34.18	3-37

ALVADON BASIL WILLIAMS

D.O.B. 21.11.1949 - Caymanas Estate, St Catherine, Jamaica
First Class Debut 19.02.1970 - Jamaica v Guyana
Test Match Debut 31.03.1978 - West Indies v Australia
Domestic O.D. Debut 13.04.1973 - Jamaica v Guyana

Test	Teams Played For		RHB
170-181	Jamaica	3	
	West Indies		
	Shell Awards XI		

SEASON	TEAM	COMPETITION	V	M	I	No	RUNS	H.S.	Av	100s	50s	CT	OV	MD	RUNS	W	Av	B.B.
1970-1985	Jamaica	First Class Matches	=	33	56	1	1790	123	32.54	2	11	10	15	2	49	0	-	-
1972-1985	Jamaica	Domestic O.D. Matches	=	17	17	0	448	89	26.35	-	1	5	2	0	10	0	-	-
1984//	Jamaica	O.A.L. O.D. Matches	J	1	-	-	-	-	-	-	-	-	-	-	-	-	-	-
1978-1979	WEST INDIES	TEST MATCHES	HA	7	12	0	469	111	39.08	2	1	5	-	-	-	-	-	-
1978-1979	West Indies	First Class Matches	A	5	8	1	439	126*	62.71	1	3	2	-	-	-	-	-	-
1985//	Shell Awards XI	First Class Matches	WI	1	1	0	4	4	4.00	-	-	-	-	-	-	-	-	-
1979//	West Indies	O.A.L. O.D. Matches	A	2	2	0	58	46	29.00	-	-	-	-	-	-	-	-	-
Total First Class Career				46	77	2	2702	126*	36.02	5	15	19	15	2	49	0	-	-
Total O.D. Career				20	19	0	506	89	26.63	0	1	5	2	0	10	0	-	-

495

DAVID WILLIAMS　　　　　　　　　　　　　　　　　　Test　201-291　　　Teams Played For　8　　　RHB / WK / LB

D.O.B.　04.11.1963 - Penal, Trinidad

First Class Debut	04.02.1983 - Trinidad & Tobago v Leeward Islands		O.D.I.	52-150
Test Match Debut	18.04.1992 - West Indies v South Africa			
O.D.I. Debut	05.01.1988 - West Indies v India			
Domestic O.D. Debut	06.02.1985 - Trinidad & Tobago v Windward Islands			

Teams Played For: Trinidad & Tobago, S/C Trinidad, West Indies, W.I. President's XI, W.I. Board XI, West Indies U23, West Indies "B", Shell Awards XI

SEASON	TEAM	COMPETITION	V	M	I	No	RUNS	H.S.	Av	100s	50s	CT/ST	OV	MD	RUNS	W	Av	B.B.
1983-1999	Trinidad & Tobago	First Class Matches	I	71	115	15	2231	112	22.31	2	6	151/39	10	3	42	0	-	-
1985//	S/C Trinidad	First Class Matches	T	1	2	0	2	1	1.00	-	-	1/1	-	-	-	-	-	-
1985-1999	Trinidad & Tobago	Domestic O.D. Matches	I	47	36	11	440	53	17.60	-	1	39/20	6	0	20	0	-	-
1991-1997	Trinidad & Tobago	O.A.L. O.D. Matches	WI	2	2	0	22	20	11.00	-	-	2/2	-	-	-	-	-	-
1992-1998	WEST INDIES	TEST MATCHES	HA	11	19	1	242	65	13.44	-	1	40/2	-	-	-	-	-	-
1987-1993	West Indies	First Class Matches	HA	25	29	3	432	51	16.61	-	1	48/6	-	-	-	-	-	-
1986-1990	West Indies "B"	First Class Matches	A	8	8	0	77	25	9.62	-	-	28/2	-	-	-	-	-	-
1988-1991	W.I. President's XI	First Class Matches	WI	3	4	0	35	20	8.75	-	-	6	-	-	-	-	-	-
1988-1991	W.I. Board XI	First Class Matches	WI	3	3	0	22	12	7.33	-	-	8	-	-	-	-	-	-
1985//	West Indies U23	First Class Matches	WI	1	1	0	13	13	13.00	-	-	1	-	-	-	-	-	-
1985//	Shell Awards XI	First Class Matches	WI	1	1	0	9	9	9.00	-	-	3	-	-	-	-	-	-
1988-1997	WEST INDIES	O.D.I. MATCHES	HA	36	23	7	147	32*	9.18	-	-	35/10	-	-	-	-	-	-
1986-1990	West Indies "B"	O.D.(I.) Matches	A	9	5	1	43	29	10.75	-	-	14	-	-	-	-	-	-
1988-1997	West Indies	O.A.L. O.D. Matches	A	9	6	4	68	21	34.00	-	-	1/1	-	-	-	-	-	-
	Total First Class Career			124	182	19	3063	112	18.79	2	8	286/50	10	3	42	0	-	-
	Total O.D. Career			103	72	23	720	53	14.69	0	1	91/33	6	0	20	0	-	-

ERNEST ALBERT VIVIAN WILLIAMS

D.O.B. 10.04.1914 - Bank Hall, St Michael, Barbados (d. 13.04.1997)

First Class Debut 21.09.1934 - Barbados v British Guiana

Test Match Debut 22.07.1939 - West Indies v England

		Test	50-21	Teams Played For	2	RHB / RM
				Barbados		
				West Indies		

SEASON	TEAM	COMPETITION	V	M	I	No	BATTING RUNS	H.S.	Av	100s	50s	CT	BOWLING OV	MD	RUNS	W	Av	B.B.
1934-1939	Barbados	First Class Matches	=	27	42	5	969	131*	26.18	1	4	11	769.2	112	2602	89	29.23	5-73
1939-1948	WEST INDIES	TEST MATCHES	HA	4	6	0	113	72	18.83	-	1	2	129.4	46	241	9	26.77	6-51
1938-1939	West Indies	First Class Matches	HA	11	15	3	397	126*	33.08	1	1	5	137.4	14	544	18	30.22	3-37
	Total First Class Career			42	63	8	1479	131*	26.89	2	6	18	1036.4	172	3387	116	29.19	5-73

LAURIE ROHAN WILLIAMS

D.O.B. 12.12.1968 - St Ann, Jamaica (d. 08.09.2002)

First Class Debut 19.02.1990 - Jamaica v England
O.D.I. Debut 30.03.1996 - West Indies v New Zealand
Domestic O.D. Debut 03.02.1993 - Jamaica v Barbados

O.D.I. 77-320

Teams Played For
Jamaica
West Indies
West Indies "A"

3

RHB / RFM

SEASON	TEAM	COMPETITION	V	M	I	No	BATTING RUNS	H.S.	Av	100s	50s	CT	BOWLING OV	MD	RUNS	W	Av	B.B.
1990-2002	Jamaica	First Class Matches	II	50	81	11	1577	135	22.52	2	5	27	127.4	319	3351	155	21.61	6-26
1993-2002	Jamaica	Domestic O.D. Matches	II	39	27	4	338	36	14.69	-	-	4	292.1	22	1178	50	23.56	6-19
1998-2001	Jamaica	O.A.L. O.D. Matches	HA	4	4	0	59	24	14.75	-	-	2	34.4	7	127	3	42.33	2-42
1996-1998	West Indies "A"	First Class Matches	HA	8	13	2	425	110	38.63	1	2	7	205.1	46	588	15	39.20	3-56
1996-2000	WEST INDIES	O.D.I. MATCHES	HA	15	13	2	124	41	11.27	-	-	8	109.4	2	556	18	30.88	3-16
1996-1997	West Indies "A"	O.D.(I.) Matches	HA	8	7	1	74	23	12.33	-	-	1	50	1	225	4	56.25	2-50
1996-1997	West Indies "A"	O.A.L. O.D. Matches	A	3	2	0	61	44	30.50	-	-	1	23	2	86	2	43.00	1-23
1999-2000	West Indies	O.A.L. O.D. Matches	A	1	1	1	11	11*	-	-	-	-	7	0	28	2	14.00	3-28
Total First Class Career				58	94	13	2002	135	24.71	3	7	34	1479.1	365	3939	170	23.17	6-26
Total O.D. Career				70	54	8	667	44	14.50	0	0	16	516.3	34	2200	79	27.84	6-19

NEIL FITZGERALD WILLIAMS

D.O.B. 02.07.1962 - Hopewell, St Vincent, Windward Islands

First Class Debut 28.04.1982 - Middlesex v Cambridge University

Test Match Debut 23.08.1990 - England v India

Domestic O.D. Debut 16.05.1982 - Middlesex v Hampshire

RHB / RMF

Teams Played For 7
Windward Islands, Middlesex
Essex, Tasmania
England, M.C.C.
English Counties XI

SEASON	TEAM	COMPETITION	V	M	I	No	RUNS	H.S.	Av	100s	50s	CT	OV	MD	RUNS	W	Av	B.B.
1982-1992	Windward Islands	First Class Matches	=	17	30	3	638	66*	23.62	-	3	8	399	51	1295	54	23.98	5-32
1982-1992	Windward Islands	Domestic O.D. Matches	=	7	6	4	129	38	64.50	-	-	1	53	2	286	13	22.00	5-65
1990//	ENGLAND	TEST MATCHES	E	1	1	0	38	38	38.00	-	-	-	41	5	148	2	74.00	2-148
1982-1994	Middlesex	First Class Matches	E	193	209	45	3027	77	18.45	-	9	46	4602.1	851	14655	479	30.59	8-75
1983-1992	Middlesex	Nat West Trophy	E	19	11	4	56	10	8.00	-	-	4	152.1	20	618	15	41.20	4-36
1982-1994	Middlesex	Benson & Hedges Cup	E	52	29	7	256	29*	11.63	-	-	6	461.3	-	1705	55	31.00	3-16
1982-1994	Middlesex	Sunday League	E	122	53	20	443	43	13.42	-	-	31	844.5	-	3764	135	27.88	4-39
1990//	Middlesex	Sunday League Cup	E	1	1	1	10	10*	-	-	-	-	8	-	32	0	-	-
1986-1987	Middlesex	O.A.L. O.D. Matches	E	3	1	1	5	5*	-	-	-	-	8	-	31	0	-	-
1995-1998	Essex	First Class Matches	E	33	49	12	548	39	14.81	-	-	8	868.1	153	3088	95	32.50	5-43
1996-1997	Essex	Nat West Trophy	E	4	2	2	17	11*	-	-	-	1	39.4	-	160	3	53.33	1-37
1995-1998	Essex	Benson & Hedges Cup	E	6	3	1	23	20*	11.50	-	-	2	45.3	-	260	6	43.33	2-26
1995-1998	Essex	Sunday League	E	5	4	1	12	12	4.00	-	-	1	26	-	153	4	38.25	2-39
1984-1985	M.C.C.	First Class Matches	E	2	-	-	-	-	-	-	-	-	54.2	7	220	10	22.00	-
1984-1985	English Counties XI	First Class Matches	N	2	2	-	75	62*	-	-	1	1	60	13	201	13	15.46	7-55
1984-1985	English Counties XI	O.A.L. O.D. Matches	N	5	5	0	69	28	13.80	-	-	2	49.5	-	211	5	42.20	2-25
1983-1984	Tasmania	First Class Matches	A	7	11	1	131	34	13.10	-	-	4	221.5	47	841	22	38.22	4-34
1983-1984	Tasmania	MacDonald Cup	A	1	1	0	19	19	19.00	-	-	-	10	-	38	2	19.00	2-38
Total First Class Career				255	302	63	4457	77	18.64	0	13	67	6247.3	1127	20448	675	30.29	8-75
Total O.D. Career				225	116	41	1039	43	13.85	0	-	48	1698.3	-	7258	238	30.49	5-65

STUART CLAYTON WILLIAMS

D.O.B. 12.08.1969 - Government Road, Nevis, Leeward Islands
First Class Debut 26.01.1989 - Leeward Islands v Windward Islands
Test Match Debut 16.04.1994 - West Indies v England
O.D.I. Debut 23.10.1994 - West Indies v India
Domestic O.D. Debut 15.02.1989 - Leeward Islands v Barbados

Test 205-305
O.D.I. 68-278

Teams Played For 6
Leeward Islands, West Indies
W.I. President's XI
West Indies U23
W.I. Board XI
West Indies "A"

RHB / RM

SEASON	TEAM	COMPETITION	V	M	I	No	BATTING						BOWLING					
							RUNS	H.S.	Av	100s	50s	CT	OV	MD	RUNS	W	Av	B.B.
1989-2003	Leeward Islands	First Class Matches	II	74	128	11	5485	252*	46.88	17	20	63	34	4	96	2	48.00	1-19
1989-2001	Leeward Islands	Domestic O.D. Matches	II	55	53	4	1591	105	32.46	1	13	25	10	0	62	2	31.00	2-62
1994-2002	WEST INDIES	TEST MATCHES	HA	31	52	3	1183	128	24.14	1	3	27	3	0	19	0	-	-
1994-1998	West Indies	First Class Matches	A	21	32	-	1083	137	33.84	3	5	13	2	0	4	0	-	-
1991//	West Indies U23	First Class Matches	WI	1	2	0	116	97	58.00	-	1	-	-	-	-	-	-	-
1993//	W.I. President's XI	First Class Matches	WI	1	1	0	11	11	11.00	-	-	-	-	-	-	-	-	-
1994-1999	W.I. Board XI	First Class Matches	WI	2	4	1	147	102*	49.00	1	2	1	-	-	-	-	-	-
1996-1999	West Indies "A"	First Class Matches	HA	5	8	1	379	170	54.14	1	2	9	-	-	-	-	-	-
1994-1999	WEST INDIES	O.D.I. MATCHES	HA	57	55	6	1586	105*	32.36	1	12	18	4	0	30	1	30.00	1-30
1996-1997	West Indies "A"	O.D.(I.) Matches	A	3	3	0	67	40	22.33	-	-	1	-	-	-	-	-	-
1995-1997	West Indies	O.A.L. O.D. Matches	A	7	7	0	186	67	26.57	-	2	5	-	-	-	-	-	-
Total First Class Career				135	227	16	8404	252*	39.82	23	31	113	39	4	119	2	59.50	1-19
Total O.D. Career				122	118	10	3430	105*	31.75	2	26	50	14	0	92	3	30.66	2-62

KENNETH LESLIE WISHART

D.O.B. 28.11.1908 - Georgetown, Demerara, British Guiana (d. 18.10.1972)

First Class Debut 31.01.1929 - British Guiana v Trinidad

Test Match Debut 14.02.1935 - West Indies v England

	Test		Teams Played For		
	42-18		British Guiana		2
			West Indies		LHB

							BATTING						BOWLING				
SEASON	TEAM	COMPETITION	V	M	I	No	RUNS	H.S.	Av	100s	50s	CT	OV	MD	RUNS	W	Av	B.B.
1929-1947	British Guiana	First Class Matches	II	15	30	2	654	88	23.35	-	4	7	-	-	-	-	-	-
1934-1935	WEST INDIES	TEST MATCHES	H	1	2	0	52	52	26.00	-	1	-	-	-	-	-	-	-
		Total First Class Career		16	32	2	706	88	23.53	0	5	7	-	-	-	-	-	-

FRANK MORTIMER MAGLINNE WORRELL

D.O.B. 01.08.1924 - Bank Hall, St Michael, Barbados. (d. 13.03.1967)
First Class Debut 17.01.1942 - Barbados v Trinidad
Test Match Debut 11.02.1948 - West Indies v England

Test 61-24

Teams Played For 8
Barbados, Jamaica
West Indies, F.M. Worrell's XI
Commonwealth XI, M.C.C.
A.E.R. Gilligan's XI
Free Foresters XI

RHB / LM / SLA

SEASON	TEAM	COMPETITION	V	M	I	No	RUNS	H.S.	Av	100s	50s	CT	OV	MD	RUNS	W	Av	B.B.
1942-1947	Barbados	First Class Matches	II	15	27	6	1547	308*	73.66	4	5	15	331.2	50	1148	43	26.69	5-32
1948-1964	Jamaica	First Class Matches	II	13	19	4	698	106*	46.53	2	4	6	220.2	47	650	20	32.50	5-87
1948-1963	WEST INDIES	TEST MATCHES	HA	51	87	9	3860	261	49.48	9	22	43	1115.5	274	2672	69	38.72	7-70
1950-1964	West Indies	First Class Matches	HA	62	89	21	3583	241*	45.93	8	20	28	1020.3	269	2465	99	24.89	6-76
1964//	F.M. Worrell's XI	First Class Matches	WI	1	1	0	24	24	24.00	-	-	1	30.1	5	81	4	20.25	3-55
1949-1958	Commonwealth XI	First Class Matches	A	60	93	8	5007	285	58.90	15	28	42	1379	450	2758	101	27.30	5-71
1961-1964	M.C.C.	First Class Matches	E	3	5	1	84	37*	21.00	-	-	2	67.3	15	161	6	26.88	2-37
1958-1959	A.E.R. Gilligan's XI	First Class Matches	E	2	3	0	180	101	60.00	1	1	1	30	7	108	4	27.00	2-27
1964//	Free Foresters XI	First Class Matches	E	1	2	0	42	42	21.00	-	-	1	27	6	72	3	24.00	2-45
		Total First Class Career		208	326	49	15025	308*	54.24	39	80	139	4221.4	1123	10115	349	28.98	7-70

BATTING

BOWLING

SECTION TWO

ADDITIONAL STATISTICS

SUMMARY OF EARLY MATCH RECORDS 1896 to 1928

Unofficial Test Match Record
West Indies XI v England XI

1896-1897	**WEST INDIES**	**P1 - W1**	
Feb 15-18	Queens Park Oval	West Indies XI v A Priestlys XI	West Indies won by 3 wkts
1901-1902	**WEST INDIES**	**P3 - W2 - L1**	
Jan 29-30	Kensington Oval	West Indies XI v R A Bennetts XI	West Indies won by innings & 4 runs
Mar 20-21	Queens Park Oval	West Indies XI v R A Bennetts XI	West Indies won by 111 runs
Apr 4-7	Bourda	West Indies XI v R A Bennetts XI	Bennetts XI won by innings & 330 runs
1904-1905	**WEST INDIES**	**P2 - L2**	
Feb 6-8	Kensington Oval	West Indies XI v Lord Brackleys XI	Brackleys XI won by innings & 17 runs
Mar 31, Apr 1-4	Queens Park Oval	West Indies XI v Lord Brackleys XI	Brackleys XI won by 4 runs
1906	**ENGLAND**	**P1 - D1**	
July 26-28	Blackpool	England XI v West Indies XI	Match Drawn
1910-1911	**WEST INDIES**	**P3 - D1 - L2**	
Feb 15-17	Kensington Oval	West Indies XI v MCC	MCC won by 5 wkts
Feb 27-28, Mar 1	Bourda	West Indies XI v MCC	MCC won by 4 wkts
Mar 2-4	Bourda	West Indies XI v MCC	Match Drawn
1912-1913	**WEST INDIES**	**P3 - W1 - L2**	
Feb 6-8	Kensington Oval	West Indies XI v MCC	MCC won by 7 wkts
Feb 20-22	Queens Park Oval	West Indies XI v MCC	West Indies won by innings & 6 runs
Mar 6-8	Bourda	West Indies XI v MCC	MCC won by 10 wkts
1923	**ENGLAND**	**P1 - D1**	
May 26-29	Lords	MCC v West Indies XI	Match Drawn (abandoned rain)
1925-1926	**WEST INDIES**	**P3 - D2 - L1**	
Jan 8-12	Kensington Oval	West Indies XI v MCC	Match Drawn
Jan 30, Feb 1-4	Queens Park Oval	West Indies XI v MCC	MCC won by 5 wkts
Feb 13-17	Bourda	West Indies XI v MCC	Match Drawn
1928	**ENGLAND**	**P1 - D1**	
May 19-22	Lords	MCC v West Indies XI	Match Drawn

MATCH RECORD   **P18 - W4 - D6 - L8**

15 matches played in the West Indies, 3 matches played in England.
No matches played against any other country.
First Test match was played on 23 June 1928 at Lords.
A total of 77 players took part in the 18 matches of which 16 went on to play Test matches.

PLAYERS' UNOFFICIAL TESTS BEFORE 1928

West Indies XI v England XI

PLAYER	I	CAREER	M	I	N	R	H	AV	100	50	CT	ST	RC	W	AV	BB
L S A'Dade	T	1896-1902	2	4	-	6	3	1.50	-	-	2	-	-	-	-	-
F L Archer	B	1910-1911	2	4	-	28	14	7.00	-	-	1	-	-	-	-	-
F E W G Austin	B	1910-1911	1	2	-	15	12	7.50	-	-	-	-	62	2	31.00	2-29
H B G Austin	B	1896-1926	8	13	1	411	83	34.25	-	4	5	-	22	0	-	-
M B G Austin	BG	1912-1913	1	2	-	7	7	3.50	-	-	-	-	-	-	-	-
C K Bancroft	B	1904-1906	2	4	1	34	29	11.33	-	-	1	2	-	-	-	-
H C Bayley	BG	1901-1911	3	6	-	141	59	23.50	-	1	-	-	-	-	-	-
N Betancourt*	T	1912-1913	1	1	-	31	31	31.00	-	-	1	-	-	-	-	-
J E Blackman	BG	1912-1913	1	2	-	5	4	2.50	-	-	1	1	-	-	-	-
W Bowring	B	1904-1905	1	1	-	5	5	5.00	-	-	-	-	-	-	-	-
C A Browne	B	1910-1913	3	5	-	134	55	26.80	-	1	1	-	-	-	-	-
C R Browne*	B	1910-1928	7	9	4	214	102*	42.80	1	1	6	-	678	20	33.90	4-43
W T Burton	BG	1901-1905	4	7	1	36	20	6.00	-	-	2	-	315	18	17.50	7-54
G Challenor*	B	1906-1928	8	12	1	365	82	33.18	-	4	2	-	124	3	41.33	3-71
R L Challenor	B	1910-1913	2	4	-	117	77	29.25	-	1	3	-	-	-	-	-
V C Challenor	B	1901-1902	3	5	-	67	49	13.40	-	-	2	-	-	-	-	-
A Cipriani	T	1912-1913	2	3	-	18	14	6.00	-	-	-	-	64	1	64.00	1-58
A B Clarke	BG	1896-1897	1	2	1	50	35*	50.00	-	-	-	-	-	-	-	-
L N Constantine*	T	1923-1928	4	7	-	42	18	6.00	-	-	1	-	154	7	22.00	4-52
L S Constantine	T	1896-1913	6	11	-	303	84	27.54	-	2	7	4	-	-	-	-
G B Y Cox	B	1904-1905	1	2	-	24	16	12.00	-	-	-	-	-	-	-	-
P I Cox	B	1901-1902	1	1	-	0	0	0.00	-	-	-	-	-	-	-	-
H A Croal	BG	1910-1911	2	4	1	74	22*	24.66	-	-	2	-	94	3	31.33	2-13
A B Cumberbatch	B	1896-1906	3	5	2	92	59*	30.66	-	1	6	-	277	15	18.46	5-67
C P Cumberbatch	B	1912-1913	2	3	-	66	63	22.00	-	1	-	-	70	2	35.00	1-8
G A Dewhurst	T	1923-1926	3	4	-	117	55	29.25	-	2	4	1	-	-	-	-
M P Fernandes*	BG	1925-1928	2	1	-	3	3	3.00	-	-	-	-	-	-	-	-
G N Francis*	B	1925-1928	4	5	3	33	14	8.25	-	-	2	-	306	8	38.25	3-57
E A Fraser	BG	1910-1911	1	2	1	11	8	11.00	-	-	-	-	16	0	-	-
W O Gibbs	B	1910-1913	5	9	-	169	39	18.77	-	-	2	-	187	4	46.75	2-43
C E Goodman	B	1896-1897	1	1	-	14	14	14.00	-	-	2	-	125	9	13.88	5-72
P A Goodman	B	1904-1906	2	4	-	75	27	18.75	-	-	2	-	32	3	10.66	3-20
H C Griffith*	B	1928//	1	D	-	-	-	-	-	-	-	-	3	0	-	-
A E Harragin	T	1901-1905	3	6	-	63	36	10.50	-	-	1	-	-	-	-	-
D C S Hinds	B	1901-1905	3	5	1	92	27	23.00	-	-	2	-	4	0	-	-
S D Hinds	BG	1910-1911	2	4	-	63	35	15.75	-	-	6	-	-	-	-	-
E L Hoad*	B	1925-1926	1	2	1	0	0	0.00	-	-	1	-	56	1	56.00	1-56
W C Hoad	B	1904-1905	1	2	-	3	2	1.50	-	-	-	-	68	2	34.00	2-68
J K Holt (sen)	J	1923	1	1	-	23	23	23.00	-	-	-	-	22	1	22.00	1-22
C V Hunter	BG	1910-1913	2	4	-	155	66	38.75	-	2	-	-	-	-	-	-
H W Ince	B	1912-1923	3	4	-	199	167	49.75	1	-	-	-	67	2	33.50	1-42
G John	T	1910-1926	7	11	3	78	27	9.75	-	-	5	-	660	29	22.75	6-93
J M Kidney	B	1912-1913	1	2	-	26	14	13.00	-	-	-	-	-	-	-	-
C H King	BG	1901-1902	2	3	-	4	3	1.33	-	-	2	-	35	1	35.00	1-35
O F Layne	B	1901-1913	8	14	1	189	59	14.53	-	1	3	-	370	9	41.11	5-104
G C Learmond	BG	1901-1906	6	11	-	135	54	12.27	-	1	2	-	14	0	-	-
F R Martin*	J	1928//	1	D	-	-	-	-	-	-	-	-	7	0	-	-

PLAYER	I	CAREER	M	I	N	R	H	AV	100	50	CT	ST	RC	W	AV	BB
D M McAuley	B	1896-1897	1	2	1	16	15*	16.00	-	-	-	-	41	5	20.50	1-11
C S Morrison	J	1904-1906	2	4	1	40	40	13.33	-	-	2	-	113	5	22.60	4-94
E R D Moulder	BG	1901-1913	4	8	1	209	104*	29.85	1	-	-	-	-	-	-	-
C A Nascimento	BG	1925-1926	1	2	1	1	1*	1.00	-	-	-	-	-	-	-	-
J M Neblett*	B	1925-1926	1	1	-	0	0	0.00	-	-	-	-	104	3	34.66	2-66
R K Nunes*	J	1923//1928	2	1	-	11	11	11.00	-	-	-	-	-	-	-	-
R C Ollivierre	WI	1904-1913	6	11	-	225	56	20.45	-	1	4	-	462	21	22.00	5-68
J E Parker	BG	1906	1	2	-	15	15	7.50	-	-	1	-	19	0	-	-
V S Pascall	T	1912-1926	4	7	2	54	21	10.80	-	-	-	-	300	13	23.07	6-77
C D Phillips	WI	1912-1913	1	2	1	1	1*	1.00	-	-	-	-	20	0	-	-
CA Reid	BG	1910-1911	1	2	-	1	1	0.50	-	-	1	-	-	-	-	-
C A Roach*	T	1928//	1	D	-	-	-	-	-	-	-	-	-	-	-	-
J C Rogers	T	1910-1913	5	9	1	156	69*	19.50	-	1	3	-	289	11	26.27	6-82
W G Sarel	T	1904-1905	1	2	-	46	31	23.00	-	-	1	-	14	0	-	-
W C Shepherd	T	1901-1905	4	7	1	15	7	2.50	-	-	2	-	171	2	85.50	2-92
W V Sherlock	BG	1910-1911	1	2	-	24	17	12.00	-	-	-	-	-	-	-	-
C Simpson	BG	1910-1911	2	4	-	70	29	17.50	-	-	2	-	-	-	-	-
J A Small*	T	1912-1928	6	7	1	82	39*	13.66	-	-	-	-	352	7	50.28	2-47
M Smith	T	1896-1897	1	2	-	2	2	1.00	-	-	1	-	-	-	-	-
S G Smith	T	1901-1906	3	6	-	77	30	12.83	-	-	4	-	235	26	9.03	9-34
S W Sproston	BG	1896-1897	1	2	-	38	24	19.00	-	-	-	-	11	0	-	-
W H St Hill*	T	1925-1928	4	4	-	141	72	35.25	-	1	1	-	-	-	-	-
P H Tarilton	B	1910-1926	4	7	-	144	50	20.57	-	1	2	-	-	-	-	-
R S A Warner	T	1896-1897	1	2	-	21	21	10.50	-	-	1	-	-	-	-	-
O E Weber	BG	1896-1897	1	2	-	7	4	3.50	-	-	-	-	-	-	-	-
W P Weber	BG	1901-1902	2	4	-	71	59	17.25	-	1	1	-	28	3	9.33	3-28
C A Wiles*	T	1925-1926	1	2	-	92	75	46.00	-	1	-	-	-	-	-	-
J Woods	B	1901-1902	3	5	3	29	12*	14.50	-	-	2	-	204	14	14.57	7.38
S M Worme	B	1910-1911	1	1	-	0	0	0.00	-	-	-	-	39	0	-	-
C V Wright*	BG	1925-1926	1	1	-	90	90	90.00	-	1	2	-	-	-	-	-

* Players that went on to play Test cricket (total 16)

Seventy-seven players took part in 15 matches: 30 from Barbados, 22 from British Guiana, 19 from Trinidad, 4 from Jamaica and 2 from the Windward Islands.

TEST MATCH RECORDS
1928-2003

1928	ENGLAND			P3 - W0 - D0 - L3	LOST SERIES 0-3	1
Jun 23-26	Lords	1	1	England v West Indies	England won by an innings & 58 runs	
Jul 21-24	Old Trafford	2	2	England v West Indies	England won by an innings & 30 runs	
Aug 11-14	The Oval	3	3	England v West Indies	England won by an innings & 71 runs	
1929-30	WEST INDIES			P4 - W1 - D2 - L1	DRAWN SERIES 1-1	1
Jan 11-16	Kensington Oval	1	4	West Indies v England	Match drawn	
Feb 1-6	Queens Park	2	5	West Indies v England	England won by 167 runs	
Feb 21-26	Bourda	3	6	West Indies v England	West Indies won by 289 runs	
Apr 3-12	Sabina Park	4	7	West Indies v England	Match drawn	
1930-31	AUSTRALIA			P5 - W1 - D0 - L4	LOST SERIES 1-4	1
Dec 12-16	Adelaide Oval	1	8	Australia v West Indies	Australia won by 10 wkts	
Jan 1-5	Sydney CG	2	9	Australia v West Indies	Australia won by an innings & 172 runs	
Jan 16-20	Exhibition Ground	3	10	Australia v West Indies	Australia won by an innings & 217 runs	
Feb 13-14	Melbourne CC	4	11	Australia v West Indies	Australia won by an innings & 122 runs	
Feb 27 Mar 4	Sydney Cg	2	12	Australia v West Indies	West Indies won by 30 runs	
1933	ENGLAND			P3 - W0 - D1 - L2	LOST SERIES 0-2	2
Jun 24-27	Lords	1	13	England v West Indies	England won by and innings & 27 runs	
Jul 22-25	Old Trafford	2	14	England v West Indies	Match drawn	
Aug 12-15	The Oval	3	15	England v West Indies	England won by an innings & 17 runs	
1934-35	WEST INDIES			P4 - W2 - D1 - L1	WON SERIES 2-1	2
Jan 8-10	Kensington Oval	1	16	West Indies v England	England won by 4 wkts	
Jan 24-28	Queens Park	2	17	West Indies v England	West Indies won by 217 runs	
Feb 14-18	Bourda	3	18	West Indies v England	Match drawn	
Mar 14-18	Sabina Park	4	19	West Indies v England	West Indies won by an innings & 161 runs	
1939	ENGLAND			P3 - W0 - D2 - L1	LOST SERIES 0-1	3
Jun 24-27	Lords	1	20	England v West Indies	England won by 8 wkts	
Jul 22-25	Old Trafford	2	21	England v West Indies	Match drawn	
Aug 19-22	The Oval	3	22	England v West Indies	Match drawn	
1947-48	WEST INDIES			P4 - W2 - D2 - L0	WON SERIES 2-0	3
Jan 21-26	Kensington Oval	1	23	West Indies v England	Match drawn	
Feb 11-16	Queens Park Oval	2	24	West Indies v England	Match drawn	
Mar 3-6	Bourda	3	25	West Indies v England	West Indies won by 7 wkts	
Mar 27-Apr 1	Sabina Park	4	26	West Indies v England	West Indies won by 10 wkts	
1948-49	INDIA			P5 - W1 - D4 - L0	WON SERIES 1-0	1
Nov 10-14	Delhi	1	27	India v West Indies	Match drawn	
Nov 9-13	Bombay	2	28	India v West Indies	Match drawn	
Dec 31- Jan 4	Calcutta	3	29	India v West Indies	Match drawn	
Jan 27-31	Madrad	4	30	India v West Indies	West Indies won by an innings & 193 runs	
Feb 4-8	Bombay	2	31	India v West Indies	Match drawn	
1950	ENGLAND			P4 - W3 - D0 - L1	WON SERIES 3-1	4
Jun 8-12	Old Trafford	1	32	England v West Indies	England won by 202 runs	

Jun 24-29	Lords	2	33	England v West Indies	West Indies won by 326 runs
July 20-25	Trent Bridge	3	34	England v West Indies	West Indies won by 10 wkts
Aug 12-16	The Oval	4	35	England v West Indies	West Indies won by an innings & 56 runs

1951-52	**AUSTRALIA**			**P5 - W1 - D0 - L4**	**LOST SERIES 1-4**	**2**
Nov 9-13	Brisbane	1	36	Australia v West Indies	Australia won by 3 wkts
Nov 30-Dec 5	Sydney	2	37	Australia v West Indies	Australia won by 7 wkts
Dec 22-25	Adelaide	3	38	Australia v West Indies	West Indies won by 6 wkts
Dec31-Jan 3	Melbourne	4	39	Australia v West Indies	Australia won by 1 wkt
Jan 25-29	Sydney	5	40	Australia v West Indies	Australia won by 202 runs

1951-52	**NEW ZEALAND**			**P2 - W1 - D1 - L0**	**WON SERIES 1-0**	**1**
Feb 8-12	Christchurch	1	41	New Zealand v West Indies	West Indies won by 5 wkts
Feb 15-19	Auckland	2	42	New Zealand v West Indies	Match drawn

1952-53	**WEST INDIES**			**P5 - W1 - D4 - L0**	**WON SERIES 1-0**	**1**
Jan 21-28	Queens Park Oval	1	43	West Indies v India	Match drawn
Feb 7-12	Kensington Oval	2	44	West Indies v India	West Indies won by 142 runs
Feb 19-25	Queens Park Oval	3	45	West Indies v India	Match drawn
Mar 11-17	Bourda	4	46	West Indies v India	Match drawn
Mar 28-Apr 4	Sabina Park	5	47	West Indies v India	Match drawn

1953-54	**WEST INDIES**			**P5 - W2 - D1 - L2**	**DRAWN SERIES 2-2**	**4**
Jan 15-21	Sabina Park	1	48	West Indies v England	West Indies won by 140 runs
Feb 6-12	Kensington Oval	5	49	West Indies v England	West Indies won by 181 runs
Feb 24-Mar 1	Bourda	3	50	West Indies v England	England won by 9 wkts
Mar 17-23	Queens Park Oval	4	51	West Indies v England	Match drawn
Mar 30-Apr 3	Sabina Park	5	52	West Indies v England	England won by 9 wkts

1954-55	**WEST INDIES**			**P5 - W0 - D2 - L3**	**LOST SERIES 0-3**	**1**
Mar 26-31	Sabina Park	1	52	West Indies v Australia	Australia won by 9 wkts
Apr 11-16	Queens Park Oval	2	50	West Indies v Australia	Match drawn
Apr 26-29	Bourda	3	55	West Indies v Australia	Australia won by 8 wkts
May 14-20	Kensington Park	4	56	West Indies v Australia	Match drawn
Jun 11-17	Sabina Park	5	57	West Indies v Australia	Australia won by an innings & 82 runs

1955-56	**NEW ZEALAND**			**P4 - W3 - D0 - L1**	**WON SERIES 3-1**	**2**
Feb 13-6	Dunedin	1	58	New Zealand v West Indies	West Indies won by an innings & 71 runs
Feb 18-21	Christchurch	2	59	New Zealand v West Indies	West Indies won by an innings & 64 runs
Mar 3-7	Wellington	3	40	New Zealand v West Indies	West Indies won by 9 wkts
Mar 9-13	Auckland	4	61	New Zealand v West Indies	New Zealand won by 190 runs

1957	**ENGLAND**			**P5 - W0 - D2 - L3**	**LOST SERIES 0-3**	**5**
May 30-Jun 4	Edgbaston	1	62	England v West Indies	Match drawn
Jun 20-22	Lords	2	63	England v West Indies	England won by an innings & 36 runs
July 4-9	Trent Bridge	3	64	England v West Indies	Match drawn
July 25-27	Headingley	4	65	England v West Indies	England won by an innings & 5 runs
Aug 22-24	The Oval	5	66	England v West Indies	England won by an innings & 237 runs

1957-58	**WEST INDIES**			**P5 - W3 - D1 - L1**	**WON SERIES 3-1**	**1**
Jan 17-23	Kensington Oval	1	67	West Indies v Pakistan	Match drawn
Feb 5-11	Queens Park Oval	2	68	West Indies v Pakistan	West Indies won by 120 runs
Feb 26-Mar 4	Sabina Park	3	69	West Indies v Pakistan	West Indies won by an innings & 174 runs
Mar 13-19	Bourda	4	70	West Indies v Pakistan	West Indies won by 8 Wkts
Mar 26-31	Queens Park Oval	5	71	West Indies v Pakistan	Pakistan won by an innings & 1 run

1958-59	**INDIA**			**P5 - W3 - D2 - L0**	**WON SERIES 3-0**	**2**
Nov 28-Dec 3	Bombay	1	72	India v West Indies	Match drawn
Dec 12-17	Kanpur	2	73	India v West Indies	West Indies won by 203 runs
Dec 31-Jan 4	Calcutta	3	74	India v West Indies	West Indies won by an innings & 336 runs
Jan 21-26	Madras	4	75	India v West Indies	West Indies won by 295 runs
Feb 6-11	Delhi	5	76	India v West Indies	Match drawn

508

1958-59	PAKISTAN			P3 - W1 - D0 - L2	LOST SERIES 1-2	1
Feb 20-25	Karachi	1	77	Pakistan v West Indies	Pakistan won by 10 wkts	
Mar 6-8	Dacca	2	78	Pakistan v West Indies	Pakistan won by 41 runs	
Mar 26-31	Lahore	3	79	Pakistan v West Indies	West Indies won by an Innings & 156 runs	

1959-60	WEST INDIES			P5 - W0 - D4 - L1	LOST SERIES 0-1	5
Jan 6-12	Kensington Oval	1	80	West Indies v England	Match drawn	
Jan 28-Feb 3	Queens Park Oval	2	81	West Indies v England	England won by 256 runs	
Feb 17-23	Sabina Park	3	82	West Indies v England	Match drawn	
Mar 9-15	Bourda	4	83	West Indies v England	Match drawn	
Mar 25-31	Queens Park Oval	5	84	West Indies v England	Match drawn	

1960-61	AUSTRALIA			P5 - W1 - D1 - T1 - L2	LOST SERIES 1-2	3
Dec 9-14	Brisbane	1	85	Australia v West Indies	Match tied	
Dec 30-Jan 3	Melbourne	2	86	Australia v West Indies	Australia won by 7 wkts	
Jan 13-18	Sydney	3	87	Australia v West Indies	West Indies won by 222 runs	
Jan 27-Feb 1	Adelaide	4	88	Australia v West Indies	Match drawn	
Feb 10-15	Melbourne	5	89	Australia v West Indies	Australia won by 2 wkts	

1961-62	WEST INDIES			P5 - W5 - D0 - L0	WON SERIES 5-0	2
Feb 16-20	Queens Park Oval	1	90	West Indies v India	West Indies won by 10 wkts	
Mar 7-12	Sabina Park	2	91	West Indies v India	West Indies won by an innings & 18 runs	
Mar 23-28	Kensington Oval	3	92	West Indies v India	West Indies won by an innings & 30 runs	
Apr 4-9	Queens Park Oval	4	93	West Indies v India	West Indies won by 7 wkts	
Apr 13-18	Sabina Park	5	94	West Indies v India	West Indies won by 123 runs	

1963	ENGLAND			P5 - W3 - D1 - L1	WON SERIES 3-1	6
Jun 6-10	Manchester	1	95	England v West Indies	West Indies won by 10 wtks	
Jun 20-25	Lords	2	96	England v West Indies	Match drawn	
July 4-9	Edgbaston	3	97	England v West Indies	England won by 217 runs	
July 25-29	Headingley	4	98	England v West Indies	West Indies won by 221 runs	
Aug 22-26	The Oval	5	99	England v West Indies	West Indies won by 8 Wkts	

1964-65	WEST INDIES			P5 - W2 - D2 - L1	WON SERIES 2-1	2
Mar 3-8	Sabina Park	1	100	West Indies v Australia	West Indies won by 179 runs	
Mar 26-Apr 1	Queens Park Oval	2	101	West Indies v Australia	Match drawn	
Apr 14-20	Bourda	3	102	West Indies v Australia	West Indies won by 212 runs	
May 5-11	Kensington Oval	4	103	West Indies v Australia	Match drawn	
May 14-17	Queens Park Oval	5	104	West Indies v Australia	Australia won by 10 wkts	

1966	ENGLAND			P5 - W3 - D1 - L1	WON SERIES 3-1	7
Jun 2-4	Old Trafford	1	105	England v West Indies	West Indies won by an innings & 40 runs	
Jun 16-21	Lords	2	106	England v West Indies	Match drawn	
Jun 30-Jul 5	Trent Bridge	3	107	England v West Indies	West Indies won by 139 runs	
Aug 4-8	Headingley	4	108	England v West Indies	West Indies won by an innings & 55 runs	
Aug 18-22	The Oval	5	109	England v West Indies	England won by an innings & 34 runs	

1966-67	INDIA			P3 - W2 - D1 - L0	WON SERIES 2-0	3
Dec 13-18	Bombay	1	110	India v West Indies	West Indies won by 6 wkts	
Dec 31-Jan 5	Calcutta	2	111	India v West Indies	West Indies won by an innings & 45 runs	
Jan 13-18	Madras	3	112	India v West Indies	Match drawn	

1967-68	WEST INDIES			P5 - W0 - D4 - L1	LOST SERIES 0-1	6
Jan 19-24	Queens Park Oval	1	113	West Indies v England	Match drawn	
Feb 8-14	Sabina Park	2	114	West Indies v England	Match drawn	
Feb 29-Mar 5	Kensington Park	3	115	West Indies v England	Match drawn	
Mar 14-19	Queens Park Oval	4	116	West Indies v England	England won by 7 wkts	
Mar 28-Apr 3	Bourda	5	117	West Indies v England	Match drawn	

1968-69	AUSTRALIA			P5 - W1 - D1 - L3	LOST SERIES 1-3	4
Dec 6-10	Brisbane	1	118	Australia v West Indies	West Indies won by 125 runs	
Dec 26-30	Melbourne	2	119	Australia v West Indies	Australia won by an innings & 30 runs	

Jan 3-8	Sydney	3	120	Australia v West Indies	Australia won by 10 wks
Jan 24-29	Adelaide	4	121	Australia v West Indies	Match drawn
Feb 14-19	Sydney	5	122	Australia v West Indies	Australia won by 382 runs

1968-69	**NEW ZEALAND**			**P3 - W1 - D1 - L1**	**DRAWN SERIES 1-1**	**3**
Feb 27-Mar 3	Auckland	1	123	New Zealand v West Indies	West Indies won by 5 wkts
Mar 7-11	Wellington	2	124	New Zealand v West Indies	New Zealand won by 6 wkts
Mar 13-17	Christchurch	3	125	New Zealand v West Indies	Match drawn

1969	**ENGLAND**			**P3 - W0 - D1 - L2**	**LOST SERIES 0-2**	**8**
Jun 12-17	Old Trafford	1	126	England v West Indies	England won by 10 wkts
Jun 26-Jul 1	Lords	2	127	England v West Indies	Match drawn
July 10-15	Headingley	3	128	England v West Indies	England won by 30 runs

1970-71	**WEST INDIES**			**P5 - W0 - D4 - L1**	**LOST SERIES 0-1**	**3**
Feb 18-23	Sabina Park	1	129	West Indies v India	Match drawn
Mar 6-10	Queens Park Oval	2	130	West Indies v India	India won by 7 wkts
Mar 19-24	Bourda	3	131	West Indies v India	Match drawn
Apr 1-6	Kensington Oval	4	132	West Indies v India	Match drawn
Apr 13-19	Queens Park Oval	5	133	West Indies v India	Match drawn

1971-72	**WEST INDIES**			**P5 - W0 - D5 - L0**	**DRAWN SERIES 0-0**	**1**
Feb 16-21	Sabina Park	1	134	West Indies v New Zealand	Match drawn
Mar 9-14	Queens Park Oval	2	135	West Indies v New Zealand	Match drawn
Mar 23-28	Kensington Oval	3	136	West Indies v New Zealand	Match drawn
Apr 6-11	Bourda	4	137	West Indies v New Zealand	Match drawn
Apr 20-26	Queens Park Oval	5	138	West Indies v New Zealand	Match drawn

1972-73	**WEST INDIES**			**P5 - W0 - D3 - L2**	**LOST SERIES 0-2**	**3**
Feb 16-21	Sabina Park	1	139	West Indies v Australia	Match drawn
Mar 9-14	Kensington Oval	2	140	West Indies v Australia	Match drawn
Mar 23-28	Queens Park Oval	3	141	West Indies v Australia	Australia won by 44 runs
Apr 6-11	Bourda	4	142	West Indies v Australia	Australia won by 10 wkts
Apr 21-26	Queens Park Oval	5	143	West Indies v Australia	Match Drawn

1973	**ENGLAND**			**P3 - W2 - D1 - L0**	**WON SERIES 2-0**	**9**
Jul 26-31	The Oval	1	144	England v West Indies	West Indies won by 158 runs
Aug 9-14	Edgbaston	2	145	England v West Indies	Match drawn
Aug 23-27	Lords	3	146	England v West Indies	West Indies won by an innings & 226 runs

1973-74	**WEST INDIES**			**P5 - W1 - D3 - L1**	**DRAWN SERIES 1-1**	**7**
Feb 2-7	Queens Park Oval	1	147	West Indies v England	West Indies won by 7 wks
Feb 16-21	Sabina Park	2	148	West Indies v England	Match drawn
Mar 6-11	Kensington Oval	3	149	West Indies v England	Match drawn
Mar 22-27	Bourda	4	150	West Indies v England	Match drawn
Mar 30-Apr 5	Queens Park Oval	5	151	West Indies v England	England won by 26 runs

1974-75	**INDIA**			**P5 - W3 - D0 - L2**	**WON SERIES 3-2**	**4**
Nov 22-27	Bangalore	1	152	India v West Indies	West Indies won by 267 runs
Dec 11-15	Delhi	2	153	India v West Indies	West Indies won by an innings & 17 runs
Dec 27-Jan 1	Calcutta	3	154	India v West Indies	India won by 85 runs
Jan 11 15	Madras	4	155	India v West Indies	India won by 100 runs
Jan 23-28	Bombay	5	156	India v West Indies	West Indies won by 201 runs

1974-75	**PAKISTAN**			**P2 - W0 - D2 - L0**	**DRAWN SERIES 0-0**	**2**
Feb 15-20	Lahore	1	157	Pakistan v West Indies	Match drawn
Mar 1-6	Karachi	2	158	Pakistan v West Indies	Match drawn

1975-76	**AUSTRALIA**			**P6 - W1 - D0 - L5**	**LOST SERIES 1-5**	**5**
Nov 28-Dec 2	Brisbane	1	159	Australia v West Indies	Australia won by 8 wkts
Dec 12-16	Perth	2	160	Australia v West Indies	West Indies won by an innings & 87 runs
Dec 26 30	Melbourne	3	161	Australia v West Indies	Australia won by 8 wkts

Jan 3-7	Sydney	4	162	Australia v West Indies	Australia won by 7 wkts
Jan 23-28	Adelaide	5	163	Australia v West Indies	Australia won by 190 runs
Jan 31-Feb 5	Melbourne	6	164	Australia v West Indies	Australia won by 165 runs

1975-76	**WEST INDIES**			**P4 - W2 - D1 - L1**	**WON SERIES 2-1**	**4**
Mar 10-13	Kensington Oval	1	165	West Indies v India	West Indies won by an innings & 97 runs	
Mar 24-29	Queens Park Oval	2	166	West Indies v India	Match drawn	
Apr 7-12	Queens Park Oval	3	167	West Indies v India	India won by 6 wkts	
Apr 21-25	Sabina Park	4	168	West Indies v India	West Indies won by 10 wkts	

1976	**ENGLAND**			**P5 - W3 - D2 - L0**	**WON SERIES 3-0**	**10**
Jun 3-8	Trent Bridge	1	169	England v West Indies	Match drawn	
Jun 17-22	Lords	2	170	England v West Indies	Match drawn	
July 8-13	Old Trafford	3	171	England v West Indies	West Indies won by 425 runs	
July 22-27	Headingley	4	172	England v West Indies	West Indies won by 55 runs	
Aug 12-17	The Oval	5	173	England v West Indies	West Indies won by 231 runs	

1976-77	**WEST INDIES**			**P5 - W2 - D2 - L1**	**WON SERIES 2-1**	**2**
Feb 18-23	Kensington Oval	1	174	West Indies v Pakistan	Match drawn	
Mar 4-9	Queens Park Oval	2	175	West Indies v Pakistan	West Indies won by 6 wkts	
Mar 18-23	Bourda	3	176	West Indies v Pakistan	Match drawn	
Apr 1-6	Queens Park Oval	4	177	West Indies v Pakistan	Pakistan won by 266 runs	
Apr 15-20	Sabina Park	5	178	West Indies v Pakistan	West Indies won by 140 runs	

1977-78	**WEST INDIES**			**P5 - W3 - D1 - L1**	**WON SERIES 3-1**	**4**
Mar 3-5	Queens Park Oval	1	179	West Indies v Australia	West Indies won by an innings & 106 runs	
Mar 17-19	Kensington Oval	2	180	West Indies v Australia	West Indies won by 9 wkts	
Mar 31-Apr 4	Bourda	3	181	West Indies v Australia	Australia won by 3 wkts	
Apr 15-18	Queens Park Oval	4	182	West Indies v Australia	West Indies won by 198 runs	
Apr 28-May 2	Sabina Park	5	183	West Indies v Australia	Match drawn	

1978-79	**INDIA**			**P6 - W0 - D5 - L1**	**LOST SERIES 0-1**	**5**
Dec 1-6	Bombay	1	184	India v West Indies	Match drawn	
Dec 15-20	Bangalore	2	185	India v West Indies	Match drawn	
Dec 29-Jan 3	Calcutta	3	186	India v West Indies	Match drawn	
Jan 10-15	Madras	4	187	India v West Indies	India won by 3 wkts	
Jan 24-29	New Delhi	5	188	India v West Indies	Match drawn	
Feb 2-7	Kanpur	6	189	India v West Indies	Match drawn	

1979-80	**AUSTRALIA**			**P3 - W2 - D1 - L0**	**WON SERIES 2-0**	**6**
Dec 1-5	Brisbane	1	190	Australia v West Indies	Match drawn	
Dec 29-Jan 1	Melbourne	2	191	Australia v West Indies	West Indies won by 10 wkts	
Jan 26-30	Adelaide	3	192	Australia v West Indies	West Indies won by 408 runs	

1979-80	**NEW ZEALAND**			**P3 - W0 - D2 - L1**	**LOST SERIES 0-1**	**4**
Feb 8-13	Dunedin	1	193	New Zealand v West Indies	New Zealand won by 1 wkt	
Feb 22-27	Christchurch	2	194	New Zealand v West Indies	Match drawn	
Feb 29-Mar 5	Auckland	3	195	New Zealand v West Indies	Match drawn	

1980	**ENGLAND**			**P5 - W1 - D4 - L0**	**WON SERIES 1-0**	**11**
Jun 5-10	Trent Bridge	1	196	England v West Indies	West Indies won by 2 wkts	
Jun 19-24	Lords	2	197	England v West Indies	Match drawn	
July 10-15	Old Trafford	3	198	England v West Indies	Match drawn	
July 24-29	The Oval	4	199	England v West Indies	Match drawn	
Aug 7-12	Headingley	5	200	England v West Indies	Match drawn	

1980-81	**PAKISTAN**			**P4 - W1 - D3 - L0**	**WON SERIES 1-0**	**3**
Nov 24-29	Lahore	1	201	Pakistan v West Indies	Match drawn	
Dec 8-12	Faisalabad	2	202	Pakistan v West Indies	West Indies won by 156 runs	
Dec 22-27	Karachi	3	203	Pakistan v West Indies	Match drawn	
Dec30-Jan 4	Multan	4	204	Pakistan v West Indies	Match drawn	

1980-1981	WEST INDIES			P4 - W2 - D2 - L0	WON SERIES 2-0	8
Feb 13-18	Queens Park Oval	1	205	West Indies v England	West Indies won by an innings & 79 runs	
Mar 13-18	Kensington Oval	2	206	West Indies v England	West Indies won by 298 runs	
Mar 27-Apr 1	St Johns RG	3	207	West Indies v England	Match drawn	
Apr 10-15	Sabina Park	4	208	West Indies v England	Match drawn	

The second Test scheduled to be played at Bourda in Guyana, on February 28 to March 5, was cancelled by the I.C.C. when the Guyana government withdrew R.D. Jackman's visitor's permit.

1981-82	AUSTRALIA			P3 - W1 - D1 - L1	DRAWN SERIES 1-1	7
Dec 26-30	Melbourne	1	209	Australia v West Indies	Australia won by 58 runs	
Jan 2-6	Sydney	2	210	Australia v West Indies	Match Drawn	
Jan 30-Feb 3	Adelaide	3	211	Australia v West Indies	West Indies won by 5 wkts	

1982-83	WEST INDIES			P5 - W2 - D3 - L0	WON SERIES 2-0	5
Feb 23-28	Sabina Park	1	212	West Indies v India	West Indies won by 4 wkts	
Mar 11-16	Queens Park Oval	2	213	West Indies v India	Match drawn	
Mar 31-Apr 5	Bourda	3	214	West Indies v India	Match drawn	
Apr 15-20	Kensington Oval	4	215	West Indies v India	West Indies won by10 wkts	
Apr 28-May 3	St Johns RG	5	216	West Indies v India	Match drawn	

1983-84	INDIA			P6 - W3 - D3 - L0	WON SERIES 3-0	6
Oct 21-25	Kanpur	1	217	India v West Indies	West Indies won by an innings & 83 runs	
Oct 29-Nov 3	Delhi	2	218	India v West Indies	Match drawn	
Nov 12-15	Ammedabad	3	219	India v West Indies	West Indies won by 138 runs	
Nov 24-30	Bombay	4	220	India v West Indies	Match drawn	
Dec 10-15	Calcutta	5	221	India v West Indies	West Indies won by an innings & 46 runs	
Dec 24-29	Madras	6	222	India v West Indies	Match drawn	

1983-84	WEST INDIES			P5 - W3 - D2 - L0	WON SERIES 3-0	5
Mar 2-7	Bourda	1	223	West Indies v Australia	Match drawn	
Mar 16-21	Queens Park Oval	2	224	West Indies v Australia	Match drawn	
Mar 30-Apr 4	Kensington Oval	3	225	West Indies v Australia	West Indies won by 10 wkts	
Apr 7-12	St Johns RG	4	226	West Indies v Australia	West Indies won by an innings & 36 runs	
Apr 28-May 2	Sabina Park	5	227	West Indies v Australia	West Indies won by 10 wkts	

1984	ENGLAND			P5 - W5 - D0 - L0	WON SERIES 5-0	12
Jun 14-18	Edgbaston	1	228	England v West Indies	West Indies won by an innings & 180 runs	
Jun 28-Jul 3	Lords	2	229	England v West Indies	West Indies won by 9 wkts	
July 12-16	Headingley	3	230	England v West Indies	West Indies won by 8 wkts	
July 26-31	Old Trafford	4	231	England v West Indies	West Indies won by an innings & 64 runs	
Aug 9-14	The Oval	5	232	England v West Indies	West Indies won by 172 runs	

1984-85	AUSTRALIA			P5 - W3 - D1 - L1	WON SERIES 3-1	8
Nov 9-12	Perth	1	233	Australia v West Indies	West Indies won by an innings & 112 runs	
Nov 23-26	Brisbane	2	234	Australia v West Indies	West Indies won by 8 wkts	
Dec 7-11	Adelaide	3	235	Australia v West Indies	West Indies won by 191 runs	
Dec 22-27	Melbourne	4	236	Australia v West Indies	Match drawn	
Dec 30-Jan 2	Sydney	5	237	Australia v West Indies	Australia won by an innings & 55 runs	

1984-85	WEST INDIES			P4 - W2 - D2 - L0	WON SERIES 2-0	2
Mar 29-Apr 3	Queens Park Oval	1	238	West Indies v New Zealand	Match drawn	
Apr 6-11	Bourda	2	239	West Indies v New Zealand	Match drawn	
Apr 26-May 4	Kensington Oval	3	240	West Indies v New Zealand	West Indies won by 10 wkts	
May 4-9	Sabina Park	4	241	West Indies v New Zealand	West Indies won by 10 wkts	

1985-86	WEST INDIES			P5 - W5 - D0 - L0	WON SERIES 5-0	9
Feb 21-26	Sabina Park	1	242	West Indies v England	West Indies won by 10 wkts	
Mar 7-12	Queens Park Oval	2	243	West Indies v England	West Indies won by 7 wkts	
Mar 21-26	Kensington Oval	3	244	West Indies v England	West Indies won by an innings & 30 runs	
Apr 3-7	Queens Park Oval	4	245	West Indies v England	West Indies won by 10 wkts	
Apr 11-16	St Johns RG	5	246	West Indies v England	West Indies won by 240 runs	

1986-87	PAKISTAN			P3 - W1 - D1 - L1	DRAWN SERIES 1-1	4
Oct 24-29	Fiasalabad	1	247	Pakistan v West Indies	Pakistan won by 196 runs	
Nov 7-12	Lahore	2	248	Pakistan v West Indies	West Indies won by an innings & 10 runs	
Nov 20-25	Karachi	3	249	Pakistan v West Indies	Match drawn	

1986-87	NEW ZEALAND			P3 - W1 - D1 - L1	DRAWN SERIES 1-1	5
Feb 20-24	Wellington	1	250	New Zealand v West Indies	Match drawn	
Feb 27-Mar 3	Auckland	2	251	New Zealand v West Indies	West Indies won by 10 wkts	
Mar 12-16	Christchurch	3	252	New Zealand v West Indies	New Zealand won by 5 wkts	

1987-88	INDIA			P4 - W1 - D2 - L1	DRAWN SERIES 1-1	7
Nov 25-30	Delhi	1	253	India v West Indies	West Indies won by 5 wkts	
Dec 11-16	Bombay	2	254	India v West Indies	Match Drawn	
Dec 26-31	Calcutta	3	255	India v West Indies	Match Drawn	
Jan 11-16	Madras	4	256	India v West Indies	India won by 255 runs	

1987-88	WEST INDIES			P3 - W1 - D1 - L1	DRAWN SERIES 1-1	3
Apr 2-7	Bourda	1	257	West Indies v Pakistan	Pakistan won by 9 wkts	
Apr 14-18	Queens Park Oval	2	258	West Indies v Pakistan	Match drawn	
Apr 22-27	Kensington Oval	3	259	West Indies v Pakistan	West Indies won by 2 wkts	

1988	ENGLAND			P5 - W4 - D1 - L0	WON SERIES 4-0	13
Jun 2-7	Trent Bridge	1	260	England v West Indies	Match drawn	
Jun 16-21	Lords	2	261	England v West Indies	West Indies won by 134 runs	
Jun 30-Jul 5	Old Trafford	3	262	England v West Indies	West Indies won by an innings & 156 runs	
July 21-26	Headlingley	4	263	England v West Indies	West Indies won by 10 wkts	
Aug 4-8	The Oval	5	264	England v West Indies	West Indies won by8 wkts	

1988-89	AUSTRALIA			P5 - W3 - D1 - L1	WON SERIES 3-1	9
Nov 18-21	Brisbane	1	265	Australia v West Indies	West Indies won by 9 wkts	
Dec 2-6	Perth	2	266	Australia v West Indies	West Indies won by 169 runs	
Dec 24-29	Melbourne	3	267	Australia v West Indies	West Indies won by 258 runs	
Jan 26-30	Sydney	4	268	Australia v West Indies	Australia won by 7 wkts	
Feb 3-7	Adelaide	5	269	Australia v West Indies	Match drawn	

1988-89	WEST INDIES			P4 - W3 - D1 - L0	WON SERIES 3-0	6
Mar 25-30	Bourda	1	270	West Indies v India	Match drawn	
Apr 7-12	Kensington Oval	2	271	West Indies v India	West Indies won by 8 wkts	
Apr 15-20	Queens Park Oval	3	272	West Indies v India	West Indies won by 217 runs	
Apr 28-May 3	Sabina Park	4	273	West Indies v India	West Indies won by 7 wkts	

1989-90	WEST INDIES			P4 - W2 - D1 - L1	WON SERIES 2-1	10
Feb 24-Mar 1	Sabina Park	1	274	West Indies v England	England won by 9 wkts	
Mar 23-28	Queens Park Oval	3	275	West Indies v England	Match drawn	
Apr 5-10	Kensington Oval	4	276	West Indies v England	West Indies won by 164 runs	
Apr 12-17	St Johns RG	5	277	West Indies v England	West Indies won by an innings & 32 runs	

The second Test at Bourda, scheduled for March 10-15, was abandoned without a ball being bowled because of rain.

1990-91	PAKISTAN			P3 - W1 - D1 - L1	DRAWN SERIES 1-1	5
Nov 15-20	Karachi	1	278	Pakistan v West Indies	Pakistan won by 8 wkts	
Nov 23-27	Faisalabad	2	279	Pakistan v West Indies	West Indies won by 7 wkts	
Dec 6-11	Lahore	3	280	Pakistan v West Indies	Match drawn	

1990-91	WEST INDIES			P5 - W2 - D2 - L1	WON SERIES 2-1	6
Mar 1-6	Sabina Park	1	281	West Indies v Australia	Match drawn	
Mar 23-28	Bourda	2	282	West Indies v Australia	West Indies won by 10 wkts	
Apr 5-10	Queens Park Oval	3	283	West Indies v Australia	Match Drawn	
Apr 19-24	Kensington Oval	4	284	West Indies v Australia	West Indies won by 343 runs	
Apr 27-May 1	St John RG	5	285	West Indies v Australia	Australia won by 157 runs	

1991	ENGLAND			P5 - W2 - D1 - L2	DRAWN SERIES 2-2	14
Jun 6-10	Headingley	1	286	England v West Indies	England won by 115 runs	
Jun 20-24	Lords	2	287	England v West Indies	Match drawn	
July 4-9	Trent Bridge	3	288	England v West Indies	West Indies won by 9 wkts	
July 25-29	Edgbaston	4	289	England v West Indies	West Indies won by 7 wkts	
Aug 8-12	The Oval	5	290	England v West Indies	England won by 5 wkts	

1991-92	WEST INDIES			P1 - W1	WON SERIES 1-0	1
Apr 18-23	Kensington Oval	1	291	West Indies v South Africa	West Indies won by 52 runs	

1992-93	AUSTRALIA			P5 - W2 - D2 - L1	WON SERIES 2-1	10
Nov 27-Dec 1	Brisbane	1	292	Australia v West Indies	Match drawn	
Dec 26-30	Melbourne	2	293	Australia v West Indies	Australia won by 139 runs	
Jan 2-6	Sydney	3	294	Australia v West Indies	Match drawn	
Jan 23-26	Adelaide	4	295	Australia v West Indies	West Indies won by 1 run	
Jan 30-Feb 1	Perth	5	296	Australia v West Indies	West Indies won by an innings & 25 runs	

1992-93	WEST INDIES			P3 - W2 - D1 - L0	WON SERIES 2-0	4
Apr 16-18	Queens Park Oval	1	297	West Indies v Pakistan	West Indies won by 204 runs	
Apr 23-27	Kensington Oval	2	298	West Indies v Pakistan	West Indies won by 10 wkts	
May 1-5	St Johns RG	3	299	West Indies v Pakistan	Match drawn	

1993-94	SRI LANKA			P1 - D1	DRAWN SERIES 0-0	1
Dec 8-12	Moratuwa	1	300	Sri Lanka v West Indies	Match drawn	

1993-94	WEST INDIES			P5 - W3 - D1 - L1	WON SERIES 3-1	11
Feb 19-24	Sabina Park	1	301	West Indies v England	West Indies won by 8 wkts	
Mar 17-22	Bourda	2	302	West Indies v England	West Indies won by an innings & 44 runs	
Mar 25-30	Queens Park Oval	3	303	West Indies v England	West Indies won by 147 runs	
Apr 8-13	Kensington Oval	4	304	West Indies v England	England won by 208 runs	
Apr 16-21	St Johns RG	5	305	West Indies v England	Match drawn	

1994-95	INDIA			P3 - W1 - D1 - L1	DRAWN SERIES 1-1	8
Nov 18-22	Bombay	1	306	India v West Indies	India won by 96 runs	
Dec 1-5	Nagpur	2	307	India v West Indies	Match drawn	
Dec 10-14	Chandigarth	3	308	India v West Indies	West Indies won by 243 runs	

1994-95	NEW ZEALAND			P2 - W1 - D1	WON SERIES 1-0	6
Feb 3-7	Christchurch	1	309	New Zealand v West Indies	Match drawn	
Feb 10-13	Wellington	2	310	New Zealand v West Indies	West Indies won by an innings & 322 runs	

1994-95	WEST INDIES			P4 - W1 - D1 - L2	LOST SERIES 1-2	7
Mar 31-Apr 5	Kensington Oval	1	311	West Indies v Australia	Australia won by 10 wkts	
Apr 8-13	St Johns RG	2	312	West Indies v Australia	Match drawn	
Apr 21-26	Queens Park Oval	3	313	West Indies v Australia	West Indies won by 9 wkts	
Apr 29 Mar 4	Sabina Park	4	314	West Indies v Australia	Australia won by an innings & 53 runs	

1995	ENGLAND			P6 - W2 - D2 - L2	DRAWN SERIES 2-2	15
Jun 8-11	Headingley	1	315	England v West Indies	West Indies won by 9 wkts	
Jun 22-26	Lords	2	316	England v West Indies	England won by 72 runs	
July 6-8	Edgbaston	3	317	England v West Indies	West Indies won by an innings & 64 runs	
July 27-30	Old Trafford	4	318	England v West Indies	England won by 6 wkts	
Aug 10-14	Trent Bridge	5	319	England v West Indies	Match drawn	
Aug 24-28	The Oval	6	320	England v West Indies	Match drawn	

1995-96	WEST INDIES			P2 - W1 - D1	WON SERIES 1-0	3
Apr 19-23	Kensington Oval	1	321	West Indies v New Zealand	West Indies won by 10 wkts	
Apr 27-Mar 2	St John RG	2	322	West Indies v New Zealand	Match drawn	

1996-97	AUSTRALIA			P5 - W2 - D0 - L3	LOST SERIES 2-3	11
Nov 22-26	Brisbane	1	323	Australia v West Indies	Australia won by 123 runs	
Nov 29-Dec 3	Sydeny	2	324	Australia v West Indies	Australia won by 124 runs	

Dec 26-28	Melbourne	3	325	Australia v West Indies	West Indies won by 6 wkts
Jan 25-28	Adelaide	4	326	Australia v West Indies	Australia won by an innings & 183 runs
Feb 1-3	Perth	5	327	Australia v West Indies	West Indies won by 10 wkts

1996-97	**WEST INDIES**			**P5 - W1 - D4 - L0**	**WON SERIES 1-0**	**7**
Mar 4-8	Sabina Park	1	328	West Indies v India	Match drawn	
Mar 14-18	Queens Park Oval	2	329	West Indies v India	Match drawn	
Mar 27-Apr 1	Kensington Oval	3	330	West Indies v India	West Indies won by 38 runs	
Apr 4-8	St Johns RG	4	331	West Indies v India	Match drawn	
Apr 17-21	Bourda	5	332	West Indies v India	Match drawn	

1996-97	**WEST INDIES**			**P2 - W1 - D1**	**WON SERIES 1-0**	**1**
Jun 13-17	St Johns RG	1	333	West Indies v Sri Lanka	West Indies won by 6 wkts	
Jun 20-24	Arnos Vale	2	334	West Indies v Sri Lanka	Match Drawn	

1997-98	**PAKISTAN**			**P3 - L3**	**LOST SERIES 0-3**	**6**
Nov 17-20	Peshawar	1	335	Pakistan v West Indies	Pakistan won by an innings & 19 runs	
Nov 29-Dec 3	Rawalpindi	2	336	Pakistan v West Indies	Pakistan won by an innings & 29 runs	
Dec 6-9	Karachi	3	337	Pakistan v West Indies	Pakistan won by10 wkts	

1997-98	**WEST INDIES**			**P6 - W3 - D2 - L1**	**WON SERIES 3-1**	**12**
Jan 29-(Feb 2)	Sabina Park	1	338	West Indies v England	Match abandoned as a draw	
Feb 5-9	Queens Park Oval	2	339	West Indies v England	West Indies won by 3 wkts	
Feb 13-17	Queens Park Oval	3	340	West Indies v England	England won by 3 wkts	
Feb 27-Mar 2	Bourda	4	341	West Indies v England	West Indies won by 242 runs	
Mar 12-16	Kensington Oval	5	342	West Indies v England	Match drawn	
Mar 20-24	St Johns RG	6	343	West Indies v England	West Indies won by an innings & 52 runs	

1998-99	**SOUTH AFRICA**			**P5 - L5**	**LOST SERIES 5-0**	**1**
Nov 26-30	Johannesburg	1	344	South Africa v West Indies	South Africa won by 4 wkts	
Dec 10-12	Port Elizabeth	2	345	South Africa v West Indies	South Africa won by 178 runs	
Dec 26-29	Durban	3	346	South Africa v West Indies	South Africa won by 9 wkts	
Jan 2-6	Cape Town	4	347	South Africa v West Indies	South Africa won by 149 runs	
Jan 15-18	Centurion	5	348	South Africa v West Indies	South Africa won by 351 runs	

1998-99	**WEST INDIES**			**P4 - W2 - L2**	**DRAWN SERIES**	**8**
Mar 5-8	Queens Park Oval	1	349	West Indies v Australia	Australia won by 312 runs	
Mar 13-16	Sabina Park	2	350	West Indies v Australia	West Indies won by 10 wkts	
Mar 26-30	Kensington Oval	3	351	West Indies v Australia	West Indies won by 1 wkt	
Apr 3-7	St Johns RG	4	352	West Indies v Australia	Australia won by 176 runs	

1999-00	**NEW ZEALAND**			**P2 - L2**	**LOST SERIES 0-2**	**7**
Dec 16-20	Hamilton	1	353	New Zealand v West Indies	New Zealand won by 9 wkts	
Dec 26-29	Wellington	2	354	New Zealand v West Indies	New Zealand won by 105 runs	

1999-00	**WEST INDIES**			**P2 - W2**	**WON SERIES 2-0**	**1**
Mar 16-20	Queens Park Oval	1	355	West Indies v Zimbabwe	West Indies won by 35 runs	
Mar 24-28	Sabina Park	2	356	West Indies v Zimbabwe	West Indies won by 10 wkts	

1999-00	**WEST INDIES**			**P3 - W1 - D2**	**WON SERIES 1-0**	**5**
May 5-9	Bourda	1	357	West Indies v Pakistan	Match drawn	
May 18-22	Kensington Oval	2	358	West Indies v Pakistan	Match drawn	
May 25-29	St Johns RG	3	359	West Indies v Pakistan	West Indies won by 1 wkt	

2000	**ENGLAND**			**P5 - W1 - D1 - L3**	**LOST SERIES 1-3**	**16**
Jun 15-19	Edgbaston	1	360	England v West Indies	West Indies won by an innings & 93 runs	
Jun 29-Jul 2	Lords	2	361	England v West Indies	England won by 2 wkts	
Aug 3-7	Old Trafford	3	362	England v West Indies	Match drawn	
Aug 17-21	Headingley	4	363	England v West Indies	England won by an innings & 39 runs	
Aug 31-Sept 4	The Oval	5	364	England v West Indies	England won by 158 runs	

515

2000-01	AUSTRALIA			P5 - L5	LOST SERIES 0-5	12
Nov 23-27	Brisbane	1	365	Australia v West Indies	Australia won by an innings & 126 runs	
Dec 1-5	Perth	2	366	Australia v West Indies	Australia won by an innings & 27 runs	
Dec 15-19	Adelaide	3	367	Australia v West Indies	Australia won by 6 wkts	
Dec 26-30	Melbourne	4	368	Australia v West Indies	Australia won by 352 runs	
Jan 2-6	Sydney	2	369	Australia v West Indies	Australia won by 6 wkts	

2000-01	WEST INDIES			P5 - W1 - D2 - L2	LOST SERIES 1-2	2
Mar 9-13	Bourda	1	370	West Indies v South Africa	Match drawn	
Mar 17-21	Queens Park Oval	2	371	West Indies v South Africa	South Africa won by 69 runs	
Mar 29-Apr 2	Kensington Oval	3	372	West Indies v South Africa	Match drawn	
Apr 6-10	St Johns RG	4	373	West Indies v South Africa	South Africa won by 83 runs	
Apr 19-23	Sabina Park	5	374	West Indies v South Africa	West Indies won by 130 runs	

2000-01	ZIMBABWE			P2 - W1 - D1	WON SERIES 1-0	1
Jul 19-23	Bulawyo	1	375	Zimbabwe v West Indies	West Indies won by an innings & 176 runs	
Jul 27-31	Harare	2	376	Zimbabwe v West Indies	Match drawn	

2001-02	SRI LANKA			P3 - L3	LOST SERIES 0-3	2
Nov 14-18	Galle	1	377	Sri Lanka v West Indies	Sri Lanka won by 10 wkts	
Nov 22-26	Kandy	2	378	Sri Lanka v West Indies	Sri Lanka won by 131 runs	
Nov 30-Dec 4	Colombo	3	379	Sri Lanka v West Indies	Sri Lanka won by 10 wkts	

2001-02	PAKISTAN			P2 - L2	LOST SERIES 0-2	7
Jan 31 Feb 4	Sharjah	1	380	Pakistan v West Indies	Pakistan won by 170 runs	
Feb 7-10	Sharjah	2	381	Pakistan v West Indies	Pakistan won by 244 runs	

Matches played in Sharjah, in the United Arab Emirates, due to unrest in Pakistan.

2001-02	WEST INDIES			P5 - W2 - D2 - L1	WON SERIES 2-1	8
Apr 11-15	Bourda	1	382	West Indies v India	Match drawn	
Apr 19-23	Queens Park Oval	2	383	West Indies v India	India won by 37 runs	
May 2-6	Kensington Oval	3	384	West Indies v India	West Indies won by 10 wkts	
May 10-14	St Johns RG	4	385	West Indies v India	Match drawn	
May 18-22	Sabina Park	5	386	West Indies v India	West Indies won by 155 runs	

2001-02	WEST INDIES			P2 - D1 - L1	LOST SERIES 0-1	4
Jun 21-25	Kensington Oval	1	387	West Indies v New Zealand	New Zealand won by 204 runs	
Jun 28-Jul 2	New Queens Park	2	388	West Indies v New Zealand	Match drawn	

2002-03	INDIA			P3 - D1 - L2	LOST SERIES 0-2	9
Oct 9-13	Bombay	1	389	India v West Indies	India won by an inning & 112 runs	
Oct 17-21	Madras	2	390	India v West Indies	India won by8 wkts	
Oct 30-Nov 3	Calcutta	3	391	India v West Indies	Match drawn	

2002-03	BANGLADESH			P2 - W2	WON SERIES 0-2	1
Dec 8-12	Dhaka	1	392	Bangladesh v West Indies	West Indies won by an innings & 310 runs	
Dec 16-20	Dhaka	2	393	Bangladesh v West Indies	West Indies won by 84 runs	

2002-03	WEST INDIES			P4 - W1 - L3	LOST SERIES 1-3	9
Apr 10-14	Bourda	1	394	West Indies v Australia	Australia won by 9 wkts	
Apr 19-23	Queens Park Oval	2	395	West Indies v Australia	Australia won by 118 runs	
May 1-5	Kensington Oval	3	396	West Indies v Australia	Australia won by 9 wkts	
May 9-13	Sabina Park	4	397	West Indies v Australia	West Indies won by 3 wkts	

2002-03	WEST INDIES			P2 - W1 - D1	WON SERIES 1-0	2
Jun 20-24	Beausejour	1	398	West Indies v Sri Lanka	Match drawn	
Jun 27-Jul 1	Sabina Park	2	399	West Indies v Sri Lanka	West Indies won by 7 wkts	

FROM 23 JUNE 1928 TO 1 JULY 2003, WEST INDIES HAVE PLAYED 399 MATCHES AND USED 253 PLAYERS.

PLAYED	WON	DREW	LOST	TIED
399	147	137	114	1

HOME AND AWAY RECORDS
Test Matches

From 26 June 1928 to 1 July 2003

ENGLAND

Home SEASON	P	W	D	L	T	SERIES		Away SEASON	P	W	D	L	T	SERIES	
1929-1930	4	1	2	1		DREW	1	1928	3	0	0	3		LOST	1
1934-1935	4	2	1	1		WON	2	1933	3	0	1	2		LOST	2
1947-1948	4	2	2	0		WON	3	1939	3	0	2	1		LOST	3
1953-1954	5	2	1	2		DREW	4	1950	4	3	0	1		WON	4
1959-1960	5	0	4	1		LOST	5	1957	5	0	2	3		LOST	5
1967-1968	5	0	4	1		LOST	6	1963	5	3	1	1		WON	6
1973-1974	5	1	3	1		DREW	7	1966	5	3	1	1		WON	7
1980-1981	4	2	2	0		WON	8	1969	3	0	1	2		LOST	8
1985-1986	5	5	0	0		WON	9	1973	3	2	1	0		WON	9
1989-1990	4	3	1	0		WON	10	1976	5	3	2	0		WON	10
1993-1994	5	3	1	1		WON	11	1980	5	1	4	0		WON	11
1997-1998	6	3	2	1		WON	12	1984	5	5	0	0		WON	12
								1988	5	4	1	0		WON	13
								1991	5	2	1	2		DREW	14
								1995	6	2	2	2		DREW	15
								2000	5	1	1	3		LOST	16
	56	24	23	9		7-3-2			70	29	20	21		8-2-6	

AUSTRALIA

Home SEASON	P	W	D	L	T	SERIES		Away SEASON	P	W	D	L	T	SERIES	
1954-1955	5	0	2	3		LOST	1	1930-1931	5	1	0	4		LOST	1
1964-1965	5	2	2	1		WON	2	1951-1952	5	1	0	4		LOST	2
1972-1973	5	0	3	2		LOST	3	1960-1961	5	1	1	2	1	LOST	3
1977-1978	5	3	1	1		WON	4	1968-1969	5	1	1	3		LOST	4
1983-1984	5	3	2	0		WON	5	1975-1976	6	1	0	5		LOST	5
1990-1991	5	2	2	1		WON	6	1979-1980	3	2	1	0		WON	6
1994-1995	4	1	1	2		LOST	7	1981-1982	3	1	1	1		DREW	7
1998-1999	4	2	0	2		DREW	8	1984-1985	5	3	1	1		WON	8
2002-2003	4	1	0	3		LOST	9	1988-1989	5	3	1	1		WON	9
								1992-1993	5	2	2	1		WON	10
								1996-1997	5	2	0	3		LOST	11
								2000-2001	5	0	0	5		LOST	12
	42	14	13	15		4-1-4			57	18	8	30	1	4-1-7	

INDIA

Home SEASON	P	W	D	L	T	SERIES		Away SEASON	P	W	D	L	T	SERIES	
1952-1953	5	1	4	0		WON	1	1948-1949	5	1	4	0		WON	1
1961-1962	5	5	0	0		WON	2	1958-1959	5	3	2	0		WON	2
1970-1971	5	0	4	1		LOST	3	1966-1967	3	2	1	0		WON	3
1975-1976	4	2	1	1		WON	4	1974-1975	5	3	0	2		WON	4
1982-1983	5	2	3	0		WON	5	1978-1979	6	0	5	1		LOST	5
1988-1989	4	3	1	0		WON	6	1983-1984	6	3	3	0		WON	6
1996-1997	5	1	4	0		WON	7	1987-1988	4	1	2	1		DREW	7
2001-2002	5	2	2	1		WON	8	1994-1995	3	1	1	1		DREW	8
								2002-2003	3	0	1	2		LOST	9
	38	16	19	3		7-0-1			40	14	19	7		5-2-2	

517

PAKISTAN

Home SEASON	P	W	D	L	T	SERIES		Away SEASON	P	W	D	L	T	SERIES	
1957-1958	5	3	1	1		WON	1	1958-1959	3	1	0	2		LOST	1
1976-1977	5	2	2	1		WON	2	1974-1975	2	0	2	0		DREW	2
1987-1988	3	1	1	1		DREW	3	1980-1981	4	1	3	0		WON	3
1992-1993	3	2	1	0		WON	4	1986-1987	3	1	1	1		DREW	4
1999-2000	3	1	2	0		WON	5	1990-1991	3	1	1	1		DREW	5
								1997-1998	3	0	0	3		LOST	6
								2001-2002	2	0	0	2		LOST	7
	19	9	7	3		4-1-0			20	4	7	9		1-3-3	

NEW ZEALAND

Home SEASON	P	W	D	L	T	SERIES		Away SEASON	P	W	D	L	T	SERIES	
1971-1972	5	0	5	0		DREW	1	1951-1952	2	1	1	0		WON	1
1984-1985	4	2	2	0		WON	2	1955-1956	4	3	0	1		WON	2
1995-1996	2	1	1	0		WON	3	1968-1969	3	1	1	1		DREW	3
2001-2002	2	0	1	1		LOST	4	1979-1980	3	0	2	1		LOST	4
								1986-1987	3	1	1	1		DREW	5
								1994-1995	2	1	1	0		WON	6
								1999-2000	2	0	0	2		LOST	7
	13	3	9	1		2-1-1			19	7	6	6		3-2-2	

SOUTH AFRICA

Home SEASON	P	W	D	L	T	SERIES		Away SEASON	P	W	D	L	T	SERIES	
1991-1992	1	1	0	0		WON	1	1998-1999	5	0	0	5		LOST	1
2000-2001	5	1	2	2		LOST	2								
	6	2	2	2		1-0-1			5	0	0	5		0-0-1	

SRI LANKA

Home SEASON	P	W	D	L	T	SERIES		Away SEASON	P	W	D	L	T	SERIES	
1996-1997	2	1	1	0		WON	1	1993-1994	1	0	1	0		DREW	1
2002-2003	2					WON	2	2001-2002	3	0	0	3		LOST	2
	4	2	2	0		2-0-0			4	0	1	3		0-1-1	

ZIMBABWE

Home SEASON	P	W	D	L	T	SERIES		Away SEASON	P	W	D	L	T	SERIES	
1999-2000	2	2	0	0		WON	1	2000-2001	2	1	1	0		WON	1
	2	2	0	0		1-0-0			2	1	1	0		1-0-0	

BANGLADESH

Home SEASON	P	W	D	L	T	SERIES		Away SEASON	P	W	D	L	T	SERIES	
								2002-2003	2	2	0	0		WON	1
									2	2	0	0		1-0-0	

| TOTAL | 180 | 72 | 75 | 33 | | | | TOTAL | 219 | 75 | 62 | 81 | 1 | | |

TEST CAREER
Batting Averages

Name	Mat	I	NO	Runs	HS	Av	100	50	Ct	St
E E Achong	6	11	1	81	22	8.10	-	-	6	-
J C Adams	54	90	17	3012	208*	41.26	6	14	48	-
F C M Alexander	25	38	6	961	108	30.03	1	7	85	5
Imtiaz Ali	1	1	1	1	1*	-	-	-	-	-
Inshan Ali	12	18	2	172	25	10.75	-	-	7	-
D W Allan	5	7	1	75	40*	12.50	-	-	15	3
I B A Allen	2	2	2	5	4*	-	-	-	1	-
C E L Ambrose	98	145	29	1439	53	12.40	-	1	18	-
K L T Arthurton	33	50	5	1382	157*	30.71	2	8	22	-
N S Asgarali	2	4	0	62	29	15.50	-	-	-	-
D S Atkinson	22	35	6	922	219	31.79	1	5	11	-
E S Atkinson	8	9	1	126	37	15.75	-	-	2	-
R A Austin	2	2	0	22	20	11.00	-	-	2	-
S F A F Bacchus	19	30	0	782	250	26.06	1	3	17	-
L Baichan	3	6	2	184	105*	46.00	1	-	2	-
O A C Banks	4	6	3	171	50*	57.00	-	1	2	-
E A E Baptiste	10	11	1	233	87*	23.30	-	1	2	-
A G Barrett	6	7	1	40	19	6.66	-	-	-	-
I M Barrow	11	19	2	276	105	16.23	1	-	17	5
E L Bartlett	5	8	1	131	84	18.71	-	1	2	-
C S Baugh	2	4	0	62	24	15.50	-	-	2	1
K C G Benjamin	26	36	8	222	43*	7.92	-	-	2	-
W K M Benjamin	21	26	1	470	85	18.79	-	2	12	-
D E Bernard	1	2	0	11	7	5.50	-	-	-	-
C A Best	8	13	1	342	164	28.50	1	1	8	-
T L Best	1	2	1	20	20*	20.00	-	-	-	-
N Betancourt	1	2	0	52	39	26.00	-	-	-	-
A P Binns	5	8	1	64	27	9.14	-	-	14	3
L S Birkett	4	8	0	136	64	17.00	-	1	4	-
I R Bishop	43	63	11	632	48	12.15	-	-	8	-
M I Black	6	11	3	21	6	2.62	-	-	-	-
K D Boyce	21	30	3	657	95*	24.33	-	4	5	-
G R Breese	1	2	0	5	5	2.50	-	-	1	-
C O Browne	14	21	6	263	39*	17.53	-	-	63	1
C R Browne	4	8	1	176	70*	25.14	-	1	1	-
B F Butcher	44	78	6	3104	209*	43.11	7	16	15	-
L S Butler	1	1	0	16	16	16.00	-	-	-	-
C G Butts	7	8	1	108	38	15.42	-	-	2	-
M R Bynoe	4	6	0	111	48	18.50	-	-	4	-
G S Camacho	11	22	0	640	87	29.09	-	4	4	-
F J Cameron	5	7	1	151	75*	25.16	-	1	-	-
J H Cameron	2	3	0	6	5	2.00	-	-	-	-
S L Campbell	52	93	4	2882	208	32.38	4	18	47	-
G M Carew	4	7	1	170	107	28.33	1	-	1	-
M C Carew	19	36	3	1127	109	34.15	1	5	13	-
G Challenor	3	6	0	101	46	16.83	-	-	-	-
S Chanderpaul	66	109	15	4155	140	44.20	8	28	28	-

Name	Mat	I	NO	Runs	HS	Av	100	50	Ct	St
H S Chang	1	2	0	8	6	4.00	-	-	-	-
C M Christiani	4	7	2	98	32*	19.60	-	-	6	1
R J Christiani	22	37	3	896	107	26.35	1	4	19	2
C B Clarke	3	4	1	3	2	1.00	-	-	-	-
S T Clarke	11	16	5	172	35*	15.63	-	-	2	-
P T Collins	19	30	6	165	24	6.87	-	-	2	-
C D Collymore	3	4	1	30	13*	10.00	-	-	-	-
L N Constantine	18	33	0	635	90	19.24	-	4	28	-
C E H Croft	27	37	22	158	33	10.53	-	-	8	-
C E Cuffy	15	23	9	58	15	4.14	-	-	5	-
A C Cummins	5	6	1	98	50	19.60	-	1	1	-
O C Da Costa	5	9	1	153	39	19.12	-	-	5	-
W W Daniel	10	11	4	46	11	6.57	-	-	4	-
B A Davies	4	8	0	245	68	30.62	-	3	1	-
C A Davies	15	29	5	1301	183	54.20	4	4	4	-
W W Davies	15	17	4	202	77	15.53	-	1	10	-
F I de Caires	3	6	0	232	80	38.66	-	2	1	-
C C Depeiaza	5	8	2	187	122	31.16	1	-	7	4
D T Dewdney	9	12	5	17	5*	2.42	-	-	-	-
R Dhanraj	4	4	0	17	9	4.25	-	-	1	-
M Dillon	34	60	2	415	43	7.15	-	-	16	-
U G Dowe	4	3	2	8	5*	8.00	-	-	3	-
V C Drakes	7	11	2	194	30	21.55	-	-	1	-
P J L Dujon	81	115	11	3322	139	31.94	5	16	267	5
F H Edwards	1	1	1	5	5*	-	-	-	-	-
R M Edwards	5	8	1	65	22	9.28	-	-	-	-
W Ferguson	8	10	3	200	75	28.57	-	2	11	-
M P Fernandes	2	4	0	49	22	12.25	-	-	-	-
T M Findlay	10	16	3	212	44*	16.30	-	-	19	2
M L C Foster	14	24	5	580	125	30.52	1	1	3	-
G N Francis	10	18	4	81	19*	5.78	-	-	7	-
M C Frederick	1	2	0	30	30	15.00	-	-	-	-
R C Fredericks	59	109	7	4334	169	42.49	8	26	62	-
R L Fuller	1	1	0	1	1	1.00	-	-	-	-
H A Furlonge	3	5	0	99	64	19.80	-	1	-	-
D Ganga	22	38	0	956	117	25.15	2	3	13	-
A G Ganteaume	1	1	0	112	112	112.00	1	-	-	-
J Garner	58	68	14	672	60	12.44	-	1	42	-
L V Garrick	1	2	0	27	27	13.50	-	-	2	-
B B M Gaskin	2	3	0	17	10	5.66	-	-	1	-
C H Gayle	32	54	2	1792	204	34.36	2	11	43	-
G L Gibbs	1	2	0	12	12	6.00	-	-	1	-
L R Gibbs	79	109	39	488	25	6.97	-	-	52	-
O D Gibson	2	4	0	93	37	23.25	-	-	-	-
R Gilchrist	13	14	3	60	12	5.45	-	-	4	-
G Gladstone	1	1	1	12	12*	-	-	-	-	-
J D C Goddard	27	39	11	859	83*	30.67	-	4	22	-
H A Gomes	60	91	11	3171	143	39.63	9	13	18	-
G E Gomez	29	46	5	1243	101	30.31	1	8	18	-
G S Grant	12	22	6	413	71*	25.81	-	3	10	-
R S Grant	7	11	1	220	77	22.00	-	1	13	-
A H Gray	5	8	2	48	12*	8.00	-	-	6	-
A E Greenidge	6	10	0	222	69	22.20	-	2	5	-
C G Greenidge	108	185	16	7558	226	44.72	19	34	96	-
G A Greenidge	5	9	2	209	50	29.58	-	1	3	-
M G Grell	1	2	0	34	21	17.00	-	-	1	-
A F G Griffith	14	27	1	638	114	24.53	1	4	5	-
C C Griffith	28	42	10	530	54	16.56	-	1	16	-
H C Griffith	13	23	5	91	18	5.05	-	-	4	-
S C Guillen	5	6	2	104	54	26.00	-	1	9	2

520

Name	Mat	I	NO	Runs	HS	Av	100	50	Ct	St
W W Hall	48	66	14	818	50*	15.73	-	2	11	-
R A Harper	25	32	3	535	74	18.44	-	3	36	-
D L Haynes	116	202	25	7487	184	42.29	18	39	65	-
G A Headley	22	40	4	2190	270*	60.83	10	5	14	-
R G A Headley	2	4	0	62	42	15.50	-	-	2	-
J L Hendriks	20	32	8	447	64	18.62	-	2	42	5
R O Hinds	4	8	1	162	62	23.14	-	1	-	-
W W Hinds	33	58	1	1871	165	32.82	4	10	28	-
E L G Hoad	4	8	0	98	36	12.25	-	-	1	-
R I C Holder	11	17	2	380	91	25.33	-	2	9	-
V A Holder	40	59	11	682	42	14.20	-	-	16	-
M A Holding	60	76	10	910	73	13.78	-	6	22	-
D A J Holford	24	39	5	768	105*	22.58	1	3	18	-
J K C Holt	17	31	2	1066	166	36.75	2	5	8	-
C L Hooper	102	173	15	5762	233	36.46	13	27	115	-
A B Howard	1	0	-	-	-	-	-	-	-	-
C C Hunte	44	78	6	3245	260	45.06	8	13	16	-
E A C Hunte	3	6	1	166	58	33.20	-	2	5	-
L G Hylton	6	8	2	70	19	11.66	-	-	1	-
R D Jacobs	51	88	17	2000	118	28.16	2	11	167	8
H H H Johnson	3	4	0	38	22	9.50	-	-	-	-
T F Johnson	1	1	1	9	9*	-	-	-	1	-
C E L Jones	4	7	0	63	19	9.00	-	-	3	-
P E W Jones	9	11	2	47	10*	5.22	-	-	4	-
D R E Joseph	4	7	0	141	50	20.14	-	1	10	-
B D Julien	24	34	6	866	121	30.92	2	3	14	-
R R Jumadeen	12	14	10	84	56	21.00	-	1	4	-
A I Kallicharran	66	109	10	4399	187	44.43	12	21	51	-
R B Kanhai	79	137	6	6227	256	47.53	15	28	50	-
E S M Kentish	2	2	1	1	1*	1.00	-	-	1	-
C L King	9	16	3	418	100*	32.15	1	2	5	-
F M King	14	17	3	116	21	8.28	-	-	5	-
L A King	2	4	0	41	20	10.25	-	-	2	-
R D King	14	19	5	50	12*	3.57	-	-	2	-
C B Lambert	5	9	0	284	104	31.55	1	1	8	-
B C Lara	96	168	5	8404	375	51.55	21	41	128	-
P D Lashley	4	7	0	159	49	22.71	-	-	4	-
J J C Lawson	7	10	1	34	14	3.77	-	-	1	-
R A Legall	4	5	0	50	23	10.00	-	-	8	1
D M Lewis	3	5	2	259	88	86.33	-	3	8	-
R N Lewis	3	6	0	26	12	4.33	-	-	-	-
C H Lloyd	110	175	14	7515	242*	46.67	19	39	90	-
A L Logie	52	78	9	2470	130	35.79	2	16	57	-
N C McGarrell	4	6	2	61	33	15.25	-	-	2	-
N A M McLean	19	32	2	368	46	12.26	-	-	5	-
E D A S McMorris	13	21	0	564	125	26.85	1	3	5	-
C A McWatt	6	9	2	202	54	28.85	-	2	9	1
I S Madray	2	3	0	3	2	1.00	-	-	2	-
M D Marshall	81	107	11	1810	92	18.85	-	10	25	-
N E Marshall	1	2	0	8	8	4.00	-	-	-	-
R E Marshall	4	7	0	143	30	20.42	-	-	1	-
F R Martin	9	18	1	486	123*	28.58	1	-	5	-
E A Martindale	10	14	3	58	22	5.27	-	-	5	-
E H Mattis	4	5	0	145	71	29.00	-	1	3	-
I L Mendonca	2	2	0	81	78	40.50	-	1	8	2
C A Merry	2	4	0	34	13	8.50	-	-	1	-
R C Miller	1	1	0	23	23	23.00	-	-	-	-
E A Moseley	2	4	0	35	26	8.75	-	-	1	-
G H Mudie	1	1	0	5	5	5.00	-	-	-	-
D A Murray	19	31	3	601	84	21.46	-	3	57	5

Name	Mat	I	NO	Runs	HS	Av	100	50	Ct	St
D L Murray	62	96	9	1993	91	22.90	-	11	181	8
J R Murray	33	45	4	918	101*	22.39	1	3	99	3
M V Nagamootoo	5	8	1	185	68	26.42	-	1	2	-
R Nanan	1	2	0	16	8	8.00	-	-	2	-
J M Neblett	1	2	1	16	11*	16.00	-	-	-	-
J M Noreiga	4	5	2	11	9	3.66	-	-	2	-
R K Nunes	4	8	0	245	92	30.62	-	2	2	-
S M Nurse	29	54	1	2523	258	47.60	6	10	21	-
A L Padmore	2	2	1	8	8*	8.00	-	-	-	-
B H Pairaudeau	13	21	0	454	115	21.61	1	3	6	-
D R Parry	12	20	3	381	65	22.41	-	3	4	-
C C Passailague	1	2	1	46	44	46.00	-	-	3	-
B P Patterson	28	38	16	145	21*	6.59	-	-	5	-
T R O Payne	1	1	0	5	5	5.00	-	-	5	-
N O Perry	4	7	1	74	26	12.33	-	-	1	-
N Phillip	9	15	5	297	47	29.70	-	-	5	-
L R Pierre	1	0	-	-	-	-	-	-	-	-
D B Powell	4	5	0	19	16	3.80	-	-	1	-
R L Powell	1	2	0	30	30	15.00	-	-	1	-
A F Rae	15	24	2	1016	109	46.18	4	4	10	-
S Ragoonath	2	4	1	13	9	4.33	-	-	-	-
S Ramadhin	43	58	14	361	44	8.20	-	-	9	-
D Ramnarine	12	21	4	106	35*	6.23	-	-	8	-
F L Reifer	4	8	0	63	29	7.87	-	-	4	-
I V A Richards	121	182	12	8540	291	50.23	24	45	122	-
R B Richardson	86	146	12	5949	194	44.39	16	27	90	-
K R Rickards	2	3	0	104	67	34.66	-	1	-	-
C A Roach	16	32	1	952	209	30.70	2	6	5	-
A M E Roberts	47	62	11	762	68	14.94	-	3	9	-
A T Roberts	1	2	0	28	28	14.00	-	-	-	-
L A Roberts	1	1	0	0	0	0.00	-	-	-	-
W V Rodriquez	5	7	0	96	50	13.71	-	1	3	-
F A Rose	19	28	2	344	69	13.23	-	1	4	-
L G Rowe	30	49	2	2047	302	43.55	7	7	17	-
E L St Hill	2	4	0	18	12	4.50	-	-	-	-
W H St Hill	3	6	0	117	38	19.50	-	-	1	-
M N Samuels	19	33	3	874	104	29.13	1	6	9	-
R G Samuels	6	12	2	372	125	37.20	1	1	8	-
A Sanford	7	10	1	35	12	3.88	-	-	-	-
R R Sarwan	34	60	5	2127	119	38.67	2	16	18	-
R O Scarlett	3	4	1	54	29*	18.00	-	-	2	-
A H P Scott	1	1	0	5	5	5.00	-	-	-	-
O C Scott	8	13	3	171	35	17.10	-	-	-	-
B J Sealey	1	2	0	41	29	20.50	-	-	-	-
J E D Sealey	11	19	2	478	92	28.11	-	3	6	1
J N Shepherd	5	8	0	77	32	9.62	-	-	4	-
G C Shillingford	7	8	1	57	25	8.14	-	-	2	-
I T Shillingford	4	7	0	218	120	31.14	1	-	1	-
S Shivnarine	8	14	1	379	63	29.15	-	4	6	-
P V Simmons	26	47	2	1002	110	22.26	1	4	26	-
C K Singh	2	3	0	11	11	3.66	-	-	2	-
J A Small	3	6	0	79	52	13.16	-	1	3	-
M A Small	2	1	1	3	3*	-	-	-	-	-
C W Smith	5	10	1	222	55	24.66	-	1	4	1
D S Smith	4	8	0	189	62	23	62	2	2	-
O G Smith	26	42	0	1331	168	31.69	4	6	9	-
G S Sobers	93	160	21	8032	365*	57.78	26	30	109	-
J S Solomon	27	46	7	1326	100*	34.00	1	9	13	-
S C Stayers	4	4	1	58	35*	19.33	-	-	-	-
J B Stollmeyer	32	56	5	2159	160	42.33	4	12	20	-

Name	Mat	I	NO	Runs	HS	Av	100	50	Ct	St
V H Stollmeyer	1	1	0	96	96	96.00	-	1	-	-
C E L Stuart	6	9	2	24	12*	3.42	-	-	2	-
J E Taylor	2	2	1	10	9*	10.00	-	-	-	-
J O Taylor	3	5	3	4	4*	2.00	-	-	-	-
P I C Thompson	2	3	1	17	10*	8.50	-	-	-	-
J Trim	4	5	1	21	12	5.25	-	-	2	-
A L Valentine	36	51	21	141	14	4.69	-	-	13	-
V A Valentine	2	4	1	35	19*	11.66	-	-	-	-
C L Walcott	44	74	7	3798	220	56.68	15	14	53	11
L A Walcott	1	2	1	40	24	40.00	-	-	-	-
P A Wallace	7	13	0	279	92	21.46	-	2	9	-
C A Walsh	132	185	61	936	30*	7.54	-	-	29	-
C D Watson	7	6	1	12	5	2.40	-	-	1	-
E D Weekes	48	81	5	4455	207	58.61	15	19	49	-
K H Weekes	2	3	0	173	137	57.66	1	-	-	-
A W White	2	4	1	71	57*	23.66	-	1	1	-
C V Wight	2	4	1	67	23	22.33	-	-	-	-
G L Wight	1	1	0	21	21	21.00	-	-	-	-
C A Wiles	1	2	0	2	2	1.00	-	-	-	-
E T Willett	5	8	3	74	26	14.80	-	-	-	-
A B Williams	7	12	0	469	111	39.08	2	1	5	-
D Williams	11	19	1	242	65	13.44	-	1	40	2
E A V Williams	4	6	0	113	72	18.83	-	1	2	-
S C Williams	31	52	3	1183	128	24.14	1	3	27	-
K L Wishart	1	2	0	52	52	26.00	-	1	-	-
F M M Worrell	51	87	9	3860	261	49.48	9	22	43	-

Totals up to 31 July 2003

TEST CAREER
Bowling Averages

Name	Mat	Balls	M	R	W	Av	Best	5	10
E E Achong	6	918	34	378	8	47.25	2-64	-	-
J C Adams	54	2853	96	1336	27	49.48	5-17	1	-
F C M Alexander	25	-	-	-	-	-	-	-	-
Imtiaz Ali	1	204	10	89	2	44.50	2-37	-	-
Inshan Ali	12	3718	137	1621	34	47.67	5-59	1	-
D W Allan	5	-	-	-	-	-	-	-	-
I B A Allen	2	282	4	180	5	36.00	2-69	-	-
C E L Ambrose	98	22103	1001	8501	405	20.99	8-45	22	3
K L T Arthurton	33	473	14	183	1	183.00	1-17	-	-
N S Asgarali	2	-	-	-	-	-	-	-	-
D S Atkinson	22	5201	311	1647	47	35.04	7-53	3	-
E S Atkinson	8	1634	77	589	25	23.56	5-42	1	-
R A Austin	2	6	0	5	0	-	-	-	-
S F A F Bacchus	19	6	0	3	0	-	-	-	-
O A C Banks	4	990	23	560	9	62.22	3-204	-	-
L Baichan	3	-	-	-	-	-	-	-	-
E A E Baptiste	10	1362	60	563	16	35.18	3-31	-	-
A G Barrett	6	1612	83	603	13	46.38	3-43	-	-
I M Barrow	11	-	-	-	-	-	-	-	-
E L Bartlett	5	-	-	-	-	-	-	-	-
K C G Benjamin	26	5132	158	2785	92	30.27	6-66	4	1
W K M Benjamin	21	3694	136	1648	61	27.01	4-46	-	-
D E Barnard	1	66	1	60	0	-	-	-	-
C A Best	8	30	0	21	0	-	-	-	-
T L Best	1	120	1	99	0	-	-	-	-
N Betancourt	1	-	-	-	-	-	-	-	-
A P Binns	5	-	-	-	-	-	-	-	-
L S Birkett	4	126	1	71	1	71.00	1-16	-	-
I R Bishop	43	8407	288	3909	161	24.27	6-40	6	-
M I Black	6	954	27	597	12	49.75	4-83	-	-
K D Boyce	21	3501	99	1801	60	30.01	6-77	2	1
G R Breese	1	188	3	135	2	67.50	2-108	-	-
C O Browne	14	-	-	-	-	-	-	-	-
C R Browne	4	840	38	288	6	48.00	2-72	-	-
B F Butcher	44	256	15	90	5	18.00	5-34	1	-
L S Butler	1	240	7	151	2	75.50	2-151	-	-
C G Butts	7	1554	70	595	10	59.50	4-73	-	-
M R Bynoe	4	30	4	5	1	5.00	1-5	-	-
G S Camacho	11	18	1	12	0	-	-	-	-
F J Cameron	5	786	34	278	3	92.66	2-74	-	-
J H Cameron	2	232	6	88	3	29.33	3-66	-	-
S L Campbell	52	-	-	-	-	-	-	-	-
G M Carew	4	18	2	2	0	-	-	-	-
M C Carew	19	1174	46	437	8	54.62	1-11	-	-
G Challenor	3	-	-	-	-	-	-	-	-
S Chanderpaul	63	1440	41	718	8	89.75	1-2	-	-
H S Chang	1	-	-	-	-	-	-	-	-

Name	Mat	Balls	M	R	W	Av	Best	5	10
C M Christiani	4	-	-	-	-	-	-	-	-
R J Christiani	22	234	1	108	3	36.00	3-52	-	-
C B Clarke	3	456	2	261	6	43.50	3.59	-	-
S T Clarke	11	2477	81	1170	42	27.85	5-126	1	-
P T Collins	19	4258	130	2218	55	40.32	6-76	2	-
C D Collymore	3	624	20	268	15	17.86	7-57	1	-
L N Constantine	18	3583	125	1746	58	30.10	5-75	2	-
C E H Croft	27	6165	211	2913	125	23.30	8-29	3	-
C E Cuffy	15	3366	145	1455	43	33.83	4-82	-	-
A C Cummins	5	618	11	342	8	42.75	4-54	-	-
O C Da Costa	5	372	13	175	3	58.33	1-14	-	-
W W Daniel	10	1754	60	910	36	25.27	5-39	1	-
B A Davis	4	-	-	-	-	-	-	-	-
C A Davis	15	894	32	330	2	165.00	1-27	-	-
W W Davis	15	2773	53	1472	45	32.71	4-19	-	-
F I De Caires	3	12	0	9	0	-	-	-	-
C C Depeiaza	5	30	0	15	0	-	-	-	-
D T Dewdney	9	1641	65	807	21	38.42	5-21	1	-
R Dhanraj	4	1087	32	595	8	74.37	2-49	-	-
M Dillon	34	7780	237	3965	123	32.23	5-71	2	-
U G Dowe	4	1014	30	531	12	44.50	4.69	-	-
V C Drakes	7	1045	37	751	23	32.65	5-93	1	-
F H Edwards	1	184	3	90	6	15.00	5-36	-	-
P J L Dujon	81	-	-	-	-	-	-	-	-
R M Edwards	5	1131	25	626	18	34.77	5-84	1	-
W Ferguson	8	2568	83	1165	34	34.26	6-92	3	1
M P Fernandes	2	-	-	-	-	-	-	-	-
T M Findlay	10	-	-	-	-	-	-	-	-
M L C Foster	14	1776	106	600	9	66.66	2-41	-	-
G N Francis	10	1619	54	763	23	33.17	4-40	-	-
M C Frederick	1	-	-	-	-	-	-	-	-
R C Fredericks	59	1187	41	548	7	78.28	1-12	-	-
R L Fuller	1	48	2	12	0	-	-	-	-
H A Furlonge	3	-	-	-	-	-	-	-	-
D Ganga	22	30	0	10	0	-	-	-	-
A G Ganteaume	1	-	-	-	-	-	-	-	-
J Garner	58	13169	575	5433	259	20.97	6-56	7	-
L V Garrick	1	-	-	-	-	-	-	-	-
B B M Gaskin	2	474	24	158	2	79.00	1-15	-	-
C H Gayle	32	1099	37	444	11	40.36	3.25	-	-
G L Gibbs	1	24	1	7	0	-	-	-	-
L R Gibbs	79	27115	1313	8989	309	29.09	8-38	18	2
O D Gibson	2	472	9	275	3	91.66	2-81	-	-
R Gilchrist	13	3227	124	1521	57	26.68	6-55	1	-
G Gladstone	1	300	5	189	1	189.00	1-139	-	-
J D C Goddard	27	2931	148	1050	33	31.81	5-31	1	-
H A Gomes	60	2401	79	930	15	62.00	2-20	-	-
G E Gomez	29	5236	289	1590	58	27.41	7-55	1	1
G C Grant	12	24	0	18	0	-	-	-	-
R S Grant	7	986	32	353	11	32.09	3-68	-	-
A H Gray	5	888	37	377	22	17.13	4-39	-	-
A E Greenidge	6	-	-	-	-	-	-	-	-
C G Greenidge	108	26	3	4	0	-	-	-	-
G A Greenidge	5	156	4	75	0	-	-	-	-
M G Grell	1	30	1	17	0	-	-	-	-
A F G Griffith	14	-	-	-	-	-	-	-	-
C C Griffith	28	5631	177	2683	94	28.54	6-36	5	-
H C Griffith	13	2663	89	1243	44	28.25	6-103	2	-
S C Guillen	5	-	-	-	-	-	-	-	-
W W Hall	48	10421	312	5066	192	26.38	7-69	9	1

Name	Mat	Balls	M	R	W	Av	Best	5	10
R A Harper	25	3615	183	1291	46	28.06	6.57	1	-
D L Haynes	116	18	0	8	1	8.00	1-2	-	-
G A Headley	22	398	7	230	0	-	-	-	-
R G A Headley	2	-	-	-	-	-	-	-	-
J L Hendriks	20	-	-	-	-	-	-	-	-
R O Hinds	4	216	5	119	0	-	-	-	-
W W Hinds	33	339	10	180	6	30.00	2-23	-	-
E L G Hoad	4	-	-	-	-	-	-	-	-
R I C Holder	11	-	-	-	-	-	-	-	-
V A Holder	40	9095	367	6327	109	33.27	6-28	3	-
M A Holding	60	12680	459	5898	249	23.68	8-92	13	2
D A J Holford	24	4816	164	2009	51	39.39	5-23	1	-
J K C Holt	17	30	2	20	1	20.00	1-20	-	-
C L Hooper	102	13794	531	5635	114	49.42	5-26	4	-
A B Howard	1	372	16	140	2	70.00	2-140	-	-
C C Hunte	44	270	11	110	2	55.00	1-17	-	-
E A C Hunte	3	-	-	-	-	-	-	-	-
L G Hylton	6	965	31	418	16	26.12	4-27	-	-
R D Jacobs	47	-	-	-	-	-	-	-	-
H H H Johnson	3	789	37	238	13	18.30	5-41	2	1
T F Johnson	1	240	3	129	3	43.00	2-53	-	-
C E L Jones	4	102	11	11	0	-	-	-	-
P E W Jones	9	1842	64	751	25	30.04	5-85	1	-
D R E Joseph	4	-	-	-	-	-	-	-	-
B D Julien	24	4542	192	1868	50	37.36	5-57	1	-
R R Jumadeen	12	3140	140	1141	29	39.34	4-72	-	-
A I Kallicharran	66	406	14	158	4	39.50	2-16	-	-
R B Kanhai	79	183	8	85	0	-	-	-	-
E S M Kentish	2	540	31	178	8	22.25	5-49	1	-
C L King	9	582	24	282	3	94.00	1-30	-	-
F M King	14	2869	140	1159	29	39.96	5-74	1	-
L A King	2	476	19	154	9	17.11	5-46	1	-
R D King	14	2485	96	1222	44	27.77	5-51	1	-
C B Lambert	5	10	0	5	1	5.00	1-4	-	-
B C Lara	90	60	1	28	0	-	-	-	-
P D Lashley	4	18	2	1	1	1.00	1-1	-	-
J J C Lawson	7	1251	38	711	29	24.51	7-78	2	-
R A Legall	4	-	-	-	-	-	-	-	-
D M Lewis	3	-	-	-	-	-	-	-	-
R N Lewis	3	585	16	318	1	318.00	1-67	-	-
C H Lloyd	110	1716	75	622	10	62.20	2-13	-	-
A L Logie	52	7	1	4	0	-	-	-	-
N C McGarrell	4	1212	65	453	17	26.64	4-23	-	-
N A M McLean	19	3299	85	1873	44	42.56	3.53	-	-
E D A S McMorris	13	-	-	-	-	-	-	-	-
C A McWatt	6	24	2	16	1	16.00	1-16	-	-
I S Madray	2	210	6	108	0	-	-	-	-
M D Marshall	81	17584	613	7876	376	20.94	7-22	22	4
N E Marshall	1	279	22	62	2	31.00	1-22	-	-
R E Marshall	4	52	2	15	0	-	-	-	-
F R Martin	9	1346	27	619	8	77.37	3-91	-	-
E A Martindale	10	1605	40	804	37	21.72	5-22	3	-
E H Mattis	4	36	1	14	0	-	-	-	-
I L Mendonca	2	-	-	-	-	-	-	-	-
C A Merry	2	-	-	-	-	-	-	-	-
R C Miller	1	96	8	28	0	-	-	-	-
E A Moseley	2	522	13	261	6	43.50	2-70	-	-
G H Munie	1	174	12	40	3	13.33	2-23	-	-
D A Murray	19	-	-	-	-	-	-	-	-
D L Murray	62	-	-	-	-	-	-	-	-

Name	Mat	Balls	M	R	W	Av	Best	5	10
J R Murray	33	-	-	-	-	-	-	-	-
M V Nagamootoo	5	1494	68	637	12	53.08	3-119	-	-
R Nanan	1	216	7	91	4	22.75	2-37	-	-
J M Neblett	1	216	11	75	1	75.00	1-44	-	-
J M Noreiga	4	1322	47	493	17	29.00	9-95	2	-
R K Nunes	4	-	-	-	-	-	-	-	-
S M Nurse	29	42	4	7	0	-	-	-	-
A L Padmore	2	474	23	135	1	135.00	1-36	-	-
B H Pairaudeau	13	6	0	3	0	-	-	-	-
D R Parry	12	1909	65	936	23	40.69	5-15	1	-
C C Passailague	1	12	0	15	0	-	-	-	-
B P Patterson	28	4829	109	2874	93	30.90	5-24	5	-
T R O Payne	1	-	-	-	-	-	-	-	-
N O Perry	4	804	24	446	10	44.60	5-70	1	-
N Phillip	9	1820	46	1041	28	37.17	4-48	-	-
L R Pierre	1	42	0	28	0	-	-	-	-
D B Powell	4	770	27	354	12	29.50	3-36	-	-
R L Powell	1	30	2	13	0	-	-	-	-
A F Rae	15	-	-	-	-	-	-	-	-
S Ragoonath	2	-	-	-	-	-	-	-	-
S Ramadhin	43	13939	813	4579	158	28.98	7-49	10	1
D Ramnarine	12	3495	169	1383	45	30.73	5-78	1	-
F L Reifer	4	-	-	-	-	-	-	-	-
I V A Richards	121	5170	203	1964	32	61.37	2-17	-	-
R B Richardson	86	66	4	18	0	-	-	-	-
K R Rickards	2	-	-	-	-	-	-	-	-
C A Roach	16	222	5	103	2	51.50	1-18	-	-
A M E Roberts	47	11135	382	5174	202	25.61	7-54	11	2
A T Roberts	1	-	-	-	-	-	-	-	-
L A Roberts	1	-	-	-	-	-	-	-	-
W V Rodriquez	5	573	10	374	7	53.42	3-51	-	-
F A Rose	19	3124	101	1637	53	30.88	7-84	2	-
L G Rowe	30	86	3	44	0	-	-	-	-
E L St Hill	2	558	29	221	3	73.66	2-110	-	-
W H St Hill	3	12	0	9	0	-	-	-	-
M N Samuels	19	1050	27	550	5	110.00	2-49	-	-
R G Samuel	6	-	-	-	-	-	-	-	-
A Sanford	7	1405	52	794	20	39.70	3-20	-	-
R R Sarwan	34	276	5	151	3	50.33	2-1	-	-
R O Scarlett	3	804	53	209	2	104.50	1-46	-	-
A H P Scott	1	264	9	140	0	-	-	-	-
O C Scott	8	1405	18	925	22	42.04	5-266	1	-
B J Sealey	1	30	1	10	1	10.00	1-10	-	-
J E D Sealey	11	156	4	94	3	31.33	2-7	-	-
J N Shepherd	5	1445	70	479	19	25.21	5-104	1	-
G C Shillingford	7	1181	38	537	15	35.80	3-63	-	-
I T Shillingford	4	-	-	-	-	-	-	-	-
S Shivnarine	8	336	10	167	1	167.00	1-13	-	-
P V Simmons	26	624	27	257	4	64.25	2-34	-	-
C K Singh	2	506	35	166	5	33.20	2-28	-	-
J A Small	3	366	11	184	3	61.33	2-67	-	-
M A Small	2	270	7	153	4	38.25	3-40	-	-
C W Smith	5	-	-	-	-	-	-	-	-
O G Smith	26	4431	229	1625	48	33.85	5-90	1	-
G S Sobers	93	21599	974	7999	235	34.03	6-73	6	-
J S Solomon	27	702	39	268	4	67.00	1-20	-	-
S C Stayers	4	636	20	364	9	40.44	3-65	-	-
J B Stollmeyer	32	990	30	507	13	39.00	3-32	-	-
V H Stollmeyer	1	-	-	-	-	-	-	-	-
C E L Stuart	6	1116	37	628	20	31.40	3-33	-	-

Name	Mat	Balls	M	R	W	Av	Best	5	10
J E Taylor	2	324	6	194	2	97.00	2-38	-	-
J O Taylor	3	672	33	273	10	27.30	5-109	1	-
P I C Thompson	2	228	1	215	5	43.00	2-58	-	-
J Trim	4	794	28	291	18	16.16	5-34	1	-
A L Valentine	36	12953	789	4215	139	30.32	8-104	8	2
V A Valentine	2	288	14	104	1	104.00	1-55	-	-
C L Walcott	44	1194	72	408	11	37.09	3-50	-	-
L A Walcott	1	48	1	32	1	32.00	1-17	-	-
P A Wallace	7	-	-	-	-	-	-	-	-
C A Walsh	132	30019	1144	12688	519	24.44	7-37	22	3
C D Watson	7	1458	47	724	19	38.10	4-62	-	-
E D Weekes	48	122	3	77	1	77.00	1-8	-	-
K H Weekes	2	-	-	-	-	-	-	-	-
A W White	2	491	27	152	3	50.66	2-34	-	-
C V Wight	2	30	1	6	0	-	-	-	-
G L Wight	1	-	-	-	-	-	-	-	-
C A Wiles	1	-	-	-	-	-	-	-	-
E T Willett	5	1326	78	482	11	43.81	3-33	-	-
A B Williams	7	-	-	-	-	-	-	-	-
D Williams	11	-	-	-	-	-	-	-	-
E A V Williams	4	796	46	241	9	26.77	6-51	-	-
S C Williams	31	18	0	19	0	-	-	-	-
K L Wishart	1	-	-	-	-	-	-	-	-
F M M Worrell	51	7141	274	2672	69	38.72	7-70	2	-

ONE DAY INTERNATIONALS
Career Batting Averages

1973 to 2003

NAME	Mat	I	NO	Runs	HS	Av	100	50	Ct	St
J C Adams	127	105	28	2204	82	28.62	-	14	68	5
C E L Ambrose	176	96	36	639	31*	10.65	-	-	45	-
H A G Anthony	3	3	0	23	21	7.66	-	-	-	-
K L T Arthurton	105	93	20	1904	84	26.08	-	9	27	-
R A Austin	1	1	0	8	8	8.00	-	-	-	-
S F A F Bacchus	29	26	3	612	80*	26.60	-	3	10	-
O A C Banks	3	3	0	44	29	14-66	-	-	-	-
E A E Baptiste	43	16	4	184	31	15.33	-	-	14	-
K C G Benjamin	26	13	7	65	17	10.83	-	-	4	-
W K M Benjamin	85	52	12	298	31	7.45	-	-	16	-
D E Bernard	4	2	0	7	7	3.50	-	-	1	-
C A Best	24	23	4	473	100	24.89	1	2	5	-
I R Bishop	84	44	19	405	33*	16.20	-	-	12	-
M I Black	5	2	0	4	4	2.00	-	-	-	-
K D Boyce	8	4	0	57	34	14.25	-	-	-	-
D Brown	3	2	1	10	9	10.00	-	-	-	-
B S Browne	4	3	2	8	8*	8.00	-	-	-	-
C O Browne	28	19	4	187	26	12.46	-	-	40	6
H R Bryan	15	8	2	43	11	7.16	-	-	4	-
S L Campbell	90	87	0	2283	105	26.24	2	14	23	-
S Chanderpaul	132	123	16	3913	150	36.57	3	25	38	-
S T Clarke	10	8	2	60	20	10.00	-	-	4	-
P T Collins	23	7	3	26	10*	6.50	-	-	8	-
C D Collymore	42	17	8	56	13*	6.22	-	-	7	-
C E H Croft	19	6	4	18	8	9.00	-	-	1	-
C E Cuffy	41	22	8	62	17*	4.42	-	-	5	-
A C Cumins	63	41	11	459	44*	15.30	-	-	11	-
W W Daniel	18	5	4	49	16*	49.00	-	-	5	-
W W Davis	35	5	3	28	10	14.00	-	-	1	-
R Dhanraj	6	2	1	8	8	8.00	-	-	1	-
M Dillon	89	44	19	195	21*	7.80	-	-	18	-
V C Drakes	30	14	5	82	25	9.11	-	-	5	-
P J L Dujon	169	120	36	1945	82*	23.15	-	6	183	21
M L C Foster	2	1	0	25	25	25.00	-	-	-	-
R C Fredericks	12	12	0	311	105	25.91	1	1	4	-
R S Gabriel	11	11	0	167	41	15.18	-	-	1	-
D Ganga	28	27	1	691	71	26.57	-	8	8	-
J Garner	98	41	15	239	37	9.19	-	-	30	-
L V Garrick	3	3	0	99	76	33.00	-	1	-	-
C H Gayle	78	76	1	2746	152	36.61	5	18	36	-
L R Gibbs	3	1	1	0	0*	-	-	-	-	-
O D Gibson	15	11	1	141	52	14.10	-	1	3	-
H A Gomes	83	64	15	1415	101	28.87	1	6	14	-
A H Gray	25	11	5	51	10*	8.50	-	-	3	-
A E Greenidge	1	1	0	23	23	23.00	-	-	-	-
C G Greenidge	128	127	13	5134	133*	45.03	11	31	45	-
A F G Griffith	9	8	1	99	47	14.14	-	-	5	-

NAME	Mat	I	NO	Runs	HS	Av	100	50	Ct	St
R A Harper	105	73	20	855	45*	16.13	-	-	55	-
D L Haynes	238	237	28	8648	152*	41.37	17	57	59	-
R C Haynes	8	6	1	26	18	5.20	-	-	5	-
R G A Headley	1	1	0	19	19	19.00	-	-	-	-
R O Hinds	11	8	3	93	18*	18.60	-	-	2	-
W W Hinds	78	74	5	2047	125*	29.66	3	12	25	-
R I C Holder	37	31	6	599	65	23.96	-	2	8	-
V A Holder	12	6	1	64	30	12.80	-	-	6	-
M A Holding	102	42	11	282	64	9.09	-	2	30	-
C L Hooper	227	206	43	5761	113*	35.34	7	29	120	-
R O Hurley	4	1	0	0	0	0.00	-	-	4	-
R D Jacobs	125	101	26	1752	80*	23.36	-	9	142	26
K C B Jeremy	6	4	2	17	8*	8.50	-	-	-	-
S C Joseph	4	4	0	57	28	14.25	-	-	1	-
B D Julien	12	8	2	86	26*	14.33	-	-	4	-
A I Kallicharran	31	28	4	826	78	34.41	-	6	8	-
R B Kanhai	7	5	2	164	55	54.66	-	2	4	-
C L King	18	14	2	280	86	23.33	-	1	6	-
R D King	48	22	13	62	12*	6.88	-	-	4	-
C B Lambert	11	11	0	368	119	33.45	1	2	-	-
B C Lara	219	214	23	8233	169	43.10	17	52	93	-
J J C Lawson	6	1	0	3	3	3.00	-	-	-	-
R N Lewis	16	12	3	157	49	17.44	-	-	5	-
C H Lloyd	87	69	19	1977	102	39.54	1	11	39	-
A L Logie	158	133	36	2809	109*	28.95	1	14	61	-
N C McGarrell	17	10	2	60	19	7.50	-	-	9	-
N A M McLean	45	34	8	314	50*	12.07	-	1	8	-
M D Marshall	136	83	19	955	66	14.92	-	2	15	-
E H Mattis	2	2	0	86	62	43.00	-	1	2	-
R S Morton	2	2	0	19	16	9.50	-	-	1	-
E A Moseley	9	6	2	7	2*	1.75	-	-	-	-
D A Murray	10	7	2	45	35	9.00	-	-	16	-
D L Murray	26	17	5	294	61*	24.50	-	2	37	1
J R Murray	55	36	6	678	86	22.60	-	5	46	7
M C Nagamootoo	24	18	6	162	33	13.50	-	-	6	-
D R Parry	6	5	1	61	32	15.25	-	-	8	-
B P Patterson	59	20	15	44	13*	8.80	-	-	9	-
T R O Payne	7	4	0	126	60	31.50	-	1	6	-
N O Perry	21	16	8	212	52*	26.50	-	1	4	-
N Phillip	1	1	0	0	0	0.00	-	-	-	-
D B Powell	2	0	-	-	-	-	-	-	-	-
R L Powell	74	68	10	1515	124	26.12	1	6	33	-
M R Pydanna	3	1	1	2	2*	-	-	-	2	1
D Pamnarine	4	3	0	5	2	1.66	-	-	-	-
F L Reifer	2	2	0	31	22	15.50	-	-	1	-
I V A Richards	187	167	24	6721	189*	47.00	11	45	100	-
R B Richardson	224	217	30	6248	122	33.41	5	44	75	-
A M E Roberts	56	32	9	231	37*	10.04	-	-	6	-
F A Rose	27	23	5	217	30	12.05	-	-	6	-
L G Rowe	11	8	0	136	60	17.00	-	1	2	-
M N Samuels	50	48	7	1345	108*	32.80	1	10	16	-
R G Samuels	8	5	2	54	36*	18.00	-	-	1	-
R R Sarwan	44	42	11	1491	102*	48.09	1	7	12	-
K F Semple	7	6	0	64	23	10.66	-	-	2	-
I T Shillingford	2	2	0	30	24	15.00	-	-	2	-
S Shivnarine	1	1	1	20	20*	-	-	-	-	-
P V Simmons	143	138	11	3675	122	28.93	5	18	55	-
M A Small	2	0	-	-	-	-	-	-	1	-
D S Smith	3	3	0	36	26	12.00	-	-	1	-
G S Sobers	1	1	0	0	0	0.00	-	-	1	-

NAME	Mat	I	NO	Runs	HS	Av	100	50	Ct	St
C E L Stuart	5	1	1	3	3*	-	-	-	1	-
J E Taylor	1	0	-	-	-	-	-	-	-	-
P I C Thompson	2	1	0	2	2	2.00	-	-	-	-
C M Tuckett	1	0	-	-	-	-	-	-	-	-
P A Wallace	33	33	0	701	103	21.24	1	2	11	-
C A Walsh	205	79	33	321	30	6.97	-	-	27	-
D Williams	36	23	7	147	32*	9.18	-	-	35	10
L R Williams	15	13	2	124	41	11.27	-	-	8	-
S C Williams	57	55	6	1586	105*	32.36	1	12	18	-

Totals up to 31 July 2003

ONE DAY INTERNATIONALS
Career Bowling Averages

1973 to 2003

NAME	Mat	Balls	M	R	W	Av	Best	4w	5w
J C Adams	127	1856	12	1499	43	34.86	5-37	-	1
C E L Ambrose	176	9353	192	5429	225	24.12	5-17	6	4
H A G Anthony	3	156	0	143	3	47.66	2-47	-	-
K L T Arthurton	105	1384	4	1159	42	27.59	4-31	3	-
R A Austin	1	6	0	13	0	-	-	-	-
O A C Banks	3	150	0	124	4	31.00	2-44	-	-
S F A F Bacchus	29	-	-	-	-	-	-	-	-
E A E Baptiste	43	2214	30	1511	36	41.97	2-10	-	-
K C G Benjamin	26	1319	12	923	33	27.96	3-34	-	-
W K M Benjamin	85	4442	58	3079	100	30.79	5-22	-	1
D E Barnard	4	24	0	28	1	28.00	1-11	-	-
C A Best	24	19	0	12	0	-	-	-	-
I R Bishop	84	4332	49	3127	118	26.50	5.25	7	2
M I Black	5	228	1	196	0	-	-	-	-
K D Boyce	8	470	4	313	13	24.07	4.50	1	-
D Brown	3	150	3	124	5	24.80	3-21	-	-
B S Browne	4	180	0	156	2	78.00	2-50	-	-
C O Browne	28	-	-	-	-	-	-	-	-
H R Bryan	15	722	5	518	12	43.16	4.24	1	-
S L Campbell	90	196	0	170	8	21.25	4-30	1	-
S Chanderpaul	132	708	0	606	14	43.28	3-18	-	-
S T Clarke	10	524	13	245	13	18.84	3-22	-	-
P T Collins	23	1235	15	946	30	31.53	3.18	-	-
C D Collymore	42	2137	19	1536	49	31.34	5-51	1	1
C E H Croft	19	1070	21	620	30	20.66	6-15	-	1
C E Cuffy	41	2153	41	1436	41	35.02	4-24	1	-
A C Cummins	63	3143	23	2246	78	28.79	5-31	2	1
W W Daniel	18	912	17	595	23	25.86	3-27	-	-
W W Davis	35	1923	31	1302	39	33.38	7-51	-	1
R Dhanraj	6	264	2	170	10	17.00	4-26	1	-
M Dillon	89	4623	58	3507	114	30.76	5-51	3	2
V C Drakes	30	1454	17	1158	47	24.63	5-33	3	2
P J L Dujon	169	-	-	-	-	-	-	-	-
M L C Foster	2	30	0	22	2	11.00	2-22	-	-
R C Fredericks	12	10	0	10	2	5.00	2-10	-	-
R S Gabriel	11	-	-	-	-	-	-	-	-
D Ganga	28	1	0	4	0	-	-	-	-
J Garner	98	5330	141	2752	146	18.84	5-31	2	3
L V Garrick	3	-	-	-	-	-	-	-	-
C H Gayle	78	2616	18	2033	67	30.34	5-46	2	1
L R Gibbs	3	156	4	59	2	29.50	1-12	-	-
O D Gibson	15	739	8	621	34	18.26	5-40	2	2
H A Gomes	83	1345	10	1045	41	25.48	4-31	2	-
A H Gray	25	1270	16	835	44	18.97	6-50	2	1
A E Greenidge	1	-	-	-	-	-	-	-	-
C G Greenidge	128	60	0	45	1	45.00	1-21	-	-
A F G Griffith	9	-	-	-	-	-	-	-	-

NAME	Mat	Balls	M	R	W	Av	Best	4w	5w
R A Harper	105	5175	47	3431	100	34.31	4-40	3	-
D L Haynes	238	30	0	24	0	-	-	-	-
R C Haynes	8	270	1	224	5	44.80	2-36	-	-
R G A Headley	1	-	-	-	-	-	-	-	-
R O Hinds	11	341	0	314	6	52.33	2-19	-	-
W W Hinds	78	329	0	284	11	25.81	3-35	-	-
R I C Holder	37	-	-	-	-	-	-	-	-
V A Holder	12	681	9	454	19	23.89	5-50	-	1
M A Holding	102	5473	99	3034	142	21.36	5-26	5	1
C L Hooper	227	9573	53	6958	193	36.05	4-34	3	-
R O Hurley	4	150	1	111	2	55.50	1-25	-	-
R D Jacobs	112	-	-	-	-	-	-	-	-
K C B Jeremy	6	192	1	163	4	40.75	2-42	-	-
S C Joseph	4	-	-	-	-	-	-	-	-
B D Julien	12	778	21	463	18	25.72	4-20	2	-
A I Kallicharran	31	105	3	64	3	21.33	2-10	-	-
R B Kanhai	7	-	-	-	-	-	-	-	-
C L King	18	744	7	529	11	48.09	4-23	1	-
R D King	48	2483	41	1696	73	23.23	4-25	2	-
C B Lambert	11	12	0	8	0	-	-	-	-
B C Lara	219	49	0	61	4	15.35	2-5	-	-
J J C Lawson	6	270	2	217	9	24.11	4-57	1	-
R N Lewis	16	715	2	614	12	51.16	2-40	-	-
C H Lloyd	87	358	7	210	8	26.25	2-4	-	-
A L Logie	158	24	0	18	0	-	-	-	-
N C McGarrell	17	859	2	681	15	45.40	3-32	-	-
NA M McLean	45	2120	18	1729	46	37.58	3-21	-	-
M D Marshall	136	7175	122	4233	157	26.96	4-18	6	-
E H Mattis	2	-	-	-	-	-	-	-	-
R S Morton	2	-	-	-	-	-	-	-	-
E A Moseley	9	330	2	278	7	39.71	2-52	-	-
D A Murray	10	-	-	-	-	-	-	-	-
D L Murray	26	-	-	-	-	-	-	-	-
J R Murray	55	-	-	-	-	-	-	-	-
M V Nagamootoo	24	1189	4	998	18	55.44	4-32	1	-
D R Parry	6	330	2	259	11	23.54	3-47	-	-
B P Patterson	59	3050	37	2206	90	24.51	6-29	1	1
T R O Payne	7	-	-	-	-	-	-	-	-
N O Perry	21	946	2	783	20	39.15	3-45	-	-
N Phillip	1	42	0	22	1	22.00	1-22	-	-
D B Powell	2	114	2	71	1	71.00	1-34	-	-
R L Powell	74	219	3	230	6	38.33	2-5	-	-
M R Pydanna	3	-	-	-	-	-	-	-	-
D Ramnarine	4	200	2	164	3	54.66	2-52	-	-
F L Reifer	2	-	-	-	-	-	-	-	-
I V A Richards	187	5644	26	4228	118	35.83	6-41	1	2
R B Richardson	224	58	0	46	1	46.00	1-4	-	-
A M E Roberts	56	3123	79	1771	87	20.35	5-22	2	1
F A Rose	27	1326	13	1046	29	36.06	5-23	-	1
L G Rowe	11	-	-	-	-	-	-	-	-
M N Samuels	50	1434	6	1184	34	34.82	3-25	-	-
R G Samuels	8	-	-	-	-	-	-	-	-
R R Sarwan	44	132	1	135	2	67.50	1-32	-	-
K F Semple	7	132	0	121	3	40.33	2-35	-	-
I T Shillingford	2	-	-	-	-	-	-	-	-
S Shivnarine	1	18	0	16	0	-	-	-	-
P V Simmons	143	3880	38	2876	83	34.65	4-3	2	-
M A Small	2	84	.	54	1	54.00	1-40	-	-
G S Sobers	1	63	3	31	1	31.00	1-31	-	-
C E L Stuart	5	258	3	205	8	25.62	5-44	-	1

NAME	Mat	Balls	M	R	W	Av	Best	4w	5w
J E Taylor	1	60	0	39	2	19.50	2-39	-	-
P I C Thompson	2	114	2	110	2	55.00	1-46	-	-
C M Tuckett	1	48	0	41	2	20.50	2-41	-	-
P A Wallace	33	-	-	-	-	-	-	-	-
C A Walsh	205	10822	185	6918	227	30.47	5-1	6	1
D Williams	36	-	-	-	-	-	-	-	-
L R Williams	15	659	2	556	18	30.88	3-16	-	-
S C Williams	57	24	0	30	1	30.00	1-30	-	-

SELECT BIBLIOGRAPHY

ASSOCIATION OF CRICKET STATISTICIANS *A Guide to First Class Cricket Matches Played in the West Indies* (Nottingham, 1984)

BAILEY, P., THORN P. & WYNNE-THOMAS, P. *The Who's Who of Cricketers* (Guild Publishing: London, 1984)

BAILEY, P., LANE, B. & THORN, P. *Jamaica Cricketers 1894/95-1994/95* (Association of Cricket Statisticians & Historians: Nottingham, 1996)

BAILEY, T.E. *Sir Gary: A Biography* (Collins: London, 1976)

BAJNATH, H. *West Indies Cricketers* (Columbus Publishers: Port-of-Spain, 1970)

BANNISTER, A. *Cricket Cauldron: With Hutton in the Caribbean* (Stanley Paul: London, 1954)

BANNISTER, J. *Brian Lara: The Story of a Record-Breaking Year* (Stanley Paul: London, 1994)

BARKER, J.S. *Summer Spectacular: The West Indies v. England, 1963* (The Sportsmans Book Club: London, 1965)

--- *In the Main: West Indies v M.C.C. 1968* (The Sportsmans Book Club: London, 1969)

BECKLES, H.MCD. *The Development of West Indies Cricket* (University Press of the West Indies: Kingston, 1998). 2 volumes

--- *A Nation Imagined: First West Indies Test Team* (Ian Randle Publishers: Kingston, 2003)

---, ed. *An Area of Conquest: Popular Democracy and West Indies Cricket Supremacy* (Ian Randle Publishers: Kingston, 1994)

---, ed. *A Spirit of Dominance: Cricket and Nationalism in the West Indies* (University Press of the West Indies: Kingston, 1998)

--- & STODDART, B. eds. *Liberation Cricket: West Indies Cricket Culture* (Manchester University Press: Manchester, 1995)

BELL, C. *West Indian Test Cricketers: A Complete Statistical Record 1928-1993* (MRC Services Ltd: Kingston, 1994)

BELL, G.O. *Sir Garfield Sobers* (Nelson: Middlesex, 1978)

BIRBALSINGH, F. *The Rise of Westindian Cricket: From Colony to Nation* (Hansib: London, 1996)

--- & SHIWCHARAN, C. *Indo-Westindian Cricket* (Hansib: London, 1988)

BOYCOTT, G. *In the Fast Lane: West Indies Tour of 1981* (Arthur Barker: London, 1981)

BURTON, C.A., HUGHES, R.G. & SANDIFORD, K.A.P. eds. *100 Years of Organised Cricket in Barbados, 1892-1992* (Barbados Cricket Association: Bridgetown, 1992)

BUTCHER, R.O. *Rising to the Challenge* (Pelham Books: London, 1989)

CAMERON, D.J. *Caribbean Crusade: New Zealand Cricketers in the West Indies 1972* (Readers Union: Newton Abbot, 1974)

CANYNGE CAPLE, S. *England v The West Indies 1895-1957* (The Worcester Press: Worcester, 1958)

CLARKE, J. & SCOVELL, B. *Everything That's Cricket: The West Indies Tour 1966* (Stanley Paul: London, 1966)

CLOSE, B. *The M.C.C. Tour of West Indies, 1968* (Stanley Paul: London, 1968)

COLDHAM, J.D. *Lord Harris* (George Allen & Unwin: London, 1983)

CONSTANTINE, L. *Cricket and I* (George Allen & Unwin: London, 1933)

--- *Cricket in the Sun* (Stanley Paul: London, 1947)

--- *Cricketers' Carnival* (Stanley Paul: London, 1948)

--- *The Young Cricketer's Companion* (The Sportsmans Book Club: London, 1966)

COTTER, G. *England versus West Indies: A History of the Tests and Other Matches* (The Crowood Press: Swindon, 1991)

COZIER, T. *The West Indies: Fifty Years of Test Cricket* (Readers Union: Newton Abbot, 1978)

---, ed. *The West Indian Cricket Annual* (Bridgetown, 1970-91)

---, ed. *Red Stripe Caribbean Cricket Quarterly* (Bridgetown, 1991-2001)

DALE, H. *Cricket Crusaders* (The Sportsmans Book Club: London, 1953)

DOBSON, D. *Records of West Indies First-Class Cricket in West Indies and Overseas 1865 to 1994* (David Dobson: Victoria, 1994)

EASTMOND, H.H. *The Nemwil Record of Test Cricket & One Day Internationals Annual 2001* (Cot Caribbean Graphics: Bridgetown, 2001)

EDMONDS, F. *Another Bloody Tour: England in the West Indies 1986* (The Kingswood Press: London, 1986)

EYTLE, E. *Frank Worrell: The Career of a Great Cricketer* (Hodder & Stoughton: London, 1963)

FIGUEROA, J. *West Indies in England: The Great Post-War Tours* (The Kingswood Press: London, 1991)

FRINDALL, W.H. *The Wisden Book of Test Cricket 1877-1984* (Guild Publishing: London, 1985)

--- *The Wisden Book of Test Cricket, Volume II, 1977-1994* (Headline Book Publishing: London, 1995)

GARNER, J. *'Big Bird' Flying High* (Arthur Barker: London, 1988)

GILCHRIST, R. *Hit Me For Six* (Stanley Paul: London, 1963)

GOODWIN, C. *Caribbean Cricketers from the Pioneers to Packer* (George G. Harrap: London, 1980)

--- *West Indians at the Wicket* (Macmillan: London, 1986)

GRIMSHAW, A. ed. *C.L.R. James on Cricket* (Allison & Busby: London, 1986)

GREENIDGE, C.G. *The Man in the Middle* (Readers Union: Newton Abbot, 1980)

GRIFFITH, C.C. *Chucked Around* (Pelham Books: London, 1970)

GIUSEPPI, U. *Sir Frank Worrell* (Nelson: London, 1969)

--- *A Look at Learie Constantine* (Nelson: San Fernando, 1974)

HALL, W.W. *Pace Like Fire* (The Sportsmans Book Club: London, 1966)

HAMILTON, B. *Cricket in Barbados* (Barbados Advocate: Bridgetown, 1947)

HARRAGIN, H. *Sixty Years of Cricket: Australia vs The West Indies* (Paria Publishing: Port-of-Spain, 1991)

HARRIS, B. *West Indies Cricket Challenge* (Stanley Paul: London, 1957)

HARTLAND, P. *The Balance of Power in Test Cricket 1877-1998* (Field Publishing: East Sussex, 1998)

HOLDING, M. *Whispering Death: The Life and Times of Michael Holding* (André Deutsch: London, 1993)

HOWAT, G. *Learie Constantine* (Readers Union: Newton Abbot, 1976)

HUNTE, C.C. *Playing to Win* (Hodder & Stoughton: London, 1972)

ISAACS, V. & ALLEN, D. *Malcolm Marshall: His Record Innings-by-Innings* (Association of Cricket Statisticians and Historians: Nottingham, 2000)

JAMES, C.L.R. *Beyond a Boundary* (Hutchinson: London, 1963)

KANHAI, R.B. *Blasting For Runs* (Souvenir Press: London, 1966)

KEATING, F. *Another Bloody Day in Paradise* (André Deutsch: London, 1981)

KUMAR, V. *Cricket Lovely Cricket* (Kumar: London, 2000)

LANDSBERG, P. *The Kangaroo Conquers: West Indies v Australia, 1955* (Museum Press: London, 1955)

LAWRENCE, B. *Masterclass: The Biography of George Headley* (Polar Publishing Ltd: Leicester, 1995)

--- & GOBLE, R. *The Complete Record of West Indian Test Cricketers* (ACL & Polar Publishing Ltd: Leicester, 1991)

--- & SCARLETT, R. *100 Great Westindian Test Cricketers: from Challenor to Richards* (Hansib: London, 1988)

LLOYD, C.H. *Living For Cricket* (Stanley Paul: London, 1980)

MANLEY, M. *A History of West Indies Cricket* (André Deutsch: London, 1988)

MARSHALL, M. *Marshall Arts: The Autobiography of Malcolm Marshall* (Queen Anne Press: London, 1987)

MARSHALL, R.E. *Test Outcast* (Pelham Books: London, 1970)

MARTIN-JENKINS, C. *Testing Time: MCC in the West Indies 1974* (Readers Union: Newton Abbot, 1975)

--- *World Cricketers: A Biographical Dictionary* (Oxford University Press: Oxford, 1996)

MCDONALD, T. *Viv Richards: The Authorised Biography* (Pelham Books: London, 1984)

--- *Clive Lloyd: The Authorised Biography* (Granada: London, 1985)

MOYES, A.G. *With the West Indies in Australia 1951-52* (George G. Harrap & Co. Ltd: London, 1952)

--- *With the West Indies in Australia 1960-1961* (Heinemann: London, 1961)

NICOLE, C. *West Indian Cricket* (Phoenix Sports Books: London, 1957)

PILGRIM, T. *The Sir Frank Worrell Pictorial* (Creativity/Innovation Services: New York, 1992)

Playfair Cricket Annual (Various presses: London, 1948-2002)

RICHARDS, I.V.A. *Hitting Across the Line* (BCA: London, 1991)

RICHARDS, J. & WONG, M. *Statistics of West Indies Cricket 1865-1989* (Heinemann Publishers: Kingston, 1990)

ROSS, A. *Through the Caribbean: The MCC Tour of the Caribbean 1959-1960* (Hamish Hamilton: London, 1960)

ROSS, G. *A History of West Indies Cricket* (Arthur Barker: London, 1976)

SANDIFORD, K.A.P. *Everton DeCourcey Weekes: His Record Innings-by-Innings* (Association of Cricket Statisticians and Historians: Nottingham, 1995)
--- *Clyde Leopold Walcott: His Record Innings-by-Innings* (Association of Cricket Statisticians and Historians: Nottingham, 1996)
--- *Frank Worrell: His Record Innings-by-Innings* (Association of Cricket Statisticians and Historians: Nottingham, 1997)
--- *Gary Sobers: His Record Innings-by-Innings* (Association of Cricket Statisticians and Historians: Nottingham, 1998)
--- *Cricket Nurseries of Colonial Barbados: The Elite Schools 1865-1966* (University Press of the West Indies: Kingston, 1998)
--- *Wes Hall: His Record Innings-by-Innings* (Association of Cricket Statisticians and Historians: Nottingham, 2001)
--- *At the Crease with Gary Sobers:His Partnerships in Test Cricket* (Cricket Lore: London, 2001)
--- *J.D.C. Goddard: His Record Innings-by-Innings* (Association of Cricket Statisticians and Historians: Nottingham, 2002)
--- *Sonny Ramadhin: His Record Innings-by-Innings* (Association of Cricket Statisticians and Historians: Nottingham, 2003)
--- & TAN, A. *The Three Ws of West Indian Cricket: A Comparative Batting Analysis* (Univers de Presse: Houston, 2002)
SEARLE, C. *Pitch of Life: Writings on Cricket* (Parrs Wood Press: Manchester, 2001)
SOBERS, G. *Twenty Years at the Top* (Macmillan: London, 1988)
--- *The Changing Face of Cricket* (Ebury Press: London, 1996)
--- *Garry Sobers: My Autobiography* (Headline Book Publishing: London, 2002)
STEEN, R. *Desmond Haynes: Lion of Barbados* (Cassell: London, 1993)
STODDART, B. & SANDIFORD, K.A.P., eds. *The Imperial Game: Cricket, Culture and Society* (Manchester University Press: Manchester, 1998)
STOLLMEYER, J.B. *Everything Under the Sun: My Life in West Indies Cricket* (Stanley Paul: London, 1983)
SWANTON, E.W. *West Indian Adventure: With Hutton's M.C.C. Team 1953-54* (The Sportsmans Book Club: London, 1955)
--- *West Indies Revisited: The MCC Tour of 1959-60* (Heinemann: London, 1960)
SYMES, P. *"Maco": The Malcolm Marshall Story* (Parrs Wood: Manchester, 2000)
TENNANT, I. *Frank Worrell: A Biography* (Lutterworth Press: Cambridge, 1987)
THORN, P. *Barbados Cricketers 1865-1990* (Association of Cricket Statisticians & Historians: Nottingham, 1991)
Trinidad & Tobago Cricket Council: Silver Jubilee Issue (Port-of-Spain, 1981)
Trinidad & Tobago Cricket Board of Control 20th Anniversary 1980-2000 (Port-of-Spain, 2001)
WALCOTT, C.L. *Island Cricketers* (Hodder & Stoughton: London, 1958)
--- *Sixty Years on the Back Foot* (Victor Gallancz: London, 1999)
WARNER, P.F. *Long Innings* (George G. Harrap & Co. Ltd: London, 1951)
WILLIS, R.G.D. *Cricket Revolution: Test Cricket in the 1970s* (Sidgwick & Jackson: London, 1981)
WORRELL, F.M. *Cricket Punch* (Stanley Paul: London, 1959)

WHITHAM, R.K. *George A. Headley: His Record Innings-by-Innings* (Association of Cricket Statisticians: Nottingham, undated)

Wisden Cricketers' Almanack (John Wisden & Co Ltd: London, 1929-2002)

WOLSTENHOLME, G. *The West Indian Tour of England 1906* (Galava Printing Co. Ltd: Nelson, 1992)

WOOLDRIDGE, I. *Cricket, Lovely Cricket: The West Indies Tour 1963* (Robert Hale Ltd: London, 1963)

WYNNE-THOMAS, P. *The Complete History of Cricket Tours At Home and Abroad* (Guild Publishing: London, 1989)

--- *The History of Cricket: From the Weald to the World* (The Stationery Office: London, 1997)

INDEX

39, 45, 97, 98-99, 100, 105, 108,
116, 120, 122, 176, 180, 208, 430
Ramnarine, Dinanath, 106, 107-108,
203, 211, 431
Ramprakash, Mark, 83, 170
Ranji Trophy, 15, 158
Red Stripe Competition, 28, 60, 80,
143, 156
Reid, A.A., 141, 142, 156
Reifer, Floyd, 60, 73, 211, 432
Richards, Jimmy, 138
Richards, Malcolm, 141
Richards, Sir Vivian, xiii, 3, 6, 26, 27,
28, 41, 80, 111, 130, 143-146, 156,
164, 188, 190-191, 192, 195, 197,
198, 199, 200, 201, 210, 433
Richardson, Richie, 3, 6, 28, 60, 111,
130, 143-144, 146, 147, 148, 156,
195, 198, 199, 210, 434
Richmond College, 164
Rickards, Ken, 24, 26, 115, 119, 120,
208, 213, 435
Roach, Clifford, 19, 37, 89, 91-92, 93,
171, 207, 213, 214, 436
Roberts, Alfie, 140, 141, 152, 209,
213, 215, 437
Roberts, Andy, 7, 8, 54, 111, 143, 144,
146, 147, 148, 150, 156, 159, 194,
210, 438
Roberts, Lincoln, 106, 211, 439
Roberts, 'Strebor', 138
Rodriguez, Willie, 100-101, 209, 440
Root, Fred, 16
Rose, Franklyn, 8, 132-133, 136, 202,
203, 211, 441
Rousseau, Pat, 137
Rowe, Lawrence, 38, 78, 15, 120, 125,
126-127, 129, 130, 136, 137, 186,
187, 188, 189, 210, 442
Rugby School, 168
Ryder, Jack, 176

Sabina Park, 21, 23, 118, 134, 172,
173, 183, 185, 187, 204
St Anne's, Trinidad, 162
St George, Barbados, 166
St George's, Grenada, 76, 154, 166

St Hill, Edwin, 89, 93, 207, 212, 215, 470
St Hill, Wilton, 89, 92, 207, 212, 216, 471
St John's, Antigua, 58, 83, 108, 137,
192, 193, 195, 197, 198, 200, 201-
202, 203, 204, 205, 206
St Kitts, 139, 142, 143, 150, 156, 157,
158, 159
St Lucia, 139, 142, 143, 156
St Vincent, 10, 41, 139, 140, 143, 157,
165, 166, 168
St Vincent & the Grenadines, 141,
152-154
Salisbury, Marquess of, 162
Samuels, Marlon, 133, 205, 206, 211,
215, 443
Samuels, Robert, 132-133, 202, 211, 444
Sandham, Andrew, 181
Sandiford, Keith A.P., 110
Sanford, Adam, 8, 136, 153, 154,
211, 445
Sang Hue, Douglas, 138
Sarwan, Ramnaresh, 28, 83, 84, 85,
205, 206, 211, 215, 446
Scarborough, 56
Scarlett, Reg, xiii, 124, 125, 209, 447
Schoult, Joseph, 16
Scotland, 31
Scotland, Rupert, 141
Scott, A.P.H., 116, 122, 209, 215, 448
Scott, Oscar, 113, 116, 117, 122, 207,
212, 216, 449
Scotts Head, 161
Sealy, Benjamin, 19, 89, 93, 207, 212,
216, 450
Sealy, Derek, 4, 12, 13, 19, 20, 21, 36,
37, 38, 62, 118, 171, 172, 208,
213, 215, 451
Sealy, Harry, 4
Second World War (see World War II)
Semple, Keith, 452
Shamrock Cricket Club, 4
Shannon Cricket Club, 4, 89
Sharjah, 62
Sheffield, 164
Sheffield Shield, 14, 169
Shell Company, 26
Shell Shield, 14, 13, 23-24, 25-26, 28,